ECONOMIC

ANTHROPOLOGY

The Economic Life of Primitive Peoples

MELVILLE J. HERSKOVITS

The Norton Library

W · W · NORTON & COMPANY · INC ·

NEW YORK

PREFACE

THIS BOOK, a thorough revision of *The Economic Life of Primitive Peoples,* is an introduction to comparative economics, in the broadest sense of the term. It would have been desirable so to entitle it, had not economic science already assigned to this designation the more restricted field of the comparison of free enterprise with communist and fascist economies. The present title, which stems from a suggestion put forward in 1927 by N. S. B. Gras, seemed a feasible alternative, especially since the term "economic anthropology" has slowly been finding a place in the relevant anthropological literature. It is to be hoped that it will gain currency among economists to define an aspect of their discipline whose significance is receiving increasing recognition from them.

The change in title represents a reorientation in point of view that goes far beyond the question of mere terminology. Ten years ago, the word "primitive" came easily to the lips. It is only with the rapid development of communications of the past decade, and the growing integration of peoples of the most diverse cultures into the world scene, that the essentially pejorative and tendentious character of this designation, like others such as "savage," "backward," or "early," when applied to any functioning way of life, became apparent. This is not the place to analyze the cultural or psychological problems of the emergent nationalisms found in expanding and newly literate communities of Africa and Asia and of other non-machine societies. Yet when their story is told, the role played by the reaction of their leaders against designations of this order will be found to be a major factor in the latent or explicit hostilities of which these movements are in many cases the expression.

The word "primitive" is open to objection, further, because it is incapable of precise definition. The presence or absence of a written language, of power machinery, of least common denominators of value—these are objectively ascertainable facts that have bearing on the study of many problems where cultures of differing historical backgrounds, institutional organization, and psychological orientations are to be compared. They are of particular relevance where economic behavior and mechanisms are under consideration, and in this context exemplify strikingly their desirability as criteria of comparison when contrasted to the essential lack of preciseness of the earlier, more inclusive designation "primitive."

The fact that this revision has necessitated what in many cases amounts to a re-writing of the original work reflects in a very real sense the developments in the study of the economics of nonliterate, non-industrial, and non-pecuniary societies that have taken place since 1940, when the earlier volume was published. The neglect by earlier anthropologists of the economic aspects of the cultures they studied no longer exists. Under present conventions of field-work, no anthropologist of competence takes as synonymous the technology of a people with their economics, or considers it sufficient if he only studies the canons of ownership, where problems of differentials in wealth and position are his concern. The change is shown by the difference in length and treatment of many topics in this volume and in its predecessor. The earlier single chapter on labor has had to be expanded into two, one on work-patterns, the other on the rewards of labor. Consumption norms now require separate treatment. Elsewhere, the new data amplify presentations and make it possible to clarify the implications of points that could only be sketched a decade ago.

The expansion and revision of the first section, which deals with theoretical and historical aspects of our subject, is likewise the result of this development, though it concomitantly represents a growing interest in the subject-matter on the part of economists. It is true that much of this interest, expressed in conversations, has not as yet yielded substantial published results; but it is apparent that the interest is there, and that systematic exploitation of the data by economists is only a matter of time. I have made it a point to discuss with economists of widely differing orientations problems of mutual concern treated in this book, and have found a receptivity and understanding that could not have been predicted ten years ago.

There will perhaps be those who will seek in these pages some treatment of the effects of contact with the economies of Europe and America on the systems with which we are concerned. This is an aspect of the contemporary scene which is focal to the problem of world adjustment. Too often, however, those who must deal with situations of this order assume that the changes that are concurring must be uni-directional, that the simplicity of the "primitive" systems on which the industrialized order is impinging makes the problem one of imposition rather than of interplay. To the extent this is the case, this book may contribute to the understanding of the historical forces at play by bringing to those having to do with problems arising out of the spread of Euroamerican technology and industrialization throughout the non-industrial world a realization of the background against which these innovations must be projected, if a workable adjustment is to be achieved. But these situations of contact, or the processes involved in them, are not within the terms of reference of this particular work. It is rather my aim to give the reader a sense of the variation that marks the manner in which all men achieve those aims of the application of scarce means to given ends that can only result from an overview of the various systems that mankind has devised to accomplish this fundamental requirement of human civilization.

The purpose of this book thus remains what it was when first written—to provide information concerning the economic life of nonliterate peoples, to consider some of the questions in economic science that can be examined by the use of these data, and to suggest lines of attack which may be profitably defined for future use. In the main, I have tried to follow the conventional categories of economics and to indicate the points at which the economies with which we are concerned diverge so sharply from our own that it is not possible to follow these conventions. I have kept to a minimum the specialized technical terms of both anthropology and economics, so that what is written may be accessible to all whose interest lies in the dynamics of culture and the variety of forms in which comparable institutions of differing ways of life can be cast.

In documenting my discussion, I have used examples from my own field research sparingly, sacrificing at times the special insight that first-hand knowledge of a culture affords in enlarging on a point, in order to use pertinent materials from other societies. The history of social science is replete with examples of students who have not learned the lesson of scientific method, that valid generalization must rest on a broad base of factual materials. On the other hand, I have not gone to the lengths of some of the older writers of the comparative school, such as Frazer, or Westermarck, or Sumner, who saw to it that every possible instance bearing on a given point was included in their discussions. For this, we have learned, means that while the reader ranges widely, he is left without any sense of cultural depth and cohesiveness. It has seemed to me to be more advantageous to cite fewer cases, and to present these more fully, than the tradition of the comparative method as classically practiced would dictate. I have therefore turned in the main to those contributions wherein economic life is adequately treated in preference to those where economic facts enter incidentally, to works representing the use of modern field techniques rather than to the older sources; and I have favored the use of less well-known data over those few instances of economic processes and institutions, like the potlatch, which have been cited so often that they need only to be referred to in order to call them to mind.

I may express again my indebtedness to the John Simon Guggenheim Memorial Foundation and to Northwestern University for the support that made it possible for me to write the original study, and to Northwestern University for funds that aided me in preparing the manuscript of the present work for the press. I may likewise repeat my thanks to those institutions, colleagues, and friends whose advice and assistance were so valuable in helping me write the earlier book. In addition I should like to acknowledge the stimulating suggestions of those, like Professor K. F. Walker of Adelaide University, Australia, whose perceptive and detailed reviews of that work I have found helpful. To those others who have read and commented on parts of this re-writing in manuscript I likewise extend my thanks— Professors Yale Brozen, Frank Fetter, Jules Henry, Elmo Hohman, Dr. Helen Hohman, Mr. Edward E. LeClair, Jr., Dr. Karl de Schweinitz, Jr., Professors Sol Tax and Harold Williamson. Finally, I take pleasure in expressing my appreciation to my friend, Professor Frank H. Knight, for his willingness to allow me to reprint his analysis of my original presentation which, with my reply, will be found in the Appendix.

MELVILLE J. HERSKOVITS

Evanston, Illinois

CONTENTS

Part IV. PROPERTY

Part V. THE ECONOMIC SURPLUS

Part VI. CONCLUSIONS

APPENDIX

TEXT FIGURES

PART I

INTRODUCTION

CHAPTER I

ECONOMIZING AND RATIONAL
BEHAVIOR

THE ELEMENTS of scarcity and choice, which are the outstanding factors in human experience that give economic science its reason for being, rest psychologically on firm ground. It is a truism that wants are capable of a degree of expansion the end of which has not been reached by any known society. Wants, that is, apparently manifest a certain dynamic quality, which seems to derive from the inventiveness and receptivity of man, and are ultimately to be referred to the cumulative nature of human culture itself. Each generation takes for granted the cultural setting of the society into which it is born. And each, because of the creative restlessness of man, adds its contribution to the total culture of the group it comprises.

It is important for us, at this point, to consider the breadth of social effort included under the term "economizing." How wide this is becomes evident in reading the many discussions of the scope of economics and its relation to the term from which the discipline derives its name. Knight holds that common definitions are too inclusive: "The term economic has come to be used in a sense which is practically synonymous with intelligent or rational." "It is in accord with good linguistic usage," he continues, "to think and speak of the whole problem of living as one of economy, the economical use of time, energy, etc.—*resource* of every sort." Yet he stresses the point that "the restrictions which mark off the modestly limited domain of economic science within the inclusive sphere of knowledge as a whole" must be clearly understood.[1]

This limitation is indicated by Benham, who states that "the rationale of economic activity is to satisfy human wants by producing consumers' goods." He explains: "People are continually deciding how they will use their time and energy and property and how they will spend their money. . . . It is these decisions which determine the nature and extent of economic activity."[2] A philosopher, assessing the nature of the economizing experience, states: "We can start with one agreed quality: Economizing is a way of doing things; first, of thinking about them, then, of acting; in sum, of arranging or choosing them. It is imposed on us by scarcity of means in relation to expanding desires. In this sense, it is purposive, a process which we direct and develop creatively; for we can agree that choice involves this."[3] This mode of circumscribing the term emphasizes conscious choice, stresses the essential role of alternatives between which to choose, and relates the whole to the problem of attaining efficiency through choosing.

Like any phenomenon that exists in time, the development of the wants of a people is irreversible. Small, isolated nonliterate societies may sometimes seem to the observer to live in terms of a degree of stability and conservatism that belies this. But there is no study of cultural change in process, or of contact between peoples having different cultures, which does not document the proposition that a people give over an item in their cultural store only when it becomes apparent to them that a more desirable substitute—iron implements for stone tools, for example—is at hand, or when circumstances beyond their control dictate this. There is nothing more difficult to accept than a lowered standard of living.

Our primary concern in these pages is to understand the cross-cultural implications of the process of economizing. We may begin our analysis by considering the concept of a free good. It is a commonplace in economic theory, for example, that no economic value can be assigned to a sunset or the view of a mountain, since these are to be had for the taking. It is only when a given good is not available in quantities to supply every

[1] Knight (1933), 1–2.   [3] Macfie, 20.
[2] Benham, 5–6.

desire for it that the economizing process comes into play. Even in the case of the utilization of what would seem to be a free good, however, some economic factors may enter. There may be more than enough animals available, and no restrictions on the member of the tribe as to where and what he will hunt; but choices will nonetheless have to be made. These considerations cannot be overlooked if the free good is not to lie, inert, as a theoretical concept and not as a functioning element in the daily life of the people.

It is generally recognized by economists that even the utilization of air, an example of a free good often cited, entails economizing. This is apparent if we consider so simple an example of economic behavior as occurs when an Australian aborigine decides to build a fire and a wind-screen. In this case, a choice is made between the cold (free) air of the night and the warmed (economic) air available only after the energy needed to collect wood, kindle the fire (no mean task where a fire-drill must be used), and build the screen, has been expended. It is apparent, in these instances, that the question of whether a resource is free or economic is not a simple concept. An understanding of these critical cases confirms empirically the economic principle that the applicability of the concept depends on the ends sought. Where choice enters so that the satisfactions derived are to be maximized, the free good becomes an economic one.

Beyond whatever free goods may be available, even to members of societies with the smallest numbers, the simplest technologies and the most direct economic systems, the far greater number of goods are not free. Even the provision of basic needs, food and shelter and clothing and implements, must inevitably involve choice; moreover, these choices are dictated not only by the alternatives between available items, but by the patterns of the culture of the individual who, in the final analysis, must do the choosing. Choice between alternatives is limited not only by the goods and services available to satisfy wants. The nature of the available goods and of the wants they are to satisfy is likewise restricted. Economizing, that is, is carried on in a cultural matrix. The matter has been phrased cogently in considering the economy of southern Bougainville, Solomon Islands: "At the present, in answer to the problem of discrepancy between needs and resources, it is sufficient to recall that these needs are *cultural* rather than *nutritional,* and to state the conviction that there will always be discrepancies between cultural needs and available resources." [4] Social conventions, religious beliefs, aesthetic conceptions, and ethical prescriptions all function in shaping the wants of peoples and the times and places and circumstances in which they can be satisfied.

We shall see how, for example, certain West African peoples conventionally and traditionally expend food so liberally on feasts that must be given during the dry season that at the beginning of the rainy season, when hard labor of breaking the ground for the new planting has to be performed, there is an actual inadequacy of caloric intake that could easily be supplied if food resources had been conserved.[5] It must be emphasized that there is no question of lack of foresight, for it is well established that these peoples are aware of the alternate possibility. It is rather a question of economic choice dictated by the drive to maximize satisfactions in terms of the traditional values of the culture.

As another instance, we may consider the utilization of land among the Kogi (or Kagaba) Indians who inhabit the Sierra Nevada range of northeastern Colombia. Because of the steepness of the mountains and the degree of erosion, this agricultural people is faced with a scarcity of land that forces each family to work patches in the lowland and highland areas, moving from one to another at considerable cost of expenditure in time and energy. In these mountain ranges, however, are many terraces, built by the earlier inhabitants, where numerous archaeological remains suggest a stable and considerable population. These terraces, each of which might provide on the average about two and a half acres of arable land, are not used, but the difficult mountain-sides and tiny patches in the valleys, often far removed from the habitation, are cultivated instead. The reason is a supernatural one: "There are many spirits of the dead there," they say. Except when they place offerings at these places, they avoid them, thus "depriving themselves of their best land" and "being forced to plant in patches far from each other, patches which at times are steep and very small." [6]

One of the principles of early economic theory was to regard

4 Oliver (1949a), 18.   6 Dolmatoff, 97–101.
5 See below, 277–80, 290–3.

the individual as the point from which all development of theoretical principles must begin. We have come to realize that the individual never exists alone; that a society, as it has been put, is more than an aggregate of Robinson Crusoes; and that social interaction in terms of cultural tradition dictates reconsideration of the earlier starting-point. The process of economizing, we recognize, is essentially based on the broader organization of society. Yet the individual cannot be left out of the picture, for all forms of social behavior, in the final analysis, must be referred to the behavior of individual members of a given society in specific situations.

This is why we must be on our guard against permitting the pendulum of reaction against the older point of view to swing to a point where we reify the common elements in the behavior of individuals into a construct that is conceived as existing by and of itself. There is much truth in the statement by Polanyi: "The outstanding discovery of recent historical and anthropological research is that man's economy, as a rule, is submerged in his social relationships." However, anyone who has had first-hand experience among nonliterate, non-machine, and non-pecuniary peoples, can but wonder at the validity of the statement which succeeds the sentence just quoted: "He does not act so as to safeguard his individual interest in the possession of material goods; he acts so as to safeguard his social standing, his social claims, his social assets. He values material goods only in so far as they serve this end." [7]

Paulme has drawn conclusions concerning this point, based on her research among the Dogon of West Africa, which depict somewhat more realistically the interaction between individual and social factors in the economic process. "It is clear," she says, "that individual advantage, understood as the realization of the greatest possible gain with the expenditure of a minimum of effort is not the sole force that causes men to work in the society we are studying. Each person is motivated, more or less consciously, in more or less indirect ways, by the desire for the well-being, wealth and prestige of the community as a whole." [8] All choices, that is, however they may be influenced by considerations of social standing, social claims, and social assets, are ultimately the choices of individuals.

[7] Polanyi, 46.   [8] Translated from Paulme, 194.

In short, we must not reject Economic Man only to substitute Society as an exclusive formula for understanding economic behavior and as a base-point for analysis. Economizing is never carried on *unilaterally*. The choices of the individual must always be limited by the resources of his society and the values of his culture. But the factors of variation to be found even within the smallest, most homogenous, and most conservative society must not be lost sight of. The economic unit, we must conclude, is the individual operating as a member of his society, in terms of the culture of his group.

This implies that any analysis of the schedule of wants of a given society which projects these wants against the supply of goods and services available to satisfy them must be supplemented by introducing a third term into the equation; the cultural definition of wants and the conventions that dictate how and when they are to be regarded as adequately satisfied. It is in terms of these factors that we will consider the economic systems of nonliterate, non-machine, and, often, non-pecuniary peoples treated in this book.

2

THE MEANS by which the ends of the economizing process, however defined, are achieved, comprise universals in human experience. They therefore provide the basis for all generalizations concerning the nature and functioning of economic systems, whatever their form and whatever the particular mechanisms they may use to convert these means into satisfying the wants that make up the socially sanctioned ends toward whose fulfillment a given economy is directed.

We may move, first of all, to those human and ecological factors that provide the goods and services which satisfy the demands of living, both biological and psychological, and that are at the core of any economic system. In some form, these factors are present everywhere; without their interaction life as we know it could not exist.

Initially, the elements that are given by the world as it is constituted must be considered: the natural resources derived from the habitat, and the labor power of men themselves, the prime mover in the utilization of what is provided by the natural setting. As Knight has phrased it, these are the "ultimate" resources, from which, through intermediate steps that vary in number with economies of different degrees of complexity, come the consumption goods that make possible the gratification of wants.[9]

But these do not tell the whole tale, for everywhere there must be the technical knowledge that permits men to take advantage of the resources to which they must look for the raw materials of their economy, and those tools they devise to permit them to utilize their labor effectively in exploiting the natural resources of the territories they inhabit. Their technologies, however crude, are expressed in the form of goods which are to be thought of, in the less complex economies, as capital goods of varying degrees of permanency. Clearing a waterhole can be interpreted in this way, despite the simplicity of the technique whereby the improvement of the natural resource is achieved, and the slight amount of time and energy that is expended in achieving this end. A bow and arrow is likewise an intermediate good of this sort. The effort capitalized in its making brings return in the greater effectiveness of its maker when hunting the game he needs for subsistence, or for prestige, or for other desired ends.

Yet while all these factors—natural resources, man-power, technical knowledge, and capital equipment—must be present in the productive processes of any functioning economy, the weighting of each in making the whole a going concern may differ widely. It is not chance that economists in their discussions have found it necessary to stress these prime factors, and especially to make explicit the role of "ultimate" resources. In a pecuniary, machine economy such as that of Europe and America, they are easily lost sight of in the face of the wealth of technical knowledge and the complexities of capital investment, with their resulting equipment which pours forth the enormous quantities and variety of goods that satisfy the needs of the people living in these societies.

In the non-pecuniary, non-machine societies with which we will be concerned, almost the exact opposite obtains. The factors of natural resources and man-power stand out in bold relief. One must search and interpret if the phenomenon of capitalization is

[9] Knight (1933), 41.

to be taken into account; the technological equipment is direct and relatively simple and at once apparent; the intermediate steps between the utilization of raw materials and the production of a consumption good are few. We shall see, in considering the simplest economies, how close to the subsistence level a society can be. Among nonliterate peoples in general, both the inventory of goods and services and the range of wants to be satisfied, as expressed in the standards of living of the people, are relatively restricted. The margin between available resources and physical survival, in the simplest of these economies, such as are found among the South African Bushmen, or the Indians of the Great Basin region of western United States, or the inhabitants of Tierra del Fuego, is slender indeed. The scarcity of available goods in societies living on this level holds the factor of choice to the narrowest of ranges; the wants are to a considerable degree biological and are of the order of survival itself. Here, in short, the need to economize does not have to be analyzed in forms of mathematical formulae; it is apparent, in all its stark biological implications, for the most casual traveler to observe.

These simplest economies, however, are few in number. They shade imperceptibly into systems in which increasing command of technology and greater capital equipment cause the factors of natural resources and labor-power again to be obscured by the secondary aspects of the total equipment for production. Even so, it is rare in these intermediate societies to find individuals as completely removed from the primary factors as, let us say, are the urban dwellers of Europe and America, though such persons are sporadically to be found. The apparatus to care for wants is capable of greater productivity, and the wants to be satisfied are correspondingly expanded. The margin which permits the expenditure of labor-power for the production of services as well as goods is greater, and this in turn leads to a greater degree of specialization.

In these societies, too, the entrepreneurial function, where it is to be discerned at all, is at a minimum. The men who, in terms of the economies of Euroamerican society, direct industrial enterprises, decide what is to be produced and how, hire workmen and direct what they shall do, borrow money to acquire capital goods or land holdings, and assume the risks inherent in their ventures, do not exist, in the sense of the word as used by economists, in non-pecuniary, non-industrialized societies. For in these societies, production and distribution involve little of the profit motive, and labor is only in special instances for hire.

Attempts that have been made to discern the entrepreneur in a South Seas chief or in a Bantu household head afford examples of this. Firth's statement, that he employs the term, "in default of finding a better," is to the point. "It must be taken in its simplest sense," he cautions, "of the person primarily responsible for an undertaking, and is not intended to imply propositions about risk-taking and profit-reception. For the Tikopia economy the term covers ownership of the final product, responsibility for payment of the workers if such is to be made, and usually some actual participation in the work." [10] In the case of the Bantu, Goodfellow, commenting on the fact that "the function of consumers to release part of their resources for further general production has scarcely existed," concludes that, "there has been little room for the function of the entrepreneur in managing such resources." [11]

We come here to a point that cannot be stressed too early in our discussion. This concerns the *generalized* nature of the mechanisms and institutions that mark the economies of all the non-literate, non-machine societies. It is a point that will recur as a basic theme of this book, and will be extensively documented in the pages that follow. It explains the difficulties that arise when we attempt to apply the more refined concepts of economics to these societies, or when we attempt to test some of the more debated hypotheses of economic theory by reference to them. The example given above of the nature of a capital good in such an economy makes the point; it could be equally well made if the question of the character of rent or interest were raised. In addition, the intimate interlarding of economic motivations with these of a religious or artistic nature further complicates the analysis.

Nonetheless, however generalized and however difficult to disentangle from their cultural matrix, the basic elements of the apparatus to care for wants are present in every economy. We may conceive of the totality of economic systems as lying on a kind of continuum. At one pole we find the societies living closest to the subsistence level, with the exploitation of natural

[10] Raymond Firth (1939), 134 n.   [11] Goodfellow, 80.

resources slight, a slender endowment of technical knowledge, and implements few and simple. At the other end we place the great literate population aggregates, with their machine technologies, producing vast stores of goods and supporting a great variety of specialists to satisfy the wants of the people. Between these extremes lie the many societies having intermediate degrees of economic complexity and technical resource. As we move from the less to the more complex, the choices that are afforded between alternative possibilities become greater, the range of wants to be satisfied wider. But in every case choices must be made.

3

THE MECHANISMS of production represent only the initial steps in the total system whereby the goods and services that meet the needs of a people are made available to them. The apparatus that utilizes the resources at hand to care for wants must be linked with some mode of distributing what has been produced if the members of a group are to be able to make their choices among the goods and services that represent the alternative possibilities presented to them. And as with the mechanisms of production, the distributive system, though a universal in human social life, takes on a vast number of forms. These vary from the highly specialized and complex modes of distribution found in the pecuniary, mechanized societies of Europe and America to the generalized and diffuse forms found among small, isolated, nonliterate groups.

How rudimentary the distributive mechanism can be is realized when we consider those societies where the economic unit is the self-sufficient family. It has, indeed, been held that there could be no distributive mechanism present at all in such situations, since "logically . . . each household would provide for its own industrial wants. No products would be exchanged in such a society. Productive effort would be directed solely to the satisfaction of the wants of the household." [12] In terms of our discussion, this implies that the distributive element of these economies is simply omitted, and the middle term of the progression from

[12] Usher (1920), 4.

production through distribution to consumption falls out. In actuality, however, this never happens. An exchange of goods and services may not occur *between* households. Yet from the fact that no human society exists wherein at least the division of labor along sex lines is absent, it follows that within the smallest, most self-sufficient households some kind of exchange of services, and of the goods produced by these services, must be postulated. For there can be no division of labor without a resulting economic exchange. The universality of the fact of division of labor, even if only on sex lines, underscores the essential soundness of the reasoning which has made of exchange and distribution basic factors in all economic theory.

This is apparent, for example, when we consider the distribution system of the Lunga and other tribes of the Kimberly Division of Western Australia, who have this kind of family-band subsistence economy.

> The husband must from time to time give kangaroo to his wife's parents and brothers; besides this he always distributes a little among his blood relatives. Most of what the woman has obtained is consumed by herself, husband and children; if she has a little extra she takes some to her mother, sister, mother's mother, father, in fact to any close relative. She on another occasion receives similar offerings from them, and also meat from her male relatives, which she shares with her husband and children. These gifts are not compulsory as are her husband's to her people. They are dictated by tribal sentiment and her own affection for these individuals; by kinship system which finds concrete expression not only in attitudes and linguistic usage, but also in the exchange of the limited food resources and the material and ritual objects which are found in the community. Kinship as seen in Australia is practical altruism or enlightened self-interest.[13]

A somewhat analagous state of affairs is found among the cattle-keeping Swazi of South Africa, where "economically the family is the unit in production and consumption" and where, in pre-contact times, trade was non-existent.[14]

The simplicity of the distributive mechanism in societies such

[13] Kaberry, 33.   [14] Marwick, 43–4, 177–8.

as these, or as are to be found in the Amazon basin, stands in
sharp contrast to the manner in which goods are distributed to
the ultimate consumer in the industrialized societies of Europe
and America. Here the economic problem resolves itself into an
analysis of market operations which are so vast and which present
such a multiplicity of choice that they seem to differ in kind
rather than in degree when compared to the household economies of many nonliterate peoples.

From one point of view, indeed, the difference actually is one
of kind. In the simplest economic systems, no pecuniary factor
enters. What elementary types of exchanges of goods and services
occur are on the basis of an immediate, *ad hoc* kind of give and
take. Because of this, the problems raised in assessing the nature
and forms of exchanges, and the kinds of choices that are made,
take on a new and particular shape. The market is present in
such rudimentary form that it exists by definition only; no least
common denominator of value obtains; there is a face-to-face
relationship between producer and consumer.

We must not, however, lose sight of the intermediate societies,
such as those of Central America or West Africa, in stressing the
economies of the simplest sort. In these more complex systems,
where the market, distinguishable as such in its institutionalized
forms, and based on exchanges involving the use of pecuniary
media—money—is present, the complexity of the process that
marks the movement of goods and services to the ultimate consumer in industrial communities is almost entirely lacking. This
derives from the fact that even among nonliterate peoples, whose
economies are of this order of complexity, the individual controls
a substantial proportion of the techniques employed by his group
in the basic tasks of getting a living, in addition to whatever
specialized skills he may possess in the production of capital and
consumption goods. Here again, then, it follows that even in such
societies, as far as the necessities of life are concerned, distribution is in large measure a process of allocating what has been
produced by members of the household to those who constitute
its personnel. Such commercial transactions as do take place,
except among social aggregates large enough to permit a degree
of specialization rare in nonliterate societies, are again personal,
direct, and specific.

Moreover, to the extent that the market in such societies does possess an objective and formal existence, it is a mechanism that facilitates the exchange of goods between members of different communities rather than between those who belong in the same group. This proposition will be amply documented in later pages.[15] Here it need only be pointed out that where the degree of specialization in production is slight, no market-place is needed to effectuate whatever few exchanges of goods may be consummated. By far the greater number of cases of market operations we shall encounter will be those in which members of different villages or tribes exchange such commodities as each produces in excess of its own needs for such other goods as its members do not themselves manufacture.

In the absence of pecuniary mechanisms and the element of profit in the transactions of the market, it follows that the problem of the relation between supply and demand takes on unexpected turns. The West African woman trader who will not lower the price of the commodity she sells when business is dull —and this is an economy where values have for centuries been expressed in the quantitative terms of the prevalent form of money—presents a difficult enough problem. But where the total supply of commodities, even of subsistence goods, available to the members of a given society is severely limited, the question of fluctuations in value becomes pointless.

Economic theory, on the whole, is not geared to consider the problem of demand schedules where the alternatives are so restricted that there is no margin between utility and disutility— or to put it in other terms, where the choices are so few that no curve of indifference can be drawn between satisfactions and costs, where costs are always maximized, since individuals must work or starve. In situations such as these, the utility of any good recognized by the culture as having utility is maximized in its mere possession, where it is a tool; or in the very opportunity to consume it, if it is a commodity such as food. There is no inducement to trade it for something else, since there are no costs (disutilities) to be taken into account.

Thus food, to a South African Bushman or a native of Tierra del Fuego, who lives always in a state of potential hunger, is always of maximum value, since it is essential to the maintenance of life itself. And since there is little surplus of energy or

[15] See below, Ch. IX.

resources available for other activities than the food quest, it follows that whatever commodities, such as clothing, weapons, and the like are produced, likewise have constant maximum value and are not subject to exchanges essential to the existence of a market in any sense of the term. Differential utilities do enter, as, for example, where an Australian aborigine cannot kill an animal that has food value for him, despite his hunger, because of a system of totemic belief that taboos the animal. Here the disutility of the animal as food is matched by its utility as a supernatural and social agent. But in setting the standards of utility in such a case no distributive mechanism, no market factor, enters, and the utilities are of the all-or-none variety.

In the vastly greater number of non-machine societies, in which people are not pressed against the iron wall of subsistence needs, and the range of choice widens, the factor of differential utility is present. A hungry man may choose between fowl and game for his meal, or between yams and taro. A less hungry one may make his choice between work and leisure, food and effort. A person confronted with a problem beyond his means of solving may employ the services of a diviner or of a worker of magic. But even here the measurement of differential utilities in terms of price based on the fluctuations of the market in response to the factors of supply and demand may be discerned but dimly, if at all. In these societies the market is not free; it is a market in which "prices"—evaluations in whatever terms— are "administered" by custom.

It is not a question of which food is cheaper, and of balancing this against a desire for a change to taro after having eaten too many yams. Both foods, in all likelihood, will be equally available; they may well be perfect substitutes, as concerns effort required to grow them as well as concerns preference in taste. But money cost will be of no importance because it is not a factor. Or again, the decision where to seek advice will be made on the basis of entirely extra-pecuniary considerations—that is, without weighing costs against satisfactions. Our man may have lost faith in the skill of his diviner, or he may have decided that the situation calls for a magic charm rather than the intervention of the gods. Choice is thus dictated by differentials in utility; but the utility is not measured in terms of alternate costs (prices) by the one who makes the choice, and is not measurable in quantitative terms by the student.

We have again reached the point where we must take into account the fact that the economic institutions and mechanisms that are sharply differentiated in the machine societies become blurred and generalized in nonliterate cultures. There can, for example, be no question that the functioning of price mechanisms in the economic systems of Europe and America can be studied in the objective terms of economic theory, which has tellingly employed it as affording a precise measure of the choices made in the market by consumers. Its place in popular thinking likewise reflects its importance as an isolate in the economy. "No judgements are more closely associated with our daily living than judgements of price and the judgements of material values that underlie the structures of market prices," Usher has observed. "Because they are commonplaces of our living we are prone to think of them as simple and obvious, though they are no less complex than any other value judgements." [16]

But what of the price mechanism in societies where cost is but one of a number of considerations dictating economic behavior? Or where it does not figure at all? Where the producer is the consumer of the goods he produces or of the greater proportion of what he produces, where market dealings are determined by all kinds of non-economic factors? Here the problem of ascertaining why given choices are made and how the economic devices that help maximize satisfactions actually function calls for an attack that will take into account the cross-cultural variations in the nature of the data.

4

WE HAVE seen that the scarcity of goods in the face of the wants of a given people at a given time is a universal fact of human experience; that no economy has been discovered wherein enough goods are produced in enough variety to satisfy all the wants of all the members of any society. This is true whether the group is small or large, the mechanisms of its economic sys-

[16] Usher (1949), 146.

tem simple or complex. More important, it is true whether the society is undisturbed and the differences in its way of life from one generation to another slight, or whether it is in a state of dynamic change. The dissimilarities between any society and any other in these respects is one of degree and not of kind. The general principle, therefore, stands, despite the many changes that are rung on the basic theme manifested in the particular forms it assumes in functioning economies.

It can also be taken as cross-culturally acceptable that, on the whole, the individual tends to maximize his satisfactions in terms of the choices he makes. Where the gap between utility and disutility is appreciable, and the producer or consumer of a good or service is free to make his choice, then, other things being equal, he will make his choice in terms of utility rather than disutility. One need not accept the hedonism of classical economics to recognize the validity, on broad lines, of the proposition, at least in the terms in which we have phrased it here.

Yet it should be apparent that the two basic postulates of economic science—the allocation of scarce resources among alternative ends and the conscious determination of the choices made in maximizing satisfactions—are not of the same order. The first is a statement of fact that can be objectively verified. In pecuniary, machine economies this can be done by means of price analysis which shows how the market responds to scarcities or overproduction of given commodities. In non-pecuniary, non-machine, and nonliterate societies we can have recourse to ethnographic descriptions of the range of goods produced by a people and record the choices that are actually reached. The empirical nature of analyses that press the point further, inquiring into the kind of resources a people can draw on, and how they are utilized in producing ultimate consumption goods, is likewise apparent. The forms taken by competitive striving for a good in short supply, if competitive patterns are present, and the degree to which this striving stimulates to further production, can also be objectively described. We can determine whether bidding will be in terms of prestige or price. We can ascertain whether a failure to increase supply is due to lack of ultimate resources, or to non-economic causes of a social or religious order. Or, where the response to increased demand is increase in supply, we can find out how this increase has occurred and, given time and resources for adequate investigation of the problem, the extent to which the supply has increased.

The second proposition, however, lies in the realm of values, not only in the technical sense of economic science, but in the broader philosophical connotation of those ultimate sanctions to behavior that give meaning to life. It is possible to bring objective proof, that is, as to *what* men do in the way of economizing; the question *why* they do it rests on subjective and cultural factors. It is significant that so much of that aspect of economic theory that bears on this latter point derives from assumptions of a psychological nature. It is more than a figure of speech when economists speak of "rationalizing" production or distribution. The usage derives logically and semantically from the prominence traditionally given the view that man, in his economic behavior, acts rationally.

The earlier concept of Economic Man, the most extreme expression of this position, has long since been given over by economists, together with any conclusions that may have been drawn concerning the relevance of this concept as indicative of Human Nature in the large. The influence of the earlier economic historians was important in bringing about this changed point of view. They indicated the need to take time and place into full account if the economies of earlier periods of western European society were to be understood. The process of refining the conception of the role of rational choice has continued, with stress being laid on non-economic choices to be made in "the business of living," or by successively eliminating more and more variables in drawing assumptions so that the choices to be made rationally are restricted not only as to time and place but to the economic as against other aspects of living, as well.

We may take as an example the case of the Kwakiutl of the Northwest Coast of North America, whose economy has been the subject of much study, earlier in terms of its dramatic prestige give-away rituals termed potlatches, and in later years concerning the productive and social system that made this institution possible. As a result of these investigations, an inner dynamic of considerable significance for the point under discussion has been revealed. Codere has phrased the matter in these terms: "In what might be called their 'economic life' the Kwakiutl are virtuoso technicians and extravagant producers and storers. It

is in their 'social life' that they 'economize'." In this society, that
is, a basic aim was the attainment and maintenance of position,
to be achieved only through the expenditure of valuable goods.
As will be seen in a later chapter,[17] this was carried on by certain financial mechanisms—investment, credit, and the payment
of interest, which, as it is phrased, "maximized the potlatch."
The underlying drive in this complex system, therefore, "is to
be found in the relation of the arbitrarily determined scarcity of
potlatch positions to the superabundance of some economic
goods." [18]

The factor of rational choice, even when its applicability is
narrowed, still remains as an element in the basic postulates of
economic science. Price movements may theoretically be predicted without reference to the behavior of individuals on the
basis of fluctuations of supply and demand in an assumed economic universe involving perfect competition, or where it is
assumed that competition is not perfect, and monopolistic factors enter. Yet underlying the argument is the human factor.
Thus Boulding, in explaining "the method of economic analysis,"
states that it begins "with very simple assumptions concerning
human behavior." He goes on "to discover what consequences
would follow for the economic system as a whole if these assumptions were true" before bringing these findings "into closer
relation to real life by introducing qualifications of our original
assumptions and seeing how they affect the picture as we see
it." [19] In other words, it is the individual, the ultimate producer
and consumer, who is the prime economic mover. His mode of
rationally choosing the economically more advantageous alternatives, expressed in price, is considered so fundamental that it
is often not even verbalized, to say nothing of being questioned.[20]

From the cross-cultural point of view, however, it is this assumption that is at the crux of the analysis, no matter how quali-
fied or restricted it may be. For the economic anthropologist

[17] See below, 226.
[18] Codere, 68.
[19] Boulding, 15.
[20] Cf., for example (512 below),
Knight's statement concerning the
categories to be distinguished in the
"interpretative aspect of social phenomena." Here, introducing his final
two categories, he writes: "But what
is finally, or almost uniquely, distinctive of human phenomena is the
aspect of conscious purpose, or rationality."

deals with the total range of human societies. Many of the questions he must ask thus arise from the fact that the economies with which he deals present a vastly greater range of differences than the earlier systems of western Europe and the Mediterranean, which themselves had enough of a special quality to cause the economic historians to raise comparable questions concerning early statements of the universality of economic mechanisms.

It is essential at this point to consider the problem of rationality in the light of our knowledge of the psychology of culture. The concept of culture, it will be remembered, includes all phases of the learned, traditionally sanctioned behavior of human beings. These phases are conceived as aspects of culture, which are universals in the ways of life of all human groups—technology, economics, social organization, political structures, religious beliefs and institutions, language, art, music, and literary modes of expression being the broadest categories. These universal aspects, in their institutionalized forms, are different in all of the many different societies found over the earth. Yet each of these *forms* represents the working out, in terms of its own particular historical stream, of universal *processes* of cultural dynamics which have brought about the results to be observed in the life of any given people at any given point in time. Thus, for example, we may say that the process of interchange of cultural items between two peoples will result from contact between them; but what forms will be taken over in a given case—whether material or non-material elements, for example—will depend on the nature of the contacts, the varied emphases laid by the two bodies of traditions concerned, and the like. It follows that since the economic aspect of a given culture is but a part of the total range of culture, any valid principles that apply to the whole must likewise apply to any part of the whole.

From the psychological point of view, culture is behavior in the broadest sense of the term—overt acts and their implicit sanctions. The mechanism that gives stability to a culture is the learning-conditioning process. An infant is born into a society that is a going concern. In his education, he is conditioned to behave, within the limits of variation sanctioned by his group, like the other members of his society. This process is called *en-*

culturation. Not only motor habits, but also modes of conceptualizing and evaluating are learned—and learned so thoroughly that, for the most part, they are taken for granted, and seem to the enculturated individual to be as immutable as the contours of his physical environment. Later in life, through the process of invention or because of contact with other peoples, reenculturation may occur. But basic motor-habits and, above all, value-systems and other sanctions are extremely tenacious, and are modified slowly, if at all.[21] More than this, these value-systems and other sanctions are taken for granted and form the basis for judgments of all sorts.

The pertinence of this last fact for an understanding of the nature of rational behavior is at once apparent. We may accept the findings of psychology concerning the role of emotions and other non-cognitive mechanisms in influencing behavior. In addition to these mechanisms, however, we find in the enculturative process a further qualifying element—the patterns of thought that are laid down in accordance with the value-systems of the group to which the individual belongs. The question of rationality, then, at once poses itself: rational in terms of what system of thought and behavior?

Granting the force of the enculturative conditioning, it is apparent that this forms the principal basis for judgment, for choice, for rational behavior in any given situation where alternatives are presented. In the light of the principle that the *process,* though universal, may manifest itself in different *forms,* we can understand why peoples hold so stubbornly to their own value-judgments. This brings us to *cultural relativism,* which stresses the validity of the most diverse kinds of value-systems for the peoples who live in accord with them. It derives from the following proposition in cultural psychology: "Judgments are based on experience, and experience is interpreted by each individual in terms of his own enculturation."[22] Its documentation is vast, and derives principally from much research that has established the devotion of every people to their own way of life, and the extent to which the malfunctioning of culture can be ascribed to a break-down in the value-systems of a people.

[21] Cf. Herskovits (1948), 17–42, for a more extended discussion of this phenomenon.

[22] Herskovits, op. cit., 63; see pp. 61–78 for an elaboration of the implications of this proposition.

The principle of relativism is nothing new. In economics, it has been present for many years, though its voice was never strong and has become stilled with the passage of time. The elder Keynes, in his classical work on the nature and method of economics, turns continually to the problem. The major presentation of relativism is to be found in a section entitled, significantly, "On the Limits of the Validity of Economic Doctrines," though various passages elsewhere are devoted to considering the "relativity of economic definitions." [23] "It is as true of economic conditions, as of social conditions in general," he says, "that they are ever subject to modification. They vary with the legal form of society, and with national character and institutions." [24]

He likewise points out how the earlier German economic historians combatted the principle of the "absolutism of theory." His analysis, in terms of "abstract" and "concrete" economics, recalls the point just made concerning the differences between process and form. He does not in any sense cede the importance of what he terms "abstract analysis"; he quite properly stresses the need to ascertain the underlying least common denominators, and then to discover how they manifest themselves in differing concrete situations. But the "inferences which possess the character of universality"—the processes assumed to occur—are to be understood through the study of the varying forms they take.[25]

This relativistic approach to the comparative study of economic behavior and institutions provides the epistemological foundation essential if the differences between different ways of life are not to be analyzed and assessed in terms of principles that derive from a single culture—in this case, our own. The point of view this latter engenders is called enthnocentrism, the roots of which, in Euroamerican cultures, will be considered in the next chapter. Here it need merely be pointed out that this

---

[23] J. N. Keynes, 293–307; see also p. 15, n. 1; p. 64; pp. 163–7.

[24] Ibid., 295.

[25] It is not without significance, in this connection, that almost the only economist who has attempted to systematize a comparative, cross-cultural approach to economics has been R. Mukerjee, the relativism of whose point of view is made explicit in Ch. XV of his work. It may, at this point, also be indicated that the phrase "comparative economics," which he attempted to study in broad terms of reference, in the terminology of economics is restricted to the comparative analysis of the economic systems of free enterprise, communism, and fascism.

is a habit of thought that must be guarded against if understanding of any modes of behavior and value-systems other than those of one's own group is to be attained.

The principle of maximizing satisfactions by the conscious exercise of choice between scarce means is valid because we find that this does occur in all societies. The cross-cultural perspective, however, gives us pause when defining "rationality."[26] We are tempted to consider as rational the behavior that represents only the typical reactions to be expected of those who order their lives in terms of the economic systems of Europe and America, where it is rational to defer the gratification of wants, to accumulate resources, to produce more goods and multiply services. Yet, as we shall abundantly see, there are many cultures, if not a majority of them, where the deferment of wants is held to be disadvantageous, where best judgment dictates that resources be expended, where there is no tradition of expanding production and increasing services. None the less, in societies having traditions of this sort, choices are not only made, but debated. It will be our task in the pages that follow, then, to discern the economic universals in human society by sampling the many forms in which they are manifest.

[26] This is implicit in a discussion of the subject by Diesing (16–23), though the question of economic relativism as regards the nature of economic rationality is not taken up as such. Yet it should be noted that in discussing the normative aspects of economic behavior, he distinguishes, as one of these, "norms of property, manners, or taste, which appear to the individual in exemplary actions and the approval or disapproval of other people."

CHAPTER II

BEFORE THE MACHINE

THOUGH man has inhabited the earth for more than half a million years, the invention of the steam engine, which introduced the machine age, occurred less than two hundred years ago. In this mere instant, as the life of the human race is counted, the machine has come to hold a place of such importance in present-day America and Europe that it is not easy for us to imagine a machineless existence.

Yet for much of mankind the machine holds little significance. Even in America and in Europe, where the influence of a mechanized technology invades all phases of life, quiet backwaters still exist where farming folk or village communities live lives relatively little touched by the machine. More important are the untold millions who today follow patterns of life almost entirely different from those by which we order our lives and who, in the Americas, the South Seas, Australia, Asia, and Africa meet their needs without the use of any of those complex mechanical aids we hold essential.

The term "primitive" has been applied to most of these folk. Because with but few exceptions, they have developed no written language, the word thus became synonymous with "nonhistoric" or "nonliterate." These terms, however, are actually to be preferred because they do not carry the connotations of inferiority, simplicity, and lack of sophistication that have come to cluster about the word "primitive," and thus to obscure its meaning. Such large differences are, indeed, to be found among nonliterate societies that to characterize them in any general manner is exceedingly difficult. Every institution shows a tremendously wide range of variation in its "primitive" manifestations. It has therefore become a truism that there is no generic difference between "primitive" societies and literate ones, but that, the world over, all cultures represent specialized local developments which have come into being as a result of the unique historical developments that, as was pointed out in the preceding chapter, mark the past of each of them.

This being the case, we may find it worth while to sketch the characteristics of the nonliterate societies that justify us in marking them off for special study. We will, in particular, consider those traits that will occupy us in contrasting and comparing their economics with those of the literate, machine cultures.

At the outset, we are struck by the differences in population size between "primitive" and literate groups. This is true not only where density is concerned, but in the numbers of those who make up the self-conscious social entities which we variously designate as "band" or "tribe" or "kingdom." Another difference between nonliterate and literate folk lies in the respective degree of contact they have with the outside world. In supplying their wants, what the nonliterate tribesman could obtain "was usually near at hand," as it has been put. On the other hand, "the whole world . . . contributes to our needs. A complicated business organization makes this possible, one that stands out in marked contrast to the simple system" of these folk.[1] Even in pre-machine days in Europe, or in the non-machine but literate cultures of Asia, the range of communication and the consequent breadth of horizon of these peoples were and are in general greater than those of an African or a North American Indian tribe, or even, for all their voyaging, of the inhabitants of the Polynesian islands. Literate societies, as we have seen, also manifest a greater degree of specialization of labor, a greater emphasis on the market and on a standard medium of exchange —money—as an expression of value to facilitate market operations, and a resultant greater economic complexity than do nonliterate communities.[2]

The machine, however, most highly developed in the cultures of North America and Europe, has been the outstanding factor in accentuating all those characteristics of an economic order that have been mentioned as distinguishing the lives of literate from nonliterate peoples. The implications of the machine for

[1] Gras (1922), 3–4.   [2] Cf. Bruijnis, 4 ff.

human society are therefore greatest in these cultures, and it is between these machine cultures and all others, especially the nonliterate ones, that the differences are widest. That is why, at the outset, the role of the machine must be emphasized as a factor in differentiating their life from ours.

2

IN CONSIDERING the influence of the machine in our lives, we must constantly bear in mind the effect the technological perfections that have gone with its development, the greater degree of productivity these have permitted, and the changes they have wrought in the economic sphere have had on some of the more important currents of thought of our day. Especially important is the fact that the achievements of the machine are objectively demonstrable, from which it follows that technological and economic gains can most readily be used when evaluating different cultures. The mechanistic philosophy of our day, when raised in the field of method to a tradition of objective observation, is readily contrasted with the mystical elements in the technology and economic order of nonliterate societies.

This is one of the principal reasons why the identification of the word "primitive" with the concept "lower" as regards social development—or its converse, the use of "civilized" in the sense of something "higher"—has been so convincing and, as expressed in the term "progress," has come to lodge so deeply in our everyday manner of thought. Here is the apparent documentation of the ethnocentrism that makes the appreciation of the values of other cultures than our own so difficult. Descriptions of our technological achievement and the multiple interrelations of our economic organization can seemingly be employed to demonstrate the more complex nature of our culture as compared with the cultures of all other peoples, especially of nonliterate folk. That such a demonstration has had so great an appeal and has been so difficult to dislodge from the popular mind is not strange. It was such an assumption that gave the attempts to establish an evolutionary sequence for human civilizations their greatest psychological force. For from this point of view—but this point of view only—the Australians could be regarded beyond question as a simpler people than the Africans; or the Africans could be demonstrably shown to be on a lower level of culture than the great aggregates that peopled Central America, Mexico, and Peru at the time of the discovery of America; or these latter, in turn, could without fear of contradiction be held less highly developed than ourselves.

In the same way, the concept of progress, so deeply rooted in our habits of thought, has derived its most important sanctions from demonstrations in the field of technology and economics. That a man, working with a machine, can produce more in given units of time with a given expenditure of energy than when working by hand, is not difficult to prove. It is not so easy, however, to show that one set of religious beliefs is more adequate than another, or one type of family organization more effective than the next. Here the validation of judgment must derive from assumptions that lie quite outside objective proof. Even in the economic and technological spheres the argument couched in terms of relative powers of productivity is by no means self-evident when the ultimate ends toward which such activities are directed —as against the values that guide day-to-day living—come to be analyzed. In all societies, that is, the technological and economic order must at least be efficient enough to permit survival. Granting this, we know enough about the psychology of culture to understand that the satisfaction of human wants is by no means dependent upon an abundance of goods. Increased efficiency in production is likewise not necessarily accompanied by a corresponding efficiency in achieving an effective distribution of what the technological system is capable of producing.

It is not alone in evaluating societies as a whole that the machine has shaped our thought. Certain concepts respecting the psychology of nonliterate peoples have been influenced by that phase of our culture which is to be broadly included under the term "science." The scientific tradition, and the nature of the problems with which scientists deal, require that every effort be made to reason from cause to effect, to work under conditions of rigid control, eliminating extraneous factors that might influence the result of any given experiment. It is not generally understood, however, that this technique, which marks scientific thinking, is by no means characteristic of the reasoning of most persons in our society, nor even of scientists in their everyday life. Yet despite this, these particular modes of thought have given rise to a concept which maintains that our ways of thinking differ from those of "primitive" peoples, who are held to be prelogical.[3] Without a tradition of reasoning from cause to effect, they are held to be enmeshed in a body of "collective representations," in which the mechanical relationship between effectuating forces and their objective results is lost in a maze of mystic associations. Life is thus lived in a world where reality, as we know it, constitutes but a portion of valid experience.

We need here do no more than enter a demurrer to this position, for many refutations of it have been written out of the first-hand experience of those who have studied nonliterate societies.[4] The significant thing for us is to realize how a mode of thought, closely associated with the basic technological processes of our culture, can be rationalized as a habit of thinking presumably followed by all those who live in this machine society, as against the habits of all who do not.

Another instance of how pervasive the indirect influence of the machine has been may be introduced here, though some of its implications for our subject will be treated at length in later pages.[5] This concerns the theory of economic determinism. The increased productivity of our technology and the accompanying complexity of economic organization has resulted in a corresponding increase in the interdependence of individuals and communities. But it was just when the industrial revolution was at its height, and the economic problems presented by it had attained an order of difficulty perhaps never before experienced, that this theory in its present form, was developed. It seems, therefore, that there might well be a discernible relationship between a point of view that holds economic phenomena to be basic in shaping other aspects of life and the historical setting of the period during which this concept was developed.

There can be little doubt that economic factors do play an important role in influencing non-economic aspects of culture; but this merely recognizes the fact that all phases of life are closely interrelated and, because of this, tend to modify each

[3] L. Lévy-Bruhl (1923), is the work which has most influenced thought along these lines. Though its author, before his death, greatly modified his original position, the point of view is still widely held by many writers who are not anthropologists.

[4] Driberg (1929), *passim.*

[5] See below, 488–96.

other. In these terms, ours is by no means the only culture where economic factors are preponderant in influencing the other facets of culture. Yet it does remain an historic fact that it was only among a people—ourselves—whose economy had become more complex than any before experienced by man, and at a time when the problems presented by the economic order were becoming most serious, that this theory made its appearance.

We must, then, be on our guard against a position that fails to take due account of modes of life other than our own, or which disregards directive forces other than those that to us appear to be of the first magnitude. Above all, we must guard against thinking of all the cultures of nonliterate peoples as one undifferentiated mass, to be contrasted with our own particular body of traditions. These reservations must be kept in mind in recognizing that the machine has made it possible for us to live in an order of society which, in its economic aspects, is to be set apart from all others because of its complexity. Only with these reservations can we achieve a workable basis for the analysis of the problems to be considered in this book. We may, therefore, in these terms, proceed to sketch the more outstanding of these distinctions. For though, in most instances, they will be found to comprise differences of degree rather than of kind, we must analyze them so that we will not lose sight of them as we later describe and seek to understand the economic processes employed by nonliterate communities.

3

THE RELATIONSHIP between the machine technology and the pecuniary organization of our economy has by no means been made clear. Yet it is apparent that this relationship has given rise to certain special kinds of economic phenomena, such as the business cycle, and the periodic unemployment that has followed on technological advances. These phenomena are the direct result of the increased productivity of the machine, coupled with a system whereby the sale of goods for profit as a technique for amassing wealth has become an end rather than a means in life. This entire complex operates so as to deprive many persons of an opportunity to obtain the basic necessities of living, no matter how willing they may be to work or how able.

Such conditions are unknown to nonliterate man. These smaller groups may live on a level but little removed from subsistence needs, where the margin between starvation and survival is slight. Yet even in such societies, the individual who, as an individual, is reduced to such straits that he must either depend on some agency set up for the purpose of preventing his giving way before the harsh dicta of the economic system, or starve, is rarely, if ever, encountered. In societies existing on the subsistence margin, rather, it is generally the rule that when there is not enough, all hunger alike; when there is plenty, all participate.

This does not mean that in cultures where the margin of available goods is greater than in those existing on such a low economic plane, an equal distribution of available resources exists. Practically all societies where life is lived on more than a subsistence level know the concepts of rich and poor, of leader and follower. But even in societies with relatively complex economies, such as those of West Africa and Melanesia, where buying to sell at a profit is of some importance and the hiring of labor is not unknown, the phenomena of the business cycle, of technological unemployment, and of malnutrition resulting from an inability to obtain the necessities of life are not found. Thus, for example, clan solidarity among the East African Baganda assured that "real poverty did not exist"; furthermore, "no one ever went hungry . . . because everyone was welcome to go and sit down and share a meal with his equals." [6] Again, the labor market, though by no means entirely absent among nonliterate groups, never attains a place comparable to that which it holds in our own economic order.

Among nonliterate folk we encounter conditions in many respects analogous to the economic system of the Middle Ages and before. As in pre-machine-age Europe, the laborer is almost invariably the owner of the means of production and to that extent is the master of his own economic destiny. That is, capitalism, as we have come to know it since the advent of power machinery, is foreign to non-machine economies. Capital goods may be concentrated in the hands of individual members of cer-

[6] Roscoe, 12.

tain communities of this type, but this merely signifies that the difference between these systems and our machine economy is one of degree rather than of kind. In nonliterate societies, we do find men who control the labor of others, whether completely, as under the institution of slavery, or for limited periods of time, under forms of employment for wages. We can even encounter, in Samoa, something akin to an organized body of workers who do not hesitate to interrupt their labor where this is necessary to enforce their demands, or even to indulge in sabotage. But the demands to be enforced are demands of prestige and not of livelihood, for among these workers there is no one to whom the return for his labor is essential to his existence.[7]

Another outstanding difference between machine and non-machine cultures is found in their degree of specialization. In the latter, as has been noted, almost every person controls all the techniques essential for his own support and for the support of those dependent upon him. Even the man who excels in building a canoe, or hunting game, or weaving, or iron-working will, with the aid of members of his family, also carry on agriculture or tend the herds, and he can, when necessary, build a house and fashion household utensils, or make the clothing that habitat and tradition dictate as necessities. Similarly, though some women may be better potters than others, or may excel in basketry or in some other occupation, yet all women will know how to do the household tasks and other kinds of work that are allotted to women under the prevalent patterns of labor. Conversely, it is rare, even where individuals surpass in certain skills, that these skills are restricted to them alone.

Thus, among the Ifugao of the Philippines,

> Division of labor is not carried further than a mere beginning. Some men are highly skilled blacksmiths. Nearly all know something about blacksmithing. Some are highly skilled wood carvers, but nearly all are wood carvers for all that. Almost the only division of labor is between men and women.[8]

In Samoa,

> The division of labor which is of importance to the mere physical well being of the people is the division of labor

<hr>

[7] Hiroa (1930), 414–16.   [8] Barton (1922), 423.

along sex lines. Every man knows how to build a small house, how to hew out a rough canoe, how to make a coconut cup, or carve a rough food bowl. The carpenters and makers of sennit lashings are essentially specialists, called in for important occasions. But upon the balance of men and women workers within the household, and upon their skill in the usual tasks in which every adult is supposed to be proficient, depends the prosperity of the household.[9]

Among the Hopi of Arizona,

> Common wants and desires, fairly standardized, simple and easily satisfied, require no diverse specialization to satisfy them. . . . It is evident that division of labor is primarily conventional, based on sex secondarily and more indefinitely on age.[10]

In Haiti,

> The life of the Haitian farmer, though hard, is simple and self-contained. With but few exceptions, he supplies all his necessities, for he commands almost the entire range of techniques known to his culture; hence Haitian economy shows a lack of specialization that in the main is only relieved by the sex division of labor.[11]

The Maori, we learn, employed

> . . . no very intricate division of labour, such as occurs in the highly complex social structure of the 'civilized' community. The fairly simple character of economic wants did not necessitate any great diversity of occupations to satisfy them, and every man was able to master something more than the rudiments of the principal crafts. Entire absorption of the working powers of the individual in one industry, or in a single process of an industry, was rare, if not unknown. At the same time division of labour on a limited scale, both as regards separation of employments and of processes, was not absent.[12]

Or, in Dahomey, a non-machine economy outstanding for its complexity, and where craft specialization is marked, "no mat-

[9] Mead (1930a), 66.   [11] Herskovits (1937), 67.
[10] Beaglehole (1937), 18.   [12] Raymond Firth (1929), 193–4.

ter what the rank of a Dahomean or what his trade, he must know how to cultivate the soil, and he will have his fields." [13]

We must recognize that all men and women in non-machine societies can control the techniques essential for obtaining a living, and, where there are specialized crafts, that the craftsmen are never dependent for their livelihood solely upon what they produce. These are sufficiently striking differences between nonliterate economies and our own. Even more striking, however, are the implications of the fact that among nonliterate peoples the extreme forms of specialization known to us, where the worker must restrict his activities to minor operations in the entire production process, is but rarely encountered. Specialization within one industry does occur in non-machine societies, as where an individual will be expert at making one special part of a canoe. But, again, almost without exception, such a worker is found to be a full-fledged member of a larger co-operative work group, and psychologically has no difficulty in identifying himself with the finished product.

The subject of industrial psychology is important in making effective the human resources needed for the kind of mass production that has been developed in our society, since the degree of specialization characteristic of the organization of our larger industries has given rise to serious problems of individual adjustment. A man who for hours on end tightens a bolt on the engine of an automobile which he will probably never see, and with which he can in no way identify himself, or who, in a packing house, makes the same cut on each of an endless procession of carcasses as they pass before him, is deprived of something that is deeply rooted in the human psyche.

It is not necessary to do more than indicate this to cause us to see why questions of this sort have been found so urgent a subject for study. Veblen put it as follows:

> The share of the operative workman in the machine industry is (typically) that of an attendant, an assistant, whose duty is to keep pace with the machine process and to help out with workmanlike manipulation at points where the machine engaged is incomplete. His work supplements the machine process, rather than makes use of it. On the contrary the machine process makes use of the workman. [14]

[13] Herskovits (1932), 266.   [14] Veblen (1918), 306–07.

In the unconscious processes of identification an infinite satisfaction is achieved if, at the end of a day or a week or a year, a worker can point to something of which he may be proud, of which he is the maker or in the making of which he has participated, and in which he retains a sense of creativeness. But this is precisely what cannot be achieved by the majority of those employed in the specialized occupations of an industrial society.

Sapir, in developing his idea of "what kind of a good thing culture is," felt that this factor of specialization was so important that it could be used as a criterion to divide cultures into those which are "genuine" and those which are "spurious":

> The great cultural fallacy of industrialism, as developed up to the present time, is that in harnessing machines to our uses it has not known how to avoid the harnessing of the majority of mankind to its machines. The telephone girl who lends her capacities, during the greater part of the living day, to the manipulation of a technical routine that has an eventually high efficiency value but that answers to no spiritual needs of her own is an appalling sacrifice to civilization. . . . The American Indian who solves the economic problem with salmon-spear and rabbit-snare operates on a relatively low level. . . , but he represents an incomparably higher solution than our telephone girl of the questions that culture has to ask of economics.[15]

We need not set up a system of comparative values in modes of living, however, to recognize that in terms of achieving a rounded life, the patterns of production in non-machine societies afford far more satisfactions to one engaged in the industrial process than in a machine society. No more apt illustration of this point could be had than in the following description of the manner of work of the Andamanese and of the drives that underlie their efforts:

> In the manufacture of their weapons, utensils, and other articles, they . . . spend . . . hour after hour in laboriously striking pieces of iron with a stone hammer for the purpose of forming spear or arrowheads, or in improving the shape of a bow, etc., even though there be no necessity, immediate

[15] Sapir, 308, 316.

or prospective, to stimulate them to such efforts. The incentive is evidently a spirit of emulation, each one priding himself on being able to produce work which will excel, or at least compare not unfavourably with, that of his neighbors.[16]

This may likewise be seen in the choices of occupation made by certain native peoples who are in contact with the world economic system. Thus, of the Malay fishermen of Kelantan, it is stated:

Popular opinion is apt to regard the Malay, in contrast to the Indian and Chinese who share his native land, as lazy, improvident, and lacking in foresight or ability to work hard and to save. . . . Because a Malay refuses to do long and monotonous work on rubber plantations away from his family, under conditions which Chinese and Indians willingly accept for the sake of the wages, it is assumed that he is lazy. No one who has seen the long, often cold, exhausting and disappointing labour of fishermen on the east coast would doubt that the Malay is capable of sustained, skilful and energetic labour. But he needs to have interest in his work, a factor which modern industrial organization has subjugated to the desire for a higher standard of living.[17]

Certainly the resources an individual in a non-machine society brings to his task must be greater and more varied, in terms of productive activity, than when he carries on the intense specialization demanded of him in a machine technology. What in the field of art has been termed the drive toward virtuosity can be given full play where every step in a process is in the hands of the producer, from the gathering of the raw materials to the finished product that may be admired by the worker's fellows.

Yet another distinction between machine and non-machine societies lies in the development of the tradition of business enterprise, as we know it. As will be shown in later pages, practically no present-day human group is entirely self-supporting, and there is good reason to believe that trade existed in quite early prehistoric times. Where tribal specialization has followed on the localization of natural resources, the needs of a people for

[16] Man, 26.   [17] Rosemary Firth, 113.

those goods they cannot produce because of a lack of essential raw materials cause them to trade for what they desire, and much of their own productive activity is devoted to the making of their own specialty for this same market. A comparable phenomenon is found within certain tribal economies, as where the makers of iron objects, to the degree that they devote their time to this work, must exchange their products for such food, utensils, or non-utilitarian objects as they need or desire if they are to have them. In a number of nonliterate societies where trading is a recognized occupation, and where, as in West Africa, trade is carried on by the use of money rather than by barter, buying in order to sell at a profit, or manufacture of goods primarily for disposal in the market, is well known. We shall also encounter cultures in Melanesia, in East Africa, and in North and South America where the trader as middleman plays an important part in the circulation of commodities from tribe to tribe. But the role which these aspects of trade play in the economic life of such peoples does not have an importance comparable in any way to that held by business in our own economy.

Though in non-industrial societies sparring between traders for advantage does, of course, mark their operations, sometimes even this seems to be absent where values in terms of goods exchanged by direct barter are fixed by traditional usage. Nonetheless, among nonliterate groups the conduct of business transactions has nothing of the impersonal quality that has come to be an outstanding characteristic of our economic system. It is well known that where a non-European has to deal with a European in a matter involving trade, both parties to the transaction are often subject to no little irritation because of differing traditions of trading. Among many who live in non-machine societies, sparring for advantage in the exchange of goods is something of a pleasurable contest of wits.

Nonliterate societies also differ from our own in the relative stress they lay on pecuniary standards of evaluation. Among ourselves, these standards assume such importance that values in terms of money not only dictate our economic judgments, but tend to invade evaluations of all other phases of our culture as well. This has brought it about that money, by and of itself, has come to have a place quite aside from its function as the least common denominator of the market-place. As a matter of fact, it is not easy for us to think of ends that are not expressed as monetary values, even though they concern art or religion or family relations. That we use phrases such as "to have a heart of gold," or to "give a gilt-edged promise," means only that our linguistic usage, like that of all peoples, reflects our standard of values—not as this standard may operate in an economic sense, but as the phrase is applied to moral and personal judgments of the broadest sort.

Now this kind of evaluation is a rarity in nonliterate societies. It is found, notably in Melanesia and in northwestern North America, where outward emblems of wealth are psychologically as important as among ourselves. Yet, in general, there are many more of these groupings where goods, to say nothing of people, are not to be bought at a price, than where the opposite is true. Many instances have been recorded where objects desired by a purchaser have been refused him in the face of fabulous offers— fabulous, that is, in terms of the values set by the people among whom the owner of the desired object lived. It is more revealing of our own psychology than that of those against whom the charge of economic irresponsibility has been laid that the basis of this charge, so often repeated in the accounts of contacts between natives and Europeans, is that these peoples are prone to accept trifles, such as beads, in recompense for objects which we hold to have the highest value, such as golden ornaments or precious stones. In reality, this merely means that in such cases the standards of value brought into play differ from our own.

One of the most widely spread traits of human beings, manifest under the most diverse types of social order, is the desire for prestige. As we shall see, there is an intimate relationship between prestige and the control of economic resources in most societies living above a subsistence level. The degree to which those who live under the regime of the machine are dependent upon others for almost every necessity of life, whether material or psychological, and the extent to which it has become necessary to translate experience into terms of those monetary units on which we are so dependent for the goods and services we find essential or desirable, demonstrate the economic consequence of extreme specialization. Here we see money assuming an importance out of all proportion to its manifestation in other cultures or at other times.

It is a commonplace that Europe of the Middle Ages stressed other-worldliness in evaluating its satisfactions and directives. This, however, is merely one way of recalling to ourselves that prestige and the resultant power associated with it can and, in most societies, is to be gained through excellence in other fields than the accumulation of wealth, that the rewards for outstanding accomplishment can be conceived in terms other than those of money.

All caution must understandably be exercised in making statements such as these. In some nonliterate groups, especially where a money economy prevails, motivations quite similar to those found in any community living under a machine technology are not lacking. On the other hand, we must not forget that many persons in our culture are not dominated by the pecuniary ideal to anything like the extent of the majority. However, granting the existence of exceptions both in nonliterate societies and our own, the broad differences in the patterned attitudes toward money in machine and non-machine cultures must be recognized.

4

A FINAL distinction between machine and non-machine societies has to do with the utilization of economic resources for the support of non-subsistence activities. Because of greater powers of production, the goods available under a machine technology to release man-power from direct concern with the tasks of producing the necessities of life are more numerous among ourselves than in any other society. The conversion of these resources into what is to be termed social leisure is of the highest importance for the understanding of many aspects of the organization of human societies, wherever they are found and whatever their complexity. As such, this point will be given extended treatment in a later chapter.[18] Here we will consider only that phase of the development of a mechanistic approach to life that accompanied the advent and growth of a machine technology, which finds its most characteristic expression in the scientific tradition.

From the beginning of the industrial revolution, the amount of economic resources devoted to the support of the scientific in-

[18] See below, 395–415.

vestigation of the world in which we live has become ever larger. This in turn has so helped to increase the efficiency of the processes of production that much more consumption and capital goods have been available than ever before. But the relationship is a reciprocal one, which has released an ever increasing measure of social leisure; and this, in turn, has permitted the investigation of a constantly wider range of problems.

Science, of course, did not begin with the machine age, as is apparent when we consider the history of physics and mathematics. Medicine, one of the scientific disciplines that has most flowered in our culture, also has a history that long antedates the coming of the machine. Those whose task it is to care for human life and assuage human suffering, whether as practitioners of scientific medicine or as magic healers, are in all societies held to be worthy of support out of the subsistence goods produced by those who are always potentially, at least, in need of them. As regards science in general, however, since there was more to consume, more social leisure has been available since the advent of the machine age to release scientists for the pursuit of their investigations. The increased efficiency of the productive processes that have resulted from the application of discoveries in the fields of the exact and mechanical sciences to industry is striking. In such matters as housing and all its related conveniences, or quantity and variety of foods, or aids to health and the prolongation of the life-span, or the wider recreational facilities and opportunities for a broader outlook on the world, the resources of machine societies are not to be compared with those where the technology does not permit an equivalent production of material goods.

There is no intention to suggest in what has just been set forth that the machine technology, by and of itself, causes the societies in which it develops to live under optimum conditions, any more than there is of indicating that the societies in which man lived or lives in what is sometimes termed a state of nature—in nonmachine cultures, that is—represent a golden age.

What is meant is that the more admirable developments of science and the multiplication of resources, like those less desirable aspects of life under this same order of society, are concomitants of the machine as against other technologies. In non-machine cultures, life, though lived at a slower pace, must be lived with far more constant regard for the demands of the natural environment, and often in actual fear of not surviving. That is perhaps why the most convincing exposition of the values of our culture to native peoples is on the technological and scientific level; and this is also why we are so prone to insist that our way of life is the best.

One further point must be clarified before we proceed to an exposition of the data descriptive of the economic aspects of non-literate societies with which we shall deal in succeeding chapters. The division of labor in the intellectual field has brought it about that students who investigate nonliterate cultures have had but little contact with those whose special concern is with the economic aspects of life; while those who study our economic organization have been so occupied with the problems of our complex industrial order that they do not customarily turn to other cultures for relevant materials against which to project their generalizations. For the problems with which we are concerned in this book, the implications of the fact that there is no established discipline of the kind envisaged by Gras under the term "economic anthropology" [19] is crucial. Hence, in probing these implications, we shall profit by a clearer view of the usefulness of the materials with which we shall be dealing.

[19] Gras (1927), 10.

CHAPTER III

ANTHROPOLOGY AND
ECONOMICS

To UNDERSTAND why anthropology and economics have not had more contact, we must first of all consider the materials with which each primarily deals. Economics derives its data not only from our own culture, but, except for economic history, from this culture as it exists today.[1] Anthropology, on the other hand, ranging the peoples of the nonliterate world, presents materials having to do with all phases of social activity in civilizations of all kinds. As concerns the economic life of these folk, it is understandable that such data are not easily assimilated to traditions of procedure based on the intensive study of the economic patterns of only one culture. Yet, as we have said, the general outline of all human civilizations is the same. If we recognize that a difference of degree rather than of kind exists between most of our economic institutions and those of other peoples, the unity of the data concerned with the problem of economizing must be apparent.

Economists and anthropologists have drawn but little on the work of each other for still further reasons. One of them arises out of the historical circumstances under which the social sciences developed. Another derives from the psychology of those who participated in this development. Finally, purely practical considerations, which have figured in shaping the division of labor between the disciplines concerned with various aspects of the study of human societies, have entered. Of these, the psychological and practical reasons are the more fundamental. They

[1] Cf. Gras (1927), 11–12.

account for the historic fact that, in studying man, we have understandably tended to attack those problems lying about us which, pressing for solution, are more obvious and, from a practical standpoint, far more accessible than those which are to be studied in the far corners of the earth.[2]

With the expansion of Europe in the sixteenth to nineteenth centuries, contacts were increasingly had with native peoples as a result of slaving and merchandising operations, missionary activities, and the growing policy of colonization on the part of European nations. The writings descriptive of the tribal cultures with whom contact was thus established eventually claimed the attention of those interested in the nature, the mechanisms, and the development of human civilization. It is not necessary here to trace the growth of this interest into scientific anthropology. It need only be pointed out that, though it became essential for the student of nonliterate societies to treat of all phases of life in describing the civilizations with which he was concerned, in one respect his work became as highly specialized as that of any other scientist. This specialization lay in the method he developed for amassing and interpreting these varied data.

This matter of method very largely resolves itself into a technique that enables the student to recognize, isolate, and analyze modes of thought and behavior taken for granted when the institutions of one's own society are studied. The student who analyzes his own economic order, his own political life, his own family organization, his own art, or his own literature is so prone to accept as given the cultural matrix in which are lodged his data that he feels no need to subject this setting to any considerable analysis. This can be a handicap, especially when generalizations having cross-cultural validity must be drawn; but it is also a short-cut for those who study any phase of their own culture. Lacking this short-cut, the student of nonliterate societies must, however, before anything else establish the nature and the underlying sanctions of the institutions in the groups he studies. It is this fact that, presenting anthropologists with their greatest challenge, forced them to develop as specialists in method.[3]

[2] "Apart from mediaeval theories, the more important modern economic theories have developed out of violent discussions of the merits of rival economic policies." Bonn (1931), 333.

[3] A vivid summary of the methodological problems presented in the study of land tenure and the use of land in a specific nonliterate

Because of their methods, anthropologists have been able to provide us with an impressive body of accounts setting forth the behavior, traditions, and customary attitudes of peoples whose cultures differ strikingly not only from our own but also, in varying degrees, from each other. It is understandably impossible for any field ethnologist, from whom our primary data concerning these cultures must come, to be specialized in the study of all those aspects of culture upon which he must touch in giving a rounded description of the life lived by a specific group. Students of economics, or politics, or art, or literature, or religion have developed theories that have the qualities of penetration and insight that can only flow from long preoccupation with data bearing on a restricted field. But those who have developed such theories have found it difficult to grasp the possibilities of submitting the validity of their assumptions to the scientific test by applying them to civilizations that are quite different from our own in terms of their historic past, their environmental setting, and their technological equipment.

When we understand, then, that the specialization of the anthropologist along methodological lines has enabled him to amass data of value for those who restrict their attention to specific fields of human activity in single cultures, we have taken an important step in establishing the basis for a greater degree of mutual give-and-take between anthropologists and economists. To this end, therefore, let us see wherein the results of specialization in the two fields have inhibited a useful degree of cooperation between them. Let us also see what kinds of data are available, and what must be made available, if the findings of the anthropologists concerning the variation in economic processes and institutions that exist the world over are to be of use to those whose techniques and problems have tended to confine their investigations to the economic aspects of our own civilization.[4]

---

community, will be found in Forde (1937), 30–1. For a general discussion of anthropological field method, see Herskovits (1948), Ch. 6, "The Ethnographer's Laboratory," 79–93.

[4] We shall take the data, methods, and theory of economics as given, and it is not proposed to suggest any criticism of work by economists in their own field. Certain comments germane to the issues under consideration that have been made by economists themselves may, however, be quoted at appropriate times.

2

Most of the earlier definitions given by economists of their field of interest related the subject-matter of economics "to the study of the causes of material welfare." Because of this, perhaps, anthropologists have tended to overlook how deeply the modern approach to the subject is concerned with the matter of choice, the "relationship between ends and scarce means which have alternative uses," [5] that has formed the basis of our discussion of the process of economizing in the first chapter of this book. As was pointed out there, this involves a universal process in human society of maximizing satisfactions. This process varies with the degree of productivity and canons that traditionally dictate desirability according to available goods or available time. Here we must return to the fact that the data on which economic theorists have based their definitions and principles pertain to a single culture, our own. This means that, from the point of view of the comparative study of culture, the "laws" derived from these data are the equivalent of a statistical average based on a single case.

This has been increasingly realized by economists, who have phrased the matter in various ways. Thus Papandreou takes the following position: "It is not sufficient to postulate the rational norm. We must further make commitment to value-systems which are 'ideally typical' in the culture under analysis." As he puts it: "The very attempt of economic analysis to build a theory of universal validity, to avoid any and all psychological and sociological commitments takes it into the path of operational meaninglessness. The only way out of the impasse, the only way for arriving at an empirically relevant science is to make these commitments. This would reduce the universality of the proposition, but at the same time it would increase their range of meaningfulness." In short, "we should extricate ourselves from the shackles of economic universalism and experiment with less general but often more useful construction." [6]

We may begin our discussion of the implications for the anthropologist of the cultural particularism that has marked economics by turning to the definition of the subject given by Alfred

[5] Robbins, 4, 16. [6] Papandreou, 721–3.

Marshall, which its author has restated in several ways. First of all, it is expressed in the following familiar terms: "Political Economy or Economics is a study of mankind in the ordinary business of life; it examines that part of individual and social action which is most closely connected with the attainment and with the use of material requisites of well-being." Some pages later we read: "Economics is a study of men as they live and move and think in the ordinary business of life. But it concerns itself chiefly with those motives which affect, most powerfully and most steadily, man's conduct in the business of life." These definitions, it is evident, are broad enough so that they easily include the economic organization of any society.

As we go farther into Marshall's book, however, we find that the promise of breadth in these definitions is by no means realized. It soon becomes apparent that this "ordinary business of life" is essentially a discussion of the phenomenon of price and its ramifications into the activities of the market as these concern the motivations behind the production, distribution, and exchange of goods and services. In other words, Marshall is concerned, in everything but his definition, with just those aspects of our economic system that are seldom encountered in other societies. We are told, for example, that the contribution of economic science to an understanding of the economic aspects of social life derives its special value from the precision it can attain in analyzing its data: "The problems, which are grouped as economic, because they relate especially to man's conduct under the influence of motives that are measurable by a money price, are found to make a fairly homogeneous group." Or, again: "*Economic laws,* or statements of economic tendencies, are those social laws which relate to branches of conduct in which the strength of the motives chiefly concerned can be measured by a money price." [7]

This tradition of economic analysis which studies economic motivation, economic processes, and economic institutions by measuring them in terms of price phenomena has continued to dominate economic thinking, whatever theoretical point of view may be held. Almost any work in the field of economic theory may be cited to make the point.

[7] Marshall, 2, 14, 27, 33; see also the series of "chief questions to which the economist addresses himself," pp. 40-1.

J. M. Keynes, for example, considers the elements to be taken as given, the independent and dependent variables in what, significantly for the point under consideration here, he calls "the" economic system.

> We take as given the existing skill and quantity of available labour, the existing quality and quantity of available equipment, the existing technique, the degree of competition, the tastes and habits of the consumer, the disutility of different intensities of labour and of the activities of supervision and organization, as well as the social structure, other than our variables set forth below, which determine the distribution of the national income.

Most of these "given" elements can, obviously, be determined for any economy, pecuniary or not, given adequate research opportunities and reasonable flexibility of interpretation of the terms employed to name them. However, this is not so apparent when we consider his further stipulations, where he says: "Our independent variables are, in the first instance, the propensity to consume, the schedule of the marginal efficiency of capital and rate of interest. . . . Our dependent variables are the volume of employment and the national income (or national dividend) measured in wage-units." [8]

Yet how are these variables to be studied in economies where the price-system is absent, where entrepreneurs exist only by definition, and where employment and unemployment are seasonal, regulated by social tradition and not the result of competition for work in the labor market? The difficulties in this may be seen from the attempt that has been made to arrive at the "economic balance" of the Nupe culture of West Africa. Despite the fact that these people have, and for many generations have had, a pecuniary economy, the results yield little more than a series of family budgets showing income and outgo, and a sense of the power of prestige motivations as well as subsistence drives in their economic system.[9] The comment of a student of another nonliterate, nonpecuniary economy concerning the well-known proposition of Keynes on saving can be cited here as relevant: ". . . his definition of 'saving' is framed in terms of the behaviour of individuals in a society with a price mechanism. Where

[8] Keynes (1939), 245.   [9] Nadel (1942), 335–65.

there is no point of price equilibrium at which transactions can take place, his terms cease to be applicable." [10]

The concept of economic equilibrium, prominent in the writings of economists of various schools, can likewise be scrutinized from the point of view of its applicability to economies other than our own. There is no reason, of course, why the following three sets of data, which we must know before we attack the problem of equilibrium, cannot be studied in any society. These three sets are "(1) the external obstacles to the production of want-satisfaction, (2) the nature of the wants and resources of the organisms concerned, and (3) the principle of equilibrium—in this case the maximization of utility, or of 'advantage.'" These, Boulding tells us, lead to "ultimate determinants . . . the physical laws of production, as expressed in the physical production functions, and the psychological laws of behavior, as expressed in the system of indifference curves." [11] Yet the type of closed economic system he envisages as the "stationary state" or his condition of "dynamic equilibrium," while conceptually applicable to the economies with which we are here concerned, are so described in terms of interest, price, stock, and the operation of firms that serious methodological problems arise in utilizing them outside the economic systems of literate, industrialized societies of Europe and America.

It is self-evident that any functioning economic system must, in the broadest sense, be in a state of equilibrium. That is, the total output of all kinds of economic goods and services, plus whatever "savings" are made in the form of capitalization of wealth, must equal its intake.[12] When this ceases to occur, as where, in undeveloped areas, economic productivity is drained off for the benefit of outside investors, without adequate return being provided the producing native society, malfunctioning sets in, with results that have been made well-known through the many studies of this particular kind of situation.

But equilibrium economics is only by implication concerned

[10] Raymond Firth (1939), 23. Firth's footnote at this point refers to Keynes, op. cit., 64, 220, 373.

[11] Boulding, 767.

[12] It is in this sense of the term that Goodfellow's chapter entitled "Equilibrium Economics and the Primitive" (72–84) is drawn. The author here is essentially concerned with establishing 1) the fact of purposive activity among the Bantu and 2) that values derive from the allocation of resources among different wants.

with the phenomenon of economic balance in this broad and general sense. The problem of how value flows from fluctuations in supply and demand, in its essentially mathematical character, needs the quantitative index of value contained in price as manifest in the market to permit its analysis. More than this, even in a price economy, a whole range of assumptions is made before the analysis is begun. Hicks, in explaining the workings of the system of general equilibrium, may be cited here:

> The laws of change of the price-system, like the laws of change of individual demand, have to be derived from stability conditions. We first examine what conditions are necessary in order that a given equilibrium system should be stable; then we make an assumption of regularity, that positions in the neighbourhood of the equilibrium position will be stable also; and thence we deduce rules about the way in which the price-system will react to changes in tastes and resources.

Again, given time and research opportunity, these are problems which, though difficult to study in non-pecuniary economies, might be susceptible of attack. Yet it would obviously not be possible even to accomplish this in terms of the clarification of method given in the next paragraph:

> In order that equilibrium should be stable, it is necessary that a slight movement away from the equilibrium position should set up forces tending to restore equilibrium. This means that a rise in price above the equilibrium level must set up forces tending to produce a fall in price; which implies, under perfect competition, that a rise in price makes supply greater than demand. The condition of stability is that a rise in price makes supply greater than demand, a fall in price demand greater than supply.[13]

It is apparent that the situation envisaged in this approach—and in the discussions of economic statics and dynamics in determining equilibrium that derive from it—affords little place for the analysis of economies not under the entrepreneurial system, where a simple technology fixes the ceiling of productivity, where demand is restricted, and where value, whether monetary

[13] Hicks, 62.

or cast in terms of consumption commodities, is determined by tradition and not by market fluctuations. The point at issue cannot be better made than by citing a comment by Schumpeter on the Keynesian approach: "What I admire most in these and other conceptual arrangements of his is their *adequacy;* they fit his purpose as a well-tailored coat fits the customer's body. Of course, precisely because of this they possess but limited usefulness. . . . A fruit knife is an excellent instrument for peeling a pear. He who uses it in order to attack a steak has only himself to blame for unsatisfactory results." [14]

This same restricted approach also characterizes the writings of Karl Marx. Here we are again confronted with an intricate economic analysis based almost entirely on data drawn from our own society, dealing with problems that arise out of the complex development of the special kind of economic system that has resulted from the invention and development of the machine. Once more, as in Marshall, the system we contemplate, in aspect after aspect, is based on our own economy, as in the discussion of money, which by definition is limited to gold and silver, and thus precludes even the application of the term to any of the numerous kinds of tokens that, as will be seen, are employed to express value in nonliterate societies.

3

CERTAIN other economists, particularly Thorstein Veblen, gave more consideration than either the neo-classical group or the Marxians to economic problems susceptible of investigation in non-machine, non-pecuniary societies. But it may be noted in passing that the problems that have claimed the interest of those who have followed Veblen touch only lightly upon the matters which are at the core of economic theory as this is ordinarily expressed in the writings of most economists. And even Veblen's followers, as their work has developed, have tended to restrict their field of interest to matters that are specifically related to our economic order. As an illustration of this we may cite the work of C. Wesley Mitchell on the business cycle. For all its brilliance of attack and the insight it yields on this particular

[14] Schumpeter, 97.

problem, these researches are but an intensive study of precisely that phase of our economy that, more than any other, is absent outside our own economic system.

Ayres, the neo-Veblenian who has perhaps most retained the point of view of what may be termed classical institutionalism, in theory, at least, continues in the tradition of recognizing the usefulness of cross-cultural terms of reference. But the matter is different in practice; one finds in his work a minimum of ethnographic documentation to supplement the historical, psychological, and philosophical arguments he employs in developing his hypotheses. This is especially true, for instance, in his discussion of the problems of price, of value, and of technology. Here the appeal to the concepts and data of the single historical stream of Euroamerican culture often makes his conclusions highly vulnerable from the point of view of cross-cultural analysis.[15]

A more striking example of how neo-institutionalists fail to take advantage of cross-cultural data is to be found in Gambs's discussion of institutionalist economics. Like Ayres, though in a more critical vein, he takes Veblen as his starting-point. But one misses completely in his work those references to "the Polynesian islanders," "the Andamans," "the Todas," and "the Pueblo communities" which at the outset of Veblen's book establish the pattern of his entire system and concern data that form the background against which his argument concerning certain aspects of our own economy is implicitly projected.[16] Gambs seems not unaware of the cross-disciplinary implications of economic science, and the arguments from psychology he brings to bear on the problems he considers are welcome contributions. But one finds among the questions he has difficulty in answering some that might prove to be considerably less formidable if cross-cultural data were taken into account along with the psychological and historical facts.

Thus we may consider the following passage:

The word "rational" has for so many centuries been associated with a false concept of the mind that we may properly discard it as having no useful meaning. Until new concepts arise to define economic behavior, we shall not advance far

[15] Ayres (1944), *passim*, but especially Chs. II, IV, VI, and X.

[16] Veblen (1915), Ch. I.

if we speak of it as being either rational, irrational or sometimes the one and sometimes the other.[17]

Yet the cultural definition of rationality, developed in our first
chapter, indicates that the problem of rational behavior, attacked from a relativistic point of view, need not lead to the
counsel of despair that yields only a negative conclusion on such
an important point.

Gambs goes to the heart of the problem of institutional economics, indeed, when he writes:

> I would say that the under-development of institutional the-
> ory results from . . . the extreme difficulty that even the
> strongest human propensities have of transcending the Ge-
> stalt in which they find themselves. In other words, the "in-
> stinct of idle curiosity" though occasionally competent
> enough and strong enough to escape from its environment,
> is normally bound down by the institutions in which it op-
> erates.[18]

Here, however, we have nothing more than a statement of the
difficulties of the student, in the face of his own enculturative
experience, of extending his analysis beyond the bounds of that
experience. But an extension of that experience, first-hand or by
reference to the ethnographic literature, into the cultures of other
societies is not difficult, and would seem to provide the path
along which institutional economics—granting its present state
as described—can move so as to "transcend the Gestalt" in which
it finds itself. We only have to recall that there are many Gestalts,
each the result of the working out, in institutionalized form, of
universal processes operative in all cultures.

Whether the approach be through concern with the pecuniary
motivations that cause men to struggle for economic betterment
or with market processes conceived in terms of supply and demand as reflected in a price structure, whether it has to do with
the productivity of labor and its reward, or is concerned with
the description and analysis of our economic institutions, an anthropologist's reaction to all these approaches must be much the
same. He can only conclude that such problems are so couched

[17] Gambs, 51.   [18] Ibid., pp. 87–8.

in terms of a single body of tradition that their investigation among nonliterate peoples can yield results only of the most general kind; where, indeed, results gained from this approach cannot be predicted in advance to be negative.

Some economists, as well as anthropologists, have reached this conclusion. Thus, one unconventional critic redefines economics as "a science of human behaviour in an exchange economy based upon freedom of contract, and upon property-rights approximating to the type that is familiar in the Western Europe or North America of our own time." The broadness of Marshall's definition is commented on in much the same vein as has been done above from an anthropologist's point of view, and it is made clear how neither Marshall nor his followers have been concerned with any but a small portion of the range of phenomena implicit in it. Their work, it is pointed out, has consisted either "of the formulation of a body of economic laws or propositions which relate strictly to market processes of one kind or another," or "of a mass of 'realistic' or 'institutional studies' which pass as economics (if indeed they are permitted so to pass at all) solely because the particular institutions or activities of which they treat have had some special importance in determining the concrete background in which at particular times or places, the laws of the market have in fact operated." [19] The fact that the attention of economists has been focused so exclusively on just those aspects of our economy least likely to be found among nonliterate folk has thus confused anthropologists who turned to economic treatises for clarification of problems and methods in the study of the economic systems of nonliterate societies. [20]

4

THE WRITINGS of the economists failed to attract the interest of anthropologists for yet another reason. In no conventional treatise on economic theory is "primitive" man depicted in a manner either in harmony with the facts of nonliterate societies as known

---

[19] Wootton, 129, 45.
[20] For a discussion of the deficiencies that have resulted from a lack of knowledge by economists and anthropologists of the work of each other in a special field, that of money, cf. Einzig, Ch. 2, 19–25.

to anthropologists, or in line with anthropological theory concerning the nature of the interaction between man, his environment, and his traditions. In all justice, it must be pointed out that since the early days of economic theory the economists, perhaps discouraged by the immensity of the task of finding out for themselves what "primitive" life was actually like, left "primitive" man severely alone. References to some hypothetical tribe living on an island and using seashells for money have, indeed, survived, at least in class discussions at one distinguished institution of learning, where an equally hypothetical investigation is undertaken to ascertain the effect of the sea-shell being a free good, so to speak, on the value of the non-existent currency.

There are some instances, however, where students of economic theory have not left nonliterate man severely alone. From the anthropologist's point of view, the description of primitive life by Bücher and his followers is an outstanding example of discussions falling in this category. These writers so misunderstood even the most elementary facts of "primitive" cultures [21] that the effect of their analyses on anthropologists was to excite derision, where it did not have the more unfortunate result of inculcating a conviction that any approach to the study of "primitive" economic life from the point of view of economic theory is futile. For to envisage "primitive" men as entirely individualistic and non-social, marked by an animal-like striving for food, without stability, foresight, or any concept of value, was to caricature what even the anthropologist most innocent of any economic training knew.

Now it is true that while Bücher decried any attempt to "exemplify the primitive (i.e., the prehistoric or earliest) condition of man by any definite people," he did maintain that "there is more prospect of scientific results in an endeavour to collect the common characteristics of human beings standing lowest in the scale in order . . . to arrive at a picture of the beginnings of economic life and the formation of society." [22] But such an approach runs afoul of elementary anthropological method. An-

[21] Even a cursory reading of the accounts of travelers available at the time would, for example, have shown the untenability of such a statement as the following: "Every- where among primitive peoples the children become independent very early in youth and desert the society of their parents." Bücher, 37.

[22] Bücher, Ch. I.

thropology has given over the search for "origins" since the time it became recognized that, except as archaeological materials can be dug out of the ground, the beginnings of any phase of human activity cannot be scientifically established. Even if anthropologists ever did accept the proposition that generalized portrayal of early life could be derived from abstracting the least common denominator of all "primitive" cultures existing at present, as was suggested by Bücher, they have long since rejected any such idea. There has been sufficient refutation of Bücher and those who have taken positions similar to his,[23] so there is not need here to repeat these critiques. But writings falling in this category must at least come in for formal recognition and some consideration if we are to understand why anthropologists have been prone to give but little weight to mention made of "primitive" life by economists.

The concept of social evolution, which was developed in the latter decades of the nineteenth century,[24] further beclouded the thinking of economic theorists, though not of all economic historians. Notable here is the criticism of Bücher drawn by Usher: "Social history does not begin at the beginning of social life. . . . Despite the brilliance of Bücher's work and the keenness of his sense of historical development, evidence is constantly forced upon our attention that he could not free himself from the disposition to describe the dawn of history as if it were the origin of organized social life." [25] It is quite possible, as has been done, to trace the "evolution" of the industrial techniques of European culture from the simplicity of its prehistoric beginnings to its present complex forms.[26] But this is neither the point of view nor the method of the earlier evolutionary or present-day neo-evolu-

[23] For the most extended critique of Bücher's approach to the economics of nonliterate peoples and his idea of the relevance of these data for the problems of economics, see Leroy, *passim*.

[24] The most recent work of this type, a curiosity in its uncritical acceptance of a pseudo-evolutionary picture of the presumed "development" of economic life, is Viljoen's volume. Published in 1936, long after the fallacies of this position had been exposed, he persists in regarding living "primitive" peoples as the contemporary ancestors, so to speak, of more "developed" folk, and in tying in their customs at the end of a sequence derived from prehistoric data.

[25] Usher (1920), 24.

[26] Dixon and Eberhart, 50–66, 80–106.

tionary approach, which held that living primitive peoples might be regarded, so to speak, as our "contemporary ancestors" and that by studying their customs the "earlier" manifestations of our own traditions can thus be traced.[27]

Both point of view and method die hard, since even where they do not significantly function, they tend to give a subtle bias to basic approaches. This is seen in simple form where "pre-literate" is used instead of "nonliterate" in writing of "primitive" folk, or where students in describing nonliterate societies employ the past tense when considering institutions that today flourish in full vigor. It is found in tenuous or modified form in the elaborate sequences of the purported historical development of types of economies set by Thurnwald.[28] It is present in a less sophisticated form in an early study of the psychology of property by Beaglehole, where it is couched in terms of the sequence "property among animals—property among primitives—property among civilized children." [29] It is to be seen in the manner in which Schmidt, Koppers and the members of the culture-historical "school" of anthropology force economic data into a mold made out of a hypothetical progression of cultural types based on the assumption of the existence of cultural "layers" resulting from the interplay of reconstructed "historical strata." [30] It is a vestige of the evolutionary approach that causes Hoyt to turn to data from "primitive" societies in order to discover the "origins" of trade and of the concept of value; [31] that places discussions of nonliterate economies, where they are found in economic histories, before considerations of the mediaeval manor and the guild system, again implying a time sequence.[32] Certainly Marshall, Marx, and Veblen, whatever differences may otherwise mark their points of view, were all strongly influenced by the evolutionary position. As a matter of fact, this approach is to be regarded as the most important single factor standing in the way of an adequate use of data from nonliterate societies by economists as a means of broadening concepts and checking generalizations.

[27] For the best statement of the neo-evolutionary approach as concerns the development of technology and economics, see Childe (1946a). His defense of the "contemporary ancestor" method will be found in Childe (1946b).

[28] Thurnwald (1932b), 59 ff.
[29] Beaglehole (1932), 22–3.
[30] Koppers; W. Schmidt.
[31] Hoyt (1926), 6–11.
[32] Cf. Gras (1922) and Weber.

5

THE FAILURE on the part of earlier anthropologists to recognize and treat fundamental economic facts in their studies of non-literate societies was extraordinary. The sections of older ethnographic monographs headed "Economics" are ordinarily more or less adequate discussions of technology. In the face of a very important tradition in anthropology, dating from the early German students, that technology and economics are not to be differentiated, it was almost entirely forgotten that "after all, fish-hooks and canoes, spears and tree traps, fire drills and bronze adzes, while constituting the technological foundation of economic activity are in reality the tools and not the life of economic activity." [33] Many elaborate studies were made of how pots are fashioned, or how houses are thatched, or how fibers are woven or wood-carving done. In these earlier, more conventional descriptions of nonliterate peoples, however, we seldom encounter statements as to the organization of those who make pottery or of the values of the finished product, in terms either of other commodities or of such money as the tribe may employ, or of what gain accrues to these potters as a result of their specialized labor. In several American series of anthropological contributions it has been customary to devote the section headed "Economic Life" to an exposition of the data dealing with technology, wherein human beings make their appearance rarely, if at all. Here details of trading, or the means of expressing value, or other more relevant economic facts are included in that part of the discussion headed "Social Organization."

That some anthropologists should eventually have themselves reacted against this consistent reluctance to study one of the most important aspects of human social life is understandable. A tradition of including the study of economic aspects of culture in programs of field study was, it is true, quietly developing, but the first explicit manifestation of this reaction took the form of a vigorous attack on the doctrine of economic man. [34] This initial volume was followed by another on the economics of the New Zealand Maori, [35] by one on the role of food in the lives of a South

[33] Gras (1927), 20.　　　　　　[35] Firth (1929).
[34] Malinowski (1921, 1922).

African people,[36] and by still further contributions where the focus of attention was fixed on economic phenomena. Finally, in this series of works, came a supplementary treatise [37] on Trobriand Island economic life.[38]

In all of these studies we had better economics than in most conventional monographs dealing with nonliterate cultures that preceded them. Yet the fact remained that if other anthropological writers held economics to be technology, this last-named group conducted their research and presented their findings on the principle that economic life in nonliterate societies could not be treated unless consideration was given to every facet of tradition that impinged on the economic institutions of a people. It is not difficult to understand how this position was reached. Economists, as has been pointed out, can take for granted the cultural matrix in which their data lodge. Early anthropologists, finding but little to stimulate their research in the highly specialized problems considered by economists, retreated into technology. Reacting against this and other aspects of earlier work, these later writers brought into the fore-conscious the cultural setting of the economic data in societies other than our own. Tersely stated, it may be observed that if for the earliest anthropologists economics was technology, for these it was garden magic and gift exchange.[39]

A development which not only combined the economic and sociological approach but injected a psychological element in terms of personality types is also to be remarked, though it has stimulated no field investigation which might test its methodological value, or the validity of the hypothesis on which it is based.

---

[36] Richards (1932).

[37] Malinowski (1935).

[38] These works have been selected for mention because, emphasizing as they did the same insistent point of view, they were characterized by one methodological attack on the problems. It must not be overlooked, however, that other studies were also being made by students employing other approaches (Armstrong, Barton, Blackwood, DuBois, Provinse) in Melanesia, Africa, and elsewhere at the same time. The data in the works of these students are of the highest importance for an understanding of comparative economics, especially since in their books and papers the ethnographic materials are not obscured by digressions on theoretical points.

[39] From one point of view this reaction, though in general highly valuable, was unfortunate. It was so violent that out of it developed a strong antipathy to carrying on studies in the perfectly legitimate field of technology or, as it is termed by the anthropologists, material culture.

Bunzel, defining economics somewhat in terms of earlier economic writing as "the total organization of behavior with reference to the problems of physical survival," stated that "fundamentally the function of any economic system is to maintain some kind of equilibrium between material needs and the potentialities of the environment." Indicating the "endless variation" of the manner in which these needs may be envisaged, she advanced three "complementary principles" which were to be discerned in the functioning economics that satisfy wants. These were (1) the material principle, which "deals with the physical relationship to the environment and with the classical anthropologist's 'material culture'"; (2) the "formal principle . . . roughly 'social organization'"; and (3) the "psychological principle . . . concerned largely with the general question of value in its widest sense, the structure of the personality that determines choice, and the attitudes that animate institutions."[40]

How to give full weight to the ways in which the institutions of a given culture are interrelated, and the manner in which they influence one another, is to take an unassailable anthropological position which is recognized as a principal aim of field research. One can also envisage problems wherein the influence of a given economic system on the personality types of those who live under it might be of importance.[41] Yet one cannot but ask whether such matters as the production, the distribution, and the utilization of goods and services cannot be studied, even where the cultural matrix and psychological traits of the carriers must be made explicit, without constant reference to all the psycho-cultural mechanisms which everywhere underlie and sanction these processes.

It is questionable if anthropologists need burden the economic theorist with all those traditional rules of social behavior, religious beliefs, and other masses of interrelated non-economic ethnographic and psychological data which are essential in a rounded study of a single culture, but are merely encumbrances in an intensive analysis of materials bearing on any given single

[40] Bunzel, 327.

[41] This is implicit in the earlier writings, and explicit in the later work of Kardiner (1939, 1945) where the economic aspects of a culture figure among what he terms the primary and secondary institutions that set the basic personality type he assumes to exist, and account for the typical psychological configurations that mark off one group from another. It is interesting to speculate to what extent his thinking along these lines may have been influenced by Bunzel's position.

aspect of social behavior. As the matter has been put: "In describing agricultural and hunting magic, must I give a complete account of these economic activities, and in mentioning magic for singing and dancing, must I describe song and dance? I think not. Everything in the world is ultimately related to everything else but unless we make abstractions we cannot even commence to study phenomena." [42] To hold that economic phenomena constitute but one aspect of culture does not mean that these phenomena cannot be studied without studying all of culture. It may be regarded as clear gain, as far as an interdisciplinary attack on the common problems is concerned, that anthropologists are coming to study economic phenomena in terms that add to the body of economic knowledge by presenting their materials without so much reference to social context and psychological consequence that these matters stand in the way of seeing the economic implications of the data that are the basis of the study.

The subsequent development of an economic anthropology, wherein economic aspects of nonliterate societies are studied in economic terms rather than as material culture, or myth or magic, or cultural psychology, has been rapid. Goodfellow's study of Bantu economics, to which reference has already been made, was one of the first of these. [43] Far more balanced in pointing the way toward an economic anthropology whereby the intensive study of a given people leads toward the analysis of economic generalizations already established, or to the setting up of new hypotheses applicable in cross-cultural analysis, is Firth's study of Tikopean economics. Here the social and religious setting of the economy is accorded full recognition as an effective force in shaping economic effort; yet the focus of the discussion remains continuously on the economic implications of the data, and on the economic institutions that document the principles of eco-

[42] Evans-Pritchard (1937), 2.

[43] As is apparent from the previous citations to this work, its tendency is to conceive of the economic anthropologist as apologist for economic theories rather than as analyst of their applicability in nonmachine and non-pecuniary cultures. His statement, "The aim of this book is to show that the concepts of economic theory must be taken as having universal validity, and that, were this not so, the result would be not only scientific confusion but practical chaos" (3) explains why the data he adduces tend to be given far-reaching interpretations to enable him to bring them into line with particular principles of economics that arise out of the study of Euroamerican economies (e.g., 90 on the entrepreneurial function).

nomic behavior.[44] In addition, an appreciable number of descriptive monographs concerned with nonliterate peoples living in North, Central, and South America, the South Seas, Southeast Asia and Africa, from which data in the chapters that follow have been drawn, have appeared, in which economic life is treated as such, or has been the primary focus of the study. It is to be anticipated that this tradition, now firmly established in anthropology, will give a sure foundation of relevant data for further comparative insights into the nature and functioning of the economic process.

6

THAT conceptual as well as methodological difficulties stand between anthropologists and economists in communicating with each other has been made apparent in this and the preceding chapter. Walker points out that anthropology, with its insistence on induction from observed fact, differs significantly from "the method of economics which, being largely deductive, is not the method of a positive science." He elaborates the point in the following passage, which returns us to a point made in the first chapter:

> Anthropologists are focused on the community rather than the individual; they view society as a system of mutually dependent elements, and emphasize the influence of social forces on behaviour. The economist, on the other hand, derives the forms of economic behaviour from assumptions concerning man's original nature. He begins by considering how an isolated individual would dispose his resources, and then assumes that the individual members of a social group behave in the same way. The "economic man" is not a "social animal" and economic individualism excludes society

[44] Firth (1939). This book appeared while the earlier version of the present work was in press. It is interesting to compare the initial chapter of Firth's study, especially the section (22–9) entitled "Lack of Coordination between Anthropology and Economics," with the first two chapters of "The Economic Life of Primitive Peoples," as a demonstration of how two students, approaching the question of the relation between the two disciplines from somewhat different anthropological points of view, can reach strikingly similar conclusions.

in the proper human sense. Economic relations are *impersonal*. The social organization dealt with in economic theory is best pictured as a number of Crusoes interacting through markets exclusively. . . . It is the market, the exchange opportunity, which is functionally real, not the other human beings; they are not even means to action. The relation is neither one of cooperation nor one of mutual exploitation, but is completely non-moral, non-human.[45] The failure of economic theory to present man as a social animal . . . is the basis of anthropologists' (and some economists') discontent with economic theory.[46]

Yet it would be unfortunate to ignore the considerable contributions of these two disciplines that are of potential or actual use to each other. Not all of economic theory is by any means as little adapted to the study of societies other than our own as caricatures of the subject drawn at one time or another by anthropologists would have us believe. As has been repeatedly indicated in preceding pages, we must allow for the inapplicability of certain aspects of current economic theory to research in non-literate, non-machine, and non-pecuniary societies. Yet we have also seen ample suggestions in the literature of economics for anthropologists to consider. In any society, for example, as has been pointed out in our initial chapter, "the adaptation of means to ends and the 'economizing' of means in order to maximize ends" are a fundamental problem to be discussed under the headings which, in one analysis, have been set forth as the "elementary factors" in the achievement of this larger goal: "(1) the wants to be satisfied, (2) the goods, uses, or services of goods and human services, which satisfy them, (3) intermediate goods in a complicated sequence back to (4) ultimate resources, on which the production of goods depends, (5) a series of technological processes of conversion, and (6) a human organization for carrying out these processes"—comprising "the social organization of production and distribution in the large." [47]

[45] F. H. Knight (1935), 282.

[46] K. T. Walker, 135. Documentation of the differing conceptual and methodological points of view sketched in this passage will be found in the critique of the earlier version of this book by Knight and the rejoinder to this critique, that comprise Appendix I, below.

[47] Knight (1924), 260.

The interests of the institutionalists [48] must lead inevitably to an ethnological position. Economists who approach their materials from the institutionalist point of view have much to give anthropologists concerned with the economic organization of non-machine societies. This is the case whether they seek to understand the possible range of variation in these institutions, to analyze the dynamic forces they exemplify for a comprehension of growth and change in culture, or merely to describe them adequately as they occur in a culture with which they happen to be concerned. What, for example, can we learn from nonliterate societies of the processes by means of which the unequal distribution of economic resources make for the formation of social and economic classes? What is the economic role of the drive for prestige, as this is exemplified in patterns of the conspicuous consumption of valuable goods and services in order to bolster social position? Translating the Veblenian concept of the "instinct of workmanship" into a generalized psychological principle concerning the satisfaction derived by the worker when he can identify himself with what he produces, and the corresponding loss of pleasure in performance when this is denied him, what can be learned by studying the relevant industrial processes in terms of the opportunity in nonliterate societies for the worker to enjoy to the full the rewards of his labor? These are some examples of what anthropologists can obtain by going beyond the emphasis laid by economists on questions dealing exclusively with our economic order.

Anthropology, too, is less remiss than might appear at first view. It is only too true that anthropologists in earlier times concealed the economic data they collected with a cunning that seems calculated. Yet in the aggregate, even in these older works, there is a great deal to reward one who will read them, to say nothing of the growing body of literature which deals with comparative economics in terms understandable and accessible to economists. Thus we can now learn for a number of societies not only how people are traditionally expected to work, and why, but how much work given individuals actually did over given periods of time. We can find not only native theories of land tenure and accounts of its manifold interrelations with social and religious custom, but also actual descriptions of land owned and

[48] Cf. Atkins, Ayres, Gambs, Harris.

transferred, with mapped and measured indications of the boundaries as they exist. Accounts have been made available of what actually was bartered in specific trading expeditions, while not only descriptions of money and the regard in which money-tokens are held are being presented, but also detailed systems of value in terms of these units of currency.

That more quantitative analyses, so important in the study of economic problems, are not available can perhaps be ascribed to the practical difficulties of method faced by those who would gather materials of this sort. But even here a beginning has been made, and data of this order will be called upon wherever possible in the ensuing pages, since we must recognize that such quantitative materials vivify discussions of any phase of economic life, in whatever culture, in a manner out of all proportion to their extensiveness. Certainly, it is a favorable omen that despite the methodological difficulties—which are so basic as to involve finding an answer to the problem of determining a stable unit in which figures may be expressed—alertness to the importance of such materials has come to be recognized by anthropologists concerned with the economic life of the peoples they study.

PART II

PRODUCTION

CHAPTER IV

GETTING A LIVING

IT IS not necessary to have an extensive acquaintance with descriptions of nonliterate societies to realize how immediate is the existing relationship between economic life and the natural environment, or habitat. So immediate is this, indeed, that in some societies the annual yield of the principal food-bearing plant or the migration of the herds upon which a people must depend for nourishment is the primary determinant of survival. Under such conditions, it is by no means unknown for a community to be restricted to an absolute maximum in size, beyond which numbers are to be increased only on pain of starvation. So rigorous a life, to be sure, is found only where the habitat is most harsh, as within the Arctic Circle or in desert regions. Yet even where nature is less difficult, and where knowledge of agriculture and husbandry have brought to man a greater measure of control, his immediate dependence upon his natural environment nay still be vastly greater than anything known to our culture, so that all other considerations must give way before the all-important food-quest.

The account of an early explorer-trader in the territory inhabited by the coastal Indians of the Gulf of Mexico affords a ready illustration of this:

> We made mats, which are their houses, that they have great necessity for and although they know how to make them, they wish to give their full time to getting food, since when otherwise employed they are pinched with hunger.[1]

[1] Myer (quoting Cabeza de Vaca), 739.

Periodic recurrences of famine afford another manifestation of nonliterate man's immediate dependence on nature. This is evidenced by the frequency with which West African stories have as their opening phrase: "It was a time of famine." In such a Melanesian island as Manam the fact that the principal crop cannot be stored without becoming unfit for consumption causes annual difficulties in providing food at the end of the dry season, difficulties which even the processes of trade cannot wholly resolve.[2] A vivid account of a great famine in another part of Melanesia, the Trobriand Islands, given by a native, shows how in times of stress, even men of rank did not disdain various despised foods and "other abominations"[3] as aids to survival.

The ability of peoples having simple technologies to manipulate their resources effectively is thus the most fundamental aspect of their economic systems. As might be expected, the most striking instances of this are to be found in those societies sometimes termed marginal, among peoples who have been forced by the superior strength of their neighbors into the least desirable portions of the earth. The Bushmen of South Africa, living in the Kalahari Desert, are one such folk. Here the paramount problem is to obtain water. To meet this need they bury water in ostrich egg-shells against the time of severest drought, or make use of their knowledge of where to find the roots, bulbs, and melon-like fruits whose moisture may spell survival. They have also developed a means of filtering water in stagnant pools by the use of a hollow reed to which grass has been fastened. Food is mainly obtained by hunting, and the insight of these people into the habits of the animals on which they prey has long been famous.[4]

The aboriginal Australians are a classic illustration of a people whose economic resources are of the scantiest. In many places their habitat is even more severe than that of the Bushmen, although this is perhaps not quite true in the northern portion of the continent. A tabulation of the foodstuffs which the aborigines of northwest central Queensland extract from the country they inhabit is instructive. Nothing seems to escape them; seeds, edible roots, fruits and vegetables, flowers and honey, insects and crustaceans, frogs, lizards, crocodiles, and

[2] Wedgewood, 393.
[3] Malinowski (1935), 163–4.
[4] Schapera (1930), 140–3.

snakes, fish caught in weirs or by poisoning the water, turkey-bustards, flock-pigeons, and other birds, emus which are driven into nets, bandicoots, opossums, kangaroos, and dingoes.[5] The variety in this list is impressive, but we must not be deceived into thinking that variety indicates plenty, for the available quantities of each element in it are so slight that only the most intense application makes survival possible.

In some areas, certain flora or fauna predominate as the primary source of food. Among the Chipewayan and the Caribou Eskimo of the far north, where agriculture is unthinkable and the gathering of wild plants restricted to a brief summer season, caribou form the mainstay of the diet. Moose, buffalo (in earlier times, before the destruction of these herds), bear, wolverines, otters, beaver, hares, and birds, particularly the ptarmigan, are subsidiary sources of food, and their knowledge of the habits of these animals, especially the caribou, is described as remarkable. They exploit their resources in game so cleverly that they never destroy or even demoralize the herds which provide them with the essentials of life.[6] The most studied inhabitants of the arctic, the Eskimo, need only be mentioned to bring them to mind as an outstanding example of efficiency in adjusting life to the difficulties posed by nature. Here no possible resource is neglected; in addition, to help them meet the demands of their difficult setting, these people have developed mechanical aids that are so delicately tuned to this setting that persons who go into the country of the Eskimo, no matter how complex the technology of the culture from which they derive, in some measure adopt the techniques of these people if they are to survive.[7]

The Indians of central and northern California, in the days before their contact with the whites, supported themselves entirely on what was available in their habitat—seeds of various kinds, roots, nuts, berries, fish, and game. The difficulties in obtaining the means with which to sustain life, and the methods by which this problem was solved, varied over the state.[8] Along the coast, especially in the north, fish were plentiful, but in the interior grasshoppers, angleworms, and yellow-jacket larvae were regularly called upon to provide nourishment, while in times of

[5] Roth (1897), 91 ff.
[6] Birket-Smith (1930), 19.
[7] Cf. Boas (1888); Jenness; Birket-Smith (1936).
[8] Kroeber, 523–6.

stress the large yellow slug was by no means scorned. Like their neighbors, the Yurok consumed the acorn extensively, and salmon that came up the rivers were an additional staple. Deer and other small game, though not plentiful, were hunted to add to the total of food resources, while bulbs were dug in early summer, and later in the season seeds were beaten out of the prairie grasses. Seaweed furnished salt. The people living on the coast gathered mussels and other crustacea, surf fish were captured when the occasion offered, and the stranding of a whale was an event.[9]

These instances show how close the association between man and nature in non-mechanized societies can be, but they should not be taken as in any sense typical of the assumed economic poverty that has sometimes been mistakenly held to characterize "primitive" societies as such. As a matter of fact, the examples given are exceptional, since the proportion of non-industrial peoples whose technological equipment is so meagre, or whose environmental settings are so severe as in the case of the tribes given here, is very small. A very large proportion of nonliterate societies engage in food-gathering and hunting to supplement what they produce by means of agricultural and herding techniques, or, in many instances, merely to provide delicacies. But even where such peoples command techniques that are substantially advanced over those of the food-gathering and hunting societies, they manifest a similar closeness to their natural environment. This is essential if they are to make the most of their technological equipment and to provide themselves with the supplementary foods to be had without cultivation or the need for domesticating animals.

The Indians of the Guianas afford a concrete illustration of the manner in which a people who are not forced to meet problems as serious as those posed by the habitats of the Australians or the Bushmen, and whose technology, though not highly developed, is more complex than that of any of the peoples who have been mentioned, effectively exploit the resources they find to hand. From the forests in which they live they obtain the agouti, the armadillo, the bush hog, the deer, the manati, monkey, otter, rat, sloth, tapir, and water haas. Of birds they

[9] Ibid., 84.

trap quail, duck, toucan, and guacharo; they have thirteen different methods of catching the fish in the rivers, while from these streams they also gather turtles, iguana, alligators—whose flesh and eggs are both consumed—frogs, crabs, and molluscs. Toads and snakes offer another food resource, as do earthworms, beetles, ants, and wasps and bees, together with the honey these last afford. Vegetable foods are mainly supplied by agriculture, which yields cassava, maize, rice, and some twenty-four "economic plants." But there are a number of "cassava substitutes" collected from natural sources—mora seeds, greenheart seeds, dakambali seeds, pario seeds, and nuts of the swari tree, besides the twenty-seven kinds of "wild fruits, berries, nuts, etc." that have been listed. In addition to all the foregoing, these Indians draw on their forested home for the materials they use to make their fermented and non-fermented drinks and, besides tobacco, which they grow, for the four other types of narcotics and stimulants they enjoy.[10]

The North American tribes of the upper Missouri may also be mentioned, among others, as further illustrating how natural surroundings can be exploited. They gathered twenty-two kinds of roots, berries, and other wild foods of these types, hunted fifteen species of animals, and trapped six kinds of birds to supplement their agricultural produce.[11] Many of the tribes that lived in the region of the Great Lakes made a major resource of the wild rice that grows there, to which they added the flesh of the fowl that fattened on the ripened stalks.[12] Or, to move to an entirely different area, we find that in West Africa, where a steady supply of food and, in addition, a considerable surplus over what is needed for primary purposes of supporting life are ensured through the complex organization of the economic order and its technological proficiency, hunting provides an additional source of food, while products of forest and stream supplement the domesticated staples in the diet. A comparable phenomenon is found in the place accorded fishing in the basically agricultural economy of Polynesia. Thus the Society Islanders know in amazing detail the habits of the numerous varieties of fish found in these waters and call on their knowledge to assure

[10] Roth (1924), 174–247.
[11] Denig, 583.
[12] Jenks, 1073 ff., 1099.

themselves the most advantageous conditions under which to seek out the schools of fish that afford the largest catch or the choicest food.[13]

2

So CLOSE, indeed, and so seemingly obvious is the relationship of nonliterate man to his habitat that one of the several determinisms which from time to time have been advanced to explain the nature of human civilization is based on this fact. The more extreme position of those who hold to this point of view, that all human culture is to be understood in terms of this need for meeting the demands of the natural environment, need not be taken too seriously. To make such a position tenable it would be necessary to establish similarity for all bodies of custom existing under a given habitat, while different cultures would always have to be found under different natural settings. Happily, this point of view is more often met with in the writings of those who set it up to disprove it than in the discussions of those concerned with the real and extremely important problem of the relationship between man and his environmental setting.

The answer given by a number of students of comparative culture is that the environment is a limiting rather than a determining force. It sets the lines beyond which a people can go in exploiting their surroundings only if their technology permits it, and dictates certain limits beyond which they cannot conceivably go at all, whatever their technological equipment. Furthermore, it is apparent that the habitat does not exert its influence equally on all aspects of culture. This is an important point for our discussion, since it is the economic modes of life that most immediately respond to the natural environment and are most obviously adjusted to it. Hypotheses concerning the relationship between a culture and its natural setting thus almost invariably, and certainly most convincingly, draw on data of this character. Yet, as has been indicated, between a people and their habitat stands their technology. Though future research must furnish full documentation, our present knowledge permits us to indicate two principles that apply in this relationship. In the first place, it is

[13] Nordhoff, 243.

apparent that in so far as the various aspects of culture are concerned, the natural environment will play a more important role where getting a living is involved than in religion, or social organization, or art. Secondly, the available data indicate that the more adequate the technology, the less direct are the demands made by their environment on the daily life of a people.[14]

The Ifugao of the Philippines afford a good instance of a people who, though possessing but a relatively simple technological equipment, extract a varied living from their habitat. Not only do they exploit what it offers of itself and employ many of its possibilities in producing their basic food necessities, but also, because of one especially developed technique, force it to yield crops of rice in seeming defiance of what would seem to be the limits set by the natural environment. A statement of the range in the sources of food-supply, in terms of percentages yielded by each of the various techniques employed, has been provided us. Produce from which peoples lacking agriculture or husbandry would have to derive their entire subsistence—hunting, fowling, fishing, and the collection of insects and wild vegetable foods—accounts for something under ten per cent. Animal-culture—chickens, pigs, goats, and cattle, of which the last two are inconsequential—provides a further four per cent. Finally, at the time when the report from which these proportions are derived was written, another two per cent was imported. This means that over four-fifths of the total subsistence produce, eighty-four per cent, comes from agriculture.

If, before considering the relationship of Ifugao processes of production to the natural environment, we sketch their setting, we find that its most striking aspect, and the one that presents these folk with their greatest problem, is the configuration of the land. The people live in narrow valleys, flanked by precipitous mountains, rising five thousand feet and more over their bases. So broken is the country that the largest single area of flat land contains no more than five hundred acres.

The two major crops are camotes (sweet potatoes) and rice; all others are negligible compared with these. Camotes grow well on the mountainsides. The steeper the slope, the more favorable the conditions for planting this crop, since here the worker,

[14] Cf. Dixon, 31–2; Herskovits (1948), 153–66.

as he clears his land and plants the roots, need not bend as he would were the slope less steep. Indeed, these plants are grown on mountainsides so precipitous that none but an Ifugao can climb them. Since the growing crops need little care, flourish in poor soil, and are not subject to the depredations of insects or other pests, it is obvious that we have here a crop admirably adapted to the environment in which it is grown.

Rice differs from the camote in every respect. It not only is a much more delicate plant, but requires irrigation. Now to be able to irrigate ricefields situated on steep mountainsides means that some device must be perfected which enables the water to be retained. The device by means of which the Ifugao defeat the limits set by these mountains is terracing. Rice does not grow above an altitude of 5,000 feet, so that the fields cannot go beyond this height, but some terraces that attain the upper limit of possible cultivation soar in sheer reaches of 2,500 or 3,000 feet. The only requirement is that there be a spring above the topmost level. The resulting flow can then be turned at will from one step to the next, until all the fields have water, a process which allows the fertile silt, that would otherwise be washed into the valley and down the river, to be retained.

The labor that goes into the construction and maintenance of the system of terraces is prodigious. In most places the earth will not permit terracing without the construction of stone retaining walls, and the stones of which these walls are built must be carried up from the bed of the river in the valley far below. Terrace walls which rise to a height of twenty feet permit fields some eleven feet in depth; elsewhere, among neighboring tribes, where the mountains are steeper, terraces rise as high as fifty feet. The details of how rice is planted, cared for while growing, and harvested need not be given here; the fact that the Ifugao have apparently achieved a contradiction in terms of what would seem to be insurmountable limitations set by their habitat, and in so doing have widened the economic base of their society, is the point that concerns us at the moment.[15]

Another illustration of how original difficulties presented by the habitat may be overcome by human effort is found in the atoll of Pukapuka, which lies some four hundred miles northeast of Samoa. This atoll consists of three islets, of which the northern

[15] Barton (1922), passim.

one, where most of the inhabitants are found, is but a mile wide. There are a number of villages on these tiny specks of land, faced by the problem of how to produce a sufficient amount of food to support life, since coral cannot be used for agriculture and the coconut trees that grew on the island when it was first settled did not provide enough nuts. The problem, however, was met by manufacturing soil in which taro, the staple in this Pacific area, could be grown. Large pits were dug, into which dead coconut fronds and other fallen leaves from the bush were placed and allowed to rot. Water seeped in through the coral, eventually forming a thick mud, in which taro flourished. As time went on, these pits were enlarged to allow for the production of more taro, and today enormous excavations yield enough to feed entire villages.[16]

This point, however, must not be pushed too far. For while culture can, and often does circumvent the restrictions of the habitat, more often we find a response to the natural setting in such matters as the rhythm of work as manifested in the annual round of economic and other activities. This is amply apparent in the analysis of Mende agricultural operations made by Little, where the production cycle and certain other phases of the culture have been projected against the average monthly rainfall for 1931–44 in the region of Sierra Leona they inhabit: [17]

Month and Rainfall (Inches per month)	Farm Operations on Rice	Other Crops	Other Activities
December (2.16)	Selection of farm sites. Brushing commences. Storing of last crop. Harvesting of inland swamps. Brushing ceremonies.	Harvesting guinea corn, millet, sweet potatoes, coco yams. Ground nut harvest complete. Cassava harvesting and planting in process.	Women fishing. Secret societies initiate.
January (0.83)	Brushing upland farms completed in some districts and commenced in others. Felling of trees in some districts commences. Harvesting of last year's crop completed.	Harvesting of guinea corn completed. Sweet potatoes, coco yams, and cacao being harvested. Cassava harvested and replanted. Planting of vegetables on wetlands.	Preparation for House Tax payments. Secret societies continue in session. Men house-building, hunting, and weaving. Women fishing.

[16] MacGregor (1935), 13. [17] Little, 231–4.

Month and Rainfall (Inches per month)	Farm Operations on Rice	Other Crops	Other Activities
February (0.37)	Brushing continues. Felling completed and burning commenced in some districts. Late swamp rice harvested.	Preparation of sites for garden crops; e.g., onions, beans, etc. Cacao plantation brushed. Coffee and kola harvested. Yam harvest continues. New season crop palm kernels gathered.	Final society ceremonies. Initiates "pulled" from the bush. House-building, hunting, and fishing.
March (4.21)	Felling trees and burning still in process. Burning completed in other districts. Preparation of sites for wetland rice and planting of hillside depressions and semi-swamp areas in some districts. Brushing of early swamps.	Sweet potatoes planted in swamps. Palm kernels, kola harvested. Yam harvest completed.	Continuation of house-building, weaving, hunting, fishing.
April (5.0)	Burning completed. Threshing of seed rice in preparation for sowing. Ploughing and sowing on some uplands commenced. Short duration varieties sown on swamps. Brushing of swamps.	Harvesting and planting of cassava. Yams and ground nuts planted. Coffee plantations brushed. Palm kernel harvest continues and late crop of cacao.	Men weaving.
May (8.1)	"Ploughing" and sowing generally in progress. Sowing finished in some districts. Preparation and sowing of swamp nurseries.	Harvest of early sweet potato crop. Cacao and coffee plantations brushed. Cassava, millet, guinea corn, etc. planted on uplands. Yams planted.	Men weaving.
June (10.2)	Sowing completed and seeding of early planted crops begins. Broadcasting on swamps.	Planting of late ground nuts. Harvest of old cassava crop and sweet potatoes. Yams staked and weeded.	Women spinning thread.
July (5.6)	General weeding of uplands. Late planting of uplands completed. Harvesting of early planted wetlands.	Harvesting of early ground nuts and early maize varieties. Planting of millet and guinea corn on uplands com-	

Month and Rainfall (Inches per month)	Farm Operations on Rice	Other Crops	Other Activities
	Transplanting of swamp rice seedlings.	pleted. Kola plantations brushed. Sweet potato harvest continues.	
August (22.9)	Weeding completed on uplands. Weeding of early planted swamps. Broadcasting on very late uplands completed. Scaring of birds general on uplands. Swamps transplanted.	Harvesting and new planting of cassava. Weeding of yams. Ground nut harvest continues, also maize. Intermediate crop of kola harvested. Palm kernel harvest slackens.	
September (17.7)	Harvesting of early upland rice. Bird scaring continues. Weeding of early planted swamps. Transplanting continues and broadcasting on late wetland still continues.	Ground nut harvest continues. Yams and coco yams weeded. Harvest of old and new cassava crops. Replanting of potatoes on swamps. Maize harvest continues. Planting of breadfruit.	
October (9.81)	Harvesting of main upland crop begins. Bird scaring on late uplands continues. Late transplanting of swamp completed. Harvest of early short season swamp rice.	Ground nut harvest completed. Main planting cassava completed. Late maize crop harvested. Planting of sweet potatoes.	
November (5.9)	Harvesting of upland rice completed.	Preparation of sites for dry season vegetables, particularly in swamps, begins. Sweet potato planting continues. Cacao harvested.	House-building begins.

In so far as the matter of obtaining a living concerns the primary problem of producing the supplies of food necessary to sustain life, then, we must conclude that while the habitat is important, the technology of a people, playing on the environmental factor, molds and shapes the possibilities offered by nature. It will therefore be apparent how significant is the statement made in the preceding chapter that while technology is not economics, we cannot escape the fact that the basis of economic life is technological. But technology is a part of culture—

that body of traditions which every group possesses. Hence we are justified in drawing the conclusion that culture plays a considerable part in dictating the forms that any given mode of obtaining a living, as any other aspect of life, may take among a given people.

3

THIS leads to the question as to the uses toward which technological devices are put, as playing on the permissive limits of the natural environment, they push these limits outward with every invention, every improvement in tools, every change toward an increased efficiency in production. Here we must look further into the question of the degree to which economic patterns are pointed toward a greater degree of efficiency in the production of goods, and to what extent the responses of a people to what is produced can be channeled by their habits of consumption so as to further or block the development of a richer material background of life.

Certainly it cannot be claimed that non-industrial peoples are not alive to many of the possibilities within their reach. Nor is their technology such as not to cause admiration for the way in which they meet the total range of the practical problems involved in obtaining their livelihood. There are numerous instances to indicate that nonliterate man has developed techniques involving a degree of foresight and of minutely detailed knowledge which not only constitute a complete refutation of the stubborn idea that "savages" lack vision and intelligence, but indicate how far these peoples will go in rationally attacking the primary tasks of gaining a livelihood. Indeed, a rich documentation is at hand not only to demonstrate the extent to which they can exercise foresight in providing for their daily needs, but also to show how effectively they are able to plan for whatever special requirements they may have to meet.[18]

The Chuckchee of Siberia depend almost entirely on their herds of reindeer for subsistence. Chuckchee herdsmen carefully select for breeding purposes does that come from hereditary lines known to produce the strongest fawns. The herd is shrewdly

[18] Mead (1937), 12.

evaluated from this point of view, the herdsman noting the lineage of each of his animals over three or four generations and determining, from his knowledge of the kind of deer each lineage characteristically produces, which does are the least desirable. When the need for meat arises, he selects those females least likely to produce the best fawns; on the other hand, in breeding he arranges the mating of his animals so that his herd eventually consists of the most desirable type.[19]

The words of an Ojibway chief may be cited to show how his people were alive to the benefits to be derived from conserving their resources:

Wherever they went the Indians took care of the game animals, especially the beaver. . . . So these families of hunters would never think of damaging the abundance or the source of supply of the game, because that had come to them from their fathers and grandfathers and those behind them. . . . We Indian families used to hunt in a certain section for beaver. We would only kill the small beaver and leave the old ones to keep breeding. Then when they got too old, they, too, would be killed, just as a farmer kills his pigs, preserving his stock for his supply of young.[20]

Among the Tsimshian, special storehouses were built during good times to conserve foodstuffs against periods of scarcity. In the myths of these people, for example, we read of a chief who possessed four storehouses full of provisions—one of salmon, one of bullheads, one of seals, porpoises, and sea lions, and one of whale meat. Another myth tells how the owner of storehouses filled them with boxes of porpoise meat and seal-blubber against the time that this food should be needed.[21]

On the Polynesian island of Mangaia, taro is irrigated by means of a race which supplies water to terraced patches. Despite the fact that only wooden digging-sticks were available as tools in earlier days, it was nonetheless possible, by means of the co-operative effort of the entire community, to achieve the completion of "public works" which attained considerable magnitude, since the race had to be dug from some distance upstream to obtain a sufficient fall of water.[22]

[19] Bogoras (1904), 70 ff., 79, 16. [21] Boas (1916), 396.
[20] Speck (1914–15), 186. [22] Hiroa (1934), 130.

However, while every culture must operate efficiently enough to ensure that its human carriers survive, it does not follow that this efficiency is as apparent when viewed from outside the culture as it appears to those who carry on the traditions under which it is sanctioned. For just as any given technological equipment can be used to extend the possibilities of the environment and thus to broaden the basis of economic and other aspects of life, so this equipment can be used to maintain traditional modes of procedure, despite objective proofs that the traditional way is more laborious and even more difficult than another equally well-known method. Many instances of this have been pointed out in our own culture. Indeed, the sociological concept of "lag" is based largely on the fact that even in our mechanistic society, a laborious operation is preferred, more frequently than we realize, to a more efficient one.

The element of tradition is thus of great importance in determining the forms of technological and economic aspects of culture no less than of any other aspects. Existing custom also profoundly influences the way in which a people will react to subsequent possible additions presented by inventions and discoveries made from within, or by ideas and techniques coming from contact with other cultures. Again we are faced with questions of the dynamics of cultural growth and the nature of cultural change—questions of the first order of difficulty, no less than of importance. We cannot help being impressed by the many different forms taken by institutions and techniques as expressed in the great variety of methods which groups of human beings employ to attain a given end. Yet when we find that in every culture the particular means evolved for solving a particular problem are looked upon as the only valid ones and that change is made with reluctance, we must also be impressed with the conservatism of human beings in modifying their customary modes of behavior.

Can nonliterate peoples, however, be said to be more conservative than literate groups? The lack of historical data on the rate of change in these non-historic societies has caused many writers to stress their conservatism. But it is doubtful whether such a position could stand a documentary test were we able to follow the course of development of some nonliterate people over a period of several hundred years. The data of archaeology testify to the ubiquity of cultural change. Furthermore, the brief histories of people without written languages of their own who have had prolonged contact with those who could write of them, give us sufficient grounds for holding that as regards their acceptance both of inner change and outer borrowings they are no different from literate peoples.

What we find is rather that in every culture change is less difficult to effect in certain aspects than others, though the element of culture most susceptible to change will vary from people to people. In our own society, the centers of sanctioned change lie in the fields of material culture and technology. But, to take only one instance, equal receptivity to change certainly does not characterize our attitude toward the intangibles of our economic organization. The vitality of the concept of *laissez faire* in the face of alterations in the mechanical basis of our economy that have deprived this point of view of all but the justification of traditional usage, bears eloquent witness to this point. Strictly speaking the terms "invention" and "discovery" describe the means by which any new elements are introduced into a body of custom, whether material or non-material. Yet we reserve the praiseworthy title of "inventor" for one who introduces a change, no matter how revolutionary, in the mechanical processes of industry, while we apply the less complimentary term "revolutionary" to the inventor of new concepts applicable to the economic structure we have raised on the industrial base.

The generalization that material culture and its concomitant economic aspects are more susceptible to change than nonmaterial-elements is not borne out, for example, by the considerable data available from Mexico and Central America. These data rather suggest that this hypothesis was drawn under the influence of observations concerning the differential rates of change found in various aspects of our own way of life. Thus, for example, we may consider the changes that have taken place in the life of the Mexican town of Tzintzuntzan, concerning which our knowledge covers a period of over four hundred years. At its initial contact with the Spanish conquerors, it was the "capital and nerve center of the vast Tarascan Empire"; today it is a small, isolated village. Though we learn that "the changes that have taken place . . . are enormous," yet "in the basic economic organization of the village, perhaps fewer changes have taken place than in any other aspect of life." That is, "a dweller in Tzintzuntzan of four centuries ago would find, in spite of great differences, more than mere traces of similarity between the outward, material manifestations of life today and that which he had known," while "the political, social, and religious forms of today would . . . be entirely unrecognizable." [23]

Whatever the case concerning change in the various aspects of culture, we are constantly presented with this paradox when we study any given culture as a whole: while human beings are strikingly conservative in the maintenance of their institutions, no body of tradition continues in living form without changing. As a result of this balancing between conservatism and change, we find a series of institutions in every culture that, held together by the sanctions given them under traditional codes of behavior, to the outsider often seem curious or quaint or inefficient. But they never seem either curious or quaint, and rarely seem inefficient, to those who live in terms of a given culture. It is the business of the anthropologist to seek out and understand this inner logic that causes a particular grouping of patterns to seem right, and most often uniquely right, to a given people. And it may be remarked in passing that this is yet another reason why those not trained in this method find it so difficult to view the customs of others with scientific detachment, especially where technology and economics are concerned. For it is in these fields that the logic of a culture is most readily to be tested by the objectively ascertainable facts of the situation in which its conventions operate.[24]

4

THIS theoretical digression has been necessary to understand the point of view that must be taken in studying even so elementary a phase of comparative economics as the methods a people employ to obtain a living. So powerful is the body of conventions that rule the lives of every folk that no people exploit the possibilities of their environment to the degree their technological

---

[23] Foster (1948), 6–15, 282–6.
[24] For a more extended discussion of the problem of conservatism and

change in culture, cf. Herskovits (1948), 479–504.

equipment permits, since sanctioned modes of behavior cut across any approach to complete efficiency in the utilization of natural resources. The members of a community, in choosing from such resources as are at hand, operate within the patterns that dictate what is and what is not permissible.

This is apparent in many instances, but as will be seen in later pages, nowhere is it more striking than in the conventions that dictate what may and what may not be eaten or worn. Even where such primary goods are not involved, taboos often exist against the utilization of certain materials for tools, or their use by certain individuals or classes of individuals within a society, or at certain periods of the year. These taboos are observed with faithfulness and fervor, despite the fact that they materially lower the efficiency of the group as a whole in wresting from their environment the means of support or survival. Many of the psychological imponderables of a religious, sociological, or artistic nature found in a given society do not, of course, bear significantly on economic patterns. But those that do concern economic life are of the greatest importance for any comprehension of this phase of existence. It is not difficult to understand how an undue neglect of such imponderables has tended to give to the speculations of those economists who have been concerned with nonliterate cultures a certain air of unreality, when the applicability of their hypotheses to life as actually lived has been put to the test of the empirical facts.

In most societies, either because of the rigors of the habitat or because of the directives given to economic effort by tradition, certain categories of natural resources are exploited far more than other equally usable elements. This is true even where no technological reasons exist for not exploiting such resources, as, for example, in East Africa, where herding and food-raising peoples in contact have failed to grasp the opportunity to learn agriculture from one another. This channeling of productive activity has been given a great deal of attention by students of the problems of the development and organization of the economic life of nonliterate peoples. Expressed in the concept of economic "types," it constituted an integral part of the evolutionary approach sketched in the preceding chapter. And since it has continued to figure in economic theory, any discussion of the way in which peoples gain their livelihood would be incomplete without mention of the classifications of types of economies that have been made.

Gras has concisely summarized in the following passage some of these classifications of types of economies:

> The old theory was that early peoples went through three stages, hunting (collectional), pastoral, and agricultural. This was the view of Dicaearchus (4th century, B.C.), of Varro (1st century, B.C.), of Condorcet (1793), List (1841), Nieboer (1900), Vinogradoff (1905), and Hobhouse, Wheeler, and Ginsberg (1915). In 1874, however, Gerland asserted that in remotest times plant culture preceded animal culture, and that later some peoples became nomads and others hunters. In 1875, Hellwald, and in 1893, Bücher, doubted whether the three traditional stages were universally true. In 1896, Hahn put different forms of plant culture before animal culture. In the same year Grosse held that the pastoral stage was not invariable. In 1897, Bos placed the hoe culture before pasturing. Pumpelly, in 1908, maintained that agriculture preceded the domestication of animals in prehistoric Transcaspia.[25]

Such a listing of contradictory progressions demonstrates the fruitlessness of seeking to establish any unilinear scheme in describing the development of economic life through various stages. The categories themselves, however, can be used to good purpose if they are considered as descriptive of the several kinds of economies that actually exist, since, as in all scientific endeavor, data must be classified as a preliminary step to any further analysis. And though such an approach is not germane to the objectives of this book, inasmuch as our interests center on the variation in economic drives and institutions in nonliterate societies, yet it will not be unprofitable to indicate some of the systems that have more recently been advanced.

Gras sets up the following categories: "Collectional economy (hunting, fishing, grubbing, and so forth), cultural nomadic economy (pasturing or planting or *both*), settled village economy (developing a true agriculture), town economy, and metropolitan economy." [26] Such a classification has several advantages. It is not evolutionary in its approach, it differentiates between

[25] Gras (1922), 44.   [26] Gras (1927), 19.

types of economies in different parts of the world, and it takes into consideration what is known of the prehistory or history of the groupings it sets up. The very fact, however, that it is projected into these several dimensions, and must include so many subdivisions, indicates the difficulties that lie in the way of attempts to classify social data of any sort when the realities of the social and historical situations are all taken into account.

Another classification of economies, which exemplifies these difficulties has been suggested by Thurnwald,[27] who distinguishes the following types of economies: "homogeneous communities of men as hunters and trappers, women as collectors" (pp. 59 ff.); "homogeneous communities of hunters, trappers, and agriculturalists" (pp. 63 ff.); "graded societies of hunters, trappers, agriculturalists, and artisans" (pp. 66 ff.); "homogeneous hunters and herdsmen" (pp. 76 ff.); "ethnically stratified cattle-breeders and traders" (pp. 79 ff.); "socially graded herdsmen with hunting, agricultural, and artisan populations" (pp. 85 ff.); and "feudal states and socially graded communities" (pp. 93 ff.). Each of these categories is illustrated by various nonliterate societies, and the series is ended by a discussion of the "familia" and "manor" in Europe, thus giving a distinct flavor of time to the progression.

This classification is open to several objections, of which the two most serious may be mentioned. It is apparent, first, that the introduction of sociological and political criteria into a classification of economies blurs the lines along which the classification has been drawn and, by confusing the objective, defeats the primary aim of simplification. In the second place the system seems to imply certain universal genetic processes in establishing these socio-politico-economic cultural types that would be difficult to establish.[28] The progression of Hobhouse, Wheeler, and Ginsberg already mentioned, is likewise amenable to use as a classificatory device. Based on "an order corresponding to the degree of control over nature and mastery of material conditions," it thus indicates a series of differences between economic types quite as much as it is a statement of evolutionary progression. It is to be noted that it has been employed in this classificatory sense by its authors.[29]

By far the most satisfactory classification of economies, how-

[27] Thurnwald (1932a), 52–84.
[28] Thurnwald (1932b), 59–102.
[29] Hobhouse, Wheeler, and Ginsberg, 29 ff.

ever, has been drawn by Forde. He first of all prefaces his statement of types with the striking caution: "People do not live at economic stages. They possess economies, and again we do not find single and exclusive economies but combinations of them." Then he proceeds to name "in the broadest way" five kinds of systems: collecting, hunting, fishing, cultivation, and stock-raising.[30] His reservation that these must not be thought to exist in pure form is most important. As we have seen, peoples everywhere are prone to utilize what is "given" them by their natural environment as their technological capability permits and within the lines set by their traditions. It is only in extremely rare instances, if in any cases at all, that they have been found to confine their efforts to one form of productive activity. Thus even where agricultural organization is advanced, hunting and fishing are carried on. We need but recall, as an example of this, the sources of the foods consumed by the Ifugao, an agricultural folk, to recognize how it was possible in the same way for the Plains Indians, whose cultures as they existed in the days of pre-white contact have been accepted as almost classical examples of the hunting type, to have grown maize as well; or how the herding culture of the Zulu of South Africa could be superimposed upon an agricultural subsistence economy.

One further point may be made here. If, in this chapter, in considering the basic economic problem of obtaining a living, attention has been centered on food, this is because food is the most essential single requirement for survival—even more than shelter, and certainly more than clothing, into whose production and use so many non-economic factors enter. Tools also fall in the category of economic essentials, but secondarily, and only when employed in producing basic needs. Other than these, the bewildering variety of goods produced by mankind is to be regarded from an objective, though never from a psychological, point of view, as a kind of economic gloss on the basic preoccupation with survival. This is especially true of cultures that do not have the machine, where, as has been seen, technologies are relatively simple and man is thus comparatively at the mercy of nature. It may be freely granted that these glosses, so to speak, once rooted in the traditions of the people who enjoy them, are not thought of as any the less indispensable. They may, in fact,

[30] Forde (1934), 461.

of themselves become so important that given individuals may find existence literally unbearable without them.

Yet the economic concerns of nonliterate peoples, especially of those who live at or near the subsistence level, do in large measure reduce themselves to fundamentals of the kind discussed here, elementary as such preoccupations may seem from the point of view of the economic complexity of our machine society. We shall, however, turn to these other types of goods as we further consider the processes of production, and we shall find them constantly recurring as we later treat of questions that bear upon the manner of disposing of what has been produced. For, survival value aside, the needs of any people, considered in the light of their own desires, include the entire range of goods and services which, with the mechanisms that exist for their production and distribution, constitutes the integrated whole of any economic system that is a going concern.

CHAPTER V

PATTERNS OF LABOR

OPINION as to the amount of work done by "primitive" man, and his ability to concentrate on a given task, has been most frequently phrased in terms of what may be called the "coconut tree" theory. This is the point of view that holds the "savage" to be a man who, commonly living in a climate where his needs are bountifully provided by nature, neither is required to exert himself nor is willing to do so when he can obtain even the necessary minimum to support life by abstaining from effort. Marshall's statement on this point may be taken as a typical example:

> Whatever be their climate and whatever their ancestry, we find savages living under the dominion of custom and impulse; scarcely ever striking out new lines for themselves; never forecasting the distant future, and seldom making provision even for the near future; fitful in spite of their servitude to custom, governed by the fancy of the moment; ready at times for the most arduous exertions, but incapable of keeping themselves long to steady work.

The passage ends with this significant sentence: "Laborious and tedious tasks are avoided as far as possible; those which are inevitable are done by the compulsory labour of women." [1]

This same point of view is stressed in the writings of Bücher. He states that ". . . man has undoubtedly existed through immeasurable periods of time without labouring," and, citing the natural growth in the tropics of the palm tree, the breadfruit tree, and similar plants, insists that "even modern research cannot dispense with the assumption that mankind was at first bound to

[1] Marshall, 723–4.

such regions. . . ." [2] The assumption here, apparently, is that the patterns of refraining from effort that mark present-day "primitive" man were laid down in the early days of human existence, and have persisted to the present because of the inertia of "savages."

Yet quite aside from the fact that prehistoric men lived much of their existence in the difficult environment of the glaciated periods, such a statement finds no support in the lives of present-day peoples anywhere. Even those "primitive" folk who inhabit that most romantic area, the South Sea islands, work and work hard, despite the fact that here, almost uniquely in the world, man is furnished by nature with practically all his needs. This fact, furthermore, also refutes Bücher's further assertion that "primitive" man not only wastes potential resources in not utilizing his environment to the full, but also wastes time—"the reproach of inertia to which primitive man is universally suspect." [3]

It is unnecessary here to argue a position of this nature, since to read any objective description of the life of peoples will show how much in error it is. Moreover, a number of effective answers have already been given to this assertion and others like it. Probably the most telling of these is that of Leroy, who, in commenting on the dictum regarding the "laziness" of "primitive" man, refers to a passage from the writings of F. W. Taylor, whose study of motor habits of workers has been fundamental in speeding up production in our great industrial plants. The founder of the "Taylor system" is effectively quoted as speaking of "the natural instinct and tendency of men to take it easy, which may be called natural soldiering"; with the reminder that Taylor was not speaking of "savages," but the workers in our own mechanized industries. [4]

As we have seen before, however, it is one thing to recognize that the need to refute an outmoded position no longer exists. But it is quite another matter to ignore the position, and thus risk not understanding how pervasive its influence has been, or how it may be present even in the thinking of those who agree with its refutation. Thurnwald furnishes an instance of this. He is entirely correct in his initial observation, regarding non-literate peoples, that "work is never limited to an unavoidable

[2] Bücher, 7.
[3] Ibid., 19.

[4] Leroy, 75–8.

minimum," but that "owing to a natural or acquired functional urge to activity" more work than is essential for survival is always done. Yet a few pages later, in a passage reminiscent of Marshall, he maintains:

> In spite of an activity which is frequently assiduous, the work of primitive peoples lacks that concentration and discipline which seems to be only acquired through working with more delicate machinery. They are quite ready to make an effort when the work requires it, but they soon relax, and as they are not compelled to make any consecutive effort toward overcoming this tendency, they yield to the feeling of fatigue.[5]

Yet knowledge of work-habits even in the most highly industrialized societies demonstrates that an ability to focus all effort on a task in hand when it is necessary to do so, to work hard when one must, and to relax when one is able, does not necessarily imply "lack of concentration and discipline," but rather a realistic sense of the physiological requirements of the human system. That concentration is possible where interest is aroused, and where it seems worth while to concentrate, is testified by many of those who have had contact with nonliterate folk.[6]

Actually, nonliterate peoples, like ourselves, do as much work as they feel they must to meet the basic demands of getting a living, plus as much more as their desire to achieve any given end not encompassed by these basic demands calls for. Unlike workers in a machine economy, however, they take their ease at their own pleasure. The Tenetehara of northern Brazil define the lazy man as "one who does not have food and necessities for himself and family."[7] In Southern Bougainville,

> There are tribal standards of minimum and maximum working hours. People who obviously spend little time in garden work are labelled "lazy.". . . It is considered a grave insult to be told: "Thy father's hand is clean; not a thing does he plant; he has no wealth in crops." And the charge of laziness is heard at a divorce hearing as often as is the charge of adultery. On the other hand, it is unusual for a native to

[5] Thurnwald (1932b), 209, 213.   [7] Wagley and Galvão, 37.
[6] Cf. Boas (1938), 134.

spend more than seven hours a day at garden work. Some individuals, of course, do; and they are praised as "industrious workers"—but are not often imitated.[8]

We shall, therefore, at the outset attack the problem of labor in non-machine societies by drawing on quantitative data to answer the questions how much, and how hard, workers in these groups actually exert themselves in the process of producing the goods and services deemed essential in the respective cultures in which they live. For it is only through quantitative analyses of our problem that we can achieve proper perspective on these important points.

2

THE ACCOUNT given for the Siang Dyak of Borneo was one of the first of this type. Like other Indonesian peoples, this folk possess an economy based on rice-culture—in this case, the non-irrigated variety—which, as the staple food, is supplemented by the wild pig and other products of the hunt, and by fishing and the gathering of wild fruits, roots, and honey. Iron-working is well developed, so that they are self-sufficient as far as the manufacture of the iron tools they use is concerned. Their hardest work is clearing the jungle for rice fields.

In this setting, the amount of work done over a period of a month was recorded for several individuals—providing a statement of how much labor a given number of individuals in this society actually performed, how much they rested, and what kind of work they did. One of these records may be given in full. It is that of a man aged about fifty, married, with a wife and a grown son.

Date	How Occupied
August 24–26	Working in his own ricefield
27	Working in Oeke's ricefield (hando) *
28–29	Working in his own ricefield
30	Home, resting (made strap for knife)
31	Working in his own ricefield

* "Pure labor exchange."

[8] Oliver (1949b), 90–1.

Date	How Occupied
September 1	Ditto
2	Home, resting; wife's uncle visiting from another village
3	Home in a.m., resting; his own field in p.m.
4	Home, resting, half day; his own field half day
5	His own ricefield
6	Sahadan's ricefield (*haweh*) †
7–12	No record (observer absent from village)
13	Home resting
14	Home; helped Kenting make coffin for dead baby
15	Home; assisting Kenting (other work taboo)
16	His own ricefield
17–18	Home, resting
19	Sahadan's ricefield (*haweh*)
20–21	His own ricefield
22	Half day his own ricefield; home resting half day
23	Half day his own ricefield; home half day—sick
24	Home—sick with dysentery
25	Ditto
26	Ditto (on his mat in the long house all day) [9]

† "Working Bee," a form of co-operative work where the beneficiary does not give any return in kind for the labor done for him.

This man's efforts, and similar summaries of the activities of others for whom records are given, may be tabulated as follows:

Activity	Number of days spent by					
	A	B	C	D	E	F
Working in own ricefield	12½	4	1	3	5	11
Working in others' ricefields	3	4	1	5	9	2
Hunting in jungle	—	10	5	—	4	—
Gathering firewood in jungle	—	—	—	1	—	—
Acting as medicine-man *	—	—	—	8½	—	—
Traveling in Siangland	—	—	5	—	3	—
At home, working	3½	6	3½	2½	2½	—
At home, resting	6	4	11½	7	3½	—
Incapacitated or ill	3	—	—	—	—	(15) †
	28	28	27	27	27	(28)

* Days or night.
† Not in original table; during these days this man was confined to his home because of an accident to his foot that did not permit him to work.

In this table, *A* is the one whose work for the month has been given above in detail. *B* was aged about forty, married, had a wife and a grown son, and was chief of the village. *C* was the

[9] Table from Provinse, 96–7; the note appended to this record for September 26 states: "Tatak died a week later."

assistant chief, about thirty-five years old, unmarried and living with an unmarried sister. *D* was a *blian,* or medicine-man, of about forty-five years, married; *E* a young man of twenty-three, married for three years, but with no children. The final case was of a man past fifty, married, whose wife, mother-in-law, and two sisters lived at his house. While this tabulation was being made, however, a falling tree so injured this man's foot that he was unable to resume work during the time observations were being set down; hence during the period of his inactivity, indicated in parentheses, he is to be regarded as an industrial casualty.

Inspection of these figures strikingly shows the variation to be expected in the amount of work done by different individuals in a non-industrial society. It indicates, further, how in this tribe, at least, the workers were able to dispose of their time as best pleased them, within the limits set by the need for providing a living. If among the Siang all must work, all may also rest. If the chief of the village spent more time hunting wild pig than any other man of the group sampled, this merely means that he was directing his efforts more toward one type of labor than another. His assistant spent more days "at home, resting" than any other man, but the chief himself is second lowest in this regard. Though the professional duties of the medicine-man prevented his working in the ricefields as much as his fellows, he is seen spending a day in the forest gathering firewood, and also, despite his other concerns, giving a day to co-operative labor. As is stressed in the original discussion of these schedules, the operation of no taboos and other intangibles seemed to interrupt the rhythm of work. Thus while custom prescribes that no work must be performed for three days after the death of a child—or for seven days, if a closely related adult dies—yet one father whose child died during the period under observation proceeded to his field the day after the death without the breach of this regulation even occasioning comment, much less punishment.

The data may be combined in a single tabulation. If the fifteen days not given for *F* are placed under the "at home, sick" heading, the total amount of time is seen to have been apportioned as indicated in the table on the next page.

The figures in this table, thus drawn on broad lines, afford some further documentation of general points that have been made. In drawing these generalizations, however, certain cau-

tions must first be indicated. Thus there is no assurance that this
sample is representative of the total population. From the information at hand, for instance, we cannot say how iron-workers
spend their time, or whether one man out of every six is a medicine-man, or how many persons might be expected to spend fifteen days out of twenty-eight as industrial casualties, or die in
any given period of four weeks. Yet even with these reservations
in mind, certain facts stand out clearly. We see how great a

Activity		Number of days
Work in ricefields		60½
working for self	36½	
working for others	24	
Work in jungle		20
hunting	19	
gathering firewood	1	
Work as medicine-man		8½
Work at home		18
		———
Total productive time		107
At home, resting	32	
At home, sick	18	
Traveling	8	
		———
Total non-productive time		58
		———
Total		165

proportion of the available working time of those whose labor
was recorded was spent tending the primary crop—more than
one-third of the total. We find confirmation of our assumption as
to the relatively great importance of the production of basic necessities in societies living on a low economic level, when we note
that almost one-half of the recorded time used for productive
activity went into growing or hunting food-supplies. On the
other hand, the assertion that non-industrial man is essentially
lazy could not be better refuted than by the fact that even if the
time put down to traveling is counted as non-productive—as has
been done because no information is given us as to the purpose
of these journeys—only one-third of the total number of days
was spent "resting." Finally, we see that more than a tenth of the
working time was lost to illness or industrial disability.

The activities of one woman have been recorded; the wife of

A in the above list, aged about fifty, sister of the chief, and mother of a grown son. Since her husband was an outstandingly good worker, she spent less time in the fields than other married women; on the other hand, being neither very old nor having young children, she did not stay at home as much as women in these categories.

Date		How Occupied
August	24	At home, pounding rice, cooking
	25	Home in morning, housework; afternoon in ricefield
	26	Tatak's field until 5 p.m.; pound rice two hours in evening
	27–29	Home, housework, pounding rice, etc.
	30	Ditto; two hours in ricefield gathering javau
	31	Ditto
September	1	With Tatak in ricefield (cooking for *haweh* group)
	2	Three hours in ricefield; home remainder of day
	3	Home, housework, pounding rice, etc.
	4–6	Ditto
	7–13	No record (observer absent from village)
	14	Home, housework, etc.
	15	Home, helping with feast after burial of Kenting's baby
	16	Home, housework, etc.
	17–26	Home, housework, pounding rice, stripping rattan, etc.

The recapitulation of how this woman used her time shows that her activities fall into two general categories:

Activity	Number of days
Home, doing housework, cleaning rice, weaving, stripping rattan, etc.	24
Helping in ricefields	3
Total	27

Here again, though, these data must be used with all caution; yet they do point to certain conclusions. One is the difference between the work of the men and the women, and the degree to which a woman is confined more closely to her home than a man. Another is the fact that while the time of the men was almost entirely taken up with the production of the basic necessities of life, an appreciable part of the time of this woman—even with all allowance for her case as a special one—went into the production of other kinds of goods, while the remainder was taken up with household tasks and the preparation of food.[10]

Comparable information, though less precisely recorded, is available from Bougainville in the northwestern Solomon Islands, where the mode of life is much easier than among the Siang.[11] We may here, however, for our second account, turn to somewhat fuller data from a comparable region, which records the actual work done in cutting and planting two gardens on Wogeo. We may consider the schedule for the larger of the two, covering an area of 2700 square yards:

Day   1.   Jaua, Sua and Kalal cutting down trees 7:58 a.m. to 12:04 p.m. and 2:02 p.m. to 4:55 p.m. They paused three times for a total of 34 minutes.

Day   2.   ——

Day   3.   Jaua cutting down trees, 7:40 a.m. to 12:13 p.m. Sua cutting down trees 8:02 a.m. to 12:08 p.m.

Days 4–11.   Timber left to dry.

Day   12.   Jaua and Sua sorting timber and fencing 7:58 a.m. to 12:15 p.m. and 2:05 p.m. to 4:06 p.m. Several pauses for total of 39 minutes. Sale and Sua's wife sorting timber and burning rubbish 7:58 a.m. to 11:55 a.m. and 2:05 p.m. to 3:16 p.m. Pauses for a total of 23 minutes.

Day   13.   ——

Day   14.   Jaua, Sua and Kalal fencing 8:08 a.m. to 12:57 p.m. Jaua and Sua marking allotments 2:25 p.m. to 3:31 p.m. Pauses for 23 minutes. Sale, Sua's wife and a young girl clearing ground 8:12 a.m. to 12:24 p.m. Pauses for 16 minutes.

Day   15.   Jaua, Sua and three youths cleared away stones 9:02 a.m. to 11:43 a.m. The two women brought along taro shoots.

Day   16.   Jaua and Sua brought banana suckers.

Day   17.   Raining heavily.

Day   18.   Jaua planted banana suckers 8:02 a.m. to 12:30 p.m. and 2:12 p.m. to 3:45 p.m. Sua planted banana suckers 11:03 a.m. to 12:30 p.m. and 1:50 p.m. to 3:04 p.m.

Day   19.   Sale and Sua's wife planted taro shoots from about 8:15 a.m. to noon. Very wet.

Day   20.   Sale, assisted by Jaua's brother's daughter, planted taro shoots and other vegetables 8:14 a.m. to 11:50 a.m. Sua's wife planted taro shoots 8:20 a.m. to 11:55 a.m. The two other women, having finished all Sale's taro, helped Sua's wife 2:04 p.m. to 4:23 p.m. Pauses for 31 minutes.

Day   21.   Kalal's wife planted her allotment 8:02 a.m. to 12:04 p.m.

[10] Provinse, *passim.*   [11] Blackwood (1935), 27–9.

This listing of hours spent in working a garden does not, of course, indicate how the remaining hours of the days listed were occupied, so that no idea of the balancing of labor and leisure is given. Yet it does show a record of consistent application to the task in hand, and a willingness to work for a sanctioned and essential end, that makes the point with which we are here concerned.[12]

We may also consider further illustrations of this quantitative approach. Here we see again not only the amount of labor an individual performs, but, when the analysis of the work done by different persons and family groups is tabulated, we can sense the variation in the degree to which members of the same society apportion their time to various tasks. Tetiev's chart of daily work performed by five Hopi men between August 7 and November 12, 1933,[13] indicates the effectiveness of the technique:

Individual	Herding sheep	Corn fields	Bean patches	Melon patches	House building	Wood hauling	Herding horses *	Miscellaneous	No Work	Total of days noted
1 †	0	10	3	9½	9½	1	0	14½	3½	51
2	49	10	1	6	8	7	1	7	9	98
3	22	9	3½	3	20	5	3½	6	10	82
4 **	17	14½	0	3	0	1	9½	3	35	83
5	22	23	0	1½	0	4	2½	5½	10½	69
Totals	110	66½	7½	23	37½	18	16½	36	68	383

* This does not include the routine care of horses.
† This man kept no sheep.
** Stated probably to be the laziest man in Oraibi.

Foster's analysis of the activities of eight families in Tzintzuntzan, on the basis of records kept over two months, demonstrates another type of insight this approach can yield. The charts he gives, which are in too great detail to permit reproduction here, show not only range of variation in work done, but also how differently, in the same community, different families can order their work-patterns—one tending toward specialization, another encompassing many activities; one, as a family, having a tradition of hard work, another being marked by their avoidance of effort.[14]

Such studies, though still not numerous enough to permit us

[12] Hogbin (1938–9), 291–6.
[13] Tetiev, 196.
[14] Foster (1948), 153–6 and Table 23.

to draw more than tentative conclusions, show, first of all, how this quantitative approach to the problem of labor in non-industrial societies brings into focus the effort put into the productive processes as can no other type of material, and how fallacious is the assumption that "primitive" man shirks labor.

3

THE AMOUNT of work done by individuals in nonliterate societies can also be studied by considering areas worked or amounts of goods produced. Here, again, the data in hand are slight, but some significant facts can be assembled. Yams are the principal food crop of the inhabitants of Umor, a settlement of the semi-Bantu Yakö of eastern Nigeria. The population of this village in 1935 was estimated at something under 11,000, of whom about 1,750 were adult males. Some 40 out of the 47 square miles included in its territory is available for cultivation, but since worked land rarely extends far from the paths that thread the bush, no large proportion of this is farmed.

The yams are planted in rows of hills which run straight across the rectangular gardens. This makes it possible to obtain fairly accurate estimates of the number of hills per plot, and of the average yield. Computing the sizes of these rectangular gardens by pacing off their boundaries, it was calculated that the average area of the farms of 97 men—later shown to be a representative sample—was approximately 1½ acres. The number of yam-hills in such an area was 2,440, planted and cared for by a "representative" household group consisting of a man, two wives, and three or four children. The mean yield was 2,645 yams, the harvests ranging from the "exceptionally low" figure of 235 to a maximum of 11,410.

The labor involved in production on this scale can be realized when it is indicated that, in addition to caring for their yams, the women grow coco-yams, corn, pumpkins, okra, three varieties of beans, sugar-cane, and peppers; while the men, who clear the fields, also plant and tend gourds, cassava, and ground-nuts (peanuts). When harvested the yams are tied in stacks, which is anything but easy work. In 1935, the totals for yams of all sizes "ranged from 350 in the case of a young man farming for the first time to 19,700, the harvest of an exceptionally large household with a farm of 8 acres." In addition to farming activities, the men gather palm-kernels from their trees, while their wives and children crack the nuts and help extract the oil.[15] Hence it is apparent that this Nigerian people, as it is in the case of the South African Pondo, where the women work gardens averaging 2.3 acres,[16] are no strangers to hard and continual labor. These instances again demonstrate that, when working within the patterns set by tradition and for objectives whose validity is acceptable to them, nonliterate folk are capable of sustained productivity of no mean order.

Data are also available on the quantities of wild rice harvested in the region of the Great Lakes of North America. In 1864 three Chippewa groups, with a total population of 3,966, gathered 5,000 bushels. This is a seasonal activity. In addition, they marketed a large quantity of valuable furs, produced 150,000 pounds of maple sugar, and grew considerable crops of potatoes and maize. An observer, writing in 1820, said: "One family ordinarily makes about five sacks of rice (5 bushels); but those who are industrious sometimes make twenty-five—though this is very rare." At Pelican Lake, Wisconsin, "they gather about twelve or fifteen bushels per family. They could gather more if they did not spend so much time feasting and dancing every day and night they are here for the purpose of gathering." Yet despite the daily interludes of recreation, the quantities of wild rice gathered are not unimpressive. It must be remembered, too, that the gathering of the crop had to fall into a rhythm of timeliness, for the rice could not be allowed to become so ripe that the grains fell off the stalks into the water, while on the other hand it was of no use if harvested too soon.[17]

4

THE CO-OPERATIVENESS that characterizes the activities of nonliterate peoples constitutes one of the most striking aspects of their patterns of labor. Co-operative work is done by groups of all sizes, and comprehends all kinds of tasks. It is obvious that

[15] Forde (1937), *passim.*
[16] Hunter, 72–3, 87.

[17] Jenks, 1074–5, 1078.

the family, the primary social unit in every society, must be a co-operative institution. The community as a whole can equally be regarded as a co-operative unit. Among the Nuer of East Africa, for instance, ". . . the members of various segments of a village have close economic relations and . . . all the people of a village have common economic interests, forming a corporation which owns its particular gardens, water-supplies, fishing-pools and grazing grounds; which herds its cattle in a compact camp in the drought, and operates jointly in defense, in herding, and in other activities; and in which, especially in the smaller villages, there is much co-operation in labour and sharing of food." [18]

But it is not co-operation of this broad kind that is meant in the present context. Here we refer to that sort of co-operation which acts as a factor in furthering the productive processes— the voluntary association of a group of men or women whose objective is the completion of a specific, definitely limited task, with which they are simultaneously concerned. Co-operative work organizations of this kind, free or compulsory, temporary or permanent, organized or informal, are found everywhere in the nonliterate world. Some of the many available examples may be called upon to document the point.

The West African type of co-operative agricultural work that has been preserved among the peasants of Haiti may be taken as a first illustration. Essentially, it is a means by which the Haitian gets the heavy work of clearing his fields accomplished quickly enough to permit him to get his planting finished at the proper time. For were he compelled to clear his lands by his own effort, the planting season would have come and gone before he could finish the task; as it is, the work is done in a day or two, and he can go on with the next step.

A working party is organized when a person having a field to be cleared passes the word about that he wishes to have a *combite*, as such a group is termed, come to do the work. At the same time the host prepares food for a feast. He slaughters an animal if the working party is large and the fare provided is to be elaborate, or contents himself with providing only a meal of cereals, plantains, and the like if he can afford nothing better. As the workers gather, their labor is supervised by one individual who sees to it that the pace is adequate to get the work done in the

[18] Evans-Pritchard (1940), 92.

time at hand, and that there are not too many shirkers. The workers, each with his hoe, form a line, and there is always at least one, sometimes two and, in a very large *combite,* three drums to mark the rhythm for the songs and to set the beat for the hoes. The stimulus of this group effort on the men is apparent in the results of their labor. In a single afternoon a field of several acres can be completely denuded of the growth of the dry season by a group that numbers about sixty-five workers.

The festive nature of the undertaking is underlined by the feast that comes as darkness falls. The one who has supervised the work also supervises the distribution of food, to make certain that the choicest tidbits and the largest portions go to the men who came earliest and worked most steadily. Where a wealthy man gives an elaborate *combite,* the hard worker may on occasion find a few small coins at the bottom of his dish as he finishes his food. That some come late and shirk their share of the labor is likewise not overlooked when the food is distributed. Should a man gain the reputation that such conduct is habitual with him, his fellows will show little enthusiasm in helping him clear his field if it be necessary for him to ask their aid.[19]

In West Africa, the region from which the ancestors of the Haitians were derived, work of all kinds is carried on co-operatively. The *dokpwe* of Dahomey not alone permits projects of considerable dimensions, such as the building of walls for large houses and compounds and the thatching of roofs, to be accomplished in manageable time. By affording a means whereby large fields can be hoed rapidly, it provides an economic foundation for the convention of this polygynous society that every son-in-law must from time to time perform a task of some magnitude for the father of each of his wives.[20] An identical function is that filled by a similar type of co-operative work among the Lobi tribes and by the *egbe* work-group of the Nupe.[21] To return to the co-operative patterns of Dahomey, we may take an instance of but one of the several Dahomean crafts, the iron-workers. Each forge here represents a kind of a co-operative society. At any one time all members of a forge will be working on the iron of one man. The product of this labor—hoes, let us say—will belong to the one whose iron was forged, and he will sell these

[19] Herskovits (1937), 70–6.
[20] Herskovits (1938), I, 71–5.
[21] Labouret (1931), 264–6; Nadel (1942), 248–251.

hoes in the market for his personal gain. While disposing of these he works the iron of each of his fellow iron-workers in turn, until the cycle swings round to him again, and the process is repeated with his iron, acquired with part of the proceeds from the sale of his hoes, again in the forge.[22]

In the Cross River area already discussed, the co-operative work which annually clears the paths to the fields of the Yakö is compulsory. A day or two sees the task finished; those who do not do their part are fined. To carry on certain farming operations—clearing and planting—work-parties are arranged by agreement with the head of the patrilineal descent group. Parties of this kind work during the mornings of the days on which markets are held—"non-farming" days, as these are termed—and each man is obligated to answer the summons and perform a morning's labor. A dozen or more men can clear "a moderate section" of land in a morning.[23] Among the Tallensi of the Northern Territories of the Gold Coast fishing is carried on co-operatively. The various pools are exploited in this manner not only because it is held to be a most efficient method, but also because of certain considerations of prestige.[24] House-building, a difficult and prolonged operation, could not be successfully accomplished among the North African Berbers of Kabylie were it not for the co-operative labor of fellow-villagers of the builder, as well as of the members of his family.[25]

The East African Kikuyu (Gikuyu) employ two types of co-operative effort when weeding gardens. One is an arrangement in terms of which four or five men, working together, care for the fields of each other. The other is the work-bee, whereby the task is done in a festive spirit of common endeavor, and food and beer are freely given to make the occasion more enjoyable.

If a stranger happens to pass by at this time of enjoyment after labour he will have no idea that these people who are now singing, dancing and laughing merrily, have completed their day's work. For after they have cleaned off the dust which they got from the fields, they look, in all respects, as though they have been enjoying themselves the whole day. This is why most . . . Europeans have erred by . . . not realizing that the African in his own environment does not

[22] Herskovits (1938), I, 75–6.   [24] Fortes (1937), 138–40.
[23] Forde (1937), 39–40.   [25] Maunier, *passim.*

count hours or work by the movement of the clock, but works with good spirit and enthusiasm to complete the tasks before him.[26]

The Lovedu of eastern South Africa have two types of co-operative agricultural work-groups—the *lejema*, a more informal one, and the *khilebe* (from *jebe*, a hoe), a local aggregate that in recent times has reinterpreted its earlier form into "ploughing partnerships." For the *lejema*, beer is brewed by the women, who are more effectively organized for the purpose than are the men who hoe; for the smaller *khilebe* no beer is provided. The social aspect of the first is outstanding, while in the second economic ends are stressed. But in both, "the value of mutual helpfulness and the necessity of minimizing the self in relation to the ends of others" is paramount.[27] In Central and South Africa numerous other instances of the same phenomenon are to be encountered —co-operation in Congo fishing, in South African Bantu herding, and in hunting operations of the Bushmen.

Co-operative labor is met with at every turn in aboriginal North America. It is described in these words by a native Hidatsa woman, recounting the farming operations of her girlhood:

The . . . day after the corn was plucked, we gave a husking feast. . . . Word had been sent beforehand that we were going to give a husking feast, and the invited helpers soon appeared. . . . For the most part these were young men from nineteen to thirty years of age, but a few old men would probably be in the company; and these were wel-comed and given a share in the feast. There might be twenty-five or thirty of the young men. They were paid for their labor with the meat given them to eat; and each car-ried a sharp stick on which he skewered the meat he could not eat, to take home.[28]

The elaborate arrangements to safeguard the interests of all in the communal buffalo-hunts of the Plains Indians are well known; in the case of the Flathead, who lived on the western border of this area, a hunt of this kind was tantamount to a "major cavalry engagement" and occupied most of the able-

[26] Kenyatta, 59–60. [28] G. L. Wilson, 43.
[27] Krige and Krige, 52–6.

bodied men of the tribe for an entire winter. So great was the sense of combined effort that even if a member of an expedition had been unsuccessful, meat was given him by his comrades so that he would not return empty-handed.[29]

In the Southwest, co-operative agricultural work is found in both the eastern and the western Pueblos. In Taos, kinsfolk co-operate in agricultural labor, helpers being given their dinners and suppers; co-operation is also found in house-building, in rabbit-drives, and, in earlier times, in deer-drives.[30] Assistance in the fields is given a Zuñi man by the fellow-members of his clan or fraternity, recompense taking the form of "an evening meal after the return from the fields each day by the family for whom they work." [31] Among the Hopi, co-operative work is carried on by three kinds of organizations: those that derive from membership in a family, clan, or society; the women's bean-planting groups; and the inter-village working parties. Springs are cleared by co-operative labor, and agricultural work is carried on co-operatively, while village groups are at times organized for the construction of houses and, in recent years, for road-building.[32] In California, instances of co-operative work include the intertribal antelope-drives in which the Yokuts and their neighbors participated, "circles that must have been many miles in diameter at the start"; the deer-drives and bear-hunts organized by the Maidu; or the reciprocal group labor of Yurok kinsmen in house-building.[33] Farther north, an elaborate system of communal work for building houses also prevailed among the Haida.[34]

No less rich is the testimony from the Pacific islands. Tasks which took more man-power than a single family could provide were completed in Mangaia with the aid of working-bees. Here again, aside from the pleasure of meeting acquaintances, the only reward was a feast, in which the family provided so generously that the workers often carried food away.[35] On Tonga an instance is cited of communal fishing where 40 specialists directed the efforts of more than 1,000 people in one of these group enterprises.[36] When it is necessary in Tanga to have large quantities of food ready for some special occasion, this is cared for by a

[29] Turney-High, 115 ff., 120.
[30] Parsons (1936a), 18, 19, 56.
[31] Stevenson, 350.
[32] Beaglehole (1937), 27–31.
[33] Kroeber, 528–9, 409–10, 39.
[34] Murdock, 5.
[35] Hiroa (1934), 130.
[36] Gifford (1929), 146.

program of co-operative work in the fields. Since all crops mature at the same time, it thus becomes possible to provide the great quantities required for such an elaborate rite as a funeral feast.[37] All the men in a Malekulan village gather to work for one another in turn, preparing the ground for gardens. Even those who belong to neighboring villages come, and all receive presents of pigs, yams, tobacco, and other goods. Their host joins them elsewhere as an ordinary worker the next day. Certain types of Malekulan fishing which involve the use of poison or are done by trapping the fish in lagoons across which fences are built can, indeed, only be carried on co-operatively.[38] Canoes are built in Bougainville by co-operative labor, as are houses, and no man refuses such help to a friend. The expected return is a reciprocal willingness to aid when called on, while, as usual, the one who benefits from the labor makes a feast—in this case a small one—to mark the completion of the work.[39] "Communal labor" in the Trobriands—as opposed, from the point of view of complexity of arrangements, to "organized labor"—figures in many places in the production cycle. It is used in building living-huts and storehouses, in transport, in certain forms of industrial work, and sometimes in fishing. As in Africa, it makes possible the fulfillment of duties toward one's relatives-in-law; as elsewhere generally, it is used in agriculture.[40]

It is understandable that the Australian horde or band must have constituted a permanent co-operating unit, but for certain kinds of hunting and fishing operations, two or three entire hordes of the Daly River tribes of the north join forces. These, by custom, are well organized, and the return enjoyed by each group is safe-guarded by well-recognized methods of dividing the catch.[41] Similarly, among the Yir-Yoront the best results in hunting and fishing are obtained by the co-operative efforts of groups of men ranging in number from a few individuals to whole tribes. Here the kill and the catch are divided among those participating in these tasks, again "according to well established usages." [42]

Indonesia also offers instances of co-operation, one of which, taken from the report already cited concerning production among

[37] Bell, 307–08.
[38] Deacon, 180, 189–91.
[39] Blackwood (1935), 450.
[40] Malinowski (1922), 159–61.
[41] Stanner, 18.
[42] Sharp, 37.

the Siang Dyak of Borneo, must suffice. Two forms of the co-operative working party are found among this people; pure labor exchange, termed *hando*, and that in which a man of means, not wishing to return the services given him, announces a working-bee called *haweh*, where he feasts and liberally provides drinks for those who participate. These two types of "exchange" and "feast" labor are used not only for clearing, planting, watching, and harvesting the ricefields, but also when a man must have help to bring in a dugout canoe or a large memorial pillar from the forest, or in house-building, or in making a coffin or digging a grave.[43]

Though the wide distribution of co-operative labor is thus apparent, little research has been done on the problem of its per capita effectiveness when compared with the accomplishment of an individual working alone. The data from Wogeo, already considered, throw some light on this problem. The clearing and planting of the garden belonging to Jaua required 79 hours' work from the men and 60 from the women. On the other hand, a garden half the size of this, worked by a smaller family group took 58 hours of labor on the part of the men and 30 on that of the women. Hogbin's comment is cogent:

> So far as the men are concerned, this would appear to establish the truth of the opinion, often expressed by the natives, that collaboration results in a speeding up of the work. "A man who toils by himself goes along as he pleases: he works slowly and pauses every time he feels like having a smoke. . . . But when two men work together each tries to do the most. One man thinks to himself, 'My back aches and I feel like resting, but my friend there is going on: I must go on too, or I shall feel ashamed.' The other man thinks to himself, 'My arms are tired and my back is breaking, but I must not be the first to pause.' Each man strives to do the most, and the garden is finished quickly." [44]

One study has analyzed the cost of voluntary as against paid labor in the quasi-pecuniary society of the Popoluca of eastern Mexico. In this case, a house, the framework of which had been constructed, was daubed by two groups, one voluntary and only

[43] Provinse, 85–7.   [44] Hogbin (1938–9), 296.

provided with food while working, the other hired for the purpose and receiving money payments. The comparative figures are as follows:

	Communal Work	Hired Help
Man hours available	120	54
Square feet completed	96	150
Time in minutes per square foot	75	20
Total labor cost in pesos	30.00	8.00
Cost per square foot in pesos	.32	0.5

Of interest here is the fact that despite the greater cost of voluntary work, the prestige factor inherent in the giving of a feast compensates for the lessened efficiency and the lower return.[45]

Whatever the case, it is not to be thought that altruism runs so rife in motivating the co-operative work of non-industrialized peoples that considerations of self-interest are lacking. It should, in fact, be quite evident from the instances cited that men and women work for others so they may have in return the labor of these others when they are in need of it. A case in point is the attitude of the Papuan Keralai man, who welcomes other men when they come and make gardens on his tract. Not only will his own garden be the more easily worked; but, for the rest, there will be ample reciprocal opportunity later to make his field on the land of these others.[46] Even more striking is the situation in the archipelago of Palau, where patterns of co-operative work are of great importance, not only as concerns the productive system as a whole, but as a mechanism which aids a family group to attain more wealth and thus improve its position in society. This mechanism, called *omulu'ul*, is described by Barnett in the following terms:

In conformance with it, a woman's brothers always stand prepared to help her husband in any way they can. If he wishes to go fishing, or if he is building a house, or if he needs labor in any way, he simply has to notify these brothers-in-law and they are expected to come to his assistance.

Yet co-operation here has a realistic aspect that is perhaps found, but not always noted, in other societies:

[45] Foster (1942), 29–34.　　　　[46] Williams, 213.

It is obvious that this system is open to abuses in the sense that men who are obliged to serve and are eager for money [47] will do far more than is necessary in their own self-interest. When this happens . . . men deliberately and assiduously press their services and food upon their nieces' and sisters' husbands in order to heavily obligate them for a money return. The pressure exerted upon a man may be entirely unsolicited and even unwanted, but he is in no position to refuse it. If he did, he would be severely criticized by everyone and in particular by those who were plying him. He would be regarded as an undesirable brother-in-law* and his reluctance to play the game might finally lead to a divorce.[48]

We should, however, likewise not commit the error of thinking nonliterate societies to be groups among whom competitive effort is unknown in conjunction with this co-operative work. Even where co-operation enters as a mechanism for survival, as it sometimes actually does, we find that within any given work group, competition for the prestige of being the best worker is seldom absent, while one group may compete with another in a spirit of rivalry that is not invariably of the friendliest. This co-operative effort, moreover, does not exclude individualistic endeavor. In the productive activities of nonliterate folk, especially where the concept of wealth is well developed and there is competition for the attainment of possessions and the prestige that accrues from them, individualism can assume a place of some importance. Co-operative work, furthermore, is not always voluntary. Group labor, performed for chiefs and priests by command, as is the case in many of the islands of the Pacific, is by no means unknown. Finally, to view the phenomenon of co-operation from all angles, it should be indicated that there is no society which does not know both the shirker and the man who, by predisposition, abstains from co-operating with his fellows, preferring to go his way alone.

[47] For a discussion of Palauan money, see below, 258–62, taken from Ritzenthaler, or cf. Barnett, Ch. III.

[48] Barnett, 59.

CHAPTER VI

INCENTIVES AND REWARDS

THE MOTIVATIONS underlying work, in terms of the rewards men seek for the efforts they put forth, have been accorded much attention by economic theorists. Here the hedonistic approach, defining a delicate balancing of pleasures and pains, has largely figured. In many discussions of the problem by economists, it has been implicitly accepted that labor is distasteful to man; that men do as little as possible, and avoid as much of it as they can contrive to escape. Conversely, it is taken for granted that to make men work, the rewards must be as great as possible; and that these rewards—customarily thought of as pecuniary in nature—must always be held before the worker like a carrot before the nose of a donkey, so that he will endeavor to attain for the future what is not possible for him to enjoy at present.

There is no reason to deny the proposition that men do not find pleasure in unremitting labor that taxes their strength unduly, or that they find no satisfaction in exertion for ends that are not clear to them, or for which they cannot see any meaningful return. But it is important to understand that to accept this proposition in no way frees us of the need to recognize the fact that the meaning of labor, the concept of hard work, and the terms in which recompense can be defined can vary greatly. For this very reason, it is only by acquiring some comprehension of the place of labor in other than the industrialized societies of Europe and America that we can understand how specialized an interpretation of the concept enters into the thinking of all of us, whether we are economists or not.

It is by no means only because of the preoccupation of economists with the labor market, and the measurement in pecuniary terms of the incentives which bring a man to accept one job and reject another, that we find it difficult to achieve this understanding. The neglect by anthropologists of the factor of labor incentives, except in the case of a few students, is noteworthy. The reasons for this neglect are, however, not too difficult to understand. For one thing, the element of degree of specialization enters. We have already seen how difficult it is to apply the concept of the entrepreneur to non-pecuniary, nonliterate societies. In an analogous manner, we find it is equally difficult to analyze the motivations that actuate the worker—in the sense of wage-worker or white-collar employee—in these less complex economic settings. Here, except where the factors of specialization in political or religious activities intervene, workers as such, in the accepted sense of men and women who are economically specialized in that they depend on wages for a livelihood, are practically non-existent. Nor are exceptions to this statement, as we shall shortly see, of any great significance in terms of the customary approach of economists to the problems of labor economics.

The second principal reason why anthropologists have so often disregarded this important question follows from what has just been indicated. Aside from their survival aspect, which in this context is obvious, the motivations to labor lie in the realm of values. Now the study of the value-systems of any people is one of the most delicate and difficult operations in the entire range of anthropological field research. It requires a sensitive balancing of what people say against what they do. In a very real sense, it is not unlike the task of the linguist, who, working from the speech-habits of a people, inductively analyzes out the grammar of a language that has never been written, but whose rules have nonetheless been followed for generations by speakers who have never realized their existence. In a similar way, the grammar of every philosophical system in which the values of a people, economic and non-economic, figure as guides to conduct, must be inducted from observing their behavior and recording their concepts of the world in which they live. Like any grammar, a value-system lies beneath the level of consciousness and only finds verbal expression when some element in it is challenged.

Why men work, then, can only be studied objectively by analyzing the situations in which they actually do perform their various tasks, and analyzing the reasons they give for working as they do. From this, we move to hypotheses concerning the underlying system of values that gives meaning to the rewards which labor brings to the worker. In a pecuniary society that has a labor market, a monetary unit of measurement exists which permits the economist to calculate choices between alternatives, and thus to draw conclusions as to motivations. From here, the social psychologist and industrial management specialist can move to test these conclusions. But for the anthropologist, lacking the pecuniary unit of measurement even in those societies where least common denominators of economic values are present, such techniques are not feasible. His probing for motivations to labor must be in the more general field of overall value-systems. And since the study of values is an area of anthropological research where relatively little work has been carried on, the data on the economic values that provide the rewards for labor held worth striving for have been overlooked, together with the evaluations that motivate behavior in other facets of experience.

Enough is known about the matter, however, to permit a certain amount of projection of our own attitudes toward work against the broader screen of the reactions that mark the orientations of other peoples. We become aware, for example, that the notion of a vacation is unique to Euroamerican society. That is, other peoples do not recognize the distinction we draw between the expenditure of time and effort in painful activity—"work"— and that which goes into pleasurable activity, or "non-work." It needs no demonstration to prove that vacations, as they are actually enjoyed, by no means represent a cessation of effort. On the contrary, vacations are largely considered as periods when an unrestricted expenditure of energy is permitted. However, and this is the important point, the expenditure of energy during a vacation is always in channels chosen solely by the person concerned. A vacation, that is, provides a release from the application of effort to tasks that are imposed by others.

Whatever the case, the data from nonliterate societies make it clear that considerations other than those of economic best advantage dictate labor and thus production. Thus among the Lobi tribes of West Africa, the small proportion of foragers to the total population of which they form a part is striking. For districts near the Volta River it is as follows:

Canton	Number of forgers	Number of inhabitants
Kpuére	7	2,144
Batié (south)	22	7,041
Batié (north)	8	3,408
Hemkoa	23	7,025
	60	19,618

Away from the stream, the numbers are:

Yolonioro	12	5,177
Tioio	2	1,644
Tiankoura	16	7,888
Bouroum-Bouroum	9	3,088
	39	17,797

Because the iron-workers are so few—a total of 99 out of a population of 37,415—local production does not suffice to supply the demand for the implements they manufacture. In consequence, for many years these have had to be imported from neighboring tribes.[1] An "opportunity" for enterprising forgers is obviously not lacking in these districts. By harder work or enlarging forges a market ready at hand could be supplied. It is apparent, however, that other than economic rewards motivate the iron-workers of these tribes and cause them to be content with but a part of the returns they might receive.

2

ALTHOUGH the economic destinies of nonliterate men are usually in their own hands, it does not follow that all members of such groups live under conditions that allow them to dictate the form their work will take, nor that the phenomenon of working for wages is unknown. Slavery, as a matter of fact, is widespread in nonliterate societies. While it was rarely the kind of institution it became in the Western World in historic times, yet except in rare instances, the time and energy of the slave was at the disposal of his master even where slavery was mildest.

In societies such as those of pre-European Peru or Mexico, or in West Africa, where dynastic political control was based on the exploitation of the great mass of the population, the worker, even

[1] Labouret (1931), 70.

where he was not a slave, but a full-fledged member of his community, was anything but a free agent. And in still other societies, where the power of rulers was not characterized by the brute force that marked it in these regions, the existence of socio-economic classes often made for the control of labor-power by those in strategic positions. Thus, in Mangaia, when powerful families had menial work to be done, poorer relatives were called on to perform these tasks, since they so needed the protection they received from their patrons that they were forced to accept what was in essence the status of serfdom.[2] Or again, in Tonga, we find that compulsory labor has existed since early times. A kind of corvée system is in operation, administered in the early days by superior chiefs and today by the government. "It was no doubt the system by which labor was requisitioned for the construction of the great royal tombs, the pigeon mounds, the great trilithons and other works for royal and public purposes." There seems, indeed, to have been a kind of labor tax, and inferior chiefs sent men two or three times a week to work for those who had higher rank.[3] Yet taking the nonliterate world in the large, these cases are not to be regarded as representative, and for that very reason they stand out against the much larger background of those societies where the worker is his own master.

Let us briefly consider some of the instances where, despite the fact that the labor market as found in our economic system is unknown, the payment of wages for labor is encountered. In the main, wages in these societies are paid in kind, since in many instances no money exists as an economic intermediary between the worker and his reward. Yet whatever form they may take, wages represent but supplementary gain to members of those nonliterate societies who earn them. Some groups, it is true, are to be found where ownership of the means of production is sufficiently concentrated to make it necessary for men and women to depend upon tasks provided by others for their livelihood, but this is emphatically the exception. A characteristic reaction to employment for wages is that set down for the Mexican town of Mitla, where "You do not work for wages unless you have to." [4] More commonly a worker hires himself out for wages to augment resources for a special end, or to make available to himself goods

[2] Hiroa (1934), 130.
[3] Gifford (1929), 181–2.

[4] Parsons (1936b), 62.

of a non-subsistence kind to enhance his social standing, or for personal gratification.

Outstanding examples of both these principles are to be found among herding folk, where ambitious young men may strike out for themselves by caring for the animals of men outside their own immediate families, receiving in payment a certain number of the young born to the herds committed to their care. This is a regular practice among such southeast African herders as the Zulu and the Ba-Ila, and their more northerly neighbors, as well as among the camel-herders of the southeastern Sahara. Several forms of wage-labor, the above-mentioned among them, as found in one of these South African peoples, the Tswana, have been carefully described. Here a man hires another to care for his cattle, the rate of payment being determined by mutual agreement. Usually a heifer is given him, though the owner of the herd may also provide food, blankets, and other necessities. The herdman may perform other services for his employer, such as digging a well, but his primary engagement is to exercise all care in watching the herd, and he is responsible for any losses incurred because of neglect of his duties.

Payment of wages by labor contract is also found among the Tswana. Basically, this is not unlike the systems of co-operative labor described in the preceding chapter. "Those coming . . . are paid . . . in beer, thick milk, . . . or tobacco, sometimes in meat, porridge, or salt." This is sufficient if the work is completed the first day, but if the task is not finished, they will come the next morning, if "there is more beer or whatever commodity has been used as payment." They can be paid in advance; should an ox die, and its owner fears it will rot because there is so much of it, he sends word that meat is available. Those willing to work for him at some future time will come and get portions of it. Or a woman "may in the same way hire labour in advance by selling beer or some similar commodity." Should a person, when called in, fail to perform the day's work for which he thus obligated himself, he may be brought before the court. However, the resulting threat of social disapproval, manifested in the refusal of others to work for such a person when he is in need of their labor, usually cares for any possible evasion of contract.[5]

[5] Schapera (1938), 253–5.

Gainful employment of this type is also common among such a Siberian reindeer-herding people as the Chuckchee, where the poorer men save their own herds in winter by working for their more wealthy neighbors, who pay them with skins and animals for slaughter. Light is thrown on the manner in which considerations of self-interest become apparent where work even on as simple a level as this is done for others by the fact that these temporary helpers habitually leave their employers in the spring before the calving season, since it is at this period of the year that the large herds prove most troublesome. Some Chuckchee families are so poor, however, that they own almost no herds at all, and such people enter the service of the more wealthy for extended periods. They receive supplies of meat and skins in payment for their services, though they must furnish their own pack-animals when they move from one camp to another. If their employer is pleased with their work, a family living under this arrangement receives about ten fawns annually, in addition to the subsistence return mentioned. In the course of five favorable years, these animals and their increase give such a family a herd of some hundred reindeer, sufficient to permit them to attain a position of independence.[6]

Another instance of how pay in kind may be welcomed by those in need of supplementary income to tide over hard times—in this instance in a non-herding society—is to be found in the practices connected with aboriginal methods of preserving squashes among the Hidatsa. Once the squashes were harvested and heaped onto the drying forms,

> The women of the family made a feast, cooking much food for the purpose; some old women were then invited to come and cut up the squashes with knives, into slices to dry. We regarded these old women as hired, and I remember that in my father's family we hired sometimes eight, sometimes ten, and sometimes only six. . . . The end slices we thought less valuable than those from the middle of the squash; and . . . they . . . were taken home by the old women. . . . About three sacks of these inferior slices would be carried home at one time by an old woman worker.[7]

[6] Bogoras, 82–3.   [7] G. L. Wilson, 68–71.

That payment, aside from the feast, was in terms of inferior portions of the squash, is perhaps significant as indicating how the need of these old women was used to further the economic interest of their employer. This is in accord with the postulates of economists regarding the manner in which the entrepreneur (a term that is, of course, not strictly applicable in this case) may be expected to act in accordance with the dictates of his own best economic self-interest.

As we have seen in discussing co-operative labor, food payments for work are common, though here there may in addition be an anticipated reward in the future benefits from reciprocal labor. An instance is given from Samoa where the chief summoned women who were experts in making floor-mats; but, as in parallel situations so frequently encountered in the South Seas, the remuneration of the workers was no more than food and lodging while they engaged in their tasks.[8] Among the Siang Dyak of Borneo, in addition to the two types of co-operative labor that have been described, work may also be done for wages, though this is not commonly found. When a man is too ill to care for his own rice field, he seeks someone outside his reciprocal work group, and pays him from one-third to two-thirds of the produce from the field, depending upon the amount of labor involved. Where this is not possible because of the economic straits of the sick man, his field will be worked by his fellows, even though his illness has prevented him from carrying out his partnership agreement for co-operative work. He will be expected later, however, either to turn over a portion of the crop he harvests, or, when he recovers, to give additional time to the plots of those who cared for his field.[9]

An interesting form of deferred payment for work, which may be thought of as a kind of old-age insurance, occurs among the Daly River tribes of Australia. Here provision is made for later maturity by accrued services expended on older kinsmen. These services are performed as obligations, and those who contribute this labor will later be the beneficiaries of the labor of young men of the next generation, who will then stand in the same relationship to them. Thus the food, tobacco, clothes, hair belts, ornaments, and other goods a young man has given are eventually

[8] Hiroa (1930), 248.   [9] Provinse, 87.

returned to him in a steady stream when he is no longer able to produce them.[10]

3

THE VALUES which dictate the attitudes of non-industrialized folk toward their work can also be analyzed by employing another approach. We may consider the implications of those precepts that are used to teach the young the role of work as the ideal of the "good way of life" finding expression in the sayings of a people. This procedure has its shortcomings, to be sure, since such data are most general in character, and often mirror idealized social sanctions rather than actual practices. A wealth of data of this type has been collected, but only three examples need be given here—one from North America and two from West Africa.

Young Omaha Indians were told by their elders: "If one does not make arrows, he will borrow moccasins, leggings, and robes, and be disliked by persons from whom he borrows." The instruction continued:

> If you are not industrious, when a herd of buffalo is slaughtered you may come across a young man whom you may consider insignificant (i.e., of no position in the tribe) but who has killed a buffalo by his own energy; you will look longingly at the best portions of the meat, but he will give them to another who is known to be thrifty and generous and you will go away disappointed.

An elderly informant, recounting the instruction he had received when a youth said:

> I was told . . . a man must be energetic, industrious. . . . An industrious man wears leggings of well-dressed deerskin; his robe is of the finest dressed buffalo skin and he wears earrings. . . . If a man is not industrious and energetic, he will not be able to entertain other people. A lazy man will be envious when he sees men of meaner birth invited to feasts because of their thrift and their ability to en-

[10] Stanner, 19.

tertain other people. If you are lazy, nobody will have pleasure in speaking to you. . . . Even when only two or three are gathered to a feast the energetic and industrious man is invited. People in speaking of him say: He is pleasant to talk with, he is easy of approach. Such a man has many to mourn his death and is long remembered. . . . Such are some of the things that used to be said by the old to the young men.[11]

Proverbs and aphorisms afford especially good insight into the traditionally correct attitudes of Africans. Comment on the canons of prudence and application is not lacking, while consideration for the worker is not overlooked. The Kru of Liberia, for instance, say: "Slowness took Tumu's canoes," when pointing out to a laggard that if, like the mythological Tumu, he does not work more energetically, he will lose what he owns. But they also say: "To be strong, a person must have more than a song to eat," a proverb that is a man's answer to a reprimand from his employer for resting while he waits for food to be brought him. Perseverance is the theme of a saying placed in the mouth of a small and greedy, but easily caught, river fish: "The blood does not dry on your bait." Since even young boys can gather in these fish, the proverb is a reminder much like our own saying: "Make hay while the sun shines." The need for being adequately prepared for one's work is stressed in the aphorism: "Rice that is not dry does not come out of the mortar unmashed" and is a comment heard when a man has failed in his task, or spoken to admonish a person who persists in attempting work clearly beyond his capacities.[12]

Still more direct statements concerning the need for work are found in the sayings of the Peul and Toucouleur. "Poverty is the elder daughter of laziness"; "He who stays in bed when he is able to work, will have to get up when he cannot"; "Dust on the feet is better than dust on the behind"; "He who cannot work, earns nothing"; "He who does not work his fields or have someone work them, him hunger will kill." [13] These few examples from the large number of proverbs current in African societies show how clearly the patterns of these cultures stress the need for application if one is to get on, the righteousness of the man who does his work

[11] Fletcher and LaFleche, 331–3.   [13] Gaden, *passim*.
[12] Herskovits and Tagbwe, *passim*.

faithfully, the reward of labor and the punishment for laziness, the necessity for aptitude in a task undertaken and the need for application to the work in hand.

4

ATTITUDES toward work are more specifically indicated in those studies where attention has been paid to this factor in the productive process. On the island of Tikopia, the motivation for labor derives from what Firth terms *positive conventions of work:*

> They include ties of loyalty to him, to neighbours, to bond friends, to a chief; the concept of labour and its implications, the explicit recognition of laziness on the one hand and of the need for rest on the other.

In addition to these, "There are a number of modes of behaviour which are conventional in the sense that they generally follow and are linked up with traditionalized concepts." These include, first, "those with a positive effect upon work, such as emulation," and second, negative factors, "such as the perception of insult, or the fear of sorcery, which lead to a falling off in productive effort."

It is made clear that the "labour situation" cannot be interpreted simply as a response to a system of reward. "Workers," we are told, "are not drawn into an undertaking from a free reservoir of labour power, their choice determined by the wage-rates offered; they come from groups attached by definite social ties to the entrepreneur. Social forces catch up and enmesh the economic factors in a wider net." The obligations of kinship and of other ties "can be contrasted with the absence of any other convention of hiring of labour. Contracting to work for another person for a reward specified in advance is not a Tikopia custom. When one person works for another their association is so governed by canons of etiquette that it assumes the form of partnership in a joint enterprise, and the ultimate reward for the labour takes on the external form of a gift." Examples of this are found in such undertakings as the repair of canoes and the extraction of sago. The matter is well summarized in these terms: a man "is not given a job because he contributes to the productive fund;

he makes the contribution because he has accepted the obligation of the job." [14]

Comment by Paulme on the point under consideration here, as concerns the Dogon of French West Africa, shows how diverse are the motivations to labor in this society:

> There is no doubt but that the primary motive for work is that of providing subsistence; but the whole of economic life by no means derives from this drive. The force of tradition, an appreciation of work well done, the desire for emulation, the wish to have the approval of his group, even when this is not expressed—all these and many more function in shaping economic activities. It would be most difficult to devise a single formula that would comprehend all the reasons which might cause a Dogon to undertake a given task.

Many of these reasons would lodge in the area of prestige-seeking. The fact that successfully completing a certain piece of work will raise a man in the esteem of his fellows would often be more important than any economic advantage which might accrue to him. Even when his own individual desires might lead him to an economically advantageous course of action, the fact that this could bring him social disapprobation turns him in another direction. Thus, we find that the need for the esteem of his group dictates expenditure of food-stuffs which will mark him as a man of wealth and position and dominates any tendency he might have to save his resources as a precaution against want. The festival which marks the end of mourning requires a family to amass great amounts of food and drink, to be consumed by those in attendance; yet the reputation for generosity this group will thus gain more than compensates for the work expended in making possible the acquisition of the goods distributed.

> It is clear that personal interest, understood as the desire to realize maximum return with minimum effort, is by no means the only drive that causes a man to work in this society. Each person is led, more or less consciously, more or less indirectly, by the desire for well-being, for wealth, and for the regard of the entire community. [15]

[14] Raymond Firth (1939), 145–50.   [15] Translated from Paulme, 193–4.

Even such a people as the Siriono of Bolivia, who live on the subsistence level, manifest a variety of reactions to the need to work. Here, where there is a constant struggle to obtain enough food for survival, immediate returns are desired against activities involving a longer-term investment of energy. The acquisition of food, moreover, so dominates the economic picture that its availability for a period of time is regarded as affording an opportunity for relaxation rather than for performing other tasks. "Labor is not a virtue among the Siriono," says Holmberg:

> They are relatively apathetic to work . . . which includes such distasteful tasks as house-building, gathering firewood, clearing, planting and tilling of fields. In a quite different class, however, are such pleasant occupations as hunting, . . . and collecting . . . , which are regarded more as diversions than as work. . . . When food, especially meat, is plentiful, little work is performed. What people like best to do at this time is to lie in their hammocks, rest, eat, indulge in sexual intercourse, sleep, play with their children, be groomed, sing, dance, or drink. Free time is rarely employed in improving the house, although rain is expected, or in enlarging a garden plot, although the supply of food is insecure.

It is of some interest to note that in this society the prestige drives that have been seen to afford so strong a motivation for labor in other groupings is at a minimum. "Besides the immediate desire and necessity for food, the incentives to labor are few." These are set forth in specific terms, as follows:

> When the immediate needs for food have been supplied, a person is neither much criticized for doing nothing, nor much praised for occupying his time in constructive labor. . . . No prestige is gained by building a better house or a larger garden, both of which may have to be abandoned in the next move. It would seem, in fact, that the nomadic character of the band is the principal reason for not working, because the results of one's labor can rarely be carried with one.[16]

[16] Holmberg, 41.

5

With this available information in hand, we may attempt to point the outstanding similarities and differences between these societies and ours in the emphasis placed on the balancing of pleasure and pain as a motivation for work. One may suspect that as far as the mass of peoples are concerned, whether living in machine or non-machine societies, life goes on without too much thought being given to distant aims. One works because one must; because everyone else works; because it is one's tradition to work. As among ourselves, labor is performed by non-literate folk with the expectation of return, and, where work is done for others, the attitude toward effort appears to be akin to that with which we are familiar. But as rewards are envisaged, we have seen how widely they differ in different societies, both in the forms they take and in the degree to which they act as drives. Among ourselves, rewards are removed one step from labor by the fact, noted above, that between the worker and the necessities of life and such luxuries as he can afford is interposed our ubiquitous pecuniary system. This means that the actual return for labor must always be translated into something else before it is directly consumable. In non-industrial societies, the rewards are direct—as witness the fact that wages, where they do exist, are almost invariably paid in kind.

There is yet another matter involved in our equation: prestige. Certainly in a vast number of nonliterate societies, as in our own, the drive for prestige constitutes a powerful psychological factor in determining economic no less than other forms of behavior. Among those groups, it is one of the most significant rewards a man can strive for. Nothing is so heady, nothing so quickly appreciated, on any level, as the recognition of ability and the measure of respect and enhancement of social standing that accompanies this recognition. How powerful is this factor in the development and maintenance of social and economic classes in many nonliterate societies will be made apparent in later chapters. Here it may be pointed out how, for example, from the admonition to an Omaha youth that was cited, this same motivation can operate as an incentive to labor. Such testimony as that from Australia, where we are told that "while there seems to be little work for work's sake, there is a real pride in craftsmanship, and any work is normally well done and brought to completion,"[17] is especially significant, just because it is given for a people whose economic system is so exceedingly simple. Or again, the discussion of the bird-snaring industry among the Maori [18] brings a realization of how many factors involving prestige constitute real spurs to effort, while lists of occupations giving the relative degrees of prestige attached to each, as are available for Tonga [19] and Dahomey,[20] further testify regarding this point.

The prestige that accrues to the hard worker, the fast worker, the careful worker, the competent worker, is thus a significant factor in motivating labor in most societies. It is doubtlessly this drive to excel and to be reputed for excellence in certain crafts that has stimulated skills that otherwise might only have remained latent. Prestige is therefore to be regarded not only an important reward for labor, but in itself a factor in encouraging production. As such, it must have played no inconsiderable part in the development of traditions for specialization in labor, to the consideration of which we now turn.

[17] Sharp, 37.
[18] Firth (1929), 128 ff.

[19] Gifford (1929).
[20] Herskovits (1938), I, 48–50.

CHAPTER VII

DIVISION OF LABOR AND SPECIALIZATION

THAT non-industrialized societies differ most strikingly from those with machine technologies in the degree to which they practice division of labor and industrial specialization has been indicated in an earlier chapter. We shall here consider, in somewhat greater detail, the forms which these aspects of the economic order take in nonliterate communities, so as the more clearly to understand this phase of the economic order of these cultures.

The terms "division of labor" and "specialization" must themselves be given some attention before we proceed with our analyses. In simplest terms, and regarded from the point of view of the total productive process of a given economic system, the amount of work required to meet the needs of a people may be performed indiscriminately by all members of the community; or this work may be divided according to the sanctions of custom and the lessons of efficiency learned from earlier generations. Thus the types of labor performed by members of each sex may be and, as a matter of fact, are always different. There may, in addition, be a division of productive function on the basis of age, or clan affiliation, or hereditary position, or caste, or guild membership. There may, moreover, also be inter-tribal division of labor, where natural resources are localized, or where differing craft traditions have been developed among the peoples who inhabit a given region.

The term "division of labor," then, is best employed when we speak of the splitting up of the total amount of effort needed to keep the economy of a given society operating at its customary rate of efficiency. Each of the sub-groups whose members perform a particular aspect of the work may be regarded as specialized in its particular calling, and the kind of labor each performs in achieving this can be denoted as its "specialization." In this sense, then, where we might speak of the *division of labor* between the sexes, we could in some societies also speak of certain woman *specializing* in pottery-making, or of some men in woodcarving. Or, in a wider sense, we might distinguish the specialization in fishing of that part of a social group which, let us say, lived near the sea-coast from the specialization in agricultural work of its inland members. However, inasmuch as pottery and wood-carvings, fish and garden produce would all represent goods desired, acquired, and consumed by members of the society, the specialized labor of each sub-group concerned with the production of any one good, or type of good, could be looked upon as representing to this extent a division of the total labor necessary to supply all the requirements of the whole.

It is necessary to bear in mind that these meanings of the terms "division of labor" and "specialization" do not carry the same significance for economists as they do for many anthropologists who have been concerned with this phase of the economic life of nonliterate peoples. In all likelihood, this divergence in meaning reflects the difference in the complexity of the economies with which each discipline deals. To economists, interested in the productive processes of industrial societies, the terms most often mean that every worker directs his labor toward the production of a very small part of a particular commodity. In this sense, the worker becomes specialized not in the production of a certain good, but of only a portion of that good. What an individual produces of itself has no utility unless it is incorporated into the finished product of which it must form a part. This does not mean that there is no division of labor and specialization as among entire industries in our society. A craftsman may make an entire chair, or a wrought-iron lighting fixture, but such craftsmen are few compared with the number of workers who turn out chair-legs or fixture-arms, which are later joined to other parts of the requisite object to make the finished product. For most economists, however, this difference in type of specialization is considered implicit and not of great relevance.

Yet it is just such elements of these concepts that have the most validity for analyzing the economic systems of non-industrialized societies. Only rarely is any division of labor within an industry—or, as it might be termed, subdivision of labor—encountered among nonliterate folk. Such intra-industrial specialization would be encountered only in the production of such larger capital goods as houses, canoes, or fish-weirs. Even here, it is the rule in such cultures that an arrangement of this sort is temporary; moreover, each worker devoting himself to a part of a specific task is most often competent to perform other phases of the work besides that on which he may at the moment be engaged. Our use of the terms here will thus have to do with that kind of division of labor and that specialized direction of effort that results in the production of commodities or categories of commodities, but not of parts of commodities.

A further qualification must be made before we proceed. It is essential for us to recognize that the degree to which division of labor and specialization are found in industrial activities of nonliterate peoples, as in the case of all other phases of their culture, varies from society to society. Thus in groups where the primary division of labor is along sex lines, every man or woman not only will know how to do all those things that men or women habitually do among them, but must be able to do them efficiently. As we move to societies of somewhat greater economic complexity, we find that certain men may spend a larger proportion of their time than others doing wood-carving or iron-working, or certain women making pots or weaving cloth; but all the members of the groups will have some competence in the techniques controlled by those of a given sex. In still other nonliterate societies, certain men and woman specialize not only in one technique, but in a certain type of product, as, for instance, where one woman will devote her time to the production of pots for everyday use and another make pottery exclusively for religious rites. It must again be stressed that, except under most unusual circumstances, we do not find the kind of organization where one woman characteristically specializes in gathering the clay, another in fashioning it, and a third in firing the pots; or, where one man devotes himself to getting wood, a second to roughly blocking out the proportions of a stool or figure, and a third to finishing it.

Our discussion of specialization and division of labor in non-literate societies will document the generalizations that have been stated, following the order indicated in the preceding paragraphs. That is, we shall first devote our attention to sex division of labor, especially important for us since in our own society this has become so blurred in the process of adjusting our traditions of labor to the machine that its significance is likely to be overlooked when our culture alone is considered. We shall then inquire into the types of industrial specialization that exist in non-literate societies and, in this connection, indicate some of the rare instances where division of labor within a given industrial pursuit makes the production of a given commodity. Finally, we shall take into account cases of tribal or regional specialization.

2

No PHASE of the economic life of nonliterate peoples has attracted more attention than has sex division of labor, and many attempts have been made to explain it. Gras, defining "the two chief concerns of mankind" as "the preservation of the individual and the perpetuation of the race," holds that "we can identify man more particularly with the latter." [1] Buxton summarizes his position by stating that, "Man is primarily the breadwinner, the provider of food in the widest sense. Woman is the distributor of loaves, that is, the purveyor of cooked foods." "In most societies," he continues, "it is the duty of the man to provide the raw materials on which the household subsists," so that, "apart from agriculture, it will be found that woman's work is complementary to that of man." [2] Durkheim, on a more theoretical level, envisages the division of labor, especially the sexual division of labor, as having "its real function . . . to create in two or more persons a feeling of solidarity." He points out that "man and woman isolated from one another are only different parts of the same concrete whole which they form again on uniting," and that "it is the sexual division of labor which constitutes the source of conjugal solidarity." Unfortunately, his discussion of how the sexual division of labor arose—a question of origin whose answer must rest on speculation—is based on unverifiable assumptions

[1] Gras (1922), 15.   [2] Buxton, 25–6, 21 ff.

concerning the undifferentiated functions of men and woman in primeval society which do not hold for any human group existing at the present time.[3]

In some instances, assumptions concerning sex division of labor among particular peoples have given rise to a portrayal of a relationship that took little account of the human factor involved. Thus Kaberry notes how Malinowski, on the basis of the existing literature concerning the Australian aborigines, stated in 1913 that though "heavier work ought naturally to be performed by the man, the contrary obtains." Because of this, he concluded that "compulsion is therefore . . . the chief basis of this division of labour, and it may be said in the Australian aboriginal society the economic fact of the division of labour is rooted in a sociological status—viz., the compulsion of the weaker sex by the 'brutal' half of society." Hence "the relation of a husband to a wife is in its economic aspect that of a master to its slave."[4] Yet Kaberry's field report shows clearly that this picture has little validity; woman's work cannot be assumed to be "more onerous" than that of the man, since "actually it is less so. . . ." The division of labor falls into fairly clear categories: "the men go out to hunt, the women to forage." If in woman's work there is less uncertainty, there is also less of the excitement the men have; if the woman's work requires more constant application to the task in hand, it also does not involve the fatiguing chase "over rugged hills" and in "the blazing sun," where "the element of sport . . . often . . . ends in the disappointment of seeing one's dinner leaping into the distance over the hills."[5]

The fact is that, as in the case of most socially sanctioned forms of behavior, we are here dealing with a phenomenon far more complex than is at first apparent. This being the case, it is futile to attempt to explain forms taken by sexual division of labor, even in a particular instance, by any one generalization. This position is implicit in Thurnwald's discussion where, in a broad way, he refers the problem to the early life of man as this has developed in the light of the ethnic contacts of any given folk—an approach whose appeal is lessened by his later attempt to ascribe sexual predominance solely to a biological cause.[6]

[3] Durkheim, 57 ff.
[4] Malinowski (1913), 287, (quoted in Kaberry, 15).
[5] Kaberry, 13–15, 17.
[6] Thurnwald (1922a), 7–8, 212.

Forde, commenting on the differences in sex division of labor present in the patterns of certain tribes of West Africa and North America, where other aspects of the industrial organization are comparable, refers the matter partly to the biological differences between the two sexes, partly to their different environmental settings, and partly to the differing historical experiences of each.[7] This type of eclectic approach to the problem would seem to be the only scientifically admissible procedure, for the social sciences, with increasingly effective techniques of analysis, are coming more and more to recognize the inadequacy of explanations of any aspect of social life among a given people in terms of any single cause.

Even where explanations of this kind have been attempted, the lack of data has made them uncertain, though they may have all semblance of validity as far as their logic goes. An instance of this is the attempt to account for sexual division of labor as found in the manufacture of pottery in Europe and literate Asia. In most cultures, pottery is the work of the women, but in this area it is done by men. The question is thus a challenging one. The answer, derived partially from inference, and partially from archaeological data, takes us back to the early days of human existence. It seems reasonable to suppose that prior to the domestication of animals or plants, the men hunted and carried on those other aspects of the food-quest that took them from home. It seems equally reasonable that the women, being closely confined to the place of family habitation, if only for physiological reasons, made their contribution to the economy of the group by searching out roots and herbs and gathering fruits and nuts.

In this way, it is further assumed, a tradition became fixed that associated men with animals and women with plants. In terms of this tradition, then, as it was carried over into later days and widely diffused, man became designated as the herdsman and, in the absence of the plow, this tradition was capable of being reintegrated in either of two ways. The old association of men with the larger domesticated animals could adhere to the new affiliation of the animal with agriculture—which was what did occur—or the animal might be assimilated to the woman-as-cultivator complex. The new association having been made, then with the discovery of the wheeled vehicle pulled by horses or

[7] Forde (1934), 171–2, 258–9.

oxen, man became identified with the wheel. And when pottery began to be turned on the wheel, pottery-making became an occupation for males.

Now, as has been said, this is a logical and, as far as can be determined, a historically correct explanation of why, among Indo-European peoples and in the Orient where pottery is made on the wheel, men are potters. But if we apply the same logic to spinning, we find it quite out of line with historical fact and observable practice. For in the same area, where the spinning-wheel was also developed, women have retained their function as spinners. It is no help to reason, as does Buxton, that "the household utensils are normally woman's work. The ancient art of pottery therefore belongs to the women, though it has passed often to men in cases where pottery has ceased to be a household industry, but has become the means of winning the daily bread, and therefore a raw material." [8] For though, under industrialization, spinning has also become a means of winning the daily bread, in this industry both men and women have always been employed.

Another example of how many factors may enter into the determination of the patterns of sex division of labor, and how important it is to control all these factors with care, is to be had in the aboriginal agricultural practices of the Kota, who live in the Nilgiri hills of India. In earlier times the men did the sowing, while the women followed after them and spread the manure which fertilized the plants. This was because the technique of manuring involved carrying a basketful of dung on the head, which, as it was moved from side to side, caused the manure to fall out over the edges of the basket. Kota men were restrained by tradition from carrying head-burdens, and hence could not employ this method, though the question why this tradition developed, or why some other method of spreading manure was not devised is, of course, aside from the point of the present discussion. Today, since the coming of the Europeans and the introduction of the potato as the principal crop, the women plant while the men manure the fields. The potato cannot be fertilized by spreading manure haphazard, but each plant must have its individual allotment of fertilizer patted over it. A large and heavy container must be carried about the field in such a way

[8] Buxton, 27.

that it can be set down beside each plant, while the manure is properly placed, and then lifted and taken to the next plant. Whether or not the native explanation that woman's strength is not equal to this task is correct or rationalized, the factor of tradition, which causes women to be unaccustomed to carrying heavy loads in their arms, is undoubtedly operative.[9]

It thus becomes apparent that the specific forms taken by sex division of labor in specific tribes must be referred to the historical development of the particular body of traditions by which a given people order their lives. This is exemplified by the changes in this phase of the economy of the Tenetehara of northern Brazil, whose culture has in recent years responded to its contact, through non-Indian Brazilians, with the broader economic order of the outer world. In earlier days, the men cleared the garden site and planted and harvested manioc—the "heavy work"—besides hunting and fishing and making houses and canoes and other utensils. The women, on the other hand, worked the gardens, being "the provider of the basic foods and . . . responsible for the necessary activities of daily life." Among her duties the preparation of manioc flour ranked high. At the present time, however, men do much of the work of planting and harvesting, and manufacture much of the manioc flour. This is to be ascribed to the fact that, "while formerly manioc flour was manufactured only for the consumption of the family group, nowadays it is often produced on a larger scale for commercial sale." Furthermore, "all Tenetehara men have seen Brazilian men of the region work at these same activities, and they have imitated the 'superior' Brazilians." As a result of the operation of such historic factors, there has been a reorientation of the older patterns whereby "the man has taken on greater importance in Tenetehara economic life" and has assumed functions which in earlier times were regarded as work for women.[10]

Such obvious factors as that women, being childbearers, are at times prevented from doing heavy work, or that the task of those who must care for children confines them more closely to the home than those who do not have this duty, must of course be taken into account. Yet the observable fact that, over the world, women work as hard as men can never be neglected—the

[9] Mandelbaum (personal communication).

[10] Wagley and Galvão, 47–8.

thesis that in "primitive" societies women work harder than men will be recalled. In addition, we must be constantly aware that the lines along which sex division of labor are drawn are so variable that it is well-nigh impossible to enunciate any principle that does not present numerous exceptions. We can say, for instance, that in general women do not care for the animals of herding peoples; but this by no means holds among the Hottentots. Among agricultural tribes it is understandable that the men should clear the fields and the women tend the growing crops; but while the first part of this statement holds for most peoples, the second does not. It seems that women almost never do wood-working, though why this generalization regarding the sex division of labor should have a wider applicability than others is difficult to account for. The only fact of universal validity that remains when special factors are counted out, is that work is everywhere apportioned between men and women. Biological or other equally broad considerations can be called on to help explain the phenomenon only in the most general terms.

Furthermore, it does not follow that the lines of sex division of labor laid down among a given people are always adhered to with anything like the rigidity often attributed to prescribed conduct among presumably "primitive" folk. The lines drawn in those communities are not so vague as in our own society; but they are nowhere as fixed as they have been stated to be. To return to the Kota, we find that while most economic pursuits are allotted to one sex or the other, no hard and fast rule is enforced. Women *usually* cook, but, as among ourselves, if a wife is ill or busy or absent, the man can and will cook a meal. Men *usually* employ the hoe, but a woman is quite competent in an emergency to take up where the man of the family left off. It is only in craft specialization that work is really, in practice, restricted to one sex or the other; but here the determining factor is the opportunity for instruction and practice. "Men do not make pottery because they have never been taught to do it. Women are not blacksmiths for the same reasons, but if someone is needed to do the simple job of operating the bellows, there is no taboo against a woman doing it." [11]

The emotional "loading" often associated with customary rules of sex division of labor is an important factor in causing it to

[11] Ibid.

be followed closely. One study of the educational development of the boys and girls, among the West African Tallensi, outlines the way in which the learning process, as applied to industrial and other economic pursuits, differs in the case of the two sexes. A synoptic chart that has been drawn of the "economic duties and activities" of the two sexes in this society can be reproduced here to indicate how early in life the conditioning of the individual to the accepted modes of sex differentiation of labor begins, and how consistently it is carried on. It will in this way help us understand how deeply may be lodged the emotional attachments of an individual to his tribal canons of sex division of labor.

BOYS	GIRLS
Economic Duties and Activities	
(3–6 Years)	
None at first. Towards end of this period begin to assist in pegging out goats; scaring birds from newly sown fields and from crops: accompany family sowing and harvesting parties; using hoe in quasi-play to glean ground-nuts in company of other siblings.	None at first. Towards end of period the same duties as small boys. Frequent nursing of infants. Accompany mothers to water-hole and begin to carry tiny water-pots. Help in simple domestic tasks such as sweeping.
(6–9 Years)	
These duties now fully established. Help in house-building by carrying swish. Assist in sowing and harvesting. Towards end of period begin to go out with the herd-boys, and to care for poultry.	Duties of previous period established. Responsible co-operation in water-carrying and simpler domestic duties. Help in cooking and in activities associated with food-preparation, such as searching for wild edible herbs. Accompany family parties at sowing and harvesting, giving quasi-playful help. Carry swish at building operations and assist women in plastering and floor-beating, but still with a play element.
(9–12 Years)	
Fully responsible cattle-herding. Care for poultry. Assisting parents in hoeing and care of crops, but without responsibility. Farming own	All domestic duties can be entrusted to them by end of this period —water-carrying, cooking, care of infants, etc. Assisting in building

BOYS   GIRLS
(9–12 Years)

small plots and ground-nuts but in quasi-play. Sons of specialist craftsmen assist fathers in subsidiary capacity—"learning by looking."

and plastering, etc., more responsibility. Often sent to market to buy and sell. Help in women's part of the work at sowing and harvest times.

(12–15 Years)

Duties as in preceding period but more responsible. Responsible care of poultry, sometimes own property. Leaders of herd-boys. Real farming of own plots and in co-operation with older members of family established at end of period. Sons of specialists experimentally making things.

Responsible part in all domestic duties of everyday life, and of those associated with ceremonial occasions. Go for firewood and collect shea-fruits in the bush, and help to prepare shea butter.[12]

How specific and detailed the accepted patterns of division of labor which call forth an emotional response may be is illustrated by an incident, trivial in itself, that is none the less illuminating. In Dutch Guiana, the Javanese, who were imported in considerable numbers to work on the plantations, continue their own aboriginal modes of life. In visiting one of their houses, attention was drawn to the variety of mats that are part of their furnishings, and the excellence of the workmanship in them was admired. As each mat in turn was commented on, the Javanese host, who was also the maker, smiled his appreciation. But when admiration was expressed at his ability as displayed in an especially fine bed mat, his smile vanished, and had he not been tolerant of the ignorance of the stranger, he would obviously have shown active resentment of the implications of the comment. For this particular type of mat, it soon was made patent, is woman's work, and to credit a man with its making is to bring into play associations that are anything but acceptable.

3

ASSUMING, then, that sexual division of labor is a universal in social life, we may turn to some specific instances of it in a few

[12] Fortes (1938), 62–4.

of the large number of societies for which it has been recorded so as to see how varied may be the forms in which it is manifested. The following account from the East African Akamba was set down by a member of the tribe:

The woman's work is to powder maize, grind flour, chop wood, fetch water, look for vegetables and cook them, cook food for her husband. . . . Her other duties are: to milk the cows and churn butter, to dig (the field), sow and plant, gather in the maize, thrash the millet and Penicillaria and the *nooko* beans; to cut and carry home grass for thatching, sweep the hut, shut the entrance to the craal and clean it after the cattle (this is seldom done, however); to plait bags and mend calabashes; feed children (a very important duty), suckle them, look after them and bring them up. . . .

The man's work is to cut . . . the framework of the house, peel off the bark to make cords of, build racks to keep maize on and other smaller ones to keep things on; to chop material for the fence around the craal, for the . . . narrow entrance to the craal and for barricading the entrances with; to cut beams to support the ceiling of the hut and wood for the sleeping-places and to build the . . . compartment in the back part of the hut; to go to Ukamba and buy cattle, goats and ivory to sell at the coast and then to buy clothes for his wife; to cut posts . . . to make brooms . . . to make the sleeping skins for the beds and the wife's skin dress and to scrape the hair off this; to sew quivers, make bows and arrow-shafts, arrowheads of iron and wood and to fix them on; to rub the arrow poison on and find small bits of goat-skin, rub these very soft between the hands, bind them on the arrow-heads and then fix the arrows in the quiver; to sew the ornaments of ostrich feathers on the quiver; to cut clubs, make swords and sheaths for these, fix the hilts on . . . to make straps for his wife to fasten bundles of wood and water calabashes with; to hollow out beehives . . . and go to hang them up; to hollow out honey jars . . . to make chairs; to look after the cattle (if he has no children); to cut out snuff-boxes and make the tweezers for pulling out the hair of the beard and eyelashes.[13]

[13] Lindblom, 543–4.

The Lamba of Northern Rhodesia hold that "the axe and the spear" are the sign of the man and "the hoe" is the sign of the woman. The lines of sex division of labor are not so stringently fixed as a mere enumeration of them would indicate: "Hoe-work is primarily women's work, though men may take a hoe to assist them. Axe-work is primarily men's work, though here again a woman may use an axe on occasion." Yet a tabulated and classified list of activities of men and women shows how, in at least the "ideal" culture of this people, the functions of each are provided for by an accepted pattern: [14]

		MEN	WOMEN
(1)	*Daily Duties*	(a) ——	(a) Draw water
		(b) Bring heavy firewood	(b) Bring kindling wood
		(c) May help sweep court-yard	(c) Sweep house and courtyard
		(d) ——	(d) Make bed
(2)	*Gardens and food preparation*	(a) Tree-felling	(a) ——
		(b) First hoeing in clods	(b) Ordinary hoeing
		(c) Burning fallen trees	(c) ——
		(d) ——	(d) Smashing the clods
		(e) May help in sowing and weeding	(e) Sowing and weeding
		(f) Scare pigs, monkeys	(f) Scare birds
		(g) Cut corn-heads	(g) Break down corn
		(h) Make stands and grain-houses	(h) Carry corn to stand; put corn in grain-house
		(i) ——	(i) Take out daily corn supply
		(j) ——	(j) Thresh, winnow, grind, pound
		(k) ——	(k) Make porridge
		(l) Search for mushrooms, caterpillars, fish, meat, etc.	(l) Search for edible leaves for relish, caterpillars, mushrooms, etc.
		(m) Gather wild fruits and roots	(m) Gather wild fruits and roots
		(n) ——	(n) Extract salt, brew beer of all kinds
(3)	*Other preparations*	(a) Making soap	(a) Preparing soap
		(b) Preparing tobacco	(b) Tobacco (old women)
(4)	*Hunting, etc.*	(a) Hunting proper	(a) ——
		(b) Trapping: game, birds, mice, etc.	(b) ——
		(c) Honey	(c) ——

[14] Doke, 96–9.

	MEN	WOMEN
	(d) Fishing: nets, weirtraps, spearing, hooking	(d) Fishing: treading, baiting string with worm-bait (no hook)
(5) *Domestic Animals*	(a) —— (b) Attention to fowls	(a) Attention to goats (b) Attention to fowls
(6) *Building*	Marking out, bringing poles, bark rope, thatching, erecting, placing bonds, treading mud for plastering, rough plastering, door	Grass for thatching, water for mud, smearing walls, preparation of floor, beating of floor, making of interior screen
(7) *Clay-moulding*	(a) (A few men mould pots) (b) Pipe-bowls	(a) Cooking and other pots (b) ——
(8) *Baskets and mats*	(a) Large baskets of bamboo (b) Shallow baskets of split bamboo (c) —— (d) Palm-leaf mats	(a) Large baskets of reeds (b) Grass meal baskets (c) Grass beer baskets, beer strainer (d) A few palm-leaf mats
(9) *Wooden utensils, etc.*	(a) Eating bowls, ladles, stamp-blocks, stools, stirring sticks, dugout canoes, drums, axe, hoe and spear handles, sticks, door-fasteners, etc. (b) Drinking calabashes	(a) —— (b) Calabashes halved
(10) *Musical Instruments*	Various	Rattles, gourds, drum (of special kinds)
(11) *Weapons and Instruments*	Spear, axe, bow, arrows, knife, hoe, adze, dancing axe, type of small knife carried in hair, wire, brass bracelets, rings, combs	Grass dancing waist fringe, stones for grinding picked up
(12) *Bark and Skin Preparations*	(a) Preparation of barkcloth (b) Sewing (c) Making skins as sleeping mats	(a) —— (b) —— (c) ——
(13) *Personal Adornment*	(a) Feather hairdresses (b) Tattooing	(a) Bead headdresses woven in girls' hair (b) Tattooing

The most detailed analysis of a given system of sex division of labor available for any people—one that is far too detailed to permit of reproduction in any degree here—has been made for the Eskimo. Every generalization that has been advanced concerning this aspect of economic life is in some measure sustained by this analysis, in some respects contradicted by it. Certain tasks are only to be done by men, others only by women; some are "prevailingly" masculine, others feminine to the same degree; while a considerable number of tasks may be performed by persons of either sex. That "a man may do any kind of woman's work and a woman any kind of man's work" if a situation is urgent enough, is merely a reflection of the common-sense manner in which the Eskimo meet the demands of the harsh habitat in which they live. That differences of detail are to be found even in the way in which members of the two sexes perform identical tasks, as where "the men avoid the working position of the women" when skin-scraping, shows how deeply the sense of the importance of differentiating the work of men from that of women may lodge.[15]

"There is little intrusion of one sex into the specific activities set aside for the other" among the Hopi of Arizona. The men "in general attend to the more energetic outdoor occupations involving hard physical labor and, formerly, danger of attack from raiding groups. . . . Men also carry on sedentary occupations such as weaving, moccasin making and the like, but this is generally done in time taken from other tasks or during the winter months." The work of each sex is as follows: [16]

MEN	WOMEN	COMMON
Hunting Trapping	Preparation of meat and carcass of animals	Men slaughter and butcher; the women dress and prepare the meat for cooking
Planting Cultivating	Husking of corn for seed; husking and grinding corn for food	Planting, harvesting, and gardening (occasionally today, frequently of old)
Harvesting Roasting of corn Gardening	Preparation of food Drying of peaches, melon, squash and chile Storing of food Cooking and baking Collection of wild food products	Girls usually assist at the roasting of sweet corn

---

[15] Giffen, 83 ff.   [16] Beaglehole (1937), 18–19.

MEN	WOMEN	COMMON
Sheep herding, shearing	Care of chickens	
Cattle ranching		
Tending eagles		
Spinning of wool, cotton		
Weaving of blankets, belts, ceremonial costumes; knitting		
Manufacture and repair of tools and weapons		
Working of silver		
Preparation of paints	Preparing and dyeing of materials for basketry	
Carving and painting of dolls	Basket making	
Manufacture of ceremonial objects		
	Preparation of clays and pottery making	
Dressing, tanning of skins		
Manufacture of moccasins		
Making and repair of clothes for both sexes		
Housebuilding	Housebuilding	Housebuilding
Assembling materials	Plastering of floors, walls	
Heavy labor	Making of outside ovens	
	Preparation of piki ovens	
	Care of house and children	
	Domestic duties	
Practice of medicinal arts	Practice of medicinal arts, especially midwifery	
Digging coal	Carrying water (formerly)	
Expeditions for firewood, salt and pigments		Expeditions to collect materials for basketry
Trade and barter	Trade and barter	Trade and barter

In addition to these tabulated accounts of sex division of labor, numerous other descriptions of the phenomenon are available, for cultures the world over, of all types of basic economies and of all degrees of economic complexity. We may, however, because of considerations of space, restrict ourselves to a few further examples from the Americas.

Men of the non-agricultural Klamath tribe usually assume the important task of fishing, although they may be aided by the woman. To the extent that hunting is carried on, the men also do this, though the women may from time to time be pressed into service to remain in the canoes during a deer-drive and kill the frightened animals as they flounder in the water. There is no evidence that the men help in such women's work as the gathering of roots, fruit and seeds, though "seeds, especially pond-lily seeds, form the second staple in Klamath life." Preparing food is exclusively woman's work, except that old men may aid them; the women also see to storing and drying foodstuffs. Houses are built by both sexes, but each sex is charged with the completion of certain well-recognized subdivisions of the work. The house pit is dug by workers of both sexes, but only the men prepare the timbers, and only women spread grass and dirt over the structure to complete it. A minor exception to the general principle that wood-working is a masculine task is to be noted among the Klamath: "Wood working and the manufacture of weapons are masculine activities. Yet the most laborious wood-working task, the making of canoes, is sometimes undertaken by women." Women care for the tanning of skins, and make all garments and moccasins; mats and baskets, mortars, metates, and other adjuncts of the cuisine are also made by them. Nets are mainly the work of men; ropes and cords are made by women.[17]

Iroquois hospitality, says Morgan, "rested chiefly upon the industry and therefore upon the natural kindness of the Indian women; who, by the cultivation of the maize, and their other plants, provided the principal part of their subsistence, for the warrior despised the toil of husbandry. . . ."[18] An early writer on the Creek declared that "the women are the chief, if not the only manufacturers; the men judge that if they performed that office, it would exceedingly depreciate them." The principal occupations of men were hunting, fighting, building houses and other structures such as corn-cribs, felling trees, and, despite the quoted statement, manufacturing canoes, mortars, drums, pipes, calumets, ball sticks, axes, arrows, bows, war clubs, and other implements of the chase and of war. Women, in addition to housework, made all the pottery and basketry and did all the spinning and weaving. Though men sometimes did the preliminary working of skins, the finishing process was in female hands. Women also made frames on which they dried peaches and other fruits and "of course pounded the corn and did the cooking." Smaller garden plots were their exclusive care, though both men and women farmed the larger town fields.[19]

[17] Spier, 144–5.
[18] Morgan (1851), 320.
[19] Swanton (1928), 384–5.

Among the tribes of the Amazon basin, the woman cares for the house and does the greater part of the agricultural labor. Her husband clears and breaks up the land, but she must plant the slips and dig the manioc while he hunts to supplement the food-supply. The division of labor is strict here, in many cases almost amounting to a taboo. The men defend the community, and do all "that calls for physical strength and skill." Besides hunting, this means making weapons and preparing arrow-poisons and cere-monial beverages; men are the foresters, making canoes and building houses with the trees they fell, while from the forest they gather fruit. Besides her housework, the woman makes "all purely domestic implements"—hammocks, pottery, and most baskets, though here the lines of sex differentiation are loosened somewhat, and the man "lends a hand" if this is necessary.[20] Similarly, among the Indians of the Chaco, the men clear the fields, hunt, fish, and make warfare, while household work, manufacturing tasks, and the care of small domesticated animals are allotted to the women.[21]

Though something of the great variety of form which this fundamental aspect of productive activity can take has been indicated, we have at the same time been able to discern certain underlying general tendencies. Thus while men in some cultures, and women in others, are found occupied with such industrial pursuits as weaving, dressing skins, making clothing, or even cooking, such a statement as the one concerning the Maori, that "in general . . . the men attended to the more energetic, ardu-ous, and exciting occupations, while the women engaged in the more sober and somewhat more monotonous tasks," [22] is much more widely applicable than just to these people. Even so broad a generalization as this, however, must be made with all care. It must involve a sense of the different forms which this phenome-non can manifest, and of the cultural flexibility which, in case of need, permits men to take up tasks commonly regarded as those of women, or women to carry on the work of the men. What is even more important, we must recognize that whatever form the division of labor by sex may take, it so operates that the work done by one sex complements that of the other. The smoothly working whole that results ensures in no small measure that the entire system will function so that the people who live by it may survive.

4

IN CONSIDERING the second aspect of the division of labor, craft specialization, we are presented with a body of data which, though almost as large as that dealing with sex division of labor, is much less specific. This is because the implications of this phase of the economic life of nonliterate peoples have been realized much less fully by those who have described their cultures. By the same token, there is no such mass of theoretical postulates as to the significance of this type of specialization as is encountered when the development and present status of the difference in types of work done by men and women are under consideration. Moreover, economists of various schools have in the main been content with the assumption that specialization is necessary for the greatest economic efficiency and have pursued the matter no farther.[23]

Certain propositions that have been advanced concerning the development of craft specialization may be indicated. Durkheim enunciated a principle that assumes a relation between specialization, population size, and economic surplus not dissimilar to that already suggested in these pages:

> The division of labor varies in direct proportion to the volume and density of societies, and, if it progresses steadily in the course of social development, it is because societies become regularly more dense and very generally more voluminous.[24]

It is not possible to document this statement, especially in its dynamic aspects, because of lack of historic control over the data from non-industrial societies. Yet if the quantitative precision it implies is not insisted upon, the position carries a considerable validity, as will be indicated later when the relation between population size and economic surplus—the basis of all release of man-power from the immediate task of supporting life—is treated.

[23] Adam Smith; Marx, 355–9.   [24] Durkheim, 289.

Thurnwald has also indicated conditions under which crafts develop:

> . . . the joint settlement of various ethnic groups under a strong government which, on the one hand, favors a wide-spread system of economic distribution (thus creating conditions requisite for the professionally specialized practice of handicrafts rendered possible by the state of peace brought about by authority) and on the other, provides the opportunity of visiting the markets to dispose of products.[25]

While cause and effect seem to have been confused here (in that strong political authority, as such, is not essential to specialization any more than is the contact of different peoples), the recognition that specialization is an aspect only of economic systems of a certain degree of complexity is one with which all must agree.

The extent to which craft specialization is practiced varies as widely as the forms it takes, as will be evident if a few descriptions of it are given. One of the cases where a sufficient division of labor exists to permit some specialization, despite a relatively low economic level, has been reported from the Yir-Yoront of northern Australia. Here, in addition to the "mild form of specialization" where some men acquire "real or fancied" reputations for hunting or fishing abilities, others who are invalids or who are otherwise incapacitated "supply the labour on provided materials and receive a special return that compensates for their disabilities in other economic endeavours. . . ." That this, though apparently making for the development of particular skills, merely foreshadows the specialization of larger and more complex communities, is made apparent when we read that "most things are made for use by the worker, and standardized techniques are followed with little variation."[26] More characteristic of cultures having simple technologies was the complete absence of craft specialization in the Andaman Islands, each man "making his own bow, arrows, adze, etc., while the wife makes her baskets, nets, and so on." This did not mean that differences in ability did not exist and exert some influence on behavior: "It happens that some men are more skilful in certain pursuits than

[25] Thurnwald (1932a), 86, 91 ff; (1932b), 115, 117 ff.   [26] Sharp, 37; see also Kaberry, 162–6.

in others. A skilful turtle-hunter, for example, may be an indifferent pig-hunter, and such a man will naturally prefer to devote himself to the pursuits in which he appears to most advantage." But the economic repercussions of the exercise of such abilities in economic systems of this order of simplicity cannot be of great importance.[27]

As might be expected, most African societies stand in sharp contrast in specialized productive activity when compared with those of Australia. Over the greater part of the African continent, iron-working constitutes a specialized activity that is striking for non-industrial cultures, since iron-workers must have a high degree of technical proficiency—which means long education and continued practice in the craft—and must thus be more than merely the best practitioners of a craft known to all persons of the proper sex in a given group.[28] In the Congo basin and in West Africa, furthermore, where the cultures have attained a degree of economic complexity outstanding among the non-literate peoples of the world, various other industries are also carried on in the same way—that is, by those who devote practically all their productive time to them. Pottery, baskets, wood-carvings, cloth, and other commodities are manufactured by those whose position as craftsmen is recognized in the organization of the community, and whose support is provided by an extensive system of markets that permit ready disposal of their wares. In addition, those other specialists whose contribution consists of services rather than of goods—chiefs, priests, and above all in Africa, practitioners of magic—are likewise numerous.

This is exemplified among the Nigerian Nupe, where many types of craft-guilds exist. Each of these organizations is "a specific social group, almost an artisan class, which enjoys official recognition and certain political privileges." The industries organized in this manner are the blacksmiths, the brass and silver-smiths, glassmakers, weavers, bead-workers, builders, wood-workers and carpenters, and butchers. This list of organized specialists is supplemented, in this society, by the individual craftsmen, men who do tailoring and embroidery, leather work, indigo dyeing, the making of straw hats and mats and basket-weaving, and, by women, a restricted amount of indigo dyeing, pottery making, and a special type of weaving. Finally, the "free

[27] Radcliffe-Brown, 40–3.   [28] Cline, 114–17, 128–9.

professions" must be indicated to complete the list—the "scholars, scientists and artists, or, in a terminology more akin to the native conception, its Mallams, barber-doctors, and drummers and dancers." [29]

In other continents societies of similar complexity also show this high degree of craft specialization, as, for instance, in Mexico. Thus, among the Tarascan peoples of Michoacán, lapidaries worked turquoise and other precious stones, doing inlay on obsidian; masons prepared building-stones for pyramids and temples; carpenters, using copper tools, made various articles of furniture, and canoes, paddles and trays; maguey leaves were fashioned into cloth or paper to which colored feathers were affixed for capes and mantles; cotton was grown, spun, dyed and woven; mats for sleeping and to be used for floor-coverings were fabricated; lacquer-work was done in certain centers. There were professional hunters, drum makers, house builders, repairers of temples, and makers of bows and arrows.[30]

Yet in early Mexico, as elsewhere, professionalism shaded into the less sharply defined group of artisans who were not professionals. Thus while the feather-workers constituted a "wealthy and honored guild," the position of the carpenters was not so clear:

Everyday objects of wood . . . were presumably not made by professional carpenters, but by the man who needed them for his own use. . . . The average man would manufacture his own spearthrower, but a skilled carpenter would be employed to carve and adorn the spearthrower carried by Montezuma or placed in the hands of some idol.

The more common situation, where the basic industries are known to everyone and are practiced by all, also obtained:

House building was not a trade, but a task in which everyone took a hand, the members of the community assisting anyone who needed a new home without reward save their food during the work and a feast when the task was completed.[31]

[29] Nadel (1942), 257, 299; cf. 257–304, *passim*.

[30] Foster (1948), 10–11. See also West, 33 ff.

[31] Thompson, 91–5.

A list of the occupations followed in the present-day Mexican town of Mitla affords an example of a rudimentary form of the more developed specialization in larger groups. Of 371 men enumerated between 1929 and 1933, 140 were merchants or men who traveled for purposes other than trade; 70 were farmers—6 or more of these also being ropemakers—and 1 was a barber; 98 were hired men, though this group included a few who were also independent farmers or ropemakers. Specialists included 3 adobe-brickmakers, 4 carters, 1 blacksmith, 6 masons, 1 thatcher, 3 carpenters, 2 woodchoppers, 3 charcoal-burners, 10 weavers, 2 tanners, 2 tailors (one of them a sandal-maker as well), 3 or 4 master brewers, 5 butchers, 8 bakers, 2 candlemakers, 1 maker of fireworks, 3 male curers (one a barber), 2 image-makers, 1 artificial-flower-maker, and 2 bandmasters. Several of these specialists, however, were also farmers and ropemakers. Most of those following such special trades were outsiders who had married into the town; "the born Mitleyeno is still a man of parts: trader, farmer, ropemaker, thatcher or brickmaker, candlemaker, or musician." Among the women, specialists were more rare, the only ones being curers and midwives, a candlemaker, and an old woman who rolled ritual cigarettes.[32]

Sporadic instances of specialization in other parts of the Americas dot the literature. Thus, among the Cherokee, medicine-men were apparently a group quite apart.[33] Certain Shuswap men were trained to become expert hunters, and, though every male in the tribe hunted and fished, "these men excelled, or were thought to excel others." [34] Well-paid Kwakiutl experts carved the totemic house-posts for the dwellings of chiefs, and exacted their fees under the threat of lessening the prestige of the employer who did not pay them well.[35] Specialization occurred even among the sparse populations of aboriginal California, most notably among the Patwin, where specific occupations sanctioned by the magic known only to the members of a given relationship group were restricted to those belonging to the proper "functional families." Certain forms of this magic aided in the performance of ceremonies, shamanism, or trade. Other families employed the same means to control salmon-fishing, the manufacture of arrow-points, goose-hunting, duck-

[32] Parsons (1936b), 63–4.
[33] Mooney and Olbrechts, 84–5.
[34] Teit (1909), 589–90.
[35] Boas (1921), 1338–40.

trapping, the making of ceremonial drums, ceremonial head-dresses and feather belts, salt-manufacture, and the making of "a variety of large coiled baskets" and "canoe-baskets." However,

> The functional family cannot be regarded as a professional group, since the activity in which it specialized did not assume the place of a sole or even chief occupation. Only at times was the individual member engaged in all the general pursuits of life customarily followed by the other village inhabitants. Even the shamans spent but a relatively small part of their time in shamanistic practice in comparison with the day-to-day routine of general work directed toward supplying the necessities of life.[36]

Among the Californian Wintu, where functional families did not exist, specialization derived from a man's "inclinations and his opportunities of learning from another." Famous craftsmen are still recalled, not only for their special gifts as makers of rope or arrows or spears, but also for their all-round ability to work with their hands.[37]

The high rank accorded the most competent specialists marked the productive economy of many South Sea islands. In Tonga, an early traveler listed the occupations of men according to rank as follows:

Hereditary: matapule (chief) and *mua*
    Canoe builders
    Cutters of whale teeth
    Funeral directors
Hereditary: *mua* and *tua*
    Stone-masons
    Net-makers
    Fishermen
    Large house builders
Hereditary or not: *mua* and *tua*
    Tattooers
    Club-carvers
Hereditary or not: *tua*
    Barbers

[36] McKern, 249–50, 255.   [37] Dubois, 21–3.

Hereditary: *tua*
  Cooks
  Peasants

In addition, experts in tying sennit wrappings brought this technique to such a high degree of proficiency that many of the products of these men rightly rank as art objects. One instance of specialization within a given industry is reported, for while the carpenter who builds a boat also wraps and ties the sennit, a house carpenter does only wood-work and leaves the ornamental wrapping to the sennit artist.[38]

The Marquesan Islanders used the term *hana* to signify work, while a specialist was called a *tuhuna*. A *tuhuna* was usually, though not always, a professional. A man became one through the training given him by his father—"the normal and simplest form of apprenticeship"—by employing a teacher, or by learning from such a specialist while in his employ. Full-fledged professionals received food, cloth, and ornaments in payment for their work, and constituted a recognized social class with special privileges and prerogatives. Major industries, carried on by male specialists, were wood-working, stone-working, house-building, and canoe-building; the minor industries, knowledge of which was not so restricted, were the cultivation of food, the pounding of tapa cloth, and work done at home such as basketry, the making of bowls, implements, and ornaments, and the carvings that adorned them.

The following list of the various kinds of *tuhuna*, "not to be regarded as complete," gives an idea of how many different specialists might be found:

Master house-builder (or master builder)	Staff maker
Stone-cutter	Skilled cloth maker
Digger of storage-pits	Fan maker
Professional skilled in making string figures and applying them in decoration such as ornamental sennit designs	Maker of tortoise-shell crowns
	Maker of ear-ornaments
	He who cuts the foreskin
	Doctor
Skilled wood-carver	One skilled in witchcraft
Skilled mat maker	Master tattooer
Maker of *popoi* pounders	Master fisher (or master net-maker)
Maker of *popoi* dishes	One learned in legends
	One learned in genealogies

[38] Gifford (1929), 142–8.

Drum maker
Master canoe-builder
Image maker
Coffin maker
Maker of hair ornaments

Ceremonial priests (three kinds)
He who composes chants

Not all these were professionals, but the tattooers, the makers of ornaments, or drums, of lashings, or those who decorated canoes and houses supported themselves in large measure on what they received for their special kinds of work.[39] Similar restriction of skills to those undergoing apprenticeships are found elsewhere in the Pacific, as, for example, in Mangaia [40] and particularly in Samoa, where specialization was accompanied by an organization of workers that is almost unique in nonindustrial society.[41]

A final example may be given—a culture where the specialist is one who has knowledge of a particular technique, not one who spends all his time making a particular object. Among the Li people of Hainan Island, though there is sex and village specialization in various crafts, are all farmers, "and they have no other full-time occupation." Two villages are known for their pottery, made by women recognized as experts. Their products are traded in the entire valley where these villages are situated. Yet pottery-making is not a "specialized full-time occupation."

> The families of these women experts are farmers and these women themselves are also farmers. They just engage in ceramics in the slack season. Second, though this skill is handed down from woman to woman it is not the duty of each woman to learn the trade and it is not a hereditary occupation. Third, though they do go out of their own villages to sell these, the earthenware was originally made to supply needs at home or, at most, needs of the village. They go out to sell only what happens to be left over.[42]

5

THE PRECEDING example can also be recorded as an instance of the third kind of specialization, wherein an entire group produces some commodity not made by its neighbors. This is a type of pro-

[39] Handy (1923), 143–5, 147–64.
[40] Hiroa (1934), 131.
[41] Hiroa (1930), 84 ff.
[42] K. Odaka, 53–4.

duction that affords the basis of much trade among nonliterate peoples. Many of our examples of this will be encountered later in the course of our consideration of that subject; at this point we may cite a few instances which emphasize local specialization in production and comment briefly on the significance of the phenomenon as an aspect of the productive processes in general. Care must be taken, here as elsewhere, not to seek out simple explanations to account for regional or group specialties. For while such environmental causes as the localization of raw materials necessary to a given commodity may explain some cases, the factor of traditional usage is as important in this as in other elements of culture. Thus, even where the range of natural resources is the same throughout an entire district, custom may still restrict the manufacture of one product to one group and another kind of good to a different folk.

This problem of regional specialization has been considered in greatest detail for one portion of Melanesia, an area renowned as a whole for the degree to which this aspect of its native economies is developed.[43] One instance must suffice here. In the Trobriand Islands the concentration of raw materials strongly influences local production. The shells used in making disks and armbands, for instance, are available only to those communities whose fishing activities make it possible for them to tap the proper beds. Stone, imported from the Woodlark Islands, is worked in the eastern Trobriands, which are nearest the source of supply. Certain baskets can only be made from grasses that grow in a few swamps, and certain wood for carving comes only from special mangrove swamps. Yet it must be emphasized that, as elsewhere, the "technical plant" in the communities from which these specialties are exported, and the "regular system of production with markets, agencies, and channels of distribution" that one accustomed to European economic organization would associate with the phrase "regional specialization," are quite lacking. Instead of a well-organized guild of workers, only a few persons carry on a given specialized tradition. Thus, the group that at one time produced the pottery for which the Amphletts are famous throughout the area consisted of seven elderly women, with three or four apprentices.[44]

Regional specialization is by no means restricted to Melanesia.

[43] Tueting, *passim*.   [44] Malinowski (1935), 21–3.

We shall have occasion later to see how in East Africa cattle, sheep and goats, and grain, the specialized products of three tribes, are associated with a complicated system of trade,[45] while in West Africa producers of tribal and local specialties dispose of their wares over a large area. In the New World, cases of local specialization are abundant; three examples may suffice here. The various Tsimshian sub-groups specialized in the articles each was called on to furnish for potlatches: carved wooden dishes, wooden boxes, wooden spoons, and horn spoons, dried mountain-goat meat and tallow, cranberries and crabapples mixed with grease, cakes of hemlock sap, mats, dried salmon, shredded bark of the red cedar, tobacco, blankets of yellow cedar, and burnt clam-shells.[46] In the Amazon basin, tribal specialties are frequently encountered. The Menimehe are renowned for pottery, the Karahone for poisons, the Boro are specialists in the manufacture of mats, plaited objects, ligatures, and blow-pipes, the Witoto in the making of hammocks.[47] Or, in Guiana, each tribe of Indians has "its own home products" for which it maintains a reputation. The Otomac were known for their clay pots, the Arekuna for cotton and blow-pipes, the Makusi for curare poison, the Maionkong and Taruma for cassava graters and hunting dogs, the Warrau for canoes (corials), the Waiwai for tucum fibers, the Guinau for hammocks, cassava graters, aprons, girdles of human hair, and feather decorations, and the Oyapock River peoples for their grinding stones.[48]

6

IF THE points that have been made in this chapter be summarized, it is seen, first of all, that the productive activity of nonliterate peoples presents far less specialization than anything found in the industrial culture of Europe and America. It is also apparent that a much greater proportion of the attention of non-industrial peoples must be concentrated on the problem of subsistence than where greater technological sophistication permits a larger degree of productivity and makes the problem of survival less

[45] Driberg, 1929, 28–9.
[46] Boas (1916), 274.
[47] Whiffen, 91.
[48] Roth (1924), 635–6.

immediate. Yet with all this difference, it is evident that non-literate peoples, even where their economies are of the simplest, follow their own ways of living not only with contentment, but, to the degree permitted by their technologies, with efficiency.

The incentives to labor and the return nonliterate man expects from his work, in their broader manifestations, have been found to show little significant difference when compared with those drives with which we are familiar. This is particularly the case when we consider the more immediate relationship that obtains in those societies between what a man does and what he gets for doing it, a condition resulting from the absence of those money values into which all return for work in our own society is cast. What does differ in nonliterate cultures from our own is the psychological compensations enjoyed by those who live under simpler economies. For, unlike workers in Euroamerican industrialized communities, the worker in these societies is occupied mainly with his own tasks and, more importantly, on his own initiative. That this initiative is not unappreciable is apparent from the variety of goods produced by most nonliterate peoples, since these goods are expressions of the drive their makers must manifest in resolving the numerous technical and other difficulties which they must surmount in wresting a living from their environment.

PART III

EXCHANGE
AND DISTRIBUTION

CHAPTER VIII

GIFT AND CEREMONIAL EXCHANGE

IN CONSIDERING the circulation of goods in non-industrial societies, it is essential that we constantly recall the significance of the difference in the degree of sharpness with which economic institutions can be distinguished within these economies and in our own. As in the case of production, forms which we differentiate quite sharply are not only indistinguishable but, in many instances, are so intimately linked with non-economic institutions that we can only discern them at all by giving the closest attention to their economic role.

The process of distribution, in many tribes, is thus set in a non-economic matrix which takes the form of gift and ceremonial exchange. Both of these institutions have received considerable attention, and there has even been some attempt made to derive all forms of exchange of goods from them. This position has been most effectively presented in an important paper by Mauss, whose work extracts the crucial point from these ritualized forms of distribution. Mauss shows that no matter how freely a gift may be tendered, or how unsought it may be, the very fact of its having been presented carries an obligation of equivalent or increased return that can be ignored only on penalty of social disapprobation and the loss of prestige. Psychologically, this principle holds for all cultures. In the less specialized economies, however, where it commonly takes institutionalized form, it is of primary economic importance.

When the institutions that involve gift exchange are observed as they actually operate, their non-economic aspects are most apparent. To the student, as to the native whose life he seeks to understand, it is the rituals and the patterned circumstances which call them forth that are important, rather than the fact that here exists a significant economic process. It is, however, the role of these institutions in stimulating the circulation of commodities that must command the attention of those primarily concerned with economic phenomena.

The purely economic aspects of the systems of ceremonial and gift exchange that are found in nonliterate societies understandably vary, as do other elements in culture. As far as the circulation of goods is concerned, it must be recognized that the mere fact that food and other perishable commodities, which everyone possesses in amounts needed to satisfy fundamental wants, are redistributed is not of itself greatly significant in the business of getting a living, however important the rite of exchange may be for the acquisition of prestige. This point becomes quite clear when the situation in Guadalcanal, the Solomon Islands, is considered:

> The same scale of comforts, or lack of them, is available to all; everyone has to spend several hours of the day at the same kind of work, all eat similar dishes prepared in the same kind of utensils from the same sort of raw foods, and all sleep on the same type of mats for beds. Wealth cannot be used therefore directly for the benefit of the possessor. . . . Every event of importance in a person's life . . . is celebrated by a feast, and the more feasts a man gives, and the more lavish he is in providing food, the greater his prestige.[1]

Many societies, however, afford striking instances of the manner in which economic and non-economic factors may combine to produce economic results. One of these may be presented in some detail, before certain further examples are indicated to show how commonly non-economic mechanisms afford the means for an exchange of goods and services.

2

FOR this example we turn again to the Kota of the Nilgiri hills of India. Here, before European contact, the following situation

[1] Hogbin (1938), 290.

obtained: The members of this tribe were musicians and artists for the three neighboring folk of their area, the pastoral Toda, the jungle-dwelling Kurumba, and the agricultural Badaga. Each tribe had clearly defined and ritually regulated obligations and prerogatives with respect to all the others. The Toda provided the Kota with ghee for certain ceremonies and with buffaloes for sacrifices at their funerals. The Kota furnished the Toda with the pots and knives they needed in their everyday life and made the music essential to Toda ceremonies. The Kota provided the Badaga with similar goods and services, receiving grain in return. They stood in the same exchange relationship with the forest Kurumba, but these latter, who could only provide meagre material compensation—honey, canes, and occasionally fruits—were able to afford the Kota supernatural protection, since the Kurumba were dreaded sorcerers, so feared that every Kota family must have their own Kurumba protector against the magic which others of this tribe might work against them.

In most of its aspects this intertribal relationship functioned on a family basis. Each Kota household had a number of Badaga families with whom it exchanged goods and services; and when, for example, a Kota died, all these Badaga families were notified so that they could provide the sacrificial animals needed. Once a year, after the harvest, the Kota women made pots which they took to the villages of their Badaga correspondents; they ritually proffered them and were tendered a feast, after which they departed, carrying away their annual provision of grain. The Kota, also, were obligated to provide the Badaga with iron tools, such as hoes, forks, and plowshares in traditional quantities. Should a Badaga wish more of these utensils, he would have to work in the field of the Kota iron-worker of whom he requested them, while they were being forged. In the event of a dispute between partners, the Kota village council considered the matter and if, as was customary, they found the Badaga at fault, no Kota might supply him with pots or tools. The Badaga's need of the Kota was thus much greater than that of the Kota for the Badaga. The Kota, that is, had fields to supply them, in an emergency, with the food-stuffs they ordinarily received from the Badaga. The Badaga, on the other hand, not only had no knowledge of the techniques the Kota controlled, but, as a matter of fact, had no desire to know them, since in the patterns of Indian life iron-workers and those who play drums are on the lower rungs of the social ladder.

The favorable position of the Kota with regard to the Badaga was reversed in the case of the Kurumba, whose exercise of magical power set at naught the material advantages the Kota enjoyed. The Kurumba exacted all the market would bear, and on occasion their demands were anything but modest. When a Kota fell ill, for example, his relatives, indicating how they had been regular and generous in sending gifts to their Kurumba worker of magic, would complain that he had not fulfilled his part of the agreement to keep them from harm. The customary reply would be that some especially powerful Kurumba sorcerer had been insulted by a Kota, or had become envious of their good fortune, and was therefore sending unusually strong magic against his victim. Only sustained effort, to be called forth by the giving of extra gifts, might counteract this influence; and since there was no other recourse, the Kota would have to give more and more lavishly. Should the patient recover, more gifts would be proffered the practitioner out of gratitude; should death eventuate, not only would nothing be returned to the family of the client, but the Kurumba "protector" would be offered sympathy for having had to grapple with so powerful an adversary.

The Toda, in their relation with the Kota, provided no essential good to these people, nor, on the other hand, were they at all dependent on Kota manufactures. It was rather the services of the Kota as musicians that was needed by the Toda. The "orchestral" instruments essential to Toda ceremonial—clarinet, trumpet, drum, and cymbals—could be played by almost any Kota, but by no Toda. As compensation, the Kota had the joy of playing and the material return of the flesh from the buffaloes that were sacrificed at the rites where they played. The Toda, for their part, obtained services that were indispensable to the ordering of their supernatural world.

Here we can clearly see how many factors enter into what, from the point of view of the student concerned only with economic phenomena, could be regarded as nothing more than an exchange of goods and services. Yet it is apparent that social position, religion, and family organization are all factors in giving a firm texture to this complex of economic relationships. From the point of view of the Kota, the ledger may be balanced somewhat as follows: They benefited materially from their contacts with the Badaga, since these were principally concerned with the exchange of commodities under social and legal sanctions. They suffered material loss in their dealings with the forest-dwelling Kurumba, since here the return was non-material, the services of a magician. As far as relationships with the Toda were concerned, neither people enjoyed any appreciable material gain. Yet because of the sanction of tradition and the pleasure the Kota derived in rendering their services to the Toda, they never slighted their part of the exchange, the performance of which was marked by a feeling-tone which strongly contrasted to that which pervaded the other types of contact.[2]

A final point to be raised in considering the mutual relationships between these three groupings concerns the nicely balanced reciprocity that has been considered a universal factor controlling exchanges in what has been termed "tribal economies" of this sort.[3] Looking only at the position of the Kota in the system, this series of exchanges seems to work out in such a way as to give them greater resources than they would otherwise have. Yet from the point of view of the way in which the system operates, as between the Kota and any of the other tribes, no such balance is to be seen, nor are motivations anything but the most diverse. "With the Todas, the reciprocity was amiable, with the Kurumba it was terror fraught, and with the Badagas it was rather competitive. Thus a Kota gave a Kurumba as much as he could afford; to the Toda he donated freely, for he liked to play; to the Badaga he gave with an eye to what he would receive."[4]

This example of reciprocal exchanges, anything but balanced in the returns they assure the participants for their contributions, again illustrates the danger of too great a readiness to generalize concerning the complex phenomena of social and economic life, especially where the total range of variation in these institutions is not taken fully into account.

3

MANY different types of exchange have been reported from southeastern New Guinea and its adjoining islands. Tueting, who

[2] Mandelbaum (communicated).   [4] Mandelbaum, ibid.
[3] Malinowski (1921), 15.

has combed the literature, summarizes the general situation as
follows:

> In Melanesia . . . commodities of great value such as pigs,
> shell ornaments, and canoes are usually exchanged cere-
> monially. Food and pots are almost always bartered. They
> are rarely exchanged ceremonially except as gifts accom-
> panying the main transaction. The same general pattern of
> ceremonial exchange, found in southeastern New Guinea,
> is also found throughout Melanesia. It is based on the recip-
> rocal exchange of gifts between groups. The exchange
> usually involves rivalry which is expressed in the quantity
> and quality of gifts displayed and distributed, in debates,
> dances, and in games. The local variations of this general
> pattern are definitely stylized and when one form becomes
> dominant in a group all classes of ceremonial exchange in
> the group conform ·to it. . . . The following classes of
> ceremonial payments are found in Melanesia: life-crisis pay-
> ments, fines, offerings, and ceremonial purchase of goods or
> services. . . . Certain life-crisis payments, such as those
> accompanying marriage, are found throughout Melanesia.
> Payments at other crises such as pregnancy, birth, ear
> piercing, or puberty have been recorded sporadically in
> the area.[5]

The numerous citations to the data which document these
points need not be repeated here. Some of the other instances
that have become available for this area since this statement and
its supporting materials appeared may, however, be mentioned
before examples of gift and ceremonial exchange from other
parts of the world are considered.

In Malekula, the idea that anything may be freely given is
unknown. "A gift is at most a venture, a hopeful speculation."
The native looks to receive "an advantage at least equal to the
value of his yam." Even though he may proffer a gift of considerable size, with the assurance no return is desired, its acceptance will eventually be met with uncomplimentary references on
all occasions and until a return is received, hints of varying degrees of broadness that it should be reciprocated are heard. On
the other hand, "to make a return equal in value to the initial

[5] Tueting, 38–9.

gift is sufficient to avoid disgrace; but if a man desires to be well spoken of he must give as repayment something of greater value than that which he received in the first place." The constant exchanges of food and pigs which serve to unify the community by binding it in "a network of obligations" also act as a mechanism for the circulation of goods. These exchanges are usually of gifts of relatively equal value, except in the rituals of certain societies, where animals are given in payment for services or for the right to display insignia. In such cases, however, "the exchanges are . . . definitely valuable as a stimulus to work and for the need to which they give rise for co-operative effort." [6]

Marriage in Bougainville, as so often elsewhere, is sanctioned by exchanges of goods which, in this case, take the form of payments in the local currency. Here, however, the natives themselves are specifically reported to differentiate the ceremonial from the economic aspects of the transaction. At the core of the festivals that constitute the marriage rite is the fact that "what we pay for is the woman's genitals." That is, the passage of these goods conveys the right to her body for procreation of children and for the satisfaction of the husband, though a woman acquired as "wife as distinct from a woman in her capacity as individual" is "not thereby prevented from being a person with any rights of her own." The exchanges that accompany marriage bring on far-reaching economic repercussions in the intertribal trade of the region. Thus the people of Petats, at the time of a given marriage, had obtained pots in exchange for women's hoods. The pots were bartered to the folk of Lontis for taro, and with these pots the Lontis group acquired pigs, which they were holding to sell as the opportunity offered for the ceremonial "currency" made of shell disks that must form the most important part of the property to be exchanged at the rite for which preparations were being made.[7]

The regular distribution of economic goods among the Australian Yir-Yoront is reported to have been cared for, as a matter of routine, by the gift-patterns of the kinship structure. Irregular giving, which "usually amounts to compulsory exchange" often occurs, as when a man who is known to possess tobacco will be sent a "gift" by a distant relative whom he rarely sees. This is tantamount to serving notice that a return of tobacco is expected,

[6] Deacon, 199–202.   [7] Blackwood (1935), 97–9, 445–6.

and in due course the return is made. "There is," however, "no abnormal liberality in giving merely for the sake of increased personal prestige, but the maintenance of a standard of prestige is apparently an important factor in gift exchange." [8] This pattern of gift exchange is reminiscent of the Daly River tribes already cited.[9] However, the return for what is given is so delayed—that is, until the donor has become an elderly man—that it is only by extending the term "exchange" far beyond its customary significance that the phenomenon can be thought of as falling in this category at all, despite its importance as a system that ensures the distribution of commodities. But we do find on the Daly River an instance where the ceremonial aspect of exchange is really subordinate to its economic end, for while the institution of trading partners is flanked by accompanying rituals, the emphasis placed by the natives on the relationship is essentially economic.

Recognizing that gift-exchange is only one form of the circulation of goods in aboriginal Australia, one none the less senses its wide ramifications, economic and otherwise, in McCarthy's classification:

(1) Gifts prescribed by kinship obligations.

(2) Gifts given to settle grievances or debts arising out of an offense or crime by an individual or group . . . to settle a blood feud, and realize a revenge. These gifts may or may not be reciprocated.

(3) Gift-exchange based on reciprocity in which gifts are given to reciprocate a service (e.g. to mine red ochre or stone, to have access to water in arid areas, to participate in feasts, to repay a guardian during initiation), or as a return for a gift of portable articles which may be of the same character.

(4) Gift-exchange of the *Merbok* type in which objects pass from one partner to another in many different local groups and may be retained only temporarily.[10]

Gift and ceremonial exchange were highly developed in Polynesia, where, as in so many other areas, the motivating factor of the process was a desire for the prestige to be derived from lavish

[8] Sharp, 37–8.
[9] See above, 116–17.
[10] McCarthy, 179.

giving. In some parts of this area, different kinds of goods are reported to have been exchanged between the interested parties and their followers, so that the economic aspect of the phenomenon must here as elsewhere be distinguished from its sociological significance. Social grade was determined in Mangaia by the quantity and quality of the gifts proffered by the family of the bride on the occasion of a marriage, and by the size of the feast marking the union. The exchange occurred some time later, when the relatives of the bridegroom reciprocated with a feast which, unless his family was willing to admit inferiority in status, had to surpass the original celebration in the amount of food available and the quantity of gifts presented.

That "reciprocal feasts and presents form the standard patterns of Polynesian weddings" [11] is a generalization entirely borne out by the descriptions of wedding ceremonies on other islands. Tongan marriage rites placed great stress on display and on the exchange of wealth—"gifts"—between the families of the principals. In distributing what had been received by his son, the father of the bridegroom kept in mind the amount each of his relatives had donated toward the gift previously given the bride. It was a matter of pride for him to see that everyone who had contributed was given twice what he had donated. In this way the distributor "often stripped his own house of all its possessions, counting the social prestige of his family of greater value than his material property." Should he fail to make everyone a return deemed adequate, the social position of all members of his family would fall, and his unmarried sons and daughters, as well as his grandchildren, would be unable to marry as desirably as they otherwise might. However, in addition to constituting a mechanism for accelerating the circulation of goods, these exchanges, as was seen to be the case in Malekula, also stimulated production, since "if the distributor had insufficient goods to meet the demands, he set his household to work making tapa, mats, baskets, and other articles required." The exchanges went on over a considerable period; beginning with the ceremonial itself, the giving of gifts might be prolonged a month or even two months. [12]

Another form of gift exchange which, operating on a prestige basis, facilitated the circulation of goods, existed on the island of Niue under the name *fakalofa*, whereby goods or services prof-

[11] Hiroa (1934), 91.   [12] Gifford (1929), 191 ff.

fered in friendship had to be returned in adequate measure. When a catch of fish was made, or taro harvested, relatives of the owner of these goods expected to receive a share "in the nature of a *fakalofa*"; but the interchanges under this system were really stabilized by feasts. When a man visited his relatives living in another village, he was honored by a feast and a dance, the most important feature of which was the exchange of complimentary remarks between the principals and the enumeration of the gifts each was about to make the other. Here deprecation of one's own contribution and extravagant praise for what was received were the order of the day. Any economic gain, however, was negated for each party to the exchange by the attempts made to outdo the other in giving; while another non-economic consideration of importance was fear of the songs of ridicule that would be composed to deride one who was "miserly in the exchange of gifts." [13] On the island of Yap, in Micronesia, this same ritualized pattern of competitive gift-giving facilitated exchange, dances being but incidental to the distribution of money and other valuables among the members of dance groups attending the festivities. These dance groups, in their songs, would specifically name what they desired. The host was here likewise subject to ridicule if mats of the type used for clothing, pandanus sleeping-mats, feathers of the frigate bird, and other goods, together with mussel-shell money of many kinds, were not at once forthcoming. The villages which benefited from these "gifts" were, of course, obligated at some later period to return what had been received; thus all profited in terms of the increased prestige that accrued to all concerned.[14]

4

IN NORTH and South America, gift-giving on the basis of an equivalent or increased return, between either individuals or groups, and the ceremonial occasions when gifts are exchanged have often been reported. It is unnecessary to make more than passing reference to the potlatch ceremonies of the Northwest Coast tribes, since these are classical in this connection and have been as carefully and specifically described as any other of the

[13] Loeb, 113–16. [14] Müller, 262.

numerous available instances of ritualized display and distribution of goods among nonliterate groups. We need only recall the competitive striving between chiefs, heads of clans, or individuals for social prestige by means of the distribution and waste of economically valuable goods on the taking of a name or on assuming a new rank, to "avenge" an insult or regain face after a mishap, to indicate the importance of this body of custom as a mechanism for the circulation of goods and, through the increased production necessitated by the requirements of the potlatch, for the stimulation of the manufacture of more commodities than would otherwise have been produced. As Codere has put it:

> Potlatching . . . is more than any single potlatch. The public distribution of property by an individual is a recurrent climax in an endless series of cycles of accumulating property—distributing it in a potlatch—being given property—again accumulating and preparing. The whole potlatch system is a composition of these numerous individual potlatch cycles and is supported and maximized in Kwakiutl by certain social and economic features. . . .

The amounts of property listed as having been distributed in potlatches held between 1729 and 1936, where this has been recorded, when taken into account in terms of the social conventions concerning the giving and receiving of potlatch goods, document the effectiveness of this institution as a factor in Kwakiutl distribution.[15]

Among the Klamath of southern Oregon, the exchange of goods at a marriage is likewise a significant factor in causing commodities to move from hand to hand. The marriage payment, which is described as "a social obligation," must be made by the family of the bridegroom, and inability to pay means that the family will be held in low social esteem. Yet though the payment is "a seal of respectability," the burden it imposes does not entirely rest upon the family of the bridegroom. After marriage, an interchange of presents occurs, in which "the advantage lies most frequently with the husband's family," who are thus reimbursed in some measure for their original outlay. The economic importance of the arrangement for the tribesmen is reflected in the

[15] Codere, 63, 90–1.

care taken by families of wealth to guard against the elopement of a daughter, since such a mishap would involve the forfeiture of the "suitable payment" that would otherwise follow. Among the poor, since they have little to lose, no such care is taken. However, even when elopements do occur, the families may preserve the amenities by making the gifts "in proper form," as is to be seen from the description of presentations that passed in one case of this type:

> It took a month to get ready to conduct a proper marriage. Leleks made the trip across the mountains . . . to get store goods. A great many people went with them to Yainax, the majority taking gifts of horses, blankets, clothing, or anything they had. One man with nothing better stripped himself of his only shirt. It must be remembered that Plains shirts were then newly fashionable and hence valuable. They gave the horses they rode there, hoping for reciprocal gifts on which to return. Horses to a total of ten were given the groom's people. They gave horses and other gifts in return. Payment having been made the affair was considered as honorably ended, and as though the groom had sent an emissary in proper order.

The amounts involved vary with the wealth of those concerned. "A chief gives a slave or more; a poor man buys with food. A chief will not give his daughter for nothing; the groom must continue to bring gifts even after the marriage." The exchanges thus could go on for a considerable time; and, as has been indicated, in the long run neither family experiences any serious disadvantage. The gifts that passed were horses, slaves, blankets, beads, food (pond-lily seeds and roots), elk and other hides, and strings of beads.[16]

Certain California Indian tribes count the rank of husband, wife, and children according to the amount given for a wife; and the marriage of a woman, in spirit if not in status, has been depicted as something not far from a strictly commercial transaction. The Yurok deemed it so important that sufficient economic goods pass in validating a match that an arrangement termed "half-marriage" was sometimes encountered; that is, a bridegroom paid what he could afford for a desired wife and main-

[16] Spier, 43–7.

tained his social status by working for his father-in-law until the remainder was considered as having been paid, thus effecting a combined payment of goods and services. Much of the property comprising the price of a "complete" marriage, carefully agreed upon beforehand, was given at the ceremony, and a large part of what was thus received seems to have been distributed immediately by the father of the bride. In addition, certain other goods which were brought with the bride by her father included such items as baskets of dentalia (the prestige currency of these people), otter-skins and other compact valuables, a canoe or two, and several deerskin blankets. These "seem to have passed in this way among the wealthy, without any previous bargaining or specification. In this way a rich father voluntarily returned part of the payment made him. . . . However, on a divorce taking place, these gifts must be returned as fully as the stipulated purchase price." The Pomo, on the other hand, effectuated marriage by quite a different pattern of exchange of gifts. No bargaining occurred until the specific amounts were to be fixed, since it was this that involved the establishment and maintenance of social position. The bridegroom gave beads and deerskins to his bride's parents, who in return might give baskets.[17]

Circulation of goods within the Hopi pueblos is almost exclusively achieved by means of gifts and the payment of forfeits in winter games, exchanges at weddings, the distribution of food to work parties, and the passing of commodities at ceremonies of birth and naming, at initiation, at funerals, and on the performance of various religious rites. Hopi trade exchange "differs from gift exchange in that the first valuation only is set by custom whereas the final contract is usually the result of individual bargaining, and much depends on personal initiative and opportunity"[18]—a statement which has a much wider applicability than in this instance alone. "As in other pueblos," the giving of presents in Taos, at fiestas or while making visits, is a deep-rooted tradition. Here, however, the line of emphasis on the non-economic aspects of the exchanges is so slight that it is difficult to distinguish this form of circulation of goods from actual trading —and it is, indeed, described as a "near form of trade." Some instances of Taos gift exchange have been provided us: one woman who went to a fiesta at Jemez was there given four silver and

[17] Kroeber, 29–32, 254–5.   [18] Beaglehole (1937), 81.

turquoise rings, two pieces of pottery, and two bread baskets by her friends, "presents for which some return will be made when the Jemez women visit Taos." For a pottery bowl a return present of money (fifty cents) was made; for two rings, a bead necklace was given.[19]

Exchanges based on gift-giving and other non-economic institutions also existed on the Plains and in the Southeast. Among the Plains tribes described by Denig, marriage was influenced and implemented by economic considerations. A man first tried to induce the girl he wished to marry to run away with him. If she acquiesced and the mating was to be made a permanent arrangement—that is, he did not discard her—he would offer her parents what he could afford when called on to satisfy the marriage requirements, being obviously in a much better bargaining position than if he had been unsuccessful in prevailing upon the girl to elope. Just how important a part of the distributive process marriage constituted is made evident by the fact that until the girl bore a child, the son-in-law had to give most of the meat and the skins of all the animals killed by him to his wife's parents. Non-ceremonial gift-giving was also an important exchange mechanism among these upper Missouri tribes.

> An Indian never gives away anything without an expectation of a return or some other interested motive. If one observes another in possession of a fine horse he would like to have he will take the occasion of some feast or dance and publicly present him with a gun or something of value, flattering his bravery, praising his liberality, and throwing out several hints as to his object, though not directly mentioning it. He will let the matter rest thus for some days, and if the other does not present him with the horse will demand his gift returned, which is done.

At times, when a horse was given as a gift and its recipient gave it to another, its return might be asked by the original donor on the ground that the gift was not to be transferred. Smaller gifts were looked upon as loans and were generally repaid—"they may be considered as exchange of necessities which they take this way to effect." [20]

[19] Parsons (1936a), 25.   [20] Denig, 510–11, 475.

Swanton reports a number of cases among the Creek, described in the early literature, where gift exchange seemed to be an important mechanism for the circulation of goods within the community. Bartram is quoted as saying:

If one goes to another's house and is in want of any necessity that he or she sees, and says, I have need of such a thing, it is regarded as only a polite way of asking for it and the request is forwith granted, without ceremony or emotion; for he knows he is welcome to the like generous and friendly return at any time. . . .

Swanton feels that at times this practice was no more than ordinary borrowing, but on occasion, borrowing was of a different kind, "in which equivalent values were exchanged instead of identical objects." His assumption, based on intimate knowledge of present-day Indian inhabitants of the region, is that each family was "pretty acutely conscious of its credit or debit as regards every other family, and that a persistent 'sponge' was looked down upon and avoided." [21]

5

GIFT-GIVING as the mechanism for the circulation of basic commodities among the South American Pilagá has been studied by Henry in one of the few quantitative analyses of distribution available for non-pecuniary societies. It is apparent, however, that this case presents some difficulties of classification. The giving, though motivated by a complex of magico-social factors, cannot be regarded as ceremonial in the sense of most of the instances cited in this chapter. The institution, that is, functions as a system of exchange only in the sense that gifts call for returns in kind.

The presentations, to an overwhelming degree, consist of food —"only about five per cent" of these distributions are of other commodities. In drawing the tables in which circulation is indicated, the problem of definition of units was faced in the following manner: "Where one object changes hands; where two people—the giver and the receiver—are involved, where several people are invited to a . . . 'dipping into the pot,' all are treated

[21] Swanton (1928), 334-5.

I

Distribution expressed as (1) number of persons receiving from and giving to specific individuals; (2) relation between number of distributions made and number of distributions received (i.e. participated in).

Name of person	Sex	Gives to [a]	Re-ceives from [b]	Distribu-tions made [c]	Distribu-tions re-ceived [d]	Difference between number of persons given to and number re-ceived from [e]
1. Adiotina	F	8	10	3	16	−2
2. Adichi *	M	10	1	4	1	+9
3. Aichotn	M	18	0	5	0	+18
4. Alpa * (UP) [f]	F	0	4	0	5	−4
5. Arana	F	22	9	16	13	+13
6. Chiyawolik * (UP)	M	5	9	3	11	−4
7. Diwa'i	F	14	9	15	14	+5
8. Hawachi *	F	3	2	3	2	+1
9. Iya'i *	F	5	1	1	1	+4
10. Iyetolik	M	9	2	3	2	+7
11. Kachina *	F	7	6	3	7	+1
12. Kadamaitn * (UP)	M	0	3	0	3	−3
13. Kalachiyoli	F	26	11	13	14	+15
14. Kiyanokaiki *	M	13	3	4	3	+10
15. Komaraik	M	16	5	5	7	+11
16. Kosiyai *	F	11	3	3	3	+8
17. Kyarai * (UP)	F	0	15	0	21	−15
18. Lorosetina	F	2	5	2	6	−3
19. Lyatarai * (UP)	F	0	9	0	10	−9
20. Nagete	F	19	10	11	15	+9
21. Nenarachi	F	8	5	6	9	+3
22. Nyorol'i	F	7	9	6	10	−2
23. Oma'i *	M	19	4	11	4	+15
24. Paranai (UP)	F	0	7	0	13	−7
25. Pasadi *	M	2	8	3	8	−6
26. Piyarasaina	F	4	10	2	18	−6
27. Pucharai	F	6	8	3	13	−2
28. Sidinki	M	40	10	37	12	+30
29. Sutaraina	F	6	14	2	21	−8
30. Waik (UP)	M	4	12	5	29	−8
31. Waina *	F	13	0	5	0	+13
32. Waluchitn *	M	25	1	5	1	+24
33. Yalachitn	F	19	13	13	16	+6
34. Yamada'i (UP)	F	1	8	1	20	−7
35. Yawotnyi	F	6	3	2	3	+3
36. Yorodaik *	M	2	1	1	1	+1

* Individuals marked with an asterisk are residents in Kiyanokaiki's part of the village.

[a] Read, "Adiotina gives to eight persons; Adichi gives to 10 persons, etc.

[b] Read, "Adiotina receives from ten persons, etc."

[c] Read, "Adiotina made three distributions, etc."

[d] Read, "Adiotina got part of 16 distributions made by other people, etc."

[e] Read, "Adiotina gave to two persons less than she received from; Adichi gave to nine persons more than he received from, etc."

[f] The notation (UP) means "unable to produce." Of those so marked numbers 4, 6, 12, 19, 24 and 30 are old and blind; 17 and 34 are old women.

as distributions, as are the cases in which an individual gives many things, like fish, to many people."

A summary of the exchanges may be presented in terms of the tables given by Henry. The first shows, for thirty-six individual Pilagá for whom "ledgers" of income and outgo were kept, the distributions made and received, and the net loss or gain as indicated by the numbers to whom food was given or from whom it was received.

It is apparent that the Pilagá gives far more than he receives. The net number of persons to whom goods were given is 206, while that from whom they were received by the 36 persons for whom the exchanges are tabulated is only 86. The range of distributions made and received is as follows:

II

Distribution ranges in terms of (1) persons giving and receiving; (2) number of distributions made and received

Number of persons receiving	Number of persons giving [a]	Number of distributions made	Number of persons distributing [b]	Number of persons received from	Number of persons receiving [c]	Number of times receiving	Number of persons receiving [d]
0	5	0	5	0	2	0	2
1	1	1	3	1	4	1	4
2	3	2	4	2	2	2	2
3	1	3	8	3	5	3	4
4	2	4	2	4	2	4	1
5	2	5	5	5	3	5	1
6	3	6	2	6	1	6	1
7	2	7	0	7	1	7	2
8	2	8	0	8	3	8	1
9	1	9	0	9	5	9	1
10	1	10	0	10	4	10	2
11	1	11	2	11	1	11	1
12	0	12	0	12	1	12	1
13	2	13	2	13	1	13	3
14	1	14	0	14	1	14	2
15	0	15	1	15	1	15	1
16	1	16	1			16	2
17	0	17	0			17	0
18	1	18	0			18	1
19	3	19	0			19	0
20	0	20	0			20	1
21	0	21	0			21	2

II—*Continued*

Distribution ranges in terms of (1) persons giving and receiving; (2) number of distributions made and received

Number of persons receiving	*Number of persons giving* [a]	*Number of distributions made*	*Number of persons distributing* [b]	*Number of persons received from*	*Number of persons receiving* [c]	*Number of times receiving*	*Number of persons receiving* [d]
22	1	22	0			22	0
23	0	23	0			23	0
24	0	24	0			24	0
25	1	25	0			25	0
26	1	26	0			26	0
27	0	27	0			27	0
28	0	28	0			28	0
29	0	29	0			29	1
30	0	30	0				
31	0	31	0				
32	0	32	0				
33	0	33	0				
34	0	34	0				
35	0	35	0				
36	0	36	0				
37	0	37	1				
38	0						
39	0						
40	1						

[a] Read, "Five persons give to no one, etc."
[b] Read, "Five people distribute never, three people distribute once, etc."
[c] Read, "Two persons received from no one, etc."
[d] Read, "Two people receive never, four people receive once, etc."

The imbalance indicated in these tables is of considerable interest, especially in the light of the discussion of economic equilibrium that has figured so largely in discussions of economic theory. For it is apparent that if outgo exceeded income in the ratio of 3 to 1 indicated in these tables, it would be impossible for the economy to function. This is rendered more complex by the fact that "although most persons receive from fewer individuals than they give to, they receive relatively often from, and so depend on, a relatively small number of people."

The point is made in the following terms:

Thus there are always some to whom the Pilagá gives but who do not give to them; while at the same time, one generally receives more frequently than one gives away. The Pilagá's "books" are therefore never in "balance," hence the common complaint in Pilagá society, "I have given to him but he gives not to me." Hence also, the anxiety one frequently hears expressed, "I have not given him food, therefore he sorcerizes me." The attitude of being at once society's creditor and debtor, of being simultaneously deprived and obligated, are . . . related to the peculiar structure of Pilagá economic relations.

The problem was further analyzed when the ratio between the quantities of food received and given away was considered. In this case, "income"—income, that is, "from sources other than one's own productivity"—equalled outgo in but three of the thirty-six cases. It exceeded outgo in fifteen instances, and was exceeded by outgo in seventeen. This figure is changed somewhat if the five persons who were "unable to produce" and made no distributions at all, are subtracted from the fifteen, in which case the ratio is ten to seventeen, or 5:8.5. Henry's comment on this is cogent: "While the productive Pilagá makes up this difference by keeping enough of his product to fill the gap between what he gives away and what he receives from others, yet, psychologically speaking, this constant gap between income and outgo becomes an important factor in the way the Pilagá experiences his economic relations." It is thus apparent that the problem of equilibrium here has two facets, one of the type customarily treated, of ratio between income and outgo over the economy of the society as a whole; the other relating to motivation and the balance felt by the individual in his functioning capacity as a member of the society.

This latter becomes the more complex when all the factors that come into play are taken into account. "A single pattern" does not determine this economic behavior. "Rather, it is determined by several lines of force, each one of which—kinship obligations, residence, expectations of marriage, dependency, fear of shamans —radiates from a different 'pattern,' a different area of traditional behavior." Thus again we are faced with inner forces playing on an economic order which, simple in character even to the degree, as among the Pilagá, that the people do not live far removed from the subsistence level, on further analysis turns out to be of a considerable order of complexity in the interrelationships among persons that constitute its essential mechanism.[22]

6

AN OUTSTANDING example of a ceremonial device for the transfer of wealth is that which, among the cattle peoples of East Africa, has variously been termed "brideprice" or "bridewealth." It is in effect a contractual relationship entered into by the families of a bride and a groom, whereby the groom, as surety of good behavior toward his future wife, and in compensation to her family for her loss, tenders his future father-in-law a payment that consists principally of cattle, but, in addition, may include other goods and services. How actual a redistribution of these valuable goods is achieved in the process is evident from the fact that in many cases the cattle, which are the really important commodities involved, are contributed by various members of the "extended family" to which the bridegroom belongs. They are in turn distributed by the father of the bride to those of his relatives who may, for example, have aided him at an earlier time in gathering the cattle he needed to make possible the marriage of a son.[23] According to Richards, who has summarized the literature for the southern part of the cattle-owning area, this spread of responsibility among the relatives of the contracting parties tends to stabilize a marriage. An early work by MacLean on Kaffir law, which she quotes to make the point, states:

> The cattle paid for the bride are divided amongst her male relations, and are considered by law to be held in trust for the benefit of herself and children, should she be left a widow. She can accordingly legally demand assistance from any of those who have partaken of her dowry, and her children can apply to them on the same ground for something to begin the world with.[24]

A detailed analysis of this institution of "bridewealth" among the Tswana describes two essentials to marriage: an agreement

[22] Jules Henry, *passim*.
[23] See Pearsall, *passim*, for a concise presentation of the various forms of bridewealth in East Africa

and their social and economic functions.
[24] Richards (1932), 124 ff.

mutually reached by the two contracting families, and a transfer of "certain livestock, generally cattle, to the bride's family by the family of the bridegroom." These cattle are termed *bogadi*. Their importance to the Tswana is that they are the mark of a legal marriage, for a man may live many years with a concubine to whom he gives free gifts of cattle without ever being regarded as married to her, since the *bogadi* will not have passed. Yet despite the fact that the institution is not recognized as an economic mechanism by the people themselves, its economic aspects make it as important in this respect as it is in the social aspects of their culture. An informal agreement, looking toward ultimate betrothal, may be concluded when a girl is still a baby or even yet unborn. Gifts are given thenceforward from time to time to the family of the girl by that of her fiancé, the formal betrothal being marked by sending an animal to the girl's people for slaughter, or by such goods as dress materials, blankets, and shawls for the girl herself to wear. The family of the girl, on the other hand, proffer a small feast to mark the occasion. Should the agreement be later nullified through the fault of the girl, all gifts received by her family must be returned; if the lad is culpable, her family not only keep what has been sent them, but demand additional compensation. At the wedding the actual transfer of the *bogadi* cattle takes place, as well as lavish distributions of food by the families of both bride and bridegroom.

Whether or not the wives of men in nonliterate societies are purchased like other articles of commerce is a question that will be considered in a later chapter. Whatever the position one takes, it is clear that among the Tswana any such interpretation of the custom of *bogadi* is quite unjustified. For it should be again emphasized that as far as the attitudes of those who practice this custom are concerned, it is a non-economic institution. Its aim is to legitimize a mating and to permit a man to lay proper claim to his children, who, without the passing of these animals, would be retained by the family of their mother. One of the beasts must be a female, so that there may be a natural increase in the herd; but the number which must pass in any given match is not fixed and there is no bargaining. Each family thus gives what it can afford. The betrothal once having been approved, the girl's family is bound to accept what is offered, the number of head varying in this tribe from six to ten. The animals are contributed here, as elsewhere in South Africa, by various members of the bridegroom's family; and upon their receipt are allocated to the proper relatives of the bride, to be held in trust to meet the demands of certain eventualities for which they may later be needed.[25]

Among the Gusii of Kenya, to the north, the transfer of cattle "provides in various ways for the maintenance of the equilibrium brought about by an initial bridewealth transaction." One lineage, which loses a woman to another, restores the balance by the receipt of the cattle given as bridewealth. Yet,

> As long as B have possession of the woman (or an adequate number of her children), they are obliged to maintain group A in full possession of the bridewealth equivalent. Conversely, as long as A have possession of the bridewealth animals (or an adequate number of their progeny), they are obliged to maintain B in possession of the woman. In neither case does the obligation cease after A have passed the bridewealth on to a third party.

Should a wife die, or the couple separate, the bridewealth must be returned, wholly or in part. Thus, a widower who had given ten cows for his wife, by whom he had one surviving child, would receive from her family nine cows and one heifer. The various systems become more complex if more of the dead woman's children survive her, but the principle of recompense is clear. Furthermore, when bridewealth is given, it passes in stages which again demonstrate the workings of the principle of maintaining equilibrium:

> 1. . . . A surrenders the rights of ownership over the herd, but retains physical possession of it. B binds himself to surrender certain rights over the girl and her offspring, but retains physical possession of her. . . . 2. . . . A surrenders physical possession of the main part of the herd but retains one or more animals. B surrenders physical possession of the girl, but retains right to take her back in case of disagreement. . . . 3. . . . A surrenders physical possession of the remaining animals: the entire herd has now been finally transferred to B. B surrenders the right to recover cus-

[25] Schapera (1938), 125–47.

tody of the girl: she has now been finally attached to the lineage of *A*.[26]

Marriage, which has appeared most often in these instances of gift exchange as the occasion on which the transfer of goods outstandingly occurs, must not be thought to be the sole vehicle of these kinds of non-economic circulation. As has been seen for New Guinea,[27] where such modes of distribution are particularly highly developed and numerous, the occasions on which exchanges can occur in non-economic ritual settings are varied in the extreme. The same is true for Africa and elsewhere; as an instance of this we may cite the elaborate funeral rites of Dahomey, West Africa. Here again, despite the fact that in the mind of the native the only economic element that rises into consciousness is the waste involved in the destruction of valuable goods and the cost of a funeral to the family that gives it, a considerable quantity of goods actually changes hands. Only the briefest mention of the economically significant elements in these involved "partial" and "definitive" burials can be given here, but they are sufficient to make the point. They include the provision, by the sons-in-law of the deceased, of the food needed by the mourning family of their wives; the cowries and drink paid the grave-digger on various occasions when he performs his functions; the repeated gifts of money, drinks, and kerchiefs presented to those who play the funerary drums; the constant stream of cloths, cowries, food, and drink that moves into the hands of the official in charge of the rites and, to a lesser degree, of his assistants; the gifts given each mourner by his best friend to console him. On the occasion of the "definitive burial," the amounts involved are increased by the spirited competition in gift-giving by the spouses of the children of the dead, where each summons the members of the mutual aid society he has joined to ensure his ability to perform adequately on just such an occasion, to "push" him, so his contribution will be honorably larger than that given by the others with whom he competes. In addition to the consumption of great quantities of food and drink, and the goods that are buried with the dead or destroyed in the course of the ritual, the distribution of much wealth in the form of gifts given

[26] Mayer, 38, 13–14, 47, and *passim.*

[27] Hogbin (1934), 98.

participants in such ceremonies must be taken into account. These gifts in some measure represent something of a process of redistribution comparable to those other instances that have been considered here, though not to any degree that would equalize return with outgo for the family giving the funeral.

7

IT IS unfortunately not possible at the present stage of our knowledge of comparative economics to be more specific concerning the degree to which these extra-economic practices affect the circulation of goods within a given society. We are told, for example, that on Ontong Java an exchange of food such as is made at betrothals, births, or funerals on one occasion consisted of two taro puddings, each almost four feet square, while the return gift included 16,000 coconuts and ten baskets of fish. An important series of annotated native drawings which represent amounts of food prepared for distribution in the feasts of the Koita of southeastern New Guinea has been reproduced by Seligman: 10 heaps of bananas, each with the figure 10 under it are indicated, and 3 paired yam-heaps of 200 each. Sugar-cane—3 uprights each supporting 4 canes, and 18 other single stalks, each with a pot of food beside it—is also shown.[28] On the Polynesian island of Uvea, again, we read that at the marriage of a woman of royal rank a pile of 500 mats was among the collection of gifts to be exchanged by the families of the principals.[29] The large quantities of valuable goods given away, later to be returned with generous increment, at the potlatch ceremonies of the Indians of the Northwest Coast indicate how important this phenomenon may be from a purely economic point of view.[30]

That those who have stressed the necessity for a careful study of the non-economic forms of exchange in nonliterate societies have taken a step toward a clearer understanding of the economics of these communities is evident, for they have brought into the foreground certain interrelations that had long gone unperceived. Yet the essentially non-economic approach implicit

[28] Seligman (1910), Pls. XV, XVI.
[29] Burrows, 57–8.
[30] Boas (1897), 341 ff. See, however, Barnett (353, quoted on 226 below), for a significant caution on this point.

in this position, oriented as it is toward the more conventional anthropological interest in social relationships, leaves much to be done. For even where the economic importance of the exchange of goods and services is emphasized, such matters as the amounts of goods exchanged in the course of rites, and more importantly, the proportion of these goods to the total amount that circulates as a result of the operation of the more routine methods of distributing commodities, are rarely touched upon. For the present we must be content with the knowledge that significant modes of distribution, not to be classified under the rubrics of conventional economics, do exist in most societies, and for the rest, recognize that the study of all these methods is essential if we are to have a valid picture of the total distributive process in the societies where patterns of this kind are found.

CHAPTER IX

TRADE AND BARTER

WE MAY now consider those instances of the circulation of goods when objects are exchanged with the primary aim of obtaining commodities, rather than to sustain or increase the prestige of the giver. In analyzing these instances of trade, properly speaking, we shall therefore be considering exchanges of values, specifically designated in terms of other goods or of such money as may circulate among the people concerned, rather than with codes of polite behavior under which bargaining may be absent, or when the procedure does not consist of a kind of patterned deprecation or the vaunting of prowess.

It may be indicated that whereas gift and ceremonial exchange usually accompany the sealing of some friendly pact, as in cases of exchange incident upon marriage, trade is often consummated with an underlying sense of hostility, none the less real for the conventionalized expressions of friendship which frequently accompany it. Even such an institution as the potlatch of the Northwest Coast of North America, wherein the ceremonial exchanges take the form of patterned hostility, does not necessarily constitute evidence against this statement. Commenting on the phenomenon, Mauss observes that the Tlingit and the Haida themselves explain the nature of the potlatch by the statement that "the two phratries show respect for each other." [1] What is meant by this can be clarified by reference to our own society when the attitudes that accompany the (delayed) ceremonial exchanges that mark a wedding or the birth of a child are contrasted with those that characterize many business transactions of any appreciable consequence. More overt in expression are comparable

[1] Mauss, 37.

phenomena among the Copper Eskimo, where trade is preceded by wrestling matches to find out which party is the stronger.[2]

This difference in the point of view regarding exchanges to achieve economic and non-economic ends leads us to another observation. The economic role of ceremonial and gift exchange seems in many, perhaps a majority of instances, to be that of achieving the circulation of goods *within* a given group. Hence, especially in economically less complex societies where little specialization of labor exists, such exchanges appear to result in the redistribution of commodities that are in some measure possessed by everyone. Trade, on the other hand, is usually *inter-tribal*, and involves the acquisition of goods not available in one's own group. A citation which clearly makes the point for a specific culture, that of the island of Tanga, may be given here:

> The whole distribution process consists of a constant exchange of gifts between individuals and between groups of individuals. . . . There is little or no barter between the natives themselves, but when they visit other groups, supplies of shell currency . . . , red dye . . . , betel nut . . . , combs . . . and such items are exchanged for pigs . . . , plank-canoes . . . , pan-pipes . . . , small log drums . . . etc.[3]

In brief, the values involved in non-economic forms of exchange are prestige values, while trade is concerned primarily with the transfer of goods whose principal value derives from their utility in meeting the demands of everyday existence. Yet how imperceptibly gift-giving can shade into trade in the same society is to be seen in a series of categories of exchange in the Trobriand Islands drawn by Malinowski:

(1) Pure gifts.
(2) Customary payments, repaid irregularly and without strict equivalence.
(3) Payment for services rendered.
(4) Gifts returned in economically equivalent form.
(5) Exchange of material goods against privileges, titles, and non-material possessions.

[2] Jenness, 49.   [3] Bell, 308.

(6) Ceremonial barter with deferred payment.
(7) Trade pure and simple.[4]

This same shading can also be seen in the various ways in which the circulation of goods and rendering of services were classified by the Puyallup-Nisqually of the Puget Sound area of western North America. These differ from the categories just given in that, being recognized and named with native terms by the Indians themselves, they do not derive from the ordering of data by the ethnographers. The Puyallup-Nisqually categories were:

(1) *i'gwis:* to swap, to exchange one article for another of the same kind.
(2) *otágc:* to exchange one article for another of a different sort.
(3) *obetsáleg*: to pay for property not yet in existence, to hire something made.
(4) *kélosad:* payment for services of a shaman in curing.
(5) *abálts:* to give something as a gift. "Giving of this type was viewed not in relation to the absolute value or desirability of the article itself but entirely in relation to the prestige of the donor. Although such giving was often reciprocal, there was no necessary reciprocity of value."
(6) *ábalıq*: to "buy their good will," gifts given to assuage a strained relationship; "when you take something to somebody so you won't be afraid of them any more."
(7) *tsólaxl:* "free" gifts proffered on visits between affinal relatives.
(8) Ceremonial distribution of property:
    (a) *opákad:* to give property at a ceremony and not expect any return.
    (b) *o'éu*: to give property for assistance during a ceremony, with no return expected, but eventually received at a ceremony given by donor.
    (c) *ogwégwe:* to give property at a ceremony with return expected.
    (d) *obtcáliq*: to bet; this was done between villages.[5]

[4] Malinowski (1922), 176 ff.   [5] M. W. Smith, 146–50.

The problems arising in the study of trade as carried on by nonliterate peoples involve many questions having to do with the determination of value and the nature of the market. How important, relatively, are utility, prestige, and the amount of labor that goes into the production of a given commodity in determining its worth? When this is expressed in terms of other goods, to what extent are these found to react to the influence of such market phenomena as supply and demand, especially as this may be evidenced in artificial control of supply as we know it by those monopolies which are occasionally encountered in nonliterate cultures? To what extent do considerations of gain influence the trading operations of peoples in these societies? What is the degree to which traders are actuated by the need to dispose of surpluses in order to obtain goods of which they have need? How extensive, indeed, are the trading activities of nonliterate peoples?

We cannot at the present state of our documentation pretend to do more than phrase most of these questions. Despite much information concerning the incidence of trade routes, the nature of the goods traded, and even the manner in which those who take part in such transactions come together, we only infrequently encounter in the literature any but the most cursory accounts of how much one commodity is worth in terms of other commodities, while we almost never find any detailed description of what actually was exchanged in any specific transaction. In short, we lack very nearly all the essential data for an understanding of the phenomena of price and value in non-industrial and non-pecuniary societies, even though some *a priori* discussion of these matters has found its way into the literature of both economics and anthropology. This is particularly to be regretted since, as the point has been phrased, "the heart of economics, both in its narrower and its broader aspects, is the theory of value." [6]

The forms of trade have in some cases been employed as designations of entire economies, and the resulting types have been used in setting up hypothetical developmental series supposedly marking off the evolution of economic life. Thus while Gras has suggested [7] that Hildebrandt's "stages" of the development of economic systems—barter, money, and credit economies—must

[6] Hoyt (1926), 4.   [7] Gras (1930), 468.

be revised into the progression of gift economy, gift barter economy, pure barter, and money barter, he nevertheless envisages them as primarily useful as marking off the stages of a sequence of growth. Yet, here again, this assumption as to the origin or evolution of institutions derived from reference to living nonliterate peoples and not susceptible of objective archaeological proof must, like others of its kind, be rejected as scientifically invalid.

With this reservation in mind, however, such a classification as this, if it is understood to represent no more than a useful device for arranging material, can be of value. The type of gift economy that Gras describes—a system held to have existed in the earliest days of mankind, when the passage of free gifts was the only means of effectuating the circulation of goods—certainly is not found in the economy of any living people, as has been demonstrated by Mauss in the work already cited. Nor can gift barter economy, conceived as a development from this initial "stage," be accepted as fulfilling the implications of the designation given it. For, as has been shown, ceremonial interchange of goods between individuals or groups often involves no bartering at all; while ritualized exchanges of this type, though providing for the circulation of goods within a tribe, frequently accompanies intertribal trade.[8]

We may therefore indicate the following *logical*—as against *developmental*—categories which can be employed to *classify* the mechanisms for the circulation of commodities that exist in primitive societies; gift and ceremonial exchange, barter, money barter, and exchange based on the use of money. Two cautions in the use of these categories must be emphasized. In the first place, it must be understood that they represent merely different kinds of exchange, carrying no connotation of "earlier," "later," or any other type of progression. Secondly, as actually found over the earth, these types so merge into one another, and any one of them so combines elements of the others, that the assignment of a given system of exchange to a given category must, in the main, be a matter of emphasis. Examples of gift and ceremonial exchange, the first type, were presented in preceding pages. A discussion of the last two categories, those of money barter and

[8] Cf. also Schmidt (1926), 178; (1920–1), II, 27; and Hoyt (1926), 115–16 for other series of developmental categories.

exchange based on the use of money, will be given in succeeding chapters. Here, then, we shall treat of barter, those instances of goods exchanged for other goods without the intervention of some least common denominator of value. We shall likewise seek to discover how extensive are the trading operations carried out on this level by non-pecuniary folk.

2

THE SO-CALLED "silent trade" is a specialized form of barter, wherein goods are exchanged without any meeting of the two parties to the transaction. The procedure is for one of the principals to deposit in a customary spot whatever commodities are to be traded, while the other, the receiver of these goods, leaves in their place some other commodity or commodities which custom has established as equivalents. This institution has aroused widespread interest and speculation among students of presumed early forms of trade, so that numerous instances of it have been recorded.[9] The classical, and probably the best-known description of the silent trade was given by Herodotus, who told how the exchanges of goods were effected between the Carthaginians and the peoples who lived on the west coast of the African continent, beyond the Pillars of Hercules.[10] Ibn Batuta, the Arabic traveler, gave some attention to the silent trade as it was carried on in the far northern "Land of Darkness." Here "goods," of a kind not specified, were customarily deposited by merchants at "the Darkness," where natives repaired during the night, taking what they found and leaving "skins of sable, miniver and ermine." Whenever the merchants were not satisfied with the payment left for them, they refused to take away the skins. On returning the next day, they would either find that more skins had been added to the number previously deposited, or that the goods originally deposited had been returned.

Similar means of effectuating "silent" exchanges occur today, or did occur until very recent times, between the Chuckchee of Siberia and the inhabitants of Alaska, between the lowland Christians of Northern Luzon and the Negritos, and between the

[9] Cf. Grierson.   [10] Herodotus, Bk. IV, Ch. 193.

Bantu of the Congo and their pygmy neighbors.[11] An instance from California of the silent trade has been given in the following passage:

The trips the Tübatulabal made beyond the borders of their own area led them, in early historic times at least, to points a hundred miles or more west and southwestward, and somewhat shorter distances north and eastward. . . . Being mainly at peace with their immediate neighbors, the Tübatulabal were able to pass through alien territory with a minimum of risk from sudden attacks. By a system of silent trade they exchanged the pinons, balls of prepared tobacco, and other commodities they had brought with them, for lengths of white clam-shell disks which passed as currency among all the tribes of this region.[12]

Schmidt cites a number of cases of trade of this type from Maylasia and elsewhere,[13] Hoyt sketches the "border line" version of it which takes place between the Siassi islanders and the Jabim of New Guinea,[14] and Thurnwald, giving instances of this form of trading between Veddas and Singhalese in Ceylon, and between Kpelle and Gola in Liberia, also refers to examples contained in a volume written about 1500 by a Novgorod merchant, entitled *Chronicle of Unknown Men in Eastern Regions*.[15] The exchange of fish for taro between the Manus and the Usiai folk of the Admiralty Islands might well come under the heading of the silent trade, though only as a border-line case,[16] while the procedures of the Kiwai Papuans, among whom this kind of exchange is an accepted method of suing for peace after hostilities, suggests that the device may have functioned at an earlier time as a more purely economic institution in this area.[17] A variant of silent exchange that exists as an adjunct to the more customary type is reported from New Caledonia. Here trading parties from the coast meet those of the inland tribes at a stated rendezvous, to exchange definite amounts of fresh and dried fish and crustacea for tubers of various sorts:

[11] Schechter, 613, 576–7.
[12] Vogelin, 3.
[13] Schmidt, M. (1920–1), II, 149 ff.
[14] Hoyt (1926), 134.
[15] Thurnwald (1932b), 149–50.
[16] Mead (1930b), 118.
[17] Landtman (1927), 216.

Each puts down his load, and chooses another in return, which he takes home with him. If by chance one of the parties cannot come at the time agreed upon, the one who has brought goods to exchange leaves his load on the ground where his tardy partner finds them later, leaving what he has to give in return in the same place. I have often admired the way these piles of goods, left at the roadside with no one to watch them, remain untouched until they are taken away by the person for whom they were intended.[18]

The questions that have been posed concerning the reasons for the existence of the silent trade need not long detain us, inasmuch as none of the hypotheses that has been advanced can be given objective proof. To hold that the existence of such an institution proves that trading in general originated in hostility between tribes, as Grierson maintains, is merest conjecture, difficult even of substantiation by the customary method of referring to the customs of living nonliterate folk.[19] It is equally a matter of guess whether or not, as both Schmidt and Grierson believe, this kind of trade developed between tribes of unequal degrees of cultural achievement, which caused them to conduct their trade on the basis of this silent exchange, since they could not meet on a plane of equality. Hoyt variously intimates that it may have been dissimilarity in language between peoples that had to be overcome, or that it was found to be convenient to leave goods where others could come upon them in following a regular route at irregular and unpredictable intervals, or that it was a device for dealing with strangers and thus avoiding possible unpleasant first-hand contacts. Yet all of these reasons, or none of them, may have been operative in particular instances; but the degree to which each or all were causal in what regions, under what circumstances, and by what methods, we can never know. What is needed to give us an understanding of the nature, if not the origin, of the phenomenon is a full description of some instance of the silent trade, including a detailed statement of what is traded, and when, and under what conditions, and how often, together with an analysis of the manner in which this particular form of trade fits into the entire pattern of tribal exchange.

[18] Leenhardt, 92–3.   [19] Numelin, 22–5.

3

THE LITERATURE on trade in nonliterate societies makes clear that barter is by far the most prevalent mode of exchange, and that it is carried on by means of giving one commodity for another, either according to established ratios or by actual bargaining. It is important that both these methods be recognized as co-existent, since bargaining by no means always accompanies barter. While haggling may, and most often does, mark the direct exchange of commodities, there is at least one case on record where this is altogether absent. It is not improbable that future detailed descriptions of actual trading operations, of which at present there is almost none drawn in economic terms, will indicate that this acceptance of established values is far more wide-spread in barter systems of exchange of goods than the common position regarding the question would imply.[20]

Whatever the process of achieving exchange, there can be no doubt of the importance of barter itself as an economic mechanism in non-pecuniary societies. This has not gone unrecognized, for even though detailed descriptions of the way in which barter is actually carried on are rare, and exact analyses of the exchanges effectuated even rarer, the information of a general nature concerning barter that has been collected is impressive. Thus the accounts of the trading operations of native peoples, recorded since the earliest times of European contact, have yielded much data, as has already been manifest. Certainly almost every modern scientific description of a nonliterate society makes some mention of the prevailing forms of trading, however cursory this mention may be. We can accordingly arrive at some idea of how great a variety of goods change hands through non-pecuniary methods of transferring commodities and over how wide a geographical area.

Most of these accounts deal primarily with intertribal trade. They serve to document the hypothesis already advanced concerning the difference between this type of exchange and the manner in which goods circulate within a group, where numbers are relatively small and the economic organization is relatively

[20] Cf. Tueting, 35, for a typical statement.

simple. It is always possible, to be sure, that intratribal barter will in the future be found to occur more frequently than has been reported, for negative evidence is at best inconclusive. But enough attention has been paid to gift and ceremonial exchange in many parts of the world to make unlikely the omission of reference to other mechanisms making for intratribal barter. In following the available data, we shall in any event find ourselves concerned almost exclusively with commercial contacts between different communities rather than with intratribal exchange.

Numerous accounts of aboriginal trade in the southeastern United States are found in descriptions of the experiences of certain early voyagers in the area. Cabeza de Vaca has set down his adventures among the Indians of the coastal region bordering the Gulf of Mexico, where, practically a prisoner, he engaged in barter to earn his livelihood.

> The Indians would beg me to go from one quarter to another for things of which they have need; for in consequence of incessant hostilities, they cannot traverse the country, nor make many exchanges. With my merchandise and trade I went into the interior as far as I pleased, and travelled along the coast forty or fifty leagues. The principal wares were canes and other pieces of sea-snail, conches used for cutting, and fruit like a bean of the highest value to them, which they use as a medicine and employ in their dances and festivities. Among other matters were sea-beads. Such were what I carried into the interior; and in barter I got and brought back skins, ochre with which they rub and color the face, hard canes of which to make arrows, sinews, cement and flint for the heads, and tassels of the hair of deer that by dyeing they make red. . . . I bartered with these Indians in combs I made for them and in bows, arrows, and nets.[21]

Lafitan, a Jesuit, writing of the transactions he witnessed in the Southeast about 1710, says:

> The savage nations always trade with one another. Their commerce is, like that of the ancients, a simple exchange of wares against wares. Each has something particular which

[21] Cited in Myer, 738–9.

the others have not, and the traffic makes these things circulate among them. Their wares are grain, porcelain [wampum], furs, robes, tobacco, mats, canoes, work made of moose or buffalo hide and of porcupine quills, cotton-beds, domestic utensils—in a word, all sorts of necessities of life required by them.[22]

Further indications of how widespread trade was in the area, and the variety of goods traded, are found in other works. Florida Indians, in their cypress canoes, went hunting and trading from the Suwanee River to the southern tip of the peninsula and on to Havana, carrying among other commodities deerskins, dry fish, beeswax, honey, and bear's oil. The Natchez and other Mississippi tribes obtained the salt they needed from the Caddoan peoples west of the Mississippi River, and bands of these folk were often met by the early explorers as they came east to trade.[23]

In the Southwest, the Tewa carried on an extensive traffic in corn, corn meal, and wheat bread with the Comanche, exchanging these products for prepared buffalo hides.[24] Taos women obtain the woven belts they wear by trading for them with the people of Isleta pueblo; their food baskets are obtained from Hopi, and yucca baskets for washing wheat from Keres. In return, the Taos folk give wheat or buckskin. They trade horses for buckskin with the Navaho, while "in 1896 the best pottery came from Tewa in exchange for wheat." [25] Jemez traders barter grapes and chile, melons, wheat, and corn for turquoise, silver belts or necklaces, dress cloths and blankets, buckskin, meat, feathers, and pottery. The intertribal exchanges as they actually work out are complex.

The women's dresses of native cloth are got from the Hopi and from Santo Domingo, pottery from Santo Domingo and Sia, turquoise from Santo Domingo, blankets and mutton from the Navaho. One trader I heard of would barter turquoise got at Santo Domingo for Navaho blankets, which he in turn disposed of at Santo Domingo for more turquoise. A man asked me to get him some red face paint from the

[22] Ibid., 737.
[23] Swanton (1928), 452–3; (1911), 78.

[24] Robbins, Harrington, and Freire-Mareco, 97.
[25] Parsons (1936a), 24–5.

Hopi; he said they had the best. What he had in his buckskin pouch he had got from the Navaho.[26]

California tribes also carried on a lively exchange of goods. The valley Maidu traded with the Wintun for beads, which represented money to them. From the lower altitudes these beads moved into the mountains, together with salt, salmon, and nuts of the digger-pine; in return, bows and arrows, deerskins, sugar-pine nuts, and "perhaps some other local food products" were obtained. From the north the Maidu received the obsidian they needed for arrow-points, and a green pigment used by them to decorate bows. Wild tobacco was traded in all directions. The Shasta received dentalia, salt or seaweed, baskets of various sorts, tan-oak acorns, and canoes from the Karok, for which they gave obsidian, deerskins, and sugar-pine nuts. For these same goods the Shasta obtained acorns from the Wintun to the south, while they sent their surplus acorn-flour to the tribes of southern Oregon, receiving for this the dentalia they so prized.[27]

Barter among the Guiana Indians of South America in earlier times was based on exchange without bargaining; or, as it has been expressed, these Indians were ignorant "with regard to the custom of presents." It is probable that in the days before contact was established with runaway Negro slaves who settled in the region and brought with them more commercially sophisticated African methods, a mode of exchange existed whereby something given, though returnable, was only casually evaluated. Today, however, instead of the "present for present" system, not only barter but bargaining seems at times to occur. Despite lack of clarity as to its exact nature the instance is important because it seems to afford an example of exchange in which emphasis determines classification, since at the present time, actual barter rather than exchange of goods accompanied by the passage of gifts is apparently the rule. This means that the economic rather than the non-economic aspects of their trading are uppermost in the minds of the natives who engage in these transactions.[28] Farther to the south, among the Amazon tribes, where no trade routes or markets have been reported, trade is an individual concern that operates across lines dividing hostile tribes. Because of

[26] Parsons (1925), 16.
[27] Kroeber (1925), 399, 287.
[28] Roth (1924), 633; (1929), 101–02.

self-sufficiency in production, "extratribal goods are distinctly luxuries," but such commodities as pottery are passed on from hand to hand so that they eventually travel considerable distances.[29]

In the Chaco, it is once more difficult to disentangle trading from gift-giving, since the transactions are reported as having "essentially the character of an exchange of presents." This appraisal does not seem to follow entirely from the data as presented, however. The fact that the Indians only trade with friends whom they habitually visit and who, therefore, can be regarded as exclusive trading partners does not seem to affect the essentially commercial nature of the transactions. The Choroti barter their own dried fish with friendly foreign tribes for maize, ceremonially valuable red paint, and certain much-prized necklaces. Barter between the Toba and neighboring tribes is of a similar nature, except that it seems to be carried on during visits between trading partners, the visitor bringing maize and the Chaco Indian returning his surplus fish. "The Indian, in conformity with his natural tact, is of course anxious not to favour one friend more than another, and thus a regular system of bartering with definite measures has gradually developed." Exchanges along these approved lines, with sanctioned return for gifts tendered, go on until the supplies of the "visitors" have been disposed of, whereupon they leave with the dried fish they came to obtain. Reciprocally, the Chaco Indian also pays "visits" to his trading partner, taking fish and returning with cereals and sugar-cane.[30]

The complexities of the trading operations of the peoples of Melanesia and New Guinea are such that only their salient points can be indicated here. In doing this, we may again profitably follow the summary of these rich materials prepared by Tueting. Pure barter exists either by itself or associated with the ritual passage of goods, and trade may be on the basis of the exchange of commodity for commodity, or some common medium of exchange may be employed for the purpose. Even where money is found, barter may continue, or the use of money may be restricted to ceremonial uses. Stated markets are found in some districts, while elsewhere casual contacts suffice to assure the proper circulation of goods. In various parts of the area, "the

[29] Whiffen, 61–2.   [30] Karsten, 99–101.

transfer of goods is usually direct and payment immediate, although goods and services may be ordered by contract and payment deferred." The kinds of goods exchanged here differ in different localities, but this variation is based on certain similarities that hold throughout. The principal articles of trade are those having economic utility,

> . . . fish, vegetable produce, sago, or goods manufactured from stone, wood, clay or feathers. Commodities of great value such as pigs, shell ornaments, and canoes are usually exchanged ceremonially. Food and pots are almost always bartered. They are rarely exchanged ceremonially except as gifts accompanying the main transaction.[31]

Since in the next chapter one of the few available first-hand descriptions of barter from this area will be cited, only two or three instances of the principles enunciated above will be briefly mentioned here. These are cited chiefly because, appearing after Tueting's summary of Melanesian trade was published, they serve to supplement her data. In Malekula, though most households are self-supporting, and exchange, as "we might expect to find," is rare on the purely economic level, markets do exist to which the inland and fishing folk of the coastal areas repair during the period between planting and harvesting yams. "It is a recognized thing that the coastal people must take everything which the bushmen bring; nevertheless, a considerable amount of bartering goes on." Nothing is paid for at the time of sale, but some ten days later the bush people come to the shore once more, where the coastal folk hand over the fish, shell-fish, and other marine produce in whatever quantities were agreed upon at the previous meeting. These markets end with the yam harvest, "presumably because . . . the coastal people are no longer dependent upon their bush neighbors for garden foodstuffs." [32]

In the area of the Huon Gulf of northeastern New Guinea, this pattern of trade based on tribal specialization has been described as seen from the point of view of the Busama. Exchanges are carried on with other peoples living along the coast as reciprocal gift-giving; it is only with the people of the interior that "a proper return" for commodities is exacted. This is because "commercialism is considered to be incompatible with

[31] Tueting, 35–8. [32] Deacon, 202–03.

blood ties," and coastal people have few relatives in the bush. Yet in trading by sea along the coast, exchanges are made only with kinsmen.

> Each type of object has its traditional equivalent—a pot of certain size being worth so many taro or mats . . . —and most of the visitors go home with items at least as valuable as those which they brought. Indeed, the closer the kinship bond the greater is the host's generosity, and some of them may be a good deal richer. A careful count is kept, however, and the score evened up later.

But the trading is never accompanied by bargaining:

> The goods are handed over as though they were free gifts offered out of friendship. Discussion of values is avoided, and each person does his best to convey the impression that no thought of a counter gift has ever crossed his mind.

So important is the factor of etiquette and the need to observe canons of generosity and so pressing the "fear of a lost reputation" as a result of this most prized quality, that return in excess of the value of a gift is frequently made. "One is ashamed to treat persons one knows like tradesmen," say the natives.[33]

Each man, in the island of Manam, has two or three or more trading partners on the New Guinea mainland, through whom all exchanges of consumption goods or valuables are made. The relationship transcends economic considerations, for the visits to the mainland are made with a lively sense of pleasure, and men who have nothing to dispose of often accompany a trading expedition merely to see their partners. Nonetheless, the primary objectives of these expeditions are economic, as is plain if the broad range of the goods bartered is indicated. Sago, cooking-pots, freshwater bivalves, colored petticoats, colored cane used in making armbands and waistbands, carved wooden bowls, "and many other things of lesser importance" are traded for the canarium nuts, areca nuts, tobacco, and bananas the Manam men bring with them. Pigs, curved boars' tusks, and headdresses and breastplates of dogs' teeth are exchanged for large slit wooden gongs, while the long bamboos used in making the Manam sacred flutes are also obtained in this manner.[34]

[33] Hogbin (1947), 244–8.   [34] Wedgewood, 395–6.

In the trading system of Australia, whose aspects of gift-exchange have been indicated and the extensiveness of which will shortly be discussed, barter played a very large part. There were definite markets (called by Roth "swapping-places") where exchanges of raw materials and finished products of various sorts were effected. This system "is barter in the true sense of the term; no medium of exchange or measure of value was or is employed anywhere in the continent. . . ." It is summarized as follows:

> It was carried on between contiguous and distant hordes and tribes to secure desired raw materials, finished articles, coroborees and songs, produced or not by one of these groups, occurring or not in their respective territories, and brought by one or more members of one group to another; such barter was carried on at recognized "market" places, feasts, ceremonies, and other gatherings, besides occasioning special journeys. Barter is thus a means whereby surplus products are disposed of, the economy of the group is balanced and its culture enriched. Barter places a high value on personal skill.[35]

Africa, where population units are large and the economic systems more complex than in most parts of the nonliterate world, presents many instances of barter, not only between tribes, but as is more rare in non-industrial communities, within a given tribe. Of the numerous cases that could be cited where both processes were carried on in the days before European control, that of the Tswana of South Africa may be summarized. The varied methods these folk employed to assure the circulation of goods reflected their specialization in production. Thus a person in need of such wares as metal goods, pots, baskets, or wooden utensils, and unable to make them himself, went to an expert and "either bought the object he wanted, if it was already available, or, as was frequently necessary, ordered it to be made." In addition, goods of this character were acquired by exchanges made between persons who chanced to have more of a given commodity than required. In times of great need, especially when there was a shortage of food, grain was obtained by the same means, as were cattle. "There was no standardized medium

[35] McCarthy, 176–9.

of exchange." All kinds of commodities—grain, meat, cattle, smaller domesticated animals, fowl, hoes, spears—were bartered, and certain rough scales of values prevailed. A pot, or milk-pail, or a similar utensil was worth its contents in grain; a sheep or a bag of cord bought two goats; a heifer was worth ten goats or five bags of corn. Intertribal exchanges of the same type also occurred. Among at least one of the Tswana tribes, the Kgatla, these were under control of the chief, to whom the outsider coming to either buy or sell had to report and give a gift "to open the way"; that is, he had to proffer an ox or a heifer if he had brought cattle with which to buy corn, or several rolls of tobacco if he had this commodity for sale.

The question of credit, without which many of the transactions could not have been carried on, does not concern us at this point, though to fill in our sketch it may be indicated that payments were often deferred, and that consequently the problems arising out of the relations between debtors and creditors were well known.[36] In this African society, then, with its economy more complex than that of most nonliterate groups, an outstanding characteristic of trade lay in its greater resemblance to business as we know it. Exchange between members of the tribe, as well as between them and those outside the tribe, was a matter of economic give-and-take, and a clear recognition existed of the difference between ceremonial exchange and commercial transactions.

4

WHATEVER the origin of trading, and whatever the earliest manifestations of exchange may have been, it is apparent both from archaeological evidence and from the ubiquity of present-day trading practices the world over that the passage of goods from one people to another is a phenomenon of great antiquity. Perhaps the most striking prehistoric find pointing how ancient are trading practices consists of a shell from upper Paleolithic deposits of southern France, which could have only come from

---

[36] Schapera (1938), 241–4; for other data from Northern Rhodesia where, as concerns the Lozi, there was intratribal trade as well as exchanges between them and other groups, see Gluckman (1941), 67–74.

the eastern Mediterranean.[37] Equally striking is the distribution of the so-called "beeswax" flints from Grand Pressigny. With central France as the only possible source of supply, implements made from this distinctive rock are found in all parts of that country, and as far east as Switzerland.[38] Instances of objects found far from their points of origin are numerous as we move into the Bronze and Iron Ages, while these become commonplace as the historic period opens.[39]

Wide areas are ranged by present-day nonliterate man for purposes of trade, as is shown both by special studies devoted to the description of trade routes in various parts of the earth, and by discussions of the trading expeditions of specific peoples found in the ethnographic literature. One significant function of trade—recognized more among literate peoples, as in the saying "Trade follows the flag," than among nonliterate groups— derives from the manner in which it makes for a kind of commercial compact, from which develop the diplomatic practices that promote those peaceful contacts so essential to economic intercourse. Trade relations, that is, as Numelin points out, in a very real sense may and often do encourage good international (intertribal) relations.[40] Some of the cases, notably in Africa, where the trader is essentially a professional, involve special factors and will be discussed later when the incidence and role of the middleman in nonliterate societies is considered. In Melanesia the trade routes and the expeditions that followed them have attracted sufficient attention so as to make it unnecessary here to go over the numerous works in which these have been made readily available. We may, therefore, restrict ourselves to the Americas, where a rich body of material exists that has had little attention from this point of view, and Australia, which presents a case of special interest as indicating the extensiveness of trading operations among peoples having an extremely simple economic organization.

Denig tells of a type of shell called "Iroquois" that was traded from tribe to tribe across the mountains from the Pacific coast until it reached the far-away Plains. These shells, about two inches long and "about the size of a raven's feather at the larger

[37] Russell, 3–4.
[38] Hue.
[39] Burkitt, *passim;* Childe, *passim;*

MacCurdy, II, 98, 211–12.
[40] Numelin (1950), 252–5; see also Chs. IX and X.

end," were hollow and curved, so they could be strung as ornaments. Some idea of the extensiveness of this trade can be
gathered from the observation that 300 or 400 such shells were
frequently to be seen on some young Crow or Blackfoot woman's
dress.[41] A study of the archaeological and ethnological evidence
of Indian trails in eastern United States also shows how widespread was the network of commercial communication between
the peoples of the region. Thus, for example, in the mounds of
Ohio, Tennessee, and elsewhere,

> . . . objects from the Atlantic, the Gulf of Mexico, and the
> Pacific, and from nearly every section of the interior of the
> United States have been found; obsidian from the Rocky
> Mountain region; pipestone from the great red pipestone
> quarries of Minnesota and Wisconsin, steatite and mica from
> the Appalachians, copper from the region of the Great Lakes
> and elsewhere, shells from the Gulf of Mexico and the
> Atlantic, dentalium and abalone shells from the Pacific
> Coast, and now and then artifacts which at least hint at
> some remote contact with Mexican Indian culture.[42]

The ramifications of Hopi trade show how closely the tribes
of the entire Southwest were knit together, and how their exchanges of goods were tied in with the commercial operations
of surrounding areas. Today they exchange corn, dried peaches,
wafer bread, hatchets, and agricultural implements with the
Navaho for mutton, firewood, wooden roof-beams, silver ornaments of various sorts, antelope-skins, sheep, and horses. This is
relatively recent, since in earlier days their northern trade was
principally with the Paiute, who would pay for the wafer bread
and corn mush they desired with wood and piñon gum, horses
and meat, bows and arrows, and sometimes, when food was
especially scarce, with children to be retraded to the Mexicans
for blankets and horses.

Trade relations between the Hopi and the Pueblos to the east
continues, though irregularly, with Zuñi, Acoma, Santo Domingo,
Jemez, and Cochiti. When at its height, for their woven goods
the Hopi received shell necklaces, indigo, blue carbonate, red
woolen blankets, buffalo-skins, hoes, and turquoise. Some of

[41] Denig, 590-1.   [42] Myer, 736-7.

these products were for their own use, while some were retraded to their commercial affiliates to the west. The Hopi also had indirect contact with the tribes of the southern Plains and of the mountains of northern New Mexico, exchanging dried meat and buffalo hide for corn and woven goods. Through the Havasupai to the west, Hopi goods found their way to the Walapai, Mohave, Halchidoma, Yuma, Kaveltcadom, Maricopa, and Pima. The trade included both goods manufactured or grown by each party, and commodities received from tribes farther removed.

The Hopi also had trading relations with the White Mountain Apache, and in recent times with the Mormons, the former bringing moccasins, arrows, mescal, and the strong green bows especially favored by the Hopi to be bartered for colored Hopi yarn, the Mormons giving horses for blankets. The Hopi themselves rarely went on trading expeditions, but were essentially middlemen, and as such will engage our attention later, since at this point we are concerned merely with their position at the center of the web of southwestern trade routes, which thus so admirably serve to illustrate the geographical range of trade and help us visualize how considerable the "volume of trade exchange" must have been.[43]

A similiar complexity of trading routes is found in other regions of the Americas. To the south, commercial intercourse between the Indian towns and villages of the Mexican state of Oaxaca gives another instance of the vigor of the trading operations recorded from the nonliterate peoples of the hemisphere. It is not possible here to detail the intricate exchanges of goods involved, or to give the local specializations that underlie these activities, but only to note their presence and importance. In Canada, the Lillooet of the west, like the Montagnais-Naskapi to the east, traveled well-worn routes, often of considerable length, along which commodities passed from group to group by means of local contacts, or were carried by those who visited one group after another for purposes of barter. Not even in the far north were these patterns of trade unknown. They existed among the Eskimo and northern Indians as they did among the Siberian aborigines. Similarly in South America, networks of trade covered the northern and central portions of the continent,

[43] Beaglehole (1937), 82–6.

while the densely populated highlands of pre-Spanish times knew a complex series of commercial relationships.[44]

Notwithstanding the slight material equipment and simple economic organization of Australia's aboriginal inhabitants, organized barter was carried on over great areas. Though the data are scattered through many works, they make an impressive picture when brought together as they have been by McCarthy.[45] Not only were various commodities widely exchanged within

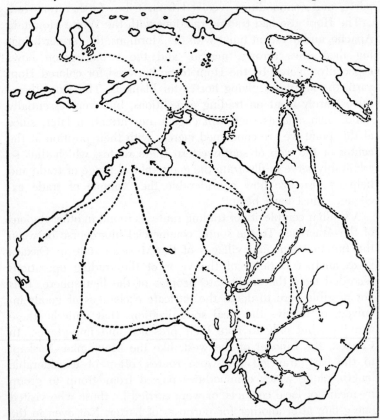

1. "Trade" in Aboriginal Australia and "Trade" Relationships with Torres Strait, New Guinea (after McCarthy, 1939–40, p. 191).

[44] Parsons (1936b), 568–70; Teit (1900–8), 231–2; Speck (1931), 578–9; Boas (1888), 469–70; Birket-Smith and de Laguna, 150–1; Bo-goras, 53, 64–5; Roth (1924), 634–6; (1929), 103.

[45] McCarthy, *passim.*

the several parts of Australia, but other goods, held to have magical qualities or prized as insignia of status, were traded throughout the continent. More than this, the aboriginal Australians had trade connections outside the continent; one from Cape York to the Torres Strait islands, another from the Torres Strait islands to western Papua, these connecting with New Guinea trade routes that in turn converged on the Torres Strait. Together with the intra-Australian "trunk trade routes," these are shown in the accompanying map. The explanation given it is worthy of note: "It is important to realize that these routes function sectionally, and that traits and ideas diffuse along their entire extent."[46]

One or two examples of the available documentation from Australia may be given here to indicate the quality of the information it yields. One student reports of the southeastern tribes:

> When at Cooper's Creek I observed that the blacks used shields made of some wood not known to me in that part of Australia. Subsequently . . . I learned . . . the Yantruwunta obtained these shields from their neighbors higher up Cooper's Creek, who got them from tribes farther to the north-east. The Yantruwunta on their part exchanged weapons made by them, and stone slabs for grinding seeds which they brought from the south. I also saw among these tribes, though rarely, a portion of a large univalve shell, worn suspended by a string from the neck, which I was told came from the north. Inquiries made later from the Deiri show that they bartered with the Mardala, or hill tribes, to the south of them, for skins.[47]

At the turn of the century, Roth described the "walkabout" of northwest central Queensland as

> part and parcel of the great trading or bartering system which is more or less continuously going on throughout the various districts. Certain trade-routes laid down from time immemorial along their own or messmates' country are followed by members of a tribe or tribes, along which each knows he is free to travel unmolested.

[46] Ibid., 191.   [47] Howitt, 714.

Along these routes, which are given in detail, pituri was traded for spears and koolamous; government blankets, pituri, human-hair belts, and other articles were exchanged for shields, stone knives, opossum and human-hair twine.[48]

More modern reports indicate the viability of these patterns of trade. In Arnhemland, another northerly region, "the Murngin and their neighbors are no exceptions" to the rule that "the Australian aborigine is a most industrious trader." Inland folk trade stone spear-heads to sea-coast tribes for red ocher and pipe clay, or for wooden spears. Gift-giving relationships enhance the exchange; a man gains prestige by having as many such affiliations as possible, so that he can obtain a present "sent from a distant people." On the Daly River, *merbok,* "an exceedingly well-organized system of intertribal exchange" has been described in some detail. For all the tribes between the Adelaide River and the Victoria River it constitutes a "basic economic network," which in earlier times and perhaps even still stretches far beyond these limits. It comprises "a series of continuous delayed exchanges of articles of intrinsic utilitarian value between individuals within the one tribe and in different tribes." These goods include red ocher, kaolin, spears, hair belts, dillybags, boomerangs, pearl shell, necklaces, armbands, girdles, wax, "and numerous other articles"; and the distances some of them travel are impressive. Thus, bamboos are sent hundreds of miles from the Daly to the Victoria River, where they are needed as shafts for shovel-spears; and "this is multiplied a hundredfold in *merbok* economy."

A similar system of "economic transactions" is found over the whole Kimberly Division, among the Lunga, and other tribes, involving a chain of partners, both men and women, called a "road," along which goods pass from hand to hand. Whether or not this organization is typical of all northern Australia cannot be said, inasmuch as in the region inhabited by the Yir-Yoront, "nothing corresponding to the *merbok*" was found. Yet trade was by no means absent, and even "the rather limited importation of goods not found in Yir-Yoront territory was governed by exchange between members of neighboring tribes following the

[48] Roth (1897), 132–6.

patterns of distant kinship, the goods travelling along recognized routes."[49]

5

IN THIS chapter, the importance of the bartered exchange of goods in nonliterate economic life has been sketched and something of the great variety of commodities that figures in these exchanges has been indicated. We must next analyze how values are established in barter, whether barter and bargaining are as closely related as is commonly conceived, and what occurs when barter gives way to a system of exchange based on the use of money. Moreover, the importance of stated markets, both within tribal precincts and when established to further intertribal trade, must also receive our attention, and, similarly, other aspects of primitive commerce such as credit and the stabilization of values. We may now proceed to consider these on the basis of the facts already presented, and of such other materials as are available.

[49] Warner, 95; Stanner, 20–1; Kaberry, 166–74; Sharp, 39.

CHAPTER X

BUSINESS ENTERPRISE, CREDIT AND THE DETERMINATION OF VALUE

THE METHODS of trading in nonliterate societies, the ends for which trading is done, and how the trader accomplishes his ends are fascinating problems. Schechter, who canvassed the literature for the available materials, concludes that as against gift exchange, individual dealings—or business, more properly speaking—are socially regulated by "various devices for the making and recording of fair bargains, for the rescission of improvident ones, and, as finally crystallized in market law, for the prevention of adulteration, short weights and measures, and other forms of overreaching and unfair trade generally." Like his literate fellow, however, nonliterate man, when attempting to enforce such rules of business procedure, becomes "frequently restless and resentful at the application of these principles to his particular case, with the consequent recurring necessity for coercing him into compliance." This phenomenon "faithfully foreshadows the conduct and necessary restraints of man in his more sophisticated, or, as we would say, in his 'civilized' economic life." [1]

When we consider motivations to trade, it is seen that those drives familiar to Euroamerican business are by no means lacking in nonliterate societies. A student of one Melanesian folk summarizes the reaction of the people he studied as follows:

[1] Schechter, 596–7.

The Malekulan is typically bourgeois and commercially minded. He is preoccupied generally with the making of deals, with bargaining and exercising his sharp wits, to getting the better of his economic rivals. Wealth, or rather the ability to display and expend wealth, is the hall-mark of rank, and a man's chief interest is to acquire wealth and yet more wealth.[2]

Because of their relative self-sufficiency, business, as such, is far less important among nonliterate groups than in the pecuniary societies of Europe and America. In these nonliterate societies, the quest for profits is by no means the fundamental drive it is conceived to be in writings on economic theory. And this fact makes for certain attitudes toward the commercial situation that are not readily comprehensible to those familiar only with our own system. Among the same Bush Negroes of Dutch Guiana who employ all their wiles to prevent the Indians and Europeans between whom they act as middlemen from having first-hand contact, are women who will part with wood-carvings their men have made for them only after long concerted pressure by relatives who urge acceptance of what in indigenous terms are fabulous offers. Or, one may encounter chiefs who, as expert carvers themselves, will not part with certain specimens of their work at any price.[3]

In pre-Spanish Mexico, the belief that it was unlucky to sell while on the way to market was so strong that it lingers on today in Central America.[4] Analogously, in Haiti, the prestige that accrues to the woman trader who can display much produce as she takes her place in the market causes her to refuse many profitable and burden-easing sales *en route*. Among certain Plains Indians, when a horse was stolen within a day or two after its purchase, or was lamed in the first race it ran for the new owner, a part of the purchase price was refunded.[5] Or we read of a certain Taos man who had gone to a fiesta in Jemez "in the hope of acquiring a blanket owing him for a deal of the year before" when he had sold a horse for two blankets, only one of which had been paid him. On going to the residence of his debtor, he "found the house full of blankets," but did nothing when in the

[2] Deacon, 17.

[3] Roth (1924), 633–4; (1929), 102; M. J. and F. S. Herskovits, 272 ff.

[4] Thompson, 130.

[5] Denig, 475.

ensuing conversation the debt was not mentioned. "The Jemez man said he was coming to Taos again, and Pablo expected that this time he would bring the blanket with him." [6]

Even these few instances demonstrate how the motives that actuate trade, and the manner in which returns from it are obtained, vary widely in nonliterate societies. Any attempt to generalize concerning the matter would thus seem to be of little profit unless our generalizations are based on the fact of this great diversity of drives in the exchange of goods and of the manner in which the attainment of objectives is furthered or impeded by the dictates of traditional patterns of behavior.

2

It is well, at the outset, to consider the way business transactions are carried on among non-industrial peoples, and some of the institutions associated with such trade. We may profitably study one of the few first-hand accounts in which barter is described in terms of its role in promoting the circulation of goods, rather than in that of the sociological implications of the process. For this we turn once more to the Melanesian community of Buka, one of the Solomon Islands off the northern coast of Bougainville. Here a "well organized and to some extent standardized system of barter takes place regularly between two villages." As is characteristic of this area, most important is the local trade, where taro is exchanged by the inland people for fish brought by the coastal folk, though when either party has a surplus, more distant trading operations are undertaken. The women, who conduct the exchanges, form a trading group, but they do not pool their goods. As a result, each woman benefits only from what she brings, so that if a trader is short of fish she must add sticks of tobacco or other goods to bring the value of her wares up to the requisite amount needed for her purchases.

Trading is carried on at stated localities and at prevailing rates. At one center off the west coast of Buka, fish are given for taro from the hill villages of the interior at the rate of 1 large fish for 12 taros, and 1 medium-sized fish for 6 taros. At another market, fish from the islands off the northwest coast of Bougain-

[6] Parsons (1936a), 25.

ville are exchanged for taro brought to the coast by inhabitants of the northern foothills, and similar trading is also done with the members of a different tribe who themselves live along the northern coast. The mountain people receive 10 fish for 10 taros, but the coastal folk must pay 6 taros for 2 fish. These prices are "said to have been fixed by . . . the 'culture heroine' from whom they trace their origin." Certainly any explanation in terms of economic advantage is difficult, since it would not be expected, in terms of economic theory or of the psychology of value, that taros would be sold at a cheaper rate (as expressed in fish) by a coastal tribe than by an interior people. An alternative explanation is understandably offered—the fear in which the mountain folk of central Bougainville are still held by those living on the coast.

These same coastal dwellers in earlier times also traded taro to still another tribe for smoked fish, when this latter people needed extra taro for special occasions, such as feasts. The rate in these cases was 1 *rabas* (a unit of 6 taros) for 1 big fish or 2 small ones. A special variant of this most common kind of exchange occurs when women from Buka fishing villages who need taro go into the hill districts to dig up the roots themselves. "In this case also fish are given in exchange," but the rate at which these sales are effected is not indicated. This is unfortunate, since here there is almost unique opportunity to measure the value given the labor necessary to dig taro out of the ground, through comparing the number of fish given for taro still in the ground with the number given for taro on which the labor of digging, or digging and transporting, has been expended.

Many other commodities besides fish and taro are bartered, all at well-established rates. The Patats women, who are expert in making the hoods of leaves worn by women in the presence of certain male relatives, exchange them for pots with the Malasang people, giving 1 large hood for 1 large pot, and 1 small hood for 1 small pot. Coral found on the beach is used to make lime, and the hill folk, who have no access to this raw material, barter taro and pots, which they also obtain from the Malasang, for this lime, though prices are in this case not specified. Pots are likewise bartered to obtain taro needed for planting, a very large pot going for 10 *rabas* (60 taros), a medium-sized pot for 5 *rabas*, and a small one for 3 *rabas*.

The trade in carrying-baskets is of unusual interest. The people of Kurtatchi possess great numbers of areca-nut palm trees, from the fronds of which they make trays or baskets, exchanging them with the people of Sōlō for taro. The baskets are packed one inside another, 6 or 7 constituting a bundle; while a load of taro is as much as a woman can carry inside one of these baskets, which is to say, as much as her strength will allow her to transport, a quantity susceptible of considerable variation. Despite this variation in quantity, the trading is load for load, and in the cases reported "no haggling seemed to occur," despite the fact that to trade baskets for the load of a strong woman means more taro for the seller than if she did business with a weaker woman. This mode of exchange at the rate of load for load is apparently well established; another instance is when breadfruit are sold for sweet potatoes. A load of potatoes—as many as a given woman can transport in her carrying-basket—is the unit on the one side, while breadfruit loads, consisting of respectively 17, 21, and 35 units, were counted. Yet again, "there was no haggling as to whether two given loads were of equal value."

Other Bougainville trading involves double and triple exchanges of goods, often transported from some distance. The data for this type of trading add but little, however, to those considered for other regions. More significant for our present problem is the description of the manner in which such transactions are actually consummated:

> I accompanied my friends from Petats on several trips to the mainland of Buka. . . . When the two parties met, packs were undone and a rapid inspection of fish and counting out of taro took place. The people of each party kept together, they went around holding out the goods they had to offer, and the buyers saw to it that the fish were of the appropriate size for the number of taro offered in exchange. I saw one women try hard to obtain two small fish for four taro, but eventually she had to be content with one. Sometimes they would get very excited and snatch the fish and taro from each other, or two women would grab the same article, almost tearing it in pieces. Two of the Buka women brought loads of dried opposum, and these also were exchanged for fish. The whole affair was got over as quickly as possible;

there was very little gossip, and it was clearly regarded as a business, not a social occasion. Both sides began their homeward journey as soon as the exchange was finished, not stopping to chat or to chew betel.[7]

Prices in terms of goods in some of the areas where modes of barter were described in the preceding chapter may also be cited. In California, the Yurok bartered tobacco at the rate of a woman's cap "full or not full" for a dentalium shell, the shortest type of shell buying the smaller amount, the second shortest the cap full.[8] The Hidatsa sold their surplus corn to the Standing Rock Sioux, taking payment in meat and hides. "They came," says the Hidatsa woman quoted, "not because they were in need of food, but because they liked to eat our corn," and would give 1 tanned buffalo robe for a string of braided corn; that is, for 54 or 55 ears.[9] When the Lillooet traded with coastal tribes, they would get 1 elkskin or 1 abalone shell for 3 goatskins or the hair of 3 or 4 goatskins. Among themselves, they valued a slave at 10 sheets of copper and 2 strings of copper tubes (generally half a fathom long), while a good hunting dog was valued at 1 large dressed elkskin.[10]

Between Navaho and Hopi, the "approximate rates of exchange" in 1932–4 for some of the articles traded were as follows: 1 dressed sheep was given for one 48-pound sack of unhusked corn, or 1 smaller sack of corn with a "moderate" bowl of sweet corn meal, or 1 small bag of dried peaches and a large plaque of wafer bread. "Portions of mutton were valued at proportionate quantities of food." A long piece of timber to be used as a house-rafter brought 10 small sacks of unhusked corn. A length of firewood was worth 1 sack of corn. The return for jewelry varied, but one example shows the value of a small ring set at a sack of corn and a plaque of dried peaches. Certain equivalents are given for Hopi trade with other tribes. A buffalo-skin obtained from the Plains tribes through retrading brought a good horse from the Navaho, Paiute, or Havasupai. A large bed-size Hopi blanket brought 2 larger buckskins and 1 other small skin from the Havasupai, who also gave a small buckskin for a small saddle blanket, a shell necklace for a white wedding blanket with red

[7] Blackwood (1935), 439, 442 ff., 480.

[8] Kroeber, 88.

[9] Wilson, 58.

[10] Teit (1900–8), 231–3.

stripes, and, for a similar blanket, a 5-pound salt-sack full of red ocher.[11]

Yet, as Hill has pointed out, "a discussion of the basic standards for exchange which prevailed between the Navaho and other peoples is subject to qualifications and non-measurable factors and is at best tentative." He goes on to elaborate on this point:

> Like other peoples, Navaho were influenced by supply and demand, and fluctuations in the estimated worth of various products have taken place throughout the historic period. In any given transaction personal whim and ability also figured in the bargain. There was no "ceiling price" and as among ourselves many individuals were recognized as shrewd business men who endeavored to out-maneuver their opponents. Such margins of success were usually attributed to ceremonial knowledge and performance and were of great concern.

At most, "certain normative ranges of values for standard goods like buckskins, buffalo robes, turquoise and blankets . . . served as points of reference in assessing miscellaneous goods and formed the basis for judgment of the success or failure of a trading venture." [12]

It is quite impossible to obtain any sense of comparable measures of value from data of this sort, and few conclusions can be drawn from them. Economic equivalents, it would appear, are often fixed where trade is continuous and the commodities exchanged are staples, so that in such cases haggling is rarely indulged in, since values are stable enough so that there is little reason for dispute. What constitutes equivalence, however, is a puzzling point that deserves far more attention than it has received. The variation in loads of taro exchanged for a fairly constant number of baskets in Buka, for example, where the unit— "a load"—depends so largely on the capacity of the individual carrier, is not easy to analyze. Or, to take another instance, the varied interpretations of which such expressions of quantity as "a small basket full" or "a cap full" are susceptible, since again the size of the container must differ considerably, seem to result from the absence of any rigid denominator of value. It is unfor-

[11] Beaglehole (1937), 83–5.   [12] Hill (1948), 379.

tunate that questions of this type have scarcely been studied in field research. Since this is the case, however, any conclusions regarding such points must be held in abeyance until enough specific materials are in hand to permit an understanding of the nature of equivalence in direct exchanges of goods and the principles that determine it.

3

THE INTRODUCTION of any symbol of value, whether in kind or in some form of money-token, materially simplifies the determination of equivalence. As has been observed, the small number of recorded instances of money-barter, where some commodity takes first rank as an indicator of value, is striking. Almost the only case of money-barter described in detail is that of the Ifugao of the Philippines, where rice is at the same time a staple food and a least common denominator in effecting exchange. This example is the more interesting because, though rice, at least until the time of this report, was employed to express value, its price fluctuated annually, regularly, and invariably according to the season. "That rice was a medium of exchange and not merely used for barter is shown by the Ifugao's hesitancy to change the price of it. For although lowland rice may be worth forty centavos a ganta, rice in Kiangan still remains at half that except during the growing season, when it doubles in value."

Rice units and their price (before 1922) in Philippine dollars were as follows:

Unit	Number of bundles	Unit	Value during harvest and spading (pesos)	Value in season of growing rice (pesos)
1 botek	1		.02½	.05
5 botek	5	1 hongal	.12½	.25
4 hongal	20	1 dalan	.50	1.00
5 dalan	100	1 bongale	2.50	5.00
10 dalan	200	1 upu	5.00	10.00
4 upu	800	1 lotak	20.00	40.00
2 lotak	1,600	1 gukud	40.00	80.00
10 upu	2,000	1 { nabukeue pigil	50.00	100.00 [13]

[13] For a table of rice currency from the neighboring Kalingas, see Barton (1949), 92.

The increase in the price of rice from 2½ cents to 5 cents at Kiangan, and from 2 cents to 7 cents at Benaue was not gradual but took place at one time; an obvious result was that most rice was bought at the beginning of the harvest and spading season. "Although the value of rice constantly increases, the price increases abruptly. And in proportion as the value of the rice increases above the price, commerce in rice decreases. This dull rice market (which is the same as 'tight' money in an American or European nation) practically stops business transactions." Yet this caused no "crisis," for just at this time of the year all hands, with the exception of the most wealthy members of the community, would be hard at work in the ricefields; it was only after the rice had been planted, which is to say when its price had risen, that commerce resumed once more.

Most transactions involving rice thus took place in the three months after the harvest; during the growing season, most rice that changed hands did so through loans to the poor, a matter that will be considered later when the institutions of credit and interest are discussed. An illustration of how rice, as used to express value, caused commodity prices to change in accordance with the changes in its own price is to be remarked in the cost of chickens:

| Name | Rice Value | |
	In growing season	At harvest
Mahin	1 hongol	2 hongol
Maduan hongol	2 hongol	4 hongol
Mahin dalan	1 dalan	2 dalan

Besides rice, pigs and carabaos were reported as "supplementary media of exchange," especially used in acquiring and computing the value of land. Pigs were designated according to size, and the following table shows their comparative worth:

Name	Value of Pigs at Kiangan Size	Money Value (pesos)
Makauayyan	Size of a bamboo: small suckling	2.50
Kinlum	Small; suckling	5.00
Bogha	Bearing first litter	10.00
Pikat	Medium size	15.00
Nungakop	Bearing third litter	20.00
Nangodi	Very large	30.00

The carabao was worth 5 or 6 pikat, or from 75 to 90 pesos, while the value of a rice field might be quoted as "5 pikat and 1 kinlum" (about 80 pesos) or "3 carabaos and 4 pikat" (about 300 pesos). Further standardized articles used in measuring value in exchanges were gold neck-oraments, amber-colored glass beads, brass gongs, rice wine jars, and death blankets. The first two were commonly used to pay fines, while the death blanket figured in various types of transactions, its value being computed at about 8 pesos.

Rice, however, was the basic medium, and the special and supplementary nature of these other expressions of value was quite clear. In the acquisition of most of these "standard" objects, and certainly in the case of rice, there was no haggling, though there might be some discussion as to what should be given for other goods, as in the instance of a chicken, where the question whether a given fowl was a *kinlum* or a *pikat* might involve argument. "Like good swappers, they usually split the difference in case of doubt. Even nowadays there is a good deal of dickering in the buying and selling of pigs. In the case of chickens there is not so much."

It must be emphasized that pure barter accompanied this system, and that the two methods of effectuating exchanges of goods were interrelated. For example, problems of paying for the services of several persons in goods not susceptible of division were resolved by computing the total in terms of rice or some other "standard" commodity. Thus a breech-clout was usually given a man for ten days' work in a rice field. But should ten men each give one day's work, as sometimes happened, the problem of "making change," which would otherwise be difficult, was solved either by exchanging the breech-clout for rice, which was then divided; or, as was more common, one of the ten paid each of the others 2 or 4 bundles of rice, according to the season, himself taking the breech-clout. Another instance would be that of a man who wished to buy a jar and possessed the three or four death blankets at which it was valued. He might not easily find an owner of a jar who cared to acquire funeral blankets, but with the blankets he could buy rice, or a pig, and with either of these it was simple to come on someone with a jar he wished to sell.[14]

The difficulty of finding other examples of money-barter may

[14] Barton (1922), 427–31.

be due to a number of causes. This type of exchange may perhaps really be as restricted as it seems to be, or, despite its existence, its importance may have gone unrecognized, or certain of the tokens that are described as "money" in the literature may actually be consumption goods. Yet the institution of money-barter in so clear-cut a manifestation and, as found among the Ifugao, is so arresting that it is difficult to see how it could be entirely missed if it existed; while, as will be seen, there are but few objects employed as money by nonliterate peoples that have use value other than to bring prestige to those who display them, as is the case of our own monetary metals when employed as jewelry. The use of iron objects as symbols of value in the African Congo, as described by Cureau—rods in the Middle Congo, hoe, axe, and shovel-blades in the Upper Ubangi, double gongs in the Middle Ubangi, iron rings, hoes, and the like in the Middle Sanga—well justify their being considered the instruments of money-barter.[15] Likewise to the point are the various commodities other than iron goods used by the Batetela, Olemba, and Sungu of the Kasai area as denominators of value.[16]

Among the peoples of the upper Katanga region of the eastern Congo, bars of salt played a similar role. On the Lualaba, the unit, called *dibanda,* was a bar weighing about 6½ pounds. On the average, one of these would purchase a hoe, or an axe, a calabash of palm-oil or a string of beads; a load of honey or eleusine was worth 4 or 5 *mabanda,* a gun, 20, while slaves had the following value: a man, 25 *mabanda,* a boy, 20, a woman, 40, a girl, 25 to 30. These bars, which were traded for goods coming from as far as the eastern coast of Africa, were thus regarded as money. The values of goods in terms of them "were responsive to the laws of supply and demand, and varied in accordance with whether the harvest [of salt] was abundant or not,[17] and with the scarcity or abundance of certain goods desired or offered." The data also show how with a symbol of value of this sort, the maximizing of satisfactions under situations of serious scarcity can find expression. In this economy, "characterized by a lack of capital and its absolute subordination to the demands of immediate need," an old man explained the relatively low values placed

[15] Cureau, Pl. XIV and 301.
[16] Torday and Joyce, 51–3.
[17] Salt was collected from pans made by overflow of saline springs during the rainy season, and by burning vegetation on which this salt-water had been deposited.

on human beings as follows: "A load of eleusine might save my life, but a female slave, no matter how strong, could at best only provide me with the hope of abundance during years to come. But I have to feed her while I find out whether she is really worth while, and she may never prove to be so." [18]

Salt is also a commodity in West Africa. In the north, sea-salt is exchanged for butter and slaves, and in the south for livestock to be used for food; while in the west, as indicating how it retains its status as a consumption good, sea-salt competes with the natural mineral from Daboya.[19] An especially striking example of the use of a commodity as a token of value is had in the case of cacao kernels in pre-Spanish Mexico, "esteemed not only for the chocolate made from it, but also as currency." Its latter role is reported as having survived until comparatively recent times in southern Mexico and Guatemala. Peter Martyr's comment on its earlier employment makes the point perfectly: "O blessed money which yeeldeth sweete and profitable drinke for mankinde, and preserveth the possessors thereof free from the hellish pestilence of avarice, because it cannot be long kept, or hid underground." [20]

It may well be that the presence of money-barter is an indication of an economic system in transition. The extent to which the Ifugao employed rice as a symbol of economic equivalence before contact with Europeans cannot be stated, but there is every indication that barter—as against money-barter—is deeply rooted in the trading traditions of the people. All the African societies cited have been in constant contact with other money-using economies, such as are found in the western parts of the continent and the Congo; or more recently, with Arabs and Europeans. In Siberia, moreover, where among the Chuckchee trade was "carried on exclusively in barter" and money was unknown, the unit of value in the Russian trade became a "bundle of tobacco 'not tampered with'" and, later, a brick of tea. Numerous instances show that these commodities involved trade with Europeans, as contrasted to the inland trade with other tribes, where values were expressed in terms such as the following: "For the hide of a large ground-seal, from 10 to 15 fawn-skins of larger size; for a coil of white thong, 5 fawn-skins; for a large bag full of seal-oil, 3 reindeer for slaughter; for a Winchester rifle with ac-

[18] Grevisse, 56 (see also section 56–9).

[19] Binger, 50 ff.
[20] Thompson, 67.

cessories, 2 sledge-reindeer, etc." [21] In other words, the introduction of European trade and the subsequent accommodation of natives to European standards of value brought about the acceptance of certain foreign commodities as measures of price—but only for European goods.

A final instance may be given, which, though not found among a nonliterate people, is of interest as adding weight to the hypothesis that trading on the level of money-barter is a transition phenomenon. In Russia during the period of "war communism" when, following the Revolution of 1917, the circulation of paper money was abolished, a system of barter quite the same as encountered among non-pecuniary societies sprang up. With the passage of time "certain goods began to play the role of media in terms of which other goods were exchanged," in this case a wagon-load of firewood and a glass of milk being the unit. Still later, owing to the unsatisfactory nature of these commodities as measures of value, flour and bread were used as indicators of price, the situation thus completely fulfilling the conditions of money-barter. [22] The use of cigarettes as media of exchange in Germany and Austria during the economic breakdown following the end of the Second World War is a similar case in point.

4

MARKETS and middlemen are frequently encountered in nonliterate societies as aids to business enterprises of various sorts. They do not by any means always go together, although stated markets of any size are rarely without professional traders. Markets for intertribal dealing are not found except among populous groups, while, similarly, merchants whose primary means of earning a livelihood comes from trade within their own group are found only in societies where a sufficiently large economic surplus is produced to support them. Except for certain instances in Africa, pre-Spanish Mexico and Peru, therefore, where markets and professional or semi-professional traders exist or did exist, such persons are almost entirely engaged in intertribal trade.

The Lobi tribes of the French Sudan, West Africa, have a con-

[21] Bogoras, 67–9.
[22] Vaisberg, 110. I am indebted   to Dr. James Bunyan for this significant reference and its translation

siderable number of markets which, because of the large variety of tribal units existing in the region, serve several different groups at once. In 1931, 40 such markets were counted. This gave an average of 1 market for 3,700 persons, though actually "those centers where from 500 to 1,000 gather are rare," since their distribution is not at all even over the various parts of the district. Generally, the maximum distance traveled by buyers or sellers is not more than 12 to 15 kilometers. Men and women leave their homes in the morning in time to reach the market between ten o'clock and noon, and leave by two or three o'clock in the afternoon to be home again before nightfall. Despite French rule, the cowrie shell, or indigenous type of money, was still employed; the women traders were especially difficult to convince of the desirability of change to European currency. Barter, however, existed jointly with the use of money-tokens, beans being traded directly for maize, and maize, peanuts, or ground peas for millet. On the other hand, such commodities as vegetable fats, yams, potatoes, gumbo, peppers, and other herb condiments used for sauces were not bartered, the explanation proffered why these had to be sold for cowries being entirely non-economic: "It isn't done; it isn't our custom; we haven't thought about it." Livestock was also customarily bartered, though on occasion cowries were given for a horse.

The amount of trade varies sharply with the season, markets showing the greatest activity during the period of the harvest. An impression of the range of this activity may be had from the estimates of attendance and volume of business transacted for three important centers of trade at the end of December, which is the beginning of the dry season and consequently the busiest time. At the market of Galgouli, an intertribal center frequented by the Lobi, the Téguessié, and some Dioula, there were about a hundred vendors in place at this period; a number which diminished during the rains to between 50 and 60. Buyers varied between 250 and 700. At Koul, frequented by persons belonging to 3 tribes from 17 neighboring communities, merchants of both sexes numbered about 150, and buyers 1,200 to 1,500 at this period of harvest; but during the rainy season there were barely 20 sellers of goods. Moulpo, in extreme northern Lobi territory, had from 80 to 100 sellers when business flourished and half that number otherwise. Taking the Koul market as an example, the commodities dealt in and their amounts, together with their value (the cowrie being equated to its December value in francs, as will be explained in the next chapter), may be given:

I. NATIVE GOODS; PRODUCE

Commodity	Number of merchants	Amount	Average number of units per merchant	Total value in cowries	Total value in francs
Beer	15	300 litres	20	30,000	75.00
Vegetable fat	20	250 kilos	12½	25,000	62.50
Gumbo	8	12 kilos	1½	800	2.00
Beans	10	30 kilos	3	3,000	7.50
Yams	4	12 roots	3	1,500	3.75
Maize	6	60 kilos	10	6,000	15.00
Millet	20	200 kilos	10	20,000	50.00
Millet seed	5	50 kilos	10	5,000	12.50
Peppers	15	10 kilos	⅔	2,000	5.00
Soumbara	6	40 kilos	6⅔	5,400	12.50
Tobacco	8	20 "heads"	2½	1,000	2.50
Total	117			99,700	248.25

ANIMALS

Cattle	6	6	1	240,000	600.00
Goats	5	5	1	10,000	25.00
Sheep	5	5	1	25,000	62.50
Guinea-fowl	10	40	4	16,000	40.00
Chickens	8	32	4	12,800	32.00
Total	34			303,800	759.50

II. IMPORTED GOODS

Salt	8	100 kilos	12½	40,000	100.00
Hoes	5	60 hoes	12	48,000	120.00
Beads		90 strings		13,500	33.75
Leather	2	20 kilos	10	40,000	100.00
Total	15			141,500	353.75
Grand total	166			545,000	1,361.50

An examination of these data, especially when the average number of units offered for sale by the individual sellers is calculated, shows that despite the importance of the market in this farming region, where population varies from 2 to 40 per square kilometer, trade must be considered an avocation. Moreover, since the amount of each commodity offered for sale is so slight, this "also demonstrates that the quantities presented must be insufficient to provide for a society having a caste structure or manifesting specialization"—which this one is not. The explanation which follows is entirely in line with the hypotheses advanced here: "Everyone has his field and lives on what he harvests, and anyone who refused to do agriculture would be liable to die of starvation, since only by hard work can a person raise the grain needed for his family and himself." [23]

In the coastal regions, where population is appreciably more dense, towns larger, and markets play a much more important role in the internal economy, the professional trader is found in large numbers. Dahomey, for example, has three types of markets, none of which is concerned with intertribal trade. These consist of the wholesale markets, which sell agricultural produce, the great retail markets, which serve as major instruments in the circulation of goods, and the small roadside stands. In addition, every village has a medium-sized evening market. The great retail markets are held in accordance with a four-day cycle, rotating between various centers in a given district, so that when any community is without a market, some neighboring town will be having its day of trading.

Though purchases of non-agricultural commodities may be made directly from the producer, or goods may be bought at one retail market to be resold at another, many middlemen, especially those who deal in produce, obtain their supply from wholesale centers. While it is a very exceptional Dahomean who does not have his farm, there are nevertheless those who specialize in the production of staple cereals; these men operate large holdings and are not concerned with retail trade. Their customers are women—for women are the merchants of Dahomey—who repair to the agricultural centers, where they obtain produce at wholesale prices regulated by a technique that accords with the broader Dahomean patterns of indirection in all kinds of relations between individuals. The procedure is as follows: Rates at which produce is sold at retail are carefully checked by these large cultivators, so that if, for example, a measure of meal sells for one franc—the use of the cowrie in commercial transactions has largely disappeared in Dahomey—the price of a measure of meal at the next wholesale market will be 80 centimes. Considerations of supply and demand may, however, seriously dislocate

[23] Labouret (1931), 56, 352–3, 356–61.

prices, as when, with unfavorable weather conditions and result-ant poor crop prospects, the large planters restrict their sales to conserve grain for seed. Prices thereupon rise sharply until con-ditions become more favorable.

The women who act as middlemen transport their produce in large calabashes carried on their heads, and many of them are known to traverse twenty or thirty kilometers on foot in order to reach the wholesale market. To these rural wholesale trading centers they may bring pottery or some other commodity made in the capital, returning the same night to prepare' for the next day's selling. Women who sell pottery at retail bring in their heavy pots between markets, while many of those who sell other goods work their fields between markets or, if they deal in cooked foods or flour, have these to prepare. The principal retail centers are of great size, and it has been estimated that on occasion as many as 10,000 persons pass through such an important market-place as that of Abomey. To detail the wares sold would neces-sitate a catalogue of all transportable goods in the material cul-ture of this people: varieties of mats; native and imported cloths; food-stuffs, both cooked and uncooked, and condiments of all kinds; beverages of various sorts; meat; iron objects, such as hoes, machetes, small knives, axes, and standards which serve as altars in the ancestral cult; calabashes for utilitarian and luxury uses; dyes, matches, kerosene, oil, needles, thread; ingredients for magic charms ranging from antelope horns and the skulls of mon-keys to countless herbs, variously twisted pieces of iron, thongs of different lengths and strips of the pelts of leopards and other felines; pots used for ritual and secular purposes. In the small roadside markets only food staples, cooked foods, and other ne-cessities are for sale; here people who are traveling or who, through oversight or neglect, have not bought all they needed at a "regular" market to last the intervening three days until the next one, can fill their immediate needs.

Retail price-fixing is done in various ways. On the coast trade associations fix the price for the commodities sold by their mem-bers. A refusal to pay an established price results in concerted physical action against one who insists on taking goods for less. In the interior, however, price-fixing is not done in so formal a manner. Prices of foodstuffs are set by the first woman to trade. What she asks is based on cost to her, which, being the same on a given day for all who have bought in the wholesale market, means that everyone who later comes with the same commodity can sell it at the same rate. These merchants obtain no advantage from price-cutting, and expressed surprise when the possibility of cutting prices to facilitate the disposal of their wares was suggested to them. Since prices are stabilized by wholesalers on the basis of retail price, the one who cut her price would not benefit beyond a single session of the market. Moreover, because the amount each woman can transport is limited by her personal capacity to carry her goods, and only rarely does she have unsold produce at the day's end, she would merely be sacrificing her own anticipated return.

Pottery sells at prices agreed on by the potters for the day, and no haggling is of any avail, for every woman must sell her pots at the stated price under fear of penalties exacted by her fellows. Palm-oil is dispensed in standard containers, and sells for a sum that varies according to the cost of a basket of palm-kernels. At present this is determined by world prices, but in pre-European days the price of palm-oil was set by local demand. Native cloth, woven and sold by men who constitute a closed guild, must bring a stated return. This is carefully based on production costs and takes into consideration the size of a given cloth, the cost of the raffia and cotton that goes into it, and the amount of labor needed to produce it. The name of each pattern, with its selling price, is known to the weavers, and here again penalties are exacted if the agreed price is cut. Those who make appliqué cloths are similarly bound; iron-workers, however, are free to set their own prices for their own goods, and much haggling results. This is also true of those who supply luxury goods such as woodcarvings, or the brass and silver figures that are classed as jewelry.[24]

There is little currency found in East Africa, nor, with a few exceptions, does one find the density of population and complex economic systems that mark the western and central parts of the continent. None the less, involved bartering operations have been reported for a number of tribes living on the frontier between the Eastern Sudan and Uganda. Here specialized tribal production and the exigencies of the natural environment make for intertribal trade, wherein certain groups act outstandingly as

[24] Herskovits (1938), I, 51 ff.

middlemen. The following diagram is given to indicate the relative location and number of days' travel from one of these tribes to another:

Tirangori (agricultural and pastoral)
(3)
Kokir (agricultural and pastoral)
(1)
D
i
d   (agricultural and pastoral)
(2)   i
Acholi (agricultural)   n
g
a
(2)
Dodoth (pastoral)

The Didinga live in the mountains, the Kokir tribe and the Tirangori who inhabit a large settlement of that name, in the foothills, while the Acholi and Dodoth are found in the plains, the latter because tribal wars have driven them from their aboriginal mountain home.

The system of exchange may be described from the point of view of the Didinga, who have many cattle, but few sheep and goats, of which they have need. The Kokir also want goats. The Tirangori, who possess sheep and goats in abundance, need cattle to replace those lost through war and pestilence. But the Didinga, "owing to geographical and political circumstances," cannot trade directly with the Tirangori, so the Kokir must act as intermediary. They buy cows from the Didinga for 28 goats each, and sell them, despite their own desire for cattle, to the Tirangori for 60 goats. "All the parties are accordingly satisfied, and ultimately get what each wants." Yet the Didinga need more goats than the Kokir can supply. For they must buy other products from other tribes, especially from the Acholi, who sell them the spears, axes, hoes, and bracelets they want, demanding for these not only the ostrich feathers and eggs and ocher the Didinga can supply out of their own resources, but also goats, for which they must trade.

The Didinga, being agricultural as well as pastoral, trade grain to the Dodoth, who "do not grow it themselves, but have acquired a taste for it since they migrated from their mountains."

The latter give sheep for this grain. Now, while in years of normal harvest the Didinga can supply the Dodoth with all the grain they wish, in poor years they must import this commodity from the Acholi to take care of the demands of the Dodoth. This, however, means that in normal years they must also buy Acholi grain, otherwise not only could they not obtain this commodity when they needed it, but the Acholi would themselves sell directly to the Dodoth, since their only reason for not trading directly for the sheep and goats they want is that the Didinga trade assures them of the disposal of their surplus grain every year, no matter what the weather.

> The upshot of all this is that the Didinga import grain from the Acholi for re-export, in order that they may get goats from the Dodoth. They also import more goats from the Kokir than they need for their own use, in order that they may re-export them to the Acholi as a set-off against the metal manufactures with which the Acholi alone can supply them. They take elaborate precautions to prevent the Dodoth short-circuiting them by maintaining an unnecessary trade in grain with the Acholi, and in the process the two middlemen, the Kokir and the Didinga, make quite a good profit every year.[25]

The wide distribution of markets, with middlemen operating in connection with them, or independently, could be documented by many more instances if space permitted; but only a few of the numerous variants can be given. In Siberia, men who on occasion acted as agents for their neighbors, carrying skins to the sea coast for disposal, and who found this life of travel congenial, became professional traders, profiting from the commissions they received for disposing of these wares in the course of operations carried on at stated times and at fixed places along the coast.[26]

For the tribes of the Pacific Northwest the market at The Dalles, described by many of the early explorers, was a center where commodities were exchanged on a considerable scale. The Wishram, "wholly middlemen," controlled this market, though not exclusively, and its presence as the focal point of trade in the area made it unnecessary for these people to go abroad to do

[25] Driberg (1929), 25–9.   [26] Bogoras, 65–7.

their trading.[27] Lewis and Clark, in 1805, observed how one of the products used by the Wishram in their considerable trade was prepared. Fish were dried, pounded, and then pressed into baskets lined with salmon-skins so as to make a cake about "two feet long and one in diameter." These baskets were stacked and kept until needed, the food remaining "sound and sweet for several years." That the "great quantities" these travelers observed being held before they were traded as far as the mouth of the Columbia River is no exaggeration is indicated by the fact that at The Dalles they "counted one hundred and seven" bundles of fish-containers, "making more than ten thousand pounds of that provision." [28]

In California, the Achomawi were intermediaries between the Sacramento Valley Wintum and the Modoc and also perhaps the Paiute who lived farther inland; "as in the civilized world, the lowlanders received raw materials and gave manufactures to the back people." [29] To the great trading centers of pre-conquest Mexico City came as many as 10,000 persons to buy and sell, while, in addition, still more business was done at its specialized counterparts. The operations of the Mexican merchant guilds illustrate not only how trade is furthered by such institutions, but also the complexity of the distributional processes in the larger social aggregates,[30] a tradition that persists to the present. This is to be seen in the detailed list of numbers of sellers, amount of business transacted, and localities of specialists selling in contemporary markets of Tzintzuntzan.[31]

Bartering between the Lhota Naga of Assam and the peoples of the plains to whom they bring their goods involves the employment of a special kind of middleman where the buying and selling of mithan (bos frontalis), ivory armlets, and boars' tushes are concerned. These commodities, it is believed, are "particularly liable to be infected with evil fortune." An old man must therefore act as intermediary for their sale, his duty being to give the final word after preliminary bargaining between the principals. "Any ill luck is believed to attach itself to him as nominal buyer, rather than to the real buyer, who pays him a commission of Re. 1 for a mithan, eight annas for an ivory armlet, and

[27] Spier and Sapir, 224 ff.; Teit (1928), 121–2.

[28] Spier and Sapir, 178–9.

[29] Kroeber, 309.

[30] Thompson, 75–7, 126–33.

[31] Foster (1948), 132–8.

four annas for a pair of boar's tushes." The striking case of a hereditary caste of middlemen in the trade between Tibet and Nepal is also to be remarked.[32]

An additional instance of the varied and complex economic interrelationships that in Melanesia have given rise to systems of trading with middlemen as constant factors, and of which examples have been encountered in previous chapters, can be given here to afford concrete documentation of this point for the area. This instance concerns the non-ritual businesslike transactions that are essential parts of the operations carried on by members of the Kula ring, wherein the natives of one island, Sinaketa, "act as intermediaries between the industrial centers of the Trobriands and Dobu." In the following table the second column shows "the prices paid by the Sinaketans to the industrial villages of Kuboma, a district in the Northern Trobriands," while the third column records what these same people receive for their purchases when they dispose of them in Dobu:

Kuboma to Sinaketa		Dobu to Sinaketa
1 *tanepopo* basket	12 coco-nuts	12 coco-nuts + sago + 1 belt
1 comb	4 coco-nuts	4 coco-nuts + 1 bunch of betel
1 armlet	8 coco-nuts	8 coco-nuts + 2 bunches of betel
1 lime·pot	12 coco-nuts	12 coco-nuts + 2 pieces of sago [33]

Only in Polynesia, of all the principal areas of the world, do we find the exchange of goods on a non-ceremonial basis almost entirely lacking. The statement made for Samoa is, however, generally valid for the other parts of the region: "With the exception of a few cases . . . all strictly commercial transactions in which goods are exchanged are of . . . [a] . . . petty, intra-familial, unstylized character." [34] Markets, as such, are thus practically unknown. The subsistence needs of all are satisfied by their own economic self-sufficiency, while the acquisition of prestige is cared for by the lavish gift-giving that marks the feasts given on occasions of special importance.

5

THE INSTITUTION of credit is widely spread in nonliterate societies, accompanies all types of exchanges, and is found in cultures

[32] Mills, 44; Pant, 217–18.   [34] Mead (1930a), 75.
[33] Malinowski (1922), 362–4.

of all degrees of economic complexity. An outstanding instance of credit operations in a society of this kind existed among the Kwakiutl of Vancouver Island, where it forms the basis of the renowned potlatch, better known for its waste of valuable goods than for its more sober economic functions.

> The economic system of the Indians of British Columbia is largely based on credit, just as much as that of civilized countries. . . . This economic system has developed to such an extent that the capital possessed by all the individuals of the tribe combined exceeds many times the actual amount of cash that exists; that is to say, the conditions are quite analogous to those prevailing in our community; if we want to call in all our outstanding debts, it is found that there is not by any means money enough in existence to pay them, and the result of an attempt of all the creditors to call in their loans results in disastrous panic, from which it takes the community a long time to recover.

This credit structure is founded on well-recognized interest rates: 5 blankets borrowed "for a period of a few months" become 6, for 6 months 7, and for a year or longer 10, which means that the lowest return is 20 per cent. Names—actual names, that is, as against "good will" such as we know in business usage, and which are not so different in their economic functioning—can be pawned. As always in pawning, however, an exorbitant rate of interest is charged, a name pledged for 30 blankets for a year requiring 100 to redeem it. A young man gets his start in life by borrowing blankets to be repaid at 100 per cent interest within a year. He distributes them as forced loans to his relatives, and these "loans" are repaid within the month at 300 per cent; lending his stock again in more normal fashion, "at the close of the year . . . he may possess about 400 blankets." [35] It is important to note, however, that while the mechanism of interest-bearing loans forms the basis for the potlatch, "lending and repayment form no part of the potlatch distribution." Rather "they are preliminary to it, and are engaged in for the purpose of accumulating the amounts necessary for the distribution." [36]

[35] Boas (1897), 341–2; (1898), 54–5; see also Codere, 68–75, for a more detailed analysis of this credit structure.

[36] Barnett (1938), 353.

Credit, as it functions in the ritual exchanges of a society having a relatively complex economic structure is to be contrasted with the forms of it found among the Australians. Here the "message-stick" system used in Queensland, and the *merbok* of the Daly River tribes are equally examples of credit structures which, though disguised by their sociological trappings, are essentially economic in their effects.[37] A not dissimilar type of delayed return existed among the New Zealand Maori, where one who "received potted birds in their season, returned the compliment by sending a present of fish when the due time came for catching them." The same was true of other commodities; that these gifts carried obligations of repayment is made clear, since one "waited, and kept his account until the other should repay." Repayment in the form of a larger gift than received was a matter of prestige, however, and hence cannot be regarded as interest in the strict sense of the term.[38]

Many accounts of credit operations in Melanesia are available.[39] In New Guinea, a type which in some respects resembles installment buying, despite its outer form as payment by the tender of gifts, centers on the purchase of canoes among the Kiwai. Canoes were traded from east to west, and "all kinds of native merchandise kept travelling in the opposite direction in payment for them." The seller received the major portion of his price on delivery; each time he visited the buyer's village, as well as "on other suitable occasions," further contributions were added. This lasted as long as the canoe was serviceable; when it broke up, the buyer sent an armshell or a string of dogs' teeth. The latter, a highly valuable item, which was traditionally looked upon as the conventional mark of final payment, emphasized its significance as an indication that no more goods would be forthcoming by attaching to it a small piece of the broken craft. If the purchaser died while the canoe was yet serviceable, his heirs were obligated to continue the payments. One especially interesting aspect of this system was that all transactions were carried on through middlemen, who took their commission not only on the initial payment, but on each succeeding installment. Their

[37] Roth (1897), 138; Stanner, 20–1.

[38] Raymond Firth (1929), 415–

[39] E.g., Seligman (1910), 109; Deacon, 196–7; Codrington, 326–7.

fees were regarded as legitimate, and the intermediaries held to strict honesty out of considerations of self-interest.[40]

Credit among the Ifugao took the form of loans on which interest, properly speaking—that is, recognized payment of debt-service over and above what was borrowed—was regularly exacted. These people even had a "form of bank discount" called *patang*, in terms of which interest was paid in advance for one year. "On a carabao (usually worth about eighty pesos) this amounts to thirty pesos a year," and was followed by an equal payment at the end of the period "for the next year" if not promptly repaid. If the loan of the animal was only for three months, ten pesos was given. Borrowing of the ordinary sort could be for ritual, non-economic purposes, but more often was done to obtain rice for subsistence until the coming harvest. Rates of interest were high; rice loaned at any time had to be doubly repaid at the next harvest, and the loan of a pig meant the return of two pigs the same size, or one twice as large, the following year, while money also commanded a hundred per cent return. If a loan was not paid on time, the interest was compounded at an almost incomprehensible rate: "If not paid the first year the debt is four times as great as the principal at the end of the second or third year. It does not take long for a chicken borrowed to become a carabao owed."

Thus a man who borrowed 3 pesos to meet the expenses of his father's funeral owed 24 pesos four years later; the creditor stated he would permit the debt to run for another year when, if it was not discharged, he would seize a rice field as payment. One wealthy man, who had loaned a poor family 200 bundles of rice worth 5 pesos at harvest time some five or 6 years previously, was demanding a carabao worth from 75 to 90 pesos as a final settlement of the debt. As may be imagined, these obligations were not met cheerfully and often were not repaid at all, though by invoking supernatural sanctions and the services of a professional collector, creditors often could obtain payment. These procedures were expensive, however, and the high rates of interest were thus partially looked upon as insurance against bad debts.[41] Interest rates in Assam are anything but low. Among the Sema Nagas the return is similar to that of the Lhota tribe, where

---

[40] Landtman (1927), 214–15.   [41] Barton (1919), 56–7; (1922), 425–6.

money brings 50 per cent, not compounded, the loan running for two years only. When rice is borrowed, four baskets per annum must be returned for each six loaned, while 100 per cent per annum, compounded, is the going rate for loans of salt.[42]

Africa, especially West Africa, where in the days preceding European control pawning was a regular feature in the economic life, furnishes numerous instances of the extension of credit. In Dahomey, pawns had to be children of the debtor, and slaves were not accepted. The labor performed by the pawns for the creditor was thought of as interest, and where the sum borrowed was not repaid at the time agreed upon, an extension was arranged under which the child continued to work for a longer period. If the pawn was a daughter, the creditor might take her as a wife in the event of too great a delay in repayment, the debt being canceled in lieu of the customary gifts and services of the son-in-law. Where the pawn was a son, protracted non-payment of the debt was ended by a final period of service, at the end of which the amount borrowed had to be doubly repaid or another mature son had to be put to work for the creditor. In such instances the lender specified how much labor was to be performed before the debt would be considered discharged and the pawn released. If the creditor was a farmer, he might calculate the number of rows to be hoed (the rate of pay for this in 1931 being 2 francs for 200 rows) to satisfy the amount due. As as alternative, the chief of the village might calculate the time needed for a man to do this work, after which the pawn was to be automatically released. Another form of pawning is still practiced in Dahomey, the pledging of palm groves. When a grove is tendered as security, the yield to be expected from it is calculated. Half this amount is pledged to debt service, the rest being applied to the repayment of principal. Regardless of the actual yield, the debt is automatically canceled and the grove is returned to its owner after the expiration of the period fixed on for the second half of the amount calculated to equal the loan.[43]

Credit in Africa does not, however, depend on the existence of a monetary system any more than elsewhere in the nonliterate world, as is indicated by the frequency of lending among the Tswana. Here nothing corresponding to interest is found; only in such cases as where a cow is purchased but delivery is not

[42] Mills, 45; Hutton, 160–2.   [43] Herskovits (1938), I, 82–5.

taken at the time of purchase does it happen that the transfer of title carried with it the obligation to render with the animal any calves it may have borne between the time when the sale was made and delivery.[44]

The instances of credit cited here, like the numerous other examples cited by Schechter in his discussion of the subject, indicate how widely distributed is the institution of credit and its concomitant, interest. It is reasonable to suppose that the explanation for its widespread incidence is to be found in the two factors suggested by Schechter to explain the mechanisms which everywhere protect the creditor: the collective responsibility of the group to whom the debtor belongs and "the absence in primitive law of any statute of limitations."[45] Certainly it becomes apparent how, in furthering the business transactions that stimulate the flow of goods from those who have them to those who need them, credit helps, in nonliterate societies no less than in our own, to give the economic structure of group life the stability that is essential to its continued efficiency of operation.

6

THE LIGHT that the materials thus far cited throw on the nature of value may now be briefly considered. Here it will be useful to turn to a classical statement of the concept in its economic implications, that of Adam Smith. "The word VALUE, it is to be observed," he says, "has two different meanings, and sometimes expresses the utility of some particular object, and sometimes the power of purchasing other goods which the possession of that object conveys. The one may be called 'value in use'; the other 'value in exchange.'"[46] It is apparent that, with the development of time, and with the concentration of the concern of economists on the price mechanism, the first of Adam Smith's two qualifications of the word has tended to be lost sight of. "This capacity which a thing has for being exchanged is called its *value*, just as the capacity which a thing has for being extended is called its 'length,'"[47] writes Boulding. Or, again, Benham and Boddy state, "The noun 'value' in modern economic writing always means

[44] Schapera (1938), 243–5.   [46] Smith, 28.
[45] Schechter, 583–90.   [47] Boulding, 256.

value in exchange. Values are nearly always expressed in money, and are then termed prices. . . . The value of one thing must always be expressed in terms of another; it is the rate at which they exchange against one another the amount of Y which can be exchanged against a unit of X; there can be no such thing as *intrinsic* value in the modern economic sense of the term 'value.'" [48]

It is apparent that while the problem of value has been greatly simplified by such a restricted approach, this has not been achieved without sacrificing flexibility and applicability. The difficulties resulting from this shift in emphasis have been recognized, even for the machine societies, by institutionalists. [49] It has also figured in the discussions of those who have studied the economies of nonliterate peoples, or who have drawn on such data to give their analysis a broad comparative base. The position of modern economists may well merit re-examination by them in the interest of greater flexibility for their conception of value, in the light of its applicability to non-pecuniary societies.

Hoyt distinguishes between "valuation," which is held to be "any expression of interest," and an "economic valuation," defined as "any such expression of interest in an economic good or service, interpreted in the widest sense." [50] Firth expresses a similar point of view when he says: "Economic value represents only a specific instance of the general concept, which is, in the widest sense, a subjective appreciation of judgment based upon the functional interrelation between a person and an object of interest." [51] Beaglehole also generalizes concerning the psychological nature of value on the basis of data from nonliterate societies:

From the subjective point of view, value is more complex than the economists would allow. Objects become values when they are desired; they are desired primarily because they satisfy major impulses; and secondly, objects are desired because they have been assimilated to, or integrated with, primary values and thus new values have become integrated with the personality." [52]

[48] Benham and Boddy, 79.
[49] Ayres (1938), 41–4.
[50] Hoyt (1926), 34; see also the exhaustive inquiry into the philosophical problem of value in Lepley.
[51] Raymond Firth (1929), 386.
[52] Beaglehole (1932), 151.

Allowing that evaluation as a psychological phenomenon, and value, as a philosophical concept, are both important subjects for discussion, and that they underlie the economic manifestations of value, such attacks on the problem are, nevertheless, so broad as to be meaningless for an analysis of specific manifestations of the phenomenon as it operates in the restricted domain of the process of evaluating goods and services incident to an exchange of goods or a payment for goods or services. Thurnwald is probably not far from the mark, certainly as concerns most cases in nonliterate societies where a given evaluation must be made in the exchange of goods or in payment for services, when he states that "economic transactions refer more to the quality and kind of real articles than to abstract values." [53] The implications of this statement, however, grouping, as it does, the manifold practices of nonliterate societies the world over, must be recognized as too broad to apply to many specific tribes. Hoyt, in another passage, envisages three psychological processes that are essential if the "perfect price" of the economists—and our own more modest aim—is to result from a judgment of value made upon the presentation of a given object: "A man must want goods; he must be able to conceive these goods in terms of the valuation of other goods; and he must be willing to negotiate with other persons for purposes of trade." [54]

On the basis of his analysis of the economic system of Tikopia, Firth writes: "Strictly speaking, . . . in a . . . community with no money, no prices in the ordinary sense of the term, and not even a thorough-going system of exchange of goods, there are no economic values. We seem to be left with simply a set of relative utilities of goods—their 'value in use' according to an older economic terminology." [55] The question is pursued further, in these terms:

> If . . . the economic value of a thing is taken in the more general sense as the amount of that thing that can be got in exchange for another having regard to circumstances of time and place, then there are many primitive economic phenomena to which the term can be applied, even though there be no single medium of exchange. . . . A concept which may help us here is that of equivalence. . . . In a commu-

[53] Thurnwald (1932b), xiii.   [55] Firth (1939), 333.
[54] Hoyt (1926), 5.

nity where actual exchange of the items against one another may never take place the idea of an imagined substitution or theoretical exchange can still allow us to construct a scale of what might be termed "economic values." This means a substantial rather than a formal use of the term. Goods are related to one another by a process of tacit comparison in which measurement is given by the possibility of substitution and not by actual transfer against one another.[56]

Firth sums up the matter when he says that "the absence of money or prices troubles the economist more than it does the native."[57]

It must be obvious at this point that values in most societies are not arrived at on the basis of considerations drawn in terms of price differentials, nor yet in terms of those hedonistic ends that have at times been held to be their principal determinant. Taking as given the psychology of evaluation, and assuming it to be fundamental to any process of evaluating anything, we may then ask the question of especial interest here: Why, in a given society, do the values attached to goods or services take the forms in which they are actually found?

Let us bring certain further materials to bear on this problem. If we refer once again to the Guiana Indians, we learn:

> In trade and barter the value of an article to the Indian depends upon his temporary want of it and not upon its intrinsic worth. . . . An Indian at one time shall require an axe, in exchange for that for which at another he will demand only a fishhook, without regarding any disproportion between their value.

These are trade goods, but apparently the principle holds generally: "In the absence of a medium of exchange an Indian has nothing to sell unless the buyer happens to be in possession of what he wants."[58] It is apparent that in this case only perceived immediate utility determines a given evaluation. Shortly before 1900 the Siberian Lamut reindeer commanded about twice the sum required to buy a Chuckchee reindeer:

> Usually, a Lamut fawn is exchanged for a grown Chuckchee

[56] Ibid., 336–7.   [58] Roth (1924), 632–3.

[57] Ibid., 35.

reindeer. A broken Lamut reindeer is worth three Chuck-chee reindeer; and the Lamut and the Tungus often break all the young bucks in their herds in order to barter them away to the Chuckchee. Therefore the larger portion of Chuckchee harness-reindeer are at the present time of the Lamut race. The Lamut, on the other hand, have stopped slaughtering their own reindeer because they can always get Chuckchee reindeer, which are cheaper, and better fitted for the purpose.

Here the labor of breaking in an animal determines its exchange value; on the other hand, that it was possible to record "the highest famine price" of a large buck would also seem to argue that scarcity can likewise enter in the establishment of relative worth.[59]

Numerous instances of valuations based on labor and scarcity have been recorded among the California Indians. To the Yurok, "even a common deerskin represented value when prepared for dance use. Besides the hide, there was the labor of stuffing the head, and woodpecker scalps were needed for ears, eyes, throat and tongue." Furthermore, "an unusually light or dark skin was worth more, and those that the Yurok call 'gray' and 'black' and 'red' are estimated at from $50 to $100. A pure albino skin, with transparent hoofs, is rated at from $250 to $500." Yet, from the point of view of value theory, it is to be noted that these highest figures are noted as theoretical only, being "given for the sake of comparison," since the value of goods of this degree of scarcity cannot among the Yurok any more than among ourselves be other than arbitrarily determined, especially since such articles practically never change hands. The values attached to individual pieces of obsidian in this tribe were similarly determined, while among the Pomo dentalium shells were evaluated according to size, thickness, and polish. Other folk living at various distances from the source of supply of this "money" not only base their evaluations of these shells on labor and scarcity, but also on such factors as "where the raw material was obtained, by whom it was worked, and by what routes transported." [60]

The prices of products sold in the Yoruba markets of Nigeria demonstrate how, in a pecuniary economy, the labor of trans-

[59] Bogoras, 73, 96.　　　　　[60] Kroeber, 26–7, 248–9.

porting goods to market can play an important part in determining values as expressed in price. Since the "gain" that accrues to the women traders depends on the differential between the various trading places, it is their business to know where to buy cheap and where to sell dear. Most of the farm produce sold in the town market of Ife is grown on the "far farms" which lie in a belt surrounding the town at a distance of some five and twelve miles. The traders, however, seldom buy at the markets regularly held in this belt because, while these markets are almost as far from town as the farms themselves, their prices are higher than at those for which produce can be bought. Therefore the market-women either go directly to the farmer, or wait on the farm paths to buy from those who carry their own produce to town. The price differentials are of the following order: farm produce costs least at the farms, becomes more expensive at the far markets, costs still more at intermediate trading points, and commands the highest price in the retail markets within town. Furthermore, the closer a given farm is to Ife, the higher the price that the traders are willing to pay for its produce; and the farmers themselves recognize that in order to attract the market-women to more distant farms, they must offer the inducement of lower prices.[61]

Another example of how a pecuniary standard makes for modes of determination of values that are in line with canons of economic theory derived from the presence of money is available in the economy of Panajachel of Guatemala. The people of this village, who "enter in minor ways, into the capitalistic world economic system" have, as far as they and their neighbors are concerned, what is described as "a domestic money economy with a strongly developed market which tends to be perfectly competitive." The unit of production is the family, and the local specialization in certain agricultural products makes it necessary to sell these so as to obtain, by purchase in the market, all subsistence and production goods. Buying and selling is for cash; credit can be extended and interest is known, but these are rarely found. What is important is that "the price of a product in a given market is fixed by the law of supply and demand." Sales, moreover, are made on the basis of cost estimates which empirical analysis shows to be remarkably accurate. Endowed with

[61] Bascom (communicated).

"the spirit of business enterprise," this example shows how, in a nonliterate but pecuniary society, we may encounter an almost classical economic system.[62]

As usual, the data from Melanesia are numerous, and it will be seen in the next chapter how carefully, for example, the Malekulans computed the value of their pigs in terms of the degree of curvature of their tusks, this being an expression of scarcity. On Rossel Island, the value of money was related to the size of the pieces and the work that had been put into preparing these shells. Among the southern Massim of New Guinea, both labor and scarcity and, in addition, certain imponderables of taste and tradition enter into the values given the ceremonial axe blades called *benam*. These evaluations vary largely, but "the larger and thinner the stones the more valuable they are; their value is also increased by the presence of light bands and inclusions which in the polished condition show as streaks. . . ." In general, in this Massim area, objects of this kind most highly valued are accorded this distinction for two reasons:

> (i) the refractory nature of the material of which they are made, necessitating prolonged work in order to produce the finished article, and (ii) durability. . . . The rarity of certain of the raw materials was also of importance as was the skill required to work them.[63]

Under famine conditions in the Trobriands, the price of seed yams became so high that a valuable stone axe, which in ordinary times was valued at 100 baskets, could be acquired for 10 baskets.[64]

There is, in all probability, no single explanation of the phenomenon of value, and certainly no single expression of it. It not only presents multiple facets to one who would follow its manifestations over the world, but it must also be regarded as determined in multiple ways in every society, and not always in

[62] Tax, Ch. 2, 1–13. For the brief description of another economy of this general area, see Wagley; and for the ecological setting and details of productive and market operations in the region see McBryde, esp. 71–124. Foster (1948), 145–7, gives an exposition of the working of Mexican markets, where, as he puts it, "in few places of the world is the exchange situation closer to the economist's ideal of a 'free market.' "

[63] Seligman, C. G. (1910), 517, 520–1.

[64] Malinowski (1935), 163.

every case by the same factors. A statement which shows how specific and individual the basis of evaluation may be among the Australian Murngin makes this clear:

> The governing principle in the evaluation of objects which will be kept permanently by their owner is the ease with which they can be transported by human carriage or dugout canoe. The amount of labor consumed in their manufacture contributes in some degree to their high value as individual property, and the relative scarcity of an object in nature or in trade also makes its contributions to Murngin economic values; but the final desideratum is the relative ease of transportation of the article, since this society has no domesticated beast of burden. Metal containers obtained in trade with white missionaries are extremely scarce and highly prized; yet if of very large size they will be given to someone remaining in camp or cut up and put to other uses.[65]

It is thus apparent that all the relevant factors operate within the limits set in any given instance by the body of tradition of the people among whom a given economic transaction takes place. These factors can be effective only in terms of a pattern of value that is a part of the larger patterning of the culture concerned. The phenomenon of value, in other words, can only be understood as one part of the wider phenomenon of culture. Lacking precise information, the problem can at least be approached with an understanding that every system of economic equivalences must be analyzed in the light of its peculiar sanctions and its own special social setting.

[65] Warner, 148.

CHAPTER XI

MONEY AND WEALTH

ALTHOUGH it is not easy to define the concept of money with precision, it is possible, if lines are not drawn too rigidly, to obtain a reasonably clear and reasonably valid delineation of it. Its function as a medium of exchange and a standard denominator of value, its characteristics of "homogeneity, portability, devisability and durability," and its subsidiary role as "a store of value and a standard of deferred payments" have long been agreed on by economists as its proper attributes. A further distinction can be made between currency, those "types of money which are subject to some form of public regulation," and other circulating media. However, we need not dwell upon this here, since in nonliterate societies there is almost never any conscious control by political authority over whatever tokens of value may circulate. The fact that these tokens, which "are generally acceptable in exchange . . . necessarily involves a tacit consent on the part of the community in which they circulate"[1] is quite reason enough why these finer distinctions can be disregarded.

We shall not be concerned with most of the many attempts that have been made to ascertain the origin and development of money, wherein much confusion is apparent as to the nature of money in presumably "early" societies. Such hypotheses as those of Schurtz, in which the rise of money is referred to the exigencies of "external" trade,[2] or the critique and development of this idea by Schmidt,[3] are too speculative to merit discussion. Certain other approaches, however, may be mentioned. Hartland has

[1] Gregory, 601–02.
[2] Schurtz, passim.
[3] M. Schmidt (1920–1), II, 157–62.

stated: "Where commercial transactions become common (and many barbarous peoples speedily acquire commercial habits) some sort of currency is necessary. Various materials have been used for this purpose . . ." [4] This indicates something of the vagueness that may be encountered. Bücher, dismissing with a phrase all the tokens used by nonliterate folk to express value, and emphasizing the rudimentary character of "the many species of money among primitive peoples," of which "much has been written and imagined," reduces the matter to the following formula: "The money of each tribe is that trading commodity which it does not itself produce, but which it regularly acquires from other tribes by way of exchange." [5] Firth calls salt and other consumption goods money, [6] while Thurnwald, noting "the point of departure" in the evolution of money as that "marked by favorite articles of barter, usually between communities of approximately equal standing," adds: "This, as a rule, involves the exchange of traditional quantities or packages, as in the case of sago or tobacco, for corresponding quantities of the other articles." In concluding his discussion, he speaks of certain consumable goods attaining "a status equivalent to real money," but the statement is documented only with instances of money-barter. [7]

Another controversial point, which illustrates the advantage of drawing flexible definitions in this field, is the extent to which "valuables" exchanged by nonliterate folk are to be regarded as money. It is evident here that either too rigid an adherence to the definitions of the economists, or too much attention given to sociological considerations, must serve to obscure the essential significance. Thus, when Malinowski, following the accepted position of the economists, indicates that objects which ceremonially exchange hands in the Kula rituals of Melanesia are not money because they are neither generally used as media of exchange, nor function as measures of value, he is on solid ground. [8] On the other hand, Mauss, insisting that objects of this type must be regarded as money despite the fact that they are "subjective and personal," have changing value, and are often used as talismans because of their magical significance, makes his case

[4] Hartland, 115.
[5] Bücher, 67–8.
[6] Raymond Firth (1929b).

[7] Thurnwald (1932b), 252–65.
[8] Malinowski (1921), 13.

by pointing to instances where such objects are used to purchase goods or services, both in the Trobriand Islands and elsewhere.[9]

The most advisable procedure would seem to counsel concentrating on the place of these objects in the economic system before classifying them as money or merely as "valuables." If they are measures of value, exchangeable for goods, or given in payment of services, they must be thought of as money, whether or not they serve in all situations as symbols expressing value, or are put to magical uses, or are worn as ornaments. Consequently, when "valuables" of the Kula ring are ritually exchanged only for each other, and never for the commodities whose barter is a concomitant of the trading rites, they are not money; but when, as Mauss states, they are accepted by the natives in payment for the pearls they fish for Europeans, they are to that extent money. Tokens like the coppers of the Indians of the Northwest Coast of North America, the great stone "wheels" of the islanders of Yap, and the cattle of the East Africans resemble in a very real sense the crown jewels to which Malinowski compares the "valuables" of the Trobriand islanders.[10] and should not be confused, as they so often are, with media of exchange.[11] But can the cowrie shells of West Africa be held any the less money because, besides their general use as a medium of exchange, they are found as decorations on the stools of rich men, or as attributes of magic charms? Are not the *ndap* of Rossel Island money when used to purchase a pig, despite the fact that ceremonial surrounds the transaction, and despite the fact that such ceremonial does not enter when humbler objects such as baskets or lime sticks are bought? Or cannot the dentalium shells of California be regarded as money, even though, in some instances, they are used only to purchase prestige and services?

The importance of the comparative study of the nature and functioning of money, as well as the obstacles to be faced in defining the phenomenon with clarity and classifying its many manifestations, is apparent in two works devoted to the subject, both of which appeared in 1949.[12] In both, the definitions advanced present a dual difficulty to the readers of these works, since the attention of the writers is so fixed on delimiting the

[9] Mauss, 68, n. 1.
[10] Malinowski (1922), 88.
[11] E.g., Mosher, 27–51.
[12] Quiggin, Einzig.

meaning of the word "money" that nowhere, in either volume, is the meaning of the term "primitive" made clear. A slight digression may therefore be of value in examining this aspect of these approaches, particularly since we have here so clear an example of the difficulties inherent in the use of this term as a significant delimiting concept, a point already discussed in earlier pages.[13]

Quiggin's work is, first of all, oriented in terms of an outmoded evolutionistic tradition in anthropology. In these terms, "primitive" money seems to include all kinds of expressions of value used by "simpler societies" or "less advanced societies," as against the tokens found among "civilized" peoples. The assumed inevitability of change toward the use of money as found in the literate cultures of Europe and America, which permeates the argument of this student, likewise obscures her meaning of "primitive." "The following chapters," she says, "are concerned with such objects as are or have been accepted by peoples before the introduction of a system of coined money."[14] The bulk of the examples of all kinds of repositories of value that are set forth in the major portion of the book is drawn, therefore, from contemporary nonliterate societies, though a chapter on Europe involves the data of prehistory, while examples are also given of barter in various early colonial areas between colonists in lieu of transactions based on the use of currency. The meaning of the term "primitive" as employed by Einzig is implied in the following passage: "The period which our enquiry must cover extends over more than five thousand years for which there is written evidence. We have also to try to probe into dark ages which lie beyond this period, and into blanks that exist, unfortunately, even in the historical period. The communities we have to deal with range from savage cannibal tribes to highly civilized nations." [15]

In his work not only is the scope of "primitive" data indicated in these terms, but an assumption is seemingly predicated of differences in quality of intellect and perception on the part of "primitive" and "civilized" man. To study the problem of money in Egypt and Greece, we are told, is comparatively easy, "because of the advanced intellectual standard of the historical races

[13] See above, 25–9.   [15] Einzig, 16.
[14] Quiggin, 4.

even in the early phases of their history." With "primitive" peoples—in this instance, it would seem, the nonliterate groupings
—the matter is otherwise:

> The real difficulty comes when we have to deal with races
> at a primitive stage of evolution. Their intellectual standard
> is inferior and their mentality is totally different from ours.
> We are, so to say, not on the same wavelength. Their atti-
> tude towards money differs fundamentally from ours in
> many respects. Unless we duly appreciate this difference,
> we leave no means of understanding primitive money.[16]

If we seek an operational definition of the word "primitive" in
Einzig's approach, the matter is not greatly clarified. In the sections headed "Ethnological," discussions often take the form of
symbols of value used in trade between natives and Europeans,
or in the dealings of early colonists among themselves. The "Historical" sections are concerned with "primitive" money among
prehistoric, early historic, and contemporary literate peoples. Perhaps here it is possible, by inference, to perceive the delimita-
tion of the word "primitive" as "customary," perhaps in contrast
to the word "legal." As will become apparent when this author's
definition of "primitive money" is considered, it is difficult to see
in his conception of the word "primitive" any other exclusive
significance, though implicit in his treatment is the acceptance
of all the value-connotations of the word that are ethnocentri-
cally derived and thus are inacceptable for the scientific analysis
of cross-cultural phenomena.

Much of the difficulty both these authors experience in defining the second word of the phrase with which they are concerned
arises from the problem of distinguishing between "money" and
"currency." This, we have seen, is a question that is not too difficult of resolution, and has been resolved by the economists in
what may be thought of as political, rather than economic terms
—currency being a common medium of exchange subject to
"public regulation." [17] Quiggin is reduced to a position where
Stuart Chase's statement is quoted as a kind of summary:

> Neither you nor I nor anyone else knows what "money"
> means or how it works. We know what it means where and

[16] Loc. cit.   [17] See above, 238.

when we use it, for here we are performing little personal operations. But its general laws, if any, are unknown to even the wisest banker or the profoundest economist.[18]

The conclusion reached by this author, however, that "for our present purpose the term money will be restricted to such forms as serve the threefold function of a recognized medium of exchange, a standard of value and a symbol of wealth," indicates that this student does not find the question of defining the word as hopeless as the quotation from Chase would imply. This is also true of the flexibility of the approach implied in a later sentence, which states that the descriptive chapters of her work will be concerned "with such objects as are or have been accepted by peoples before the introduction of a system of coined currency," which fulfil the functions previously indicated.[19]

Einzig, moving toward the problem of defining "primitive money" from the side of economics rather than that of comparative ethnology and the question of museum display, is also faced with the need to differentiate between money and currency, though this point bulks less important in his work than in that of Quiggin. His definition takes into account various implications of the term that have been discussed by economists, and attempts to reconcile them with broad, cross-cultural usage. Money, he concludes, is

> . . . a unit or object conforming to a reasonable degree to some standard of uniformity, which is employed for reckoning or for making a large proportion of the payments customary in the community concerned, and which is accepted for payment largely with the intention of employing it for making payment.[20]

In addition, a series of criteria is given for determining limits between "primitive and modern money." Thus, all "non-metallic money with the exception of paper money and credit money" are to be classified as "primitive," and all money of metal which is not guaranteed as to weight and fineness by a State. Further, paper currencies "issued in terms of primitive currencies" are to be regarded as "primitive," and so are coins that "change hands

[18] Quiggin, 3, citing Chase, 197.   [20] Einzig, 326.
[19] Op. cit., 4.

by weight," together with cut coins. Similarly, commodity currencies are "primitive," and credit-money also, since, "if . . . granted in terms of goods, then it is nearer to natural economy than money economy and must be regarded as primitive." [21]

Much of the difficulty in deciding whether a given medium of exchange and store of value is money or not, found in the discussion of both these special treatises on "primitive" money, might have been avoided if the functional significance of the many indicators of value given in their rich documentation was treated more fully. Particularly is this true with reference to the role of these indicators in prestige as over against subsistence economies, the two categories that make up the dual economic systems, to be considered later, of so many societies. In these terms, "treasures" of various sorts, as will be seen, which have been considered generally as money, and are so classified by both Quiggin and Einzig, fall into their proper place as indices of wealth rather than media of exchange. Money, it will be seen, can be employed in this way to validate position in society and accord prestige. But, again, cross-cultural reference indicates that the importance of money as a single factor in attaining prestige and furthering the acquisition of subsistence goods tends to be exaggerated because of the usages of the pecuniary society to which the students of the problem have been enculturated.

The importance of clarity in distinguishing the different functions of "valuables" in assessing the nature of money will be seen if a passage taken at random from Quiggin's works on the subject is cited. Thus, the function of certain valuables of New Caledonia is described as follows:

Throughout New Caledonia and the Loyalties trading is almost all by barter, and money rarely changes hands save in the more costly purchases such as canoes and valuable ornaments. Nevertheless, money is all-important in native life, though its significance is far more ceremonial, religious or magical than economic. It enters into all functions from birth and marriage to death, and the accompanying rites and ceremonies; it takes part in all feasts, all alliances and peace-makings, it is used for the accomplishment and atonement of crimes, and is essential in all ceremonial presentations.

[21] Ibid., 329.

Consisting of shells, and accompanying ornaments, this type of valuable takes on several forms. *Miu bwarre,* or "black money," is "most valued and extremely fine." It was "used more for presents for great chiefs, and for fines, than for trading, and many natives had never even seen a string of it." On the other hand, *miu me,* or "white money," was of a value that "an ell would buy a wife, and a half a fathom a canoe." A cheaper kind of this white money was used by whites in trading with natives, at the rate of one franc a meter.[22] The difficulties of classification here are obvious: the impossibility of discovering the actual role of these different types of tokens—some never seen except by a few persons, and in an economic system where trading is predominantly by barter—renders judgment as to their economic function equally difficult.

The interpretations of Einzig are similarly broad, though here the distinction between items that represent a store of value and those that constitute media of exchange is in most cases drawn. This work, like that of Quiggin, thus holds primary value as showing how varied are the objects to which men can attach particular worth, and how different can be the means employed to establish equivalences of desirability.

Essentially, it would seem that we are once again confronted with a principle concerning the economic life of nonliterate peoples with which we are already familiar, that its institutions and mechanisms take on generalized outlines in contrast to the specialized and sharply differentiated forms of the economic systems of industrialized societies. That is why many field anthropologists, not appreciating the controversial implications of their data for the problem of the nature of money, have shown an unwitting wisdom in reporting the tokens of value used in any given society as they have found them, without considering whether or not these tokens are to be thought of as money in the economist's sense of the word. In order to achieve a synthesis of economic theory and ethnological fact, therefore, we shall accept as money *any kind of least common denominator of value,* whether it be of metal, shell, stone, or other material, or, indeed, even if it itself is a consumption good, so long as it is regarded as a part of a system of graded equivalents, and is used in payment for goods and services.

[22] Op. cit., 168–70.

That such tokens will almost invariably exhibit the subsidiary function of "a store of value" is self-evident, and as such will in most societies be found to act as instruments in the attainment of prestige. In these cases, where value is stored in goods not used as least common denominators in the purchase and sale of commodities or services, as in the case of cattle in East Africa, or the stone "money" of Yap, these valuable commodities will not be regarded as money. But if the use of the tokens is embedded in a ceremonial setting of a sociological or a religious nature, or other non-pecuniary forms of exchange are found in conjunction with their employment, they will none the less be considered as money, provided that their use in certain instances is such as to stamp them as valid indices of value, given and accepted in exchange for commodities not so regarded.

2

THE USE of money, as just defined, by nonliterate peoples, is outstanding in three parts of the world: West Africa and the Congo,[23] Melanesia and Micronesia, and western North America. Tokens that indicate value are not by any means unknown elsewhere, as, for example, the "wampum" of the Indians of eastern North America[24] or the fine mats used in Samoa, in terms of which "everything was valued" and some things paid for.[25] But the distribution of such instances is scattered, and it is often questionable whether the term "money" is being applied in the reports to media of exchange or depositaries of value, which, as expressions of wealth, must be considered under a distinct heading.

The cowrie shell, as has been indicated, is important in all West Africa. Little information is available regarding the internal economies that were based on the use of this token, for none of the early travelers who visited West Africa were equipped to do such a study, even had they been interested. Thus most of the evaluations in their writings are given in terms of cowries trans-

[23] For Africa as a whole, Tucci (73–103) classifies money into five types—cowries, iron, salt, copper, gold dust and a miscellaneous group of forms.

[24] Cf. Swanton (1906), and Hewitt.

[25] Cf. Hiroa (1930), 319; Mead (1930a).

lated into European currency, though the fact that these sea-shells were so readily equated to the money of Europe is in itself a justification for regarding them as true currency. For specific tribes in the area, a number of tables of values have been set down, and the one from Dalzel's *History of Dahomey* (1793) may be quoted as an example:

Unit		Number	Value		Weight		
			s.	d.	lb.	oz.	tenths
40 cowries	1 tockey, or string	40	0	1⅖	0	1	7
5 tockeys	1 galhina	200	0	6	0	8	4
5 galhinas	1 ackey	1,000	2	6	2	10	0
4 ackeys	1 cabess	4,000	10	0	10	8	0
4 cabess	1 ounce, trade	16,000	40	0	42	0	0

Explaining the final item, the author states: "Now from this ounce, weighing on experiment about 45 lb. troy, or 42 lb. avoirdupoise, the weights in the last column are determined." [26] That we are dealing with actual money is apparent from the fact that the value of the cowrie shell reacted to changes in values of related currencies in quite the manner that any currency would be expected to react. In the case of Dahomean money, an example of this is had in the following statement from Forbes dated 1851:

> The currency of the Dahoman kingdom is the cowrie shell, of which 2,000 are calculated to form one "head" to which a nominal value of one dollar is attached. Such, however, is the scarcity of metallic currency, that, in exchange, the silver dollar is eagerly taken at 2,400 to 2,600 cowries; and other metals, as well the lower as the higher, are freely taken in barter.[27]

It has been seen how the cowrie, as late as 1931, was still being used as money by the Lobi tribes. The changes in value of this shell, concerning which data are available since 1883, is striking. The first report, by Binger, which evaluated certain articles in terms of cowries, quoted it at 1,000 for 2 francs. After the occupation of the country by the French the rate fell, and in the region of Gaoua remained stable until 1918 at about 800 to the franc.

[26] Dalzel, 135.   [27] Forbes, I, 36.

After the armistice and during the period corresponding to the fall of the franc, the cowry continually rose, indicating that it was good money in native eyes, who considered nickel tokens and local small bills as being valueless and only to be used in paying taxes and fines.

Even at that time there was a considerable manipulation of the market, and these induced fluctuations have persisted, despite attempts to suppress such operations.

After silver pieces disappeared from circulation, a five-franc note was exchanged for 600 cowries, and this remained its normal value until the time the report being used here was written.[28] Beginning in November, however, and until February, European money appreciated, since at this time taxes to an aggregate of some 500,000 francs, payable only in French money, would come due. To obtain the necessary currency, the natives turned to the Sudanese peddlers who travel the region, and who make a considerable profit from such transactions. The annual accretion in value of the franc was gradual; from the standard quotation of 600 cowries for a five-franc note in October 1931, the rate rose to 800 in November, to 1,500 in December, and finally to 2,000 in January, dropping abruptly to the "normal" value at the end of the month, when taxes had been collected and the need for French money was no longer pressing. The result of this fluctuation on prices may also be noted. The natives during this period would charge six times as much for goods bought with cowries as with metal tokens or paper money; it is on the increased (December) value of the franc that the calculations of the values of goods sold in Lobi markets, reproduced in the preceding chapter, were based.

Because of this need to exchange cowries for European currency, or the reverse—since from relatively early times guineas, shillings, louis, and francs had drifted into this territory—professional money-changers are a familiar part of the economic scene. After 1914, when taxes were no longer collected in kind, a *bourse* developed, especially in the markets of Dapola and Nandol, near

---

[28] An explanatory point must be noted here. In West Africa north of the forested strip, European currency is principally nickel or bronze, since silver has been found unsatisfactory, apparently both from the point of view of the government and of the natives.

the Volta River, as well as on a less professional scale in other centers. Here Mossi and Mandingo money-changers would sell notes for cowries while the franc was appreciating, and with the same shells would buy back the French currency when the cowrie had returned to its customary value. However, the peace enforced by European occupation seems to be accomplishing what governmental fiat could not do. With the introduction into the area of traders who buy produce with European money, the natives are learning how to obtain the francs they need for taxes without recourse to money-changers. Indeed, the use of the cowrie itself in commercial transactions seemed to be going the way it has gone elsewhere in West Africa.[29]

A recrudescence of the use of cowrie shells in Northern Nigeria in 1932 gives further evidence that this token is actually money. This recrudescence, brought about by the world economic crisis and arrested by improved economic conditions, occurred in the large Nupe markets of Bida and Agaie, to which cowries acquired in other regions were brought by traders for disposal. The effects of this crisis were felt by native peoples wherever they were in contact with Europeans, so that, for example, in Northern Nigeria, the smallest coin, the *anini*, worth a tenth of an English penny, was still too large a unit for petty trade in these hard times. The rate of exchange in Ajuba (Gbari country), where the cowries were largely acquired, was 500 to the penny, and they were sold in Bida and Agaie at twice that amount, or 250 to the penny, the rate of exchange obtaining when their legal use was outlawed by the British colonial government. Many of the cowries showed traces of having been buried in the ground since they had been declared valueless, for this shell has never been entirely abandoned by the natives, who have continued to use it in making ceremonial payments. Among the Gbari, for example, women are always on hand at funerals to sell cowries to mourners and guests, who present them as gifts and use them to pay for the services of grave-diggers and musicians. The effect of this is that "cowries represent today something like a ritual currency reserved for the symbolic payment of certain services of a ceremonial and religious nature." The custom that decrees only cowries to be valid in discharging obligations at funerals or

[29] Labouret (1931), 326–3; see also Tauxier, 423.

weddings and in paying diviners is economically important in that it has perpetuated their use, and explains why in a time of economic stress quantities of these shells are available.

These data from Nigeria are the more significant, since they not only indicate how deeply an economic pattern of this sort can lodge in a culture, but also demonstrate once again how a definition drawn too closely makes it difficult to understand this phenomenon where it is desirable that the economic role of a token be regarded in economic perspective. It is maintained, for example, that cowries are not "proper money at all; that is to say they were never exclusively an instrument of economic transaction, nor more specifically a means of exchange," but were rather employed "for certain magical purposes, for 'medicines,' ritual ornaments, and such like." Leaving aside the question whether their use in providing compensation for ritual goods and services would not to this extent justify their designation as money— here the confusion between the concepts of "money" and "currency" will be noted—certain internal evidence in this brief report seems to controvert the interpretation given the use of these cowries:

> In a small way cowries are still used in local trade, between two villages or two compounds, but not for the main trade of the country, agricultural products, and not on a large scale. Buying and selling of millet, yams, or corn is only done in real money ("for must we not pay our taxes in money?"). But if you are buying a little beer from your neighbor's house, a little fruit, or an odd calabash of corn you may have run short of, you pay in cowries instead of the "anini" or two this would cost. The women, the traders *par excellence* of the country, thus collect the scattered hoards of cowries in their hands, keeping them for the occasion when a supply of "ritual currency" will be needed.[30]

3

WE MUST conclude, then, that in West Africa the cowrie is money. Yet a point arises in this connection that has considerably troubled those concerned with the nature of money in

[30] Nadel (1937), 489-91.

nonliterate societies. Here the generalized character of economic institutions not only causes the concept of a legal and exclusive currency to be unknown, but also directs the use of such tokens of value toward the payment of ritual goods and services or toward the establishment of prestige in a manner which effectively masks the economic significance of the process. This problem is clarified if we consider certain data gathered in the study of the numerous kinds of tokens of value that circulated in aboriginal California and other regions of western United States.

If the Yurok be taken as a first instance, it is seen that here, as among other northwestern California tribes, the accumulation of wealth is a passion, and payments are exacted in every conceivable type of social situation. Native Yurok media of exchange are principally dentalium shells, though subsidiary tokens of value may also be employed—woodpecker scalps, obsidian blades, and certain ritual objects, which are essentially depositaries of value to be equated with our jewels rather than with our currency. Dentalium, though, is recognized by the Indians as money; the native term translated as "human beings their dentalium" is employed in the sense of "Indian money," and the shells are readily equated with American coins.

The value of a shell depends on its length, and hence dentalia are graded with care. Whatever their size, they are strung on cords that reach from "the end of an average man's thumb to the point of his shoulder," and all effort is made to have only shells of uniform size on a string. The names and sizes of these shells, and their number per string, are as follows:

Length of shell in inches	Yurok name of shell	Yurok name of string	Shells to strings
2½	Kergerpitl	Kohtepsis	11
2⁵⁄₁₆	Tego'o	Na'apes	12
2⅛	Wega	Nahksepitl	13
2	Hewiyem	Ta'anepitl	14
1½	Merostan	Tsepupitl	15

As might be expected, the largest dentalia are scarcest, and the price of a string appreciates in proportion to the increase in size of the individual units. The following table of values in American dollars, based on the prices that prevailed in the early days of white contact, shows this:

Shells to string	Value of shell	Value of string
11	$5.00	$50.00
12	2.00	20.00
13	1.00	10.00
14	.50	5.00
15	.25	2.50

The values of these shells, about 1920, were roughly one-half of those given; yet the principle of earlier times, that "an increase in length of shell sufficient to reduce by one the number of pieces required to fill a standard string about doubled its value," continued to be operative.

Some of the valuations of goods in terms of dentalium strings can be given; presumably they would be sold for the amounts indicated, though this is not explicitly stated, and it will be noted how substitute evaluations in terms of other goods are also given. The values are estimated on the basis of a twelve-shell string being worth ten American dollars.

Commodity	Value
1 large boat	2 12-shell strings, 1 full and 1 short, or 10 large or 60 small woodpecker skins
1 small boat	1 13-shell string or 3 large woodpecker heads
1 very small boat	5 shells from a 13-shell string
1 small boat	A blanket of 2 deerskins sewn together and painted; or a quiver of otter and fisher fur, with bow and 40 arrows
1 eagle skin	1 shell of smallest size
1 woman's capful of tobacco	1 small shell
1 house	3 strings
1 well-conditioned house of redwood planks	5 strings
A tract bearing acorns	1 to 5 strings
Meat from a "small" section of a whale	1 string, presumably of small shells
A "black," "red," or mottled deerskin, dressed for dance use	5 strings
A light gray skin	6 strings
A white skin	10 strings
Obsidian or flint blades	2 to 10 strings
1 slave	1 to 2 strings

For the services of a doctor, the charge was one to two strings of "good money"; dentalium shells were also used to meet marriage

payments—for a wife from a wealthy family ten strings of varying lengths were given—while they were similarly used to discharge what might be termed fines.[31]

Various kinds of money-tokens were found among other California tribes—the Shasta, Wintun, Yuki, and others used dentalium, while farther south clam-shell disks were current among
the Miwok, Yokuts, and Chumash. Yet, with the exception of the
Yurok, it is no easy task to reach a conclusion how these tokens
functioned as money under the usage given this term here; while
even in the case of the Yurok the attention of students has been
so fixed on the valuables themselves that whatever role dentalia
may have played as a medium of exchange in everyday use appears in the literature only as a kind of after-thought. It seems
not unlikely that what is found here is a type of money that,
while operating to some extent in the acquisition of capital and
consumption goods, is oriented principally toward the purchase
of services and prestige. As has been indicated, this would not
make these tokens any the less money, inasmuch as in the case
of dentalium, at least, what is used as an index of value is not a
consumption good, but is part of a system of graded equivalents
used to pay for services and to acquire prestige. This point is
clarified by reference to an analysis of the pecuniary mechanisms
employed by the Tolowa-Tututni.

These northern California peoples used the dentalium shell
and other "treasures" as indices of value much like the Yurok.
As among other tribes of the region, though great emphasis was
laid on wealth, subsistence was cared for by a generous supply
of natural resources, so that the use of money to acquire subsistence goods was at a minimum. How, then, were these tokens
employed? "Money was serviceable in the purchase of social
protection and prestige, in sex, and in maintaining familial status,
but it entered hardly at all into the subsistence equation." To
phrase it differently, Tolowa-Tututni money was a "device for
dealing in a limited set of social recognitions."

These tribes, therefore, did not translate the value of a basket
or a given quantity of dried salmon into dentalium shells and
then do their trading in terms of dentalia equivalents, for where
subsistence products were involved, trade was entirely on the
level of barter. Only where the acquisition of prestige was a

[31] Kroeber, 23–8.

factor—the payments of a rich man to compensate for wrongs committed by members of his village, or payments made to the family of a bride, or upon the death of a child, or for insults, or for the services of a shaman—was this currency called upon. The matter has been expressed in diagrammatic form comparing the role of money in obtaining subsistence and prestige in our own society and in this one. The equation to be drawn for Euroamerican culture is: subsistence⇆money→prestige. For the Tolowa-Tututni it is: subsistence—(money⇆prestige). That this approach elucidates much that has hitherto been obscure in the treatment, not alone of the use of these tokens, but of comparable materials elsewhere, again demonstrates the importance of not drawing lines too rigidly in defining the concept of "money."[32]

4

MELANESIA, with a bewildering variety of tokens of value,[33] offers another example of how flexibility in approach simplifies the problem of whether or not, in any given situation, we are dealing with money. Let us take a typical statement:

> The natives manufacture a form of currency (amfat) from large clam shells. These amfat, although made in the fashion of bracelets, are never so worn, being kept solely for exchange purposes. An amfat is a measure of values, but only of certain goods and services; it is also a medium of exchange, but only in respect of certain items. One must be wary, therefore, of calling it "money." [34]

It is somewhat difficult, even from this brief summary of the nature of these valuables and the uses to which they are put— made as bracelets but never worn, used solely for exchange and as a measure of value—to see how they can be considered as

[32] DuBois, 50–3. To this dual classification of subsistence and money economies, Bascom (1948) has added the concept of the "commercial" economy where a cash crop is grown for sale in a world market to enable natives to obtain goods otherwise unavailable to them. Attention should also be called to the classification of "business" economy used by Codere (13–23) in her discussion of Kwakiutl economics.

[33] Lewis; Codrington, 323–8.

[34] Bell, 308.

anything but money. Yet, apparently, one must be wary of calling these *amfat* by this term, though the word "currency," which in its technical sense is obviously not at all applicable in this instance, is used to name it.

That a less restricted point of view is decidedly in the interest of clarity is evident from the analysis of the Melanesian data by Tueting, who approaches the material from a point of view somewhat analogous to that advanced here:

> Trade, barter or ceremonial exchange, may be effected by "valuables" . . . objects which serve as the instrument by means of which value can be accumulated . . . which serve as a measure of value but measure the value of specific objects only, as greenstone adzes which pay for canoes in Panniet . . . or . . . which fulfill wholly or in part any of the other functions of money.[35]

That is to say, these ceremonial emblems of value, in so far as they aid in the economic evaluation of either goods or services or both, must concern us as money, whatever other role they may play in ritual and gift exchange carried on for non-economic ends by means of non-economic institutions.

A revealing suggestion why such great difficulty obtains in determining what constitutes money in Melanesia appears in a discussion of the use of shells and dogs' teeth in the Admiralty Islands. These tokens have "all the requirements of a good money base." They are rare, the supply can be increased only with ordinary expenditure of labor, they are small and hence portable, and they are "extremely divisible—a respectable enough list of orthodox requirements to please any economist." Dogs' teeth are the basic standard of value, and "the value of every object sold or exchanged in the Admiralty Islands can be expressed in terms of dogs' teeth or shell money." Ten taro are valued at one large dog's tooth; and so are ten coconuts, or forty betel nuts, or one bundle of bark fiber. "The idea of a common medium of exchange is perfectly clear to the native mind," and the natives possess the linguistic symbols for calculating their commercial transactions in terms of their monetary units. The same reaction to manipulation of the money market is shown by dogs' teeth as by our own currency or the cowries of West Africa. When early traders, for

[35] Tueting, 36–7.

example, imported large quantities of these teeth from China and Turkey, immediate inflation followed, with a consequent rise in prices, so that "a pot formerly worth one dog's tooth now sold for ten." Once this importation was checked by decree of the administering authority, dogs' teeth settled back into financial equilibrium.

Are dogs' teeth and shells, then, money? Under definitions that insist that a given medium shall be a universal and sole instrument in determining value and effectuating exchange, they clearly cannot be so considered, inasmuch as such tokens are not used "as much as a quarter of the time." Indeed, the situation is comparable to that of the Lobi of West Africa, who, as will be remembered, despite their preponderant use of cowries, also actively engage in barter. And so in the Admiralty Islands, too, "barter, the method of exchange which is considered so much clumsier, so much cruder and more primitive, is constantly resorted to out of preference." The reason for a restricted employment of these tokens—whose use, it may be pointed out, is mandatory in ritual exchanges—is to be found in the general patterns of production which hold not alone for this region, but "all over the archipelago" and throughout Melanesia. As in almost every other nonliterate society, "no one is dependent upon money for existence," and only in that class of needs that are secondary and do not involve subsistence requirements can the risk be assumed of trusting to "money" to provide them.

The special case of a widower who lived with his sister and turned over to her, as a return for his maintenance, some of the dogs' teeth paid him for his services as magician, is instructive. The sister could use these teeth as marriage payments of a nephew, who meanwhile would provide her with fish which she could use in part to feed herself and her brother, and barter what remained for taro. But she "could not have taken the dogs' teeth to market and bought taro with them except in most unusual conditions." For she would have had to compete with those who had fish to barter, and no matter how keenly the man from the interior might desire the dogs' teeth she offered, his children could not eat them. He might give his taro for them, hoping that he could use them to buy fish at an advantage, but in the main those who brought fish would not part with them except for taro or sago or betel nuts or bark fiber. "So dogs' teeth and shell money often go begging in the market," and only the rich man who controls the labor of many young people can afford to take advantage of opportunities to acquire the money, "which the unsuccessful fisherman or bad gardener brings to market."

Clearly we are here again confronted with a dual economy—with barter where the necessities of life are involved, and a pecuniary orientation in matters involving the discharge of ceremonial obligations, the purchase of prestige, and the associated drive to acquire wealth. Here, where "every one is close to the subsistence level for food," it is understandable that "food is bartered against food," especially when to obtain a particular kind of food it is necessary to go to a particular community whose members are as hungry for one's special product as one is for theirs. Yet the elaborate system of indicating values, it must again be recalled, does figure in purely commercial transactions involving the purchase of non-edible goods such as bowls, lime gourds and spatulas, bags, mats, thatch, spears, fish-nets and the like, as well as in ceremonial exchanges. To refuse to recognize these tokens of value as money, therefore, would merely indicate a greater attachment to a definition than to the realities of the economic system in which they function.[36]

The instances of the use of spondylus shells and giant clamshell disks on Rossel Island, respectively termed *ndap* and *nkö*, have been cited so frequently and accorded such wide recognition as money, even in the restricted sense of the term, that it is not necessary here to enter into any extended exposition of their use. The intricacy of this system, in which tokens of varying size have varying values, and the complexity of computing interest on the loans in which they figure have taken the imagination of students of comparative economic institutions from the time the data were first published. Briefly summarized, these tokens are employed "primarily as media of exchange and standards of value"; they are "systematically interrelated as regards value"; and "any commodity or service may be more or less directly priced in terms of them." That they play a most prominent part in ritual exchange does not lessen their right to be considered pecuniary instruments. If there is a suggestion in the phrase which states that commodities "may be more or less directly priced in terms" of this money, and that barter, which is entirely

[36] Mead (1930b), 121–30.

unmentioned in the work from which our data are derived does exist together with this money as a means of effectuating exchanges, this assuredly does not diminish the applicability of the term "money" to the *ndap* and *nkö* that symbolize value for the Rossel Islanders.[37]

From this point, where money exists as conventionally defined, Melanesian economic systems can be graded as to their modes of exchange through all degrees of applicability of a rigid definition of the term until non-pecuniary folk are reached, where the circulation of goods is effected only through barter, and valuables are only used for display, rarely figuring in effectuating the circulation of economic goods. Thus the tokens of value used in New Ireland are employed almost as much in the payment of goods and services as on Rossel Island; the "money" of the Solomon and Admiralty groups is removed from purely economic concerns; while among such folk as the New Caledonians, what is called "money" consists merely of valuables exchanged to regulate certain social situations and as equivalents for precious objects such as jade axes, "all other goods being obtained by barter."[38]

5

ANOTHER example of a dual economy is available from the Palau Islands, the westernmost group of the Carolines in the South Pacific. Here the tokens of value are essentially instruments for the maintenance of position and prestige; yet at the same time they function in this area of experience as money. The place of this system of tokens in the total culture has been summarized in the following passage:

> Money is, or was, involved in such institutions and social phenomena as marriage, divorce, death rites, birth rites, politics, war, status and prestige, reciprocal relations and religion. That the people themselves regard money as of paramount importance is shown by the fact that its acquisition is a major goal, that money and recent transactions in-

[37] Armstrong, 59 ff.
[38] Powdermaker, 200 ff.; Thurnwald (1934-5), 134-9; (1937), 26 ff.; Blackwood (1935), 446-9; Leenhardt, 127.

volving it is a primary topic of conversation among the men, by the fondling care with which it is handled and stored in the sacred section of the house, and by the high regard accorded the money expert.[39]

The fact, however, that this money functions only in one aspect of a dual economy is made clear by the following explicit statement:

Palau economy had no actual need for a money system. It was an artificial and superficial system from the standpoint of actual need, for Palau was a subsistence economy and the rich resources of the islands provided plentiful materials and foodstuffs and obviated the need for trade. The monetary system was specifically geared for social uses and penetrated nearly every phase of the social system. In fact, money was so closely integrated with the social system that it is hard to imagine the social system at a period when money was not used.[40]

The tokens themselves were all imported, and consisted of "polychrome and clear glass beads, and crescentic bar gorgets and beads of pottery." They had, apparently, been traded through many hands, some of the polychrome beads appearing to be from India or elsewhere on the Asiatic mainland. The various categories are classified into nine basic kinds, called "families" by Ritzenthaler, according to the nature of the materials of which they are made, their color, and their shape. Each "family" contains a number of different types, into which the individual pieces are grouped. In the case of the more valuable pieces "the individual histories . . . are known to certain of the money experts, who can relate the origin and subsequent transactions along with the names of the persons through whose hands the piece was passed down to the present time." That these experts in money have extensive and specialized knowledge is apparent from the fact that the most competent of them was able to give the names and numbers of almost 3,000 pieces falling into 282 types and belonging to the various "families." It is indicative of the place that this money holds in the patterns of thought of the Palauans that information of this scope can be obtained despite the fact that "not all these types, or even all families, are in

[39] Ritzenthaler (1949).   [40] Ibid., 1.

circulation at the present time," though "money which has gone out of circulation"—because of the circumstance of foreign control—"is kept rather than . . . discarded by the owner." [41]

The factor of scarcity in maintaining the value of the money-token enters here as elsewhere. For many years, none of this imported money has been coming in. Unlike the case where dogs' teeth brought into the Admiralties caused inflation, the experiment of the ethnographer of offering Venetian polychrome glass beads as a substitute for one class of native money met with complete indifference on the part of the chief to whom these beads were presented. They would be accepted as a gift, it was stated, but they would never pass for money. On the other hand, though inevitable breakage reduces the total amount of money available, the values of the remaining pieces have not changed. This, however, would seem to be the result of contact with the Germans and the Japanese during the long period of their occupations, and with Americans during the Second World War and since. "The increasing desirability of foreign money tended to lessen somewhat the demand for native money," it is reported. "The reduction in number of pieces, plus the impact of foreign money, has resulted in the decline in fluidity of native money from pre-contact to modern times." [42]

Yet this problem of value, though in Palau related to scarcity in the supply of money, is by no means here to be resolved by reference to this single factor. Again, the matter of prestige enters:

The value of *ba'al* money [the most valuable type] as of all Palau money, is based on quality, size and history. Such money was traditionally owned by only upper rank families, and was never used in ordinary economic transactions. In former times the important use of it was for war reparations, but it was also used in important social customs such as the payment to the wife's family upon the death of the wife. . . . At the present time such money functions as prestige money symbolic of rank and power. Every effort is made to keep it within the family, and considerable intrigue goes on in the attempt by a family to acquire important pieces of money largely through the agency of judicious marriages.

[41] Ibid., 6–7.   [42] Ibid., 7–8.

The bead money, unlike the *ba'al*, is used in everyday transactions, the standard value for all money being the opaque polychrome glass bead called *kluk*. The "theoretical worth" of the best pieces of *kluk* is 100 *swalo* of taro, a *swalo* being a coconut-leaf basket holding about ten pounds. But "whenever the *kluk* is valued in terms of foreign money it is at 100 to 1. Thus in German times a *kluk* was worth 100 marks, in Japanese times 100 yen, and at the present (1948) has an unofficial, but operating value of 100 dollars." Within the system, values as between types are not fixed, but overlap in accordance with the quality of a given piece and its history. This, for instance, is seen in the increase in value of a piece that has been used in an important economic transaction. It is because of this fact and of the fact that is is considered good practice to "fool the other person if you can," that a group of money experts has emerged. For where pieces may be misrepresented to the unwary not only as to their value but as to their class, and where money is so important, it is not difficult to see how significant is the role of these experts, and why they are called "wise men."

Money can be earned or acquired through the various rites that mark birth, marriage, divorce, and death. Money was also counterfeited, but the penalty for this was death in earlier times; since the period of Spanish occupation "a counterfeiter was forced to forfeit the largest pieces of money in his possession, and if he had no large valuable piece he forfeited all his small pieces." Money in earlier times was loaned at interest, the rate being about 50 per cent; the penalty for losing or spending a piece held as security was serious, since all the property of a lender who did this was destroyed by his fellow-villagers, and his taro-patch confiscated. Money is earned by making such items as canoes, and wooden bowls, and building houses. Prestige is lost if, for example, one were to build his own house or construct his own canoe. Money, when obtained in this way, is individually owned, but one Palauan estimated that three-fourths of the money extant is owned by families, while Useem is reported as indicating that only about one family in four possesses any money at all.[43]

It is impossible here to do more than list the situations in which money enters in the life of the Palauans. It figures in the

[43] Ibid., 13–16; ref. to Useem, 16.

rites of birth, and naming; it is paid for tattooing; it enters into concubinage arrangements, and is basic in marriage-payments and the exchanges between families that follow a marriage and endure as long as the couple live together. It is used for adultery payments, to obtain the return of an angered wife, and in divorce. It is basic in all aspects of social mobility, since only by expenditure can an individual achieve higher rank, or succeed to a chiefly position. It makes possible the building of a communal men's house; it is given as a gift in inter-village dancing competitions; it is used for fines. Fees for divination and some offerings to the gods take the form of money. Finally, as has been indicated, it was the indemnity paid by a district defeated in war or could be used to assure the aid of an ally in attack or defense.[44]

The importance of this money in the life of the people is so great that "the acquisition of money" becomes "the primary goal of the individual." That it is kept in the sacred portion of the house underscores this fact. It has maintained itself in the face of contact with four currency-using cultures, during the sixty-five years of foreign control that began with the Spanish regime in 1885. This is the best indication that this complex is a monetary system, in all senses of the term. At the same time, its place in the culture and its actual uses indicate once more the advantages in analysis that derives from differentiating the prestige from the subsistence economy. This obtains no less here, where the two are marked off by the use of differing expressions of value, than in those economies where both are channeled through a common medium of exchange.[45]

6

IT HAS long been a truism of economics that the concepts of wealth and money are only related in so far as money can be used as an index of those values which at a given time are ascribed to the various kinds of goods held in a society. Wealth, as Carver showed early in the century, can only consist of scarce goods, since things "that are so abundant that no one needs to

[44] Ibid., 17–28.
[45] Barnett (1949, esp. Chs. III and IV) is in essential agreement with Ritzenthaler's discussion of Palauan money, as is indicated by his statement (49) that "Palauan money is more like our jewels than it is like our money."

give himself any concern about getting them . . . have no value and are not classified as wealth." Such things are non-economic goods—goods which can be used without economizing. Wealth, therefore, consists entirely of goods that are not free, and thus have economic value for their possessors. Any measure of this value is thus a measure of wealth. But, just as it is "a mistake to assume coal is weight or that lumber is bulk," so wealth and its measure in our society, money, are by no means the same.[46]

Granted the distinction between money and wealth in economic treatises, the evaluations of our culture in terms of pecuniary considerations has nonetheless brought about an understandable confusion of the two concepts in the usage of laymen. This makes it pertinent to raise the question whether, in nonliterate societies, one finds those unequal concentrations of values in the possession of some and not other members of a given community which constitute the essence of the popular meaning of the term "wealth" as applied in the phrase "a wealthy man"; and whether such concentrations are found irrespective of the presence of money as an index of the values involved. In whatever terms wealth is conceived, the economists cannot be held entirely blameless that money and wealth, or the terms "wealth" and "wealthy," are not differentiated more effectively by those who, like some anthropologists, are not trained to handle the concepts of economic science. For it is apparent that the existence of money permits a mobilization of resources which more effectively furthers the accumulation of valuable goods by an individual than where wealth is only measurable in produce or cattle or some other commodity. It also follows that where values can be expressed in terms of money, wealth can be manipulated with greater ease to attain desired social, political, or other ends than where it is absent.

It will be recalled that one of the primary functions of money is to act as "a depositary of value." But this does not mean that it is necessarily the only depositary of value, even where the use of money is most highly developed. Precious stones are no less precious because we have currency which can represent their preciousness with equal efficacy. This was roughly paralleled by the "copper" of the Indians of northwestern North America, the equivalent among them of a valuable jewel, valued in terms of

[46] Carver, 101–04, 119–20.

blankets just as the jewel is thought of in terms of dollars, or guineas, or francs. A similar case is that of the so-called "stone money" of Yap, those great cartwheels which, even though under the sea, continue to symbolize value. Yet in Yap the functioning tokens of exchange are tridacna shells, used where large amounts are involved, or, in more humble transactions, mother-of-pearl.[47]

Actually, in all societies possessing goods which are "valuables," whether these have an auxiliary function of money or not, their possession constitutes the equivalent of wealth. Let us consider at this point how wealth is manifested in societies where money is not found, or where tokens used in effectuating the exchange of goods are subsidiary to other objects deemed of highest worth. In Polynesia, though money was not found to any significant extent, the concept of wealth was highly developed. In Mangaia, for example, adzes were prized "not only as necessary tools but as material property and wealth." They could be used to ensure life and safety in the event of conquest, when they would be given to a powerful chief in return for his protection. An adze-maker could create wealth "by making sets of adzes and hiding them for future use and trade." On the same island the owner of a set of fishing nets was a man of wealth, especially if he owned one of the wide, finely meshed type.[48] The Tongan concept of wealth was equally clear: this consisted of mats, tapa cloth, and other manufactured articles, which at the death of the owner had to be divided according to carefully drawn rules.[49] On the island of Ontong Java coconuts, timber pandanus palms, and a few other fruit trees gave value to the land, and those who possessed large stores of these products were persons of wealth.[50] And in Samoa, whether or not the fine mat is to be regarded as currency, there is no question but that the possession of many of these fine mats, accompanied by the ownership of fiber mats and bark cloth in quantity, was the recognized mark of a man of wealth.[51]

In East Africa, where currency in any form is absent, cattle constitute an almost exclusive hall-mark of wealth. The subsistence economy of these tribes is based on agriculture; but the number of cattle owned by a man correlates highly with his

[47] Müller, 126–33; Senfft, 151.
[48] Hiroa (1934), 133, 145.
[49] Gifford (1929), 181.
[50] Hogbin (1934), 130–2.
[51] Hiroa (1930), 80–1; Mea (1930a), 73–4.

position. That is, among these peoples, as in most societies, position is related to wealth, and cattle are the sole expression of wealth. It is of no consequence how much cultivated land or other goods a man possesses, for should he not have adequate resources in cattle, he can have no place of respect in his society. As among the Gusii: "Young men as well as old acquire cattle greedily and part with them reluctantly, and the size of a man's herd is . . . one of the best indices to his social standing.[52]

Notwithstanding this, cattle can in no sense be considered money; for nothing can be acquired with them except wives, and a long time has elapsed since competent students have held to the earlier naïve concept that the giving of cattle by the family of the suitor to a family of his bride constitutes an act of wife-purchase. A cow is eaten only on certain ceremonial occasions, or when an animal dies; nor have cattle any other subsistence utility aside from that of supplying milk, since they are never employed as beasts of burden. They are merely possessed and esteemed for the prestige their possession brings. But they are not money.[53]

A few instances of what comprises wealth in one or two North American non-pecuniary societies may also be given. In all the Plains area, after the introduction of the horse, these animals furnished almost the only index of wealth. This has been clearly shown for the marginal Flathead; among the Crow and other Plains tribes the act of highest valor, and consequently that which brought the greatest prestige, was that of the warrior who, unaided, cut a horse from the enemy's picket-line. Among the tribes of the Upper Missouri, "a man's wealth is estimated by the number of these animals he owns." [54] The Klamath of Oregon, in another area, counted many kinds of goods in the category of wealth: slaves, horses, beads of various types, food, bows and arrows, furs, hides, especially of elk, Plains type garments, armor, large houses, buffalo hides, canoes—"In a word, articles of value in foreign commerce, articles of dress and adornment, of war, ritual and sustenance." Descriptions of wealthy men include that of a war leader owning five quivers, going into battle with one under each arm and one on his back, with extra bowstrings; while elsewhere such a one is designated as a man possessing

[52] Mayer, 1.
[53] Herskovits (1926), *passim.*
[54] Turney-High, 105; Denig, 474-5.

fur blankets, coyote and wolf pelts.[55] Turning to an American society known for its pecuniary orientation, we find that besides the copper plates that were the most valuable goods of the Northwest Coast Indians, they counted elk-skins, marten garments, sea-otter garments, canoes, raccoon-skins, and spoons made of elk and antler horn as marks of wealth. This is reflected in the folk-tales of the Tsimshian, where in one account we see how an outstanding hunter or fisherman, by amassing goods needed by others, could become a wealthy man.[56]

For final examples of non-pecuniary wealth, we may turn once again to Melanesia, where, on Malekula, a wealthy person is described as one "who possesses many boars with finely curved tusks and one or many houses filled with yams." Of these categories, it is essentially to the acquisition and care of pigs that a man gives his attention. It is not, however, the number of his pigs but their quality that is of moment, especially as this relates to the more prized growth of the tusks of boars. In Seniang, 23 names for grades of these tuskers have been recorded; in Lambumbu, 11 grades.

Though it is not possible here to detail the manner in which the growth of a borrowed pig affects the return on the loan, it is instructive to reproduce the diagram showing how these tusked animals become increasingly important as depositaries of value with the development of their tusks as these describe a complete circle and begin a second curve: In Figure 2, if we take 3 as the unit of value for the smallest size pig, the first four grades increase by 1 point each. The fifth grade, where the tusk is seen projecting through the flesh, increases by 2 points, the seventh is 4 points higher, the ninth is 12 points higher than the seventh, while the eleventh is 24 points higher than the ninth.[57] Of similar importance in the determination of wealth is the part played by the "valuables" of the Kula ring. They constitute an instance that is especially striking, however, since, though they are not money, as the term is conventionally used, their exchange for each other is an invariable concomitant of the barter that goes on along with the ritual of their passing. Moreover, their importance for the point being considered here is that while one who does not possess these "valuables" cannot be accounted wealthy, no man may

[55] Spier, 42–3.
[56] Boas (1916), 435–6; 225 ff.

[57] Deacon, 196.

retain the "valuables" he has at a given time, but must trade them along their well-regulated path.[58]

It is apparent, then, that while the concepts of money and wealth are closely related, money is in no way indispensable to the existence of wealth, or to the existence of socio-economic

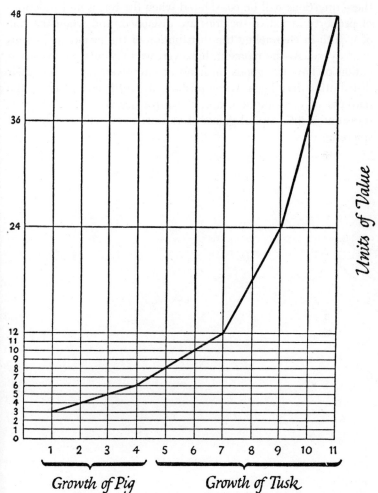

2. *Value of Pigs and Tusks on Malekula (adapted from Deacon:* Increase of Values of Pigs with Growth of Tusks, *p. 196).*

[58] Malinowski (1922), 81–3.

status as comprehended in the concept of a wealthy man. But to indicate the nature of money in nonliterate societies, the place of wealth, and the relationship between the two only opens the door to further questions concerning the disposal of the wealth of a community as it is represented in what is produced. Many of these questions will be considered when the forms and functions of property in native societies are discussed, and when the role of wealth in channeling the distribution of the economic surplus is analyzed. At the moment, however, we may turn to an examination of how the goods on hand at any given time, once their distribution has been accomplished, are utilized. That is, the patterns of consumption, and the processes by which effort is transmuted into capital goods of various sorts, will next be considered.

CHAPTER XII

CONSUMPTION NORMS
AND STANDARDS
OF LIVING

THE CONSUMER has received relatively little attention from economists, whose interests have from the earliest times of their discipline been so focused on the production, distribution, and exchange of goods that this phase of the economic cycle has tended to have only passing recognition.[1] It is not strange, therefore, that the economics of consumption in nonliterate societies is a subject to which anthropologists have turned only relatively lately. This, however, has not only been caused by the absence of a lead from the economists; it has developed out of the nature of the data.

A major factor that has rendered difficult the study of consumption in nonliterate societies has been the absence of a pecuniary standard of value, whereby the worth of resources assigned to various ends can be calculated and the resultant planes of living of a people effectively described. Hogbin indicates some of these methodological problems in his "attempt to calculate the exact quantity of food the household consumed, how much was given away or wasted, and how much received" among the Wogeo of the Schouten Islands, north of New Guinea.

> It was sufficiently difficult to find out the number of taro and bananas put into the vegetable stew which provides the basis of the evening meal on four days out of seven, for I was fre-

[1] Cf. Hoyt (1938), 3–71.

quently away from the village while it was being prepared; but by comparison this was an easy task when I attempted to record the exact number of persons who were given a share and how much they ate; moreover, I was never certain whether the members of the household had had a snack elsewhere.

On the other side of the ledger, it is to be noted that the figures Hogbin did obtain give a picture which, for all its deficiencies, is an improvement over the completely unquantified guesses often encountered in the literature. For a household of three, one member of which was an infant, and where two and a half taro are estimated as weighing one pound, and the same weight is assigned six bananas, the following figures are given:

Cooked daily: 18 lbs. taro and 3¼ lbs. bananas
Given away or wasted daily: 5½ lbs. taro and 1 lb. bananas
Eaten outside the house daily: 1 lb. taro and ¼ lb. bananas
Total amount eaten by household daily: 13½ lbs. taro and 2½ lbs. bananas
Daily diet of one person: 4 lbs. 8 oz. taro and 12 oz. bananas.

This, however, excludes bananas eaten raw and other fruit used in season; nor does it consider the fact that during the month of June breadfruit replaces taro, nor take into account the nuts, coconut flesh, and occasional bit of wild pig consumed when available. The estimate for consumption of the two staples given above may be compared with the following record, which covers a period of six months (183 days):

Produced .... 7,000 taro and 4,200 bananas
Received as gifts .... 1,000 taro and 750 bananas
Gave away or wasted .... 3,000 taro and 2,300 bananas
Ate .... 5,000 taro and 2,600 bananas

This gives a daily diet for one person of 3 lbs. 10 ozs. taro and 12 ozs. bananas, the difference "to be accounted for, in part at least, by the fact that in the latter instance no account has been taken of the substitution of breadfruit for taro during June."

On Wogeo, unlike in other parts of the world, "the agricultural year . . . has no well-marked rhythm," so that we find no set times of feasting and famine such as obtain elsewhere. Yet the problems of consumption are present, in allocation of time and energy in the production and utilization of staples and delicacies, as well as in the discharge of those obligations which a man or woman must fulfil as members of the society. The basic factors of any system of consumption are thus present, though in generalized form, and can be estimated without utilizing those mechanisms of evaluation that give precision to description in pecuniary societies.[2]

2

IF WE turn to the traditions which determine the consumption of goods in non-industrial cultures, we are confronted at the outset with a fact that, like others already adduced, contravenes conventional preconceptions of how "primitive" man lives. It will be remembered that in discussing the manner of getting a living, the closeness of these folk to their natural environment was emphasized. At the same time, it was pointed out that although the existence of a simple technology makes the problem of survival acute, there is still no human group that exploits to the fullest its environment, even within the competence of its technological equipment.

Food, the most fundamental necessity of life, offers the most striking case in point. For what is more logical than to expect that resources would be exploited to the utmost to meet this most vital of all needs? Yet this is not the case; and data from many societies demonstrate that the reasons for this are most often to be found in aspects of culture that lie entirely outside the economic sphere. For the consumption even of this elementary necessity is found to be influenced, if not actually determined, by all manner of traditions of what is and what is not suitable for human nourishment. Taboos ranging from individual prohibitions to proscriptions of a totemic order, and quite irrational ideas holding that certain consumable products should not be eaten—irrational, that is, from the point of view of the assumptions underlying native reasoning—are found among all peoples.

So strong, indeed, are the convictions regarding the fitness of certain foodstuffs for human consumption that the violation of

[2] Hogbin (1938–9), 289–91, 131, and *passim*.

accepted patterns arouses the strongest emotions. Mention to a layman in our society of some of the foods we taboo, that are consumed by other peoples, such as ant larvae or roasted beetles, "high" meat or the contents of the digestive tract of an animal that has been killed, is enough to bring on a strong negative reaction. Yet when rationally considered, from the point of view of the food values of these delicacies—which is what they usually are considered by those who consume them—they do not greatly differ from certain delicacies of our own that would be and, in some instances, have actually been found distasteful to those outside our own culture. Thus it is well known that to the Chinese milk is something emphatically not to be drunk as meat to the Hindu of India is something not to be eaten. A proposal among ourselves to substitute the meat of a horse for that of a cow, or of a puppy for that of a lamb, would scarcely be entertained.

This same reaction is found among other peoples. An example may be taken from the customs of the Siriono of Eastern Bolivia, who so literally live on the subsistence level, that the two most frequent expressions heard among them are "my stomach is very empty" and "give me something." [3] These people do not eat snakes, because they believe that the meat is poisonous, even in the case of non-poisonous serpents. Holmberg recounts how having killed one of these, he fried a large steak of snake-meat in front of the Indians, offering some to them after demonstrating by eating it that it had no ill effects. Not only was it refused, but when later the chief learned that he had eaten some muffins Holmberg had fried in snake-fat, "he immediately jumped out of the hammock, put his finger down his throat, and threw up every bit of the muffin he had eaten." [4]

A comparable selectivity is found in clothing. One need consider the differences not alone in style but in the materials that often differentiate the clothing of the two sexes in a given society to recognize how arbitrary are the selections made from the available supply of goods. On a larger scale, entire peoples follow their traditional concepts of what materials may properly be worn, so that folk to whom weaving is known neglect available resources in hides, or, on the contrary, where skin clothing is worn, greet the introduction of more pliant materials with disapproval.

[3] Holmberg, p. 30.   [4] Ibid., 33.

This is particularly true when certain types of clothing are associated with social status, a point effectively illustrated by a situation that at one time developed in the Gold Coast of West Africa. In a volume dealing with the art of the Ashanti, a detailed analysis was given of the warp and weft counts of the great cloths made by these people.[5] These diagrams were somewhat different from similar analyses which appear from time to time in anthropological works, having been made by an English weaving company with the object of reproducing cloths for sale to the Ashanti themselves at a much lower price than that set by native craftsmen. The reproductions of the originals were of such excellence that without close inspection they could not be told as such either in design or in technical finish; yet the first shipment was the last, and only Europeans who know no better or do not care have bought them. For the right to wear these intricate patterns, each with its special name, goes with rank and can only be conferred by the king of Ashanti. When a man appeared wearing an imitation cloth, he was greeted with such ridicule that no Ashanti dared be seen wearing one in public.

Thus, as far as could be determined, a considerable economic advantage to the consumer was given up without regret, since economic advantage was at variance with accepted traditions of seemly behavior and vested rights. With the passing of the years, however, the economic pull of the less expensive imported cloth asserted itself in a compromise. Cloths made in Europe are now generally worn, but the patterns do not in any way resemble the native designs, which are still found only on cloths of native manufacture, used by chiefs and men of wealth on occasions of social and ceremonial importance.[6]

The factor of variation in wants within a given society also enters in determining standards of consumption. Firth, who approached the problem of consumption norms in Tikopia from the point of view of its "complex scheme of social relationships," has made the point for this group. He found variation in consumption according to age and sex and status, so that the "wants of single individuals or households" differ to a considerable degree "from the waxing and waning demands of intermittent ceremonial—initiations, marriages, or funerals—and the seasonal demands of religious ritual." Translating this, in general terms, into degree

[5] Rattray (1927), 252–63.   [6] Lystad (communicated).

of elasticity and inelasticity of demand for various products, Firth further indicates how the variation in demand due to the operation of these factors in establishing consumption differentials here affects the schedule of production in the economy. In this way, the groundwork is laid for the satisfaction of differing wants according to the need of individual or family in terms of age, sex, status, and situation.[7]

3

IT WOULD not be difficult to range the other forms of primary consumption goods and indicate how similar traditional values are factors of the first importance in shaping the economics of consumption. At this point, however, we may attempt an exposition of some of the available materials that bear on the matter.

One or two specific instances of data of a general kind, which are available to the student of the economics of consumption among nonliterate peoples, may be cited. Thus, among the Omaha, the conventions observed in butchering game were such that, except for the portion of the animal allotted to the one who had killed it, it was divided according to the order in which those engaged in the work reached the carcass. A buffalo was divided into seven parts, comprising eleven portions, each of a different degree of desirability. The meat, when "jerked," was placed with the available ears of corn in the caches found near each dwelling—pits, carefully dug to a depth of some eight feet, rounded at the bottom and sides, and lined with split posts to which bundles of grass were tied to absorb moisture and assure the preservation of the contents until needed.[8]

Or, again, commenting on the habits of the wild rice gatherers, Jenks observes that "the food of primitive man varies with the season of the year and the section of the country in which they are," and that "they frequently live upon one staple at a time." On this basis, he provides a timetable of consumption that has considerable usefulness. In the region of the upper Great Lakes those Indians principally consumed maple sugar during March, April and May; then they ate early berries, and then

[7] Raymond Firth (1939), 33–5.   [8] Fletcher and LaFleche, 271–5.

green corn, until in the autumn the wild rice became available. In spring and summer they supplemented their diet with the vast number of wild fowl to be found near the rice fields, while in winter the people lived on the meat of the animals they hunted and the pemmican they made from this meat. Against these facts the consumption of wild rice is projected. The rice was eaten mainly after the harvest, though some of it was stored for later use. The Indians whose hunting grounds became "fruitful" about the time the harvest ended saved a considerable proportion of the grain for later use.[9]

In the literature on peoples inhabiting other portions of the globe, hints of this same general character are also found. Thus a considerable amount of a man's substance on the island of Niue was apparently used in gambling.[10] Consumption of certain foodstuffs in the Marquesas Islands could effectively be stopped for a time if a chief invoked his right to taboo the gathering of produce or the killing of pigs so as to ensure an adequate provisioning of fresh breadfruit or taro or coconuts or pigs for a future feast.[11] In Buka, the consumption of pork is "reserved for special occasions," when pigs are slaughtered for feasts at which the prestige of the host depends on how much pork he can provide. This practice is followed in Malekula [12] and elsewhere in Melanesia.

The utilization of goods for ritual purposes and, in particular, ceremonial consumption so as to gain prestige, are among the most important and consistent elements in the use of available food resources in primitive societies. This obtains in Melanesia and Polynesia, as has been indicated; its presence in America, though not everywhere in as dramatic a form as in the Pacific Northwest, and in Africa, as among the Baganda or Zulu or Ashanti or BaLuba, is equally well known. A common expression of ritual consumption of goods clusters about the complex of death and burial customs, when valuable commodities are disposed of. So important is this phenomenon of the drive for prestige, as it impinges on the economic order, that consideration of it must await the special attention to be given them when, in a later chapter, the economics of prestige and its role in main-

[9] Jenks, 1095–7.
[10] Loeb, 50.
[11] Handy (1923), 59.

[12] Blackwood (1935), 281; Deacon, 16–17.

taining social position is considered. For the present, and to the extent the materials will permit, let us seek to understand something of the quantitative significance of such institutions in stimulating the consumption of goods. Among the available data is a list of the amounts of foodstuffs consumed at certain specific feasts witnessed by early observers in the islands of New Zealand:

Date	Quantity of Food Consumed
1829	462 baskets of potatoes counted
1831	Upwards of 1,000 bushels of potatoes in as many baskets. Joints of beef and shark.
1831	3,000 bushels of *kumara* as presents; 2,000 to be consumed, 290 pigs killed for occasion
1836	About 2,000 bushel baskets *kumara;* 50 or 60 pigs cooked
1837	6 large albatrosses, 19 calabashes shark oil, several tons fish, principally dried young shark, 20,000 dried eels, great quantity pigs, and baskets of potatoes almost without number
1844	11,000 baskets potatoes; 100 large pigs, 9,000 sharks; liberal supplies flour, sugar, rice, and tobacco
1846	Several pigs, 6 canoes full of flour and sugar, besides potatoes and *kumara*
1846	Several tons potatoes and *kumara* in rows; 500 pigs, quantity of eels, 16 casks tobacco
1849	Potatoes, cooked pigs, dried shark, pumpkins, *kumara*, etc. Hard to ascertain quantity. At one stage 200 pigs arrived. About 2,000 baskets of potatoes by then collected—40 tons. Supplies continued to arrive.[13]

Food consumption can be studied on the qualitative as well as quantitative level. This involves the manner in which a people continuously adhere to accepted modes of procedure in respected, though modest, forms of daily living. "Beside the questions of nourishment and of individual taste or preference," says Bascom of the Nigerian Yoruba, "patterns of food consumption also involve the factor of prestige. . . . The dishes that are prepared and even the staple food which serves as the basis of subsistence vary with economic means, while in order to maintain a particular social status certain foods must be served to guests, regardless of what may be eaten in private." Meat stew and yam loaf are the foods that are kept on hand to serve those who may come to visit a man, or who may be present when he sits down to eat. Relative desirability of foods is ex-

[13] Firth (1929a), 298, 318–20.

pressed in such a proverb as, "Yam loaf is real food; yam porridge is just nourishment; if we do not see either, we eat cornstarch porridge; to keep the mouth from being idle is the purpose of toasted corn." This numerous people have many markets where cooked foods are to be purchased. But here again the prestige factor enters, for it is held shameful if a man has to send to the market for food with which to entertain unexpected guests. The stew-pot of a man of standing must always be amply filled to care for these emergencies.[14]

The factor of prestige can thus operate on a small or a large scale in the economy of a given society. Yet, whether entailing modest or lavish expenditure, on a day-to-day basis or on special occasions, the facts regarding expenditure of this kind, even though incomplete and despite their not being projected against the total economic system, suggest the resources that can be summoned to aid in meeting the overall consumption needs of the society. Understandably, these accounts do not present the negative aspects of this phase of distribution and consumption, except by inference, in terms of loss of prestige where an inadequate reserve of foodstuffs does not permit the proper procedure to be followed. That this is a significant factor in the total economy should, however, not be forgotten, despite the difficulties in obtaining and presenting data of this order.

4

AN ANALYSIS of the use of foods among the Tallensi of the Northern Territories of the Gold Coast, West Africa, projects the patterns of food-consumption against the productive activities of the people. The approach thus affords a picture of the food resources that are at the disposal of the native at a given time of year, and his use of these resources in the light of his immediate needs:

Productive cycle	Food cycle
April: First planting—rain fell on March 26, and early millet and some cow-peas and *neri* was planted in the valley settlements. Rain again in	Food stores very low in average households and being rationed. Many dependent upon supplementary sources of supply. People buy-

[14] Bascom (1950), 51–2.

Productive cycle

mid-April enabled most people to plant early millet, etc. Women sowed their vegetable patches. Hoeing begun; but not more than one day in three devoted to agriculture. Communal fishing expeditions.

May: Rains continue erratically. Early millet planted in the stone and hilly areas. Others inter-planting guinea-corn and late millet on compound farms and some ground-nuts. Work on bush farms preparatory to planting commenced. Tempo of agricultural activity increasing rapidly.

June: Height of agricultural season. Men completely absorbed in hoeing and weeding, planting guinea-corn and late millet on bush farms, rice, ground-nuts and minor crops. Hiring labour for help in hoeing and weeding. Women plucking nangena.

July: Early millet harvested by those who planted first on valley land. Hoeing and weeding of compound and bush farms in full swing. Some still planting subsidiary crops. Poultry breeding begins.

August: Late planters harvest early millet. Invited collective labour for hoeing and weeding coming

Food cycle

ing grain abroad for re-sale. Ample food supplies in market and many buying grain. Market-prices average. Children gleaning ground-nuts. Wild fruits . . . being consumed to stave off hunger.

Food stores deplenished and severe rationing. "Hunger" commences. Poorer households suffer two or three days' hunger a week, living on vegetable soup, ground-nuts and wild fruits. Householders send their wives to purchase grain abroad for consumption and re-sale if they have money. Many selling livestock bit by bit to buy grain in market. Prices of all commodities rising. Visits being made to relations in more fortunate areas to get some grain.

Peak of "hunger" reached. Granaries empty among poorer households. Much livestock sold or bartered for grain very cheaply; grain scarce and dear. Much ground-nuts for sale. Small groups of children wander about hungry, feeding on wild fruits and small animals they find near the settlements. Toward the end of the month many people are staunching their hunger by cutting the ripe or half ripe heads of early millet which they roast on the embers and nibble at.

Early millet eaten by those who harvest. Relatives from the later-planting areas come to beg again. Wild fruits still eaten and hunger prevalent in late-planting areas. Ground-nuts, beginning to ripen, plucked and chewed as snacks.

Almost everybody has early millet; hunger appeased for a time.

Productive cycle

Food cycle

to the fore, but hired labour still in evidence. Fresh hibiscus leaves used in soup.

September: Harvesting ground-nuts and other subsidiary crops (roots and legumes) begun. Hoeing and weeding of bush farms continue. Women plucking green ocro and burning early millet stalks for *bakaa*. Ritual festivals commence.

Those who harvested in July already reaching end of supplies of early millet, and resort to market and relatives. Early millet very expensive in market. New ground-nuts (partly green), roots, and legumes supplementing diet largely.

October: Harvesting of guinea-corn, rice, root crops, legumes, etc., general. *Neri* lifted. Women frying and storing vegetables.

Food becoming plentiful. Price of grain falling rapidly in market. Cooked food cheap and plentiful in market. Marriage season begins (with ritual and social expenditure of food).

November: Harvesting late millet on bush-farms, cow-peas and Bambara beans. Women burning valley grass for *ziem*. Children gleaning ground-nuts in play, not because of hunger. Height of festival season.

All kinds of food plentiful. Harvest festivals, during which enormous quantities of food are consumed and circulated and many animals sacrificed, giving the maximum meat supply of the year, and root crops including purchased yams especially in demand for the festivals. All foodstuffs abundant and cheap in the market.

December: Agricultural work over.

Height of ritual season: funeral ceremonies, children's dedication ceremonies, many marriages; all involving consumption of livestock and grain, in sacrifices, as cooked food, and beer.

January: Period of secondary activities such as housebuilding, cutting grass and timber for roofing, handicraft work. Young men begin to go abroad temporarily.

Grain rationing begins. Grain and other foodstuffs, including imported maize, plentiful and cheap at market.

February: As in January.

Grain issued for only one meal a day. Many purchasing grain rather than use up their own supplies. Ground-nuts and cow-peas regular and important supplements to cereal food. Women finding grain to augment supplies, by trading, etc.

Productive cycle	*Food cycle*
	Market supplies still plentiful, prices average.
March: As in February. Sporadic cleaning of fields and hoeing.	Grain supplies sinking and more carefully rationed. Children and women gleaning ground-nuts to stop hunger. People going to Mampuru and Nabte countries to purchase grain for re-sale. Grain still plentiful in market, also other products, e.g., yams (imported).

The conclusions that are drawn from this table may profitably be quoted: "A striking correlation emerges from the above synopsis of the cycle of food economy. It will be seen that domestic food-supplies are at the lowest at the time—recognized as such by the natives—of the most arduous output of physical labour, i.e., in May-June, and highest when there is least agricultural work. In other words, it would seem that food consumption is inversely correlated with food requirements, if we may assume that more food is needed to sustain the arduous agricultural labour of the rainy season than the leisure months of the dry season." One reason for this mode of ordering things must be sought in traditional habit, for it is plain that they lack neither the technique of storing foodstuffs nor the concepts of thrift and frugality. Apparently, therefore, we not only have here an example of the organization of the consumption patterns of a nonliterate people, set forth so as to indicate its regularity and orderliness, but a demonstration of how, in relation to physiological needs, these patterns may be determined by custom in a manner not at all calculated to serve the greatest physical good of the consumers.[15]

Another attack on the problem of consumption can be made by analyzing the possessions of individuals. This yields some notion of how much a given native has obtained for himself out of the total productive processes, how much he has to dispose of, and, to the degree possible to be inferred from what he possesses, what use he may potentially, at least, make of his goods. For this we turn once again to the Lobi tribes, and reproduce inventories of the goods owned by members of two households, one poor and one well-to-do.[16] The values given in francs are cal-

[15] M. and S. L. Fortes, 253–61.   [16] Labouret (1931), 349–51.

culated on the basis of January prices,[17] when these lists were made:

Household of Kidyo Botoro

I. Kidyo personally possessed:

Millet, 2,000 kilograms at 0 fr. 25	500 fr.
Maize, 400 kilograms at 0 fr. 25	100
Yams, manioc, peanuts, etc.	40
Tobacco	5
3 goats at 5 francs	15
7 chickens at 1 franc	7
5 guinea-hens at 1 franc	5
1 dog	5
3 hoes at 2 francs	6
Iron for arrows	3
Axe	2
Various utensils	5
Copper ornaments	10
Cowries	15
	718

II. Yafokona, wife of Kidyo, owned:

Baskets	4 fr.
Pottery	12
Beans	3
1 chicken belonging to her child	1
Ornaments	15
Cowries	20
	55

III. Dinekoni, co-wife of the preceding and somewhat older, owned:

Baskets	4 fr.
Pottery	12
Guinea-hens	5
Ornaments	15
Cowries	35
	71

The holdings of this family thus came to 844 francs. In the case of the wealthier family, whose possessions totalled 2,728.50 francs, the distribution was as follows:

[17] See above, 247–9.

Household of Nomiré

I. Nomiré owned:

Millet: 4,000 kilos at 0 fr. 25	1,000 fr.	
Maize: 700 kilos at 0 fr. 25	175	
Yams, peanuts, etc.	100	
Tobacco	10	
7 head of cattle at 100 francs	700	
5 sheep at 12 fr. 50	62 fr. 50	
4 goats at 5 francs	20	
10 hoes at 2 francs	20	
Tools and utensils	15	
Copper ornaments	25	
Cotton clothing	50	
Cowries	200	
	2,377 fr. 50	

II. Tonagniem Palé, first wife of Nomiré, owned:

Baskets	10 fr.
Pottery	30
Personal provisions	40
2 goats at 5 fr.	10
6 chickens at 1 franc	6
4 guinea-hens at 1 franc	4
Copper ornaments	25
Cotton clothing	30
Cowries, profits from selling beer	10
	165

III. Lompo Da, second wife of Nomiré, owned:

Baskets	6 fr.
Pottery	10
1 goat at 5 francs	5
3 chickens at 1 franc	3
Ornaments	20
1 small cloth	10
Cowries	25
	79

IV. Bayine Palé, son of Nomiré and Tonagniem, owned:

1 hoe	2 fr.
1 axe	2
3 chickens	3
	7

The other members of this household owned nothing.

It is apparent from these tables that the differences in the possessions of these two groups must validly reflect a real difference in their respective standards of living. This, in turn, suggests that further tabulations of this kind, on a wider scale, based on data derived from peoples in various parts of the world, must throw as significant a light on the economics of consumption in non-literate societies as they must on the distribution of tribal wealth.

5

OTHER DATA bearing on consumer economics that have been collected in Africa take two forms, the study of budgets and of nutrition. The basic question of balance between income and outgo, the difficulties in assessing which in non-pecuniary societies were exemplified in the opening pages of this chapter, are here alleviated by the presence of a money economy—in pre-European days based on the cowry shell and other media, and at present on European currency.

In a study of the budgets of sixteen individuals of the Ibo people of Eastern Nigeria, Harris has summarized the data in tables which give a concept of pattern and variation about these norms as concerns intake and expenditure. We may, first of all, consider the annual income and outgo of a man about thirty-three to thirty-five years old, a member of one secret society, with a household consisting of two wives, two children—a boy of ten and an infant daughter, and his mother.

Income

	£	s.	d.
1. Shares of bride-price of various girls of his kindred		1	9
2. Sold no yams (small crop)		0	0
3. Sale of coco-nuts		1	0
4. Sale of fowl		1	6
5. Profit from trade in European cloth, bought at Port Harcourt and sold at local markets	5	10	0

Income

	£	s.	d.
6. Shares from fees of new members of *Akan* secret society		1	6
TOTAL CASH INCOME	£5	15	9

Expenditure

	£	s.	d.
1. Government tax		4	0
2. School tax			6
3. Contribution for purchase of cows eaten at Bende Divi-			

Expenditure	£	s.	d.
sion Union meeting			2½
4. Contribution for sacrifice to *Kamálu*			2
5. Contribution for annual sacrifice to *Aleúkwu*			3
6. Food for household		6	0
7. Food for self when away trading		3	0
8. Clothing for children (in addition to above profit on trade in clothes, takes one cloth each for self, two wives and mother)		2	3
9. Meat, palm wine, kola to greet visitors		5	6
10. Contributions to burials of those in his kindred, and affinal relatives			4½
11. Stockfish, meat, and money to those women who gave him food during "famine" period		2	0
12. Soap		2	0
13. Made fetish so that his young wife would become pregnant		7	0

Expenditure	£	s.	d.
14. Calendric ceremonial sacrifices to ancestors, deities and other supernatural agencies		1	6
15. Kerosene		8	0
16. Tobacco, potash, and snuff		12	0
17. Paid entire brideprice for his second wife this year. It was necessary to pay this entire sum at once because the man who had been previously paying for this girl had to be completely repaid before the girl could become the wife of this man	5	10	0
18. Six contributions to sib council meetings			6
19. Contribution for bribe money given by sib to policemen who arrested two sib members on charge of illicit distillation of gin			6
TOTAL CASH EXPENDITURE	£8	5	9

Such budgets, like the others presented in the analysis under discussion, "represent only *monetary* income and expenditure." Thus they give "no picture of economic reserves . . . of these individuals, nor of the consumption of food not purchased in the market but which has been obtained through food gifts or exchanges or gotten directly from the farms." Nonetheless, "because so much of the life entails monetary transactions of one sort or another, these budgets present not only a sharp insight into the economic life of the Ibo individual but they cast into relief many other aspects of his culture." This is apparent in the figures given above, which, for example, demonstrate the value assigned such intangibles as are evidenced by contributions to kin groups and associations, for religious purposes, or for such ends as the acquisition of a wife or the provisions to be made for visitors.

As in most African societies, the economic position of women is here high. It is thus essential, for any analysis of the consumption economics of this people, that the activities of members of this sex likewise be taken into account. We may thus consider the case of a woman about forty to forty-five years old, the first of her husband's two wives, who had two children by a previous marriage, but none by her present spouse.

Income

	£	s.	d.
1. Purchases large pot of palm-oil for 6d. or 9d. and resells it in small quantities of ½d. or 1d. Makes approx. 3d. profit on each pot. Disposes of about 15 pots per year		4	0
2. Sale of crops grown on her farm	1	5	0
3. Sale of crops gathered in bush		5	0
4. Money received from men to whom she sent food during "famine" period		2	6
5. Profit from trade in smoked *mbása* fish, pepper, coco-nuts, and other native foods. Buys food at local markets and resells at markets where prices are somewhat higher		10	0
6. Sale of fowl		4	0
7. Profit from trade in tobacco		6	0
8. Profit from trade in salt. Sells approxi-			

Income

	£	s.	d.
mately 280 forms of salt during year		3	6
TOTAL CASH INCOME	£3	0	0

Expenditure

	£	s.	d.
1. Food for household		10	0
2. Contributions for burials		1	0
3. *Úri*, camwood, chalk, and other cosmetics		1	0
4. Contributions for purchase of cows at Bende Division meeting			½
5. Stockfish, meat and other food sent to men during "famine" period		2	0
6. Contributions to annual sacrifices to *Aleúkwu*			2
7. Contribution for sacrifices to *Kamálu*			1½
8. Clothing for self; headkerchief, 2s.; dress, 1s.; 3 cloths, 7s. 4d.		10	4
9. Various sacrifices for well-being		1	3

Expenditure	£	s.	d.
10. Gave 5s. to husband when he had court case		5	0
11. Her son by previous marriage is a trader in cloth at Aba. He often sends her gifts of cloth. When he visited her this year she gave him £1.10s.	1	10	0

Expenditure	£	s.	d.
12. To daughter of her sister who married this year she gave: mortar and pestle, duck, palm-oil, fish and other food delicacies		5	0
TOTAL CASH EXPENDITURE	£3	5	11

It is to be noted that in the two accounts of cash income and outgo cited here, expenditure exceeds income. In the case of this man, the large payment of bride-wealth accounts for this discrepancy; the deficit in the second, the only woman's budget where this was the case, is not explained. It is apparent that this type of discrepancy must sooner or later be compensated for, and when the accounts are considered for the total series of cash budgets presented, we see that the need to balance budgets is actually not neglected.

It would be beyond the point to reproduce here tabulations of consolidated income and expenditures for men and women, but some consideration of the principal items will be worthwhile. The sale of yams accounts for 16.7 per cent of the total income of all the men. This is followed by profit from the sale of palm-oil and kernels (11.2 per cent), profit from trade in European articles (9.8 per cent), interest on loans (6.6 per cent), money received from mothers, sons, daughters or other relatives (5.0 per cent), and bride-price received on behalf of daughters (4.2 per cent). In the case of the women, the largest source of income was from sale of crops grown on their farms (29.4 per cent), followed by money received from trade in native foods, salt, pottery, and tobacco (23.1 per cent), profit from the sale of palm-oil and kernels (12.5 per cent), sale of crops gathered in the bush (6.9 per cent), money from men to whom women sent food during the institutionalized "famine" period (6.2 per cent) and money received from "lovers"—men who live with women for whom bride-wealth has not passed, and whose children are not under their control—(4.0 per cent).

As against this, the most important expenditures for the men are bride-price and presents for a new wife (20.8 per cent), clothing (10.3 per cent), food for the household (8.8 per cent), court fees, fines, and bribes (5.7 per cent), meat, palm wine, and kola for visitors (5.5 per cent), wages and food to farm laborers (4.8 per cent), repayment of principal and interest on loans (4.5 per cent), and diviners' fees, blood-suckings, fetishes, and miscellaneous sacrifices (4.1 per cent). In contrast to these stand the priorities in the list for women: food for the household (23.7 per cent), money given to older sons (13.6 per cent), clothing for self and children (10.7 per cent), diviners' fees, medicines, blood-suckings, fetishes, and miscellaneous sacrifices (6.7 per cent), *urí*, chalk and other cosmetics (6.3 per cent), money given to husband or dead husband's brother (6.3 per cent), wages to women who help in weeding the farm (6.1 per cent), and the purchase of stockfish and meat given to men during the "famine" period (6.0 per cent).

Two unpublished family budgets collected by Professor Henri Labouret, may likewise be given. The first is that of a Bambara family living in the Buguni district of the French Sudan, the second of a cultivator living in the Adaou district of Indénié, Ivory Coast.[18]

The Bambara family consisted of fifteen persons, four men, four women, and seven children, who consumed eleven full and four half rations, or a total of thirteen. The relatives who made up the group worked six days out of seven in their common field, where they raised millet, peanuts, fonio, and some maize. In addition to the communal fields, each of the men and women in the component households of this extended family had his own private holding, worked mornings and evenings and the whole of each seventh day. Their resources assured the family its subsistence without making it necessary for them to purchase anything until a period in June, when those in charge of the houses sold certain products such as shea-butter and soap, improving upon their available food supply by utilizing the receipts from their sales to this end. Since the cost of the daily ration was 1.50 francs, this involved a daily expenditure for the family of 19.50 francs, compensated in part by sales, which came to about 8

[18] Other materials of this kind, from East Africa, presented in somewhat more general terms, are to be found in A. T. and G. M. Culwick, 282–9.

francs, leaving a net of 11.50, which, multiplied by twenty-five days—the period in question—equalled 287.50 francs.

Routine expenses were sufficiently heavy, even though work clothes were made of cotton which was spun, woven, and sewed at home. The total budget may be broken down as follows:

I. ORDINARY EXPENDITURES

A. *Clothing*
  1) *Men*

4 caps of European materials at 5 francs	20.00	
4 large tunics at 3 francs per metre	120.00	
4 pairs shorts at 10.50	42.00	

  2) *Women*

3 cloths at 10 francs	30.00	
3 handkerchiefs at 3 francs	9.00	

  3) *Children*

Miscellaneous	20.00	
		241.00

B. *Supplies*		
Soap, starch, and bluing	70.00	
C. *Lighting*	90.00	
D. *Miscellaneous*	50.00	
		451.00
E. *Obligatory ceremonial expenditures*	90.00	
F. *Medicine and consultations*	20.00	
G. *Taxes*		
8 adults at 22 fr.	176.00	
4 subscriptions to the Société de Prévoyance	4.00	
H. *For supplementary cost of food, as noted above*	287.50	
Total of ordinary expenses		1,028.50

II. EXTRAORDINARY EXPENSES

(In 1936 the cost to the head of the family for the circumcision of young Seriba, one of the members of this household, was as follows)

1 ox	150.00	
Gift to iron-worker	5.00	
Soap	5.00	
Vegetable fats	5.00	
Food for 10 guests over a period of 4 weeks, at 3 francs per day each	840.00	
Miscellaneous	50.00	
		1,055.00
Total family expenditures in 1936		2,083.50

We now turn to the receipts and expenditures of the forest-dwelling family of Kwaku Duao, of the Ivory Coast. This group consisted of two households totalling three men, four women, and nine children less than ten years of age. Their farms assured food for these persons, as well as for the workers they hired to aid in working the thirteen hectares of land planted in cocoa trees, and the one hectare of coffee shrubs possessed by Kwaku Duao, which produced the following amounts:

13 tons of cocoa at 1,000 francs	13,000.00	
504 kgs. of coffee at 3.25	1,637.00	
144 kgs. of bird-lime at 4 fr.	576.00	
Total		15,213.00

Against this amount, expenses were:

A. *Food*		
Meat, fish, preserves, salt, oil, condiments, at 250 fr. per month	3,000.00	
Food at 1 fr. per day for 12 laborers during 8 months	2,880.00	
B. *Clothing*		
Men	1,131.00	
Women	490.00	
Children	125.00	
C. *Supplies*		
a) Lighting, soap, starch; b), annual repairs to the metal roofed cement house	700.00	
D. *Obligatory ceremonial expenditures*	1,400.00	
E. *Medicines and consultations*	400.00	
F. *Expenses of working cash crops*	3,480.00	
Total		13,606.00
Receipts		15,213.00
Apparent profit		1,607.00

In the above accounting, no note is taken of what members of the family may have earned on their own account, whether by working for others or in personal business transactions. Furthermore, it would seem that the amount stated as having been paid out for the exploitation of cash crops is greater than it should be. The actual profits of a family comparable to that of Kwaku Duao may therefore be assumed to have been in the neighborhood of about 3,500 francs, instead of the 1,607 credited above.

It is apparent from a scrutiny of both these family budgets that there was a balancing of receipts and expenditures in terms of needs. Aside from the subsistence requirements, provision was made for the expenses incurred in meeting the demands of the supernatural. The figure for this in the first budget is striking, since an amount greater than that expended for all regular living costs was required to support the cost of the circumcision rite for which the group was responsible. How serious an obligation of this character can be is thus clearly demonstrated.

6

ANALYSES of the diet of nonliterate peoples are especially enlightening in the study of consumption patterns among nonliterate peoples because of their quantitative material. One such study has been made for certain communities of the Bemba tribe living on the Tanganyika plateau of northeastern Rhodesia. This group inhabits an area lying from 3,000 to 4,000 feet in altitude; their economy is based on agriculture. Their diet is fundamentally one of millet and other cereals, roots and vegetables; meat and fish play a minor part.

The consumption of food may be indicated by two sample entries from the records:

VILLAGE OF KUSAKA, FAMILY E

Date	Men	Women	Children	Infants	Food	Meals
Sept. 15	6	1	3	2	7½ lb. flour; 4 lb. cow-pea leaves; 1 lb. dried pumpkin; 1 lb. groundnut sauce	a.m. porridge; stewed pumpkin. p.m. porridge; stewed cow-pea leaves
Sept. 21	1	1	1	2	14 lb. potatoes	4 p.m. potatoes
Sept. 24	1	2	3	3	4½ lb. flour; 6 lb. meat	a.m. children roast their own potatoes. p.m. porridge and stewed meat

VILLAGE OF KUNGU, FAMILY B

Date	Men	Women	Children	Infants	Food	Meals
Feb. 28	—	1	1	0	3 gourds (3½ lb.) ¾ lb. Livingstone potatoes	p.m. only
Mar. 2	—	1	1	0	2 gourds	p.m. only
Mar. 7	—	2	2	0	2 lbs. flour 2 dried fish 2 pumpkins	a.m. pumpkin, p.m. porridge and fish

The calculation made of food at hand in these villages gives some idea of the amounts of food "available in a typical village at a plentiful season of the year." Despite the methodological difficulties in making this calculation it was found that the sixteen granaries measured,

> . . . showed an average supply of about 2,804 lb. of millet per family for the next six months. The relishes stored in the granaries showed that . . . six of fourteen families had a supply of ground-nuts, one owning about 60 lbs., and the others in the neighborhood of 20; seven families had bundles of dried leaf relishes; six had beans, ground beans and peas in small gourds; and six had dried potatoes. Two had no supply of relishes at all, and one householder had only sufficient seeds left for sowing.

These averages, however, must be considered in the light of the fact that there are strong seasonable differences in the amounts of food available at any given time. It must also be remembered that the rate of consumption may be affected by the amount of work done at a given season of the year, or by the sudden arrival of guests, or unexpected demands from kinsmen in the village.

An attempt was made to reckon the "man-value" of the daily diet: "The average intake of each constituent of the diet per single 'man-value' per day was obtained by dividing the total amount eaten over the whole period by the total 'man-value' of the people eating the food." The reduction of the data in terms of work done in two villages by men and women of the families selected for study, though bristling with further methodological questions that cannot be overlooked in evaluating the results, throws novel light on the value of the native diet in terms of an ideal caloric supply. The findings are given on p. 292.

Though interpretations of these data must await more comparative materials, their significance for the study of the problems with which we are concerned is obvious. How essential work can be carried on in the face of the dietary deficiencies indicated in the table given above is a problem that naturally arises, but to this question there seems at the present to be no answer. The explanation should be noted that

> . . . while some of the hardest agricultural work of the men

—the clearing of the bush—takes place during June, July, August and September, the most plentiful months of the year as regards food, yet the heavy hoeing of the old millet gardens before planting them with ground-nuts, and the re-hoeing of the village beds, should take place in the rainy months when food is short. During the season under observation there was no doubt that this work was insufficiently done, and the productivity of the gardens consequently diminished, and less ground put under cultivation.

CALORY INTAKES AND REQUIREMENTS

Village	Family	Calory intake per man-value per day	Calory requirement per man-value per day	Intake as a percentage of the requirement
Kasaka	A	2,293	3,200	72
	B	3,164	3,300	96
	C	1,685	3,460	49
	D	1,440	3,280	44
	E	1,725	3,350	52
Kampamba	A	941	3,190	30
	B	2,510	3,160	79
	C	2,181	3,010	73
	D	1,544	2,970	52
	E	1,508	2,960	51
	F	2,642	3,120	85

The relation between adequacy of food and the energy displayed by the people is reflected in the small number of dances held during the rains, the manner in which "the children sit still instead of playing noisy, singing games," and the way "men lie about idly waiting until the evening meal late in the day." [19] It even affects the psychological "set" which this people have toward situations in which control of their economic needs is involved:

> In a society in which people regularly expect to be hungry annually, and in which traditions and proverbs accustom them to expect such a period of privation, their whole attitude toward economic effort is affected. In some primitive tribes it is considered shameful for an individual or a whole community to go hungry. It is something unexpected, and to

[19] Richards and Widdowson, 174–8, 188–90.

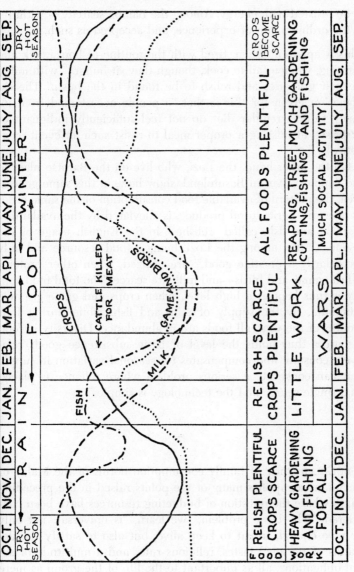

3. *Seasonal Variation in Food Resources of the Lozi (after Gluckman, 1941, p. 19).*

be resisted with energy. Among the Bamba scarcity is within the ordinary run of experience, and accepted as such.

This is apparent when, tired with the routine of housework and farming, women fail to cook, though they sit hungry "with millet in their granaries and relish to be found in the bush." The explanation given for this is that "a people accustomed from infancy to an irregular diet do not feel sufficiently indignant or surprised at missing a proper meal to resist such an event energetically." [20]

On the other hand, the Lozi, who live on the Barotse plain of the Zambesi river in Basutoland, show how, in this same general area, the pattern of available food consumption of the same order as concerns agricultural produce, is alleviated by the availability of meat and fish, called "relishes" in the English usage of the region. Cattle, among the Lozi, being a food resource and only secondarily a prestige good,[21] are utilized, when other proteins —fish, game, and birds—and milk are scarce. The total food supply is thus kept at a high level, when crops and game are at a minimum, by the supply of milk and fish, while during four months of the year, all foods are in abundance. Diversity in food resources thus holds the level of basic subsistence goods relatively constant and compensates for seasonal variation in supply that can constitute a serious problem where reliance is placed on a single source and the technology is simple.[22]

7

A DETAILED study of family consumption norms of the Malay of Kelantan exemplifies many of the points raised in the preceding pages where the question of budgeting resources have been considered. "The basic problem," we learn, "is universal: not only to have enough to eat to keep alive, but also to satisfy the demands of personal tastes, religious rules and a multitude of social obligations, all as important to the life of the group as mere subsistence is to the life of the organism."

This demands varied employment of resources in terms of the wants that are felt:

[20] Richards (1939), 37, 105.   [22] Gluckman (1941), 18–19.
[21] See above, 264–5.

The degree of knowledge, skill and energy, combined with the relative valuation by the individual of personal and social needs, will determine the extent to which the problem of managing resources is efficiently solved. In different conditions, the different "pulls" of demand will take a different strength and direction. But the reasons which underlie this can be analyzed. Different conceptions of housekeeping are not haphazard, accidental, due entirely to stupidity or avarice. They are the result of different social evaluations of time, leisure, hospitality, display, tradition, initiative, and a host of other considerations. The resulting pattern of behaviour, in conjunction with the level of resources determined on the productive side, results in the standard of living of a people.[23]

It is in these terms that the expenditures of the families of the fishermen studied must be considered, together with "the considerable choice in details of consumption" of these units, which none the less can be seen as "conforming broadly to certain patterns of consumption." This is at once apparent in the graphic presentation of the seven groups of " main items of daily expenditure" based on detailed tabulations gathered in the course of field research, and reproduced on the following page.

These are the standard expenditures. In addition there are various "non-recurrent" items—soap, needles, clothing, and the like, calling for "negligible" amounts and "ceremonial payments and gifts," which are anything but negligible. These are classified as private and public obligations. The former are to finance the expenditures that mark the "crisis rites"—birth, death, marriage, and circumcision. As in other societies where the margin of income over subsistence needs is slight, these are financed by contributions from others. This, however, is reciprocal, and merely means that costs are spread over a considerable period before a feast, when a backlog of reciprocities is built up, and afterwards, when initial gifts are returned in equivalent amounts. Gifts given are characteristically greater than expenditures on a given occasion—one wedding which produced $295 in cash contributions and some $60 worth of rice cost $190, leaving a balance of about $165. "This of course," we are told, "is really only a

[23] Rosemary Firth, iii–iv.

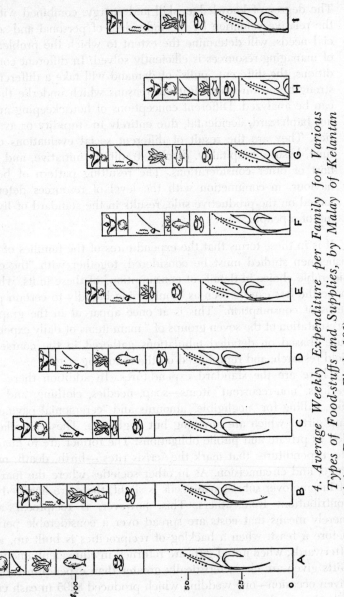

4. Average Weekly Expenditure per Family for Various
Types of Food-stuffs and Supplies, by Malay of Kelantan
(after Rosemary Firth, 181).

realization of assets, and a mortgaging of the future." The advantage comes through the command of a surplus, which even if only temporarily in the possession of an individual, can be used to acquire land or to buy a boat or fishing net. But his obligation remains, and it is noteworthy that "the future prospects of the host are a definite factor in the consideration of the guest in deciding how much to give."

Public ceremonial obligations are incurred on Moslem feast days. Thus during Ramadan, the daytime fasts are offset "by indulging in mighty meals all night," when commodities, the price of which goes up for the period, are consumed. At the end of the month, there is a three-day holiday, when visits are exchanged, pilgrimages to the graves of ancestors are made, and presents of cakes are given friends. On another holiday, celebrating Mohammed's journey to Mecca, "the ideal is for a family to have a share in a bull to be killed ceremonially, the flesh of which is to be given away to the poor or, more usually, either divided raw among friends and relatives or eaten at a party to which guests are invited." Still another occasion is a religious holiday on which a group of people prepare a special kind of pudding for distribution.

Here, as in Africa, the yearly round has periods of plenty and those when resources are scarcer. Yet as far as the fisherman of this region is concerned, "with perhaps a few exceptions, he is not, even during the difficult period of the monsoon" when fishing cannot be carried on, "living on the margin of subsistence." His diet is fairly well balanced at all times; "from the point of view of nutrition, . . . it seems probable that the fisherman's family enjoys a diet which at most times of the year is sufficient for the energy needs of the people, not too unvaried, and, prima facie, not badly balanced." [24]

[24] Ibid., 76, 127, 129, 131, and *passim*.

CHAPTER XIII

CAPITAL FORMATION

THE PRODUCTIVE activities of men are directed toward one of the two possible ends of the economic process that have been set forth, with various phrasing, by economists. The first is the production of consumption goods, such as food, clothing, and other commodities that provide subsistence wants, or those goods that fill psychological needs and validate social status. The second end is the making of what has been termed by Marshall auxiliary or instrumental capital,[1] by Ely production goods,[2] and by Seligman productive capital,[3] which in non-mechanized societies would include implements such as hoes, knives, nets, traps, canoes, forges, looms, and similar instruments to further production. Goods in this second category, moreover, can be further subdivided. The expenditure of labor on larger group projects such as terraces, temples, irrigation ditches or on roadways—"public works," that is—can be distinguished ethnologically, if not from the point of view of economic theory, from the tools and other production goods employed by individuals.

Whatever divisions may be marked off, we must always guard against drawing hard-and-fast lines in making our classifications or arbitrarily assigning a given good to any single category, where differentiations in form and function are as generalized as we have found them to be in non-industrial economies. Food clearly falls in the first class, whether grown to be eaten by the individual cultivator and his family or as a response to patterns of prestige in terms of which a large proportion of a crop will have no other use than to be displayed so as to acquire an intangible good, prestige. A hoe, on the other hand, though it

[1] Marshall, 75.
[2] Ely, 110.
[3] Seligman, E. R. A. (1905), 313.

would seem to fall equally clearly in our second class, may take on a sacred character and have lavished on its blade and handle all the ornamentation that can go into embellishing sacred objects, thus defeating its primary aim, since it can probably never be productively employed, and making of it a prestigeful consumption good.

Unlike the study of consumption norms, capitalization of effort has had wide discussion, although it has perforce been directed toward a specialized variety of the phenomenon, one which is largely inapplicable to non-pecuniary societies. Early in the history of economics the term "capital" came to have the restricted meaning not only of those tools and other means of production, but also of the investment resources controlled by an individual called a "capitalist." The returns on this man's investment, the reward for his abstention from immediate enjoyment —that is, consumption—of whatever resources were available to him, were called "profits" if his participation in an industry was direct, or "interest" if it was indirect. This return was thus equated with that earned by the worker for his expenditure of energy, or by land in reason of its value; and thus no concepts are more fundamental to economics than those comprised in the triad "land, labor, and capital," the resources of a people, and its companion triad "rent, wages, and interest," the corresponding return for each.

From the point of view of economic theory, the question of capital formation can in principle, and for any society, be approached in various ways. In the final analysis, all capital derives from the interplay of the factors of labor and available resources that, in a given economic system, provide for the needs of living, and by diverting a certain proportion into production rather than consumption goods, further the processes of maximizing satisfactions.

The classical economists envisaged this in terms of the denial of present satisfactions so as to achieve future gain. As Adam Smith put it,[4] "Capitals are increased by parsimony, and diminished by prodigality and misconduct." In a pecuniary economy, this means the investment of savings in the term of money in permanent installations and production goods that will yield to the investor return on his capital, while providing the society as

[4] Adam Smith, 321.

a whole with more consumption goods that result in raising the standard of living. This theory dominated most of the earlier capitalization of resources in the industrialized countries of Europe and America. And it is not without interest, in terms of intellectual no less than of economic history, to speculate on the degree to which this same theory, taken over from the classical economists, in modified form, by Karl Marx and from him by the economists of the Soviet Union and other countries wherein communism prevails, may not underlie the various "Plans" that have been instituted there. It is equally interesting to observe the reflex of these back into the planning that has come to mark the operations of large-scale private and governmental enterprises in capitalist economies.

Another approach to the problem of capitalization is the Keynesian attack, which envisages the development of capital in terms of the utilization of the continuing pool of unemployed labor-power that marks the large-scale industrialized production system in the pecuniary machine economies of contemporary capitalist societies. Because of its striking departure from earlier positions in its underlying assumptions and in its implications for the formulaton of economic policy, it has been the subject of much controversy. Like all of Keynesian theories, however, this one is specifically oriented toward the problems of the society out of which it has grown. It has little relevance for the non-pecuniary, non-machine societies with which we are here concerned. For, as has been amply demonstrated, the utilization of available man-power in such societies presents no difficulty. Unemployment, in the sense of the term as used in the industrialized economies of the historic world, is almost literally unknown.

A third approach, which similarly stems from the conception of deriving capital accumulation out of excess labor power, envisages an economy in which the production of consumption goods—food, clothing, and shelter, let us say—requires less than the total labor available to the society. In this case, capital goods can be acquired by the society if this surplus labor is diverted away from the subsistence activities, where its utility is negative, toward other forms of work. This is the mechanism that has been in operation where technological change has made for greater efficiency in the production of subsistence needs and has thus released labor-power to be applied in the making of capital goods.

Something of a combination of the first and third of these alternatives is to be seen in the economies of nonliterate people; here as elsewhere, however, the generalized nature of the institutions in such cultures preclude the degree of fineness in differentiation that characterized the analysis of those in literate, pecuniary, and industrial cultures. This is apparent in Firth's discussion of Tikopean economics, where he comments on a "marked feature" of this system, "the ease with which many goods ordinarily used for direct consumption are converted into goods used for production and vice versa." He illustrates this in the following passage:

Pandanus mats used for sleeping purposes, and bark-cloth, used for blankets and clothing, are employed to facilitate the production of such articles as canoes, troughs and sinnet cord; food, both cooked and raw, and food-plants such as coco-nuts, are essential elements in the maintenance and reward of producers. On the other hand sinnet cord, used in fishing and for the lashing of canoe and house timbers, and wooden bowls, used in the preparation of food, are sought and accumulated for transfer in large amounts on such nonproductive occasions as funerals, marriage, and initiation ceremonies. Even such apparently fixed productive items as canoes, troughs and bonito hooks can be handed over as indemnity for services of a non-economic kind. It is as if in our society clothing, bedding and plates and dishes were poured into the productive system to pay for the making of tables, chairs, boats, and motor-cars; while on the other hand the habit of giving kitchen utensils as wedding presents were extended to embrace the presentation of ploughs and workmen's tools, and business men accumulated machinery partly for the purpose of meeting their social obligations.[5]

The factor of co-operative labor, discussed above,[6] and part-time work, enters here also. It will be remembered how, in Dahomey, the way in which those affiliated with a given forge in turn work on the iron of each fellow-member. This, in a very real

[5] Raymond Firth (1939), 237-8.   [6] Ch. IV, Section 4, *passim.*

sense, compounds the combined productive ability of the individual members of the group by making for a greater degree of smoothness of operation and presumably a greater production of the hoes that are so important a form of production good in the native economy. More than this, however, is the fact that about one-fourth of the time and effort of each worker actually goes for the production of subsistence goods, one day of each four-day week being given over to agricultural and other similar work. The rationale for this is religious; it is believed that on the day sacred to Gu, the deity of iron, the forge must rest. This frees the iron-worker for these other tasks and, from the point of view of the total economy, feeds the labor-power he expends on that day back into the production of primary consumption goods. This subtracts by so much from that part of the whole his labor-power contributes in extending the capital resources of the total economy.

The question of capitalization of resources in nonliterate societies has in part been given little attention for much the same reasons advanced to account for the lack of data concerning their patterns of consumption, and in part because of the direction of anthropological interests toward other aspects of group life than its economic phases. Especially important, again, is the absence in these societies of a ready measure of value. Lacking this, almost any approach not wholly qualitative presents ever-present problems of method which are formidable in scope and have, as far as detailed analysis is concerned, yet to be solved. Our discussion here, therefore, will be focused essentially on problem, though such data as are available will be utilized.

2

If we probe some of the implications of the conceptual triad of land, labor, and capital, with their postulated returns of rent, wages, and interest on profits, added reasons will become apparent why students of non-pecuniary economies have been reluctant to become enmeshed in what appears to be a resulting dialectic. It should be evident that no society exists where all of these three—land, labor, and capital—are not found, where any of the three, indeed, can conceivably be absent. That land is basic to production is too obvious to need elaboration; its importance as property will be treated in the next section of this book. Labor is equally fundamental, no matter how idyllic the mode of life. As for capital, there is no people who live so close to nature that they do not employ tools of some sort—the definition of man as a "tool-using animal" will be remembered—and consequently, at least to that degree, the phenomenon of capitalization is present. Moreover, it is only the poorest cultures where more permanent works are not found, and instances are not lacking where even the more specialized use of the term "capital" can be applied, as has been demonstrated in the discussion of credit and interest in those nonliterate societies where money capital is present.

Since land, labor, and capital are ever-present forces in non-industrialized economies, it is apparent that they must yield some returns. The question for the economic theorist thus concerns the extent to which these returns can be classified in prescribed manner and under approved headings. Examples will be encountered where rent, as such, is charged for the use of land. Wages have been found in the form in which they are known in Euroamerican society—a definite pecuniary return, or specified pay in kind, for work performed for another person over a given period of time. Interest exists as return on loans, and profits as the reward for an investment of labor or wealth, or both, in goods destined for the market. But nearly all such examples can be regarded as exceptional among nonliterate peoples. Even where they are found, it is often only by compressing the data into the mold of concepts derived from economic theory that any recognizable resemblance to the rent, the wages, the interest, or the profits of the industrialized economies of Europe and America can be extracted.

Most peoples recognize the boundaries that are indispensable adjuncts to any system of land tenure; but it will be seen [7] how private property rights in land—individual ownership—is a rarity. No land-hunger exists, and there is thus no reason to lay stress on private ownership; land is customarily held for use only, with the title theoretically vested either in the group as a whole, or in a headman as its representative and responsible head. What, then, of rent? Should it be said that the grain a man

[7] Pp. 331–70 below.

harvests from the field he has worked represents his return from his land, and hence is to be regarded as rent? Or is this a return for his labor, and thus his wages? Or is it yet but a kind of interest on "that particular form of capital" which it constitutes "from the point of view of the individual cultivator," [8] the man who has improved the land by working it? Furthermore, in the matter of wages, is the feast given by a man for whom co-operative work is performed to be looked upon as payment to those who, by expending their labor, have helped a neighbor? That this, as most instances of what can conceptually be classified as wages in nonliterate societies, is rather a return for incidental work than the major instrument for obtaining a livelihood is theoretically aside from the point. But what of the fact that this feast is but a part of a reciprocal agreement?

Similar considerations must be kept in mind when we try to apply to non-industrialized economies the current concepts of capital and its return. Granted that the tools of a worker constitute his capital in such cultures, or that an irrigation ditch, a more permanent improvement of the land, represents a capital investment of the combined effort of the community that has made it, how shall the return be classified? When the iron-worker uses bellows, hammer, and anvil on which he has lavished hours of labor, is his gain from the goods he produces to be regarded as a return on capitalized investment, or a reward for labor? When the members of a community come to have at their disposal additional quantities of food because they have dug an irrigation ditch, is this interest, or a kind of rent, or wages? To show how data from nonliterate cultures must be distorted to make them fit into the matrix of concepts developed from the study of our complex society, we need but cite one example where this has been tried. Thurnwald maintains that "the increase of cattle . . . suggested the idea of productive possessions and of interest on capital. Similar conceptions apply to the possession of a wife." [9] But he is obviously applying concepts to a situation where, in terms of the culture concerned, they have no applicability.

In a few studies of nonliterate groups, the phenomenon of capitalization has received a somewhat more explicit treatment. Thus, among the Popoluca of Eastern Mexico "essential" capital

[8] Marshall, 535.   [9] Thurnwald (1932b), 205.

goods are listed as "machetes, axes, chahuaste (a flat-bladed cultivating tool), gunny sacks, rope, crude pack saddles, bows, arrows, fish-nets, hatchets, guns, powder, shot, carrying nets, and pocket knives." [10] Later, other items, such as digging sticks, fences, and pack animals are added to the list. Yet even in an economy as little complex as this, the question of category presents itself:

> Food on hand for family consumption offers no problem. But take the case of 1000 kilos (or whatever the exact figure is) of beans in the store house of Fidel Hernandez. His family will consume 100 kilos, and these obviously are not to be classed as capital. The remaining 900 kilos will be converted into clothing, flashlights, axes and other items he is unable to produce directly, and thus should be classed as capital. It is clear that many Populuca items, as Western items, are fluid, and constitute capital depending on how they are used." [11]

Or, again, we may turn to the Kwakiutl of the Northwest Coast of North America, whose "plane of living," we are told "was one of the highest of any North American Indian group." Though known best for the dramatic ceremonies of the potlatch wherein wealth was redistributed or destroyed, it is apparent that their daily life had no lack of support. "They were wealthy not only in the material necessities of everyday living, but also in the possession of numerous objects, tools, utensils, houses and canoes. . . ." The interplay between natural and human resources and capital equipment is made apparent in a further statement: "Although Kwakiutl wealth was closely related to the great natural wealth of the region in which they lived, it was actually produced by their magnificent technical and artistic virtuosity and by their unusual energy." Food-getting techniques, especially those employed in fishing, were numerous and, together with modes of gathering wild foods, produced surpluses, to retain which different techniques of storage were used.

Texts gathered from the Kwakiutl by earlier students have been drawn on by Codere to make up a list of the "economic activities" of this people. Fifty-one "industries" are listed, such as making dishes, boxes, and other objects used in caring for food

[10] G. M. Foster (1942), 16.   [11] Ibid., 39–40.

or storing it, and the manufacture of canoes, paddles, sails, traps, nets, hooks, and other items employed in fishing, in addition to various techniques of obtaining and preserving food-stuffs. These give some indication of the capitalization of effort and resources required to produce the goods needed for carrying on the seasonal subsistence and prestige economies of this society. And this is made even more evident by the fact that "the Kwakiutl definition of an economic activity was the making of a single product or tool with specialized planned functions, or the procuring of a single natural product, often, as the presence of specific storage techniques and containers indicated, in anticipation of a storable surplus." [12]

It is revealing of the problem inherent in studying capital formation, use, and return on investment in societies such as the preceding one and those a part of the larger economic system of the literate world, to compare the preceding data with those gathered among the Malay peasant fishermen of the states of Kelantan and Trengganu. With a well-defined industry, having capital investment paid for in money, strictly speaking, with returns computed on the basis of a catch sold for export, the precision that derives from analyses based on an instrument of this kind for measuring value can be achieved. Variation within the society in terms of individual control of capital goods can be assessed; the distribution of available resources between different courses of action studied, and returns computed. Here, however, we enter the area of economic history and economic analysis in the customary sense. We are at that point on the continuum that stretches from non-pecuniary economies to those of the literate, industrialized peoples where the circumstance of culture-contact intervenes to create problems of a character not envisaged in the terms of reference of this work. [13]

3

THE INADEQUACY of the data concerning capital goods in nonliterate societies thus remains to plague the student, rendering it difficult, when considering them, to know just when a given

[12] Codere, 4–5, 14–20.   [13] Raymond Firth (1946), 126–183, and *passim*.

object may be classified as a capital good. There is little question that the irrigation ditches of the Pima Indians, for example, represent capitalization of effort and were so viewed by native opinion, however ambiguously phrased. "When a tract was newly brought under irrigation a committee of six men was chosen to make allotments to those who had assisted in digging the ditches," and the right to use this productive land was thus held to be a reward for the effort put into constructing the improvements on it.[14] If, however, we turn to a list of the "domestic implements and utensils, fire sticks and yam sticks, huts and shelters," of the Australian aborigines of Queensland, and ask which of these are capital goods and which are merely secondary consumption goods, the problem becomes much more complicated:

1. Elongated wooden trough
2. Native chisel (of wood with flint blade)
3. Native cementing substance
4. Water-bags
5. Dilly-bags
6. Grind-stones
7. Pounding stone
8. Fire-sticks (2 kinds)
9. Yam-stick
10. Huts and shelter (3 kinds) [15]

Perhaps the first two items, the fourth to seventh, and the ninth and tenth might be classified as one or another possible type of capital goods; but the other two are patently consumption commodities.

What may be learned of the incidence of capital goods in nonliterate societies is probably best to be inferred from discussions and descriptions of material culture and technology. Some idea can in this way be had of what a people possess and, in some cases, what the productive effort of the group has accomplished in the way of public works. This is to be seen in the elaborate listing of material culture traits that has been made for one of the peoples of the North American sub-arctic, the Ingalik of the lower Yukon River, a Northern Athapaskan group. Three hundred and thirty-three items manufactured by this people are described. These include, first of all, primary tools, such as knives, awls, adzes; lines of sinew, bark and grass; containers; and such

[14] Russell, 87–8. [15] Roth (1897), 101.

things as fire-drills, stretchers, and wood pestles. Then come weapons; fishing implements; snares, deadfalls, and other traps; clothing; shelters, caches, and racks; items incident on travel, from bridges to boats; dyes and paints. Forty-nine of the total number of items comprise toys and games, dyes and paints, puberty paraphernalia, and objects used at funerals and for religious ceremonies. Of the items in the classifications given above, perhaps fifty more might be queried as to their inclusion in a list of capital goods—objects such as labret plugs, nose beads, soap, medicine, and the like. The culture is one of the "simpler" ones, being based on hunting, fishing, and food-gathering. It is not without significance to realize that, in such a culture, two-thirds of the material objects produced by the people are in the nature of instruments which further the production of basic necessities of life and promote physical survival. But only by inference does such a fact help solve the problems raised when questions concerning the capitalization of resources are under consideration.[16]

There is little point in reproducing here any of the numerous other listings of material goods, instruments of production, and public works such as can be found in almost any ethnographic work, inasmuch as, lacking their economic setting, relatively little would be gained by doing so. It can be shown, for example, that tribes living in more favorable environments, or having complex technologies or with relatively extensive human resources, produce more goods and have more to show for the labor of their members in the way of means of further production and of permanent structures than other peoples who live in less favorable settings, or whose technical equipments are simpler, or whose populations are smaller. It would not be unprofitable, indeed, to compare from this point of view two such lists of the goods produced by groups living in different parts of the same general area, both of which have been studied by the same competent student. These detail the elements in the material culture of the inhabitants of the small South Sea island of Tongareva, where resources are comparatively slight and economic organization is comparatively simple, and of Samoa, which has a large population, a highly developed social structure, and a more favorable

16 Osgood, *passim*.

environment.[17] But even were this done, we should then only be enlightened on the very general points just mentioned, while of the many further important problems arising out of the presence and use made of these goods and the manner of their control, such an exercise would tell us almost nothing.

At some future time, it is to be hoped, students who stress the economics of capitalization in nonliterate societies will turn their attention to these tribes whose technological basis of production and whose material equipment is well known. Building on these essential data, they may then proceed to investigate the problems arising from the fact that these folk have invested their labor-power in more or less long-lived goods. Until this is done, however, the incidence and significance of capitalization in non-industrial societies can be discussed only in terms of problems to be studied and of possible procedures to be followed, as has been the case in this chapter. This much, nevertheless, we can say: once such data are collected and made available, there is little doubt that they will provide comparative materials that will enrich our understanding of comparable processes in our own economy.

[17] Hiroa (1932), *passim;* (1930), *passim.*

PART IV

PROPERTY

CHAPTER XIV

THE PROBLEM
OF OWNERSHIP

WE HAVE thus far been concerned with the dynamics of the economic systems in nonliterate societies, especially as these manifest themselves in their productive and distributive mechanisms. At this point, however, we must shift the focus of our attention from process to institution. We therefore move, first of all, to the analysis of those concentrations of wealth which, as property, are based on what is produced. These concentrations, in their functional role, reflect the utilization by the community of goods and services either for ends determined by all its members, or for ends dictated by those to whom, consciously or through traditional usage, this task is delegated.

The realism of the anthropological approach to economic phenomena is best seen in the very fact that, in the study of comparative economic systems, both processes and institutions must receive consideration. Here, too, the underlying unity in the interests of analytical and institutional economists becomes apparent. For in the detachment gained through the study of the economic life of non-industrial societies it becomes clear that economic institutions are everywhere the end result of economic processes, while processes must be studied the better to comprehend those institutions that develop out of their operation.[1] In the analysis of our own economy, it is possible—though according to institutional economists not desirable—to take the end result of the processes of production and distribution as these affect the non-economic phases of social life, which are more or

[1] Knight (1924), 258, 259-60.

less taken for granted. These economic by-products are thus either disregarded or are accorded only cursory mention. In the
case of nonliterate economies, this is not possible. For even
though the cultural matrix is well in hand, no clear picture can
be gained of economic organization unless we know both the
means taken by peoples to get a living and to produce what
wealth they may have, and the manner in which the disposal of
this wealth influences the form and operations of institutions
which, in turn, affect the life of a given group.

2

THE DIVERGENCE in focal concerns between anthropologists and
conventional economists is nowhere more immediately discernible than in those problems that cluster about the concept of
property. From the point of view of economists whose concern
is with economic processes as they may reveal economic laws,
property, as such, is too static a phenomenon, too much the result of an interplay of forces the majority of which are non-economic, to be of any great interest. Some attention is occasionally
paid to hypothetical "stages" through which the evolution of the
institution of ownership is assumed to have reached its present
forms. More commonly, however, when property is discussed in
the orthodox textbooks, it is treated merely as an end result of the
disposal of those goods whose accumulation is a phase of the
processes of production, distribution, and exchange. The problems of property, being essentially legal, sociological, or ethical,
are more often ignored than not. Economists, it is true, do devote
some attention to the questions of how the ownership and use
of producers' goods affect further production, or how the drive
toward the accumulation of wealth influences distribution and
exchange. But the orientation of such discussions toward these
phenomena is almost invariably to consider them as phases of
production, or distribution, or exchange, and is generally not related to the study of property as such.

This orientation is the more evident when we examine definitions and discussions of property, of which the following may be
taken as an example: "Property and wealth are respectively the
personal and impersonal, the legal and the economic, aspects of

productive agents." In another passage of the same text we read: "Property is ownership, the legal control over the sources of economic income." The discussion of the phenomenon thereupon proceeds to analyze further the legal aspects of ownership and ethical considerations inherent in statements such as: "Property rights must meet the test of social expediency." [2] That is to say, what is held to be of interest to economists in this aspect of social life is the production of wealth, the manner in which it is distributed among the members of a community, the use to which such resources as individuals may acquire are put, under existing sanctions, and the further productive or distributive or consumptive activities that result from this process of accumulation. By the same token, economists are not concerned with such matters as the sanctions themselves, or the manner in which the holding of wealth may influence the social structure as a whole, or the far-reaching political, religious, and artistic consequences that may issue from the varied concentrations of wealth in the hands of individual members of a given society.

The anthropological position, on the other hand, lays emphasis on the very factors that least interest the majority of economists who have treated of property. The logic of this is inescapable. The forms which social definitions of property may take are so manifold, the bases on which ownership of wealth may be sanctioned are so varied, and the modes of ordaining the use of property are so different that the description of these facts is essential if we are to be provided with a setting that will enable us to see the institution in its proper perspective. This is why the approach most frequently encountered in anthropological discussions of property, whether among a particular people or as it exists in the nonliterate world in general, is so often purely descriptive. This is also why anthropological interest in the institution of property has been so largely dictated by its close relationship to the social structure under which it exists.

Lowie,[3] whose consideration of property has considerably influenced anthropological thought concerning the value of studying property in nonliterate societies, sets the tone when he states

[2] Fetter, 361–3, 370.
[3] Lowie (1920), 205 ff. In a rewriting of this earlier work (1948), Lowie discusses the problem in somewhat less rigid terms, but in no way revises his basic point of view enough to invalidate what is stated here.

that "notions of property tinge every phase of social life." This sentence is found at the outset of a chapter on property in a volume which, appropriately enough for the point being made here, is devoted primarily to the analysis of the forms of human social life and thus is entirely outside the literature of economics. The need to assess the validity of the hypothesis that "the transmission of property has been a potent factor in the creation of sib organization" is indicated as the immediate reason for the inclusion of the discussion at all in the volume, and this point of view is reflected throughout the pages devoted to land tenure and the ownership of material and non-material goods, and, as might be expected, to modes of inheritance. The question whether or not wives are to be regarded as property is examined in the light of this theoretical postulate; and the problem of the existence or non-existence of "primitive communism" is considered from the same point of view.

Schmidt, who has devoted a volume to the forms of property in what he terms the "simplest" societies—the *Urkulturen*—makes his analysis from a point of view which would more nearly approach that of an institutional economist than does that of Lowie. More elaborate in its treatment, and stressing psychological, sociological, and religious factors in ownership, he nevertheless gives in each case something of the environmental setting of the cultures he considers, and of the manner in which these folk, with their meager technological equipment, go about obtaining their living.[4]

To round out our discussion, the position of the institutional economists should at this point be examined. Commons makes very plain the importance of the study of property and ownership for those who follow this approach when he says:

Going back over the economists from John Locke to the orthodox school of the present day, I found that they held two conflicting meanings of wealth, namely: that wealth was a *material* thing, and again that it was the *ownership* of that thing. But ownership, at least in its modern meaning of intangible property, means power to *restrict* abundance in order to maintain prices; while the material things arise from power to *increase* the abundance of things by efficiency of

[4] Schmidt, W., *passim*.

production, even in overproduction. Hence, ownership becomes the foundation of institutional economics, but material things are the foundations of the classical and hedonic economics, whose "corporeal" meaning of property was equivalent to the material thing owned.

Later in the same work we find passages that, especially germane to the point under consideration, clarify and extend this point of view. Thus at one point we read: "The term 'property' cannot be defined except by defining all the activities which individuals and the community are at liberty or are required to do or not to do, with reference to the object claimed as property." At another, we find the statement: "Property is not only a claim but is also a conflict of claims to whatever is scarce, but rights of property are the concerted action which regulates the conflict." [5]

Hamilton and Till analyze the concept of property in these terms:

A creature of its own intellectual history, the word belongs to a culture, to a society, and to a vocabulary. The hazard of reading the associations of the word into the subject of inquiry constantly attends its use; at best it is a darkened glass wherein to exhibit passing systems of ownership. . . . About every great need—food, sex, work, parade, worship, defense—a group develops its own unique ways of accomplishment. Such usages endow object and office with worth and fix the conditions under which wealth may be appropriated. In essence property is a conditional equity in the valuables of the community.

They observe that "if the word is to be employed away from home, property must be exalted into an abstraction," something which entails great difficulty, since one must "find the least common denominator for a series of facts which sprawl across diverse societies." Anthropologists, to be sure, would ask for a qualification of the over-emphasis of these students on the tribe as "an overgrown family rather than a state in microcosm," and would take exception to the assumption that "the compulsion of blood makes the terms 'public' and 'private' singularly inappropriate when applied to ownership in primitive societies." They

[5] Commons, 4–5, 74, 303.

would, however, turn with renewed approval to another definition of the concept offered in the same discussion: "Among different peoples personal and communal rights are put together after
many patterns; but, always and everywhere, property is an accepted medley of duties, privileges, and mutualities." [6]

The institutional approach is thus seen to underscore the cultural determinants of a non-economic nature that, together with
economic causes, result in the great variety of practices and attitudes toward ownership found in human societies the world
over. In practice, however, stress is laid on the study of forms of
the phenomenon taken in one civilization, our own. Yet it must
be emphasized that the understanding of economic institutions
can only be enhanced by ranging all types of economies. Such an
attack will fill in the canvas of human economic effort, just as
the study of institutions themselves gives point to the analysis
of the economic processes that have brought them into existence
and make for their continuation.

3

FAILURE to recognize the fact that in the course of its development every society has devised a special mold in which to cast
its traditions of ownership is one of the primary reasons for the
misunderstanding of the nature and significance of "primitive"
property that is evidenced in the earlier works on the subject and
in most of their more modern counterparts. For here is where
the specialized technique of the anthropological field-worker
must come into play if these patterns of ownership, so widely
divergent from our own, are to be described not only in terms
that have meaning for ourselves, but also with full emphasis on
their significance for those among whom they are operative.
Firth states the difficulty in these words:

> It must be realized in considering the problem of the control
> of man over material goods that such terms as "property"
> and "ownership," which are employed to indicate a certain
> set of relationships in our own society, do not necessarily
> preserve the same connotation when applied to a native com-

munity. The essential factors in the situation—the individual, the goods, and the other members of his community—
remain unchanged, but the set of concepts by which these
are related has been formed against a different cultural background. Hence the impression that is conveyed to a European by the simple and satisfying statement that an object
is "owned" by a certain person may be entirely divorced
from reality through his ignorance of all those rights and
qualifications which to the native form an integral part of
the situation." [7]

The importance of considering the social matrix in seeking
to understand the phenomenon of property has likewise been
stressed by Hallowell. "Property, considered as a social institution," he says, "not only implies the exercise of rights and duties
with respect to objects of value by the individuals of a given
society; it also embraces the specific social sanctions which reinforce the behavior that makes the institution a going concern."
These sanctions and their operation comprise the fourth of a
series of variables "to be considered in any comprehensive view
of systems of property relations," the others being the following:
(1) "The nature and the kinds of rights exercised and their correlative duties and obligations"; (2) "The individuals or groups
of individuals in whom rights and privileges, powers, etc., are
invested and those who play the correlative roles in the whole
complex scheme of relations"; and (3) "The things, or objects,
over which property rights are extended." [8]
The flexibility of approach that is essential if we are to consider questions of property-rights in cross-cultural perspective is
to be seen in the position taken by Hogbin in discussing the
rights exercised over land by groups or by individuals on the
island of Wogeo. Explicitly stating that he has deliberately omitted all reference to "ownership," he continues:

To say that anyone "owns" land in Wogeo would in fact be
untrue, for this concept is properly applied only when the
whole context of rights is the same as in our own society.
When we hear that one of our fellow citizens "owns" a block
of ground we know exactly what is meant, since we are familiar with the various rights involved, those claimed by the

[7] Firth (1929a), 330–1.   [8] Hallowell (1943), 121–30.

community at large as well as those exercised by the individual concerned. But in Wogeo the situation is profoundly different—allotments are neither sold nor leased for rent, inheritance is more rigidly prescribed than amongst ourselves, and the conventions regarding cultivation and the location of dwellings are dissimilar. The only alternative would be to define these differences every time the expression was used . . . a method . . . both cumbersome and misleading. . . .[9]

In an essay on the development of the property concept, Hobhouse underscores the caution that must be observed when drawing on observations made even by those whose reports are based on long experience with a given people. He considers the single case of land tenure among Australian tribes. Here, first of all, such competent observers as Spencer and Gillen have stated that "there is no such thing as private property in land" among the aborigines. Yet equally competent observers, Grey and Eyre, say of the same folk that "land neither belongs to a tribe nor to a group of families, but to a single male." As one goes further into the data, it becomes apparent that both these statements are perhaps but reflections of a social arrangement that admits of either interpretation. For Howitt, who carried on studies in the southeastern part of the continent, found that here the right to hunt over land is acquired by the circumstance of having been born in a given locality. This land "belongs" to the tribesman forever—but it also "belongs" to all others who, like this individual, were born in this region, since they have the same right to hunt over it. Thus any of the numerous persons who might be questioned regarding the ownership of this particular land could rightly claim it as "his"; to the inquirer who might try to assess the situation on the basis of a less searching analysis the system of tenure might in all justice appear to be communal.[10]

The difficulty in assessing the nature of ownership among nonliterate peoples is also enhanced by the fact that custom and law are everywhere rigid in statement when compared with the elasticity of social practice actually found in a given society. This fact has provided the basis for the generalization that "ideal" culture may be quite different from behavior as actually ob-

[9] Hogbin (1939–40), 149–50.   [10] Hobhouse, 4–5.

served, or the "real" culture. Even in the study of our own ways of life this fact is often disregarded, despite the commonplace nature of the assertion that laws may be nullified in practice when they are out of line with customary behavior, or that where sanctions are accepted by a people the actual limits of permissive behavior are in practice anything but rigid. One reason why the variation in custom does not figure more prominently in the literature is that the student who is aware of the methodological problem recognizes that to perceive deviations in social behavior, he may need greater familiarity with what the people themselves regard as a proper course of action than he possesses. More often, however, the reason is merely that a nonliterate or, indeed, any foreign society presents a unified front to an investigator not alive to the tendency for behavior to vary about a sanctioned norm. If he asks about a given procedure, he is told its approved form; where this is not followed, he may either tend to identify such behavior as deviant or be satisfied with an explicit assurance that he has merely witnessed an exception.

From such rigidly formulated descriptions have sprung the conception of the extreme conservatism of "primitive" society and the image of members of a nonliterate community as composed of men and women living in a kind of cultural strait-jacket. In reality, where such an institution as property, for example, is under consideration, there are not only many interpretations possible as to what constitutes property in a given society, but even where a consensus has crystallized into law, the customary requirements of ownership may be disregarded when personal relationships, difficulties in obtaining a living, or the stresses of conflict so dictate.[11]

As an illustration of this principle of flexibility of custom in the light of legal requirements, we may consider the status of food as property among the Bushmen of South Africa. The rule in this society, recognized by everyone, is that all kinds of food, whether animal or vegetable, and water as well, are private property. This rule stands the test of usage in that one who takes food or water without the permission of the owner is liable to punishment for theft. Yet the Bushmen, it will be recalled, living in one of the harshest natural environments known to any group

[11] For a fuller discussion of these theoretical and methodological points, see Herskovits (1948), 86-8, 573-9.

of human beings, lead a most precarious existence. It is thus understandable that while the man who shoots a buck or a bird, or who discovers a terrain where vegetable food is to be gathered, is acknowledged as owner of his kill or of what he has found, he is, nevertheless, expected to share with those who have nothing. The one who is successful in the hunt, therefore, divides his kill with those who are present, but "the dividing is done by him, and the skin, sinews, etc., belong to him to be done with as he pleases." As a result, all available food, though from the point of view of customary law privately owned, is actually distributed among the members of a given group. But it would not be difficult for one cursory observer to deduce "communism" from this situation, while another, having access to different information, or merely being more legalistic in his approach, might maintain that in this primitive society considerations of private property are supreme.[12]

Another instance of variation in customary behavior may be taken from Africa—an example which, moreover, may give thought to those students of social organization who tend to attribute to the rules of property-ownership a preponderant role in originating, maintaining, and perpetuating the larger relationship groups found in many nonliterate societies. In Dahomey, West Africa, the inheritance of the spiritual qualities that give to a person his social affiliation is in the male line, and the system of relationship is thus dominated by the patrilineal principle. In this region, furthermore, as in most of Africa, ancestor-worship is an important element in the religious life. Sacrifices given by members of each relationship grouping descended from a given male ancestor to their forebears who, as spirits in the other world, continue to look out for the well-being of their descendants, thus figure prominently in the rituals of this cult. Yet not only in this part of West Africa, but elsewhere over the continent where the same descent principle obtains, the personal relationship between a man and his mother's family (to which he does not belong, and to which he is not related, from a sociological point of view) can be very close. The animals designated as sacrifices to the ancestors are contributed by the paternal descent-group and become the property of these forebears. Yet this rule of ownership is often violated in favor of the child of

[12] Schapera (1930), 148.

a woman belonging to a relationship group, when such a child visits the ancestral rites of his mother's line—to which, it must be emphasized again, he does not appertain—and takes for himself certain of the sacrifices intended for his mother's ancestors.

The explanation of this seemingly aberrant behavior, in the light of the concept of ownership of the sacrifice as related to the system of social groupings and descent, lies purely in the realm of sentiment. The ancestors are believed to be flattered when the child of a daughter, whose father's family constitutes his only legally and socially recognized affiliation, cares to notice them. Consequently the violation of customary rules of property is not only condoned but appreciated, and resentment against what would ordinarily be held to be punishable interference with goods belonging to another is changed to approbation.[13]

4

MOST discussions of property, and in particular of property among nonliterate peoples, turn on a relatively small number of questions. The nature of the institution must inevitably be a subject for clarification. Frequently, both in the older anthropological literature and in the writings of economists, the "origin" and "evolution" of property are hypothetically sketched in some form or other. As has been indicated, anthropologists are most generally concerned with the role of property in stabilizing such social groupings as the family and the clan; while, almost without exception, everyone who has discussed any aspect of the subject takes some position regarding the problem of private as against group ownership of wealth.

Hobhouse has given one of the most careful analyses of the concepts which cluster about the term "property." In the introductory sentences of his brief discussion of the topic, he enumerates the general characteristics of the institution.[14] Beginning with the broadest possible definition, that property is "to be conceived in terms of control of man over things," he points out that to meet the demands of the natural environment, man must

[13] Herskovits (1938), I, 154.   Westermarck, II, 2, Lewinski, 5-6.
[14] Hobhouse, op. cit., 6-8; cf. also

have at least some measure of control over the implements he uses to wrest his living from nature. Temporary control, however, is not a property right, for this only appears when control is not subject to challenge by others, and "a certain permanence" is assured it. In recognizing that property can exist without being private, Hobhouse is careful to utilize the concept of "common property" employed by earlier writers, under which a man and those associated with him exercise a given control "to the exclusion of the rest of the world."

It may be objected, with some justice, that this category of "common property" is used in so broad a sense that it must lead, and perhaps already has led, to confusion in the study of the patterns of ownership among nonliterate peoples no less than among ourselves. The difficulty is not serious, however, and can be met by refining the use of the terms one step further. For as it stands, there is no differentiation between "common property," representing, for example, the absolute ownership of a canoe by a group of men within some Melanesian tribe, and common ownership of land. But a tribal theory of land tenure which holds that the right to certain land is inviolate only while it is being worked or occupied, after which it reverts to the tribe for reallotment, is certainly not analogous to the absolute rights over the canoe conceded the men who own it in common. In the same way, no distinction is made under this definition between the ownership in our society of a factory by a group of partners or stockholders, let us say, and the ownership of a public park, which all members of a community may use unrestrictedly.

The term "common ownership" is thus helpful, but it is obvious that to apply it to the instances cited, either for a Melanesian society or our own, would be to violate the spirit in which the ownership of such kinds of property is conceived. We may, however, limit the term "common property" to those objects and rights jointly possessed by some restricted group within a given society, to the exclusion of the other members of this society. Under this heading, we would include not only the Melanesian canoe and our factory, but family and clan property and those things possessed by members of secret and other types of associations, whether this be clubhouse, regalia, or songs and rituals. We can then designate as "public property" that which in theory or practice is the possession of an entire people. We shall in this way give recognition to an important category of property, which, where the canons of ownership among nonliterate peoples is concerned, has far-reaching significance.

Property cannot be defined, however, without giving attention to the factor of variation in ownership which has been stressed in the preceding pages and which must be recalled here. Hobhouse fully recognizes the importance of this factor when he states that "property is a principle which admits of variation in several distinct directions." He points out that control over property

> . . . may be more or less fully recognized and guaranteed in society. It may be more or less permanent, more or less dependent on present use and possession or enjoyment. It may be concentrated in one hand, or common to many. It may extend to more, or fewer, of the purposes to which a thing may be put. But that the control may be property at all, it must in some sort be recognized, in some sort independent of immediate physical enjoyment, and at some point exclusive of control by other persons.

The concept of property may be clarified further by making more explicit than does Hobhouse certain of its connotations in the various societies in which it is found, and in the different types of goods and intangibles that constitute it. Those aspects of ownership, for example, which more than the objective fact of possession often determine whether or not a given object may be considered as property, are the privileges that accrue to an owner over his goods. Variously recognized in various societies, they may, in the broadest terms, be classed under three headings: the privilege of use, the privilege of disposal, and the privilege of destruction. In the strictest sense, ownership is conferred only when all three of these forms of privilege are enjoyed with regard to something owned, though in most societies ownership on these terms is seldom countenanced. In our own culture, there are many ways in which society, as embodied in the state, stands between a man and complete control over his possessions. Certainly no discussion of the institution as it exists in nonliterate cultures will be realistic unless it is recognized that varying degrees of totality of possession are reflected in the extent to which totality of control is permitted owners of goods or rights.

This will become apparent when the manner in which land and natural resources are held is discussed. It will be the more emphasized when, in the course of our consideration of the ownership of other types of goods, it will be necessary to inquire into the question whether or not wives are "bought" and, by that token, become the property of their husbands—a question discussed perhaps more than any other when the nature of "primitive" property is being considered.

All this is but to stress a point always to be held in mind that whatever absolute criteria of property may be set up, *the ultimate determinant of what is property and what is not is to be sought in the attitude of the group from whose culture a given instance of ownership is taken.* If this makes generalization the more difficult, the difficulty must be accepted and taken into account. For only as an institution, in conjunction with all the other institutions that comprise a given body of custom, plays its role of helping to give purpose and meaning to the lives of those who live in accord with it, does it have the cultural reality that makes it a valid object for investigation by those interested in ascertaining the forms taken by human civilization and the mechanisms that have given these civilizations their present form.

5

DESPITE the intellectual fascination of the problem of how social institutions originated, and the many speculations—all of which invite discussion—of the manner in which human beings developed the concept of ownership and the sense of property, we will not be concerned with questions of this order. For here, no less than in other segments of man's social life, to attempt to draw specifications of the first forms of property, to search out the dawn of a property sense in man through the study of forms of property in the "rude" civilizations of contemporary nonliterate man, is but an academic exercise doomed to scientific futility by the simple fact that no hypothesis of this order is subject to the ultimate test of reference to relevant data.

The ownership of wealth may have arisen from the exploitation of the weak by the strong; it may have arisen from differences in privileges possessed by the two sexes; it may be the result of differences in energy and foresight between members of the earliest human community. Or it may have been none of these; or again it may have been one of them in one part of the earth, and another in a different locality; while in still other areas it may have been any one of several combinations of these possibilities. From the point of view of modern anthropology we must be content to observe that the phenomenon is a universal one, since there is no group who live so precariously that there is not some tool, some weapon, some bit of ornament or clothing that is not regarded as indisputably the possession of its maker, its user, its wearer. We must, therefore, ascertain from the facts the variations in the institution as it exists and analyze its social and economic role.

How difficult any other approach can be is to be seen in Seagle's attempt to consider the nature and origins of property by use of the "contemporary ancestor" method, whereby the customs of living nonliterate peoples are held to constitute valid proof of early practices. Quite aside from the question of an assumed "primitive communism" which this student, like many others, purports to establish on the basis of such evidence, the question of priority is answered in a manner anything but convincing. "Even in the law of the culture peoples," he states, with what would seem to be reference to literate societies, "such an abstract conception as ownership is a relatively late development." He resolves the difficulty by suggesting that it is better "to consider the control over chattels as a phase of the law of persons rather than of property inasmuch as the chattel is considered only an extension of the person." The fallacy in this extension of the concept of the "primitive mind," arising from the extreme ethnocentrism of its conception, will be obvious and needs no further consideration here.[15]

The ubiquity of the institution of property has given rise to other explanations of it, and attempts have been made to refer the widespread nature of the phenomenon to an innate, instinctive tendency of proprietorship. This approach is understandable and persuasive. All things considered, when one is presented with a universal in human culture, there are but two explanations possible. Either the phenomenon must have been invented very

[15] Seagle, Ch. V, especially 51.

early in the history of man and diffused with him, or it must be the result of some instinctive, innate drive.

Psychological explanations of property are varied. One of the most influential was that of Letourneau,[16] who interpreted the universality of the phenomenon as evidencing a direct property-holding instinct, found in beast and man. Yet that explanations of this order are too simple was seen many years ago when, in his preface to the English translation of Laveleye's work on primitive property, Leslie said:

> Property has not its root in the love of possession. All living beings like and desire certain things, and if nature has armed them with any weapons are prone to use them in order to get and keep what they want. What requires explanation is not the want or desire of certain things on the part of individuals, but the fact that other individuals, with similar wants and desires, should leave them in undisturbed possession, or allot them a share, of such things. It is the conduct of a community, not the inclination of individuals, that needs investigation.[17]

The approach of Beaglehole was comparable to that of earlier students. He called on a kind of extension of the Jamesian concept of the "me," whereby objects outside an individual become psychologically assimilated to his personality, to explain why property is so universal in human cultures. "I think it is probably not far from the truth to suggest that personal property is, by the native, believed to be part of the self, somehow attached, assimilated to or set apart for the self," he stated. Beaglehole thus envisaged a generalized innate drive toward ownership—"a blind instinct to keep that which satisfied fundamental needs"— over which play those traditional concepts of property, found among every people, to produce the "social canalization" that results in the patterned form the institution invariably takes.[18]

It is clear that any hypothesis that is advanced concerning the drives that make for the acquisition and retention of property depends largely upon basic approach. If the fact is stressed that things are held for the specific use of the possessor, and the universality of ownership in terms of possession, whether in the

[16] Letourneau, 1–2.
[17] Laveleye, xi.

[18] Beaglehole (1932), 134, 197; see also Hoyt (1926), 73–4.

case of humans or animals, is thus emphasized, the position that an inborn "property sense" must exist will inevitably be congenial. On the other hand, the differences between the traditional modes of withdrawing some goods or natural resources from use by all members of given human groups—what may be so withdrawn, and the moral and legal aspects of this withdrawal—may be contrasted with the absence of traditional usage among animals, as evidenced by the inflexibility of their behavior. In this case, the ubiquitousness of the phenomenon recedes into the background. An instinctive basis for ownership in animals can be likened to the drive for possession in man, just as techniques of communication, found among social animals, are sometimes interpreted as being derived from another "instinct" which, in man, finds expression in language. In both of these instances, however, the relationship between the phenomenon in animals and human groups is tenuous. As far as the range of form of these phenomena in human societies is concerned, this is so broad when contrasted with their restricted manifestations in animal societies that for purposes of scientific study the hypothesis of a possible instinctive basis can be regarded as of negligible value. Indeed, as with theories of absolute origins of human institutions, acceptance, in the final analysis, rests on faith that reinforces assumption.

6

THE SOCIOLOGICAL implications of the institution of property, in so far as these impinge on the form of family or clan, will receive but limited attention in this book, despite their importance. That the relationship exists has been shown in innumerable monographic and general discussions where the interaction between property concepts and social structure have been analyzed. In this respect, the role of the canons of inheritance is of the greatest importance. The ways in which property is handed down from one generation to the next often help greatly in determining what, in a given culture, is regarded as falling in this category, and in establishing relative values for different types of property. Among a given people it may be necessary to range widely over these interrelationships to ascertain existing rules of ownership.

This, however, again involves the problem, already touched upon, of determining the form of the cultural matrix as a preliminary to studying any particular institution or process which lodges or is operative in the setting. In this general discussion, we will confine ourselves to the form of the institution of property and, except in those cases considered in the next section, where the relevance is immediate, leave to one side its ramifications in non-economic fields.

In much the same way, the question of the presence or absence of "communism" or of "private ownership," as these terms are commonly used, will only concern us in passing here. This dichotomy is soon discovered to be meaningless in the face of analyses of property relationships as they actually exist in nonliterate societies, but the vitality of the dispute is such that it will be referred to in later pages. The real importance of the controversy, which has had wide historical implications, derives from its place in political polemic; but symbols which have become slogans are blunted tools in scientific investigation. It is difficult to see how the fact of the total absence among a given tribe of private ownership of any good, should it be established, could serve as the basis of an argument to abolish individual tenure in our particular society. Conversely, the fact that everywhere individuals own some thing or things they do not share with anyone else, and are perhaps never asked to share, scarcely constitutes proof of the desirability, in our culture, of maintaining in private hands vast and far-flung enterprises or valuable natural resources.

The concepts "private property" and "communism" are too general, too heavily charged with emotional content to be anything but liabilities where scientific objectivity is sought. Our task, rather, is to obtain a sense of the variation possible in this, as in other aspects of the economic life of the folk with whom we are concerned and to seek to determine the mechanisms operative in bringing about such property arrangements as exist among nonliterate peoples. With this orientation, then, we move to a consideration of the forms taken by property in these societies and their economic significance.

CHAPTER XV

LAND TENURE:
HUNTERS, HERDERS AND
FOOD-GATHERERS

THE LAND holdings of peoples who have never developed agri-culture or herding have been carefully studied, primarily because of the challenge presented by one of the most widely accepted tenets of the older evolutionary school of social theorists, that in earliest times hunters and food-gatherers recognized no ownership of the land from which they drew their subtenance, and that not until agriculture developed was the allotment of land regularized in customary law. This proposition, however, overlooked the fact that agricultural peoples hold in common large portions of their available land—even land that is worked. Perhaps because of the inertia of the wide acceptance of this point of view, the growing body of testimony from hunting and herding tribes which went to the contrary went unnoticed for a considerable period. Eventually, however, cases presumed to be "exceptions" to the rule were given new significance by the results of research carried on among the hunting tribes of north-western North America. It then became evident that the earlier hypothesis, if not entirely untenable, needed at least to be largely revised. In this manner, the older position thus came to be almost entirely abandoned by anthropologists, though it has persisted in the writings of those not conversant with these other findings.

Because of this inertia, the facts may be reviewed here. This review, however, will hold a dual significance for us, since these facts will aid us in clarifying the economic problem of the determination of value in land and at the same time have a bearing on the more important problem of the nature of land-tenure in hunting and food-gathering economies. The materials are, of course, not of a type to permit detailed testing of the validity of such economic tenets as the role of marginal utility in determining land values, or the bases on which the return from property in land is established. These concepts, derived from pecuniary societies, are only capable of being adequately analyzed where the returns from land can be reduced to pecuniary standards. None the less, though such standards are quite lacking in societies where the level of technological achievement is simple and economic complexity is slight, certain fruitful conclusions can be reached, even where no least common denominator of value obtains.

Intra-tribally, in cultures such as those of the Great Basin area of North America or within the territorial limit of each of various tribes of Plains, land was a free good. This is made clear, in the case of the Comanche, by Hoebel's statement concerning their attitude toward the land on which they lived:

> The Comanche had no concept of land value. As herding hunters, land was a matter of unconcern for them, being held neither individually, jointly nor communally. One may merely speak of land as having been communally occupied. . . . Trespass by persons of enemy tribes meant death, unless it was a woman whom they cared to take as a captive, or unless the warrior escaped by display of cunning or bravery. "Friendlies" could visit with impunity and partake of Comanche game without danger.[1]

On the other hand, in the case of the Indians of the Pacific Northwest, where "the economic resources—fishing, hunting, and gathering grounds—pertained to the local group as a whole, titularly they belonged to individuals." The two "overlapping and apparently not well differentiated concepts of property-right" involved here are explained in the following terms:

> Characteristically, a man is said to have "owned" an economically important tract. This "ownership" was expressed by his "giving permission," as natives usually put it, to his

[1] Hoebel, 118.

fellows to exploit the locality each season. At the same time fellow-members of his local group—his relatives—had an inalienable right to exploit the tract. The present writer time and again has heard statements by informants from northwest California to Tlingit country to the effect that a certain man "owned" a particular place, for example, a fishing-site, and that his permission was required before other members of his society could use it. Nevertheless no instance was ever heard of an "owner" refusing to give the necessary permission. Such a thing is inconceivable to the natives. . . . Actually, individual ownership in these cases does not mean exclusive right of use, but a sort of stewardship, the right to *direct* the exploitation of the economic tract by the local group. The latter it was who held exclusive right.[2]

What, then, gives land its value? The emphasis of economists on the phenomena of our own culture makes their principles difficult to apply to nonliterate societies, except in the generalized form already known. Though the situation of land may figure in determining its desirability, land is rarely valued for its accessibility to a market, so important a factor among ourselves. Considerations of marginal yield constitute but a minor determinant in societies where no quantitative expression of value exists, and return in the form of rent or marketable goods is of little importance where, indeed, it is present at all. The psychological elements in land-ownership among nonliterate peoples, as among ourselves, intervene in the resolution of questions involving alienation of particular plots.[3] The emotional attachment of men to the districts where they were born and to the particular localities over which they have exercised proprietary rights, as well as magical and religious considerations, are powerful noneconomic forces that must always be taken into account.

Thus, we can see how a number of elements, among the Mexican Popoluca, enter in giving land its worth. Among this people, the value of land

. . . is expressed neither in terms of money nor any other commodity, and it is never bought, sold, or traded. This situation cannot be explained on the grounds that land, since

[2] Drucker, 59.   [3] Cf. Firth (1929a), 361–6.

it loses its fertility after several years, is of temporary value. The Popoluca are perfectly aware of the potential value of exhausted land, and jealously guard their rights to it. Good land near a village is the most valuable possession a man can have, and probably nothing another man could offer him would induce the owner to part with it. Conversely, an hour's walk usually brings a man to good land upon which he has a claim, and the possible fruits of the two extra hours a day would not be sufficient to induce him to attempt to purchase land lacking the distance handicap.

The conclusion reached by the writer of this passage will not be surprising: "This inability to give land value in terms of a market constitutes a fundamental difference between Popoluca and Western economies." [4]

Prestige may enter as a major consideration, as is seen in the canons of evaluating land among the Kalinga of northern Luzon, Philippine Islands:

Cultivated lands are either . . . irrigated rice fields, or . . . hill farms—clearings on the mountainsides that are cultivated for a year or two and then abandoned to revert to jungle and regain their fertility. The greater part of the Kalinga's wealth and that which gives the highest prestige is his irrigation systems and rice lands. Lubwagen is a wealthy region: it is said that every household has at least one rice field. The prestige value is so great a factor in boosting their price that the return is very low as compared with interest rates on money. [5]

From the point of view of a broad least common denominator of the factors entering into the evaluation of land, then, only certain points can be made, and these tentatively, awaiting their documentation. First of all, as with any type of property, land must not be a free good, if value is to be assigned to it, but some sense of scarcity must be present. In the second place, it must figure consciously in the general economic life of the people. That is, it must lend itself to exploitation, which means that labor must be expended in connection with its use, though this need not involve permanent improvements such as mark off

<hr>

[4] Foster (1942), 54–5.   [5] Barton (1949), 91–2.

farmed from uncultivated land in an agricultural community. Finally, it must yield some recognizable return, economic or psychological.

2

THE INITIAL challenge to the doctrine of communal ownership of land among hunting and food-gathering peoples was contained in the research of Speck among the Timiskaming Indians, a "modified branch of the Algonquin group of the Ojibwa" and other tribes in eastern Canada and the United States.[6] Among the Timiskaming, the social units consisted of the families that made up a given band, "individuals related by descent and blood together with other women married to men of the family." They were not only held together by membership in a common socially recognized group, but, more importantly, welded into a unit by control over a common hunting territory, which was "the main bond of union and interest."

These hunting "lots" or territories comprised well-recognized stretches of land, with natural boundary marks such as rivers, lakes, swamps, or clumps of cedars and pines. The test of trespass applied here, since it was forbidden to hunt outside one's own territory. Trespassing was either punished with death, or revenged by the use of sorcery. Permission might be given to hunt in the territory of another band, especially if reciprocity for an earlier similar permission was involved. The privilege was never permanently extended, however, and was intended only to aid friends to provide themselves with food when game was scarce in their own hunting grounds. Permission also had to be obtained if, when traveling, the land of another family had to be crossed. Where animals were killed for food by the traveler, the pelts had to be brought or sent to the owners of the land, and the reciprocal right of passage in this case became automatic. The yield of a tract was not only safeguarded by rules of trespass, but care was taken within the family to see that no more of each type of game animal was killed during a given season than could be taken and still maintain the supply.

The right to share in the family's land was inherited in the

[6] Speck (1915).

paternal line. A given hunting ground was sometimes subdivided "to adjust matters" when there were several sons, though all those who controlled these new independent territories would extend mutual privileges to those who had had the right to hunt over any of the original tract. Nevertheless, "for the most part, the territories were fairly rigid and permanent" and "only a few changes are remembered to have taken place within the range of tradition."

The limits of the hunting lands of each band were so well recognized that it was still possible at the turn of the century to map the hunting territories claimed by each family group. This represented a striking achievement, especially when it was pointed out that the tribes where this was done included, for example, the Penobscot of Maine, whose land had long since been lost to the dominant white population. In all this area the "land philosophy" was essentially the same:

> The ownership of land is not accompanied by any sense of power or prestige derived from it, either in a social or in a political way, in proportion to the size of the territories or the number of them possessed. While there is a definite belief in the ownership of the land itself, as is exemplified in the trespass prohibition, it is the game and more properly the fur-bearing game which is the ultimate motive in land ownership.

Thus in this case it was the resources of the land which gave it value, rather than its acreage, and no competitive drive to acquire more land existed, for the simple reason that "it is possible for a man to utilize in trapping only so much land."

The range of variation in size of these hunting territories, the population-density of their inhabitants, and the ratio of hunters to non-hunters has been tabulated for the Grand Lake Victoria Indians of Quebec and the Berens River Indians of Manitoba, both Ojibwa-Ottawa Algonkian peoples.[7] The consistency of the ratio of active hunters to non-hunters is striking and leads Hallowell to analyze the "controlling factors in the size of hunting territories." He points out, first of all, that "there is nothing in the economic culture of these people to motivate the accumulation of large tracts of land." In accordance with the principle stated

[7] Hallowell (1949), 39–41.

immediately above is his further explanation that "the products of the land are a primary source of wealth rather than the ownership of land in the sense of 'real estate.'" Moreover, "there is also no prestige whatsoever that accrues to the man who hunts over a large tract of land as compared with the man who traps over a smaller area." Since inheritance rules are also ruled out as a

Name of Group	Size of Hunting Grounds			Size of Hunting Group		Density of Population	
	No.	Range (sq. mi.)	Av. (sq. mi.)	Range (no. persons)	Av. (no. persons)	Range (sq. mi. per person)	Av.
Grand Lake Victoria	31	64–1716	316	2–17	5.6	13–146	55.6
Berens River	43	13–212	93	4–49	14.9	1–245	6.2

Name of Group	Ratio of Active Hunters to Other Persons					
	Active Hunters		Other Persons		Ratio	
	Range	Av.	Range	Av.	Range	Av.
Grand Lake Victoria	1–3	1.3	1–14	4.3	1:0.5–1:65	1:3.1
Berens River	1–10	3.3	2–39	11.6	1:1–1:8	1:3.5

factor in stabilizing the boundaries of land hunted over by the bands, he urges that ecological factors be brought more prominently into account than has previously been the case in seeking to understand this particular man-land relationship.

In Australia a comparable type of land-ownership existed in pre-European times among the folk who are so often cited for the simplicity of their economic system. These bands are nomadic hunters and food-gatherers, but nomadism does not mean that they are "unrestricted wanderers." Each group, in this case, as among the North American tribes studied by Speck, is divided into local units that are the counterpart of the American family hunting band. Their pattern of land tenure has been summarized, in the following terms:

1. There is a concept of actual land ownership by individuals or families.
2. A family hunting territory is enclosed by well defined boundaries.
3. Trespassing is forbidden (with certain exceptions).
4. A district is inherited from father to son.
5. Ownership is realized to such an extent that a proprietor may dispose of land as he chooses.
6. The family districts are patrilocal.[8]

Recent reports are in line with these generalizations, though they stress the variations that must be expected. The land holdings of the Murngin clans have been mapped by Warner, who emphasizes at the same time the religious and sociological sanctions of these common holdings and underscores the fact that they are inalienable.[9] The reciprocal aspect of the use of land figures prominently in the account of tenure patterns among the Daly River tribes. Among the Yir-Yoront the data, though "indicating that one of the chief functions of clan ownership is the apportionment and conservation of natural resources," also indicate that the reciprocities obtaining here are not permanent, for all the freeness with which they are granted.[10] The accounts of those who knew the life of the aborigines before disintegration had set in, of particular importance where they are in agreement, tend to substantiate the generalizations that have been cited. Even in the writings of those who do not grant the Australian a tradition of individual ownership of land are found statements, such as one that comments on the desire of natives "to die and be buried on their own inherited hunting ground." [11]

That the value of land to hunting and food-gathering peoples lies principally in its resources is made clear also from evidence on the Selk'nam of Tierra del Fuego, a people whose economic organization is likewise outstandingly simple:

Land only means something to the Selk'nam in so far as game range over it; for the special kind of existence led by

[8] Davidson (1928a), 627; (1938), 658–61.

[9] Warner, 17–19, 40, 389–90.

[10] Stanner, 403–4; Sharp, 23.

[11] Davidson (1928a), esp. 627 and n. 37, 629.

these folk and the daily round of their communal life depend on these animals. . . . It is because of this that the formula of communal tenure overlying basic private ownership can be derived.[12]

Each group, both in this tribe and in others related to it, possesses land over which it hunts and wherein members of other family groups may not hunt. The pattern of hunting territories in North America and Australia is thus also apparently found here, and the conclusion of a survey of the literature, that "the evidence is sufficient for considering the Fuegians as the possessors of a family hunting territory system very similar to that noticed for the other hunting peoples," seems valid.[13]

An analogous type of land tenure, noted for the Vedda of Ceylon even before Speck's analysis for the North American hunting tribes, is so well known that it would scarcely require mention were it not that it extends the distribution of this type of ownership to still another area. Here, too, strict tenure by families and even within family groupings is found; boundaries are recognized, and trespass is severely punished, while transfer of land and its resources, even within a family, can only be made with the consent of all members of the group.[14] In the Andaman Islands the local group "owing or exercising hunting rights over a certain recognized area" was semi-nomadic within the boundaries of the land it possessed. Trespass was forbidden; and though in some cases "boundaries between two neighboring groups were not very clearly defined," yet on the whole the pattern sketched for these other hunting folk also seems valid in this case.[15] The Punan of Borneo, nomadic hunters without crops or domesticated animals, apparently parcel out their territory in similar fashion. For though, as it is stated, they are "perpetually wandering in their exploitation of the forest," yet any given band will "commonly attach itself to an undefined general area." Similarly, each group of Malayan Negritos "has its own recognized beat or territory," outside which its members rarely move except to visit other tribes.[16]

The Bushmen of South Africa may afford a final instance of

[12] Gusinde, 424.
[13] Davidson (1928b), 410.
[14] C. G. and B. Z. Seligman, 105–15.

[15] Radcliffe-Brown, 26–7, 29–30.
[16] Hose, 40; Evans, 21.

nomadic peoples who have definite allocations of land. Here the basic grouping is what Schapera terms the hunting band which, possessing its own territory, exercises authority and has rights only within this territory. Boundaries, constituted by natural landmarks, are clearly recognized. In some cases, areas belonging to different bands may be separated by "neutral zones"— forest belts or open flats or watercourses—where no one ventures except transiently. The most important designating element of the property of a given group consists of the water-holes, the "real property of the band." In this desert land, these are jealously guarded, and trespass is here most vigorously resented and repulsed. Encampments are usually located close by, and the game that drinks at them or the wild vegetable foods that grow adjacent to them may not be hunted or gathered except by their owners.

In certain parts of the Bushman territory, there are areas over which the members of several groups may hunt at will. But even here the division of the land is not forgotten, and each band retires to its own property when the more difficult seasons set in. On the other hand, in certain Bushman groups (such as the Auen) a somewhat more restricted, almost private, ownership of land has been reported, "in the sense that when a man burns a patch of veld in order to promote the growth of veldkos (wild vegetable foods) on it, he alone has a claim to its products." Both of these are, however, special instances. In general, what may be thought of as a characteristic family hunting-band pattern,[17] that differs in no significant way from those found elsewhere in the world among hunting folk, is rather the typical form of land tenure here.[18]

3

IT IS clear, then, that among hunting peoples, common rather than communal ownership of land is the rule. It is equally apparent that among such folk land is valued not for itself, but because of the game animals or wild plants or watering-holes or other es-

[17] References to the family hunting-band system among the so-called "marginal" peoples elsewhere may be found in Cooper (1939), 80–5.

[18] Schapera (1930), 75–7, 127, 155–6.

sentials found on it. To what degree does the feeling that such natural resources constitute property persist among groups that are essentially food-gatherers rather than hunters? The data bearing on this point may be taken from western and central North America, where some of the fullest studies of land tenure among food-gathering folk have been made.

Here some tribes are found which have no sense of real property at all. Though, for instance, Klamath families do return to permanent winter encampments, their summer residences, while they may be reoccupied from year to year, are not held with any sense of vested right. Furthermore, no individual ownership of fishing places or dams exists, nor are proprietary rights recognized to hunting territories, berry or seed patches. A chief neither owns nor controls the use of fishing places, nor do those who live near the dams have any special claim to them. Those living near a dam may be asked to fish for one coming from elsewhere, but this is only because they know best how to use the site.[19]

The food-gathering, fishing, and hunting Kwakiutl of the Northwest Coast have a highly-developed sense of property in land and resources. Each relationship group (*numaym*) has its own hunters, who hunt only on their own land. When a mountain-goat hunter is caught in the act of trespassing, he may be pushed down the mountainside and killed. Each group owns its own viburnum-berry ground, and land where it alone can harvest crab apples, cranberries, elderberries, currants, huckleberries, and other food plants. The owners of such land defend their rights so strongly against trespassers that fatalities often eventuate. Salmon streams, where no non-member may fish, are likewise owned by these groups, while the right to exploit the sites best fitted for fish-traps is also reserved to members, whose possession of such localities is recognized.[20]

Among the Shuswap, important fishing grounds, berry patches, and root-digging grounds were available to all tribal members. Deer-fences were private property and could be inherited, and it was only on their abandonment that another could establish his claim by rebuilding them; eagle-cliffs were likewise privately owned and inheritable.[21] Among the neighboring Lillooet, on the other hand, "the right to fish at places where large and important

[19] Spier, 11, 149.   [21] Teit (1909), 572.
[20] Boas (1921), 1345–7.

fish-weirs were located, was considered the property of the clan that erected the weir each year." In some places carved and painted totem-poles were put up to give notice of this property right. Hunting grounds and berry patches were commonly owned, with the reservation that in the case of the latter, clan chiefs supervised the picking of berries, so that none would be taken too early in the season.[22]

The Maidu of California held that "land as such was not really owned," since its use was free to all members of a community. Though early reports are not entirely clear, "it does appear that fish-holes were sometimes owned and that fences for deer-drives could be erected in particular places only by certain families." Yurok land "of any value for hunting" was privately held as far as a mile or more back from the river along which a community lived, and in these tracts rights were strictly enforced and poachers were liable to be shot. Otherwise no claims were laid to land. Fishing rights were held jointly, and "all prolific eddies" were pre-empted, the several owners using these each in rotation for one or two days.

> It was forbidden to establish a new fishing place or to fish below a recognized one. This provision guaranteed the maintenance of the value of those in existence, and must have very clearly restricted the total number to those established by tradition and inheritance.[23]

The Southeastern Pomo restricted land-holdings to those tracts yielding vegetable food; and it was possible for Gifford to list eighty-five tracts held by families during the days of aboriginal occupation. Property rights were only exercised as far as acorn-gathering was concerned, however, and not in the case of deer-hunting, since a man might roam wherever game was to be found. Nevertheless, during the acorn season a deer-hunter refrained from trespassing on the territory of families not his own, lest he be suspected of having designs on the acorns. In flagrant cases of trespass, the culprits were set upon and beaten by the families owning the land.[24]

Such instances make it clear that societies with such simple economies as these, where private or even family tenure is otherwise absent, may, by assigning desirable land to the category of individual or common property, safeguard the exploitation of resources. In addition, these data document further the postulate that in these societies, where ownership is concerned, not land but what the land yields is important.

4

THE ANALYSIS of conditions under which land is held and used by herding peoples is limited by the fact that less is known about land tenure among such folk than among either those with hunting and gathering economies or among agricultural tribes. It is possible, and from hints here and there in the literature even probable, that the application of a concept analogous to that of the family hunting band might point the way to a more adequate understanding of their systems of ownership. As among hunting tribes, there seem to be almost no cases on record where, under aboriginal conditions, any shortage of suitable land for grazing existed in the territories of nonliterate pastoral folk. It seems too often to be taken for granted, however, that the use of all available land was free to any members of a tribe or group of tribes whose herds roamed a given region.

In pre-European times the Hottentot of South Africa valued land both as pasture and as hunting ground. "It is clear from the accounts of the early Dutch and other travellers that every Hottentot tribe in the Cape had its own territory, into which strangers might not intrude for hunting and pasture without first obtaining permission." Hottentot tribes moved about freely in search of pasturage for their cattle, and boundaries between territories were at best but vaguely defined. In Southwest Africa, where water rather than grass is the major problem, each pool or "fountain" was thought to belong to a specific people, who, however, did not refuse its use to the members of other tribes, even though the strangers might camp there for long intervals. Land was inalienable, and every member of a tribe had full right to the use of whatever tribal land he needed for himself and his family and their herds, though he might never lay exclusive claim to any portion of this territory. Among a few tribes, certain trees were considered exclusive property. A person who dug a water-hole or opened a spring made this his property, and all who wished to use it had to have his permission; but he was under obligation to see that no stranger or the stranger's stock was denied access to it. A share of a hunter's kill had to be given to the chief as compensation for having killed the game which, in theory, was held to be the property of this leader; and a certain control was exerted over grazing land by a chief who might order a given section left ungrazed for a period. The man who found a swarm of bees likewise acquired rights of ownership over the honey, but he was required to give some combs to the chief and also to guard against so disturbing a young swarm that it flew away.[25]

Among the cattle-keeping Bantu peoples of South and East Africa, who combine herding with hunting and agriculture, land tenure derives from the theory that all land is vested in the head of the tribe. In South Africa, "anybody may graze his cattle and hunt wherever he pleases" though "people living in the same area tend to assert exclusive claims over its grazing. . . ."[26] Among the Tswana peoples of Basutoland we see how this works out. Here a system of cattle-posts obtains, whereby the animals are maintained away from the villages, sometimes at distances of fifty to a hundred miles or more. They range freely, wandering about the open country in the rainy season when water is plentiful, or they are herded to wells for watering during the remainder of the year. With considerable variation in the number of cattle owned by a given individual, demands on available grazing land likewise vary. This has given rise to the role of the chief, as the instrument whereby this land is allotted, though in no case is there exclusive allocation to any individual. "At best he must share with a number of other people the pastures of the place where his cattlepost is situated, although no one else may bring his cattle there without permission." Yet occupation does give a certain prior right. Thus "if a man builds a hut or good kraals at his post, and so indicates that it is not merely for temporary use, he established a form of lien over the place, and can return to it any time. 'His ruins . . . will be there to validate his claim,' say the Tswana."

In the case of hunting, which both aboriginally and today has economic importance, tribal members may freely utilize this resource without reference to occupation or use for other purposes. There are, in most tribes, no "private hunting lands of any description. People may hunt wherever they like, even over the fields or grazing districts of others," the only restriction being that traps may not be set in the fields of another or on public roads. However, in some parts, where tributary peoples were under the charge of a member of conquering tribes, hunting preserves were known. "This man alone was . . . entitled to hunt there, with the aid of his serfs, for skins and ostrich feathers, and trespass by others could be punished. But there was no such prohibition against outsiders hunting in the area for meat." [27]

Farther north, among the Nyakusa of southern Tanganyika, "pasture, unlike garden land, is jointly owned by the whole village group and no individual has any exclusive rights to any portion of it." That is, "every member of a village has the right to graze his cattle on the village pastures," but with the reservation that "when any member of a village takes up new garden land by hoeing it he must not, in so doing, encroach unduly on the village pastures." [28] Still farther to the north, in Ankole, pasture land was so plentiful that it was free to all Bahima herders. As in Bechuanaland, however, tribesmen who dug a watering-hole regarded it as their property as long as they lived near it and watered their stock there; but on their departure it was available to all who needed it, sites of cattle kraals being held only during occupation. It is a commentary on the manner in which a scarcity value of land may emphasize ownership and restrict use, that among the Hima cattlekeepers of Ruanda, a neighboring tribe, a developing land shortage following upon European occupation has given rise to family ownership of the tracts on which the cattle graze.[29]

Among one of the most northerly of these East African cattle folk, the Lango, land is today owned by villages which also control grazing and water rights. However, "indications are not entirely wanting to show that in the remote past land was held communally by the clan within the sphere of tribal occupancy, and that such clan-land was at the disposal of the individual members of the clan for their use as long as they required it." Both the group as a whole and each individual in it have com-

[27] Schapera (1943), 223–38, 255–8, citations from 223, 228–9, 258.

[28] Godfrey Wilson, 47.

[29] Oberg (MS.), 11.

plete rights over cultivated village land during occupancy, but ownership in any sense of the word involving privilege of disposal is not conferred thereby. Interestingly enough, hunting land is the only kind admitting of private ownership, though the owner of a tract of hunting land may more properly be said to own "the hunting rights over the land rather than the land itself, and with closer settlement following on an increased population even these rights will one day inevitably disappear." The owner of such a tract may thus not refuse permission to any group desiring to build a settlement and cultivate land in the area he controls. Grazing land and the essential water rights that go with it, as well as the privilege of fishing in these waters, are communally held by villages, and no individual tenure within this common form of ownership is permitted. The violation of these rights by outsiders, whether for the purpose of grazing or watering cattle, or for fishing, is severely punished.[30]

The Kazak (Kirghiz), who inhabit the steppes between the Caspian Sea and the Altai Mountains, were a nomadic, stock-breeding people at the time of their conquest by the Russians. They lived in units called the *aul*, defined as "mobile villages" or nomadic encampments, each consisting of the scattered dwellings of the individual families comprising it. Seasonal migration to obtain proper pasturage for the herds still marks the yearly round of these folk, and many groups make a circuit of between 200 and 300 kilometers. Considerations of land-ownership, then, arise in connection with grazing land, winter habitations, and agricultural and meadow land. Since in this herding culture the raising of crops is a subsidiary occupation, it is but necessary to settle on a plot and to plant it to have the use of it; the winter habitations, more permanent in nature, are privately owned. The customary usage where tenure of pasture land is concerned does, however, present some difficulties. The use of such land seems to be relatively free at the present time, and has been for an extended period. Certain testimony indicates that this accords with the theory of tenure that the use of steppe pastures is based on "occupancy and the right of the first comer." Informants tend to give conflicting testimony, however, which is not clarified by observed practice.

From the older literature it seems possible that each relation-

[30] Driberg (1923), 170–2; cf. also Evans-Pritchard (1937), 42–9.

ship group (*uru*) had pasture lands which non-members were pro-
hibited from using. One writer goes so far as to maintain that the
very routes by means of which the several groups reached their
traditionally owned pasturage were fixed and not to be violated.
Within the area of grazing land owned by the *uru*, the allocation
of specific ranges may have been the task of the elders, or traditional usage may have given certain localities to certain families
or groups of families, or the entire range may have been freely
available to all members. In any event, the question was not a
pressing one to the Kazak, since the pasturage is extremely rich.

The precise manner in which ownership of meadow lands was
determined is also not easy to discover; but it is evident that it
was restricted and that trespass was severely punished. It is
stated by some natives that ownership was private. On the other
hand, a given individual could say on separate occasions that
such lands, "belonged to an entire *uru*, to the rich men in the *uru*,
and finally that in theory they belonged to the *uru* but were for
all practical purposes divided among its wealthiest and most important members." Hay for the winter was cut and stored by
workers hired by an owner of meadow land or by his poorer relatives. In the latter case, these might glean what was left after the
harvest, or cut the hay from the poorer portions of the meadow as
a return for their work. A man who owned no meadow land
either would have to turn his animals out to graze for themselves
during the winter, or, if his resources permitted, would rent land
on which to raise the necessary hay, or might buy the hay from
someone whose meadow produced more than his herds required.[31]

It can be understood from the preceding instances how the
study of land tenure among herding folk is made difficult by the
many complicating factors that enter into it, since even where a
people do no agriculture or have no settled habitations, other
considerations than just those having to do with retention of desirable pasturage may enter. A further example may be given
which makes this particular point. Among the Siberian Chuckchee, breeders are careful to keep the area about their summer
camps clear, since the herds must be taken there for ceremonials
and slaughtering in the fall. Trespassing is therefore "a grave
offense" which gives rise to serious quarrels. Even during the

[31] Hudson, 20, 32–5.

winter season, when land is not subdivided and trespass is not possible, difficulties apparently arise because the animals of two herds grazing close to each other become mixed and their separation offers many opportunities for dispute. This is especially the case when one herd is much larger than the other, since the possibility of changing the identifying ear-marks carried by each animal is always present.[32]

The status of land tenure among herding peoples given here could be indefinitely amplified by citing more of the many general statements which report only that people wander at will, or that certain areas belong to separate clans, or that possession of a certain pasturage over a period of years gives the approval of customary usage to continued retention. "The range of the wanderings of a Chuckchee camp," we read, "extends from a hundred to a hundred and fifty miles, and in most cases covers the same or nearly the same territory every year; but any camp that becomes dissatisfied with its range may pick out a new one wherever it chooses, the only condition being that it may not trespass on any ground already occupied by others for the season running." Twelve of these "groups" are listed, each with thirteen to one hundred camps; and the geographical district occupied by each group is given.[33] This is one of the clearest statements available concerning the patterns of land tenure among a herding people. Yet how boundaries are marked, how sub-units of the larger group allocate the vast territory grazed over by each, and other related questions are not answered.

The reason data bearing on the land-tenure of herders are so slight may be the result of practical difficulties in field procedure. In part these difficulties, which should not be insurmountable, have not been resolved because of the tendency on the part of anthropologists to treat land tenure and other aspects of property primarily as a phase of social organization. Here the remedy lies in a simple redirection of interests. More serious is the possibility that European control has tended to destroy the traditional divisions of pasture-ranges, and that boundaries, possibly vague at best when the system was in full operation in aboriginal times, cannot be reconstructed as readily as those of family hunting bands.

The urgency of such work as can still be done on the problem

[32] Bogoras, 78.   [33] Ibid., 25–6.

of land-ownership among herding folk is thus apparent. Until more precise studies are made, however, it can merely be said, in summary fashion, that grazing land as such is rarely if ever owned by individuals, and that a presumption of group owner-ship is strong. It also seems probable that the vagueness of the boundary-lines where restriction of tenure exists is a result of the seasonal nature of grazing and the large resources of land avail-able to most herding peoples. This in turn must lower any scar-city value it may possess, making it a matter approaching in-difference where a given herd grazes, since all herds can be adequately cared for.

CHAPTER XVI

LAND TENURE:
AGRICULTURAL PEOPLES

THE VARIETY of forms of land tenure that can exist at a given time among a single people is seldom recognized. The problem here is not the methodological one, already considered, of exercising all caution against the misinterpretation of the rules of ownership. There the difficulty was in proving the assumptions underlying the system of reasoning that is employed. We are rather confronted with the task of understanding how more than one way of doing the same thing may be found in the same society. It is on this, as a matter of fact, that the discussion of the validity or invalidity of primitive communism founders, for it is rare that a given people either hold land exclusively in common or privately, since in most societies both private and group ownership operate simultaneously. That the two types of tenure have existed concurrently for millennia is proved by excavations of Danish Bronze Age sites, where within the confines of a single village territory the boundaries marking individually owned strips and communally held grazing land are clearly to be seen.[1]

Instances of how many and varied forms of land tenure may simultaneously be found in an agricultural society are so numerous that only a selection of the available documentation can be indicated here. Nine distinct categories of those who have an interest in the land have been recorded from the Trobriand Islands. These include, first of all, the district chief, to whom some of the produce comes as tribute. The village headman also has an interest as a recipient of tribute, and so has the "garden magician,"

[1] Hatt, 76 ff.

who as "master of the soil" receives a return of prestige for his services on the land. The head of the sub-clan gives permission for a plot of land to be worked, and the members of a minor sub-clan, whose ownership of definite lands is granted, even though these lands are worked by others, are likewise concerned. In addition, there is the village community as a whole, which cultivates the land about the village and whose members have the full right to "use its public approaches, its water-holes and most of its territory in the search of wild fruits, in hunting and collecting, and to cultivate the soil," and the individual members of a community, each of whom has an allotment to cultivate. Finally we come to the actual gardener, who, whether owner or not, is absolute master of his garden while cultivating it, and the sister, or other female relative of a gardener, who has a stake in what he produces through the operation of the reciprocal gift exchanges of taro that mark the harvest. Ownership, as such, is thus determined by what are described as "the general principles of land tenure, citizenship and rights of residence." Three categories of land are distinguishable—village sites, uncleared forest, and garden plots. Of these, the first and third are restricted, while the second is available to every member of the community. The garden land is divided into fields, each worked by an individual or by a gardening team; for one village these numbered fifteen fields containing between 500 and 560 plots.[2]

Three distinct kinds of land-ownership are also found on the Polynesian island of Uvea. The first category has to do with public land, which consists of the uncultivated desert region near the center of the island and the forest about the crater lakes. Here any member of the tribe may gather wood or exploit whatever other resources the forest offers. The second category concerns village property. Where the shore is wide enough to permit cultivation, patches of taro are worked on land belonging to the whole village, the individual plots being redistributed at intervals by the village council. Public thoroughfares are owned by the community, as is the land on which stood the public building each village possessed in pre-European times. The third class of ownership, by far the most important, is that of lineage. These holdings should theoretically be concentrated in districts, and, to a considerable extent, according to villages. This clear-cut

[2] Malinowski (1935), 328–30, 430–4.

system has, however, become confused with time, since changes of residence, marriages between persons of different lineages, and the consequent splitting of these relationship groups have brought about a reapportionment of the land. "Each lineage owns at least one house site in a village and plantation land in the interior," this latter type usually consisting of a number of scattered tracts.

Lineage property is administered by the head of the group as a unit, rather than as a congeries of individual units. As a consequence, sales of such land only rarely occur, and tenure, which is constant, only changes with births and deaths. Even gifts to individuals or groups within the lineage are infrequent, except where a line becomes so large as to be unwieldy, and fission within the group results in splitting its holdings. Tenure is assured every member of a lineage as his inherited right, despite the fact that the title to the land he is using vests in the group of which he is a member. In addition to the right to a part of the land possessed by his own—that is, his father's—lineage, each person has also a "subsidiary right" to the land of his mother's line, though the exercise of this latter right is usually regarded as a "resource in case of need." Women as well as men are entitled to lineage land, so that even though a woman's principal means of subsistence is the produce of her husband's garden, she does not by the fact of her marriage forfeit her right to a portion of what is grown on the land of her own lineage.[3]

In general, land tenure among the Ibo of eastern Nigeria, West Africa, takes four forms: sacred or tabooed lands, virgin forest, farming land held commonly by villagers, members of a "kindred," or of an extended family, and individual holdings. The first type consists of sacred groves about shrines of public deities and the "evil bush." Such land is considered to be the property of the deities or spirits concerned, and it is only since European control that adventurous souls, under the urge of economic necessity, have dared interfere with this spiritual proprietorship by farming such land. When no misfortune comes to a farmer after two years of trespass of this sort, the land is regarded as his own. The reasons why virgin forest is not farmed vary. There may be more land than is needed; or it may be that its conservation has been decided upon by the village for purposes of shade or de-

[3] Burrows, 66–8.

fense, or to serve as a source of wood or fiber. In the first case, anyone needing land may clear a farm which will henceforth be his own, transferable to his heirs or available to him as a pledge for a needed loan, as he sees fit. But where doubt arises whether or not the village requires a plot chosen by a man from unworked land, the prior claim of the group to this land must be acknowledged, and permission of the village elders must be sought and obtained before work is begun.

The category of communal holdings of farm land, which comprises all land "held in reserve for the benefit of the whole group," includes three subdivisions. Village-held farm land is called "land of the people" or "land held in common." In certain districts all such land has been apportioned, and none remains in the hands of the community, but other villages hold such large tracts that no need of apportioning has arisen. Usually such land is at some distance from the villages, however, and all acreages suitable for farming which are situated nearer the settlement are the property of individuals or small family groups. In still other instances, village lands held in common consist only of the poorer tracts, where nothing but cassava can grow. Land held by the relationship groups—the "kindreds" and "extended families"—is called "ancestral land," and can only be alienated by the consent of the entire membership. When one of these families divides, its holdings are divided between the newly formed groups. An important element in this general category of family land is that on which a compound stands. The household which occupies the site owns such land, to be alienated only under conditions of severe stress. To sell or even to pledge such land (or, in more recent times, to rent it, as is done by certain Christian families) is believed to bring on the resentment and hence the punishment of the ancestors buried there. This feeling persists even where household sites are no longer occupied; "for religious . . . or, at any rate, for sentimental reasons" full rights to these are retained by the family that once lived there.

The most important form of land tenure, if only because it is the most common, is private ownership. "In many village-groups there is scarcely any land at all within the recognized boundary of the group which is not held by individuals." Such land is acquired in several ways, as already mentioned; that is, by clearing a forested tract, by inheritance, or by having it pass into one's possession through default on a loan. Such land is private property in every sense of the term, carrying the right to lease, sell, or pledge it, the last method being the one under which most land changes hands. Rent, however, is nominal, since most often the use of a plot is given a friend for a pot of palm-wine or a feast at harvest time, or, indeed, for no return at all; though if the amount of land thus "rented" is considerable, the owner may ask twenty or thirty yams for its use.[4]

2

THOUGH the institution of property has often been designated as a stabilizing force in society, the validity of this statement when it is applied to the landed holdings of non-agricultural tribes is not entirely clear. The statement is far more cogent in the case of agricultural peoples; yet even here it is subject to some reservations. If it is true that no community lives by agriculture, or hunting, or herding, or food-gathering alone, it follows at once that where agriculture is but one of a number of techniques for exploiting the food resources of a given area, this principle of stability will apply merely to the extent that other methods do not require the group to move about in order to obtain fresh game or new pasturage. Settled villages are, as a matter of fact, almost never inhabited by non-agricultural peoples. Yet while fields tend to cluster about the settlements of agriculturists, they may, because of progressive exhaustion of the land, be steadily pushed farther and farther from the central location. Thus, in Borneo, villages move periodically with the need to farm virgin land, while epidemics or other emergencies frequently cause a village site to be shifted to what is considered a more propitious location.[5]

Among nonliterate cultivators, scarcity of land is almost unknown, except occasionally in such thickly settled portions of the nonliterate world as West Africa or Mexico or the highlands of Peru or Indonesia. What makes for stability, therefore, would not seem to be the fact of land-holding as such, but rather those attachments to land which derive from the fundamental fact that

[4] Meek, 100–04; see also J. S. Harris (1942b), 90–1.   [5] Hose, 36.

it takes more initiative to move than to continue routine living. This is an important reason for not seeking newer habitations when technology permits rotation of crops, or where, land being plentiful, fields lie fallow when exhausted and no religious or magical beliefs encourage a shift in residence when evil omens manifest themselves. Whatever the reasons—and we may be assured that there are far more of them than suggested here—it is undoubtedly true that among agriculturists less shifting occurs, more stress is laid on the importance of land, greater feeling exists against trespass, and boundaries are delineated much more sharply than in hunting societies or among food-gathering or herding peoples.

With these general points in mind, we may now turn to further specific instances of land tenure in agricultural communities. We shall indicate how property in the form of cultivated land is acquired, how it is held, under what conditions it changes hands or is abandoned, and how this ownership fits into prevailing schemes of land tenure when agriculture is but one of a number of modes of getting a living.

3

AMONG such a Melanesian agricultural community as Lesu, in eastern New Ireland, holdings of clan and village are found. Land owned by clans was not worked in former days, as it was held to be the abode of certain supernatural beings who, offended, would wreak their vengeance on those who dared use it. Today, however, as a result of observations that no harm has come to the whites who planted coconut trees, such land is worked. Where these plots are situated too far away from the village of the clan owning it to permit them to farm it conveniently, it is cultivated by members of other clans, who may give a portion of their crop to the "real" owners. Should such land as is worked by non-clan members be sold to the whites, those who are engaged in tilling it most often share in the proceeds. Yet "they are not considered its owners," nor may they transmit their gardens to their heirs, for such land goes automatically to the next generation of clan members.

The second and economically more important category consists of village land. A village in this part of New Ireland is made up of a series of "hamlets," the houses of which follow the beach for several miles. Each settlement has its own land, running back in a strip from the beach to the uncut forest. The available data do not make explicit whether this land has special value or differs in the way it is held from other farm lands worked by villagers. Since, however, "with the exception of clan land," both the extension along the sea and the land going back for five or six miles from the shore are owned jointly by members of the village group, this latter is probably not the case.

As so often in nonliterate communities, much of the village land is uncultivated, and a villager may plant any unoccupied plot he wishes. Most couples, however, prefer to farm the land worked by their parents. So strong is this feeling, in fact, that though village land is free to all village members, a man would hesitate to plant land once used by persons of the preceding generation without the permission of a son or daughter of the earlier tillers. When a man and his wife are both members of the same village, they may cultivate two plots, though if they work but one, or if the man is from another village, they generally work the plot of the wife's parents. Title to this village land is not alienated when a man moves away, for he retains his full rights to plant there. He also shares in the proceeds from any sale of this land, to which, indeed, he must give his consent as a member of the group.[6]

The land of each clan in southwestern Malekula, whether under cultivation or not, is clearly delimited by boundaries which, near the coast, consist of walls built of coral blocks. As in the Trobriands, these tracts are subdivided into plots "each of which 'belongs to' a certain kinship group," representing a subdivision of the clan. Every adult male has "his own" patch. In those localities where there is any scarcity of land, this patch is inherited from his father. If land is plentiful, it has been wrested from the bush. Women work the plots of fathers, brothers, or husbands. The rule of tenure is that no man retains more than a life interest in his garden. Even though his sons continue to work the garden after his death, this does not imply the existence of a right to inherit the land itself, but merely the continuation, in one spot, by members of one family, of the exercise of every clansman's right to a plot on clan land. Land is "leased," generally for no

[6] Powdermaker, 31–2, 157–60.

more than one agricultural year, by giving an outsider "temporary rights of tillage" in return for half the harvest, but emphasis on the temporary nature of the arrangement prevents any effective invasion of the principle of common ownership. On the death of a debtor, land can be claimed by a non-member of the clan in payment of an undischarged debt incurred by the deceased. In this case, however, surviving fellow-clansmen make all effort to redeem the land so that it will not pass out of the group holdings.[7]

Comparable, but not identical, is the situation obtaining in Tanga. The island of Boieng is divided into eight districts, each owned by a clan. These divisions are partitioned into sub-districts, which in turn are owned, occupied, and jealously guarded by sub-sections of the clan, from which individual families or extended family groups within every sub-section freely select garden and dwelling sites. The principle of clan ownership, which is not explicitly stated, must, however, be deduced from the distribution of the holdings of clan members, for the native does not recognize an area of this sort as "a synthesis of smaller areas definitely owned and occupied" by such a sub-clan group. Aside from this aspect of the rules of ownership, the tenure pattern follows, in a general way, that with which we are already familiar. A family has complete control over the crops from the land it works, and the feeling against trespass is so strong that "not even a brother would take food from this garden unless he has first obtained the owner's permission." Division of rights within a family plot follows the rule that a man and each of his wives hold and work separate gardens and store their crops separately. Trees that are individually planted are the property of the one who plants them, but other trees on clan ground are free to all members of the group.[8]

In Manam, the village-clan type of ownership recurs, each village possessing land that is subdivided among its patrilineal clans, these tracts, in turn, being "owned" by individual clan members. This land, "owned" by women as well as men, is inheritable, so that "proprietors" of land sometimes do not live near their land. In this event, they are brought a part of the harvest by clansmen who cultivate such gardens for them. Chiefs control more land than commoners. The principle of common owner-

[7] Deacon, 172–4.   [8] Bell, 307.

ship, with individual rights to specific plots held over many generations, does obtain, but the alienation of land by an individual, for all that, is countenanced no more here than elsewhere in this general area.[9]

The complexity of the relationships and rules that govern land tenure in these Melanesian islands is revealed in Oliver's account of the methodological problem he encountered in unravelling them in southern Bougainville, where the ownership of land is important and the "land-puller" a well-known phenomenon. In general, however, the Melanesian pattern is followed, with land being held by kin-groups of various orders—immediate and extended families and clans, as these are recognized as belonging to local groupings—together with rare instances of individual ownership.[10]

The examples cited in the preceding pages are sufficient to indicate that the principle of Melanesian land tenure in general, stated by Codrington,[11] that "there is no strictly communal property in land," is acceptable if revised in the light of more modern findings. Actually, Melanesian agricultural communities seem, in general, to recognize rights to work certain plots of land through the circumstance of residence or birth rather than rights to land itself—that is, they admit the ownership of produce rather than of the garden where it is grown. It is a commentary on the assumed validity of the wider hypothesis that private land-ownership is universal among agricultural peoples when we find that here, where farming is the primary occupation, common tenure exists, such as might be expected in a hunting or food-gathering tribe. And, as we proceed with an examination of land-holdings among agriculturists elsewhere, we shall repeatedly find this emphasis on the ownership of usufruct. The recognition of trespass as an offense thereupon merely becomes evidence of a recognition of the right to own crops, and not of the ownership of land itself, as is sometimes concluded.

4

POLYNESIAN land tenure veers sharply toward private ownership when compared with the prevalent patterns of Melanesia, though

---

[9] Wedgewood, 391–3.
[10] Oliver (1949b), 4–8, and *passim.*
[11] Codrington, 59 ff.

instances of group control are by no means lacking. In Pukapuka, for example, large tracts of the land where most of the food-crops are raised, are divided among villages and set aside as commonly owned reserves. Other land is apportioned among the lineages of the village, whose members retain the ownership of certain portions of their allotment in common, and, for the rest, divide it into homestead plots which appear to be the private property of those who have their dwellings there. Trespassing, a serious offense, especially when the productive village reserves are entered, is severely punished, and great care is taken that the boundaries between all tracts, by whomever owned, are so well marked that no questions arise as to their limits. Emphasis is laid on the punishment of trespass because talo and other essential subsistence crops grow there. Similarly, private ownership within lineage boundaries is based on the benefits that accrue from the talo beds, coconut trees, "bush timbers," and other resources of such land.[12]

An outstanding example of private land ownership is had from Mangareva, where individual holdings of the mountainsides "up to the top of the ridges went with the cultivatable land of the shore and valley flats. Ownership also applied to the sea and the coasts." Except for certain small freehold estates, the land was divided between about ten aristocratic "large landowners," who leased most of their holdings to farmers. In a few instances, of rare occurrence, squatters might settle on unworked tracts, and if not removed, the land they farmed became theirs. Boundaries were well known, though constantly in dispute as each owner or tenant sought the opportunity to increase his holdings. Lease-holds were inherited, and a farmer made every effort to retain the plot his ancestors had worked; a man who leased large tracts might sub-lease to others or work his land with servants. Manga-reva offers one of the few instances among primitive cultures where land was rented. A farmer gave the first and second crops of breadfruit to his landlord, retaining the third, together with the fallen fruits of the first two crops, for himself. War, leading to a change of ownership, might also lead to a change of tenants. Otherwise, a farmer was expelled for failure to turn over the produce expected of him, or if he neglected to weed his garden

[12] E. and P. Beaglehole, 32–44.

or otherwise failed to care for the estate, or if he himself or some member of his family offended the landlord.[13]

Individual ownership of land in Samoa, on the other hand, is described as being "rare and sporadic." Most frequently a man obtains a portion of land for himself when he clears some ground and becomes recognized as its cultivator. "A claim to new land is easy to establish, but difficult to perpetuate." In essence, to do this it is necessary that the land be continuously farmed. If the cultivator does hold his land, however, he may on his death leave it to anyone he wishes, though the ultimate jurisdiction over land always lodges in the village group, and anyone who works land within this jurisdiction may be assessed on his crops or his labor. Land is regularly alienated in the exchanges incident upon marriage, but returns as a rule under the control of the village in which it is situated after an interval of not more than one or two generations.[14]

Tongan land belonged to the ruler, who allotted it to his various chiefs. Since each succeeding holder of the title was confirmed in his tenure of the holdings of his predecessor, however, such grants were for all practical purposes permanent, and in effect constituted private holdings not unlike those in Mangareva. These chiefs, in their turn, parceled out plots to minor officials and commoners. Each man, as far as possible, lived on the same land as his father, though a chief could dispossess commoners to transfer them more or less arbitrarily to other parts of his holdings. Boundary marks were carefully set and were permanent, for especially in more recent times there has been considerable land-hunger.[15] A not dissimilar form of land tenure is reported from the Marquesan Islands, though here private ownership is stressed more than in Tonga. Theoretically, "the land on which the tribe lived was owned by the chief in the same way that with us family property is legally owned by the head of the family." In time, however, most tribal land came to be regarded by the chiefs as their personal possessions. Within this framework of tenure, land was apportioned by a chief to the families under his rule, in accordance with the importance of their social position. In addition, however, a family could settle on unoccupied land, plant its breadfruit and coconut trees and taro plots there, and

[13] Hiroa (1938), 161–4.   [15] Gifford (1929), 171 ff.
[14] Mead (1930a), 70–2.

henceforth have "primary right" to it.[16] In Niue, private land tenure in any form was subsidiary to family property, for land could not be alienated from the family group. It could be bequeathed, but in the absence of heirs the family head would reallot it to other members of the group.[17] A not dissimilar system marks the patterns of land-holding in Tikopia.[18]

Two final instances of Polynesian land tenure may be given, the first to show how the private ownership of trees, important in all this area, could be extended to include the land on which a man's trees grew, and the second to indicate how a factor such as war might act to promote individual tenure. In Tongareva, the coconut tree, which must be planted by man, served as a factor in accentuating "the sharp definition of individual rights to land." Since the person who planted trees on land he occupied had the right to their fruit, he was also regarded as having an exclusive right to the land on which his trees grew. So strong was this principle, indeed, that "the planting of coconuts, if allowed to go unchallenged, established the right to land even without occupation. . . ." The entire emphasis, it is true, was on the trees and the nuts they bear, yet ownership of the land was also implied.[19]

In Mangaia, a system based on the allotment of tribal tracts by the chief to the individual families under his control, and the subsequent passage of these tracts by inheritance to the next of line, was disturbed by the frequency of intertribal wars. Here the pattern of warfare laid emphasis on individual valor rather than on inherited chiefly position, and land tenure thus "came to depend upon conquest, which obliterated the rights of previous occupation and cultivation." This brought about the redistribution of conquered land among the conquerors, the principal warriors receiving the largest shares. In this way a class of large landowners grew up. The conquered, who took refuge in the poorer uplands, gained what sustenance they could. They eventually developed into a kind of half-serf class, whose members, though nominally undisturbed in their tenure, ensured to themselves the protection of a powerful chief by wooing his favor with gifts.[20]

[16] Handy (1923), 57–8.
[17] Loeb, 67.
[18] Raymond Firth (1936), 373 ff.

[19] Hiroa (1932), 41, 58–9.
[20] Hiroa (1934), 129–30.

5

AMONG New World agricultural peoples, rules of tenure of the tribes in southwestern United States have been subjected to the most careful study. The Navaho who first farms a plot, whether man or woman, retains possession of that plot, though with his permission members of his family, relatives, or friends may plant on a part of it. More than this, however, anyone who wishes to plant on land adjacent to a field already established has to obtain consent of the owner of the plot already worked. Boundaries are carefully set, so that no misunderstanding can arise as to where a field terminates. In earlier times land was inherited according to the matrilineal principle; more recently the sons of a male owner have been permitted to inherit. Once established, rights to a given tract were permanent, so that even though the original user or his heirs abandoned it for a period of years, they might evict anyone who had moved on it in their absence. None the less, prudence dictated that a relative be placed on land when one had to be away from it for any length of time. Until recently, land was neither bought, sold, nor rented, and there was no private ownership of wild shrubs or trees, roots or berries, or springs. If a man planted a tree it was his, but should a tree that grew of itself be needed for firewood, anyone might enter a field to chop it down without being guilty of trespass. In analogous manner, pasture land might be used by anyone, but where a range was already being grazed to capacity, one who ran his sheep on the same range would incur resentment.

The lack of agreement found among authorities who have dealt with Navaho ownership is undoubtedly due to a failure to recognize that no land, as such, is owned, but that it is the yield from land which is important in matters concerning tenure. The phrase that has been used to describe their mode of tenure, "inherited use ownership," can, indeed, be applied with profit far more widely than just to these people, as is apparent when land tenure is considered not only among agricultural folk, but also among hunting, herding, and food-gathering peoples. Asked directly concerning customary usage, a Navaho tends to reply: "We do not own land, we simply use it." Actually, unworked land was in the nature of a free good, and only with the addition of improvements incident upon cultivation was there an accretion of value such as to make exclusive possession desirable. Yet once again, it must be emphasized that such "improvements" are not the equivalent of those permanent "capital" changes in land that give the term its economic significance in our culture, nor does "exclusive possession" mean permanent holding.[21]

Among the neighboring Hopi, the clan is the important agent in dictating the control of land, village boundaries being merely limits within which assignments according to clan affiliation are made. Clan lands are not contiguous, but are distributed in patches. This reduces the risk of crop failure from floods, which rarely go beyond the confines of a single wash. Such lands are divided among the maternal lineages and sub-divided among the households of each of these groups. In addition, an adequate reserve of land is held outside cultivation, so that a household whose fields have been washed out or which have been covered by the drifting sands of the desert, will not become destitute. In addition to these clan lands, certain sections are set aside, planted, and cultivated for political and ceremonial officers, by working parties drawn from the membership of the village or society over which a given officer has charge.

Fields belonging to individual households are not sharply delimited, but to the degree title is recognized, it is lodged in the hands of the women, through whom descent is counted. As the matter is summarized: "Ownership is vested in the clan, the individual women have the usufruct and also the right of disposal subject to the veto of the clan expressed either by mass opinion or as a decision of the clan mother." In addition to this common tenure, certain provisions for individual ownership come into force when a man initially prepares land that was previously waste, plants fruit trees on it, or cultivates beans and squash there. This land is usually, though not always, a part of the village land not allotted to the clans represented in the community. The one who reclaims it may ordinarily bequeath it to a nephew or to his son, which prevents it from relapsing into its original status as village land. If he allows it to go out of cultivation while he is yet alive, someone else may take it over, though the consent of the original cultivator is required, and he can recover his land if he wishes to resume its cultivation. It is thus apparent that

[21] Hill (1938), 20–3.

among this sedentary people, as among the less settled Navaho, attention and interest focus on the produce of the fields rather than on the ownership of land as an end in itself, though accounts of tenure among the neighboring Zuñi indicate private ownership, with the right of alienation, was the rule.[22]

A similar point of view is seen to prevail as we range farther in agricultural North America. The Plains Indians who did some cultivation, such as the Mandan, the Gros Ventre, and the Arikara, held that even though a man set out a plot of ground, tilled it consistently, and fenced it in, he was merely using tribal land. Should he leave it idle even for a year, anyone in the tribe had the right to take it, though "there being no scarcity" of land in the days when Denig wrote, there occurred "no difficulties . . . upon this point."[23] Exactly the same arrangement is reported for the Omaha, whose land was cultivated by families. Fields left uncultivated for a season became free land, and trespass on a new occupant was not permitted.[24] Even among the Hidatsa, where family boundaries were marked with care and fields were separated from one another, land that went unused on a woman's death might be taken over by someone else, though it was felt that permission of the heirs of the dead should be obtained before crops were set out on the abandoned field. The same principle of ownership of usufruct rather than of land obtained among the Creek of southeastern United States and in pre-Spanish Mexico.[25]

6

THE FORM of land-ownership most widely encountered in agricultural Africa is one by which individual tenure, during use, derives from the allotment of land by the representative of the tribe or of the clan, who acts as trustee for the group as a whole. This fundamental fact is sometimes obscured where a concentration of people exists, but analysis almost invariably shows that the general rule is operative. "All land occupied by the tribe is

[22] Forde (1931), 371, 373–83; Beaglehole (1937), 14–17; Lowie (1920), 217.

[23] Denig, 476–7.

[24] Fletcher and LaFleche, 269.

[25] G. L. Wilson, 110–14; Swanton (1928), 336, 443–4; Thompson, 60–2.

vested in the Chief and administered by him as head of the tribe," is the principle of tenure among the southeastern and eastern Bantu. This does not mean that the chief is owner of the land; Junod cites an example of this in telling how, after land had been allotted to his mission by the local representative of a chief, this same man later came to ask permission to take the fruit of a tree not being used by the missionaries.

Everywhere in this area the natural resources are available to all tribal members. They may graze their cattle anywhere on the pasture lands, all may use the springs, cut wood, dig clay for pots, and gather wild fruits and edible roots. Only land used for residences and for cultivation is restricted, but it is significant that what is "owned" with regard to such land is "private rights," which means that such land is not "private property." It is assigned by the chief, and while in use is exclusively reserved for those who live on it or work it. It may be handed down to a man's heir, and the head of a household has the word as to how it will be subdivided among his dependents. Here again, however, when land has once been assigned to a wife or son, it cannot be alienated any more than the entire grant can be withdrawn by the chief who made it. Except to be transferred to a friend, with the permission of the headman, land is never sold or disposed of "in any other way in return for material consideration." It can be reassigned if abandoned, otherwise it must remain in the hands of the assignee or his heirs, and it can only be taken away by a process of confiscation operative if the holder is guilty of some serious crime.[26]

As we turn to the Congo and West Africa, we find that holdings may be sanctioned by village or clan assignment, though in the area as a whole the ruler more frequently figures as the eventual source of a given grant. A typical expression of Congo practice is had in the following statement:

The land surrounding a town belongs to the people who live in the town. Certain landmarks, as streams, forests, etc., are agreed upon as boundaries. . . . Within the boundary the people of the town are free to make their farms and build their houses where they like, provided the land is not al-

[26] Schapera and Goodwin, 156–7; Junod, II, 5–9; Stayt, 166–7; Schapera (1938), 195–213; Gutmann, 302–3; Godfrey Wilson, *passim*.

ready occupied by someone else. Priority of occupation is the only title recognized.[27]

This principle is apparently contradicted by the occurrence of private ownership among the Ibo, to which the right of alienation attaches. Yet such a conclusion does not necessarily follow. It will be remembered from the discussion of Ibo land tenure in earlier pages, that this people also have much land which is subject to the control of village councils. The apparently exceptional nature of the Ibo system of private tenure perhaps arises from the fact that they have little or no surplus land, so that the pressure of population is such that a man, having begun to cultivate a tract, dare not give it up. We are not informed as to the Ibo theory of land tenure; from the data as given, however, it is easy to see how continuous rights to usufruct over a series of generations might have developed into a vested interest in the land itself, and thus here have transformed the theory as well as the nature of land tenure.[28]

The Cross River area is not far removed from the Ibo country, but here ownership of land belonging to the "patrilineal kin group" and farming rights derive either from a man's membership in one of these groups or from permission granted an outsider by such a group to farm a plot of their land. The assignment of land is primarily made to the "wards" of a village, the residents of each ward having the right to large tracts of land, and the kinship group holdings being scattered over these tracts. Since only a fraction of the available farm land is worked, a given garden constantly changes by a process of "piecemeal accumulation or abandonment," but there is here no question of absolute ownership.[29] In Dahomey, where most of the land close enough to habitations is cultivated, the idea that a man has a permanent individual title to land as such is unthinkable, and no holding may be alienated except with the consent of the chief. A native king no longer reigns here, but the French colonial government has, with respect to the land, merely stepped into his place as trustee.[30]

A similar concept of ownership obtains in the Gold Coast.

[27] Weeks, 109.
[28] Meek, loc. cit.
[29] Forde (1937), 36.

[30] Herskovits (1938), I, 78; II, 15.

"The hoe is the one to lay claim to the land," goes one Ashanti proverb, and another states: "The farm (meaning the farm produce) is mine, the soil is the Chief's." Tribal ownership of land is translated into individual and family rights to usufruct. Provided a man continues to use the soil and to pay his dues to the Stool from which he derived this right, his possession is undisturbed.[31] Among the Akan peoples, south of the Ashanti, the rules are almost the same:

> Previous cultivation of, and in some cases, occupation with a definite intention to cultivate, a forest-land, entitle the cultivator and occupier to a privilege of private ownership over the particular land in so far as agricultural rights are concerned. . . . But his title stops here. He can make use of his *farm* in any way or form. But he cannot alienate the *land*.[32]

The Lobi tribes likewise envisage occupation of the land during use only, the Earth being regarded as the source of the contract by which men are permitted to benefit from working the land. Tribal territories are well differentiated, and a member of one tribe is liable to punishment if found trespassing on the land of another. Within the tribe, the land is parceled out among families, each family head being responsible for the equitable distribution of what he controls. Land, though passing by inheritance from one generation to the next, cannot be alienated; conversely, a family group occupying a tract by right of birth cannot be dispossessed except for the gravest offense. Yet should a man have no heir, his field automatically becomes communal property, and may be allotted to a new tenant "as though the land had never been cultivated." So important is it to understand this special kind of religio-legal sanction among the Lobi of holding land for use only that Labouret, from whose account these rules have been taken, refuses to use the terms "usufruct" or "property." He prefers to substitute the phrase "ground-rights" (*droits fonciers*), in the sense of "possession and withholding, under the condition of contributing to religious offerings and of rendering certain fixed services."[33]

---

[31] Rattray (1929), 340–58. [33] Labouret (1931), 367–73.
[32] Danquah, 206.

7

ENOUGH cases have been encountered in previous pages where generalizations concerning the form of an institution are valid only to a point, that to find another instance of a departure from a rule will not be surprising. Thus, it has become apparent that among agricultural peoples the concept of private property in land, as such, exists but rarely, and that what is prized is the exclusive right to benefit from produce raised on a given plot. Yet it would be doing less than justice to the question of the ownership of land if the fact was not recognized that the range of variation among nonliterate peoples runs the gamut from group possession to private ownership.

This is to be seen among the Nigerian Nupe, where five traditional methods of acquiring land reflect the types of holdings found there. These are as follows: a member of a land-owning family can acquire a parcel of the land "held jointly by the family group, the apportionment of which is controlled by its head"; or he can "enter into an arrangement with an individual landlord (using the term here in the widest sense)," [34] leasing land on a temporary basis and paying rent in kind. This second form, called "borrowing," is much like the third method, whereby a man leases a plot "for life or for an indefinite period." There is also hereditary—or secondary—tenantship, a kind of sharecropping system whereby the tenant has absolute right over his land, and may even sublet it or otherwise dispose of it provided the original owner, or his descendant, continues to receive the share in the produce of this land that had been agreed on. The final and fifth form is primary tenantship, whereby "a landlord who himself owns the land by the right of conquest or appropriation may cede complete and absolute right over land to another person." This individual may be a Nupe or a stranger who has performed political services to the owner; it is an aspect of the feudal organization of the Nupe state, since the one who cedes it none the less continues to receive a share of the produce.

These modes of acquiring land fall into two categories— *(1) Acquisition in virtue of membership of a group (kinship group or village community), holding 'corporate' right to land.

[34] The meaning of this phrase is not explained.

(2) Acquisition of land in virtue of a contract between individual landowners—a short-term contract such as the 'borrowing' of land, or a long-term, or indefinite, contract such as is embodied in tenantship and in the granting of land for services rendered." The complexity of this system is not lessened when one considers "its historic roots in war and conquest, and the fact that, in consequence of this, not all these forms are to be found in all parts of the territory inhabited by the Nupe." [35]

Yet when we analyze the data from the Nupe, we find the familiar pattern of village land ownership held in trust and administered by the village head in behalf of its members, native or adopted, and family ownership, for which the head of the family is trustee. This is not to deny the importance for the present-day scene of the other forms of "private" ownership that have been noted. Yet it is apparent that they represent a gloss over the underlying tradition resulting from the conquests of recent centuries.

If this is taken into account, the pertinence of the phrase "inherited use ownership" that has been cited as descriptive of Navaho land tenure is thus seen to have no less significant applicability because we find that among certain nonliterate peoples, historic circumstance has extended the range of variation in modes of tenure to the pole of private holdings. As a matter of fact, the principle of "inherited use ownership," as found among these American Indians is perhaps best described by the following statement of the principles governing the holding of land among the West African Ashanti:

It appears . . . essential that we should cease to regard land . . . as a single immovable entity or possession; it is necessary to consider it as comprising three distinct attributes, or as having three distinct aspects:

1. The land itself, in its most literal sense, i.e., the soil, the earth.
2. The usufruct, the use to which the soil may be put; in other words, *the right of occupation* as distinct from *the property in the soil.*
3. The all-important fact that crops, trees, and even

[35] Nadel (1942), 181–3; for details concerning these types of acquisition and ownership of land see the sections that follow the summary cited, 183–201.

houses, were not regarded as "part of the realty," to use the legal phrase, or, in plain words, were not looked upon as being inseparable from the soil in which they had their roots, or upon which they stood.[36]

The concept of land tenure in nonliterate societies as a kind of "inherited use ownership" would seem to clarify a good many points. It explains, for instance, why rent is so rarely encountered, while it resolves the controversy regarding private as against communal holding of land. For as far as the land itself is concerned, though it is in the vast majority of instances tribally controlled or, where this is not the case, owned by families, the right of the individual to retain it for his use gives tenure the complexion of ownership. Private ownership of land, however, implies greater rights than are generally accorded in the systems of nonliterate peoples, while fully communal tenure assumes that the individual has fewer rights than are found in practice. Nonliterate folk, that is, are concerned with the products of the land, not with the land itself. This is perhaps a reflex of the lack of economic surplus, production thus being for use, and attention being focused on yield rather than on the source from which the yield is derived.

[36] Rattray (1929), 340.

CHAPTER XVII

GOODS, TANGIBLE
AND INTANGIBLE

THE DISTINCTION to be drawn between land and natural resources and all other objects held as property has important implications. Property falling in the first category, a "given" of the natural environment, need only be worked in order to reap what is at least potentially already offered by it. But other possessions, whether these be tools or works of art, songs or magic formulae, are the creations of man himself. This is not the case for domesticated animals and slaves, it is true, but even here the conditions under which the animals live and the slaves attain their status are primarily cultural. Their relationship to their owners, as to all other forms of property, is subject to considerations that differ from those arising out of the physiological necessity that binds man to land and to natural resources.

In most non-industrial societies, with their comparatively slight degree of specialization, the greater part of every man's possessions have been created by himself. Thus the facts that trade among such peoples is in the main not concerned with goods essential for living, and that, but for those exceptional instances where it is necessary to import food, commodities acquired from outside the tribe are but a veneer on necessity, come to have fresh significance when translated into terms of property. In societies where every person, man or woman, within the terms of the dictates of sex division of labor, controls all the techniques of his culture, it is apparent that most of the tools he employs in his daily work, the clothing he wears, and the shelter in which he lives will be made as well as owned by himself. In every respect, therefore, the resulting object is as much a part of him as is the song he likewise owns, or a design he may likewise have created.

As always, we must exercise care not to push any explanation too far. Culture is far too complex a phenomenon to permit any simplistic explanation to have more than partial validity. It is precisely in our own society, for example, where the degree of specialization is more developed than in any other culture and the possibility of personal creation of what we own is reduced to a minimum, that the concept of private property is most highly developed. It can, of course, be reasoned that any pattern, once established, is capable of infinite elaboration and refinement, and it is possible that this has occurred in our own society on the basis of an early identification of a man with what he himself made. Our interest here, however, is to note the fact that in all groups personal ownership of some goods and rights exists; that private property, in this sense, is known everywhere; and that these aspects of ownership can, as a class, be contrasted with the ordinary regard of nonliterate peoples for their land and natural resources.

2

THE MANNER in which the property relationship between an owner and his possessions rests on psychological processes of this kind may best be investigated by considering the ownership of tangible goods among peoples with little-developed technologies, living under difficult environmental conditions, where cooperation in labor and equality in the distribution of available resources must be observed on pain of extinction. Two principles are observable among them: what a man makes and uses in obtaining his livelihood is his personal property; and what he has in excess of his needs, or is not using, must be made available to other members of his group.

"The first great unwritten law of the [Eskimo] settlement," it has been stated, "is that no one may without reason avoid the struggle for food and clothing." The conception of private property becomes clear in the light of this principle. Clothing, sleds, skin boats, hunting weapons, and the like, which are used by individuals, are privately owned, and no one would presume to contest their ownership. On the other hand, large communal houses, or stone structures employed in fishing salmon or caribou-hunting are never owned individually, but belong to the community that built, maintains, and uses them. The matter becomes clearest, however, when we consider the cases in which a man owns more than one of a given kind of production good. Here the well-known Eskimo principle that "personal possession is conditioned by actual use of the property" comes into play. A fox-trap lying idle may be taken by anyone who will use it; in Greenland a man already owning a tent or a large boat does not inherit another, since it is assumed that one person can never use more than one possession of this type. It is apparent, therefore, that here the concept of private property is more a formal than a functional element in Eskimo economics. That is, though what a person himself uses is generally acknowledged to be his alone, any excess must be at the disposal of those who need it, and can make good use of it.[1]

The Great Basin area of western North America is inhabited by Indian tribes whose standard of living is likewise but slightly removed from the subsistence level. They include migratory food-gatherers like the White Knives Shoshoni, whose technical equipment for meeting the environment is incomparably less developed than that of the Eskimo. Having few possessions, their property concepts are simple, and, as might be expected, "production and use were the determining criteria of ownership" in the days before European contact. A person's clothing, which was his private property, was made by the wearer for himself; likewise the baskets and pots made and used by the women, and the bows and arrows, clubs, and flint tools made and used by the men were, in the main, the exclusive property of their makers. Capital goods such as large fishing and hunting nets, which were made and used by the members of a camp group acting co-operatively, were jointly owned; where a net was individually manufactured it was the property of its maker, who, however, was expected to permit a fellow-tribesman to have it when it was not in use.[2]

Similarly, in Tierra del Fuego, personal goods—those things made and used by a man or woman—constitute private property.

[1] Birket-Smith (1936), 148–51.   [2] Harris (1940), 69.

A Selk'nam man's personal possessions include his skin mantle and other articles of clothing, his bow and quiver full of arrows, his knife and scraper, drill and other tools, objects used for ornamental purposes, raw materials, traps and fish-nets, his fire-making tools and his hunting dog. The property of a woman consists of her clothing and ornaments, baskets and carrying-strap, knife and scraper, the container in which she carries her child, her leather bag, and her sewing materials. Children's clothing and toys are their personal possessions, and the familiar tale of the refusal of a parent to sell his child's property without permission from his offspring is encountered here. Such an item of property as the family shelter belongs to its occupants and is used and owned in common, and this is also true where two families construct a hut together. Food belongs to all family members, but here the absence of surplus food dictates immediate consumption, and the situation is thus not comparable to one where a local group or the members of a co-operative organization make, use, and own in common some kind of capital good.[3]

The institution of private property is weaker in Australia than among any of the preceding folk. Among the Murngin, articles of technology are individually owned; but where co-operative labor is necessary, there is "a feeling of collective ownership" of the product. Among the Yir-Yoront, property may be acquired in several ways—by "working or using," by borrowing or appropriating, by stealing, by gift and inheritance, or by exchange. The principal objects of "exclusive control of owned property" are certain clan property and a man's fighting and certain hunting spears. Gifts, once bestowed, are no longer given a thought, and borrowing and appropriation go on without exciting a great deal of interest. Permanent ownership of goods is rare; that "this appears to be correlated with the simplicity of native material equipment" makes it the more understandable why individual ownership is recognized and practiced to this slight degree.[4]

The concept of private property in goods of all types is well developed among the South African Bushmen. All portable objects are individually owned, and theft is severely punished. Huts, which incidentally have but little value, are family prop-

[3] Gusinde, 429–34.   [4] Warner, 146–7; Sharp, 38.

erty. The clothing of a man, however, his weapons, skins, ornaments, utensils, "and indeed everything that he makes" are owned
by himself alone and are entirely at his disposal. Similarly, everything a woman makes is her property, and not even her husband,
who may have given her much of what she owns, may dispose
of her belongings without her consent. Among certain Bushmen
tribes, indeed, the sense of private property is consciously in-
stilled in children by their parents, who make small bows, digging-sticks, and other objects for them, and impress upon them
that since they now themselves own these things, they may no
longer turn to their playmates for them.[5]

3

It is not possible to detail the forms of property to be found in
societies whose technologies permit their members to amass
resources beyond the necessities of life. Not only are all types of
possessions owned, but they are owned in all manner of ways
and under all kinds of sanctions. Yet, like a thread running
through the entire fabric of ownership, the same principle is to
be discerned that has been set forth for property other than
land and its resources in societies with the simplest economies,
the least-developed technologies, and the most exacting environments.

This principle has been clearly expressed by a number of
writers. Junod states: "The Bantus are agriculturalists. They
believe that the products of their labour belong to them and that
no one else is entitled to appropriate them. The notion of property is in direct relation to the work accomplished." Among the
Tswana, "personal effects are the private property of the people
by or for whom they were made or acquired, and by whom they
are habitually used." The private property of the Upper Missouri
tribes is described as follows: "All clothing, skins, arms, etc.,
made by themselves are the sole property of those who make
them, and this is the only general right among them that admits
of no dispute." Among the Creek, the tools made and used by
the man of the house belonged to him. Firth, in listing Maori
forms of personal property, summarizes the underlying principles

[5] Schapera (1930), 147-8.

of ownership among these people in the following terms: "Very often such things were collected or manufactured by the person possessing them, in which case the labour involved gave a strong prescriptive right to the sole use of the article—especially as it was open to any other member of the community to acquire similar goods, provided that he was willing to expend the necessary time and labour." [6]

The same principle comes out very clearly in the conventions of ownership found among the Siriono of Bolivia. "The native concept of property may best be expressed," [7] we are informed, "by saying that the environment exists for the exploitation of all members of the band, and that society recognized the rights of ownership only so far as this exploitation is pursued. In other words, the preserve of the Siriono is communally owned, but its products become individual property only when they are hunted, collected, or used." And though "holdings in movable property are few," yet "individual rights of ownership are recognized and respected." A man owns the bows and arrows he makes, the game he kills, the maize or manioc he raises. A woman owns the pots she fashions, and her baskets, calabashes, and "all of the things which she herself makes or collects." Or, among the Havasupai of northern Arizona,

> Items of personal use other than land are clearly owned by the individual, and objects which are *on* the land—houses, crops, horses, and the few cattle—are also individually owned, for there is abundant evidence that a person can dispose of these items largely as he wishes. When he dies, much of his personal property is buried with him, his house is burned or abandoned, and the crops he planted stand in the fields and rot or are destroyed. These things are so clearly his that it seems disgraceful that anyone should consider using them after he is dead. The land, however, is not so closely associated with the man who uses it. . . . The individual proprietor's rights are largely rights to *use* the land. [8]

In suggesting that the forms of private property most widely spread in nonliterate societies are those things made by their

[6] Junod, I, 446; Schapera (1938), 229; Denig, 474–5; Swanton (1928), 337; Firth (1929a), 334.

[7] Holmberg, p. 21.
[8] Service, 361–2, 365.

owner, most constantly used by him, and most intimately related to him, no implication of any general theory of property akin to a labor theory of value is involved. For one thing, too many exceptions exist to permit a generalization of this kind to be regarded as universally applicable. Nor here, as in previous cases, may we fail to give full weight to the fact that means of acquiring private property include a great variety of devices in which creative labor may play no part. All these other devices can, of course, be regarded in a sense as derivatives of primary ownership, since except in those societies where vested interests and motivations of profit and prestige make for human exploitation, a man must either have earned what he owns by the expenditure of his labor, or have inherited what another has labored to produce. Only land and natural resources are provided him by nature. Even here, any exploitation of these involves work—something not without significance in the light of the concept of land tenure prevalent among nonliterate folk—that the yield from land is owned rather than land as such.

The principle of ownership that has been advanced is strikingly exemplified in cases wherein the right to land is held distinct from the ownership of trees planted on it. We have even seen, in the instance of one Polynesian island, how the right to land is held a development from the ownership of the trees a man planted there, though, to be sure, this is an extreme instance. Of significance is the point that ownership of trees, quite independent of land tenure, exists most often where the tree is of a domesticated variety that must be planted and cared for until it matures. Coconut trees in Polynesia are of this type, and so are the palm trees of West Africa.

Not so well known as either of these examples are the conventions regarding the ownership of trees in East Africa. The member of the Wabena tribe, for example, regards his fruit trees as inalienable property, whether or not he retains the land he has worked when he planted them, and even if he moves to a distant village. Nor are trees inherited in the same way as the right to land under cultivation. For while traditionally a man's son inherits his field, trees are disposed of at will and may be bequeathed to a brother. In such a case, the son who succeeds to the field may not take the fruit that grows in it without permission. Consistent neglect of trees does eventually vacate title to them, as it does to land, but in the instance of trees the process is much longer. Examples are cited where, in villages, trees are allowed to go on bearing for years after their owners have moved to another part of the country without their ownership being challenged.[9] Among the Nyakyusa and neighboring peoples, the same principles have taken on reinterpreted form with the introduction of economically valuable trees, notably the bamboo. Here, when the man who plants bamboos moves to another part of the tribal territory, the bamboos he planted pass to his kinsmen.[10]

In the New World trees are similarly held. Concerning tree holdings of the Popoluca of Mexico, we learn that "ownership comes from planting and inheritance"; and no instance was discovered "of claiming trees already growing in a wild state, though it is possible this practice exists." [11] The pre-European Ojibwa patterns of ownership of maple-sugar trees likewise makes the point. Here an individual marked by blazes the limits of his claim, which comprised as many trees as he could care for. He always knew the exact number that were his, and this was important, for unclaimed trees were free until worked, when they became private property. Trees were inherited like other goods, could be given away or loaned, and were treated in all respects like any private possession.[12]

The Melanesian who plants trees holds them as property distinct from land, and the knowledge of who owns the trees on a given plot is "most minute and accurate." Codrington, in recounting his purchase of some land in the region, states that after the transaction was completed the owner of a fruit tree on land acquired earlier "put in his claim, which he had before omitted to make. He was accompanied by the owner of the ground on which the tree stood, who testified that the claim was good, for the claimant's grandfather had planted it." [13] In Assam bamboos, like trees marked by a person, when small are private property, "belonging, as a rule, to the man who planted them and his heirs, irrespective of the ownership of the land on which they are planted." It is common for bamboos to be planted near the village on land belonging to someone other than the planter,

[9] A. T. and M. G. Culwick, 263–4.
[10] Godfrey Wilson, 43–45.
[11] G. M. Foster (1942), 82.
[12] Landes, 96–7.
[13] Codrington, 65.

and if this was not forbidden before the planting was done, the owner not only might not uproot the bamboos but was required to clear a fireline to protect them when he burned over his land. It was only away from the village, where fear of detection was slight, that such bamboos would be torn up and thrown away.[14]

A point raised in an earlier chapter may now be considered further. As has been indicated, the temptation has been strong to explain the identification existing between a man and his property by reference to some mystical, non-realistic, "pre-logical" assumption arising out of the special thought processes of "primitive" man. Instances are cited where a growing object is believed related to the growth of its owner, or where ritualistic observances are performed to make a tree the property of the one for whom the ritual has been carried out. But in Dahomey, for example, where the umbilical cord of every child is buried under a palm tree which thereupon becomes his inalienable property, no mystic relationship exists between the man and the tree that is his. He owns the tree merely because his umbilicus, which is a part of him and partakes of a certain character related to some of the supernatural beings that rule his life, is buried here.[15] The discussion by Hiroa of the analogous ownership of coconut trees in Tongareva makes the same point:

> When the women conceived, the human fruit was growing . . . on the "land" within the woman, for when the child was born, it was accompanied by the afterbirth. The afterbirth . . . was the portion of the land upon which the child had grown. . . . With this concept in mind, it is easy to understand that the subsequent planting of a coconut on the buried placenta is a natural continuation of the metaphorical idea into material reality. The child which grew on the hidden placental land reaches maturity on the external terrestrial land and the coconut tree also reaches maturity after being planted on the buried placenta. The coconut yields its fruit to the grown-up child and the circle is complete. The relationship of the boy to the tree is one of exclusive ownership combined with a certain amount of sentiment. . . . There is nothing in the nature of a mystic bond between him and the tree. . . .[16]

14 Hutton, 68.   II, 250-2.
15 Herskovits (1938), I, 261-2;   16 Hiroa (1932), 31.

As is so often the case, the matter resolves itself into a question of the categories drawn by a people, and of the assumptions that underlie a given system of thought. In holding that identification through labor and use makes for ownership, then, one need go no further than common-sense, day-by-day observation of human behavior to conclude that those things a man uses most constantly, those things of immediate importance to him as a means either to biological survival or to maintain his proper place in society, become almost a part of him, both in his own mind and in that of his fellows. Hence these are the objects which, more than any others, he conceives as particularly and peculiarly his own.

The widespread incidence of private ownership among non-literate peoples makes it unnecessary to discuss a problem that assumes such importance where land is concerned—whether or not tenure has a communal or an individualistic basis. On occasion, the point is made that, as has been seen for the Eskimo, commodities of which there is some surplus are available to all members of a community, regardless of ownership. Among peoples hard-pressed for subsistence, the act of sharing what is available does not necessarily imply any absence of a sense of ownership. Hoyt has put the matter cogently: "In almost all groups the more fortunate will, in times of necessity, share with their neighbors who have less. Such practices as these are familiar to us today; we are here on the border-line of charity." [17] Certainly, among peoples who live above a subsistence level, it is often no more than considerations of customary behavior that dictate the division of a kill, or those of prestige which require that one member of a community share his harvest with his fellows. Co-operation must never be construed as evidence that individualism is non-existent. And this statement is as true concerning ownership and distribution of property as where aspects of production are involved.

4

LIVING and inert objects must be differentiated where the ownership of material property, other than land and natural resources,

[17] Hoyt (1926), 107–08.

is under discussion. As regards inert objects, the very fact that they figure in a culture is enough to indicate that they are owned, whether individually, or commonly, or tribally. Faunal and human property present special cases, however, since they give rise to different attitudes on the part of those who own and use them. They must be cared for in a special manner, they arouse especially strong sentiments of affection or antipathy, and they must often be acquired in special ways. In the class of living property, several divisions may be distinguished—the herds of a people come at once to mind, while slaves are likewise an obvious category. The most disputed division, which most students would no longer make at all, is that of wives. However, even though disputed, it continues to be frequently urged that in many parts of the world wives are "bought" and "sold" and are therefore to be considered property, so that brief attention must be given these assertions before returning to the manner in which slaves and animals, indisputably forms of property, are held.

The analysis by Beaglehole may be taken to indicate how the problem of the status of women as property has been approached: "I will first consider," he says, "the basis of one of the most fundamental property values of both savage and civilized society. I refer to woman as a property object." Stating that "marriage by purchase is the prevalent form of primitive marriage," he says, "it is exceedingly rare to find tribes where women inherit on equal terms with the man of the group. Mostly the wives are regarded as property and inherited with the rest. . . ." Insistence on premarital chastity is ascribed to a property taboo, for "unfaithfulness and laxity before marriage may result in property complications incident to notions of illegitimacy." [18] Since this assumption is developed to a point where it is maintained that "the woman in savage society may be looked upon as a value of considerable importance," it is not difficult to comprehend how but a further step is needed to conclude, as we have seen Thurnwald does, arguing from another premise and without explicitly subscribing to the position of woman as a chattel, that: "Wives are the oldest form of 'profitable capital' not only on account of their offspring and because the husband profits from having his food supplied, but also because of the

[18] Beaglehole (1932), 158 ff., 215–16.

woman's skill in handicrafts." [19] It is far more in consonance with the facts to hold, with Bunzel, that where an exchange of goods is involved, the acquisition of a wife in a nonliterate society is "an economic arrangement between the two contracting families, which may or may not accord to the husband and the husband's family certain rights over the woman and certain claims upon her family." [20] This is undoubtedly the clearest and most valid summary of all those facts that are implicit in the varied phrases, "wife purchase," "bride price," "bride wealth," and the like.

Africa is perhaps the last refuge of those who hold for purchase as the primary means of acquiring wives. Specialists on the ethnography of other areas, when indicating that wife-purchase is not found in the American or Polynesian tribes with which they are familiar, tend to refer to Africa as a contrast. Thus we read of one western North American tribe:

> Bride purchase is as inapplicable a term as can be found for the Klamath practice. Payment constitutes an obligation, a seal of respectability. This is the well-nigh universal situation in North America if payments enter at all; it is a far cry from the commercial, contractual bride purchase of Africa, for example. [21]

The reports of modern field-workers from Africa, however, are replete with denials that the acquisition of a wife has any element of commercial transaction connected with it. Reference has been made in a preceding chapter to the real nature of the transfer of cattle in East and South Africa, and elsewhere in the world, incident upon marriage. This need here only be supplemented by the citation of one or two from the many express denials of wife-purchase that have been entered.

> According to Tswana law, no marriage is regarded as complete unless *bogadi* has been given by the husband's people to the wife's people. This transfer has often been looked upon by missionaries and others as constituting a purchase of the woman, and as involving her in many humiliating consequences. . . . This conception of *bogadi* is altogether wrong. . . . The Tswana themselves speak of *bogadi* as a thanksgiving (*tebogo*) to the wife's parents for the care they

[19] Thurnwald (1932a), 156; (1932b), 180.

[20] Bunzel (1938), 382.
[21] Spier, 43.

have spent on her upbringing, and as a sign of gratitude for their kindness in now allowing her husband to marry her. . . . But the main function of *bogadi* is further said to transfer the reproductive power of a woman from her own family into that of her husband. This fact is of considerable importance, for upon it rests the whole Tswana conception of legitimacy.[22]

Similarly, among the Gusii to the north, we learn:

It is bridewealth payment that distinguishes a merely biological family—a group of little significance in Gusii society —from a legitimate family, a group that is all-important for inheritance and succession, legal and mystical alliance, and membership of all politically significant groups. . . . The great equitable principle from which all specific rules of Gusii bridewealth law will be found to derive is that all men ought to have equal opportunities for founding their own *ebisaku*.[23]

Thus as in the case of the Tswana, it is made plain that "bridewealth payment determines legitimate filiation," and lays the grounds on which the individual takes his place in the social network in which his life is lived.[24]

From across the continent the testimony of another student of African law is in full accordance with this. Concerning "wife purchase" among the Ibo, Meek states that "it is hardly necessary to remind readers that this well-established term does not imply that a wife is purchased from her parents and becomes a mere chattel of her husband." Its main purpose "is to regularize and give permanence to the union of a man and woman, and so to distinguish marriage and the foundation of a family from a mere paramour relationship and the promiscuous begetting and rearing of children." Its other functions all tend toward stabilizing the marriage, and none of them is economic—indeed, some of them are distinctly to the contrary, since should it become necessary to refund what has been given, the family of the bride might easily suffer serious financial embarrassment.[25] Fortes has demon-

[22] Schapera (1938), 138–9.
[23] Mayer, 4. *Ebisaku* is the plural form of *egesaku*, the name for the door of the traditional Gusii living-house that opens into the central cattle pen of the head of the household, and hence stands for the lineage with its legal issue.
[24] Ibid., 64.
[25] Meek, 266.

strated how, among the Tallensi, though it is said that "a man owns his wife, has he not bought her?" to call a married woman a chattel would bring on a prompt denial. The concept "to own" means that the man has authority over his wife and is responsible for her. Analysis of the economics of the household demonstrates the reciprocal nature of the claims spouses have on one another.[26] The idea that brides are bought in West Africa was perhaps most adequately reduced to proper proportion when a sophisticated Dahomean inquired whether or not the French institution of the dowry did not imply that the father gives a *dot* to purchase a husband for his daughter.[27]

The fact of the matter is that the economic position of women, like other facets of culture, can be placed in proper cross-cultural perspective only by an empirical analysis of the facts. A *priori* assumptions and accepted semantic orientations must be subjected to scrutiny in the light of the interplay of personal relationships in a given society. "The Malays are Moslems," we learn of the fishing people of Kelantan, "but this does not prevent the women from playing an extremely important role in the social system." Of 101 women whose economic status was studied, it was found that "approximately half follow . . . occupations for a definite livelihood of their own, with or without dependents to support, whereas approximately half are engaged in supplementing their husbands' incomes." The implications of this are significant: ". . . in most cases here it is the desire not for subsistence, but for a higher standard of living, which impels them to work, and with this in a number of cases is associated the desire for some independence of action and income." Even where fishermen are the primary earners, their money is given to the women "both to spend and to save." To this people, this is as it should be—"for who should guard the money when we are away all day, if not the woman?"[28]

5

IF WOMEN are not property at all, slaves in many nonliterate societies may be regarded as what, in the case of the Lango of

[26] Fortes (1949), 101–04.   [28] Rosemary Firth, 17–23.
[27] Herskovits (1938), I, 85.

East Africa, has been termed limited property. As a matter of fact, the ownership of slaves is here so limited that the lot of the slave is almost indistinguishable from that of the freeman. On the payment of the usual dowry an enslaved girl is given in marriage by her captor, who stands in the place of a parent to her, and her only disability is that in the event of continued conflict with her husband she has no family to summon to her aid. Male slaves are usually adopted by their owners; they marry Lango wives and are in no way discriminated against.[29]

Farther south, among the Wabena, slaves were war captives, criminals, debtors, and the children of slaves. The family life of a slave was disturbed only on the death of a master, when, through the processes of inheritance, the group to which he belonged might be broken up; but this was avoided wherever possible by arrangement between the heirs. To sell a slave needed the consent of the owner's tribal superior, and to obtain this an important reason, such as the need to liquidate a pressing debt, had to be given. If cruelly treated, a slave could be awarded by a chief to a new master. A slave could sue in the courts, though this seldom occurred, since to win, the evidence had to be overwhelmingly in his favor, and he was exposed to the vindictiveness of his master if he lost. The economic advantage in owning slaves was that the owner profited from their labor; yet a slave worked no harder than did free young men under the prevailing matrilocal system of residence. Slaves might even own slaves, and any other property they might have on their death was inherited in the same way as was that of freemen; and, what is of paramount importance in the native conception of status, they were also accorded as careful burial as freemen. They did labor under two serious disabilities, however, for a slave, if so ordered, was required to submit to the poison ordeal in place of his master; while at the death of a tribal chief, one male and one female slave had to accompany his spirit to the next world.[30] The same sort of slavery prevailed in Uganda and the Congo, where, if anything, slaves were more favorably situated than among the Wabena.[31]

A similar picture is painted of slavery among the Ibo for the period preceding European occupation. A member of the tribe

[29] Driberg (1923), 173.
[30] Culwick, ibid., 133–7.
[31] Roscoe, 14; Weeks, 110, 112 ff.; Cureau, 149, 155.

might be enslaved for infractions of recognized customs, or if he fell in the class of "children whom the group did not consider as normal human beings" and had been born with or developed some unusual physical or physiological trait. Inability to pay debts was cause for selling a man, or he might be taken and sold as a result of a political struggle for power. A stranger—trader or traveller—or even a child of a neighboring family might be kidnapped and disposed of to slavers. Slaves were utilized in farming and trading and might be sacrificed at the funeral of a powerful slaveholder. They served as conspicuous evidence of wealth and they were at times dedicated to the service of a diety. The slave could not marry a free person, nor could he become free by his own efforts; and he was without any of the civil rights accorded free Ibo. However, his economic position might become most advantageous, and "many slaves determinedly utilized their capabilities . . . to achieve a position of wealth and consequent power which would compensate for their disabilities as members of the lowest caste." [32]

This type of what is called household slavery is characteristic of most forms of human ownership among nonliterate peoples. Slaves, as in the instances cited or among the Lobi people, are members of the family; or, as among the Yurok of California, the number of slaves owned by any one family is so small that the personal element in their supervision bulks large. Even where, as among the Flathead Indians, the lot of the slave was far from enviable, the children born to a female slave might take the social position of the free father. The lower Chinook owned slaves in considerable numbers, but these made their homes in the same quarters as their masters; "their opinions were often sought; their ridicule was deeply felt." In some instances, as in certain Amazonian tribes, a male slave was eventually accorded full membership in the tribe, except that "the chief would consider that he had a lien of sorts on such a man, and this would be commuted by payment of perhaps half his shooting bag, probably until the time that he married." [33]

It is difficult to evaluate the economic advantage that accrued from slavery of this kind. There was, indeed, another hand in the fields or at the traps, but the slave had to be watched so that

[32] J. S. Harris (1942a), *passim.*
[33] Labouret (1931), 373–5; Kroe-   ber, 32; Turney-High, 131; Ray, 51–3; Whiffen, 69–70.

he did not escape, and, at all events, there was another mouth to feed. This is no negligible factor where, as among the East African Bachiga, slaves produced little more than they consumed and were rarely discriminated against in terms of the tribal standard of living.[34] Profit did accrue from slavery where there was a large market for slaves, as in West Africa while the New World slave-trade flourished, or in East Africa while Arabia was an available market, but these conditions were in no way typical. To be sure, among certain tribes, such as the Maori, "the economic value of the slave to the community was considerable," since slavery permitted the necessary social leisure to enable others "to develop the finer arts of life"; yet this is one of the few instances on record in the nonliterate world where such an attitude, reminiscent of the point of view of the Greeks of classical Athens toward slavery, has been noted.[35] In other exceptional nonliterate cultures, such as Dahomey, where mass slavery obtained and the master profited from slave labor on the plantations, an economic advantage is clearly to be seen, but in the majority of nonliterate societies, the economic gains from slavery must have been slight indeed.

Considered as property, then, a survey of slavery in these nonindustrial cultures indicates that whatever the manner of acquisition of slaves, and whatever the work required of them, their status as human beings invaded to a considerable extent their status as property. As a result, some limitations on free use and on unrestricted right of disposal were always present, and in many communities this operated eventually to take slaves out of the category of property, or at least to mark them off from other forms of property.

6

THE DATA on the role of the larger domesticated animals as property are as sparse as is the information on the land-holdings of herding folk. Concern with the purely sociological aspects of ownership of herds, as manifested in their inheritance, their place in ceremonial exchange, and the like, marks reports on the life of such folk to the neglect of the strictly economic aspects

[34] Edel (1937), 142.   [35] Firth, ibid., 201–04.

of this ownership. A further difficulty is presented by conventions that obscure the actual possession of animals, whereby the herds of relatives are pooled and cared for according to the dictates of a family elder.

An example of such pseudo group ownership is to be found among the Siberian Koryak. Every individual has his own reindeer, marked by a special notch cut into the ears of his animals. One or two fawns are set aside for each child at birth, and the natural increase gives the recipient, when grown, either a herd of his own or the beginnings of one.

> Of course, the original herd belongs to the father; but considering that each child has its own reindeer, and that the wife and daughters-in-law retain as their property the reindeer which they brought in marriage, the whole herd of a large family belongs to a group of interrelated proprietors, under the direction of the eldest male.[36]

The ownership of the Kazak herds in Turkestan was similar:

> Cattle were all held in the individual ownership of members of the group, usually by male heads of families. There is some indication, however, to suggest that they could be considered as belonging to the family as a whole but held in trust and utilized for their benefit by its head. Such a situation, for example, might be implied by the right of sons to demand from their father a portion of his animals on coming of age.[37]

Little is known of the size of herds held by nonliterate folk. This is perhaps because these herders are not accustomed to think in terms of numbers, but in many instances consider their animals as individuals, each having its own name and special attributes. Such a disregard for numbers characterizes the relevant attitudes of the Chuckchee, who are reported as not caring a great deal how many animals they have in their herds, showing concern only for the more important animals, such as the breeding-bucks, the harness reindeer, old dams, and the like.[38] Taboos against counting, or reluctance to reveal numbers to a

[36] Jochelson, 747.   [38] Bogoras (1904), 51.
[37] Hudson, 31.

stranger, also often make it difficult to obtain quantitative data, as was the case in connection with a detailed study of the place of cattle among the East African Nuer, where only a limited amount of enumeration was possible. This count showed, however, that though herds were smaller than in previous years because of repeated attacks of rinderpest, yet one village possessed 165 head, or an average of some 11 head per household, in addition to some 6 sheep or goats; in another village, eleven byres housed 76 "adult cattle," 20 calves, 33 sheep and goats, or an average of 8.7 cattle and 3 sheep and goats per family. At one camp a group of fifty-five men and boys herded about 100 head. This gives an average of approximately 2 head per male, or of about 10 head of cattle and 5 goats and sheep to a byre. Since each byre belongs to a group of about eight persons, the per capita of cattle for the Nuer is slightly more than one head per person—that is, "the cattle population . . . does not greatly exceed the human population." [39]

Among these same people, whose cattle figure so importantly in the economy—twenty-five uses of the "bodies or bodily products of cattle" are noted—it is striking to remark how non-economic factors enter into every aspect of their ownership, though they are in no sense sentimental about their animals and value them entirely on the basis of utility. None the less, their preoccupation with their herds is intense. As it is put: "He who wishes to live or understand their social life must first master a vocabulary referring to cattle and to the life of the herds." The cattle play an important part in determining affinal relationships, and many disputes arise óver their disposal. Such facts as these, and the manner in which they enter into the religious life together with their essential place in various rituals, all differentiate them from other kinds of property among this people.[40] Whether this is characteristic of herding cultures in other areas cannot be said. But the importance of the problem, as indicating the manner in which economic and non-economic phenomena are intimately related, and particularly as showing how considerations of a non-economic nature can invade the immediate advantages to be derived from following an economic path of least resistance, must be obvious.

[39] Evans-Pritchard (1937-8), 244.   [40] Ibid., Part II, *passim.*

7

THAT intangibles can be important as property is a commonplace in our own culture, for many valuable businesses have been
reared on foundations no more substantial than a patented process, a copyrighted trade-name, and a subsequent accretion of
goodwill. It is also evident that intangibles have an importance
in the dynamics of the economic life of non-industrialized peoples
equal to their place in our own economy, especially where land
tenure is involved. Many instances of other kinds of intangibles
held as property by nonliterate peoples, much as we hold patents
and copyright, have been given. Bunzel, in a brief passage, extends this by indicating that these rights form the basis of monopolistic production, and stresses their role in the establishment
and maintenance of class and caste divisions. To apply the term
"monopolistic" to those techniques restricted to certain groups
found within nonliterate cultures would seem to be stretching the
meaning of the word farther than is desirable in the light of its
implications in terms of the monopolistic controls our own society knows. The point raised is none the less a suggestive lead
for more detailed investigation.[41]

Many instances of intangible property are available, some of
which may be mentioned. The crest rights of the Indians of the
Northwest Coast of North America are well known. Here, as has
been pointed out many times, a name must be validated by an expenditure of economic goods subsequently returned to the holder
through the enhancement of his wealth as well as his social position, the two being inseparable.[42] A great variety of Nootka
topati have been observed—those "various kinds of ceremonially
recognized property . . . whose use is restricted to a given
family and is subject to certain principles of ownership, inheritance, and transfer." [43] The *topati* include knowledge of family
legends, which are transmitted like other property to the holders'
heirs, a ritual for spearing fish which is more freely owned and
thus available as a gift at the owner's will, names of many kinds
that are exclusively held and applicable at the pleasure of the
owner, rights to carve certain designs on totem-poles and grave-

[41] Bunzel, 348–9.   [43] Sapir and Swadesh, note to p.
[42] Boas (1916), 500 ff.   222.

posts, to sing certain songs, to dance certain dances, and many other rights of a highly specialized ceremonial nature, such as the privilege of performing certain minute portions of fixed rituals. The specialization of the "functional families" among the Patwin of California was almost entirely based on the rights to pursue their specialties because these were owned as property by each family.[44] Among the Ojibwa, such intangibles as dances, the power to doctor, hunt, fish, divine, make war, gamble, and give names are obtained through dream experience, the dream being "the most highly personal property" and of the greatest value.[45]

Membership in the Melanesian men's societies is a valuable asset that can only be acquired through the expenditure of considerable wealth. In Malekula, entrance into a grade of the Nimanghi society necessitates large payments which are regarded as purchasing the privileges and outward ornamental marks of a given rank.[46] Many intangibles are held valuable by the Samoans. Thus, as an instance, one family in Satupaitea, Savaii,

> has a monopoly or patent right over the very crude *malauli* hook made from a fish bone tied at an angle to a piece of wood. Anyone wishing to fish for malauli with such a hook made his request with an accompanying present to the head of the Nuu family.

Trade-marks are important, and should a builder use the sign of a society other than his own, he is reported to the guild and, if found guilty, is fined. Sometimes when a chief cannot afford to have his house finished all at once, he will employ different builders at different times. In one such case, at least, a marker was used by the second builder to distinguish his work from that of the first, to draw attention to his neater work "and to thus advertise himself." [47] In the Marquesas, personal names were family property; in Mangaia the incantations employed by a man to give him success were carefully treasured and transmitted to his son; while in Niue, songs, charms, names, and family traditions were important elements in family wealth.[48]

The exclusive rights to their calling held by iron-workers,

[44] McKern, 254–7.
[45] Landes, 109 ff.
[46] Deacon, 373.

[47] Hiroa (1930), 86, 89–90, 522.
[48] Handy (1923), 87; Hiroa (1934), 148; Loeb, 67.

especially in East Africa, have been commented on many times; not so well known are some of the intangibles valued in other parts of the continent. In Dahomey and elsewhere in West Africa, magic charms, when purchased, become the property of the buyer. Each charm carries the knowledge of its composition and of the formulae that actuate it, and this is quite as valuable as the actual outer manifestation of the power or protection desired by the purchaser. For this knowledge, once acquired, can be resold without any spiritual loss to an owner of a charm. Hence while there is a guild of professional practitioners of magic, what a man knows concerning a charm he counts as his property and he benefits economically from his right to sell it to others.[49] Titles are valuable economic goods all through West Africa. Thus among the Ibo of Nigeria, a title can only be obtained by the expenditure of much valuable goods. Once bought, it confers not only social position but economic advantages as well.[50]

[49] Herskovits (1938), I, 81–2; II, 263.   [50] Meek, 165 ff.

PART V

THE ECONOMIC SURPLUS

CHAPTER XVIII

POPULATION SIZE, ECONOMIC SURPLUS AND SOCIAL LEISURE

IT HAS become apparent that non-industrial peoples are by no means incapable of producing an excess of goods over the minimum demands of necessity, even though possessing technical equipment and economic systems that tend to leave the output of their productive processes much nearer the level of subsistence and survival than is the case in the industrialized societies of Europe and America. The very fact that means of effectuating the circulation of goods within and between tribes do exist signifies that something more than just enough to feed, clothe, and shelter a people is available. Such phenomena as the delayed exchange of goods on a ceremonial basis, or the extension of credit by one tribesman to another, show that not only entire groups, but individuals within these groups possess a surplus over immediate need. The existence of property and the recognition of wealth in themselves offer a further demonstration, if one is needed, that an economic reserve is at hand when requirements of survival or the desire to establish or maintain prestige dictate its use.

This being the case, the problems of the degree to which such surpluses over subsistence needs are found in various societies, and their manner of disposal as indicating certain ways in which satisfactions are maximized, come to the fore as among the most important elements in the study of the economics of nonliterate peoples. In studies of the Euroamerican economy, whether of the more conventional order or made from the institutionalist point of view, these alternatives are recognized as being present, at least by implication. Yet a knowledge of how the economic surplus is allocated in terms of alternative uses is basic to any attempt, in any culture, to assess the limits of economic inequality; for our own culture, the matter is vital in all efforts to understand the social disequilibrium arising out of this inequality.

In what size populations, we may ask, and within what limits of productivity does an economic surplus appear? In those societies existing above a subsistence level, what disposition is made of the goods in excess of the demands of survival? To what extent does this excess widen the range of uses for satisfying new wants, in terms of new social orientations? Does it go toward raising the standard of living of the entire community? Is it concentrated in the hands of a few persons? When it is thus concentrated, what disposal is made of it by its possessors? What is the manner of life of those who do not participate in its distribution?

Because of the complexity of our own economic organization, it is difficult, if not impossible, to obtain a clear view of the operation of these forces. Here, consequently, perhaps more than in any other aspect of economics, recourse to the materials from nonliterate societies is of immediate significance. For if these questions are familiar to us as a result of unsatisfactory attempts to understand their implications for our own life, it may be suggested that they may with profit be taken into the laboratory of the social scientist. Here they can be studied in terms of their variation under differing conditions of life, different historical antecedents, in different-sized groups and under variously equipped technologies. In this way, their analysis may conceivably lead to a more objective reconsideration of analogous phenomena in our culture.

The one significant attempt to analyze the distribution of the economic surplus on a comparative basis is that made by Thorstein Veblen.[1] Writing at the turn of the twentieth century, Veblen took certain positions with regard to psychological and ethnological theory that definitely "date" these aspects of his work, especially where he concerns himself with instinctivist psychology and the classification of cultures according to an evolutionary scheme. Attention has already been drawn to the un-

[1] Veblen (1915), *passim.*

tenability of such a concept as the "instinct of workmanship." In the same way, the "stages" of society Veblen took over from Lewis H. Morgan—savagery, lower and higher barbarism, and the like—and the attempt to indicate a unilinear scheme of development for the leisure-class institutions which he treated, are today quite outmoded.

None the less, it was Veblen's genius to be able to penetrate through the evanescent quality of his supporting theses to the hard core of tenable postulate. It is quite possible to rephrase his "instinct of workmanship" as a principle having to do with the pleasurable identification of a craftsman with the product of his labor, accompanied by a drive toward perfection that often results in virtuosity. It is in similar fashion possible to read "degree of complexity of economic organization" for Veblen's "evolutionary stage" and thus bring his assumptions into line with present-day knowledge. It is in this more acceptable sense that Veblen's concepts will be employed in our attempt, in this and succeeding chapters, to understand and document the manner in which the economic surplus is distributed in nonliterate societies, and how, transmuted into social leisure, it makes for the development and maintenance of those differentials in status which are reared on the foundation of economic inequality.

2

No DETAILED research has as yet been made into the factors that enter into the production of an economic surplus. Far more data than are at present in hand will be needed if the operation of these factors is to be understood. The problem is first of all complicated by the fact that its variables make their relative weighting in a given situation difficult to assess. In addition, these variables are so numerous that they make proper control almost impossible. We shall, however, here consider the nature of these variables and, in broadest lines, draw certain generalizations regarding their interaction.

The physical environment is an extremely important factor. It provides the setting within the framework of which the struggle for life goes on, and, as has been indicated in earlier pages, sets the limits for the exploitation of its potentialities. However, it constitutes a relatively passive element, which is played on by the technological capacities of a given people. The possibilities of wresting from a favorable environment more than enough to support a community are naturally much greater than where a group live in an unfavorable one; and when the technological equipment of both peoples is equal, this factor must be decisive. In the study of culture, however, things are rarely equal. It is only necessary to recall the effectiveness with which peoples who know irrigation, or terracing, or the rotation of crops, or other such techniques exploit what would at first glance seem to be most unpromising environments to realize that the role of the natural setting of a culture cannot be evaluated without taking into consideration the equipment which a people bring to the task of shaping it to their needs.

The relation of population size to environment and technology on the one hand, and to per capita productivity on the other, offers the greatest challenge in investigating the conditions which make for an economic surplus among a given people. The difficulties in the way of meeting this challenge perhaps explain why the problem has received so little attention at the hands of investigators. Thus, so elementary a question as that of determining just what is meant by such designations as "tribe" or "band" or "people" and how such a grouping is to be distinguished from its neighbors, assumes major proportions here. This problem solved, however, the task is by no means ended. Is it justifiable to take gross numbers as a criterion when making assumptions as to the relation between the size of a group and the amount of economic surplus its productive system achieves? Or should density of population be the test? And even where clear differences in population size and density exist, will not a smaller group with more highly developed techniques for exploiting their environment surpass the productivity of a larger group less competently equipped?

In view of these initial difficulties, only certain tentative statements of a general nature can be made concerning the relationship between population size, productivity, and the resultant available social leisure. On the whole, it seems that the problem of survival is most pressing in the smallest societies. Conversely, it is among the larger groups, where the specialization appears which is instrumental in producing more goods than are sufficient to support all the people, that the enjoyment of social leisure is made possible.

3

THE QUESTION of per capita productivity can, perhaps, be best approached by considering how different societies support those individuals whose contributions to the total economy arise from the functions they perform as rulers or controllers of the supernatural. Such persons are dependent on the capacity of a group to furnish them with the economic goods they require if they are to provide for their basic needs. Marginal peoples, numerically small, generally inhabiting difficult environments and, with perhaps the exception of the Eskimo, equipped with technologies of an inferior order, offer an advantageous point of departure. One such group are the Bushmen of South Africa, who can be compared with respect to their capacity to support specialists in political administration and the care of the supernatural with the Hottentot, living in an environmental setting not dissimilar to theirs, but whose level of economic life is slightly higher.

In the southern reaches of Bushman territory no one enjoys economic advantage because of any special position in society. The head of a band is accorded deference, "but his authority in general is very limited," and the direction of hunting activities which are carried out in common, or of migration, is in the hands of those whose experience and ability are informally recognized. In the northwestern part of the area, where tribes are somewhat larger, a hereditary chief is acknowledged. Here, however, the office is most rudimentary, and since "no tribute or services are rendered to the chief, nor are there any special signs of chieftainship, such as a particular dress or mode of life," it is apparent that his position brings him no added participation in the total store of goods produced by his group. The reason is simple: the Bushmen produce no surplus. Consequently, the chief is "a leader rather than a ruler," and it is by force of his personality rather than by his control of tribal resources that he makes effective such authority as he may theoretically possess. There are no priests, and though the special magic powers of some members of the community are recognized, these persons are in no way differentiated from their fellow-members of the community. The only apparent return they receive from the practice of their craft is an occasional gift.

Now over the areas inhabited by the Bushmen ranged groups whose total in pre-European times has been conservatively estimated at 10,000 for the Cape province. On the other hand, the Hottentot, despite ravages of disease and war, and with allowance made for those of European ancestry, were officially estimated on the basis of the 1904 census as numbering some 50,000. It is, therefore, instructive to compare the two groups. Like the Bushmen, the Hottentot were organized into small bands, but unlike them, their bands recognized allegiance to larger clan and tribal groupings. Each tribe was headed by a chief, whose cattle-kraal was the most important in the tribe, and who was attended by councilors, the headmen of the various local groups in the tribe. Hottentot chiefs wore no special insignia, "except that their karosses were made of leopard and wild cat skins." But the chief "is generally the wealthiest man in the tribe," and among the Nama Hottentot fines levied in criminal cases either are given him alone or are divided with his councilors, while, in addition, he may also receive a share of damages awarded in a civil suit. Though this matter will be treated at length in later chapters, it may also be noted at this point that the obligations to expend wealth ostentatiously, which accompany rank in societies economically more secure, are foreshadowed here. For Hottentot chiefs, like rulers the world over, are expected to "have an open hand and an open house," and parsimony is "the worst thing" a chief can be accused of. As among the Bushmen, the members of Hottentot groups who were competent in the control of supernatural powers were in the main workers of magic. Yet ritualistic observances not found among their less numerous Bushmen neighbors are to be noted, as where, in the worship of the great Hero, large feasts are held on the occasion of the expected onset of the summer rains.[2]

Other cultures of this marginal type reflect in a comparable manner the absence of an economic surplus, in that those specializations, which in more complex economies mark the activities of a class composed of those who produce services rather than

<hr/>

[2] Schapera (1930), 149–51, 197– 8, 39–40, 50, 329, 332–5, 378–9, 389 ff.

goods, are wholly or almost entirely absent. The Nuer, who inhabit the difficult swampy terrain of the upper Nile, have a society where "there is little inequality of wealth and no class privilege." A man does not accumulate goods, for if he acquires more
objects than he can use, he can only give them away. Cattle can
be amassed, but this is not done except for "a few sacred herds
kept by prophets." Actually, when a herd reaches a given size,
its owner—"if one may speak of an owner of a herd in which
many people have rights of one kind and another—is morally
bound to dispose of it by either himself marrying or by assisting
a relative to do so." [3] Yet so classless is this society, and to so great
an extent is its political structure based on opposition of kinship
and local groupings, that it has been described as an "anarchic"
state.[4] Though "leopard-skin chiefs" do exist and play "a minor
role in the settlement of disputes other than homicide," their
political powers are limited to intervention between groups and
derive solely from their "sacred association with the earth." As
such, the "leopard-skin chief" is a "ritual expert," whose social
position is no greater than that of any other respected man, and
whose economic position is no more favorable.[5]

In the arctic, Central Eskimo settlements respect the authority
of a man who has special knowledge of the haunts of game. Yet
when the question of moving the camp or apportioning work
arises, though such a respected person may indicate what he
considers the best course, "there is not the slightest obligation to
obey his orders." These communities know a type of "servitor"—
one who having no ties of his own, or who is not competent himself to make his living, joins the household of another—but the
relationship is based on mutual consent. The prestige of the
master of the household and his place in society is enhanced no
more because he has a retainer than is that of the "servant" lowered because of his subordinate position. The shaman acts as a
doctor, but is economically no better off than his fellows.[6] Among
the Chipewayan tribes of northern Canada, as among the Eskimo, the "chief"—provided such an office ever existed—enjoyed
the confidence of his equals only by virtue of his achievements
and capabilities. The medicine-men of these tribes were like-

[3] Evans-Pritchard (1940b), 92.   [5] Ibid. (1940b), 172–6.
[4] Ibid. (1940a), 272.   [6] Boas (1888), 581.

wise full participants in the productive life of the community and were in no manner supported by it.[7]

The only authority exercised among the Selk'nam of Tierra del Fuego is within the family; among the wider community, life is lived in "unhindered freedom and equality." Group leadership exists only on the basis of moral force. The role of the medicine-man is important, but not from an economic point of view; though the calling is far more sharply defined than that of leader of a group, those who follow it are by no means supported by the community in return for their services.[8]

These tribal groupings of Tierra del Fuego have long been famous for the paucity of their technology and the harshness of their natural environment. "The *Alacaluf*," we are told, "live from day to day on available food. They store none because even carefully dried foodstuffs mildew in the great humidity." They practice no agriculture, nor do they have any domesticated animals except the dog. Their material culture is simple. As concerns status, we are informed that "there are, apparently, no clans or chieftainships. The families that live and hunt together are generally blood relations. The advice of the oldest individual may be asked, but is not always followed." The account speaks of "shamanism," which would indicate, as in the case of the Yahgan and Ona, a certain degree of specialization in the manipulation of the supernatural.[9]

Among these two other Fuegian peoples, the same lack of resources is found, and there are the same specific statements concerning the total absence of persons having political position. Among them, however, curers, who also "influenced weather, helped in hunting, prognosticated and so forth" were trained by older shamans, and went through a "shaman's institute and feast, which could last several months," and which functioned to "condition and school young candidates." This group training was not present among the Ona, the knowledge each candidate had to have usually being taught "by a shaman father to his son" over a period of two or three years. Because of the general economic picture, it may be assumed here again that the return to these men, which is not indicated, was meager.[10]

[7] Birket-Smith (1930), 66.
[8] Gusinde, 421–3, 718–19.
[9] Bird, 63, 71, 78.

[10] Cooper (1946a), 94, 103–04; (1946b), 116–17, 124.

Another poorly endowed, marginal people, the Shoshoni of the Great Basin area, similarly lack chiefs or economically significant specialists in the supernatural. The band, a family group, is the social and political unit. It is directed by its head; in larger temporary gatherings only those with specific supernatural power for the task at hand are accorded authority over the proceedings, and they receive no reward for their services. Shamans administer to the needs of the sick, but they become no wealthier because of their specialized skill, since whatever remuneration they may receive is dictated by the caprice of spirit that gives them their power, and this return is as likely as not to be worthless.[11] In the same region, while the Paviotso shaman has all opportunity to amass wealth, there is no point in his doing so, inasmuch as objects so classed are rarely accumulated. Moreover, since the tribe has no system of exchange, the shaman must work to supply his subsistence needs like any other person. "In short, his supernatural power does not offer the opportunity to gain marked economic privileges." [12]

The absence of an economic surplus is strikingly correlated with an absence of economically privileged status among the Australian tribes. The smallness of their bands, the crudeness of their technological equipment, and the sparseness of population over their area, are too well known to need restatement. "The organized tribe with its use of chiefs does not exist" among the Murngin. The highest social status in the camps of the aborigines of Queensland is accorded the elder, whose opinion is most highly respected; but "there is no single individual chief to direct affairs." Older men are also recognized as leaders among the Yir-Yoront, and these, informally organized into a kind of "community gerontocracy," direct the affairs of the group to which they belong, and carry on the ceremonials demanded in the worship of the supernatural. But other than this there are no distinctions of rank.[13]

The Siriono of Bolivia, it will be recalled, live close to the subsistence level. Because "the Indians are forced to devote most of their time and energy to the immediate struggle for survival," they have neither priests nor shamans. However, they do have chiefs of a sort, men who are "nominally the highest official"

[11] J. S. Harris (1940), *passim*.   [13] Warner, 9; Roth (1897), 141;
[12] Park, 66–71.   Sharp, 20.

of each group. Yet power is casual: "To maintain his prestige a chief must fulfill, in a superior fashion, those obligations required of everyone else." The prerogatives of the chief are not many, but he does have the right, with his family, to occupy the communal house, and, as an indicator of status, he will have more than one wife. The chief is said by all to be "entitled to a share of every catch of game," but an empirical check demonstrated that this rule was rarely observed. "Their requests (for food) more frequently bear fruit than those of others, because chiefs are the best hunters and are thus in a better position than most to reciprocate for any favors done them." On the whole, such returns as the chiefs receive are in the nature of prestige. They are referred to as "big" men and command more respect than ordinary individuals.[14]

Each of the three semi-independent sub-tribes of the Chiroti of the South American Chaco is markedly smaller than its neighbors. None of these units numbers more than 1,000 souls, and the total figure for all three is estimated at about 2,000. Hence it is profitable to compare such small groups, in respect to their ability to support those who do not produce subsistence commodities, with the neighboring Toba, who have a population of between 3,000 and 4,000. The Choroti have almost no effective chiefs; the picture, indeed, reminds one of the Australians and other marginal folk. Even the so-called "great chief" cannot enforce his will, and a village chief is "nothing but a *pater familias* enjoying a certain esteem." It is not surprising to learn that these officials do not appropriate resources of the community in the way of their more powerful fellows in societies having a more numerous population. Workers of magic are found, but since every old man "is more or less expert in the act of magic and considered able to handle the rattle gourd or the drum," it is not possible to point to professionals who are the equivalent of those specialists in other societies whose skills are used as an economic asset. In this culture, then, "social classes do not exist," since "all members of this primitive society are equally rich or equally poor."

What, then, of the Tobas? In terms of our hypothesis, the difference that might be expected between the absence of economically effective segmentation in a very small group and a

[14] Holmberg, 90, 59–60.

rudimentary segmentation in one somewhat larger, is at once apparent. For though among the Toba the tribe is "in its essence only a group of families united by the tie of blood relationship" and "social ranks and classes do not exist," yet a "germ of nobility" is to be discerned, and the real power possessed by Toba chiefs is backed by a certain control of economic resources. The chiefs, that is, are distinguished "by having several wives and by being richer, since of the spoils taken in war the main part is allotted to them." Thus while the categories of rich and poor are of but minor importance in view of the prevalent patterns of economic equality, yet it does happen, though rarely, that a great chief who has waged war successfully against other tribes will have larger flocks and more wives than his subjects.[15]

4

It is hardly necessary to compare these groups having sparse populations with the societies which represent the other extremes of numbers and resources among nonliterate peoples. One finds moving through the accounts of those who, in Peru and Mexico, West Africa and Malaysia, witnessed the functioning of the so-called "high cultures" not only rulers and priests, but corps of assistants and servitors and craftsmen whose duty it was to provide ornaments, regalia, and settings worthy of their masters. Well-defined procedures are also often recorded whereby a considerable part of the labor of the group went for the upkeep of royal and priestly establishments.

More important for our purposes are those societies that fall between the extremes, such as those of Polynesia. Varying in size and technological achievement, the production of an economic surplus is facilitated by the favorable environmental conditions in which for the most part they live. In Tahiti the rulers, who also exercised important priestly functions, were the highest of the three existing social classes, the others being the "gentry" and the "plebeians." Chiefs from this social stratum were regarded as descendants of the highest class of gods. They wore the costumes of these gods, and were themselves held to be gods incarnate. "Their lands were extensive, their dwellings were spa-

[15] Karsten, 18–19, 43–6, 94–5.

cious . . . and they always had a large retinue of retainers chosen from the lower classes." The humbler members of the royal family lived in much the same way as the more important personages of the group, "but on a smaller scale." Royalty of all ranks engaged in the more gracious forms of productive activities; it was deemed shameful not to excel "in all the arts and handicrafts of their time, feeling it a disgrace to appear ignorant or clumsy before their people." The gentry were farmers, working their own lands and acting as faithful keepers of the lands of their sovereign. Their standard of living was less elaborate than that of royalty, but higher than that of the lowest class, who did most of the actual labor on the land.

The social status of each class, and, what is more important for the present discussion, its economic position, were well recognized. No more effective formulation of the economic role of each and the return each could expect from the store of total goods produced could be had than the native phrasing of the situation: "The types of men are three. Take a breadfruit. When it is cooked, take off the skin, that is for the people. The meat, that is eaten by the *arii* (the rulers). The core is given to the manahune (commoners without property)." To the ruler certain things were *tapu*, and none other than he could partake of them; in this category came the cavalla fish, the chest and filet of the hog, and the first fruits of the land.[16]

Though class structure throughout the Pacific area was not always as marked as in Tahiti, it was present in some form almost everywhere, and everywhere its economic base is readily apparent. In the Marquesas, the chief had the right to the first fruits of the gardens, especially the breadfruit, and to the first fish of each catch. In Tonga, the burden of supporting the upper classes was appreciable, as can be seen from one report, which gives some idea of the comparative numbers in each class. In Lifuka as a whole, among the male heads of families in 1920 were numbered 33 chiefs, 116 matapules—officials appointed from the higher non-chiefly families—and 275 commoners; in Foa the numbers were 8, 53, and 110 respectively; in Uiha, 3, 23, and 109; in Kolovai Tongutalu 18, 10, and 74. Mangaia also had three social grades, the lowest a population of serfs, the descendants of captives, who survived only through the goodwill of their

[16] T. Henry, 229–30; Handy (1930), 42–4.

overlord, from whom they purchased security by bringing to him what they produced.[17]

Maori chiefs were invariably wealthy men, and the sources of the liberal support given them by the community have been set down in some detail. They owned private gardens and rights over bird-trees and fishing grounds, which were better worked than those of ordinary men because of the labor-power of their households, which were much larger than those of commoners. The principal chief of a district, in addition, held special rights to any sea mammals cast ashore within his territory, to flotsam and jetsam on uninhabited neighboring shores, and to any hidden goods that might be dug up or otherwise discovered. Here, as elsewhere, he was presented by his subjects with the first fruits, and in addition, received offerings of food from their annual harvest. Those who asked a favor of a chief showed prudence if their plea was accompanied by a gift, while tribute from vassals and those living on the land belonging to a chief also increased his income. The freemen of neighboring settlements were often called on to work his forests, or to obtain birds or fish for him, while presents were sent him from time to time by his relatives in other districts, and travelers who passed through his territory expressed their appreciation in tangible form.[18]

In the Melanesian Trobriand Islands, the chief, the wealthiest man in his community, supports the expenditures required of one in his position by means of the tribute paid him by each "vassal" village which he controls through his political marriages. From each of these villages he takes a wife, who is always related to the village headman, so that, in effect, the entire community must work to supply him with the produce that is his due as the affinal relative of their local ruler.

> In olden days, the chief of Omarakana had up to as many as forty consorts, and received perhaps as much as thirty to fifty per cent of all the garden produce of Kiriwana. Even now, when his wives number only sixteen, he has enormous storehouses, and they are full to the roof with yams every harvest time.

This food is expended by the chief "for the many services he requires." Thus it is used by him to acquire objects of wealth, to

[17] Handy (1923), 58–9; Gifford (1929), 108 ff.; Hiroa (1934), 109 ff.   [18] Raymond Firth (1929a), 285–8.

underwrite the expenses of great feasts or of overseas expeditions, and to purchase the supernatural controls needed to maintain himself in power. Here, it must be remarked, appears a mechanism frequently encountered; the support by the chief, or ruler, of specialists in the supernatural. The only way in which a Trobriand chief can punish his subjects is by recourse to supernatural forces, and consequently some of his wealth must go to the workers of magic, since their very presence is a threat to any challenge to his power. It is thus apparent that "the chief's position can be grasped only through the realisation of the high importance of wealth, of the necessity of paying for everything, even for services which are due to him, and which could not be withheld. . . ." [19]

In Bougainville, Solomon Islands, where there is "no established tradition by which a leader is succeeded in office by son or nephew," there are none the less "social-political hierarchies" which, as in the Trobriand Islands, are based on the ability to control and manipulate wealth—in this case pigs and shell-money. According to Oliver, "the real leader is the one who originates action in traditionally accepted ways. He is the feast-giver, the wealth-distributor." He attains his position "at the top of the social-political ladder by building up prestige with frequent distributions of food. *Giving away* food and riches rather than accumulating and displaying it is the key to social and political success in Siaui."

The relationship between the average number of pigs held by men who were heads of households, and the ages of these men, may be indicated. It is apparent that in a system such as this, as in other societies with similar arrangements for the acquisition of status through the display and expenditure of wealth,[20] the relationship actually found might be anticipated, since only with increasing age can the wealth needed to achieve status be obtained. The tabulation is given on the following page, while on p. 410 a graphic presentation of them will be found (in Figure 5).

It may be pointed out that factors other than the ownership of pigs enter in the determination of status. As between villages, for example, one group may give more feasts, and thus have less pigs on hand, than another. Again, the number of wives possessed by a man will be related to his resources—the average holdings

[19] Malinowski (1922), 62–5.   [20] See below, 461ff.

Age of householder	Number of householders	Average Number of pigs
19–21	7	1.8
22–24	8	3.2
25–27	18	3.6
28–30	16	3.8
31–33	16	3.4
34–36	15	3.5
37–39	10	3.8
40–42	10	4.3
43–45	12	4.1
46–48	9	5.0
49–51	5	5.4
52–54	9	4.1
55–57	4	4.7
58–	9	4.2

of pigs by 186 monogamous households sampled in Siuai was 3.6, of 13 polygamous units, 5.0.

Whatever the force of the various factors involved, the economic base of the position of the man of status in this society is clear:

> The native leader has certain rights and obligations *vis à vis* his followers. His house is frequently larger, but his diet is no better. He is relieved of the onerous tasks of climbing palms and carrying heavy burdens, but he continues to work in his garden. He is treated with respect and deference wherever he goes, but in return must be a generous host. He frequently calls upon his followers to labor for him, but must repay their efforts with pork meals. Nowadays, he has no armed force to back up his orders, but he can control the opinions of most of his followers and thereby make life fairly unpleasant for a disobedient one. And, on top of all this he has supernatural sanction for his position.[21]

For the Bantu of South Africa, it has likewise been shown how power and prestige derive from control over economic surplus. A man is here liable to his chief "and other political superiors" for labor as well as tribute in kind, and these obligations can be enforced in the native courts. The commoner can be sent on er-

[21] Oliver (1949a), 13–14; (1949b), 59–60.

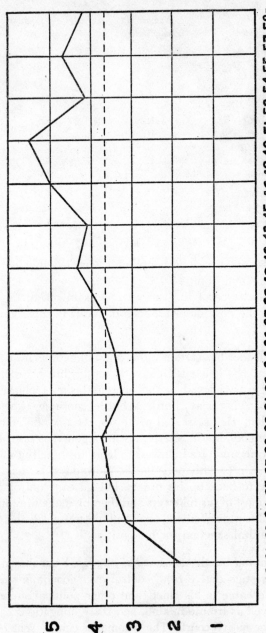

5. *Total Number of Pigs Owned by Households in Noronai Village, northeast Siuai, Solomon Islands (after Oliver, 1949a, p. 14).*

rands for his overlord, or can be summoned to perform "various tasks" either for him or for some member of his household, such as helping build and thatch royal dwellings, rounding up stray cattle, and destroying wild beasts. Tribute may take the form of the crops from special fields worked for the chief by the people, or, as among the Sotho, of a basket of corn from each woman, when she harvests her field; he also benefits from the hunter's bag. His wealth is always considerable. He has "by far" the largest herds of cattle in the tribe. All animals captured in raids must be brought to him for redistribution at his pleasure, and stray cattle are taken to him and must be reclaimed within a certain period if he is not to retain them. Upon his installation, he is given cattle by the head of every family, and in some parts of the region the father of each lad undergoing initiation must pay him one animal. Fines for certain crimes are retained by him, while, in addition to all these sources of revenue, there is a constant flow of gifts from those who desire his favors, or who wish to remain in his good graces. He is priest as well as ruler, and plays an especially important role in rain-making ceremonies; but this function has little economic significance, since he merely acts as would any family head. In this area, too, are healers, magicians, and diviners. These are professionals whose support is also a charge upon the community.[22]

Yet lacking the conceptual framework employed in this discussion, the relationship between resources and social status in this area can be confusing. Thus, concerning the Swazi, we are first informed that "though differences of wealth exist, no class structure similar to that of industrialized Europe has developed. There is no capitalist class with the monopoly of the means of production, no proletariat from whom these means are debarred, and no self-conscious, leisured class that maintains itself on the labour of others."[23] This is not entirely consonant with the later statement: "Swazi accept economic and social inequality and approve of wealth as the privilege of men of noble birth";[24] or that "the cattle of kingship," held by the king in trust for the nation, "exceed those of any individual"; or that "within the principalities chiefs usually, but not inevitably, own larger herds

[22] Schapera and Goodwin, 166–70; Hoernlé, 226 ff.   [23] Kuper, 137.
[24] Ibid., 153.

than their subjects." [25] Figures of the distribution of ownership of cattle show the inequalities that are found among this people of one district:

No. of cattle									
0	0–5	5–10	10–20	20–30	30–40	40–50	50–60	60–70	Over 70
No. of owners									
6	0	2	7	9	4	3	2	3	1

The underlying validation of social position would seem to be expressed in this sentence: "Obligations as well as benefits accrue from wealth: rich men gain prestige and security, not by hoarding, but by judicious distribution."

Numerous societies in the Americas, lying between extremes of size and resource, show that in the New World the distribution of the economic surplus among the members of a given tribe was by no means equal. Among the Natchez of southeastern United States the apportionment of wealth strongly favored the nobles, whose display of goods to enhance their position will be treated in a later chapter. To the north, Iroquois economic structure made for a tripartite grouping, often overlooked because of interest in the political and social organization of these people. In addition to the mass of free citizens of the community, who, though varying in social position, were not of significantly different economic status, there were the medicine-men, whose "monopolistic part in production . . . gave them a certain control over the surplus of the clan, which they were not slow to perceive," and the servile groups, who "stood below . . . the [members of the] clan in the distributive system." Just as the former group obtained their wealth "in the form of a tax . . . rendered in return for the supposed services of the medicine man in controlling the forces of nature," so the underprivileged group "received nothing but 'food and shelter in exchange for their ceaseless labor and sweat.'" [26]

5

FROM all parts of the world materials are thus on hand to make clear that nonliterate societies everywhere, producing more goods

[25] Ibid., 151.   [26] Stites, 76–8.

than the minimum required for the support of life, translate their economic surpluses into the social leisure which is only afforded those members of the community who are supported by this excess wealth. Just why the surplus is produced remains obscure. As has been suggested, this question will only be resolved when further research produces quantitative data to give us a clearer picture than we now have of the relationship between natural environment, technological equipment, and population size.

Yet if we collate our materials, it is possible to formulate this problem more sharply than has hitherto been done, and such a formulation may at least serve as a basis for future investigation. It is to be recalled that the societies having the simplest economies, crudest technologies, and surpluses either nonexistent or so slight as to be of little significance, also have the smallest populations. On the other hand, it is evident that among the most populous nonliterate peoples, the surplus is large enough to enable these groups to support considerable numbers of persons not engaged in the production of subsistence goods. This point is the more striking if the literate historic cultures are included, since these comprise both greater populations, greater economic surpluses, and larger leisure classes than are found elsewhere.

It thus appears that whereas in the smallest groups life is a real struggle for existence in which man is barely the victor, in larger groups there is more than enough to go around, and this surplus becomes proportionately greater as populations are more numerous. The factor of superior technology must, of course, enter. Yet why, we may ask, should large groups have superior technologies? Is there some bio-statistical reason which brings it about that by chance more persons of an inventive turn may make their appearance in larger groups than in smaller ones, and thus create the means whereby the labor of their fellows and their descendants is rendered more efficient? Does mere chance dictate the result? Does the accident of invention encourage a tendency for human groups to breed toward the limit of their productive capacity? Or does the process of directing the surplus goods produced into the hands of a few members of the community, as noted even among groups living only slightly above the subsistence level, create a condition that encourages the thought and reflection which can only come with the leisure enjoyed by some persons? And is it this opportunity which not only makes possible inventions in the technological sphere, but also encourages the development of those aspects of culture commonly described as "civilization"?

Whatever the case, the almost universal inequities which seem to mark the distribution of surplus economic goods is striking. This surplus wealth, it is apparent, goes to two groups, those who govern, and those who command techniques for placating and manipulating the supernatural forces of the universe. The members of these groups are, therefore, to be regarded as belonging to a leisure class in that they, like their families and their retainers, profit from the social leisure which this economic surplus represents. They are, to be sure, members of a leisure class—certainly in so far as they are encountered in most nonliterate societies—only in the sense that the goods they deal in consist of intangibles whose production does not require the exercise of the manual labor their less privileged fellows give to the production of the essentials to life they produce. Obviously, members of the leisure class do not occupy their time purposelessly, for they are often hard driven by the cares and preoccupations of their obligations toward the groups from which they derive their support. As it has been put for certain African societies, "Economic privileges, such as rights to tax, tribute, and labour, are both the main reward of political power and an essential means of maintaining it. . . . But there are counterbalancing economic obligations no less strongly backed by institutionalized sanctions. It must not be forgotten, also, that those who derive maximum economic benefit from political office also have the maximum administrative, judicial and religious responsibilities." [27]

Having attempted to sketch the conditions which make for the production of an economic surplus and the social leisure it represents, two further points must be considered. The first concerns the manner in which non-producers of subsistence goods obtain the support of their fellows and entails a description and analysis of the devices employed to ensure them command of the surplus they must have in order to live and function. The second point bears on the measures taken by those who benefit from the economic surplus to ensure that those who do not so benefit remain content with their lot. Here we are at the heart of the

[27] Fortes and Evans-Pritchard, 8–9.

matter. For we find that people the world over are not only content, but often proud to yield a portion of what their labor produces for the maintenance of their superiors on a plane of living that surpasses their own.

In attempting to answer these questions, we enter the topsy-turvy realm of prestige economics, where the greatest aid toward the production of esteem is the economic waste of useful goods. Here, as we shall see, the more conspicuous the display of economic advantage by the group in power before those whose duty it is to provide them with the means of supporting their position, the greater the assurance that their power will be continued and that they will be able to maintain control of the economic surplus on which this power rests.

CHAPTER XIX

THE COST OF
GOVERNMENT

THE FACT that public finance must constitute an essential phase of the administration of nonliterate communities is not commonly recognized when their processes of government are discussed. None the less, the regulation of group life cannot be carried on without cost, and this cost must be deducted from any surplus that may be produced by a people over their subsistence needs. The proportion of the surplus devoted to this purpose, and its use by those in whose hands it is placed, will obviously vary greatly from one culture to the next. But, as has been demonstrated in the preceding chapter, no society can afford a government whose available resources are insufficient to relieve those charged with the direction of affairs from the necessity of themselves producing all their primary wants.

As in any analysis of public finance, income and expenditure must be primary considerations, though it must be made clear that much more is known of how income is assured rulers in nonliterate societies than of how they dispose of what they receive. Accounting is a recent development even in Euroamerican culture; in these other societies the absence of record-keeping, to say nothing of an almost universal lack of stable currency in which to calculate receipts and expenditures, makes it possible only in exceptional instances to bring even the most rudimentary bookkeeping devices to our aid. Hence, though what a chief may levy as taxes or receive as gifts can, in a general way, be ascertained from the literature, as can his rights to command the labor of his subjects and the circumstances under which he may confiscate their possessions for his own or public use, our information is vague indeed as to what he does with these goods and services. Some of the goods available to the ruler, as we shall see in a later chapter, are redistributed to win the loyalty of his subjects, or they may be destroyed to enhance his prestige. The cost of the mechanisms which assure tranquillity in times of peace and security in time of war is usually a charge against the income of the ruler, particularly in more populous and highly organized societies. The dictates of *noblesse oblige* necessitate that lavish hospitality be dispensed by those in high position, while, in addition, they are often called upon to make what can be termed philanthropic donations. But to balance these and other forms of expenditure against what is received can only be done, if at all, in the generalized terms which by now stand in familiar contrast to the sharpness that marks the similar but more clearly differentiated phenomena in literate pecuniary societies.

However generalized public finance in nonliterate societies may be, and however difficult to reduce to quantitative statement, the means whereby rulers are assured of support by those they govern must none the less be regarded as taxation. Any attempt to understand how the economic surplus is diverted into the hands of those who govern may thus be best furthered by an attack from the point of view implicit in this designation. We accordingly proceed, to the degree our data permit, to note those devices that are employed to assure revenue to those who rule, and, where possible, the reactions of those taxed. We shall at the same time attempt to indicate as well the expenditures made by governments of nonliterate groups for socially useful purposes, rather than for purposes of individual advantage, leaving the latter to the discussion of the relationship between spending and prestige.

2

THE MOST sharply differentiated systems of taxation and public expenditure are understandably to be found in those societies having the most complex political organization. Two West African kingdoms falling in this category that have been the most carefully studied for materials of this type may therefore be dis-

cussed at the outset. Not only do these materials demonstrate
how in certain nonliterate societies the problem of supporting
the regime was solved, but they also serve as a stepping-stone to
an understanding of the less specialized forms of comparable
phenomena among groups lacking such intricate types of governmental organization.

In analyzing the levies laid by Ashanti rulers, Rattray stresses
the fact that

> "onerous and no doubt irksome as these taxes may sometimes
> have been, they nevertheless constituted the lesser impost
> levied by a Stool [1] upon its subjects. By far the most onerous
> duty placed upon the Ashanti landholder in olden days does
> not appear on our schedule, i.e., the obligation imposed upon
> a subject to give life and limb, fighting in the service of his
> overlord, when called upon to do so.

The taxes themselves were, however, sufficiently burdensome.
First in the order of their yield were the death duties, which accrued to a given Stool slowly, as they moved stage by stage up
through the appropriate hierarchy. Thus when a man of substance died, the elder who was his immediate superior succeeded
to a specified proportion of the "private personal property" of the
deceased—movable assets, gold-dust, slaves, cloths. Upon the
death of this elder, his superior took a similar proportion, and it
was only upon the demise of this third man that the ruler of the
territorial division received his share of the estate from which the
chain of deductions had commenced. The manner of collecting
these dues varied. A chief might legally send his treasurer to seal
the rooms and boxes of his dead subject, but if "a more delicate
and tactful way of going about the collection of this tax than the
other more forcible method" was desired, payment could be left
to the discretion of the relatives of the dead man. This, it seems,
"practically amounted to the same thing in the end" because in
such cases the social sanctions acted to reinforce the political
ones.

The second most important source of revenue to a Stool was
the trade monopolies and the taxes on the transportation of com-

[1] The word "Stool" is employed
in the Ashanti literature as the
equivalent of "throne." This term
will therefore be retained in discussing Ashanti public finance here.

modities. Kola was exported to the north, and slaves, livestock, and shea butter were acquired in return. Southward slaves and gold-dust were sent to the coast, and the carriers returned with rum, guns and gunpowder, metal rods, salt, and "soft goods." Roads to the north were closed when the trading operations of the Stool were being effected; when these roads were reopened, all other traders who passed were assessed twenty-five kola-nuts per load, twenty of these going to the principal chief. While porters carrying goods from the north were not taxed, those who returned from the coast with commodities for sale were assessed gold-dust to the amount of three or four shillings before they were allowed to proceed to their home markets.

A third source of revenue was what Rattray terms court fines and fees. One type of fee, foreign to European legal procedure, was given by the party acquitted of a charge; this was a thank-offering and also "served the purpose of securing witnesses to attest to the judgment of the court should the trial ever be questioned." The death penalty could be remitted by a chief upon payment of a fine. Unlike other fines, this type was not divided among his subordinates, and since such fines were in amounts that ranged to an equivalent of about four thousand dollars, they offered an appreciable source of income. Taxes on gold-mining operations comprised a fourth form of revenue. This tax generally amounted to two-thirds of the gold mined, the miner retaining the other third. There were, in addition, further ways of caring for the needs of the treasury. A special levy met the funeral expenses of a chief; spoils of war were apportioned among the chiefs; assessments were imposed to care for the ceremonies of the enstoolment of a new chief; national levies for other specific purposes were authorized from time to time; there was a war tax; treasure trove was reserved to the ruler; while foodstuffs, game, and fish could be confiscated as need for them arose.

Appreciable decentralization marked Ashanti political organization, each unit in the system having its own jurisdictional right to assess those it governed. The hierarchical system of great and petty chiefs was responsible for the procedure of having revenues paid into the head chief's treasury filter through the treasuries of his subordinates. For example, the total amount to be collected when a specified tax was decreed was divided into two equal parts, the Stool of the paramount chief being responsible for half, and the subordinate chiefs for the other half. The paramount chief's quota was thereupon subdivided into five parts. This chief assumed responsibility for one of these fifths, which was in turn divided equally between himself, on the one hand, and the queen mother, the heir apparent, and other members of the royal family, on the other. This tenth, then, that the paramount chief had accepted as his personal quota was again divided into nine unequal parts, which the heads of the various groups of palace officials were charged with collecting. Each chief profited from the process of collecting his required quota, his subjects being the ones to pay what was ostensibly demanded of chiefs. The Ashanti proverb cited by Rattray: "A chief may 'eat things,' but he does not pay a debt," reflects long experience.

To what degree did the taxpayers benefit from levies? Certain taxes imposed for specific purposes—to buy guns and powder, to defray funeral costs, or to furnish regalia—were applied at once to the specified ends. The demands of hospitality took a large proportion of the sums collected, for anyone might eat in any chief's palace as a matter of right. Consequently, "many of the food taxes . . . went in keeping open house, thus finding their way back again to the people who had supplied them." The palace of a chief was built and kept in good repair by the elders of his district and the men under them, who also cleared paths and bridged streams. For these services "presents" paid for out of the public funds were proffered in lieu of wages, which were practically unknown in this culture. Fines, especially thank-offerings, were divided and subdivided until they were widely dispersed, this being the manner in which palace attendants received their remuneration. Weavers, or makers of metal objects, or carvers of stools for the chiefs were fed while at work, and in addition they received gifts "corresponding approximately to the market values of their wares."

A sufficiently effective method of accounting assured probity in the workings of this system, despite the absence of writing. Receipts and disbursements were balanced at the end of each day by the use of cowrie shells, and any discrepancy was investigated until responsibility was placed on the proper shoulders. The financial checks and balances essential to the smooth functioning of any fiscal agency were thus provided, and the assessments in money, labor, and kind collected from those at the bottom of the social scale assured support to minor and central governing bodies for the fulfillment of their roles as the acknowledged leaders of the community, in a manner traditionally sanctioned for the ruling group.[2]

3

IN THE kingdom of Dahomey, a system of social stratification similar to that just described among the Ashanti to the west was marked by sharper delineation and greater rigidity of structure. At the base of the pyramid were the slaves, the majority of whom labored on the royal plantations or on those of the great chiefs. Next came a group roughly comparable to European serfs; the children of slaves who, born in Dahomey, might not be sold outside the country, yet did not enjoy such liberties as were accorded free Dahomeans. Comprising the third stratum are the families of free farmers and artisans, such as iron-workers, weavers, jewelers, potters, and other specialists. This class furnished the soldiers; and it was also from this class that the higher ranks of officialdom were filled, since political expediency dictated that those to whom power was entrusted be of humble origin so that attempts at rebellion would not find potential leaders of royal blood in strategic positions. Finally, atop this pyramided structure were the senior members of the priestly hierarchy and the rulers, with whom we will be particularly concerned here.

Control over the collection of taxes and other revenues was maintained through the operation of a unique system, whereby a female bureaucracy within the royal compound duplicated the hierarchy of male officials who actually administered the affairs of the kingdom outside those walls and served as checks upon the reports of these men. For each officer there was a "mother," a titular wife of the king who lived in the royal compound and was always present whenever the official gave any report. This woman also received the reports of the "control" officers sent out to obtain independent accounts of the matters concerning which official statements had been or were to be made. In addition, eight "wives of the leopard" who always accompanied the king, listened to what was said by a given official, and they were sec-

[2] Rattray (1929), 107–19.

onded by another group of the same number whose presence was also required on such occasions. It is thus to be seen that with the various outer controls and the triple "inner" control exercised by the women of the royal household, the opportunities for peculation were not plentiful.

Two principles were operative in all taxation. The first was that the control exercised by the monarch—that is, the "external" control—must always be indirect. Thus, no one was questioned concerning the number of cultivators in a given village, but the count was quietly obtained when these farmers, village by village, brought their "gifts" to the king before the annual rites for the royal ancestors. The second principle, which throws considerable light on attitudes toward the taxing process, was that for purposes of what among ourselves would be termed propaganda, the king himself paid the same taxes as his subjects, especially on the produce of his fields. He thus sought to create in the minds of his people the impression that he himself was subject to the same rules as all other Dahomeans, and he seems to have resorted to much ingenuity to foster this belief.

We may now consider some of the products which were taxed in this kingdom, and to the degree possible, the amount of tax that was levied. In the case of agriculture, a given proportion, varying yearly, of the harvest of each village had to be turned over to the officials from the palace, where the produce was transported and, in the main, held for the army. Palm groves were assessed approximately one-third of their total yield; the palm-oil, which with the declining slave-trade became increasingly the most important source of revenue of the monarchy, was shipped to the sea-coast and traded for guns, ammunition, and other European goods. Livestock was taxed only every two or three years, the size of the assessment varying according to calculated need and available numbers. Cattle, which were not numerous in Dahomey, presented no problem, but sheep and goats were counted without the knowledge of their owners by means of ruses in which the priesthood co-operated with the officials of the monarchy in a manner to be detailed in the next chapter. The census of livestock was taken by village, and on this basis the number of animals demanded of each settlement was fixed. In one instance where the residents in a given village possessed 800 goats, the levy was 12.5 per cent—"five from each forty," or

100 animals. Horses, which were rare, were in effect "registered," since only men of high position might ride them, and then only with the express permission of the monarch. Four thousand cowries per year was the approximate license fee for each animal, though early first-hand accounts of rituals of the royal ancestral cult make it appear that those who rode horses were also expected to meet supplementary charges in the form of "gifts" to the king. One pig was demanded of each person who owned these animals; butchers paid an "occupational" tax according to the number of head handled, in addition to a quarter of an animal as a gift to the king on the occasion of the annual ancestral rites.

There were numerous other occupational taxes. Hunters were counted—by subterfuge—during rituals for the gods of the hunt. They worked in groups, each under its chief, these chiefs being assigned to thirteen divisions, each of which was required to furnish meat for the palace during one of the Dahomean native months. In other words, one-thirteenth of each hunter's efforts went as a license fee. Since the heads of all the animals had to be sent to the palace, the amount of game killed, as well as the number of hunters, was controlled, and a complete return of everything due was assured. Salt, evaporated from sea-water, was manufactured at the coast, and since this industry was in the charge of the "Viceroy of Whydah"—as the subordinate who ruled this important town has been termed—an especially careful check was maintained. Inasmuch as salt was held a necessity, tradition has it that royal policy dictated that no revenue was to be obtained from its manufacture. Each salt-maker was therefore assessed but ten small sacks annually, an amount calculated only to supply the actual needs of the palace.

Iron-workers were required to make cartridges as their contribution to the needs of the government. After a complicated process of indirect counting, based on control at the forges and in the market-places where they disposed of their wares, they were assessed on the basis of the amount of iron each forge had not disposed of and thus had on hand. Each iron-worker was presented with a token bar of iron by the king, and told to return after a given time with a specified number of cartridges. The number, however, was carefully based on the amount of iron represented by the unsold hoes or other goods a forge had on hand after the year's operations, which is to say, on the basis of the year's surplus, as represented by the current inventory. Similarly, weavers were levied on against the products of their looms, and wood-cutters were assessed on the basis of how much wood they had gathered.

Certain commodities were royal monopolies. All honey was reserved by the king, to be used for curing the meat required by the troops on campaign. In the two districts set aside for the purpose, those who cared for bees also cultivated red and black pepper and ginger for the palace; otherwise, pepper, which was highly prized, could only be grown for commercial purposes in seven districts near Allada. However, the monarch did not make the mistake of alienating his people by forbidding them to grow the condiment for themselves, for each farmer was permitted to cultivate enough plants to yield him a raffia-sack full. But this was not adequate even for the needs of the simplest households, so that a man was compelled to buy the remainder in the open market. Revenue came from the duties levied on the transport of pepper; forty-six cowrie shells were assessed against each sack which passed through each customs post, thus assuring an appreciable return to the treasury.

Sales taxes were also a profitable source of income. As has been indicated in an earlier chapter, Dahomean markets, following a cycle based on the native four-day week, did a large amount of business. The taxes were levied in kind and were not high, but in their aggregate they bulked large. The tax on the sellers of meat has been mentioned. In addition, all other traders were held liable for a measure of whatever commodity was offered for sale. This levy, well documented by those who visited the kingdom before its conquest by the French, is said today to be so deeply lodged in tradition that voluntary contributions are still made by those who do business in the markets for the upkeep of the old palace and the maintenance, in so far as circumstances permit, of the pre-European ceremonies for the royal ancestors. The toll system offered a further means of taxing marketable products, and many early travelers commented on the toll-gates they encountered at intervals. On the main road between the capital, Abomey, and the principal port, Whydah, there were four of these posts, and all goods shipped in either direction had to pay duty at each gate. Porters who carried the goods paid a tax based on the number of trips made, these being recorded for each carrier at every toll-gate passed. Grave-diggers and those who directed funeral rites were also taxed, as were the heads of the various religious cult-houses, but the revenues from these taxes were of relatively minor economic importance and were levied mainly because of the political control they afforded.

What was received went for the lavish support of the king and his entourage; for maintenance and equipment of the army; for compensating the numerous administrative officials that ruled the kingdom; and for defraying the cost of the expensive ancestral rites of the royal family which were held to assure the continued survival and prosperity of the kingdom. As among the Ashanti, every male taxpayer was liable to serve in the army, or, when summoned, to work on roads or at other communal tasks. Unlike the Ashanti, however, there was no obligation laid on the ruler to compensate those who thus gave of their time and labor. For it is in the impersonal nature of its administration, in the care with which expected yield was balanced against actual receipts, and the check on those who handled the moneys of the king, that the Dahomean monarchy is distinctive among nonliterate societies. That there was political acumen as well as economic efficiency in the system emerges from the fact that the counts on which levies were based, and the controls exercised, were effectively masked. On the other hand, the liability of royalty and subordinate chiefs to the same taxes as were levied on their subjects made for further psychological assuagement of what must at least have been a heavy burden upon all.[3]

4

OTHER data from West Africa, such as in the case of the Nupe,[4] might be cited to further document the support of government in nonliterate societies. However, since the general pattern has been indicated in the two examples just given, we may present materials from different regions of Africa before proceeding to other parts of the world and to societies with simpler forms of political organization. The Baganda supported three more or less independent royal establishments: those of the king, who was the

[3] Herskovits (1938), I, 107–34.   [4] Nadel (1935), 285–7.

effective ruler of the entire country, of the queen, and of the king's mother. When taxes were to be levied, the king appointed a special representative for each district. The prime minister, the keeper of the royal umbilical cord, the queen, and the king's mother each similarly named a representative, district by district, while the representative of the local chief completed the tax-collecting group in each section. Taxes, on the basis of a count of houses, were assessed *pro forma* by the king's agent against each sub-chief. "The amount usually demanded was a fixed number of cattle from each sub-chief, and a fixed number of bark-cloths and one hundred cowry-shells from each peasant; of the smaller chiefs each paid a number of goats and also a few hoes."

To assemble the levy took two months and more, since such goods as bark-cloth and hoes had to be made especially for the purpose, and the cattle had to be gathered. When ready, each responsible officer took his portion to the district chief, who forwarded the entire amount to the capital. Here the prime minister examined it, checked the total against the number of houses and people in the district as reported by his enumerators, and, if correct, sent the tribute intact to the king. Should the total not be correct, the king's agent was required to return to his district and obtain what was lacking. The total was then divided into two halves. From the first, each district chief received for himself a part of what had been collected from those under him and his subordinates, and the queen, the king's mother, the prime minister, and the keeper of the king's umbilical cord were also allotted their shares. The remaining half was taken over by the royal treasury. High officers and subsidiary royalty not only retained their shares of the taxes paid by the entire kingdom, but kept for themselves what was assessed on their own estates and districts. States tributary to Uganda forwarded their tribute through the chiefs ruling them; this consisted of cattle, slaves, ivory, cowrie shells, salt, hoes, and other local products.

The king imposed other levies. The possibilities of sales and occupational taxes were not overlooked:

Not only in the capital, but also throughout the country districts, there were market-places under the supervision of the authorities, with regular market-fees for the wares which were offered for sale. Moreover, people in the capital, who tried to evade the market-dues by selling their goods privately outside the market-place were liable to heavy fines and to the confiscation of the goods which they tried to sell. The market-places in and around the capital were under the supervision of a special chief appointed by the King, who collected the dues; these amounted to ten per cent of the value of each article sold or bought.

Boys and girls were liable to be chosen for service in the palaces of royalty and of the highest officials. Labor for building the royal enclosure or new houses in the royal compound, or for repairing the buildings already there, might also be requisitioned, and road-making was a charge against the labor-power of the country.

Court cases were a never ending source of revenue for chiefs as well as royalty. A fee of twenty cowrie shells was paid by a plaintiff when making his plea, and both he and the defendant each paid a goat and a bark cloth before the case was tried. Appeals could be taken from lower to higher courts, but each involved the payment of correspondingly heavier fees, while bribery was so rampant that a system of indicating by signs what would be given for a favorable verdict had been developed to facilitate this aspect of the administration of justice. Inheritance taxes also helped the royal budget, since the king received a share of the property of the deceased. Even more lucrative was the royal power—also found in Dahomey—to "break" any chief who gave the appearance of becoming too rich or too powerful; a new appointee was expected to show his gratitude in a fitting manner.[5]

To the south, the BaVenda of Rhodesia, despite their less impressive governmental structure, show the same principles of control of economic surplus by the governing group, and they possess just as efficient mechanisms for the concentration of this surplus in the hands of those in power as was seen in the preceding instances. "Venda chiefs," says Stayt, "are generally rich out of all proportion to their subjects, obtaining a large revenue from their lands, taxation, proceeds of justice, and the fees levied on social functions, as well as many other perquisites." Free labor to work a chief's fields makes of them a profitable enter-

[5] Roscoe, 244-5, 452, Ch. VIII.

prise, while, as elsewhere, an official may call levies to build or repair his dwellings. Where the great chiefs have land within the domain of lesser officials, persons who reside in these districts may be called on to do double work, since both categories of those in authority must be served. With the consent and approval of the ruler's council, taxes in hoes and goats may be levied after "prevailing conditions and the ability of the people to pay" are taken into consideration. Petty chiefs, responsible for collecting this tax within their districts, receive a part of what they gather, though what they receive depends upon the goodwill of the ruler. Today, when a money tax is levied, citizens who are absent from the land are liable, and special messengers are sent to collect their share from the men working in the gold-fields of the Rand.

Fines, here as elsewhere, add to the revenue of a chief, who as judge is entitled to a part of what is paid by the loser in a suit; where a considerable amount is involved, the gratitude of the winner is shown by a gift of several additional head of cattle. In pre-European days, "large windfalls" came through the conviction of murderers and sorcerers, whose families and property were forfeit to the chief. Skins of all lions and leopards had to be given to chiefs and petty chiefs, who also received a hind leg of all cattle or wild game killed near their seats of government. Puberty ceremonies, even today, bring revenue in cash or services; perhaps the only revenue which Venda chiefs do not receive when compared with their fellows in other parts of Africa is that derived in connection with the inheritance of property. For, as far as is reported, no inheritance tax is found.[6]

5

IT IS all but impossible to find materials concerning the fiscal policies of tribes outside Africa comparable to those available for that continent, though it is clear that some part of the economic surplus is everywhere allocated for the support of those who rule. As has already been pointed out, one of the methodological problems derives from the fact that the less complex the political organization, the less specialized are the institutions and

[6] Stayt, 105, 217 ff.

the mechanisms that ensure their perpetuation, and consequently the more difficult it is to segregate them for purposes of study and analysis. This difficulty is enhanced where the economic system is of a similar generalized character, or where, as in the Pacific area, the problem of getting a living is relatively simple. Yet taxes or their equivalent are almost always to be found. Even though they may take the form of labor rather than goods, or consist of goods which all produce and have, the underlying process corresponds to that which has been observed in more specific form among African peoples and is still more sharply distinguishable in historic civilizations.

Some of the hints in the literature regarding the manner in which the taxing process operated in the South Seas can be given here to supplement the evidence presented in the preceding chapter, where the existence in the area of a leisure class, whose economic function is that of consumer rather than that of producer, was considered. When a large house was to be built for a chief in Mangaia, he summoned the members of his tribe to do the work, though on occasion another tribe might be called to work while the host's subjects provided the essential feasts. That this latter was a shrewd move is attested by the observation that the visitors "usually did harder work than they would at home, being stimulated by the desire to make a name for themselves."[7] In the establishment of a Marquesan person of rank, tasks necessitating manual labor were performed by his dependents, who were given food and shelter. However, when there were not enough dependents to perform a given piece of work, supplementary labor was conscripted. Whenever such a servitor became dissatisfied with his forced labor and ran away, a war leader was sent to seek him out and kill him.[8]

All Tongan land, and its products, were ultimately the property of the supreme ruler; and the same was true of the land ruled by each of the lesser chiefs, though the areas under their control were subject to the demands of their superior. First fruits, or the first of any catch of fish, were the prerogative of the chiefs. The Tui Tonga received the direct tribute of those farmers who lived near him, while those at a distance delivered their contribution to the local chief, who forwarded the prescribed portion to this supreme head of government. One of the important

[7] Hiroa (1934), 130–1.   [8] Handy (1923), 47–8.

chiefs, the Tui Kanokupolu, appointed inspectors to see that he obtained his due. All foodstuffs in his district were *tapu* to him, so that such a sign as a sharp stick thrust into the trunk of the banana tree, or some coconut leaves hanging from the branches of a breadfruit tree, warned the commoner not to touch what had been reserved for this grandee on pain of being thrashed, or of death itself. All large pigs were reserved for those of high degree, while "a fisherman caught eating a large fish might have his tongue pulled out, or be thrashed, or even killed." Pigeon-snaring, like other sports, was reserved to chiefs, and they pre-empted all the birds that were caught, since whipping or death was the penalty for a commoner caught eating a pigeon.[9]

Tapu on Tikopia, while here not the exclusive prerogative of chiefs, can have serious economic repercussions; though some of these taboos may be imposed by individuals, their sanctions in the main can be referred to fear or reverence of the chief. Four types are distinguished:

Taboo	*Economic Effects*
Imposed by throwing the firestick	Inhibits the felling of sago palms in Uta for nearly two months.
Funeral prohibitions: (a) on richer foods (b) on plucking coco-nuts (c) on reef fishing (d) on canoe fishing	Diversion to poorer foods, accumulation of reserves to small extent, diversion of productive energies from sea to land.
Restriction of access to taro land or individual cultivations.	Retention of individual advantage; limitation on general freedom of utilization.
Restriction on taking coco-nuts.	Restraint on immediate consumption with increased future consumption. Immediate diversion in part to other food-stuffs.

To this, and other influences of the chief on production are to be added his economic role as consumer. "He is the recipient from his people of periodic gifts of food and special types of raw material which, sporadic in the case of any individual contributor, nevertheless form *in toto* a steady stream of additions to his wealth." Much of what he receives he redistributes; as among the Ashanti, the obligations of the chief toward his people are

[9] Gifford (1929), 102–6, 117.

heavy, and must be met under terms of the duties of his office.[10]

Perhaps the clearest statement of the relationship between commoners and chiefs in the South Seas is one which protests a proposed suppression of the custom of "begging" on Fiji, where in earlier days the power of the nobles to draft labor for their own purposes was considerable. Championing the old custom, an article in the Native Gazette of July 11, 1905, pleads its case in the following terms:

> What is Fijian begging? Begging is the requisition of the common folk. See, the commons in Fiji cannot make requisitions, for requisitions are the chief's part. But what are requisitions? Requisitions are begging on a very big scale; they have not ceased, but are allowed by the law. Well, the commoner has begging as his only requisition. . . . The chiefs, they are free to go on putting levies upon us but then we are undone by it since we are forbidden to beg. Who is the commoner to approach you nobles and say, "Please pay me, Sir, for what I have done, or for the food I have brought," or whatever it be? Impossible. If your requisitions cease, your calls on us, your proclamations, your pomp, then will begging cease.[11]

6

THE ADMINISTRATION of the Inca empire of pre-Spanish Peru represents the most highly developed governmental system in the aboriginal New World. Seconded only by the Aztec and Mayan states, the methods of control and the efficiency with which the business of the state was managed are famous. We need here, therefore, only outline those methods which bear on the problem of how in Peru the support of a ruling class was achieved through the diversion of the economic surplus, to supply their needs, before examining a few further instances of this process in aboriginal North America.

[10] Raymond Firth (1939), 202, 212 ff. The table given here omits the two central columns of the original, "Social Context" and "Sanction," which are not germane to the point under discussion in these pages.

[11] Hocart, 100–02.

Essentially, the Inca state was a federation of a large number of conquered local political entities. Because of the close control necessitated by this manner of growth, there gradually came into being an ever increasing bureaucracy, which in time was charged with seeing that production was maintained and that commodities were distributed in accordance with the regulations set down by the ruling powers. As in some African kingdoms, a census was kept of population and resources, *quipus*, or knotted cords, being used. Tribute in goods and, more importantly, in services was levied against each province on the basis of this count. In some regions the labor draft took the form of agricultural work, elsewhere work in the mines was commanded, while each craftsman was required to produce a specified quota of goods—cloth, stone-carvings, and the like—from materials supplied him by his overseers. Accounts had to balance; they were kept in duplicate so that the provincial governors might be protected against peculation after the tribute required of them had been delivered. One of the early writers has given a list of those exempt from tribute, which is significant for our discussion: all persons of royal blood and all rulers of provinces and their families; all officers of the army, except those of the lowest rank, and the sons and grandsons of these officers thus exempted; all minor officials "if sprung from the people" while in office; soldiers on active duty, though these might be regarded as paying their tribute by means of their army service; "youths" below twenty-five years of age and "elderly men" over fifty, though both these groups were expected to help kinsmen who might be liable to the tribute; women, sick persons, and those incapacitated; and the priests of the Sun.

What was the disposition of the goods collected, and the use to which the man-power was put? In essence, the political supremacy of the rulers, exerted in the economic sphere, was utilized not only to maintain the ruling group in luxury, but also to assure those who supported them an adequate standard of living. This necessitated a controlled redistribution, when necessary, of the goods produced, and also implied a program of public works; and both of these were efficiently realized, if contemporary observers are to be relied on. Included in the latter was the remarkable system of roads that connected the principal centers and outlying districts of the country, the bridges that carried these roads over streams and canyons, the aqueducts that guaranteed a supply of water where it was needed, storehouses where surplus food was held for use in times of famine, the dwellings of the rulers and headquarters of administrative officials. As for the receipts from the taxing process, what remained after the wants of royalty had been satisfied were stored and drawn on when required. In the main, however, the directed agricultural work provided all with food, and other activities supplied the remaining needs. It is recounted that while thieves were severely punished, a man who stole because he needed food or other necessities of life went unpunished, while the jurisdictional official whose task it was to see that such needs were met suffered the penalty.[12]

7

THE ESSENTIALLY democratic tradition of most American Indian tribes and their relatively simple economies has made the existence of a well-defined class of rulers the exception rather than the rule among them. Where chiefs direct the life of the people, they function more as leaders among equals than in the manner of African or Oceanic or Asiatic rulers, or those of the pre-Spanish societies of Peru, Central America, and Mexico. In Taos, a governor and a council constitute the ruling body, controlling the war captains whose chief function is today to police the pueblo. Fines or confiscated properties are divided among the officers, but other than this there is but little return to them for their services.[13] Chiefs of Hopi villages and clans and their households were, and in some cases still are, supported in some measure by their followers, who cultivated their fields for them. And while "the chief did not himself demand and organize these services," which were voluntary, they constituted a generally recognized duty, and made it possible for these leaders not to "engage directly in any economic activity." [14]

Among such California tribes as the Nisenan (southern Maidu) and the Patwin, the chief was characteristically a wealthy man, who used his wealth to maintain his prestige. The return such a

[12] Joyce, 102 ff.; Means, Ch. VIII. [14] Forde (1931), 376.
[13] Parsons (1936a), 71–2.

chief enjoyed for his services was appreciable in the light of the resources of his people, even though from an absolute point of view what he received was not a great deal, consisting of gifts of game or fish, or pre-emptive rights to especially productive groves of oak trees. The Patwin chief and his family did not have to hunt, fish, or gather foodstuffs; in addition he could also levy upon his people to satisfy special wants, such as calling the young men to gather firewood; while his daughter could summon young women to collect grass seeds.[15]

The chief of the Californian Nomlaki, "aside from the social prestige of the office itself, . . . gained status through his wealth." The sources of this wealth, in general terms, were as follows:

He was in a position to trade with outside persons as well as with villagers. Furthermore, he apparently used the supplies brought in by other people for his trading activities. The chieftain also enjoyed an immunity from the more menial tasks, such as rope-making and hunting, and lived from the produce of his fellows' labors, just as he enhanced his wealth by using their goods as capital in trading. Also because of his position he was expected to marry rich wives—usually several of them—which in turn improved his economic position.

His duties were varied. He exhorted the people: "Do right, don't get into trouble, help your neighbor." He apportioned communal tasks. He was arbiter of disputes and ruled on decisions by the villagers to embark on a given project, such as building a dance house. As concerns the more strictly economic aspects of his role, we learn:

He kept on hand a supply of perishable necessities of life for use when visitors came to trade. It was his duty to be always in a position to trade. Thus a war might be ended by an agreement to barter goods, and it was apparently necessary for the prestige of the group to make a good showing in these postwar negotiations. Furthermore, any family falling short of food replenished its stock from the chief's larder. Such loans from the headman's supply were either paid for with beads, rope or some other item of fairly standard value,

[15] Beals, 360; McKern, 242–6.

or later returned in kind. Acorns were, however, kept in a common granary to be drawn on by each family. They were not the property of the headman, but it was his duty to see that no person took more than his reasonable share. The role of the chief as an economic stabilizer was reflected in a similar pattern in connection with feasts. The rabbits killed for a ceremonial occasion were placed in a common pile and redistributed by the chief to the family heads according to their individual needs. Each family would roast and pound their rabbits, making patties of the pounded meat. A youth was sent around to collect one of the patties from each family head for the chief, who thus had a supply of meat for any latecomers, or for children who became hungry later in the evening.[16]

The essential democracy of Plains Indian life inhibited any marked development of economically privileged classes. The Omaha had a Council of Seven Chiefs who, with the aid of officers to keep the peace, organized communal buffalo hunts, confirmed leaders, made peace with other tribes, and were generally charged with the administration of tribal affairs. But membership in the council was not hereditary, entrance to the order of chiefs being only possible through the performance of certain prescribed acts and the giving of certain gifts. These gifts "were not only in recognition of their high office and authority as the governing power of the tribe but to supply them with the means to meet the demands made upon them because of their official position." Since chiefs did not have the time to hunt as did ordinary men, and thus could not secure "a large supply of food or . . . the raw material needed for the manufacture of articles suitable . . . as gifts to visitors, the gifts made by aspirants to tribal office therefore partook of the nature of payment to the Chiefs and Keepers for the services they rendered to the people."[17]

Certain tribes of southeastern United States were marked by the unusual development, for North America, of a highly developed class structure. The Natchez were divided into two classes: the nobles, headed by the Great Sun, and the commoners,

[16] Goldschmidt, 324–5.

[17] Fletcher and LaFleche, 206 ff., 212–13.

or stinkards. "What distinguishes them," said Charlevoix, "is the form of their government, entirely despotic; a great independence, which extends even to a kind of slavery in the subjects, more pride and grandeur in the chiefs." The chief, according to Le Petit, was blindly obeyed by his people. From the point of view of the public support given him as agent of government, the comments that he was "absolute master not only of their property but of their lives," and that "whatever labors he commands them to execute, they are forbidden to exact any wages," reveal a mechanism by now familiar to us. Subjects were obliged to yield up "the best of their harvest, and of their hunting and fishing," in addition to being liable for services. The reaction to these obligations was not unlike that in other societies, as is attested by the statement of Charlevoix that the royal settlement was not populous because the people, realizing that the great chief could take for himself any of their possessions, formed their villages "at some distance" from the seat of government.[18]

The only detailed account of taxation in any North American tribe is that given for the Kwakiutl Indians of the Northwest Coast. The contributions levied for this purpose have been set forth with a vividness only possible when such material is given in the aboriginal statement. This can be profitably quoted at length, and needs no comment:

> This also was asked by you about the early Indians. Indeed, they work for the head chiefs of the numaym. When the hunter goes out hunting, and he gets many seals, the hunter takes one of the seals and gives the seals as a present to the head chief of his numaym; for he cannot give one-half of them (to the chief)—even if the hunter has obtained many seals—and give a feast with the other half left from what he had given to the chief. Therefore, the hunter takes one seal for food for his children and his wife. The hunter, who does so, is treated well by the chief. If a stingy hunter gives half of his seals to the chief because he prefers the price offered by another chief of another numaym, then the chief of the hunter's numaym tries to kill the hunter, and often the chief strikes the hunter so that he dies, if the chief is a bad man; and, therefore, the chiefs of the various numaym own

[18] Swanton (1911), 101–02, 110.

hunters. The seals are all given to the chiefs by the hunters, for the meat of the seal is not dried.

Mountain goat hunters, when they get ten goats by hunting, give five goats to the chief of the numaym, and the goat hunter keeps the other five goats and dries the meat. Sometimes the chief cuts up the goat meat for his numaym, when he wishes to do so. If he wishes to dry it, he does that way. When the chief is a good man, he does not take the goat away from the hunter by force, and the good chief never thinks that one-half given to him by the hunter is not enough. If a chief is bad, he wishes more than half to be given to him by the goat hunter, and if the goat hunter does not wish to give more than half of the goats, then the bad chief will take them away by force. Then the bad chief may kill the goat hunter, but generally the goat hunter kills the bad chief, if he overdoes what he says to the hunter.

Now . . . I will talk about dry salmon obtained by the salmon-fisher. If one hundred are caught . . . he gives twenty salmon to the chief of his numaym, and sometimes more than twenty, if the chief and the salmon-fisher are both good-minded, but when (both) are bad, then the salmon given to the chief is less, for there are only ten salmon given by the fisherman to the chief. Sometimes, the salmon-fisher has more than a thousand dry salmon caught in the river. Then generally the chief and the fisherman quarrel and often fight until one of them is killed. . . .

Now I will talk about those who dig cinquefoil. When the woman and her husband go to dig cinquefoil roots in their garden-beds . . . the woman . . . takes her digging stick and her two baskets and . . . throws the short roots into the larger basket and she throws the longer roots into the smaller basket. . . . As soon as (she is) done, she goes home to her winter house. The cedar-bark baskets which are to be given to the chief are put in a canoe in a separate place. As soon as the woman . . . and her husband arrive on the beach of their house, the man shouts to the chief and asks him to come to meet him, and the chief usually comes down at once to meet the woman who has dug the cinquefoil roots, and when she arrives at the beach, the husband . . . shows the cedar-bark baskets with long roots to the chief. He says to him, "These are given to you by my wife, chief," and the chief thanks him for his word. . . . He does not give any of the baskets with the short cinquefoil roots, and the common men eat the short cinquefoil roots.

And this is the way with all kinds of berry cakes. When there are five bundles of berry cakes obtained by the woman who has picked the berries, she gives one bundle of berry cakes to the wife of the chief. . . . Often the wife of the chief thinks that one bundle of berry cakes is not enough; that is, if the wife of the chief is a bad woman many times the two women quarrel. . . . If the woman is strong when picking . . . berries . . . when the berry picker has two hundred bundles of dried berry cakes, she gives forty bundles to the wife of the chief. . . .

Of all the different kinds of food, a little is given to the chief by those who belong to his numaym: clams, mussels, small mussels, and horse clams. Of all of these, a little is given to the wife of the chief by the woman who digs shell fish. . . .

. . . About the hunter. When he has shot three bears, he gives one to the chief of his numayn and he keeps two bears; and when a sea hunter has killed three sea otters, he gives one to the chief of his numaym. This is done with everything that is obtained by hunters and sea hunters and canoe builders. The canoe is generally given to the chief.[19]

8

It is apparent from the preceding pages that the cost of government is a substantial charge upon the productive capacities of those societies where the services of a governing group are employed. It will be remembered, however, that in discussing the economic surplus and its partition, it was stated that those relieved in whole or in part of the necessity of providing their own primary subsistence needs included the intermediaries between man and the supernatural world as well as the rulers. We must, therefore, proceed to an examination of the mechanisms which assure support to those concerned with the world of the supernatural in the societies where they act as mediators.

[19] Boas (1921), 1333 ff.

CHAPTER XX

THE SERVICE OF THE SUPERNATURAL

WE HAVE seen that to estimate what may be termed the national budget of nonliterate societies is difficult. At most, what can be indicated is an estimate of the participation of rulers in the wealth produced by the community as a whole, and the return in the way of public works and security that the people enjoy for their contributions. In the case of priests, workers of magic, diviners, and others who manipulate the supernatural powers of the universe, the problem is even more perplexing.

One of the major difficulties derives from the fact that, in so many nonliterate cultures, the functions of the ruler and of the mediator with the supernatural are discharged by the same individual. This has been clearly expressed by Landtman, where, in his attempt to account for the origin and persistence of social classes, he considers the differentiation of priests as a group:

> The union of the highest sacerdotal and civil dignities may have taken place in connection with the general development of leaders. In an early state of society there exists little or no contrariety between the spiritual and social or political powers; thus, as a rule, a certain civil authority is always attached to the priesthood. The same superiority which raised a man to the position of a chief may make him a spiritual headman as well.[1]

We are, of course, concerned here no more than we have been elsewhere in this book with the matter of origins. But if we

[1] Landtman (1938), 136.

rephrase "in an early state of society" to read "cultures having simple economies," the matter resolves itself into the problem of the degree of specialization permitted by the technology of a given group.

In terms of accounting concepts the problem we face is that of discovering what part of their resources a people devote to meeting the costs of management and social and psychic insurance. Where there is little surplus, the personnel susceptible of being diverted from productive activities is so small that in some instances no one individual can devote his full time to the duties which correspond to those of rulers and priests in more prosperous communities. In such cases, or even where one or two persons can in part be supported by their fellows, these officials will therefore execute the functions of both types of specialists. It is possible that the rule of elders, such as is found in the gerontocracies of Australian tribes, actually represents a device whereby those who can no longer provide for themselves are compensated for the services they can still perform in directing the affairs of men and in assuring benevolence on the part of the supernatural.

The question of the nature of religion, and the extent to which its subjective and ceremonial manifestations are determined by the economic setting in which it occurs, cannot be considered here. Whatever the role of the professional in religious matters, and whatever the degree of his devotion to the beings he serves, the fact remains that even those most attuned to the supernatural world must provide for their mundane wants. It is thus understandable how professionals, especially in more complex cultures, number among them those to whom ease of living is an important objective. This fact, and the fact that a certain *esprit de corps* is often found among those whose position in society releases them from manual labor, account for the active co-operation existing in many nonliterate societies between the rulers and their priests, shamans, diviners, or medicine-men. This point offers us the most promising lead to an understanding of some of the ways in which those who are in the service of the supernatural obtain their economic support from the community they serve, and yields some insight into how their identity with the rulers gives a further instance of the less specialized form which institutions take in nonliterate societies when compared with ourselves.

2

A STUDY of this phenomenon among the Yokuts and Western Mono tribes of California will make the point.[2] Here the supporting economic system was relatively simple. No impressive economic surplus existed, though "before white intrusion, game, acorns, seeds and tule roots formed an abundant food supply in the San Joachim valley." There was little property in land, an absence of codified law to guard nonexistent special privilege, and "equality of rank among the people at large, that is, the absence of a class system." There were certain lineages which were "mildly aristocratic," but differences in social status grew out of the recognition of individual abilities, such as the power to obtain goods which were destroyed or given away, or the ability to acquire supernatural power, or to be an orator of distinction.

The power of the chief derived from the prestige of his office and the wealth his position brought him. His house was larger than the houses of commoners, and he was provided with food by the young hunters of his village. His storehouses had always to be well filled, since he was expected to entertain any outsider who might come to the village and also to support the poor and aged. He alone might have two wives, since only he could afford to support them and since his duties as dispenser of hospitality made their assistance necessary. His "monetary wealth," which surpassed that of any of his subjects, was derived from his monopoly on the trade in eagle products and his control over intertribal commerce. He shared, moreover, in the payments made doctors of his tribe when dances were given for entertainment, since an invitation, with a gift of money, was sent a chief when it was desired that he come and bring his shamans. The latter received the donations of the audience, and both chief and shamans thus profited. This same system of holding dances was the means of levying taxes, the mechanism operating as follows:

The chief requested certain performances, sanctioned others, that cost money: doctors and dancers did not dance and *winatuns* (messengers) did not run errands for nothing.

[2] Gayton, 372–7, 398–401, 407 ff.

But it was the spectators who paid the expenses. The chief was, and was regarded as, the ceremonial leader of his community of whom it was said "he gave this dance, he made that mourning ceremony," etc., in spite of the fact that it was the public at large who paid for them. No public taxes were levied and placed in a general fund, but the more simple expedient of having the persons present at any ceremony contribute on the spot produced the same result.

Since the main duty of the chief was to see that the ceremonial activities of the tribe were properly carried out, this "tax" was thus a means of ensuring return to him for his services to the community.

The shaman was able to manipulate the supernatural for both good and evil. This left him "in an equivocal position" so that whether he was more feared than respected depended on his character and reputation. His power, which was "exclusively occult," came from his dream experiences. Anyone might have these dreams, but some persons had more of them than others and each dream brought him closer to supernatural power and gave him the ability to do the doctoring that made of him a professional. Some of those whose dream experiences entitled them to doctor did so with hesitation, or refused to exercise their power, because of the danger of being killed if they failed in a cure, for a failure laid the practitioner open to the suspicion of witchcraft.

When a patient fell ill, a fee was sent the shaman when he was summoned. He received an additional amount when he began his curing, and this, often a considerable sum, was not given back even if the patient failed to recover, for the relatives of the dead man preferred to allow the fee to be retained rather than incur enmity by asking for its return. "This custom of retaining the fee increased the shaman's wealth and augmented the belief that doctors made people ill just to get their money." Curing was believed to be essentially a contest between two shamans. One had caused the sickness, and another, because of his superior power, attempted to overcome the baleful influence of his rival.

It is apparent that the controlling forces in Yokuts life were the chief and the shaman. Since they co-operated more often than they came into conflict, it is important to understand the mechanisms and results of this co-operation, which, in summary, "greatly increased the wealth of the chief on the one hand, and protected the shaman from the violence of avenging relatives on the other." An instance to show what happened when a man of means exercised his theoretical right not to contribute to some ceremony ordained by his chief may be taken by reproducing these passages from the account of a native:

> If a man, especially a rich one, did not join in a fandango, the chief and his doctors would plan to make this man or some member of his family sick. The doctor would sicken his victim . . . [and would] . . . see to it that he is called in to make the cure. He makes several successive attempts to cure his victim, each time being paid for his services. He withholds his cure until he has finally broken the man and got him into debt. . . . The money which the shaman has collected as fees in the case he divides with the chief. Should the victim's relatives seek vengeance, for which they must obtain the chief's permission, the chief refuses his sanction on the ground of insufficient evidence.

Other situations in which chiefs and shamans might collaborate to the economic advantage of both are also indicated:

> The chief always had money. People made him presents when he was going to give a ceremony. If he got short of money he would have his doctor kill somebody who was rich. If the victim chosen belonged to another tribe he would send a gift of money to the chief of that tribe asking that he have his doctor kill the man. If the chief accepted the money he had his doctor proceed with the process of sickening and killing the man. The money received was divided between the chief and the doctor. Doctors who killed this way made sure that the patient would finally send for him by making him more sick for every other doctor that the sick man sent for. Usually we had good chiefs with good doctors, but sometimes even a good chief would bribe a doctor to kill some man he thought ought to be killed.

This picture is not as sinister as might seem at first glance. For if shamanism was a force that destroyed life, it also preserved it; if the chief abused the power he derived from his alliance with those who manipulated supernatural forces, he would suffer censure in a subsequent loss of prestige and the possibility of untimely death. There was even some "moral" justification for the intrigues of chiefs and shamans:

> A chief who hired a shaman to sicken a rich man who did not join in the expenses of a fandango or mourning ceremony was setting a public example at the same time that he was enriching himself. To the chief and to his shaman, who shared the money paid in fees by the sick man, it was unquestionably a matter of financial profit. But from the point of view of the public at large it was a fair punishment. Thus: a man of money who neglected or refused to bear his share of a public expense was placing a heavier financial burden upon his fellow-citizens. . . . In the absence of any law or system of taxation, it behooved each citizen, especially those of wealth, to participate in the sharing of public expenses, lest he incur the displeasure of the chief and of the public, and sickness or death be visited upon him.

Thus the law was upheld, and assurance was given that the obligations of every member of the community were properly met. In the process those who enforced the law and provided it the sanctions needed for its enforcement were enriched. If, because of their law-enforcing power, they sometimes co-operated so as to enrich themselves, this is merely due to the fact that in the elaboration of the patterns underlying any institution, an increasing variation in behavior may eventuate in what in terms of the culture appears as abuse of power.

3

THE PRECEDING instance of co-operation between rulers and those who control the supernatural world has been taken from a culture of slight technological achievement and of simple economic and political organization where the highly personal nature of the religious life causes little attention to be given cult organization. How, in comparison, co-operation between rulers and priests is effected in a much more complex society, and the economic consequences of such co-operation, may next be considered. For this we shall return to Dahomey.

As with the rulers of this kingdom, the economic role of the priest is principally that of a consumer. Every priest has his cult-house, where the novitiates are lodged who come to him for instruction in the nature of the gods they are to worship, and for training in the cult-practices they will follow. While in the cult-house, novitiates are fully provided for by members of their families or their spouses. Those responsible for the maintenance of a person in training must also render gifts to the priest in charge, and in addition must see to it that someone gives the equivalent of fifteen days' work in his fields. The gods themselves must likewise be given sacrifices on ceremonial occasions, or when suppliants come to ask for favors. These sacrifices, which take the form of animals, cooked foods of various kinds, and money, are for the support of the deity. The support of a shrine, however, includes the maintenance of those attached to it, and since they consume the flesh of the sacrificial animals, these sacrifices can be regarded as operating to swell the income of the priest in charge and of his more important subordinates. During the great rituals, large numbers of animals, considerable gifts of money, many fine mats (that can only be employed once in the service of the gods), and large quantities of food are proffered by those who attend. It is thus to be seen that the not inconsiderable return to the priesthood takes its place beside the cost of maintaining the monarchy as a substantial charge against the income of this people.

It will be remembered that in discussing the taxation policy of the Dahomean monarchy, the indirection which marked the collection of census and other data was stressed as a major factor in policy. It will also be recalled that, in the case of certain goods, especially livestock, it was stated that the technique of indirection was in certain cases implemented through active collaboration between priests and taxing authorities. This point may now be documented.

At times, on a market-day, a crier would be dispatched by the chief priest of the feared and powerful spirit of a sacred river, the Halan, to apprise the populace that this spirit had threatened a poor harvest and an epidemic among the livestock. Every man and woman was, therefore, instructed to bring to the palace within three days a cowrie shell for each of his animals to appease the wrath of this being—one shell for each goat, one for each head of cattle, and one for each sheep—and to deposit the shells for each kind of animal separately. Before the cowries were brought, each animal was to be touched with the shell representing it, in order that the threatening danger might be transferred to the shell. A ritual fringe of palm-fronds was also to be placed about the neck of each beast to make the spiritual quarantine more effective.

Since the people complied in all haste, these results were achieved: as something having value was given, there was an assurance that no more than the correct amount of cowries would be accumulated; as the value of one shell was extremely slight, no economic burden that might of itself have been resented was imposed. The shells thus collected made an impressive total, and the king, not unmindful of its effect, demonstrated his concern by doubling this number before the entire sum was sent to the chief priest who had issued the warning. All benefited, therefore; the royal bureaucracy, by retaining an equal number of pebbles as the number of shells forwarded to the priest, had an accurate count of the animals kind by kind and village by village, on which to base their fiscal computations; the people received reassurance that a threatened danger would be avoided, and at an extremely low cost; and the priests received their due in remuneration and gratitude from the monarch with whom they co-operated and from the people whom they served.

The identical device could not, of course, be employed time after time. Variations were introduced on the principal theme. For instance, a different category of gods would become incensed with the people, and for differing reasons. Or different methods of making the supernatural ill-will known, often in themselves indirect, were employed, as when dead animals were found at various crossroads, and their owners, seeking out the diviners, discovered "independently" why these misfortunes had come upon them. The procedure in averting continuing disaster was invariably the same; the process of assuring income to the kingdom was facilitated, the support of the king, in so far as this type of tax was concerned, was aided, and the priests were the more richly rewarded for their services in directing affairs according to supernatural will.[3]

4

THE OFFICES of political headman and spiritual leader may be merged even where a considerable surplus over the subsistence needs of the people is present. In Polynesia, to cite an outstanding instance, though the economic system afforded adequate support for an impressive number of persons engaged in nonproductive activities, the distinction between chief and priest is often not clear. Handy envisages this as the result of an emergent differentiation of function in the area—"the development of the complicated polity of the larger social and political groups out of the simple patriarchal family." In its "simple rudimental form" the three religious functions found in the islands—the divine chief, the prophet, and the priest—were combined in one individual, as in Samoa and Tahiti. The next step finds the village or tribal chiefs, heads of "but expanded families," serving as diviners and priests. Finally, in more complex Polynesian cultures, chiefs and religious leaders were completely differentiated except at the apex of the system, where, as in Hawaii, the ruler was head of the religious cult. Differentiation throughout the entire system existed in Tonga and the Marquesan Islands.[4]

Williamson, in surveying the social and political systems of the islands on the basis of the earlier literature, is explicit regarding the vagueness of the distinction made between secular and religious officials:

> So far as chiefs are concerned . . . there can be no doubt that in many . . . of the islands the chiefs did engage largely in religious acts and ceremonies. Many of them were in fact . . . priests also, and it is probable that writers often refer to people as chiefs who were really priests, and *vice versa,* whilst in a number of cases they were probably both.[5]

This is apparent from Firth's analysis of the role of what he terms "economic ritual" in Tikopia. He regards such ritual as

---

[3] Herskovits (1938), I, 102–03, 118–20.

[4] Handy (1927), 135–8.

[5] Williamson (1924), III, 32.

"essentially a conservative force" which "helps in the perpetuation of the system of production and distribution in vogue in the society, and in particular, in the maintenance of the economic position of people of rank." This operates in the following manner:

> The titular ownership of lands, springs of water, and canoes by the chiefs; the assistance that is given to them in many of their undertakings; the gifts of food brought to them, hang upon the belief of all members of the community that the chiefs are the representatives of the gods and the ancestors in whose power the fertility and efficient functioning of the system of production lie.[6]

Returning to Williamson, we find him speaking of "certain priests, who appear to have belonged to the classes which I am calling official and hereditary priests," who "in one or two cases . . ." were

> appointed by the chiefs to act as priests; some of them were themselves chiefs; in some cases their priestly offices had probably been for long past hereditary in their aristocratic families. . . . In most cases we find an association between sacred and secular offices in the fact that these priests were themselves orators or secular officials.[7]

The religious establishments were afforded generous support in these islands. Even though the offerings to the gods, and of gifts of food in particular, were either consumed by the worshippers or, at the larger festivals, were redistributed to them in substantial part, an appreciable residue was left for the upkeep of the ecclesiastical establishment. Thus, at the ceremony for the first fruits, "large quantities of food were brought to the public assembly ground and piled into an immense heap." This food was then divided "between the gods, the priests, the *marae* attendants, the chiefs and the commoners."[8]

Mangaia was one of these islands where the functions of priests and rulers were differentiated. We need but consider the roster of the more important priests to recognize how substantial

[6] Raymond Firth (1939), 171.
[7] Op. cit., III, 46.
[8] Williamson (1937), 121–2, 252–3.

a charge against the resources of the community their support must have been. There was an "inland high-priest" whose sanctity "held so long as he restricted himself to his religious duties"; for such specialization he was "rewarded for his services with liberal grants of land by the Temporal Lord," and "also received official shares of food at public feasts, besides presents of food on ordinary occasions." The "shore high-priest" defended the coast against the spirits that were believed to come from the west; he also received grants of land "confirmed or added to by the various Temporal Lords in recognition of the priest's services." This priest also had a special right to all the turtles that were caught. The "ruler of food" controlled the fertility of fields, and was charged with the imposition of closed seasons over agricultural districts and fishing grounds that had been used to excess. At public feasts held during peace-times, he controlled the distribution of food, and even in times of war conquest did not affect his position so long as he attended only to the provisioning of the warriors of his tribe.

Tribal gods had their own priests, who wielded much power within their own groups. As learned men who controlled the voices of the gods, they acted as a court of last resort in settling "knotty problems with regard to war and tribal politics." "Some priests," we are told, "used the voice of the god to further their own personal ends . . . [but] . . . the voice of the god was used for humane purposes as well." This was especially true where it was a question of professional solidarity: "Some priests protected people from death by secreting them in the curtained chamber of the house set apart for the second image of their god . . . the men recorded as so saved were priests of other gods. . . ." Feasts, important elements in worship, were given "by powerful families or by a whole tribe," who contributed vegetable food from their own gardens. The food was displayed to as great advantage as possible, a familiar method in all the island region for attaining prestige, and was carefully divided so that those ministering to the deities would not be slighted. At such feasts the tribal priests were given three allotments, the *ariki* priests three allotments, the Temporal Lord one allotment, the district chiefs one allotment each, and the sub-district chiefs one allotment for each district group, while finally "a long single spread" where the commoners were fed "was laid for those without any title or distinction." [9]

The expense entailed in the support of the Tahitian priesthood may be inferred from the elaborateness of the aboriginal sacerdotal and ceremonial organization as set forth in a contemporary account. The only direct statement of this cost declares: "Priests of all kinds were well paid for their services, and lived comfortably." Such an assertion, however, when taken together with the description of the intricate rites and formulae that had to be learned by every candidate, makes it evident that the priests had of necessity to be freed from the routine duties of making a living in order to discharge their functions. As a matter of fact, these priests seem to have been specialists of a kind unique in nonliterate society. The subjects taught in "teachers' schools" were history, heraldry, geography, navigation, astronomy, astrology, mythology, time, numbers, seasons, genealogies, and the study of enigmas and similes, while in addition there existed what we would term vocational schools. A further economic note is here of interest: "The students of both classes of schools paid their teachers with the best of food, with birds' feathers, images of wood and stone, rolls of tapa, choice mats, and every kind of wearing apparel of the time." Studying for the priesthood meant learning many kinds of formulae, but that this long preparation was necessary is apparent from the description of such a ceremony as that of "uncovering the gods" on important state occasions or in times of great distress. Here are to be noted the elaborate decoration of the priests, their withdrawal even from their customary activities, the great quantities of food and other commodities given as gifts to the gods, and the taboos imposed on the common folk, such as the threat of death if one of them unwittingly strayed on the scene. All these not only clearly demonstrate the economic role of the priesthood as consumers of subsistence goods produced by the community as a whole, but also show how this class, in the performance of sacred duties, was maintained in a fashion that must have necessitated the appropriation of a considerable portion of the wealth of the community. [10]

The pre-contact culture of Palau offers another example from the Pacific area of the economic worth of those who serve the

[9] Hiroa (1934), 112–20, 138–40.   [10] T. Henry, 152–4, 159 ff.

supernatural powers. These powers were all conceived as ancestral spirits. One category, the forebears of a given clan, were proffered small offerings by the individual and larger ones by the clan head. The second category was made up of the deities, properly speaking. Each clan worshipped a god and goddess carrying titles "that were the supernatural counterparts of the titles of the man and woman who were the leaders of the clan." These leaders, as priest-chiefs, conducted the rites deemed necessary when the ordinary spirits of the dead were not believed to be powerful enough to function in a given situation. But just as some clans were wealthier and more powerful than others, so the gods of these clans were believed to be more powerful than those of lesser groupings and were accorded the rank of village or district deities. Their shrines were larger and these gods had intermediaries, termed *korong*, who, unlike the clan priest-chief, were specialists.

These *korong* were "called" to serve when they were first possessed by a spirit, their behavior being such as to give them recognition as "the selected vehicle of a god on the basis of performance." But the position of such a person could not be inherited, and he himself held it only so long as he gave value for services rendered—that is, as long as his performance indicated that he had not been "abandoned" by his deity. His position was important, sometimes as important as that of a principal district chief. Since his services were paid for, and offerings made to his god were kept by him, he became wealthy. He was thus both politically powerful and a man of means, "two attributes" that "had to go together" in Palau.

He lived usually in an ordinary house, but in some cases distinctive high dwellings were built for him. Some of the ceremonies decreed by the *korong* took the form of feasts, which on occasion were lavish. Significantly, these latter could be given only by the wealthiest families and afforded such a group "an opportunity to increase its prestige and to further involve itself in the ramifications of wealth manipulation." Thus the *korong*, himself becoming a power in the community, was instrumental in perpetuating the position of those who already held power. And "because it often happened that a *korong* was by birth a low class individual, there can be no doubt that the chiefs had considerable discretion in according a man the recognition of being the medium of an important god. The assumption of the role of a *korong* was therefore not as wholly fortuitous as it would appear to be on the surface." [11]

5

ADDITIONAL materials to document the economic rewards of priests, shamans, diviners, workers of magic, and others in this general category are to be found in the literature bearing on the ways of life of many other tribes. Among the Yoruba of West Africa, appeal is made to the diviner on every conceivable occasion by anyone who has to make a decision, or who must approach the gods with a request for help. The process of divining as carried on by these *babalawo*, as they are called, employs two methods. Each method involves the permutations of eight or sixteen seeds, which, by the way they fall either when thrown or appear when juggled in the hand, give a result that indicates a series of "verses" appropriate to the combination wherein the answer to a specific question asked by the inquiring client is to be revealed. The number of verses that must be mastered reaches several thousand, and the calling of diviner is thus a profession in every sense of the term. The system itself is termed Ifa, after the spirit that guides those who manipulate the mechanisms of divination. The "verse," with its parable, indicates not only the solution of a difficulty, but the god who will give aid, the sacrifice to be given this deity, and the remuneration of the diviner.

In some cases the petitioner is directed to become a worshipper of a given god, or to "give" his child to a deity. The "verse" appropriate to this situation clearly demonstrates how a person thus chosen must devote himself exclusively to his new calling, thus depending upon it for his support. In the following translation, Ifa is the spirit that would actuate the diviner who might recite the "verse," *eda* are the palm-kernels he uses, and Alumo another name for Ifa, whose question and its answer point the response to the query of a client now before his diviner to ask, let us say, for supernatural aid that will assure a cure to his sick child.

[11] Barnett, Ch. VII, esp. 205–07.

The water of the forest is like dye,
The water of the grassland is like oil from palm-kernels,
The palm-kernels imbedded in the path are polished like
    those of Ifa,
But they do not drink the blood of sacrifices like Ifa.

They divined for Alumo when he was going to buy *eda* as a
slave. They said he must serva his *eda*, his slave. . . . Ifa says
this boy is a *babalawo*. This boy was serving Ifa when he
came from the sky. The rising of setting sun must not see
him in the farm, and his feet must not brush the dew from
the farm road. And Ifa says that we are about to buy something. The person in question should not resist the thing he
is about to buy; if his money is not sufficient, he must add to
what he has. This thing he wants to buy will benefit him.
This is the day when a person must pay for his Ifa palm-
kernels.

Then I cannot go to the farm, Alumo;
    Won't you come and see what my *eda* are doing for me?
Then I cannot go to the river, Alumo;
    Won't you come and see what my *eda* are doing for me?
Then I cannot go to the market, Alumo;
    Won't you come and see what my *eda* are doing for me?
Then I cannot go to a distance, Alumo;
    Won't you come and see what my *eda* are doing for me?

Ifa says that it is the destiny of this person to do no other
work than divining; he must do no farming except to garden
a plot inside the town. This person must return to that which
he has abandoned and become a diviner, or at least learn
to recite the verses of Ifa. He is to bring a female goat and
20,000 cowries, no less, as an offering; when he has done
this, he is also to go and sacrifice a female goat to Ifa.

Despite the symbolism of the ritual language, it is clear that our
client, or his son, is to renounce ordinary labor and neither farm
nor sell in the market nor transport goods like others, but only
to serve his god and derive his livelihood from the payments of
those who come to him seeking the advice his supernatural
powers permit him to give them. And in this case a goat is offered
Ifa, the deity that sanctions divination, while the fee of the diviner

is another goat and cowries to a sum calculated in 1938 at five shillings.[12]

In South Africa, the absence of a "sacerdotal caste," as Junod terms it, is marked. Here the fact that much of the religious life centers on the ancestral cult is responsible for the absence of the guild of priests that, for example, exists in West Africa or among the Baganda of East Africa. Among the Bemba of Northern Rhodesia "the fundamental . . . beliefs in the powers of the ancestors . . ." are ". . . one of the most important sanctions of the chief's authority, and hence were unfailingly performed at the latter's court." This, in turn, is associated with the tradition that the position of the chief is to be maintained by the aid of labor performed for him by the men and women over whom he rules, and to whom he must give food, as he must to others who come to him. That is, "the giving of food . . . is an absolutely essential attribute of chieftainship . . . and the successful organization of supplies at the capital seems to be associated in the Bemba mind with the security and well-being of the whole tribe itself." The fact that the "sacred kitchen" is the first house to be built with special rites at the founding of a chief's new village underscores the economic importance of this complex of ancestral cult, chieftainship and control of food, taken as a whole.[13]

Junod states that among the Thonga "the right of officiating in religious ceremonies is strictly confined to the eldest brother. . . ."[14] A similar observation has been made for the entire region of Bantu South Africa: "The person considered most competent to offer up a sacrifice is the senior living representative of the ancestors." Of particular interest for us here is the added statement that "the Chief in the same way is the priest of his people. Only he can approach his ancestors directly on behalf of the tribe: he is the natural link between them and the powerful spirits of dead Chiefs governing their welfare. . . ."[15] In the preceding chapter it has been indicated how, in this same area, chiefs were rewarded by means of their control over the taxing power and through their right to levy upon the labor as well as the goods of their subjects. But in paying for the services of their

[12] Bascom (communicated).
[13] Richards (1939), 351, 148–9.
[14] Junod, II, 411.
[15] Eiselen and Schapera, 258–9.

secular officials, the South African tribesmen appear to have a more advantageous economic arrangement than is the case in many other nonliterate societies, since for the same amount they benefit from those services necessary to care for the demands of the supernatural powers that make for good or evil in their lives.

Though explicit statements regarding the economics of supernatural control are as rare for this area as elsewhere, it is safe to conclude that the only form of supernatural service which carries with it an economic return, in the restricted sense of the term, is the practice of magic and medicine. These specialists are called in when specific needs call for their aid, and they are paid a retainer as well as the fee agreed upon, once their work is done. The Tswana worker of magic, like the West African diviner, serves a long apprenticeship, not alone under his father, from whom he inherits the art, but also "under several different magicians, to each of whom a fee of one or more cattle must be paid." Furthermore, he must have permission of the chief of his district before he may practice; if a stranger, he may be ordered to leave the tribal territory and forbidden to collect such fees as are owing him. In earlier days the retainer was the skin of a goat or a sheep or a little corn; today it is one or two shillings in cash. The charge varies with the nature of the work. For curing minor illnesses the practitioner receives a sheep or a goat, while for "more serious cases, or for such major tasks as charming cattle, fields or huts, it is usually an ox." The fee is waived if the end agreed upon is not achieved, but where the work is conscientiously performed and the desired result is obtained, an unpaid fee can be recovered in court. In this particular tribe, however, once a substantial fee, such as an ox, has been paid a practitioner, his continued services are available to the client and his family without further charge from that time onward.[16]

The most detailed study of African magic on which we can draw deals with the Azande, a tribe living on the Nile-Congo divide, where magic is property and, as such, can be bought and sold like any other alienable good. How these magic forces are manipulated is taught a beginner during a long initiation, wherein the essential element is "the slow transference of knowledge

[16] Schapera (1938), 255–6.

about plants from teacher to pupil in exchange for a long string of fees." It is imperative that each step be adequately compensated, since a medicine for which too little is given leaves its seller dissatisfied, thus weakening its effectiveness and rendering it valueless to the buyer. The pupil, normally a young man, frequently does not have the means to satisfy the high cost of tuition, and in consequence is permitted to make his payments in installments. But in any event he is expected to give his teacher the first fees he receives after he begins to practice and an occasional present from time to time afterwards.

Naturally such expensive training must carry an assurance of future return. This return is of a dual character, partly material, partly psychological. While many men attempt to become professional practitioners, and a fair proportion succeed in establishing themselves as such, the ablest among them also come to hold an important place in society. The interplay of their interests with those of the governing group is of some significance. The worker of magic has what would be termed commoner as against aristocratic status, and his activities comprise and evoke "entirely a commoner practice and mainly a commoner interest." Yet princes respect these men and do not disdain to give them the patronage that assures to themselves the services of efficient informants about possible unrest in the kingdom and protection against possible female witches in their own harems.

Owing to demands on their time, workers of magic are withdrawn from the ordinary round of economic activities here, as in other societies where these and other specialists in the supernatural function. For example:

A first-class witch-doctor is constantly being summoned to court or to the homes of affluent commoners or to those of friends and relatives, and in consequence he is not able to give the same attention to economic pursuits as laymen can give to them. He makes up for his loss by his earnings as leech and diviner, which are either paid to him in food and tools or in metal wealth which can be exchanged for the one or converted into the other.

The value of these returns is not told us, but that they adequately support the specialists in magic is self-evident. To this extent they represent a further instance of that particular aspect of the utilization of the economic surplus with which we are here concerned.[17]

6

TURNING to the New World, it may be recalled how, among the Yokuts-Mono folk of California, the specialized activities of shamans and chiefs were co-ordinated so as to strengthen the social and economic position of each. Yet, aside from the study of this single instance, as one discussion of shamanism has put it, "we know almost nothing about the role of the shaman in the social systems of the greater number of tribes in the Plateau, Great Basin, and California." Since the sociological aspects of shamanism have thus been ignored, or have "emerged only as a by-product of the investigator's preoccupation with religion," [18] it is not strange that our knowledge of the economic aspects of shamanism or other forms of religious leadership are even more fragmentary. One or two statements which imply that a return was made to the shamans in various western tribes may, however, be cited. Narratives obtained from surviving Nomlaki indicate that the shaman was a person of moment, whose control of the supernatural rendered him returns of economic as well as of psychological value. He was "a man of power and wealth," whose prestige was "compounded out of fear of his power, respect for his ability, and recognition of his wealth." [19] According to Spier: "it is clear that the shaman is the most important individual in Klamath society, taking precedence over rich men, the chiefs. Shamans' houses are the largest in the village, and they have at least as much property as the wealthy layman." Or among the Tsimshian: "In other cases (than, e.g., selling meat and other provisions) people became wealthy by their shamanistic art, for which they are well paid." This statement is documented by reference to a passage from one of the myths, that, "the shaman prince did what his supernatural power told him. . . . Then she (the chief's daughter) came back to life . . . and the chief, the father of the girl, paid him much property—slaves, costly coppers, canoes, and all kinds of goods." Whether the humbler mem-

[17] Evans-Pritchard (1937), 213–15, 251–3.

[18] Park, 102–03.
[19] Goldschmidt, 357–8.

bers of this society rewarded the successful practitioner according to their means is not stated, but it may be supposed on the basis of our general knowledge of the area that these men did not do their work for nothing.[20]

Our scant knowledge of the economic position of the religious leader in North America may be a reflection of the fact that, over the continent, specialization of any kind is relatively weak. It is not possible, therefore, in most instances even obliquely to infer the nature of the economic return to practitioners of this sort. Thus, among the Cherokee:

> To have an adequate idea of the social status of the medicine man we should bear in mind that in his person we find cumulated such professions and pursuits which in our society would correspond to those of the clergy, the educators, the philosophers and the historians, the members of the medical profession in its widest sense . . . and finally, to a certain degree, even to those of the politicians and of the press.[21]

The Iroquois had "Keepers of the Faith," men and women who constituted a "select class appointed by the several tribes to take the charge of their religious festivals and the general supervision of their worship." Yet it is specifically stated that they had no special privileges. They were "common warriors and common women," and their office was "without reward." [22]

Elsewhere in North America we find indications that religious specialists received some return for their services, even though they may not have been entirely supported by their communities. Despite the marginal nature of Eskimo economic life, we are specifically informed that "the angakut (shaman), who must be paid at once for curing a sick person, receives pretty large fees for services of this kind." Among the Natchez, offerings of first fruits and other products were brought to the temples of the gods and taken by the priests to the political leader, who redistributed them as he saw fit. Here, however, the matter was complicated by a situation analogous to that in Polynesia, for the Natchez political leader was also the head of the religious estab-

[20] Spier (1930), 107; Boas (1916), 436, 328.

[21] Mooney and Olbrechts, 91.
[22] Morgan (1851), 177, 179.

lishment, and himself sacred; hence any return to him as ruler may well have been at the same time an offering to him in his capacity as supreme priest.[23]

A word may be said regarding the support of the large religious establishments that functioned in Mexico and Peru. Both these areas had established sacerdotal orders, numbering many initiates who gave their entire time to their religious duties, and who received training in schools where their support was assured during the period of their studies. In each region the wealth thus withdrawn from the general store was supplemented by the appropriation of human resources to the temples and the rituals conducted therein—support given not only in the form of the labor of those who worked the priestly gardens and saw to the upkeep of the sacred places, but also in the form of human sacrifices. The offerings came both from the population at large and from the ranks of captives, who themselves might otherwise have been productively employed as servants, serfs, or slaves. These religious establishments, indeed, approximate the religious structures of literate cultures in their richness, the involved character of their organization, and the implication of extreme specialization in the esoteric nature of their rituals, recalling forms that otherwise are known only in societies having a far greater degree of complexity than marks nonliterate communities.

7

THUS despite all the accounting difficulties, or the confusion that arises from the fact that the role of priests and rulers in many cultures of nonliterate peoples performed by the same individuals, it can be concluded that in such societies those in accord with the supernatural are rewarded for their services out of the economic surplus produced by the people they serve, in the same way as are those who direct everyday affairs. Both rulers and priests, moreover, in discharging the services that constitute their responsibility, must have assistance adequate to the dictates of their social position and the requirements of their duties. Hence

[23] Boas (1888), 594; Swanton (1911), 166.

in those societies where the existence of a large population creates heavy administrative difficulties, and a sophisticated world-view makes for a crowded ceremonial round, the numbers of persons involved in this withdrawal of potential man-power from the production of subsistence commodities is considerable and their support a major charge against the total income of the group.

CHAPTER XXI

WEALTH, DISPLAY, AND STATUS

WE HAVE seen that in nonliterate societies the goods produced over the demands of necessity are not equally distributed, but are channelled into the hands of specialists who constitute a small proportion of the total population. It remains to inquire what use is made of this surplus by those individuals whose economic role is to collect, consume, and redistribute the goods that have come to them. This means that we must consider that aspect of the consumption of goods which, in all societies, constitutes the core of prestige economics. We therefore return to an analysis of the drives underlying the economic functions of those groups in nonliterate societies, which, following Veblen, have been designated as leisure-class groups. It is an engrossing and important problem. For what Veblen terms "differentiation in consumption" through the "specialized consumption of goods as an evidence of pecuniary strength" is achieved in many societies by experts whose specialization permits them to develop techniques for utilizing goods and services that make of this phase of their socio-economic role an end in itself.

This was what Veblen had in mind when he used the phrase "conspicuous waste," a phrase which, because of the "undertone of deprecation" accompanying its use, he himself recognized as not entirely satisfactory. If, however, Veblen's own alternative, "conspicuous consumption," is substituted for "conspicuous waste," the implications for an understanding of the economic and social psychological problems of the unequal disposition of the economic surplus and the resulting social leisure this affords are of the first importance. As a matter of fact, it seems likely that Veblen, in coining this phrase and in indicating its dynamic and institutional implications, hit upon one of those principles which, in generalized form, are applicable to human societies everywhere. For in the vast majority of cultures the position of those in power is established, continued, and constantly strengthened by the prestige that derives from elaborate display and consumption of economically valuable goods.

An example of how this mechanism of prestige competition operates is found in the socioeconomic system of Ponape, one of the Caroline Islands, in Micronesia. Here Bascom distinguishes (1) a subsistence economy, which cares for the immediate needs of the producing household; (2) a commercial economy, which since contact with the outer world produces goods sold for export; and (3) a prestige system, concerned with the goods "through which social approval and social status are gained."

This prestige economy, associated with feasting, is based on yams, pit breadfruit, kava (a native drink), and pigs, yams being the most important prestige commodity. Of the Ponapean, we learn

> . . . his motivations and attitudes towards work cannot be explained simply in terms of a desire to earn enough money to purchase necessary imports and to produce enough food to keep himself and his family from hunger. Not infrequently families go hungry at home when they have large yams in their farms ready for harvest.

When a feast is given, kava and pigs are offered, besides pit breadfruit and yams. Prestige goes to the man offering the oldest breadfruit, but this is secondary to that accorded the one whose yam is largest. That this is a stimulus in yam production is seen in the classification of yams, the largest being that which requires from four to twelve men to carry, the other two sizes being those requiring two men to transport, and those which one man can handle. Shape and variety count as well as size and weight, but the latter, which may be up to 220 pounds, is the predominant consideration.

"Success in prestige competition," we are told, "is regarded as evidence not only of a man's ability, industry and generosity, but also of his love and respect for his superiors." The men who consistently bring the best yams are selected by the Section and District chiefs to fill "titles" that may be vacated, and thus enhance their social status by their ability in prestige competition. Yet, as is often the case in situations of this sort, ostentation in display must be accompanied by patterned modesty in behavior. To boast of having the largest yam would expose a man to pitiless ridicule if, another year, he were bested by a rival.

The secrecy that accompanies the planting and growing of yams, and which stresses their importance to the Ponapean, is marked. It is the height of impropriety to question even a friend about his crop. The importance of the yam is also reflected in the knowledge of varieties of yams shown by Ponapean men. "Without by any means exhausting the subject, one hundred fifty-six varieties of yams were recorded, together with their shape, size, color, and other characteristics, and in many cases the periods when they were first planted on Ponape, the names of the men who first planted them, and the Districts and Sections in which this was done." This is in contrast to bananas, which are a primary subsistence food. Only three varieties of these are cultivated, and for none of them could the time of introduction be given.

The most important type of prestige is that which accrues to the man who develops a new variety of yam. Such plants are cultivated in the greatest secrecy, and a man will sometimes wait several years before he announces his achievement, since "he would be ashamed if he had to refuse requests for cuttings because he did not have enough." He may, with calculation, let out his secret, so that the rapidly spreading news of the event will arouse speculation and make his presentation the more dramatic at the time he gives the new variety its name, is known as its introducer, and is the undoubted winner in the competition at which it is, so to speak, unveiled.[1]

The nonliterate complex West African culture of Dahomey may also be drawn on for a further instance of how the prestige economy operates. Here the ancestral cult is of the utmost importance, and every family or larger relationship group sacrifices regularly to its deified forebears. The culmination is the royal ancestral rites, whose lavishness, in the days before the resources flowing from the taxing power were diverted to a European ad-

[1] W. R. Bascom (1948), *passim*.

ministration, greatly impressed all eyewitnesses. Now, while the relationship of the king to his ancestors was like that of any other Dahomean, there was this difference—the king alone might offer sacrifices of human beings. And the explanation of this fact has direct bearing on our discussion, so direct, indeed, that it might have been taken from Veblen's work itself.

Everyone, reasons the Dahomean, no matter what his position, must begin a sacrifice to the ancestors with beans and corn meal, the "food" given the forebears of those who are so poor they can afford nothing better. This principle is in recognition of the fact that since fate is capricious, prudence dictates that the human-like ancestral gods not be permitted to lose their taste for humble fare which, under less happy circumstances, might be all that a once well-placed descendant could afford. Those higher in the economic scale add chickens to this, those in still better circumstances give a sheep or a goat. Chiefs in the olden times, and members of the royal house today, possessing still greater resources, might offer their ancestors a bullock. But the king alone, in the days of native autonomy, could sacrifice the most expensive animal known to the Dahomeans—a human being, a slave. To grasp to the full the relevance of the example it is merely necessary to understand that the explanation is that of Dahomeans and not of the student. A further relevance is given, however, by the fact that in advancing this explanation Dahomeans of lesser social position manifest all that prideful identification with royalty which is so much the concomitant of the Veblenian concept.[2]

The Kwakiutl offer still another instance of prestige-giving display. This may be best presented by citing without comment a relevant passage from a native text:

Not long after [a princess] has been married [to a chief] . . . her father pays the marriage debt, and she has for her canoe mast an expensive copper. And he gives as a marriage-gift a name to the husband of his princess, and much food with it, and also canoes. This is what is called "paying-the-marriage-debt, sitting-in-the-canoe-of-the-princess"; for generally there are twenty who sit in the canoes of the princess of a real chief, when they put down the copper bracelets and the small coppers and many dishes and the anchor-line of

[2] Herskovits (1938), II, 55–6.

many spoons; when all this has been put down (the) chief
. . . says, "Now I will go and call my princess that you may
see her come." Thus he says, and goes into his house. And
before long he comes back walking ahead of his princess,
and the chief stands outside of his house, and his princess
comes and stands by his side. She wears a blanket covered
with abalone shells and entirely covered with abalone shells
is her hat. Then the chief . . . speaks and says, "Come and
look at this weight which originates with our family history,
when the chieftainess carried the copper. Now stand up, son-
in-law, I will dress you." Thus says the chief and takes the
abalone-covered blanket of the chieftainess and her abalone-
covered hat and promises to give them to his son-in-law,
and he takes his copper and gives it also to his son-in-law.
Then he calls his son-in-law to come and take them. . . .
Then the chief says to his son-in-law, "O son-in-law! now
I have changed your chief's dress, son-in-law. Now go!
It is finished. You have my chieftainess for your wife." Thus
he says, and takes off the large ear-ornaments of abalone
shell on each ear of the chieftainess and the nose-ornament
of abalone shell and attaches the ear-ornament to his son-in-
law, and he also puts the nose ornament of abalone on him.
Then his son-in-law goes back and stands where his *numaym*
is standing, and he speaks, and says, "Look at me! Now my
whole chief's dress has been changed by my father-in-law.
Now the chieftainess my wife, has no dress." Thus he says as
he walks along and goes into his house and the property with
which the marriage debt has been paid is carried into his
house. When everything has been carried in, it is given away
to all the tribes, when day comes.[3]

The phenomenon of conspicuous consumption has thus by no
means gone unrecorded by those who have studied the valida-
tions of status in primitive societies. What has been stressed in
these accounts, however, as in the case of discussions of property,
are sociological rather than economic implications. That is, anthropological concern with the canons of ownership derive principally from the fact that the holding of property, particularly in
land, is one way in which aspects of the social structure such as

[3] Boas (1921), 777–9.

the clan or the family are validated. In a similar manner, the concern of anthropologists with the phenomenon of the acquisition of prestige by the display, conspicuous consumption, and even, in terms of native evaluation, waste of valuable goods tends to center on the role of these in maintaining social institutions rather than in their economic expression. However, inasmuch as there is this crossing of the sociological and economic lines of interest, the data upon which to draw for documentation of this phase of economic life are relatively full. It is consequently possible to reassess the materials and analyze tribal patterns of unequal allocation of surplus goods, so as to understand how their lavish expenditure helps establish and continue the class distinctions which in industrialized societies are at the core of many pressing social and economic problems.

At the outset we may consider how institutionalized processes of conspicuous consumption establish and maintain position in a society where political organization is simple, rank is an expression of esteem for a person as an individual, and the structure of society is less marked by class differences than among larger groups where greater wealth permits social stratification. We will thus see how prestige is attained in one of these smaller groups, before ranging more widely over the earth and examining societies less simply ordered.

2

Such a society is that of Guadalcanal, Solomon Islands, consisting of villages divided into hamlets of minute size—one village, having a total population of 171 persons comprises seven such subdivisions. The clans in any given village are split into what is termed sub-clans, or, if we employ a more apt designation that has been applied to similar groupings elsewhere, into extended families. Each of these latter is called by the native term meaning "tributary," and each "tributary," whose members live together, have their gardens in adjoining plots, making up a co-operating unit, headed by a leader. His position is not hereditary, and his "authority depends on personal qualifications and generosity in providing feasts and otherwise distributing wealth."

"Ambition rarely shows itself," we are told, "until a man is in his early thirties and has settled down to the responsibilities of married life." If, at this time, he desires to become a person of position in his "tributary"—a *mwanekama*—his first move is to increase the size of his gardens. Since the help he obtains must be paid for by feasts which themselves demand adequate resources, at first he moves with care, calling on a few close relatives and neighbors to aid him. As he continues the process of expansion, more workers are needed, and these are fed by the produce from the land he has hitherto cultivated; for "the food available soon exceeds that given away, and no serious embarrassment is caused." At the same time, the ambitious man accumulates as many pigs as he can by begging sucklings from litters of sows belonging to friends or near relatives, and being especially careful to bring to maturity all the animals he himself breeds.

After a few years he "allows it to become known that he intends to erect for himself a fine large house." This is the necessary first step in progressing toward the status of *mwanekama.* Friends and relatives assist in the long task of constructing the framework, being glad to do this "partly on account of the excellent food which is always available, and partly because they really enjoy working together," plus the fact that "by giving their labour they lay an obligation on the owner of the house to make a contribution to their bride-price." Gathering and preparing the material for thatching is difficult because the leaves are full of small thorns; preparation of the thatch may therefore require the services of as many as one hundred men, all of whom have to be well fed. The actual thatching takes place a few days later, after the leaves have dried, and is the occasion for further distribution of food. When the young men and the women of the hamlet have built the walls and floor of the house, using flat stones brought from the beach, the time has arrived for the "feast to remove the thorns," which celebrates the completion of building operations.

Preparations for one such festival occupied about two weeks. They began when the wife of the giver of the feast and the other women of the hamlet brought many loads of yams to the village; these yams, estimated to weigh about five tons, filled the old house in which the young man had lived. In the meantime the prospective host, the men of his "tributary," and all his young helpers were busy catching fish to be smoked and preserved until needed.

When the date for the feast had been definitely set, one day was spent collecting firewood, and another chopping these logs and branches into usable lengths. The day before the festivities was occupied with making yam cakes. Final preparations took the early morning of the next day. The amount of work involved in cooking the great quantities of food, in scraping the tubers, in gathering areca nuts and betel pepper, in decorating the food-bowls that the food gifts might be admired, and in slaughtering, cutting up, and cooking the pigs was most impressive.

The presentation of the food affords a clear view of the quantities involved and the ritual setting:

By about three o'clock everything was ready and the villagers began to assemble in Atana's hamlet . . . each woman brought with her a basket of yam cakes. Several bowls of pudding were also contributed, and the other *mwanekama* of the village sent along a pig each. Bunches of areca nuts and betel pepper were distributed to the guests, and the young men busily piled the food into heaps. First there was a gigantic mass of yam cakes, containing between 3000 and 4000, then a pile of meat—13 pigs had been provided, four of them of enormous size—then 19 large bowls of pudding, and last about two hundredweight or more of smoked fish.

All those present who had actually worked on the house were counted, and a pebble was placed in a coconut shell as each was named. When all were accounted for, the host, with some helpers, each with an armful of cakes, repaired to a level clearing. As he called each name, he threw away a stone, and a cake was placed on the ground, each cake about two feet from the next. These cakes were arranged in rows, and on each more cakes, fish, and a joint of pork were heaped. When the food had been distributed, the host called out the name of each guest to receive a portion from the hands of an aide, until the presentation to this group was completed. Next the leading men of this and surrounding villages received yet more generous allotments of food, each being given "a very large joint of pork, as well as a bowl of pudding." The distribution of food ended with extra gifts to the young men and women who had acted as laborers, or who had helped the wife of the host. "By this time 257 separate presentations had been made, and Atana was left with the mere remnants for himself, just a few bones and one or two cakes."

The reaction of those in attendance is important. The feast was obviously a great occasion, and was attended by strangers from other villages. It was marked by gaiety and an interchange of gossip and it afforded an opportunity to wear one's fineries and permitted those who received gifts to obtain prestige for themselves by passing on some of this food to relatives coming from a distance. All remained in the hamlet until the

> last morsel of food had been distributed, and . . . an immense amount of satisfaction was derived from the sight of the food, and whenever an opportunity presented itself it was handled and admired. . . . "We shall eat," they said, "till we sicken and vomit." [4] They related to one another accounts of previous feasts and compared the amounts of food provided. When I expressed amazement at the sight of so much food they told me how sometimes at marriages . . . so great is the quantity of food that a good deal is rotten before it can be eaten and has to be thrown to the pigs.

It is apparent that here, in any event, the phrase "conspicuous consumption" is applicable to the processes employed in terms of goods accumulated and utilized solely to the end of attaining prestige. For the rest, the attitudes indicated in the passage just cited make the point that the greatest possible display is in the psychology of this group inseparable from the establishment and maintenance of social position.

His house-feast given, the aspirant for social honors has only started on a career of continuous expenditure. Impoverished by his effort, he begins anew, cultivating ever larger gardens, incessantly striving to increase the number of his pigs, exchanging yams and pigs for the strings of shell disks that are the local form of Melanesian depositaries of value. He may wed one or two extra wives to help him cultivate his gardens and, more importantly, to prepare the food he must always have on hand for visitors. His

---

[4] Almost exactly the same phrase is employed by inhabitants of the Trobriand Islands in describing their feasts. Malinowski (1922), 171. On Wogeo, also, similar expressions of attitude toward ritual overeating are heard: "It would be better for my stomach if I finished now, but I shall go on till the pains become intolerable." Hogbin (1938–9), 325.

wealth is constantly at the disposal of his fellow-villagers, and less elaborate feasts given by more humble members of his community must be aided with generous contributions, while he must also have on hand enough strings of shell disks to contribute to the bride-price of the young men who aided him in building his house.

Despite these obligations, he gradually rebuilds a surplus, until he comes to be in a position to give a dance festival, where the display and expenditure are even greater than in the preceding instance, if only because it requires a longer period of time. As a result, "the whole community thus owes every *mwanekama* who holds a dance a very great debt, and his reputation is always enormously enhanced"; once such a feast has been given, a man's reputation as a *mwanekama* is established. From then on, this reputation need only be sustained by a continuous flow of gifts and feasts, which the *mwanekama* is in better position than ever to afford, until he advances in years, becomes less active, and thus relapses into obscurity. While his prestige remains high, however, he has many psychological and material advantages to repay him for his efforts. He wears special ornaments associated with his rank, he is looked upon as the leader of the community, at his feasts he is assisted by his kinsmen, who help with the work necessary to create the wealth he must dispense.

We thus see clearly exemplified in this small Melanesian community the processes by means of which an economic surplus is created and redistributed. We also see how hard work, the drive to achieve status, and the co-operation of kinsmen and neighbors make possible the acquisition of prestige. Finally, it becomes apparent how the factor of conspicuous consumption permits a man to achieve the highest recognition and the most desirable social position his society affords.[5]

3

THIS pattern of attaining prestige by means of conspicuous consumption and display underlies Melanesian custom everywhere. The exhibition of yams, the gift-giving, and the lavish feasting

[5] Hogbin (1938), 289–305.

that accompany trading expeditions and mark other ceremonial occasions in the Trobriand Islands, where the economic role of competitive productivity, consumption, and waste is striking, have been set forth at length.[6] Again, though it is stated of the person of rank among the Solomon Islanders that "the prestige of a *tsunaun* was never distinctly a matter of the possession of property," it is also recorded that he owns more strings of ceremonial currency than other men; that he must provide "more than a commoner" in making the marriage payments of the younger members of his lineage "who, being themselves *tsunaun*, should marry women equal to them in position," and that in most instances he has several wives, which fact, though "not in itself a sign of rank," is none the less a sign of wealth. If a bride is of *tsunaun* lineage, the number of strings of ritual currency changing hands is much greater than when she is a commoner, a fact emphasized by the sound of the ceremonial gong, which punctuates with a single beat the giving of each string of currency. A child who is a *tsunaun* must be cicatrized more elaborately than one of common stock, and, as might be expected, the specialist who does the cicatrizing is paid more generously.[7]

Malekula likewise follows this pattern. "In the northwest," Deacon informs us, "the chiefs owe their influence and power, in part at least, to opportunities of acquiring greater wealth than ordinary men; wealth which they can expend profitably on gifts and feasts." This wealth also helps them in their quest by enabling them to "purchase the services of highly skilled magicians by whose arts they can inflict damage and suffering on those who oppose or threaten them, and in this way they are able to wield power beyond the reach of men of lesser means." Wealth, as a matter of fact, is here acquired only to spend, and a person who retains his wealth is looked on as less worthy than another who spends it by purchasing high rank in the men's societies. Value even determines which of the several forms of killing a pig is to be used in any given instance, for only low-grade animals—in terms of the intricate system of evaluating the tusk growths—are clubbed to death, while those of higher status are killed in more honorific fashion. "To be stingy," as the matter is summarized, "is to sink in public esteem; to be open-handed

[6] Malinowski (1922), *passim;* (1935), *passim.*

[7] Blackwood (1935), 51, 85–6, 428.

is to acquire fame, honour and influence." The Suque club of the
New Hebrides, with its graded ranks wherein membership is
gained only through the expenditure of increasingly large
amounts of goods, is but the counterpart of the societies which
flourish in southwestern Malekula. Here, beginning with the
lowest rank, the novice must make "appropriate payment" to his
sponsor, each successive grade involving heavier expenditure and
greater display, as befits the rising prestige that goes with
membership in each higher order.[8]

4

The conspicuous distribution of goods as an element in ceremonials is as important in Polynesia as in Melanesia. Modes of
ceremonial display such as are found in Ontong Java have been
effectively compared to similar procedures elsewhere—to the
potlatch of the Kwakiutl Indians, the Suque of the Banks and
New Hebrides Islands, the public exhibiting of crops in the
Trobriands, and to the lavish gift-giving throughout Polynesia.[9]
Since these particular manifestations of conspicuous consumption have been shown to be distributed over the whole Pacific
area, it is of interest to turn to another aspect of display in this
region, wherein rank is validated and confirmed by a display of
valuables which, as evidence of position and concentrations of
wealth, emphasize the economic power of their wearers. These
valuables function in this sense either because of their scarcity
value, or because of the labor that has been lavished on them,
or through symbolic representations of useful objects so elaborately worked as to render them useless for practical ends. A
striking example of this latter type of validating symbol has
been reported from the island of Mangaia where "Tane-mata-ariki
was represented by finely lashed adzes on special carved handles
which . . . because of the size and shape of the hafts . . .
could not be used in practical woodwork." [10]

The elegance of the guest-house of a Samoan chief, which reflects his position, was determined by the way in which the

[8] Deacon (1934), 49, 198–200;   [9] Hogbin (1932), *passim*.
Codrington (1891), 103; Layard   [10] Hiroa (1934), 144–68.
(1928), 142–3.

guild of carpenters were entertained while it was being constructed. It was "no light financial undertaking, but pride and
prestige had to be adequately housed." To this end the entire
family, and all the retainers of the chief, for months ahead
busied themselves with growing additional food, preparing
sennit for lashings, and gathering other materials. At feasts of
other kinds, questions of prestige constantly invade those of
utility in the preparation and cooking of the pigs, an all-important item of the ceremonial diet. The actual cooking has become
secondary to ritualistic considerations. "If the pig is too well
done, the flesh is liable to tear away and the exact boundaries of
the ceremonial divisions cannot be maintained. This creates
adverse comment and criticism on the part of those watching."
As a consequence, ceremonially prepared pork is undercooked,
the meat being often merely warmed through, to be recooked
at the homes of the recipients. "A failure in ceremony cannot be
remedied, but underdone pork can be recooked."

Clothing is so important a distinguishing mark of status that
the drive to possess valued articles of wearing apparel is held
to have stimulated ever greater refinement in technological
processes, as in the plaiting of mats. These prized mats "were
not needed and could not be worn as everyday clothing. They
were purely an expression of rank to be worn during ceremonies
and discarded as soon as possible afterwards for the sake of
comfort." Their everyday use was discouraged by the sanctions
of customary usage. "A person wearing a fine mat on ordinary
occasions would be regarded much in the same way as a person
. . . appearing at breakfast in a dinner suit with his breast
emblazoned with orders and decorations."

Samoa affords a further instance of leisure-class preoccupations in the activities that are closely akin to those sports which,
in our own culture, have been associated with class status. Fowling—pigeon-netting—in Samoa, as a matter of fact, bears a
striking resemblance to falconry, the sport of the European
feudal nobility. Originally prestige was derived from intervillage
competitions, but as interest grew in the success of a particular
pigeon-netting champion and the sport became more specialized
and costly, the chiefs took over. Only they could command the
labor necessary to erect the special platforms used in pigeon-
netting, and they enlarged these platforms to make the sport

more difficult, which in turn made it necessary to expend more time to achieve the desired proficiency. Eventually the prestige of the game, through its identification with those of high status, became associated with everything used in it. Therefore, while a section of a tree-trunk was an adequate seat on ordinary occasions, it became necessary when fowling to have "the neat seat with legs lashed to projecting lugs with a decorative design." In addition to pigeon-netting, the rituals of the kava ceremonial, the existence of special "courtesy language," and many other forms of privilege enjoyed by the several "status groups" on this island further indicate how fully the canons validating position and prestige by conspicuous consumption were established and were carefully followed.[11]

It is impossible to detail the wealth of available material from other parts of Polynesia bearing on these processes. On Tonga, for example, the kava etiquette is but one manifestation of it. Other instances to be cited from this island alone include the special houses inhabited by sons and daughters of chiefs, the great care given by specialists to the complexions of daughters of chiefs, and the cushions on which a young woman of this rank sat, "to keep the skin of her upper legs and buttocks soft and smooth"; when taking part in games a chief was given a handicap over an opponent of lesser rank; the food of a nobleman was prepared in a particular manner; and many nobles supported bards to soothe them with song and praise of their largesse. Some of the excesses of these chiefs, such as the feature improvised by one host of presenting naked dancing-girls to his guests, or cutting off an arm of each of the cooks who had prepared a certain feast to divert those of high position in attendance, were no less ingenious than the diversions of the leisure classes as recorded for the historic cultures.[12]

It has been seen how, in Tahiti, the elaborateness of the rituals and the leisure enjoyed by the priests indicate that display accompanied an allocation of a part of the economic surplus to them. This, it was shown, allowed the specialists to see that worship was carried on in a manner befitting the high position of the gods, and to train their successors in office. Other char-

[11] Hiroa (1930), 9–10, 19–20, 81, 119 ff., 316–17, 542–4; Mead (1930a), 102–11, 113–16, 129–30.   [12] Gifford (1929), 122 ff., 128 ff., 153, 156 ff.

acteristic marks of a leisure-class tradition were, however, also to be found on this island. Sports were divided into categories following the rank of the participants. Boxing was a lower-class diversion and, from the point of view both of setting and of the manner in which contests were carried on, is to be contrasted with archery. The special ceremonies of purification that marked archery competitions, the distinguishing dress worn by the participants, the "nicely kept lawns on public property" where the contests were held, and the retainers who acted as scorers and umpires cause this sport to stand out markedly from the rough-and-ready setting of the boxing bout, where the greatest prestige came to the boxer who could boast of the number of opponents he had maimed or even killed. The customary outward marks of political or sacerdotal rank were also found on this island, and all members of the upper classes exercised the meticulous care of their bodies that is possible only when those who do this are not required to perform manual labor.[13]

The training of bards and other practitioners of the arts who, "because they recorded events and human relationships . . . were valuable to the aristocracy in establishing claims to the physical, social, and religious prerogatives of rank," was extensive and must have been a heavy charge on the resources of Polynesian economies. "New Zealand and the Society Islands," we are told, "had famous houses of learning, really primitive universities, at which ancestral lore, genealogies, traditions, religion, magic, navigation, agriculture, literary composition, and all the arts and crafts were taught by learned priests." Elsewhere, there were other "courses of higher learning," such as the "famous college of heraldry" in Hawaii. In Samoa, the "talking chiefs," the spokesmen, "were gifted orators skilled in protocol, traditions, genealogies, and composition." The accomplishments of the man of power are summarized as follows:

In general, the hallmark of any well-born and well-trained chief was his ability to give orations with an abundance of religious and historical allusions, metaphors, similes, and proverbs. He must also be able, when occasion demanded, to compose suitable poetry.[14]

---

[13] T. Henry (1928), 276–8; Handy (1930), 44.

[14] Luomala, 773–4; see also above, 450.

5

THE POTLATCH of the Indians of the Northwest Coast of North America has become the classic instance of the utilization of wealth for purposes of validating position and ensuring prestige. This has been described in such detail, especially for the Kwakiutl, that it need be no more than sketched here, despite the fact that it affords us an almost perfect illustration of the principles with which we are concerned. So well known has the Kwakiutl potlatch become, indeed, that it is necessary to stress the observation made in the opening pages of this chapter, where it was pointed out that the conspicuous display of wealth among this same people can take other forms; that, for example, the daughter of a chief on the occasion of her marriage is literally covered with valuable shells to stress her high position. The tradition of the potlatch, it must also be indicated, is widespread. It is practiced not alone by the Kwakiutl, the neighboring Tsimshian, among whom the waste which marked these rites and their sanctions have been recorded in native myth, the Tlingit, and the Haida, but in addition is found among inland tribes to the east and those living south and even north of the coastal belt where its best-known forms are found.[15]

Among the Kwakiutl, and perhaps also among the Chinook and the Tlingit, the potlatch was the means of validating inherited position, and reinforced a relatively stable class system composed of nobles, commoners, and slaves. Murdock holds that among the Haida this acquisition of status was solely a matter of potlatching, wherein no considerations of hereditary rank were operative. For the point with which we are here concerned, this interpretation merely makes our hypothesis the more cogent. For according to this analysis, position is attained only on the basis of potlatches given by one's parents, who themselves benefit but little by the goods they expend. Hence if a person of low degree does in some manner obtain the necessary amount of property and potlatches with it, his children will be higher in social position than himself. On the other hand, a man who

---

[15] Boas (1921), 786 ff., 1340 ff.; ibid. (1916), 276–7, 439, 537–42; Swanton (1908), 438–43; ibid. (1905), 162–70, 176–80; Murdock (1936), *passim;* Birket-Smith and de Laguna (1938), 475, n. 1–4 for full references.

because of his parents' efforts was himself born to high status, but who, through laziness or shiftlessness, has not himself accumulated goods for the purpose of potlatching, penalizes his children, though such a man does not lose his own status.[16] In this sense, the goods expended in the potlatch may most fully be regarded, as Barnett puts it, as "prestige investments." For these goods, which "consist almost entirely of treasure items . . . have an arbitrary value unrelated for the most part of physical human needs," since "their consumption utility, especially in recent times, has been negligible." [17]

One of the earliest visitors to the coast of California has left an account of the regalia and entourage of a chief which, though subject to all qualification on the score of naïvete and exaggeration, does none the less present a picture that is of value. The description is that of Drake, who touched the coast just south of Point Reyes in 1599. It presumably concerns the Pomo Indians, showing their use of "money and class distinctions" in dress:

A while after, their King with all his Train appeared in as much Pomp as he could. . . . In the Front before him marched a tall Man of good Countenance, carrying the Sceptre or Mace Royal, of black Wood, about a Yard and a half long, upon which hung two Crowns, one less than the other, with three very long Chains oft doubled. . . . The Crowns were of Knit-work wrought curiously with Feathers of divers Colours, and of a good Fashion, the Chains seemed of Bone, the links being in one Chain almost innumerable, and worn by very few, who are stinted in their number, some to ten, twelve or twenty, as they exceed in Chains, are thereby accounted more honourable. Next . . . came the King himself, with his Guard about him, having on his Head a Knit work Cawl, wrought somewhat like a Crown, and on his shoulder a Coat of Rabbet Skins reaching to his Waste. The Coats of his Guard were of the same Shape, but other Skins, having Cawls with Feathers, covered with a Down growing on an Herb, exceeding any other Down for Fineness, and not to be used by any but those about the Kings Person, who are also permitted to wear a Plume of Feathers

[16] Murdock, op. cit., 18–19.
[17] Barnett (1938), 353, 351. See also Drucker, *passim*, for certain broader social and areal settings of the prestige complex.

on his Head, in sign of Honour, and the seeds of this Herb are used only in sacrifice to their Gods. After them followed the Common People almost naked, whose long Hair tied up in a Bunch behind, was stuck with Plumes of Feathers, but in the forepart, according to their own fancy, their Faces were all Painted, some White, others Black, or other Colours. . . .[18]

In this area, rank and prestige are today marked by outward symbols of wealth as they were at the period of initial contact. Among the Yurok, where wealth was synonymous with status,

> . . . rich women ornamented their dress heavily. Haliotis and clam-shells jingled musically from the ends of the fringes, and occasionally a row of obsidian prisms tinkled with every step. Poor women contented themselves with less. They may sometimes have had recourse to a simple skirt of fringed inner bark of the maple, which was standard wear for adolescent girls and novitiate shamans.

At dances, "the beautiful skins or headdresses or obsidians displayed at a dance by one rich man excite the interest and envy of visitors of wealth. . . . Such wealthy spectators return home determined to exhibit an even greater value of property the next year." The further comment, that "poor men take notice but are not stirred" by these displays, is eloquent. In the southern portion of the state, the Mohave are reported as regarding the display and destruction of property as essential for the maintenance of high social position.[19]

As has been indicated, the most complex political and sacerdotal organizations found in North America north of Mexico were those of the Natchez of southeastern United States. The "Great Sun" as the supreme ruler and priest, and the officials who surrounded him, enjoyed numerous special costly privileges which were denied commoners, while their dress and manner of life reflected their wealth. When the Great Sun so desired, a deer dance was ordered, and a hundred of his retainers were detailed to bring in one of these animals alive so that they might "exercise themselves pleasantly" with it. When the successor to the Great Sun was born, every family with an infant at the

[18] Barrett (1908), 32.   [19] Kroeber, 76, 40, 745.

breast was compelled to pay him special homage, and a certain number of these infants were chosen for his future service, which meant that when of age some hunted and fished to supply his table, some cared for his fields, and some became members of his retinue. "If he happens to die, all these servants sacrifice themselves, with joy, to follow their dear master . . ."—an instance of the control of manpower and its withdrawal from productive uses. Representatives of other tribes were generously entertained by the Great Sun by being quartered with subordinates. The economic implications of this arrangement were tersely summarized by one contemporary when he stated: "for it is at the cost of his subjects that he defrays the expenses of the embassage." Polygyny was permitted, but only men of high position could support plural wives, since, again in the words of an observer, "having the right to oblige the people to cultivate their fields for them without giving them any wages, the number of their wives is no expense to them." Yet the prestige obtained from thus having a large establishment understandably reinforced their position in the minds of their subjects.

Insignia were worn which set off men of rank from those of low status. The Great Sun, as "a mark of his preeminent authority" wore a feather crown, beautifully worked by a process that demanded the labor of an appreciable number of persons; others of the noble class wore valuable feather mantles. On ceremonial occasions the dress of officials and priests was especially elaborate. The ruler, in addition to his feather crown, wore "a necklace of large pearls and feathers"; he was seated on a special stool, covered with a buffalo robe and "many peltries." The accounts of rites of all kinds, especially religious ceremonies, further illustrates how display marked every phase of the life of the privileged class. All of this, it may again be stressed, must be regarded as representing a charge on the productive labor of the community as a whole, laid by those whose place in society represented a vested interest in the surplus produced by the people they ruled or served as priests.[20]

Though the great resources of Mexico and Peru permitted more extravagant display than anywhere else in the New World, the underlying principles that directed this are no different from those operative for the Natchez or, indeed, for any of the cultures

[20] Swanton (1911), 70–1, 142–3, 106–07.

previously cited. This is evident if a description by Torquemada of the intricate rites performed on the occasion of the death of a Mexican ruler be compared with the terse statement that "for the common people the ceremonies were, naturally, very much simpler." In life as in death, prestige was furthered by conspicuous consumption and display. Noses, lower lips, and ears of nobles were decorated with plugs of jade, crystal, obsidian, or other precious stones or metals; persons of lesser rank wore plugs of pottery. Necklaces worn by the upper classes were of jade or gold or of gold in combination with semi-precious stones, and one of these, of elaborate design, sent by Cortez to Charles V, represents a great concentration of value. As everywhere, feather-work was expensive, so that feather mantles could be owned only by those whose wealth and position permitted. Montezuma was always borne in a litter by four chieftains; a canopy of green feathers whose fringes were ornamented with gold, silver, pearls, and jade was held over him by four more chiefs; his feet were never permitted to touch the ground, but he walked on mantles laid in his path; the soles of his sandals were of gold and adorned with precious stones.

The symbols of rank borne by the warrior class take those forms associated with membership in such classes. Thus the induction of young men into the warrior group involved an initial degradation, familiar in rituals which validate membership in privileged groupings. This heightened the contrast of status upon their eventual emergence from training amid the great display of wealth that brought to an end this ceremonial deprivation. The young warrior was compelled to undergo various tests in consolidating his position, but once established, there were many degrees of advancement he could achieve on the basis of successive exploits, each of which brought with its recognition highly prized privileges of special dress and ornament. Warriors of common status, besides cotton armor, carried shields as part of their defensive equipment, round wooden disks covered with skins. For more important members of the warrior class, however, distinctions in rank were designated by the decorations of feather-work and sometimes of jewelry on their shields. When troops returned triumphant from a campaign, they were given an impressive welcome to the capital. The wealthier warriors were visited by poor people who sang songs in their honor, receiving in return gifts of food, drink, and clothing and a small share of the spoils. Warriors of noble status who had died as sacrificed prisoners, or whose bodies were not recovered after a defeat, were represented by wooden effigies, which were dressed according to the rank of the dead, decorated with jewels, and burned as the actual body of an Aztec noble would be; and slaves were sacrificed, as at any cremation ceremony.[21] An equivalent display also marked the functioning of the religious orders of pre-Spanish Mexico.

In Peru, where the head of the state was at the same time the supreme religious head, the economic validation of the position of priests and rulers was accentuated by the concentration of both functions in the hands of this single personage. Here the materials which document these practices are so rich as to make it impossible to review them even in fragmentary form. Their epitome, contained in a description taken from the contemporary sources of the way in which the art of the gold- and silver-smiths was utilized to create for the priest-ruler a worthy setting, sufficiently makes the point:

> Gold and silver were cast, soldered, hammered and inlaid, and the finer examples of the goldsmith's art excited the wondering admiration of the conquerors. The Inca even possessed gardens in which the trees and plants were imitated "all in gold and silver, with their leaves, flowers and fruit; some just beginning to sprout, others half-grown, others having reached maturity. They made fields of maize with their leaves, heads, canes, roots and flowers, all exactly imitated. The beard of the maize-head was of gold, and all the rest was of silver, the parts being soldered together. They did the same with other plants, making the flower or any part that became yellow, of gold, and the rest of silver." [22]

6

IN THE great political groupings of Africa and Indonesia, as well as in the less complex societies in these and other areas, the

[21] Thompson (1933), 53 ff., 82–3, 91 ff., 114–24.   [22] Joyce (1912), 209 and *passim;* cf. also Means (1931), 284–417.

same mechanisms found to be operative in the cultures of Oceania and the Americas are also active.[23] With but rare exceptions we find that, to the extent to which the economic system, the technological level of achievement, and the natural setting permit, some men enjoy more favored positions than others; that those who have a vested interest in the surplus goods produced by others have obligations of generosity that take as their form ceremonial lavishness, display and the ritual destruction of property; and these in turn set in operation sanctions that make the position of such persons more secure.[24]

It must again be made explicit that this hypothesis does not imply that obligations are not scrupulously fulfilled. It is, moreover, true that in regulating the political order, keeping affairs attuned to the supernatural world, contributing to the store of knowledge, or elaborating the setting of government or religion, those so occupied make contributions which, in the end, have resulted in a higher standard of living and a greater enjoyment of life to the people as a whole. Again, the fact that in certain societies there is active co-operation between the two principal types of beneficiaries of the economic surplus which results in their mutual advantage is not to be viewed either as impugning all motives that lead to this co-operation or as denying the satisfactions to be derived from it by the group as a whole. For if the objective of social behavior is furthered by mutual helpfulness of this kind, it can only be argued that those who pay the price receive full value in the direction and assurance made available to them for the cost to them of these services. It cannot be maintained, on the basis of our existing knowledge that, from either a psychological or an ethnological point of view, attitudes of blame are held by those who contribute to the support of their superiors. Rather we find far more frequently a lively pride in display, a drive toward emulation, a joy in following sanctioned leadership, and pleasure derived from the fact that adequate

[23] This relationship will be apparent in South Africa, for example, if the discussions of it as concerns the Swazi (Kuper, 154–7) and the Bemba (A. I. Richards, 1939, 211–16) are consulted.

[24] One such exception would seem to be the Popoluca of Mexico, where motives of conspicuous consumption to validate status "appear to be minimized." However, even here, a "set norm of status" is maintained by a house-raising party, though this is non-competitive. Cf. Foster (1942), 36, 75–6.

direction is being given political or religious matters by those whose competence is based on the divine order, or inherited position, or special training.

What is important from the point of view of those whose interest centers in either the economic or the sociological implications of the phenomenon is its widespread distribution and its effectiveness in institutionalizing socioeconomic differences within a given population. This economic force, it must be repeated, is not the unique cause of class differences. Military operations support and further the institution of slavery. There is also the vast problem, barely attacked as yet, why women participate so disproportionately in the outward manifestations that distinguish the males of privileged groups from all other members of society.

Yet allowing for the constant effectiveness of these and other non-economic factors, an explanation of the widespread fact that some members of so many societies are relieved from the cares of manual labor in order to direct or ensure physical and supernatural protection, is to be sought on the economic level. Psychological factors, in the nature of acquiescence and identification of those with the least to gain from the arrangement, constitute puzzling concomitants of the phenomenon. These, however, bring out only the more clearly the underlying socioeconomic drives and the institutions arising from them. It may be suggested that if these important psychological concomitants are to be understood, the problem will have to be attacked through an intensive comparative study of nonliterate groups possessing such institutions. From such research, it is anticipated, fresh light will be shed on some of the perplexing problems which arise out of the unequal distribution of wealth in our own society.

PART VI

CONCLUSIONS

CHAPTER XXII

SOME PROBLEMS AND POINTS OF VIEW

WE HAVE seen how men everywhere, impelled by the circumstances of their existence, wrest a livelihood from their natural environment, devise implements to give them technological competence, set up systems of exchange and traditions of consumption, and develop concepts of value that determine those choices between the alternatives inherent in the productive and distributive process. Whether we consider the motivations underlying the economic activities of peoples without writing or a machine industry, or the institutions that are the framework of the economic systems of nonliterate, non-industrialized societies, it is clear that these are directed toward the same ends and utilize substantially the same means to attain those ends, as do peoples who are equipped with-writing, and with the superior technologies of the historic societies.

In discussing all such matters full weighting must be given the point raised at the beginning of this book, wherein the significant differences between the economies of nonliterate societies, taken as a whole, and the dominant economic order of present-day America and western Europe were set forth. Considerations of sound analysis dictate that no comparison between our own and other economies be attempted without full realization of the effect on the main lines of economic development and the shaping of economic institutions exerted by the presence of a machine technology, the invasion of the evaluative processes by pecuniary considerations, and the high development of business enterprise.

Yet practically every economic mechanism and institution known to us is found somewhere in the nonliterate world. Division of labor and the specialization this represents, the multitudinous forms of money, the various aids to business such as credit and interest, the investment of labor-power and other resources in capital goods—all these, so important in our own culture, have been found to exist in numerous non-machine, nonliterate economies. Similarly, the institutional aspects of these economic systems are comparable to those of our own, as where the control of wealth, resulting in socioeconomic class differences, interacts with other non-economic institutions to influence their form and affect their role in everyday life.

The distinctions to be drawn between literate and nonliterate economies are consequently those of degree rather than of kind. Restated, this merely re-emphasizes the point that the economic processes and institutions of nonliterate folk, being more generalized and less sharply differentiated than are their counterparts in our own culture, thus present special methodological problems to those who would describe them and analyze their nature and functioning.

Certain further points that were merely touched upon in early chapters may now be considered at greater length. One of these concerns the extent to which economic elements in a culture influence the non-economic aspects of its social life. This, as customarily phrased, is the problem of economic determinism. Another has to do with the degree to which in general individualistic as against collectivist activity prevails in "primitive" societies. Both are important, if only because of the polemics that have marked their discussion; both are peculiarly susceptible to analysis and appraisal on the basis of data from nonliterate societies. Hence we shall direct our attention to their analysis before we address ourselves, in closing, to certain other less controversial matters of concept and method which arise out of the subject-matter of this book.

2

ECONOMIC determinism, like those other determinisms of an environmental, racial, or cultural nature, has at one time or another had much appeal for students of human social life. This is primarily because by reference to a single factor that is powerful enough to supply arresting instances, attractive explanations are provided for the difficult problems raised in the search for the genesis and development of human institutions. Unfortunately, simplistic approaches of this sort encourage the neglect of those other influences which, at any given time and in any given society, also function, and thus inhibit the fullest analysis of these problems.

As occurs so often, the very act of advancing postulates of this sort has had varied results. On the one hand, the assertion that a single given factor in human experience is all-powerful has at times led to a serious re-examination of the data, to the end that a new conception of its role has emerged as an improved tool for further investigation. Frequently, however, the claims of extremists have tended to render counter-suggestible those whose materials do not support the universal validity such a theory may be asserted to have, so that, in all too human a manner, they bend their energies to the negative task of refutation.

For purposes of illustration, we may for the moment return to the postulate of environmental determinism. This point of view seems to have passed through the phase of refutation, and to have arrived at a point where serious examination can be given the problem of the relationship between human institutions and their natural setting. For many years it was thought necessary by anthropologists merely to recall how the Chuckchee and the Eskimo, though inhabiting the same difficult arctic environment, not only posses different social, political, and religious institutions, but even differ significantly in their material culture, where environmental influence might be expected most forcefully to manifest itself. In a similar manner, appeal was made to the difference in basic economic systems, technologies, and art-forms of the Pueblo and Navaho inhabitants of the desert area of southwestern United States to prove that different cultures can exist in the same setting, and that hence environmental factors are not to be considered determining ones.

Today the point that "human geography demands as much knowledge of humanity as of geography" can be regarded as no longer debatable. Anthropologists, like geographers, are tending to turn from assertion and protest to the assessment of the relationship between culture and its natural setting. By those whose focus of attention is the setting of culture, it is recognized that "between the physical environment and human activity there is always a middle term, a collection of specific objectives and values, a body of knowledge and belief; in other words, a cultural pattern. . . ." [1] Reciprocally, it has been established among anthropologists that the environment plays its limiting role—a view quite different from the negative phrasing of this statement, that the natural setting does no more than impose limits on a culture. It is thus possible at the present time to draw the two conclusions regarding this relationship that were stated in an earlier chapter:

> The natural environment will play a more important role where getting a living is involved than in religion, or social organization, or art. . . . the more adequate the technology, the less direct are the demands made by their environment on the daily life of a people. [2]

The postulate of economic determinism, however, still calls forth a negative response from most anthropologists. In view of the anthropological tradition which considers economic phenomena in sociological or technological perspective, it is understandable that the problem of the amount and kind of influence exerted by economic factors on other aspects of culture should have received little attention. What is here so striking, however, is that anthropologists have not only not been similarly unmindful of this hypothesis of economic determinism, but that, on the contrary, they should have gone to some lengths to indicate its lack of validity when applied to nonliterate cultures. In the sense that it is important to have it clearly understood that no unilateral explanation is valid for the complex phenomenon that is human tradition, these efforts have not been unimportant. One may, however, well ask whether it is essential, the point once made, to labor it beyond the dictates of necessity.

There is little need to have recourse to the findings of modern psychology any more than to the findings of present-day anthropology to demonstrate the untenability of the theory of economic determinism in its cruder, more extreme statement. It is of little help to assert, as some economic determinists have asserted, that

[1] Forde (1934), 465, 463.   [2] See above, 73.

because man must eat to live, his life is determined in all its aspects by this fact. This position, indeed, uncomfortably resembles assertions of uncompromising environmental determinists that man must breathe if he is to survive. The problem, in its simplest form, involves some rough kind of correlation, as when the question is raised of the degree of consistency between hunting or herding or agricultural economies and various types of religious, social, artistic, and other institutions—problems that can only be posed in the present state of our knowledge. Certainly any attempts to explain institutions primarily in terms of an appraisal of economic advantage, whose rationality is judged in other than relativistic terms, are doomed to failure.

The economic waste found among many tribes of western North America, arising out of quasi-religious beliefs in the contamination of death, may be cited to illustrate how folk living but slightly above or even on a subsistence level can permit a non-economic factor to stand in the way of their own best interests. Among the Northern Shoshoni of the Lehmi Valley, "at death, a person's . . . clothes, blankets, and cherished articles were buried with him, a few things being given to his children. . . ." [3] Before the days of European contact, the Chipewyan tribes left nothing of a man's goods when he died. "On the death of a relative they destroy guns, blankets, bottles, everything, in short, they possess, concluding the havoc by tearing their lodges to pieces." [4] The Klamath, whose resources were somewhat greater, not only heaped the property of the dead man on the funeral pyre, his beads, arms, and skins, but valuables contributed by others to honor the dead were also consumed.[5] "The amount of property destroyed" at the anniversary rites for the dead carried out periodically by the Maidu and other California tribes "must have been immense by aboriginal standards." The resources of these folk are small; yet "as late as 1901, 150 poles of baskets, American clothing, and the like, were consumed at a single Maidu burning." [6] Nor is such wastefulness confined to the American Indians. In Melanesia the ceremonial destruction of valuable property at death, or at rites for adolescent boys, or as a method of showing anger is quite comparable from the point of view of the respec-

[3] Stewart, 194.
[4] Birket-Smith (1930), 77, citing Simpson.
[5] Spier, 72–3.
[6] Kroeber, 429–32.

tive economies to these North American instances. In many parts of Africa, funerary rituals offer outstanding instances of the consumption of wealth to no utilitarian end.

Do not those who destroy goods in this way run in the face of economic necessity, to say nothing of their personal economic best advantage? An elementary knowledge of the psychology of culture should serve to assure that a culturally realistic answer be given this question. Behavior of this sort is accepted since, as a part of the entire cultural equipment of a people, the enculturative conditioning of the members of the society in question will be such as to make this economic waste outweigh considerations of the most effective utilization of available resources.

We must look, then, beyond mere negation if we are to ascertain just where the economic organization most strongly exerts its influence, where it is weakest, and what processes are involved in setting the configurations and relationships to be encountered in studying a given society. One or two instances may be given to make clear how such an approach might be employed. The Menomini Indians "absolutely refused" to plant wild rice because of a mythological prohibition; the Dakota, with no such prohibition, also refused to sow this grain; while, on the other hand, the Ojibwa, who like the Dakota knew no sanction against the practice, planted wild rice "from purely economic motives." [7] Such facts may be adduced as proof that economic considerations will not prevail over mythological ones if the latter are strong enough; but this is a conclusion admitted even by extreme economic determinists in their contention that religion, in our own culture, is primarily an institution which, by its very nature, stands between men and their economic best interests. It would seem that the question *why* mythical sanction dictated practice in the first instance, and "economic motives" decided the matter in the last case, is the important one to be answered if the real significance of the processes involved is to be assessed.

Another example is afforded by three tribes in the Peermade hills of Travancore, southern India, who live in similar habitats, possess similar economies based on crude agriculture, and whose most important rituals are related to their major occupation. Among the Paliyan and Mannan, two of these tribes, the rituals are "casual and haphazard" in contrast to their rigidity and

[7] Jenks, 1019.

complexity among the Urali, whose ceremonial calendar "imposes a strict schedule of operations on Urali economy and makes the tribesman more efficient cultivators than their neighbors." Because of this fact,

> the Urali follow a successful one-year plan; the Mannan and Paliyan follow their own fancies, with the result that the Urali are by far the most prosperous of the Periyar tribes. . . . All the energy and time and wealth that the Urali lavish on the performance of rituals is not fruitlessly squandered, but bring ample returns through the constraint which the ceremonies impose on the tribesmen and which enforces more efficient cultivation. The manifold Urali rites may not bring rain, or favorable winds, or keep the wild pig away from the fields, but they do make a better farmer of the Urali.[8]

Here again it would not be difficult, were one ferreting out instances where a non-economic factor exerts a striking influence over an aspect of economic life, to cite this case. The statement that ". . . the ceremonial factor is a paramount one in which the Urali pattern stands in bold contrast to the traits of the other two tribes" could be tellingly quoted to demonstrate how one can "refute" economic determinism. Yet it is apparent that while the Urali ritualistic pattern of agricultural ceremonies has been important in giving this people greater wealth than their neighbors, the economic factor of hard and regular work has also been significant in achieving this end.

3

IT MAY be well at this point also to consider the theory of economic determinism in the light of the historical setting out of which it emerged. Today associated principally with the name of Karl Marx, it was developed as an integral part of his political philosophy, which in turn was based on his analysis of the economic system of his time. The most precise statement of Marx's position is found in the preface to his *Critique of Political Economy*, where it takes the following form:

[8] Mandelbaum (1939).

Men, in the social production which they carry on, enter into definite relations which are indispensable and independent of their wills; and these relations correspond to a definite state in the development of their material powers of production. The sum-total of these relations of production constitutes the economic structure of society—the real foundation on which rise legal and political super-structures and to which definite forms of social consciousness correspond. The method of production in material life determines the general character of the social, political, and spiritual processes of life. It is not the consciousness of man that determines their being, but, on the contrary, their social being determines their consciousness.[9]

It is not hard to see from this how the reaction of a sensitive, socially conscious man to the working conditions and standards of living of the wage-earners during the early days of the industrial revolution took the form of an explanation assigning a preponderant and even an exclusive role to the economic factors in the historic process.

As was pointed out in the case of Marshall's statement concerning the nature of economic science, its interests and problems, there may be a wide divergence between a point of view as defined and the treatment an author accords his materials in developing his position. It is striking how little stress is laid in the writings of Marx, and even Engels, his collaborator and literary executor, on the influence exerted by the economic aspect of a culture on other than its political and social structure, despite Engel's attempt to establish certain broad principles of social evolution along the lines of Lewis H. Morgan's stages of culture as given in *Ancient Society*.[10] It was those who came after Marx and after Engels who employed the theory to account for every vagary of human behavior, individual as well as social; who held that, as it has been phrased by one non-Marxian economist, "all social life is nothing but a reflex of the economic life." [11]

In the hands of its originator and his colleague, stress is laid almost entirely on the influence exerted by economic elements in culture on those mechanisms and institutions which, based on

[9] Marx (1933), xvi, also 392, n. 2.   [11] Seligman, E. R. A. (1902), 382.
[10] Engels, esp. 191 ff.

economic inequalities, are most responsive to the modes of exploitation and the vested interests of special privilege. The theory, in short, was employed by Marx and Engels in a manner far more restrained, far more congenial to those who today search out the interrelations between the various aspects of culture, than its caricature defended by many of its later enthusiastic proponents. It is this more extreme form of the theory that has rendered it a ready, though specious target for the simulated engagements of the mimic intellectual warfare in which its critics have too often engaged.

In one respect, moreover, the works of Marx and Engels give an impression strikingly akin to that gained from reading any textbook or work on theory written by adherents of the classical school of economists, especially in the manner in which interest is exclusively centered on our culture. It is, therefore, not surprising that in discussions of economic theory Marx's allusions to the economic life of "primitive" peoples are almost as rare, certainly no more acceptable, and as much incidental to the establishment of some postulate bearing on our own economic order as are those in the writings of Adam Smith, or Marshall, or Bücher when these students turn to supposed modes of behavior, or to motivations, or to presumed economic mechanisms in "savage" societies.

A complicating factor enters at this point. This concerns the difficulty often encountered in distinguishing between the theory of economic determinism, and the point of view summarized in the phrase "the materialistic conception of history" or, as it is often expressed, "historical materialism." Why it has been so difficult to separate the two concepts is perhaps understandable when it is seen how both can be inferred from the passage quoted from Marx, though if we scrutinize this same passage, we see that even here they are separated. "The method of production in material life determines the general character of the social, political, and spiritual processes of life"; this is clearly economic determinism. The sentence that follows it, however, constitutes an equally succinct statement of historical materialism: "It is not the consciousness of men that determines their being, but, on the contrary, their social being determines their consciousness." If we rephrase these statements, it becomes apparent that the first maintains that in the historic processes by means of which institutions are founded and perpetuated, the economic factors are decisive in determining the forms they take. The second sentence, on the other hand, states what is today the most generally accepted position of social scientists—that no force extraneous to man's bio-psychic reaction to his total situation can be called on to account for the outer manifestations and inner sanctions which give to every culture the organized and stable forms that permit it to function continuously over succeeding generations.

With the hypothesis of historical materialism, therefore, no social scientist can quarrel. It is, on the contrary, an expression of method toward the realization of which all effort is being continuously directed. Economic determinism, on the other hand, must be rejected as must any other simplistic explanation of culture. This does not mean that the influence of a given economic system on other aspects of the culture of which it is a part is to remain unstudied. On the contrary, this is the crux of one of the most important problems in the entire repertory of the social sciences. We can understand the genesis of the theory with greater insight if its classic statement and the extreme restatements of it encountered from time to time are regarded as the reactions to a particular culture, our own, wherein economic factors are actually of primary importance. That the passage of the years has put finer conceptual and methodological tools in the hands of students of society and has given them wider horizons is aside from the point. Just because they have these improved devices, it is all the more incumbent upon them to assess the relative weight, in various cultures, at various times, of the several aspects of culture, as their most effective lead in the analysis of the plural factors in social causation.

4

THE QUESTION of the extent to which economic activities of nonliterate peoples are based on collectivist or individualistic effort derives its importance primarily from the appeals made to instances of one or the other type of organization as justification for proposed changes in the economic and political structure of our own culture. That what is done in these societies is not, however, necessarily pertinent to discussions of this sort has already been indicated. For if it is granted that every culture is the product of its own historic past, then even if a given institution or form of behavior is encountered frequently, it does not follow that it is impossible or undesirable to establish innovations that differ from all existing types, or that it is impossible or undesirable to maintain an institution or mechanism already in operation, however unique it may be.

It is worth noting, however, that in most discussions on this level, emphasis is placed on "proofs" that have to do with the forms of property-ownership rather than with other phases of economic life. So marked is this tendency that it is not easy, at first glance, to see how the problem relates to the production, distribution, and consumption of goods as well as to the manner in which the end-results of the productive and distributive processes are held and administered. Further analysis, however, shows the necessity of extending the scope of the problem to include all aspects of economic life, which, in turn, adds complexity to what is already sufficiently involved.

It will be remembered that in any investigation of communal versus individual ownership the data must be divided into relevant categories. Different types of property and the various forms taken by each type must first be considered. Only after this can the legal aspects of the manner in which a given good is held among a given people, and the extra-legal sanctions under which, in common practice, the control of any good or plot of land is reserved to its owner alone, or informally permitted to be used by others, be studied. With these data in hand, the question of what others enjoy this privilege, and under what circumstances, can then be further considered. A specific instance from the South American Chaco may be given at this point to recall the varied documentation of this problem, as presented in earlier chapters:

> In spite of the liberality which appears in the relations of the different members of the community to one another, private property is strictly respected in all the tribes. . . . The land . . . is considered to belong to the people in general; no Indian, not even a chief, has a direct claim to any part of it above his fellows. The flocks of sheep and goats

feed on the common pasture. Similarly the natural products of the country, such as game, fish, wild fruit, honey, and fire-wood, are common property. But as soon as an individual family has taken possession of a piece of this common land for cultivation, its ownership is acknowledged and respected as long as the family actually cultivates it. What the Indian collects of the natural products of the country and what he produces or acquires through his own work—such as clothes, ornaments, weapons and implements, magical instruments, etc.—is also regarded as his exclusive property, although, as soon as food is in question, an unwritten moral law and social sympathy largely induces the individual owner to share it with others. The flocks of course also belong to individual families. The sheep and goats always wear property marks, so that when they are taken home from the pasture in the afternoon the Indians can easily determine who is the owner of each animal.[12]

Here we find no simple formula of ownership. Land is communally owned but restricted as to use by tenure as long as cultivated; private herds, which belong to individual families, graze on this communal land; foodstuffs are privately held but generously shared because of traditional considerations; the results of a man's labor are his own. It is apparent that any attempt to analyze such a series of property concepts—or other similarly complex systems from which data in our earlier discussion were drawn—in terms of the simple categories of private and communal holding, will result in misinterpretation, if not in utter confusion.

Attention has been given to the place of co-operative labor in the productive activities of non-industrial societies. The data amply prove that a spirit of comradeship and mutual aid of a kind not unlike that suggested by Kropotkin[13] does exist as a significant factor in assuring the functioning of the processes of production with a degree of efficiency and a smoothness that, it is reasonable to assume, might otherwise not be attainable. The types of co-operative labor considered in the discussion of production were concerned chiefly with the means of obtaining the food and other goods essential to the maintenance of life. There are,

[12] Karsten, 94.　　　　　　　　　　[13] Kropotkin, 63 ff.

however, many other kinds of co-operative effort in the production of goods which, though of equal psychological importance in the schedule of wants, do not have the physiological urgency of food or shelter. In Tonga, for instance, tapa cloth is manufactured by co-operative associations of women, each of whom brings an equal number of white strips that have been prepared by herself. The finished product is shared by all the members of the group. These work together in a special house under the direction of an old woman who, presumably, is especially competent in the techniques employed.[14] On the island of Tikopia, canoe-building and repairing, net-making, and the extraction of turmeric are all done co-operatively.[15] The functioning of the co-operative principle among the Dahomean iron-workers' and other guilds, or among the canoe-builders of Melanesia, will also be recalled.

It is to be noted that mechanisms are not lacking to enforce the rule that those who pool their labor must not shirk if they are to share. Mention of this has already been made, when the work societies of Haiti were described. In comparable fashion, on Ontong Java, where fishing is carried on in groups, zeal and skill are rewarded and malingering penalized. The man who for some days pretends he has fever, or that he has children to look after, or who offers some other excuse to permit him to eat without working is sooner or later discovered, and the members of his group no longer set aside a portion of the catch for him. The anger of his wife and neighbors when he does not fulfill his duties as producer and provider is an effective spur to a change of heart.[16]

Just as in the ownership of property, the fact that some productive activities are carried on communally, or by groups within the community as a whole, does not imply that individualistic effort is lacking among nonliterate producers, or that individual initiative is not spurred by the hope of individual reward. In many non-pecuniary societies, it will be recalled, the production and sale of certain goods are the right of one person alone, and drives both of prestige as such, or of prestige masked by the pecuniary terms in which reward may be couched, cause a man to seek to outdo his fellows. Facts of this character prove that

[14] Gifford (1929), 147. [16] Hogbin (1934), 226.
[15] Raymond Firth (1939), 115–38.

though the principle of mutual aid is widespread among nonliterate folk, it is by no means universal or exists to the exclusion
of competition based on individualistic striving for economic
gain.

It must thus be re-emphasized that the entire discussion of
communism versus individualism, in so far as reference to "primitive" societies is concerned, seems to be but a kind of intellectual
shadow-boxing. Verbalistic blows are dealt without command of
adequate knowledge either of the actual forms taken by economic
institutions of primitive groups, or of the significance of the
terms "socialistic" or "communistic" or, indeed, even "individualistic." The Inca are one people who for many years were cited
as a supposedly perfect example of "socialism" [17] or "communism"
—where a beneficent ruler, through the wise and efficient administration of his kingdom, saw to it that while all contributed
to the common store, none was permitted to want. Yet though
all may have been cared for from the cradle to the grave, the
designation "socialistic" is valid only if one disregards the fact
that the surplus produced by the labor of the citizens went not
for the common good, but for the support of those who exercised
the functions of governing and of controlling the supernatural
world. The picture, indeed, resembles the totalitarian regimes
of the present day much more closely than the outline of the
socialistic state as customarily drawn. It is, moreover, by no
means even assured that the picture itself is justified, since at
least one close student of pre-Spanish Peruvian culture has
termed the "supposed communism" of the Incas a "myth" and a
"fiction." [18]

We may do well, in seeking to understand this controversy,
to bear in mind the statement of one French student concerning
the matter:

"Communism" and "individualism" are formulae too vague
and too loose to give us a grasp on reality. Everywhere, it
is true, we find individual right to property, because man is
a person and this right is a direct, spontaneous manifestation of his personality; everywhere also this individual control limits and adapts itself in accordance with the necessi-

[17] E.g., Baudin, vi.   [18] Latcham (1927), 48; (1929),
                        5–6.

ties of group life: of family, clan, tribe. From this derives the fact that [among primitive folk] we find individual ownership pure and simple, family property, communal property, while finally we encounter cases where the right to individual ownership, as a result of imperious economic circumstances, finds itself subordinated to a system of borrowing and sharing without ever, nonetheless, completely vanishing.[19]

In production and distribution, even in consumption, no less than in the case of the property rights with which this citation is concerned, the permutations and combinations of degrees of individual effort and reward, of group labor and the sharing of produce, are of an infinite order not to be subsumed under any formula of unilinear development, of inner correlation, or of economic law. Only when it is fully realized that in no society is the individual entirely subordinated to his group, that in no group is complete individualism the rule, can the problem be solved of the extent to which, over the world, common effort is directed toward the achievement of common ends, and where and in what situations men work and save for themselves alone.

5

IT IS apparent from the data of the preceding chapters, and the questions raised there, that much work in the study of the economics of nonliterate societies remains to be done before our knowledge of the mechanisms and institutions of this aspect of these cultures is to be brought to a state of knowledge in any degree comparable to the information at hand concerning social organization, or religion, or art. The problems for future research need not be repeated here, for they have been stressed in the appropriate pages.

Two or three major points on which anthropologists and economists alike can profitably clarify their postulates and revise their methodological approaches may, however, be again emphasized. Certainly once and for all it must be made clear that

[19] Leroy, 45–6.

economics and technology are not identical; while the two are intimately related in that the latter is the basis of economic organization, they nevertheless deal with different problems, require different techniques for study, and thus constitute separate bodies of material. This being understood, it must also be understood that economic problems may be studied without the need to give a complete account of all the interrelations between an economic system and other aspects of social life, or the need to consider all the sanctions on which a given body of economic custom rests. In other words, it is as important that anthropologists divest themselves of a sociological bias when studying economic phenomena as it is that they turn aside from a preoccupation with technology. The economic phases of non-industrial societies must be considered as constituting a body of data dealing with a major aspect of culture in the same way as art or religion or folklore or linguistics are generally so considered.

It has become increasingly imperative that a quantitative approach to studies of economic life must be employed wherever possible. The practical difficulties of obtaining materials of this order in cultures where the counting tradition is at best secondary, and where units for the measurement of goods, to say nothing for measuring value, are absent, may be granted. Yet counting can be done, as has been seen in the illuminating instances in the pages of this book where it has been possible to cite quantitative data. Hours of labor have been counted, and garden areas owned or planted. The return from a given amount of labor can also be computed if sufficient patience and diligence are directed toward this important point. We have seen how rarely we are told the precise quantities of goods displayed where prestige is based on display, or how even more seldom we are permitted to learn the actual amounts consumed in the countless feasts that have been described. What a man keeps in his house for everyday use, what he puts aside as a reserve, what he gives in taxes or to his priests —these, in definite quantitative statement, will be more rewarding than even the most meticulous non-quantitative descriptions.

As for the economists, certain revisions in the use they make of comparative data, and in their attitude toward phenomena from cultures other than their own, would be highly desirable. It is understandable that much of any change in this direction must await the collection by anthropologists of more materials which can be used by them and presented so that the data can be readily found and analyzed. It would be a distinct gain were economists to divest themselves of their concern with origins, of the concept of "stages" in the development of culture, of the idea that there are "types" of economies based on hunting or herding or agriculture, and instead avail themselves of the opportunity to test almost any conceivable theoretical postulate by reference to the differing customs of non-industrial societies. In this way, they could take their hypotheses, so to speak, into the laboratory afforded by nonliterate societies, and thus give a firmer base than is now accorded the refinement of concept that is a primary concern.

For just because economic theorists may test their points of view by reference to procedures and institutions which are more generalized and less sharply differentiated than those of an industrial society, they will perceive factors not directly apparent when only their own culture is considered. For the economist, therefore, the study of non-industrial economies must eventuate in the development of a technique of testing approaches that has up to the present been all but neglected. When nonliterate societies are studied in their economic manifestations, not as a developmental series and thus a part of economic history, but as offering this methodological opportunity, there will, moreover, inevitably be a stimulating reaction on the anthropologists in which they, in their turn, will be the more adequately guided in their quest for field materials.

For the rest, the study of the economic life of nonliterate folk, like the study of any aspect of human civilizations other than our own, will give perspective and breadth of vision that must otherwise be lacking, not alone to specialists but to all those who are concerned with broadening their general understanding of the mechanisms of human civilization. Especially at the present time, when as never before the need of men to find ways and means of controlling the historical processes which shape their institutions has become apparent in all its urgency, the knowledge that our own traditions, our own beliefs, our own techniques are not the only valid ways of meeting the demands of life comes as a stimulating vision of the infinite possibilities open to man in achieving his goals and perpetuating his group. That the economic phases of this endeavor are everywhere and always of paramount importance in the effort is self-evident. Hence the wider our range of vision in this, as in other fields where the battle of existence and survival is waged, the greater may be the chance, slender at best, that men will eventually attain that direction of his own destiny that for millennia, however unexpressed, has been a primary aim of human aspirations.

APPENDIX

DEDUCTION AND INDUCTION IN ECONOMICS

SHORTLY after *The Economic Life of Primitive Peoples* was published, Professor Frank H. Knight wrote a critique of the book, a rejoinder to which was invited by the Editor of *The Journal of Political Economy*. Critique and rejoinder were published together in the issue of the *Journal* for April, 1941 (vol. xlix, no. 2), Professor Knight's discussion being entitled "Anthropology and Economics," the reply, "Economics and Anthropology, a Rejoinder."

In the succeeding years, the suggestion has several times been made that these two articles, which contrast the deductive and inductive approaches to the analysis of social phenomena—in this case, the phenomena of economics—might with profit be reprinted in a later edition of the book. Its re-writing offered the opportunity to do this. Despite the fact that the revisions are so extensive as to make certain points in the pages that follow no longer entirely applicable, the two papers are reproduced here as written, except that three paragraphs of Professor Knight's article, which comment on statements that were carried on the dust-jacket of the book, have been deleted. The page references in his article, which have been retained, are to "The Economic Life of Primitive Peoples." No attempt has been made to relate them to corresponding pages of the present book, the re-writing of which has made this pointless. The pages indicated in the second article have been deleted, since these referred to passages in Professor Knight's critique here reproduced and can readily be found there if desired.

* * *

1

ANTHROPOLOGY AND ECONOMICS

FRANK H. KNIGHT

IT SHOULD be said at once that this reviewer discusses this book from the standpoint of his own specialty—economic theory, including economic methodology and pedagogy. Those interested in a review from the standpoint of the author's own specialty will naturally consult the appropriate anthropological mediums. It should also be said that the discussion will be frankly critical in tone. This is justified, in the writer's mind, by the importance of the book itself, as an able pioneer effort in a field which has long been crying for cultivation. That field, in general terms, is the interrelations of the different social science disciplines, and the objectives clearly in the mind of the author are more effective collaboration, and less mutual misunderstanding and criticism, between the workers in the different branches of social science. It is the reviewer's hope, by a critical examination of this work, and specifically by pointing out what seem to be errors and shortcomings, in nowise to "blame" the author but to contribute something to the promotion of the cause in the interest of which the book itself was written.

* * *

The opportunity for usefulness of this review essay is that of considering what contribution to the solution of general economic problems might be derived from a study of anthropological data, presented in such a way as to bring out their relevance. It is to be admitted, and even emphasized at the outset, that there is no great clarity, to say nothing of unanimity, among economists themselves, as to the nature of the problems. Consequently, no severe criticism of Professor Herskovits is involved in saying that he did not achieve such clarity through the study of economic writings, which he obviously undertook, at some length, as preparation for writing his book. He may well even have been confused by it. He can hardly be "blamed," either, for leaning heavily upon the definition of economics given by the outstanding authority in the past generation among economists themselves, namely, Alfred Marshall, or for taking toward economics and its methodology the general position of numerous members of economics faculties—the "institutional economists" (but cf. pp. 41, 275). Marshall's is quoted as "probably the best known definition" (p. 29): "Political Economy or economics is a study of mankind in the ordinary business of life; it examines that part of the individual and social action which is most closely connected with the attainment and with the use of material requisites of well-being." The author proceeds to comment on the generality and inclusiveness of the definition and to remark that the promise of Marshall's definition is by no means realized, that his actual treatment is centered upon price phenomena and the activities of the market, and that "Marshall is concerned in everything but his definition with just those aspects of our economic system that are seldom encountered in other societies" (pp. 29–30). True enough; but the question is, in the first place, whether it is Marshall's definition or his treatment which correctly represents the modern science of economics. Herskovits assumes that it is the definition; the verdict of a critical appraisal from a standpoint of economics itself must certainly be the opposite. But the most careful study of Marshall will hardly yield any clear conception of the nature and objectives of economics as an analytical science.

When we turn to Professor Herskovits' specific criticisms, we find the statement: "That economic theorists have based their definitions and principles solely on data from one culture means that from the point of view of the comparative study of culture their 'laws' are the equivalent of a statistical average based on a single case" (p. 28). Since a comparative study of cultures was the farthest thing from Marshall's intention, this is sheer nonsense; and our author's own further discussion is a tissue of contradictions. The beginning of any rational approach to the problems must be recognition that there are universal principles of "economy"—as indeed our author recognizes in his next sentence, which contrasts "the general principle of maximizing satisfaction which is valid" and "everywhere works in practice" with "more particular and less general propositions," the validity of which in cultures other than our own remains in question. It also goes without saying that there are such less general propositions, such as those relating to markets, enterprise, etc., which apply where they do apply; and the habit among economists of making the bulk of the content of their treatises deal with those which apply in our own culture misleads no one and hardly calls for defense.

As already suggested, the error, in so far as there is an error, on the part of an economist like Marshall is primarily in his definition, but the use of such an all-inclusive definition has no doubt helped to obscure the argument itself. A satisfactory definition should certainly indicate something of the hierarchy, as to generality, of the "principles" to be developed and the vast range of subject matter to be excluded in arriving at the actual content of the main field to be considered in detail. A definition like that of Marshall would, on the face of it, include the whole of technology and all the empirical details of "economic" activity, meaning virtually all activity, over the whole world, and over all time, as far as any data exist for such "study" and "examination." Marshall's main error is failure to conform to the title of his book itself which (in all editions from the very first—in 1890) reads *Principles of Economics*. It is too universally understood to require encumbering the title of a book on the subject by specification that a treatise with such a title deals with the principles of economics, distinctively as exemplified in "modern" culture. Undoubtedly the concept of "economy" in general usage includes technology; but in our culture no one would think of reading a book or attending a course on "economics," without a modifier, for the purpose of learning either about any technical, concrete, or descriptive aspect of our own economic life, or about the way in which the "principles" are exemplified in any other culture.

The first essential weakness of Professor Herskovits' opus is that it explicitly sets out to make anthropological data "intelligible to economists" in the absence of any clear grasp on his part of *any* of the principles in which economists are interested and with which they deal, whether the most general principles involved in "maximizing satisfaction" or the "more particular and less general propositions" applicable to organized competitive markets or to "business enterprise as we know it." Naturally, these less general principles do not apply where the phenomena to which they relate are absent; and, on the other hand, the most general principles are not different in different culture situations—exactly as the principles of mathematics are not different.

It is the last point which needs emphasis, particularly in the present connection. Economics, in the usual meaning, as a science of principles, is not, primarily, a descriptive science in the empirical sense at all. It "describes" *economic* behavior and uses the concept to explain the working of our modern economic organization and also to criticize and suggest changes. It is, of course, of some interest, in connection with the description, to point out contrasts between economic behavior and actual behavior, in our own and other culture settings, which does not conform to the principles as stated. But the interest in this contrast itself arises primarily out of the fact that the conceptual ideal of economic behavior is assumed to be, at least within limits, also a normative ideal, that men in general, and within limits, wish to behave economically, to make their activities and their organization "efficient" rather than wasteful. This fact does deserve the utmost emphasis; and an adequate definition of the science of economics, as treated in modern textbooks, might well make it explicit that the main relevance of the discussion is found in its relation to social policy, assumed to be directed toward the end indicated, of increasing economic efficiency, of reducing waste. This practical objective requires that the discussion deal with principles as they operate in the setting of our own institutions. But an adequate definition of economics would require at least a long chapter in a book, if not a volume, and the task cannot be further pursued in the scope of a review article.

It is interesting to compare with Marshall's definition of economics one cited from an anthropologist and presenting the anthropological point of view. Professor Herskovits quotes (p. 39) from an especially authoritative recent volume [1] the definition of Dr. Ruth Bunzel: "The total organization of behavior with reference to the problems of physical survival." Such a conception can produce nothing but confusion; and, as further matter quoted by Herskovits shows, the author herself is immediately involved in contradiction by referring to "material needs" and especially by stating as one of three " 'complementary principles' which are to be discerned in the functioning economics that satisfy wants" a "psychological principle" which is "concerned largely with the general question of value in the widest sense, the structure of the personality that determines choice and the attitudes that animate institutions." The confusion here is surely too obvious to call for detailed comment. Economic activity in the inclusive meaning certainly must include all activity which involves the economy of means, quite regardless of the end or purpose which is in view and motivates the action. The cost of living, even in the narrowest sense of the term "cost," always depends on the "standard" of living, which is chiefly an aesthetic category, and in a sense in which aesthetics includes all values; but discussion of these problems is not the task of economics.

The very first "crying need" of social science in general, at the present juncture in history, is clarification on the old, old question of the relations between induction and deduction. The point of this observation just here is that to no small extent this means in practice the relation between other social sciences and economic theory. For the latter is the one social science which effectively uses inference from clear and statable abstract principles, and especially intuitive knowledge, as a method. In contrast with it, all other social sciences are empirical, including those which use the word "economics" (or "economic") in their designation—though it should go without saying that no science can be at once social in any proper sense and empirical in at all the sense of the physical sciences. This relationship between observation, induction from observations, and inference from "a priori" principles forms the very pivot of the problem of collaboration between the social sciences, and specifically of collaboration between economic theory and the "quasi-empirical" sciences of history, socio-

[1] *General Anthropology,* edited and partly written by Professor Franz Boas (New York, 1938).

logy, and anthropology, including institutional—one might say anthropological—economics. An essential feature of the situation is that all these sciences are distinguished primarily not by differences in the subject matter, in a designative sense, with which they deal, but rather by centering upon different features or aspects of the *same* phenomena. The principles of economy are known intuitively; it is not possible to discriminate the economic character of behavior by sense observation; and the anthropologist, sociologist, or historian seeking to discover or validate economic laws by inductive investigation has embarked on a "wild goose chase." Economic principles cannot even be approximately verified—as those of mathematics can be, by counting and measuring.

One of the main obstacles to effective co-operation is the hostility to principles, and specifically to economic principles, which is a universal bias on the part of those who work with the more empirical aspects of social phenomenon. This bias appears in Professor Herskovits' book in the form (among others) of several rather scornful animadversions to the "economic man" (pp. 33, 37, 57, etc.; and note Index!). Now the concept of the economic man is merely an analytical, essentially terminological, device for referring to the economic aspect of behavior, an aspect universal to all behavior in so far as it is purposive (or even unconsciously telic, since we can speak of plant economy). The convenience of the concept amounts to necessity, if economists and other social scientists are to avoid the sort of confusions in their thinking that are here pointed out. Yet the scientific and logical "morals" of theoretical economists themselves, not to speak of divergent and more or less antagonistic "schools," have been so corrupted by the bias for empiricism in our intellectual mores that the term, which was current in the literature a century ago, has virtually disappeared from usage even in that speciality.

The philosophical problem of the distinction of categories, or interpretive aspects of social phenomena, cannot be developed at length here. But it may be useful to observe briefly that at least four or five quite "fundamental" categories have to be recognized. The first is physical mechanism, though the fact that man is first of all such a machine is no doubt rather to be taken for granted as a substratum than explicitly brought into the discussion of social phenomena. And the same is partly true of the second category, the biological view of man, the distinctive notion in which is unconscious teleology. In a critical-philosophical sense, this category includes a considerable range, from the features which man has in common with the lowest plant life, through the "instinctive" behavior (individual and social) of animals and the "institutional" aspects of human social life itself. But a workable classification should probably separate at least the last, as a third evolutionary and logical level of existence, because it is virtually distinctive of human phenomena.

But what is finally, and almost uniquely, distinctive of human phenomena is the aspect of conscious purpose, or rationality. However, clarification of notions, even at an elementary level, requires emphasis upon a sharp differentiation between two main aspects of rationality itself. At a "lower" level (fourth in our series) rationality means economic rationality, which again means the deliberate, problem-solving, designed, or planned use of means to realize *given* ends. But human behavior or conduct also involves a "higher" form of rationality, namely, deliberation about ends. This is also a virtually or quite universal aspect of conduct, along with the economic. Purely economic behavior, in which ends are given and only the use of means in realizing them is "problematic," is rather an analytic abstraction, a "limiting case" hardly exemplified in reality, though indispensable for discussion, because discussion must proceed analytically. Deliberation about ends as problematic takes many forms, but they do not call for analysis here.

Another vital consideration in connection with co-operation between social sciences is the "human equation" in the scientists themselves. Any social scientist should early learn to recognize the fact that "man" (in our culture, if not universally) including himself and his fellow-scientists, is a competitive, contentious, and combative animal, given to self-aggrandizement, and inclined to make this end justify nearly any means. We are all anxious to co-operate, provided it means having others co-operate with us and learn from us! This human trait is copiously exemplified in most social science writing, especially that which comes in contact with methodological problems in any way, and Professor Herskovits' chapters dealing with general problems are no exception. A conspicuous example is his quotation of economic generalizations from fellow-anthropologists (e.g., on p. 29) and from such "economists" as Karl Bücher (see references in Index—incomplete as usual), who, if he was either an anthropologist or an economist, was decidedly the former, with the evident motive of putting "economists" in the wrong. And this same "human, all too human" motive is also the natural explanation of many confused, contradictory, and absurd general statements in the author's constructive argument.

Naturally enough, the same type of argumentation, *ad hominem,* is also used against fellow-anthropologists as such. Early in the book, as would be expected, we encounter the characteristic scorn of the modern "enlightened" anthropologist for the notion of evolutionary "stages" in economic life and systems, which is extended to the distinction between "types" of economy (e.g., pp. 61, 457). The author cites, as a bad example, the use of the term "preliterate" instead of "non-literate" (p. 35). Does he really think that serious scientific error will result from implying that men were nonliterate *before* they were literate? Similarly, in a late chapter (p. 357, also p. 399), he insists upon using the notion of "degree of complexity of economic organization" instead of "evolutionary stage," and the same question applies. Of course, such notions must be used "intelligently," as in general they probably have been, though doubtless not always. But surely no serious student needs to be warned against the implication that human development has proceeded by a uniform linear serial sequence, with exact uniformity over the whole earth at a particular date in evolution or history. Rather, what he does need to be warned against is the disposition, already hinted at, of imputing stupidity to other writers, when at least a moderate degree of intelligence would be a more reasonable assumption. It is, however, important to emphasize that practically all "early" features of human nature and social organization persist in the modern, most highly civilized peoples. Evolution, prehistoric and historic, has for the most part taken the form now familiarly referred to as "emergent" in which new developments are superposed upon and incorporated into the older pattern, adding cumulatively to the degree of complexity and pluralism.

The list of kinds of emotional bias which corrupt scientific study and exposition, and which are exemplified in this book, cannot be left without mentioning one in particular, which is perhaps the most serious of all. The author illustrates traditionalism and unwillingness to change in our own economic organization by referring to "the vitality of the concept of *laissez-faire* in the face of changes in the mechanical phases of our economy that have deprived this point of view of all but that justification which psychologically, is the strongest of all, the appeal to traditional usage" (p. 61). As a matter of fact, this statement illustrates at the same time two fundamental forms of bias. On the one hand, it exhibits a *political* position, or attitude, not to say a prejudice; and, on the other hand, it is surely questionable to bring such evaluations into descriptive exposition without considering (*a*) the conceivable alternatives of the institution condemned, (*b*) their merits and demerits in terms of all that would be involved in any hypothetical substitution, and (*c*) the concrete possibilities and costs of change.

Another example of the corruption of scientific morals by political romanticism is found in our author's repeated statement that "planned scarcity on the scale on which it exists among ourselves is indeed unique" (p. 448, also p. 10). The merits of the political position exhibited or insinuated in these statements is not a subject for discussion in this review; the question of fact involved will call for notice later.

But it is interesting to note the emotional appeal which the conception of a well-managed penitentiary or orphan asylum as a social ideal (the meaning of a planned or regulated economy) so commonly exercises upon the minds of writers about society from any point of view other than serious and competent study of the problems of social betterment through social self-transformation by political action along economic lines. The second romantic bias illustrated (if it is not a form of the same one) is perhaps even more interesting, since it is the precise antithesis of the one which the author's statement is intended to illustrate; it is the emotional disposition to *iconoclasm*. This is perhaps as common and perhaps also as serious as the prejudice in favor of conservatism, or the rationalizing adulation of the institutions and usages of a writer's own culture.

Discussion in further detail of the anthropologist's failure to understand the meaning of economic concepts must be omitted here because of limitations of space. It can only be set down as a dictum, from the point of view of the special student of economic theory, that Professor Herskovits, in constantly making use (as he must) of such general concepts as production, wealth, capital, money—and especially the treacherous notion of an "economic surplus," which constantly recurs —shows a conspicuous lack of understanding of what such terms have to mean if they are to be fruitfully employed in economic discussion or if their use is to result in clarity rather than confusion. To be sure, it should again be noted, by way of extenuation, that a writer from any other field would find the greatest difficulty in getting adequate light on these matters from any sampling of the writings of economists such as he could readily make, or without intensive study of carefully selected recent literature. The notion of "labor" as a measurable magnitude (intrinsically an aspect of the general economic problem of value) should be added to the list, as an especially egregious case, from both points of view, i.e., the confusion in this book and also in a large proportion of the recognized authorities in the main tradition of economic theory itself.

It would be natural and proper to ask which, if any, of the "errors" referred to really make a serious difference for the argument as a whole, for such conclusions as may be said to follow from it, and for its general usefulness. To some extent, certainly, they are relatively "harmless," at least to economists. Their significance, as confirming belief in man-in-the-street economic prejudices in the minds of non-economic social scientists, is more important. Similar observations no doubt apply, *mutatis mutandis*, to the errors of economists in making use of references to "primitive society" in economic exposition, on which anthropologists are fond of dilating. Such discussion of this problem as is allowable here can best be given by discussing the more general question as to "what use" anthropology can be to the economist, either in his own thinking and investigation or especially in the teaching of his subject.

The first observation under this head must be to emphasize the point as to harmlessness just mentioned in the opposite relationship. One thinks immediately of Adam Smith, whose "romantic" archeology has been satirized in particular by Veblen, posing as an anthropological specialist (with what justification is not in question here; the question would raise large issues as to the relation between science and satire in Veblen's work as a whole). As to the significance of such allusions in economic exposition, the answer must be that it usually makes little or no difference whether the comparisons are anthropologically authentic or not. Indeed, we probably should not stop here; it would seem to be definitely requisite in the teaching of economics to bring out principles affecting our own institutions by means of comparisons between our own and "simpler" societies and at the same time out of the question to make the comparison refer to any particular society or social type as reported by anthropological investigation. The reform which would be in order from this pedagogical point of view would be to make it clear in all such comparisons that the situation used for contrast *is* a hypothetical one, and to describe it clearly as such, in the points actually significant for the purpose in view. In fact, all that is really called for is a "reasonable" interpretation of the literature as it stands, in line with the suggestion already made. But teachers and writers in economics might be admonished to make it explicit, perhaps by the use of some such phraseology as a *"hypothetical* primitive society," what they are doing—in so far as they consider it important to avoid contributing to the entertainment of anthropologist-critics or nourishing their "superiority complexes."

The chief requisite for better mutual understanding between economists and anthropologists is that the latter should have some grasp of the categorical difference emphasized above between economics as an exposition of principles—which have little more relation to empirical data of any sort than do those of elementary mathematics —and as a descriptive exposition of facts. From the opposite point of view, there is this important difference—that any intelligent or useful exposition of facts imperatively requires an understanding of principles, while the need for facts in connection with the exposition of principles is far more tenuous, and the "facts" which are really in question need not be facts at all in the sense of actuality for any particular point in time or space, provided they are realistically illustrative.

Beyond the admonition mentioned, it would be highly desirable on general grounds for economists to know more about the facts of economies other than their own. Even if no direct use is made of it, such knowledge would be fertile in suggestion of facts, relations, and principles in one's own economic system which might otherwise escape observation because of the well-known psychological principle that what is too familiar is very likely to be overlooked. From this point of view, again, "authentic" facts are not necessarily more useful than travelers' tales based on superficial and largely false impressions —the bane of modern anthropological science—or even outright fiction or poetry. A good economist certainly needs both the proverbial "broadening" effect of actual travel and a wide range of reading in history and all branches of literature; and knowledge of scientific anthropology will be useful in much the same way.

It is undoubtedly true that, *if* economists are going to teach anthropology, they should know something about it and not teach too much that "isn't so." But, again, the main sin of this sort calling for expiation and reformation is on the other side. The teaching of utterly false and misleading economics (and putting economists in their place) is a favorite practice in the classrooms and textbooks of the other social sciences. Moreover, until such time as a sweeping reformation shall be accomplished in the understanding and use of economic principles by historians, sociologists, and anthropologists, in the presentation of their own subjects, it will be difficult to the point of impossibility for the economist to make much use of "authentic" data from these other fields. For, in the absence of such understanding—and of much more caution in making statements whose meaning depends upon it—the economist cannot trust the statements of fact and can, after all, use them only as hypothetical or imaginative and suggestive.

One important fact which the economist can really learn from even a cursory perusal of the volume before us is the virtually infinite variety in the ideas and institutions of primitive peoples which are connected in one way or another with the economic side of their lives and problems. Even a moderate dose of this material should suffice for the admonition already mentioned—that the economist should distinguish between authenticity and the hypothetical character of primitive or simpler social situations used for purposes of comparison and contrast. He should at least realize that practically any simple generalization in this field, which would be significant for his purposes, is probably indefensible as a descriptive statement in the absence of an understanding of the culture context as a whole. He would then avoid any appearance of teaching anthropology as such, unless he uses, in its entirety, some actual and full report of a particular society at a particular date by an anthropologist accepted in his own profession as reliable.

The need of the economist (as pedagogue) for simpler conditions to contrast with those of our own culture suggests the question as to what general contrasts, if any, can be made between the economic life and organization of "non-literate" peoples and our own, beyond such commonplaces as the fact that they did not have modern machinery and technology. Professor Herskovits discusses this topic of differences in his introductory chapter, entitled "Before the Machine" (already referred to). Perhaps the most important specific question has to do with stability versus change and progress and with the closely related contrast between the individual liberty in economic matters which is a characteristic of modern Western civilization and the commonly reported and accepted prevalence of a fairly rigid control by *custom* in "early" economic life. On this point, Professor Herskovits has a good deal to say, but it is difficult to interpret. In his general chapter on production (chap. iii, "Getting a Living") he makes the following categorical statement (p. 60): "As a matter of fact, the brief history of these peoples in contact with those who could write of them, has given us quite sufficient grounds for holding that as regards both their willingness to accept inner change and outer borrowing they are no different from other people." And this is the view which is chiefly emphasized whenever the question comes up explicitly—notably in chapter x on "Consumption and Capital Formation" and chapter xi on "The Nature of Primitive Property." (This last and the three following chapters, dealing with various forms of property, are the most informative and illuminating of any in the book for the student of economics and particularly of "institutional" economics.) The emphasis is on the fact that in different societies, including our own, "taboos" differ chiefly in being effective in connection with different activities or aspects of social life.

But the general argument is largely contradicted by specific data; and, in particular, it is rendered dubious by statements regarding taboos in our own society which clearly cannot be taken at their face value, which at best might be defended as literary exaggeration for the sake of emphasis. For example, in the paragraph following the citation just given (in connection with the reference to the institution of laisser faire, already cited in another connection) the statement that our culture is receptive to technological innovations but not to those of an organizational sort can only be characterized as false to the facts and based on political prejudice. It is enough to mention the proliferation of corporate and other forms of business enterprise, revolutionary reorganization of market institutions, etc. And at the level of social-political action there has been a corresponding growth of public enterprise, while the volume of regulatory legislation and case law is such that, as legal authorities tell us, it would tax the utmost capacity of any human being to read it all. The outstanding fact of the history of the past two generations is not the dominance of taboos against change but, on the contrary, the growth of a general and uncritical clamor for revolutionary change in our fundamental economic institutions and organization as a whole. This situation goes back to and overlaps in time the preceding revolutionary period in which the doctrine and system of economic freedom called laisser faire became established. On the issue as to primitive society, a smatterer in the literature cannot help noting a radical change in the tone in recent years in the direction of Professor Herskovits' position, i.e., indicating that the degree to which primitive society is custom bound and in consequence problem free was previously exaggerated. Common-sense reasoning leads one to suspect a tendency now to swing to exaggeration in the opposite direction.

In relation to the same problems we are also brought back to the question of fact raised by Professor Herskovits' references to planned scarcity as a unique feature of our own economic civilization. As to conditions in the United States specifically (and other countries are different only in detail and in degree) it is a commonplace among competent economic analysts that the great bulk of the planned scarcity which is real is either the direct and intended effect of governmental policy (the "New Deal") or is a consequence which any such economist would have predicted of economically indefensible policies intended to alleviate the condition of depression during the past decade (hence going back of our New Deal administration). That such policies were advocated by economists of repute merely points to the sad state of economics as a science and incidentally to what is perhaps the major problem of free society; we mean the problem of any intellectual leadership being effective or getting attention which stands for ideas or policies very different from the conceptions and prejudices of the man in the street. Apparently Mr. Herskovits regards the N.R.A. and the A.A.A., and the wages-and-hours law, as exemplifying the prevalence in our society of taboo against any departure from the policy of laisser faire!

The only economic meaning which planned scarcity can have in private business is monopoly. Data scattered through Professor Herskovits' book itself, as well as "common knowledge" about conditions in pre-industrial society, above the most primitive level at least, make it fairly clear that, in relation to totality of economic life, monopoly is more important in such societies than it is or has ever been in our own.

This is surely true if we except monopolies created or fostered by governmental action and "natural" monopolies which have always been recognized and treated as calling for public action of some sort. The writer does not need to be reminded that this is not the view of the man in the street, or even of many "economists," and he takes it for granted that his own statement will be imputed to political prejudice by those who do not agree with it. It is not, indeed, implied that planned monopoly does not present a significant problem, actually and potentially. But unquestionably the most serious phase of this problem itself is the kind of action to which it moves the public mind in the effort to do something about it—on the basis of a wildly exaggerated opinion of the amount of monopoly power possessed and exercised by producers and a gross misconception of the nature of the real evils of monopoly and of the problems raised. The real, root problem is again found in a well-recognized trait of human nature, the urge to explain any supposed evil by finding an "enemy" and to deal with it by "liquidating" somebody.

The problem of change versus stability presents a major issue of policy on which the study of primitive society might conceivably throw some light. This is the question of the gains and losses involved in individual economic liberty, in comparison with a greater stability which, in theory at least, might be had through a greater emphasis on the folk wisdom presumptively embodied in the traditions of the past, enforced by authority. Perhaps we ought educationally and in our laws to emphasize the sanctity of tradition as such—including the authority of functionaries whose authority rests upon tradition or upon religious grounds. Obviously, this is a political rather than a distinctively economic problem, and beyond that is one of social psychology and the mechanics of institutional permanence and change. The present writer has no opinion to put forward here in this field; he merely suggests the possibility of drawing some "inductions" from the widest possible view of the experience of the race as to the nature of man and institutions (or the absence of any such "nature") for ascertaining the given conditions of the problem of change, including the prevention of undesirable changes.

As a last observation, we return again in a sense to the meaning of the "economic category" as an element in individual and social life and specifically to the fact that it is an element or aspect of varying meaning and importance in all conscious activity whatever. Professor Herskovits repeatedly and almost constantly convicts himself of accepting another naïve conception of the man in the street as to the meaning of "utilitarian" considerations. Of all the fallacious and absurd misconceptions which so largely vitiate economic and social discussion, perhaps the very worst is the notion—exemplified in extreme form in the citation from Dr. Bunzel, given above (but later, as pointed out, contradicted in the same passage)—that an interpretation of utility, or usefulness, in biological or physical survival terms has any considerable significance at the human level. A discussion of human society, even if restricted to "economic" life in the narrowest meaningful interpretation, must unquestionably relate as much or more to what may be called the "higher values" as to "subsistence" in the sense of physical nutrition and protection from the elements. As all anthropological data themselves clearly show, such a conception of "subsistence" in connection with man is meaningless to the extent that man is human. One thing that must strike the attention of any critical reader of this book is the absence of any consideration of the economic side of the distinctively human aspects of life, such as the universal craving for beauty and for play or recreative activity.

Indeed, the general impression given is rather worse than this statement indicates. The author (following Veblen!) virtually treats all interests and activities above the purely animal level as wasteful and as expressing an immoral struggle for domination and display. He devotes a full-length chapter (chap. xviii) to "Wealth, Display and Status," and it is the main theme of another chapter (xv) on "Population Size, Economic Surplus and Social Leisure." In the latter chapter we read the following remarkable statement: "From all parts of the world, materials are thus on hand to make clear that primitive societies everywhere, producing more goods than the minimum requirement for the support of life, translate their economic surpluses into the social leisure which is only afforded some members of the community—persons of privilege supported by this excess wealth" (pp. 369–70). And the same thought pervades two further chapters—chapter xvi on "Cost of Government" and chapter xvii on "The Service of the Supernatural."

To be sure, a writer of intelligence could hardly be so blinded by a theoretical prepossession as to be quite so consistently wrong as we have indicated. Near the end of chapter xv, we do find the following: "Nor is it intended to suggest that members of the leisure class [two groups, those who govern and those who command techniques for placating and manipulating the supernatural forces of the universe] occupy their time purposelessly, or that they are not often hard-driven by the cares and preoccupations of their obligations toward the groups from which they derive their support" (pp. 371–72). But surely the statement is primarily interesting for the ambiguity of its implications! Incidentally, what is meant by population size in chapter xv is the size of the social or political unit; this is rather incidentally treated in two paragraphs, and there is no consideration anywhere of population density or of the relation between population and resources, hence none of the vital question as to how population comes to be limited so that there is an "economic surplus." We are certainly justified in saying that politics and religion, as well as art and recreation are practically viewed in Veblenian terms, as nonutilitarian and "invidious" activities.

As to the aesthetic side of life, we have noticed the word "art" just once in the book. This is in the concluding chapter (p. 465), where social organization, religion, and art are contrasted with economics as aspects of primitive life about which our knowledge is already relatively satisfactory. (Neither this word, nor any close synonym appears in the Index.) As to recreation, there are two references to sport (pp. 389, 483), in both cases as a leisure-class activity in Polynesia.

In conclusion, it is in order to repeat and re-emphasize the statement that this review has been written with the exclusive aim of making some constructive contribution to the problem of collaboration between social science disciplines in a particular case—economics and anthropology—where the opportunity and perhaps the need for collaboration is especially obvious. If apologies are in order for making the discussion excessively critical in a negative sense, they are offered unstintingly. But however unconventional, and quite possibly wrong, the view may be, the writer does not consider the main usefulness of a book reveiw to consist in the dispensing of praise and blame. Our strictures, in so far as they are such, would apply as well to a similar discussion as it would be written from the point of view of any social science other than economics (and in part including economics, *mutatis mutandis*). Indeed, much more damage is actually done in the way of lending scientific and scholarly sanction to economic fallacies and popular prejudices by sociologists, and especially by historians, than is done or threatened from the direction of anthropology. Professor Herskovits himself has not been sparing of criticism; but, while his language often borders on the scornful tone, it is all in good temper, read in the total context.

As already stated, the book is a pioneer effort in its field, and as such has the merits and the shortcomings to be expected in a "pathbreaking" work. Moreover, a perusal of it will prove of great value to economists in many ways. As also suggested, the damage it is likely to do, if any, is rather to readers from the other social sciences, notably anthropology itself; but the danger is probably not very great of making the situation worse than it was before. Moreover, let us also repeat that the errors which we think we have found, and which we have endeavored to point out, solely in the hope that doing so in the clearest terms may contribute to their correction or mitigation in later work (we may hope especially in a later re-working of the material by the same author) are not at all "original" with Professor Herskovits or peculiar to him. And we have also tried to emphasize that, if they are to be blamed upon anyone, it should be, above all, on economists as a group. As is well known, this profession is largely a shambles in consequence of the activities of men of the cloth who clamor for the substitution of history or sociology or anthropology—or "most anything"—for economics. The tragic failure of social scientists in all branches to see that the disciplines and "approaches" are complementary and that the problem is more effective co-operation, not mutual destruction, is merely an aspect of the naïve positivism consequent upon the triumphal march of physical science in the modern age.

Thus the errors and prejudices of this book are an integral part of the prevalent mores of social discussion, which social scientists have made little headway in overcoming. It is a sobering commentary that they have largely grown out of the development of "science" itself. By a false analogy the spectacular success of the natural sciences has inspired a misdirected endeavor to apply the same empirical categories in the field of social phenomena, where the relevant data and the problems are of an entirely different character. The resulting prejudice against intuitive knowledge and against deductive reasoning and the recourse to interpretation is the root of the main difficulties in the way of social science in general becoming either true or useful. There will be little hope of overcoming them until they are clearly brought to attention; and a review of Professor Herskovits' notable volume seemed to present an appropriate occasion for making an effort in that direction.

2

ECONOMICS AND ANTHROPOLOGY
A REJOINDER

MELVILLE J. HERSKOVITS

Proffessor Knight's critique of my book, *The Economic Life of Primitive Peoples,* is so much a profession of scholarly faith that it is not easy to comment on what he says without indicating something of the fundamental point of view implicit in my own approach to those problems of social science with which I have been concerned. This is not to say that his comments are to be regarded as other than gratifying, or than having the potentialities which any well-conceived, constructive criticism must have. Too often interdisciplinary studies are permitted to remain unilateral attempts to understand subjects which impinge on several disciplines and are thus doomed to fail of their purpose, since only discussion by many specialists concerned with such problems can achieve a true cross-disciplinary attack. Hence what Professor Knight has to say is to be regarded as an important step toward establishing the study of comparative economics, to which both anthropology and economics must make their contributions if work in such a field is to constitute a significant development in our search for knowledge.

I am convinced, however, that it is going to be extremely difficult to attain this objective if the deductive point of view stressed by Professor Knight comes to be the accepted approach. For no social science, it seems to me, can accomplish its ends if it disregards the first commandment of science in general—that only through constant and continuing cross-reference between hypothesis and fact can any understanding of problems and valid interpretations of data be had. Furthermore, I hold that this fundamental approach must be implemented not only in the practices of scholars, but in the way they teach their subjects. Deduction has played its part and will continue to play its part in scientific work; and this is true whether it be called utilizing working hypotheses or "playing hunches." Only for training purposes do we impress upon the graduate student the principle that the answer to a problem may not be assumed before the data are in. As a scholar grows in experience he comes to understand that the most fruitful attack on a problem is an approach motivated by a flash of insight telling him that a certain body of data should throw needed light on a given problem of his concern in terms of certain derived results. It is the way such intuitive flashes are used, rather than the fact that they are used, that differentiates the scientist from the nonscientist. For the latter, the flash is the answer; for the scientist, it but indicates the outlet of a road to be traversed in search for the truth. Yet does not Professor Knight, by implication at least, exalt the intuitive flash into the method best employed? What other conclusion can be drawn from a statement such as the following?

> The very first "crying need" of social science in general, at the present juncture in history, is clarification on the old, old question of the relations between induction and deduction. The point of this observation just here is that to no small extent this means in practice the relation between other social sciences and economic theory. For the latter is the one social science which effectively uses inference from clear and statable abstract principles, and especially intuitive knowledge, as a method.

What does this amount to when translated in terms of one of the "intuitional" economists' more cherished concepts, that of "economic man"? I am, for example, taken to task by Professor Knight for my "rather scornful animadversions" to this concept. Yet, if one believes that theories should be based on data—a point of view which I am certain I am not alone among social scientists in holding, and in which I should believe that I am even joined by some economists—what other attitude can be taken toward a concept that has been more largely responsible than any other for that complacent intellectual provincialism to which I refer in my book, manifested by so many of those who profess a discipline of the vast importance of economics? We may grant, for purposes of discussion, that the concept of economic man is "merely an analytical, essentially terminological, device for referring to the economic aspect of behavior, an aspect universal to all behavior in so far as it is purposive," and that in the past this concept has had a convenience that made it "amount . . . to necessity" if clarity of thought was to be achieved. Yet can its continued use be defended when investigators of human societies all over the world are unanimous in testifying that no such creature exists or, as far as the data indicate, ever did exist? To disregard such findings is not the counsel of clarity, but of confusion; and the proof lies in the fact that the untenability of the concept of economic man has made itself so manifest even to economists that its use by them has in recent years steadily diminished.

Such usage, indeed, becomes even less defensible as the actual materials of comparative economics, such as I attempted to set forth in my book, become available. For what is the pedagogical and analytical purpose of such a construct if not to offer a background against which to project observable economic behavior such as is to be witnessed all about us in our own culture, and thus bring to us a better comprehension of our own modes of economic life? Would Professor Knight hold it advisable to set up a fiction for purposes of illustrating a point, when the point can be adequately illustrated by reference to what actual social groups really do in the way of getting a living and maximizing their satisfactions through the production and distribution of the goods made available to them as a result of the interaction between their natural environment and their technological equipment? Certainly the description of "man" which he gives—"a competitive, contentious, and combative animal, given to self-aggrandizement, and inclined to make this end justify nearly any means"—cannot be regarded with any degree of equanimity by those acquainted with data which demonstrate the wide range of human personalities found in the many societies where this problem has been studied. And if Professor Knight's description of human nature—or "man," as he terms it—is thus far out of line with the facts, how can one be sure that the lay figure named Economic Man he will erect for his students will not, under the canons of the intuitive approach, fail equally to give any sense of the variation we know in fact exists in the forms of human economic behavior?

It is because of the general point of view indicated in the preceding paragraphs that I regard with something akin to dismay Professor Knight's proposal that "in economic exposition" it "usually makes little or no difference whether the comparisons are anthropologically authentic or not." I have, for some years, protested against the opinion expressed by many anthropologists that economists are to be held at fault because they have used concepts of man's social and psychological life untenable in the light of modern findings; it has been my feeling that anthropologists must first learn to speak in terms that are at least understandable to some economists before they can charge disregard of their data. Yet a statement such as I have just quoted makes me feel that I have perhaps been wrong in my position. Perhaps economists will persist, however anthropologists phrase their findings, in living in their world of logical unreality, disregarding the contributions of those whose training makes them competent to describe and interpret the customs of peoples who live differently from ourselves. Of course, Professor Knight enters his caution—but what a caution it is!

. . . it would seem to be definitely requisite in the teaching of economics to bring out principles affecting our own institutions by means of comparisons between our own and "simpler" societies and at the same time out of the question to make the comparison refer to any particular society or social type as reported by anthropological investigation. The reform which would be in order from this pedagogical point of view would be to make it clear in all such comparisons that the situation used for contrast *is* a hypothetical one, and to describe it clearly as such, in the points actually significant for the purpose in view.

The caution is carried further, in terms, however, which are no more reassuring:

> . . . teachers and writers in economics might be admonished to make it explicit, perhaps by the use of some such phraseology as a *"hypothetical* primitive society," what they are doing—in so far as they consider it important to avoid contributing to the entertainment of anthropologist-critics, or nourishing their "superiority complexes."

For my part, I can only reaffirm my conviction that, where comparisons must be made in the teaching and writing of economic theory and principles, a fanciful picture of human life that is unlike any human existence known to us is bad pedagogy and bad scholarship. It seems to me that no matter how explicit the hypothetical nature of an example employed to document an argument may be made, it is essentially in terms of the objective reality of the documentation that the point stands or falls, and not through the recognition of its hypothetical character. In a word, my point of view concerning scientific method is that findings must be based on fact; and that to depart from reality is to vitiate the tenability of conclusions and later statements of policy that may be based on them.

By the same token, I hold it as an article of scientific faith that clarity of thought is to be attained only by the greatest possible precision of linguistic usage in expressing thought. And this is why I am glad also to reaffirm my belief that the use (by economists, or anyone else) of such a concept as "stages of development" implies a belief in a type of social evolution that cannot, on the basis of objectively verifiable data, be established as valid; and that to use the term "preliterate" instead of "nonliterate" is bad—even for economists. The effect of this practice can only be to bolster a point of view which persists in regarding "early" man as a type exemplified by modern primitive folk. But those who speak and write of such people, historically unrelated to ourselves, as our "contemporary ancestors," as Professor Knight himself certainly understands they are not, will stand convicted of the employment of the logical fallacy implied in such usage, while conclusions drawn by them, to the extent that they are based on such conceptualization, will be open to attack. And while I would be the last to "impute stupidity to other writers," or to do other than to make "the more reasonable assumption" of "at least a moderate degree of intelligence" on the part of such persons, I should at the same time be doing less than my duty as a scientist were I to fail to protest at a position which so many economists take out of lack of familiarity with the materials and theoretical assumptions of the field in which such competence as I possess happens to lie—a position which is encouraged by Professor Knight's argument concerning terminology.

I must re-emphasize that the foregoing paragraphs are not intended to disparage all elements in the position taken by Professor Knight. It is inevitable that in drawing critiques certain points must be over-emphasized; and I realize that just as I, for example, indicate that in science deduction can never be more than an adjunct to the inductive method, so Professor Knight, in stressing the importance of deduction, would, I am sure, be the first to deplore such a departure from reality as is involved when a student turns his back on available data dealing with a given problem. It should be pointed out, moreover, that Professor Knight's discussion includes a critique of schools of economic thought which differ from his own point of view quite as much as it comprises an analysis of certain points made in my book. Now it would be presumptuous of me, as an anthropologist, to permit myself to be drawn into a controversy of this character. What is important is the conclusion to be drawn that, by this very token, it is evident that the approach I have employed in my discussion of comparative economics and the concepts I have utilized are perhaps neither as foreign to the total field of economics, nor as uncongenial to all economists, as they may be to the system which Professor Knight so brilliantly espouses. And if I must plead extenuating circumstances for such lack of clarity as may be found in my treatment of economic data in my book, I can point to Professor Knight's own statements concerning the absence of any considerable degree of clarity "among economists themselves as to the nature of the problems."

A few of the specific points brought up in the discussion of my book may be profitably examined at this point. Perhaps the most important has to do with the criticism lodged against my use of Marshall's definition of economics. As Professor Knight remarks, I can "hardly be 'blamed' . . . for leaning heavily upon the definition of economics given by the outstanding authority in the past generation among economists themselves." What Professor Knight seems most to object to in my comment is my assertion that the promise of Marshall's definition is not realized—that the book itself is centered upon price phenomena and activity of the market, which are phenomena unique to our society, and that, because of this, the universal applicability of his conclusions is to be challenged. The fact that Marshall's book is called *Principles of Economics,* which is regarded by Professor Knight as of major importance, does not seem so significant to me; what is perfectly clear, however, is the fact that Marshall himself recognized the validity of the position that economic "laws" are not tenable as such unless they can be shown to be applicable to more societies than just our own. I have not, of course, made a critical analysis of the various editions of Marshall's book as Professor Knight has done; this is outside my field. The edition which I own is the eighth, the printing that of 1936. But I can point to Appendix A in this edition (pp. 723 ff), entitled "The Growth of Free Industry and Enterprise," as proof of the validity of my contention. For here Marshall is at pains to document his position by sketching the outlines of what he conceived to be the economic life of "savages" and "early civilizations," as a prelude to his tracing the development of these phenomena in Greek and Roman times and in Europe during the Middle Ages.

Once again, in this connection, I must underscore my refusal to acknowledge that economic "laws" drawn from the consideration of a single culture, even one so complex as our own, are other than "equivalent to a statistical average based on a single case," as I put it in my book. This criticism I did not level against Marshall in particular, as Professor Knight would seem to indicate, but against the economists of the classical and neoclassical school in general. I do not consider it necessary to take account of Marshall's intent, or the intent of any other economist who indulges in this practice. It is not intent that is important in science; it is the approach to a problem in terms of the way conclusions are reached that is significant. If there are those "universal principles of 'economy'" that, according to Professor Knight, are "the beginning of any logical approach to the problems" of economics, then they must be verified by study of the actual facts concerning the economic life of as many different societies as can be reached. In other words, I must disagree entirely with the statement that "economics, in the usual meaning, as a science of principles, is not, primarily, a descriptive science in the empirical sense at all," if by this is meant that principles are to be divorced from facts. The laboratory of the theoretical physicist may be comprised in a pencil and a pad of paper; but, unless the astronomer working at his telescope achieves results that are in accordance with the hypotheses of the theorist, his conclusions will be held inacceptable.

A demurrer must also be entered to Professor Knight's citing against me the definition of economics given by Dr. Bunzel, which I myself quote only as an example of how anthropological training is not conducive to phrasing economic problems in economic terms. I agree with him that, as regards her definition, "detailed comment is hardly called for," and this is the reason why my own comment on the definition was as brief as it will be found to be in my book. The matter goes further than just this, however, for it merely exemplifies the way in which Professor Knight has misread my chapter on the relationship between economics and anthropology. Professor Knight's discussion of my point of view ascribes to me a position that I should be the last to take—and, indeed, did not take. If I indicated certain reservations to certain procedures that have been followed in the theoretical discussions of economists, I think it should also be said for the record that I was faithful in stating, as I saw them, the shortcomings of my anthropological colleagues in their presentation of economic data. I can but wonder why this matter received no mention; as I must similarly wonder why no mention is made by Professor Knight of my insistence that anthropologists learn to think quantitatively in planning the gathering of economic data in the field and no longer content themselves with the type of broad, general statement concerning economic life they have been prone to make in the past.

The matter of bias, which is discussed at some length by Professor Knight, likewise deserves attention. The concept of our economic system as one of "planned scarcity" is most certainly not of my creation; by the same token, I suspect that there are many competent economists who would not agree that this is "another example of the corruption of scientific morals by political romanticism." The fact of the matter is that no society, other than our own, exists where human beings starve because there is too much food, or where they cannot build houses because there is too much lumber, or where they cannot afford to have shoes because the productive capacity of the shoe industry is too great. I dislike the *argumentum ad hominem,* but I doubt if my conclusions from such facts as these are motivated by a drive any more emotional than that which causes Professor Knight to read into my words the meaning that I hold to "the conception of a well-managed penitentiary or orphan asylum as a social ideal." The whole discussion of bias, indeed, seems to be a little pointless in the light of our present knowledge of psychology. It is difficult to envisage a human being, no matter how scholarly or how committed to scientific method, who does not exhibit some kind of bias most of the time. In the exact sciences, where data are measurable, we recognize this fact and allow for it, and we call it by the statistical term "error." In the social sciences, particularly in social theory, we cannot achieve this, and too often merely call names.

These special points, like many others which call for comment are, however, really more or less aside from the major issue. This, I feel, is whether or not the disciplines of anthropology and economics can join in contributing to a deeper understanding of the range of variation in man's methods of getting a living, and in documenting any general principles to be drawn from such facts, which will help us the better to understand our own economic motivations and behavior. I am happy that on this fundamental point there is no disagreement between Professor Knight and myself. Such matters as the importance of specialization of labor, the significance of gift exchange, the role of prestige, and the nature of property seem to be points of interest to the comprehension of which anthropology can contribute tellingly to economics. I should even persist in feeling, despite Professor Knight's disagreement, that the concept of the economic surplus over subsistence needs, and the idea of the translation of this surplus into social leisure, can also be of use to economists in aiding us to understand the working of certain important aspects of our own economic system. On the other hand, economists possess conceptual and methodological tools and a range of problems which anthropologists cannot ignore if their studies of culture, which must include its economic aspects, are to be at all complete.

In the final analysis, the value of a discussion such as Professor Knight and I have joined in lies in the stimulus it may give for continuing consideration of the issues that have been raised. It is my hope that the future will see further analysis of the points that have been taken up here, so that the science of comparative economics may eventually emerge as a structure based on a foundation that is equally solid in its anthropological and economic postulates.

BIBLIOGRAPHY

NOTE: *The titles in the following list include only those works to which reference has actually been made in the text of this book.*

ARMSTRONG, W. E. (1928): *Rossel Island, an Ethnological Study.* Cambridge.

ATKINS, WILLARD E. (1932): "Institutional Economics, a Round-table Discussion." *Am. Econ. Rev.*, suppl. to vol. xxii, no. 1, pp. 111–12.

AYRES, C. E. (1938): *The Problem of Economic Order.* New York.

—(1944): *The Theory of Economic Progress.* Chapel Hill, N. C.

BARNETT, H. G. (1938): "The Nature of the Potlatch." *Am. Anth.*, vol. xl, pp. 349–58.

—(1949): *Palauan Society.* Eugene, Ore.

BARRETT, S. A. (1908): "The Ethno-Geography of the Pomo and Neighboring Indians." *U. Cal. Publ. Am. Arch. and Eth.*, vol. vi, pp. 1–382.

BARTON, R. F. (1919): "Ifugao Law." *U. Cal. Publ. Am. Arch. and Eth.*, vol. xv, no. 1, pp. 1–186.

—(1922): "Ifugao Economics." *U. Cal. Publ. Am. Arch. and Eth.*, vol. xv, pp. 385–446.

—(1949): *The Kalingas, their Institutions and Custom Law.* Chicago.

BASCOM, WILLIAM R. (communicated): *Notes on the Yoruba of Ife, Nigeria.*

—(1948): "Ponapean Prestige Economy." *Southwestern Jour. of Anth.*, vol. iv, pp. 211–21.

—(1951): "Yoruba Food." *Africa*, vol. xxi, pp. 41–53.

BAUDIN, LOUIS (1928): *L'Empire socialiste des Inka.* Tr. et Mém., Inst. d'Eth., vol. V.

BEAGLEHOLE, ERNEST (1932): *Property, a Study in Social Psychology.* New York.

—(1937): *Notes on Hopi Economic Life.* Yale U. Publ. in Anthrop., No. 15.

BEAGLEHOLE, ERNEST and PEARL (1938): *Ethnology of Pukapuka.* B. P. Bishop Museum, Bull. 150.

BEALS, RALPH (1933): "Ethnology of the Nisenan." *U. Cal. Publ. Am. Arch. and Eth.*, vol. xxxi, pp. 335–414.

534 BIBLIOGRAPHY

BELL, F. L. S. (1933–4): "Report on Field Work in Tanga." *Oceania,* vol. iv, pp. 290–309.

BENHAM, FREDERIC (1936): *Economics.* London.

BENHAM, FREDERIC and BODDY, FRANCIS M. (1947): *Principles of Economics.* New York and Chicago.

BIRD, JUNIUS (1946): "The Alacaluf." *Handbook of South American Indians,* vol. I, pp. 55–80. Bull. 143, Bureau of Am. Eth. Washington.

BIRKET-SMITH, KAJ (1930): *Contributions to Chipewyan Ethnology.* Rep. 5th Thule Exped., 1921–4, vol. vi, no. 3.

—(1936): *The Eskimos.* London.

BIRKET-SMITH, KAJ and DE LAGUNA, FREDERICA (1938): *The Eyak Indians of the Copper River Delta, Alaska.* Copenhagen.

BLACKWOOD, BEATRICE (1935): *Both Sides of Buka Passage.* Oxford.

BINGER, L. G. (1892): *Du Niger au Golfe de Guinée.* Paris (vol. I).

BOAS, FRANZ (1888): *The Central Eskimo,* 6th Ann. Rep., Bur. of Am. Eth.

—(1897): *The Social Organization and the Secret Societies of the Kwakiutl Indians.* Report of U. S. Nat. Museum for 1895. Washington.

—(1898): *Twelfth and Final Report on the North-Western Tribes of Canada.* British Assn. for the Adv. of Sci., Bristol Meeting, Section H.

—(1916): *Tsimshian Mythology.* 31st Ann. Rep., Bur. of Am. Eth.

—(1921): *Ethnology of the Kwakiutl.* 35th Ann. Rep., Bur. of Am. Eth.

—(1938): *The Mind of Primitive Man* (2nd ed.). New York.

BOGORAS, W. (1904): *The Chuckchee, Material Culture.* Publ. Jessup N. Pac. Exped., vol. vii, part 1.

BONN, M. J. (1931): "Economic Policy." *Encyclopaedia of the Social Sciences,* vol. V, pp. 333–44.

BOULDING, KENNETH E. (1941): *Economic Analysis.* New York.

BRUIJNIS, N. W. (1933): *Ethnologische Economie, en de Studie van het economisch Leven der inheemsche Bevolking in het oosten van den Indischen Archipel en Nederlandsch Nieuw-Guinee.* Arnhem (Holland).

BÜCHER, KARL (1901): *Industrial Evolution* (transl. from the 3rd German edition by S. M. Wickett).

BUNZEL, RUTH (1938): "The Economic Organization of Primitive Peoples." *General Anthropology* (F. Boas, ed.), ch. VIII. New York.

BURKITT, M. C. (1926): *Our Early Ancestors.* Cambridge.

BURROWS, EDWIN G. (1937): *Ethnology of Uvea* (Wallis Island). B. P. Bishop Museum, Bull. 145.

BUXTON, L. H. D. (1924): *Primitive Labour.* London.

CARVER, THOMAS NIXON (1904): *The Distribution of Wealth.* New York.

CHILDE, V. GORDON (1925): *The Dawn of European Civilization.* New York.

—(1946a): *What Happened in History.* New York.

—(1946b): "Archaeology and Anthropology." *Southwestern Jour. of Anth.,* vol. ii, pp. 243–51.

CLINE, WALTER (1937): *Mining and Metallurgy in Negro Africa.* Gen. Series in Anthrop., No. 5.

CODERE, HELEN (1950): "Fighting with Property, a Study of Kwakiutl Potlatching and Warfare, 1792–1930." *Monographs of the American Ethnological Society*, XVIII. New York.

CODRINGTON, R. H. (1891): *The Melanesians, Studies in Their Anthropology and Folklore*. London.

COMMONS, JOHN R. (1934): *Institutional Economics, Its Place in Political Economy*. New York.

COOPER, JOHN M. (1939): "Is the Algonquian Family Hunting Ground System Pre-Columbian?" *Amer. Anth.*, vol. xli, pp. 66–90.

—(1946a): "The Chono." *Handbook of South American Indians*, vol. I, pp. 47–53. Bull. 143, Bureau of Am. Eth., Washington.

—(1946b): "The Yahgan." *Ibid.*, pp. 81–106.

CULWICK, A. T. and G. M. (1935): *Ubena of the Rivers*. London.

CUREAU, AD. (1912): *Les Sociétés Primitives de l'Afrique Équatoriale*. Paris.

DALZEL, ARCHIBALD (1793): *The History of Dahomey, an Inland Kingdom of Africa*. London.

DANQUAH, J. B. (1928): *Gold Coast: Akan Laws and Customs*. London.

DAPPER, O. (1670): *Umbständliche und Eigentliche Beschreibung von Africa*, Amsterdam.

DAVIDSON, D. S. (1928a): "The Family Hunting Territory in Australia." *Am. Anth.*, vol. xxx, pp. 614–31.

—(1928b): "Family Hunting Territories of the Tribes of Tierra del Fuego." *Indian Notes*, vol. v, pp. 395–410.

—(1938): "An Ethnic Map of Australia." *Proceedings, Amer. Philosophical Soc.*, vol. lxxix, pp. 649–78.

DEACON, A. BERNARD (1934): *Malekula, a Vanishing People in the New Hebrides* (C. H. Wedgewood, ed.). London.

DENIG, EDWIN T. (1930): *Indian Tribes of the Upper Missouri*. 46th Ann. Rep., Bur. of Am. Eth.

DIESING, PAUL (1950): "The Nature and Limitations of Economic Rationality." *Ethics*, vol. lxi, pp. 12–26.

DIXON, R. A. and EBERHART, E. K. (1938): *Economics and Cultural Change*. New York.

DIXON, ROLAND B. (1928): *The Building of Cultures*. New York.

DOKE, C. M. (1931): *The Lambas of Northern Rhodesia*. London.

DALMATOFF, GERARDO REICHEL (1950): *Los Kogi, una Tribu de la Sierra Nevada, en Colombia*. Bogotá.

DRIBERG, J. H. (1923): *The Lango, a Nilotic Tribe of Uganda*. London.

—(1929): *The Savage as He Really Is*. London.

DRUCKER, PHILIP (1939): "Rank, Wealth and Kinship in Northwest Coast Society." *Amer. Anth.*, vol. xli, pp. 55–65.

DuBois, CORA (1935): "Wintu Ethnography." *U. Cal. Publ. Am. Arch. and Eth.*, vol. xxxvi, no. 1, pp. 1–248.

—(1936): "The Wealth Factor as an Integrative Factor in Tolowa-Tututui Culture." *Essays in Anthropology presented to A. L. Kroeber*, pp. 49–66. Berkeley.

DURKHEIM, ÉMILE (1893): *De la Division du Travail Social*. Paris.

EDEL, MAY M. (1937): "The Bachiga of East Africa." *Cooperation and Competition among Primitive Peoples* (M. Mead, ed.), pp. 127–52. New York.

EINZIG, PAUL (1949): *Primitive Money in its Ethnological, Historical and Economic Aspects.* London.

EISELEN, W. M. and SCHAPERA, I. (1937): "Religious Beliefs and Practices." *The Bantu-Speaking Tribes of South Africa* (I. Schapera, ed.), pp. 247–70. London.

ELY, RICHARD T. (1918): *Outlines of Economics* (3rd revised ed.). New York.

ENGELS, FREDERICK (1902): *The Origin of the Family, Private Property, and the State.* Chicago.

EVANS, IVOR H. N. (1937): *The Negritos of Malaya.* Cambridge.

EVANS-PRITCHARD, E. E. (1937): *Witchcraft, Oracles and Magic among the Azande.* Oxford.

—(1937–8): "Economic Life of the Nuer: Cattle." *Sudan Notes and Records,* vol. xx, pp. 209–45; vol. xxi, pp. 31–78.

—(1940a): "The Nuer of the Southern Sudan." *African Political Systems* (M. Fortes and E. E. Evans-Pritchard, eds.), pp. 272–96. London.

—(1940b): *The Nuer.* Oxford.

FETTER, FRANK A. (1905): *The Principles of Economics.* New York.

FIRTH, RAYMOND (1929a): *Primitive Economics of the New Zealand Maori.* New York.

—(1929b): "Currency, Primitive." *Encyclopaedia Britannica,* 14th ed.

—(1936): *We, the Tikopia, A Sociological Study of Kinship in Primitive Polynesia.* London.

—(1939): *Primitive Polynesian Economy.* London.

—(1946): *Malay Fishermen: Their Peasant Economy.* London.

FIRTH, ROSEMARY (1943): *Housekeeping among Malay Peasants.* London.

FLETCHER, A. C. and LA FLECHE, F. (1911): *The Omaha Tribe.* 27th Ann. Rep., Bur. of Am. Eth.

FORBES, FREDERICK E. (1851): *Dahomey and the Dahomans* (2 vols.). London.

FORDE, C. DARYLL (1931): "Hopi Agriculture and Land Ownership." *Jour. Roy. Anthrop. Institute,* vol. lxi, pp. 357–405.

—(1934): *Habitat, Economy and Society.* London.

—(1937): "Land and Labour in a Cross River Village, Southern Nigeria." *Geographical Jour.,* vol. xc, pp. 24–51.

FORTES, M. (1937): "Communal Fishing and Fishing Magic in the Northern Territories of the Gold Coast." *Jour. Roy. Anthrop. Institute,* vol. lxvii, pp. 131–42.

—(1938): "Social and Psychological Aspects of Education in Taleland." Supplement to *Africa,* vol. xi, no. 4.

—(1949): *The Web of Kinship among the Tallensi.* London.

FORTES, M. and S. L. (1936): "Food in the Domestic Economy of the Tallensi." *Africa,* vol. ix, pp. 237–76.

FORTES, M. and EVANS-PRITCHARD, E. E. (1940): *African Political Systems*. London.

FOSTER, GEORGE M. (1942): "A Primitive Mexican Economy." *Monographs of the Amer. Eth. Soc.*, v. New York.

—(1948): *Empire's Children, the People of Tzintzuntzan*. Pub. No. 6, Inst. of Soc. Anth., Smithsonian Institution. Washington.

GADEN, HENRI (1931): *Proverbes et Maximes Peuls et Toucouleurs*. Tr. et Mém., Inst. d'Eth., vol. XVI. Paris.

GAMBS, JOHN S. (1946): *Beyond Supply and Demand, a Reappraisal of Institutional Economics*. New York.

GAUD, FERNAND and VAN OVERBERGH, CYR. (1911): Les Mandja (Congo Français). *Collection de Monographies ethnographiques*, vol. viii. Brussels.

GAYTON, ANN H. (1930): "Yokuts-Mono Chiefs and Shamans." *U. Cal. Publ. Am. Arch. and Eth.*, vol. xxiv, no. 8, pp. 361–420.

GIFFIN, NAOMI M. (1930): *The Roles of Men and Women in Eskimo Culture*. Chicago.

GIFFORD, E. W. (1923): "Pomo Lands on Clear Lake." *U. Cal. Publ. Am. Arch. and Eth.*, vol. xx, pp. 77–94.

—(1929): *Tongan Society*. B. P. Bishop Museum, Bull. 61.

GLUCKMAN, MAX (1941): "Economy of the Central Barotse Plain." *Rhodes-Livingstone Papers, No. 7*.

—(1943): "Essays on Lozi Land and Royal Property." *Ibid.*, No. 10.

GOLDSCHMIDT, WALTER (1951): "Nomlaki Ethnography." *U. Cal. Pub. Am. Arch. and Eth.*, vol. xlii, no. 4, pp. 303–443.

GOODFELLOW, D. M. (1939): *Principles of Economic Sociology . . . as Illustrated from the Bantu Peoples of South and East Africa*. London.

GRAS, N. S. B. (1922): *An Introduction to Economic History*. New York.

—(1927): "Anthropology and Economics." *The Social Sciences and their Interrelations* (W. F. Ogburn and A. A. Goldenweiser, eds.), pp. 10–23. Boston.

—(1930): "Barter." *Encyclopaedia of the Social Sciences*, vol. II, pp. 468–9.

GREGORY, T. E. (1933): "Money." *Encyclopaedia of the Social Sciences*, vol. X, pp. 601–13.

GREVISSE, F. (1950): "Salines et Saliniers Indigènes du Haut-Katanga." *Bull. du Centre d'Etudes des Problèmes Sociaux Indigènes*. No. 11, pp. 7–85.

GRIERSON, P. J. H. (1903): *The Silent Trade*. Edinburgh.

GUSINDE, MARTIN (1931): *Die Selk'nam*. Anthropos-Bibliothek, Expeditions-Serie I. Mödling bei Wien.

GUTMANN, BRUNO (1926): *Das Recht der Dschagga*. Munich.

HALLOWELL, A. I. (1943): "The Nature and Function of Property as a Social Institution." *Jour. of Legal and Political Sociology*, vol. i, pp. 115–38.

—(1949): "The Size of Algonkian Hunting Territories: A Function of Ecological Adjustment." *Am. Anth.*, vol. li, pp. 35–45.

HAMILTON, WALTON H. and TILL, IRENE (1934): "Property." *Encyclo-paedia of the Social Sciences*, vol. XII, pp. 528–38.

HANDY, E. S. C. (1923): *The Native Culture in the Marquesas*. B. P. Bishop Museum, Bull. 9.

—(1927): *Polynesian Religion*. B. P. Bishop Museum, Bull. 34.

—(1930): *History and Culture in the Society Islands*. B. P. Bishop Museum, Bull. 79.

HARRIS, ABRAM L. (1932): "Types of Institutionalism." *Jour. Pol. Econ.*, vol. xl, pp. 721–49.

HARRIS, JACK S. (1940): "The Acculturation of the White Knives Shoshoni." *Acculturation in Seven American Indian Tribes* (R. Linton, ed.), New York, pp. 39–116.

—(1942a): "Some Aspects of Slavery in Southeastern Nigeria." *Journal of Negro History*, vol. xxvii, pp. 37–54.

—(1942b): "Human Relationship to the Land in Southern Nigeria." *Rural Sociology*, vol. vii, pp. 89–92.

HARTLAND, E. SIDNEY (1924): *Primitive Law*. London.

HATT, GUDMUND (1937): *Landbrug i Danmarks Oldtid*. Copenhagen.

HENRY, JULES (1951): "The Economics of Pilagá Food Distribution." *Am. Anthrop.*, vol. liii, pp. 187–219.

HENRY, TERUIRA (1928): *Ancient Tahiti*. B. P. Bishop Museum, Bull. 48.

HERODOTUS: *History* (transl. by G. Rawlinson). New York, Everyman's Library.

HERSKOVITS, M. J. (1926): "The Cattle Complex in East Africa." *Am. Anthrop.*, vol. xxviii (n.s.), pp. 230–72, 361–80, 494–528, 633–64.

—(1932): "Some Aspects of Dahomean Ethnology." *Africa*, vol. v, pp. 266–96.

—(1937): *Life in a Haitian Valley*. New York.

—(1938): *Dahomey, an Ancient West African Kingdom*. New York.

—(1948): *Man and His Works*. New York.

HERSKOVITS, M. J. and F. S. (1934): *Rebel Destiny; among the Bush Ne-groes of Dutch Guiana*. New York.

HERSKOVITS, M. J. and TAGBWE, SIE (1930): "Kru Proverbs." *J. Am. Folk-Lore*, vol. xliii, pp. 225–93.

HEWITT, J. N. B. (1908): "Wampum." *Handbook of American Indians*. Bur. Am. Eth., Bull. 30.

HICKS, J. R. (1948): *Value and Capital* (2nd edition). Oxford.

HILL, W. W. (1938): *The Agricultural and Hunting Methods of the Navaho Indians*. Yale U. Publ. in Anthrop., No. 18.

—(1948): "Navaho Trading and Trading Ritual: a Study of Cultural Dynamics." *Southwestern J. of Anth.*, vol. iv, pp. 371–96.

HIROA, TE RANGI (PETER H. BUCK) (1930): *Samoan Material Culture*. B. P. Bishop Museum, Bull. 75.

—(1932): *Ethnology of Tongareva*. B. P. Bishop Museum, Bull. 92.

—(1934): *Mangaian Society*. B. P. Bishop Museum, Bull. 122.

—(1938): *Ethnology of Mangareva*. B. P. Bishop Museum, Bull. 157.

HOBHOUSE, L. T. (1913): "The Historical Evolution of Property, in Fact and in Idea." *Property, Its Duties and Rights*, pp. 1–31. London.

HOBHOUSE, L. T., WHEELER, G. C. and GINSBERG, M. (1915): *The Material Culture and Social Institutions of the Simpler Peoples*. London.

HOCART, A. M. (1929): *Lau Islands, Fiji*. B. P. Bishop Museum, Bull. 62.

HOEBEL, E. ADAMSON (1940): *The Political Organization and Law-Ways of the Comanche Indians*. Am. Anth. Ass'n., Memoir 42.

HOERNLÉ, A. WINIFRED (1937): "Magic and Medicine." *The Bantu-Speaking Tribes of South Africa* (I. Schapera, ed.), pp. 221–45. London.

HOGBIN, H. IAN (1932): "Polynesian Ceremonial Gift Exchanges." *Oceania*, vol. iii, pp. 13–39.

—(1934): *Law and Order in Polynesia*. London.

—(1938): "Social Advancement in Guadalcanal, Solomon Islands." *Oceania*, vol. viii, pp. 289–305.

—(1938–39): "Tillage and Collection, a New Guinea Economy." *Oceania*, vol. ix, pp. 127–51, 286–325.

—(1939–40): "Native Land Tenure in New Guinea." *Oceania*, vol. x, pp. 113–65.

—(1947): "Native Trade around the Huon Gulf, North-eastern New Guinea." *Jour. of the Polynesian Society*, vol. lvi, pp. 242–55.

HOLMBERG, ALLAN R. (1950): *Nomads of the Long Bow, the Siriono of Eastern Bolivia*. Pub. No. 10, Inst. of Soc. Anth., Smithsonian Institution. Washington.

HOSE, CHARLES (1926): *Natural Man, a Record from Borneo*. London.

HOWITT, A. W. (1904): *The Native Tribes of South-East Australia*. London.

HOYT, ELIZABETH E. (1926): *Primitive Trade, Its Psychology and Economics*. London.

—(1938): *Consumption in our Society*. New York.

HUDSON, ALFRED E. (1938): *Kazak Social Structure*. Yale U. Publ. in Anthrop., No. 20.

HUE, EDMOND (1910): "Distribution Géographique de l'Industrie en Silex du Grand-Pressigny." *6ᵉ Cong. Préhist. de France, Tours*, pp. 390–419.

HUNTER, MONICA (1936): *Reaction to Conquest, Effects of Contact with Europeans on the Pondo of South Africa*. London.

HUTTON, J. H. (1921): *The Sema Nagas*. London.

JENKS, A. E. (1900): *The Wild Rice Gatherers of the Upper Lakes, a Study in American Primitive Economics*. 19th Ann. Rep., Bur. of Am. Eth.

JENNESS, D. (1922): *The Life of the Copper Eskimos*. Report of Canadian Arctic Exped., vol. xii, 1913–18.

JOCHELSON, W. (1908): *The Koryak*. Publ. Jessup N. Pac. Exped., vol. vi, part 2.

JOYCE, T. A. (1912): *South American Archaeology*. London.

JUNOD, H. A. (1927): *The Life of a South African Tribe* (2 vols.). London.

KABERRY, PHYLLIS M. (1939): *Aboriginal Woman, Sacred and Profane*. London.

KARDINER, ABRAM (1939): *The Individual and his Society*. New York.

—(1945): *The Psychological Frontiers of Society*. New York.

KARSTEN, RAFAEL (1932): *Indian Tribes of the Argentine and Bolivian Chaco.* Soc. Scien. Fennica, Comment. Hum. Litt., vol. iv, No. 1.

KENYATTA, JOMO (1938): *Facing Mount Kenya, the Tribal Life of the Gikuyu.* London.

KEYNES, JOHN MAYNARD (1939): *The General Theory of Employment Interest and Money.* London.

KEYNES, JOHN NEVILLE (1897): *The Scope and Method of Political Economy* (2nd edition, revised). London.

KNIGHT, FRANK H. (1924): "The Limitations of Scientific Method in Economics." *The Trend of Economics* (R. Tugwell, ed.), pp. 229–67. New York.

—(1933): *The Economic Organization.* Chicago.

—(1935): *The Ethics of Competition and other Essays.* London.

KOPPERS, W. (1924): "Die Menschliche Wirtschaft." *Der Mensch aller Zeiten,* vol. III, *Volker und Kulturen,* pp. 377–630. Regensburg.

KRIGE, E. JENSEN and J. D. (1943): *The Realm of a Rain-Queen, a Study of the Pattern of Lovedu Society.* London.

KROEBER, A. L. (1925): *Handbook of the Indians of California.* Bur. Am. Eth., Bull. 78.

KROPOTKIN, P. (1916): *Mutual Aid, a Factor of Evolution.* New York.

KUPER, HILDA (1947): *An African Aristocracy, Rank Among the Swazi.* London.

LABOURET, HENRI (1931): *Les Tribus du Rameau Lobi.* Tr. et Mém., Inst. d'Eth., vol. XV.

—(communicated): *Native Family Budgets from French West Africa.*

LANDES, RUTH (1937): *Ojibwa Sociology.* Col. Univ. Contr. to Anthrop., vol. XXIX.

LANDTMAN, GUNNAR (1927): *The Kiwai Papuans of British New Guinea.* London.

—(1938): *The Origin of the Inequality of the Social Classes.* London.

LATCHAM, R. E. (1927): "The Totemism of the Ancient Andean Peoples." *Jour. Roy. Anthrop. Institute,* vol. lvii, pp. 55–87.

—(1929): *Las Creéncias Religiosos de los Antiguos Peruanos.* Santiago de Chile.

LAVELEYE, EMILE DE (1878): *Primitive Property* (transl. by G. R. L. Marriott, with an introduction by T. E. Cliffe Leslie), London.

LAYARD, J. W. (1928): "Degree-Taking Rites in South West Bay, Malekula." *Jour. Roy. Anthrop. Institute,* vol. lviii, pp. 140–223.

LEENHARDT, MAURICE (1937): *Gens de la Grande Terre.* Paris.

LEPLEY, R., ed. (1949): *Value, a Cooperative Inquiry.* New York.

LEROY, OLIVIER (1925): *Essai d'Introduction Critique à l'étude de l'Economie Primitive.* Paris.

LETOURNEAU, CH. (1892): *Property, Its Origin and Development.* London.

LÉVY-BRUHL, LUCIEN (1923): *Primitive Mentality.* New York.

ST. LEWIŃSKI, JON (1913): *The Origin of Property, and the Formation of the Village Community.* London.

LEWIS, ALBERT B. (1929): *Melanesian Shell Money*. Field Museum Anthrop. Series, vol. xix, no. 1 (Publ. No. 268).

LINDBLOM, G. K. (1920): *The Akamba*. Arch d'Études Orientales, vol. XVII. Uppsala.

LITTLE, KENNETH L. (1951): "The Mende Rice Farm and its Cost." *Zaïre*, vol. v, pp. 227–273.

LOEB, EDWIN M. (1926): *History and Traditions of Niue*. B. P. Bishop Museum, Bull. 32.

LOWIE, ROBERT H. (1920): *Primitive Society*. New York.

—(1928): "Incorporeal Property in Primitive Society." *Yale Law Jour.*, vol. xxxvii, pp. 551–63.

—(1946): *Social Organization*. New York.

LUOMALA, KATHERINE (1946): "Polynesian Literature." *Encyclopedia of Literature* (J. T. Shipley, ed.), vol. II, pp. 772–89. New York.

LYSTAD, ROBERT A. (communicated): *Notes on the Ashanti of the Gold Coast and the Agni of the Ivory Coast, West Africa*.

MACCURDY, GEORGE GRANT (1924): *Human Origins*. New York.

MACFIE, A. L. (1949): "What Kind of Experience is Economizing?" *Ethics*, vol. lx, pp. 19–34.

MACGREGOR, GORDON (1935): "Notes on the Ethnology of Pukapuka." *B. P. Bishop Museum, Occas. Papers*, vol. xi, no. 6.

MALINOWSKI, B. (1913): *The Family among the Australian Aborigines*. London.

—(1921): "The Primitive Economics of the Trobriand Islanders." *Economic Journal*, vol. xxxi, pp. 1–16.

—(1922): *Argonauts of the Western Pacific*. London.

—(1935): *Coral Gardens and their Magic* (vol. I). London.

MAN, E. H. (1932): *On the Aboriginal Inhabitants of the Andaman Islands* (2nd ed.). London.

MANDELBAUM, DAVID (1939): "Agricultural Ceremonies among Three Tribes of Travancore." *Ethnos,* vol. iv.

—(communicated): *Notes on fieldwork in India*.

MARSHALL, ALFRED (1936): *Principles of Economics* (8th ed.). London.

MARWICK, BRIAN ALLAN (1940): *The Swazi*. Cambridge (England).

MARX, KARL (1933): *Capital*. London, Everyman's Library.

MAUNIER, RENÉ (1926): *La Construction Collective de la Maison en Kabylie*. Tr. et Mém., Inst. d'Eth., vol. III.

MAUSS, MARCEL (1925): "Essai sur le Don; Forme et Raison de l'Éxchange dans les Sociétés Archaïques." *L'Année Sociologique,* (n.s.), vol. i (for 1923–4), pp. 30–186.

MAYER, PHILIP (1950): Gusii Bridewealth Law and Custom." *Rhodes-Livingstone Papers,* No. 18.

MCBRYDE, FELIX W. (1947?): *Cultural and Historical Geography of Southwest Guatemala*. Pub. No. 4, Inst. of Soc. Anth., Smithsonian Institution, Washington.

MCCARTHY, F. D. (1938–9; 1939–40): " 'Trade' in Aboriginal Australia and

'Trade' Relationships with Torres Strait, New Guinea and Malaya." *Oceania*, vol. 9, pp. 405–38, vol. 10, pp. 81–104, 171–95.

McKern, W. C. (1922): "Functional Families of the Patwin." *U. Cal. Publ. Am. Arch. and Eth.*, vol. xiii, pp. 235–58.

Mead, Margaret (1930a): *Social Organization of Manua*. B. P. Bishop Museum, Bull. 76.

—(1930b): "Melanesian Middlemen." *Natural History*, vol. xxx, pp. 115–30.

—(1937): "Economic Control in Primitive Society." *Planned Society* (Findley Mackenzie, ed.). New York.

Means, Philip Ainsworth (1931): *Ancient Civilizations of the Andes*. New York.

Meek, C. K. (1937): *Law and Authority in a Nigerian Tribe*. Oxford.

Mills, J. P. (1922): *The Lhota Nagas*. London.

Mooney, James and Olbrechts, F. M. (1932): *The Swimmer Manuscript, Cherokee Sacred Formulas and Medicinal Prescriptions*. Bur. Am. Eth., Bull. 99.

Morgan, Lewis H. (1851): *League of the Ho-dé-no-sau-nee, or Iroquois*. Rochester.

—(1877): *Ancient Society*. Chicago.

Mosher, Stuart (1936): *The Story of Money*. Bulletin of the Buffalo Soc. of Natural Sciences, vol. xvii, no. 2.

Mukerjee, Radhakamal (1921): *Principles of Comparative Economics*, vol. I.

Müller, Wilhelm (1917): *Yap*. Erg. der Südsee Exped. 1908–10, edited by G. Thilenius. II. Ethnographie. B. Mikronesien. Bd. 2, 1 halbb. Hamburg.

Murdock, George P. (1936): *Rank and Potlatch among the Haida*. Yale U. Publ. in Anthrop., No. 13.

Myer, William E. (1928): *Indian Trails of the Southeast*. 42nd Ann. Rep., Bur. of Am. Eth.

Nadel, S. F. (1935): "Nupe State and Community." *Africa*, vol. viii, pp. 257–303.

—(1937): "A Ritual Currency in Nigeria—a Result of Culture Contact." *Africa*, vol. x, pp. 488–91.

—(1942): *A Black Byzantium, the Kingdom of Nupe in Nigeria*. London.

Nordhoff, C. B. (1930): "Notes on Offshore Fishing of the Society Islands." *Jour. Polynesian Society*, vol. xxxix, p. 243.

Numelin, Ragnar (1939): "Den Primitiva Handeln och dess Geografiska Utbredning." (With French abstract.) *Geogr. Sällskapets i Finland, Tidskrift Terra*, vol. li, pp. 1–25.

—(1950): *The Beginnings of Diplomacy*. London and Copenhagen.

Oberg, K. (MS.): *A Comparison of Three Systems of Primitive Economic Organization*.

Odaka, K. (1950): *Economic Organization of the Li Tribes of Hainan*

Island. Yale Univ., Southeast Asia Studies, Translation Series, New Haven.

OLIVER, DOUGLAS L. (1949a): "Economic and Social Uses of Domestic Pigs in Siuai, Southern Bougainville, Solomon Islands." *Papers, Peabody Mus. of Am. Eth. and Archaeology,* vol. xxix, no. 4.

—(1949b): "Land Tenure in Northeast Siuai, Southern Bougainville, Solomon Islands." *Ibid.,* vol. xxix, no. 5.

OSGOOD, CORNELIUS (1940): *Ingalik Material Culture.* Yale Univ. Pub. in Anth., no. 22.

PANT, S. D. (1935): *The Social Economy of the Himalayans.* London.

PAPANDREOU, A. G. (1950): "Economics and the Social Sciences." *The Economic Journal,* vol. lx, pp. 715–23.

PARK, WILLARD (1938): *Shamanism in Western North America.* Northwestern U. Studies in the Social Sciences, No. 2. Evanston.

PARSONS, ELSIE CLEWS (1925): *The Pueblo of Jemez.* Papers of the Southwestern Museum, No. 3. New Haven.

—(1936a): *Taos Pueblo.* Gen. Ser. in Anthrop. No. 2. Menasha.

—(1936b): *Mitla, Town of the Souls.* Chicago.

PAULME, DENISE (1940): *Organization Sociale des Dogon.* Paris.

PEARSALL, MARION (1947): "Distributional Variations of Bride-Wealth in the East African Cattle Area." *Southwestern Jour. of Anthrop.,* vol. iii, pp. 15–31.

POLANYI, KARL (1944): *The Great Transformation.* New York, Toronto.

POWDERMAKER, HORTENSE (1933): *Life in Lesu.* New York.

PROVINSE, JOHN H. (1937): "Cooperative Ricefield Cultivation among the Siang Dyaks of Central Borneo." *Am. Anthrop.,* vol. xxxix, pp. 77–102.

QUIGGIN, A. HINGSTON (1949): *A Survey of Primitive Money, The Beginnings of Currency.* London.

RADCLIFFE-BROWN, A. R. (1933): *The Andaman Islanders* (2nd ed.).

RADIN, PAUL (1937): *Primitive Religion, Its Nature and Origin.* New York.

RATTRAY, R. S. (1927): *Religion and Art in Ashanti.* Oxford.

—(1929): *Ashanti Law and Constitution.* Oxford.

RAY, VERNE F. (1938): "Lower Chinook Ethnographic Notes." *U. Wash. Publ. in Anthrop.,* vol. vii, pp. 29–165.

RICHARDS, AUDREY I. (1932): *Hunger and Work in a Savage Tribe.* London.

—(1939): *Land, Labour and Diet in Northern Rhodesia; an Economic Study of the Bemba Tribe.* London.

RICHARDS, A. I. and WIDDOWSON, E. M. (1936): "A Dietary Study in North-eastern Rhodesia." *Africa,* vol. ix, pp. 166–96.

RITZENTHALER, ROBERT E. (1949): *Native Money of Palau* (mimeographed for submission to the Pacific Science Board, Washington, D. C.).

ROBBINS, LIONEL (1935): *An Essay on the Nature and Significance of Economic Science.* London.

ROBBINS, W. W., HARRINGTON, J. P. and FREIRE-MARRECO, B. (1916): *Ethnobotany of the Tewa Indians.* Bur. Am. Eth., Bull. 55.

ROSCOE, JOHN (1911): *The Baganda*. London.

ROTH, W. E. (1897): *Ethnological Studies among the North-West-Central Queensland Aborigines*. Brisbane and London.

—(1924): *An Introductory Study of the Arts, Crafts and Customs of the Guiana Indians*. 38th Ann. Rep., Bur. of Am. Eth.

—(1929): *Additional Studies of the Arts, Crafts and Customs of the Guiana Indians*. Bur. Am. Eth., Bull. 91.

RUSSELL, FRANK (1905): *The Pima Indians*, 26th Ann. Rep., Bur. of Am. Eth.

RUSSELL, J. TOWNSEND (1932): "Report on Archaeological Research in the Foothills of the Pyrenees." *Smithsonian Misc. Coll.*, vol. 87, no. 11, publ. 3174.

SAPIR, EDWARD (1949): "Culture, Genuine and Spurious," in *Selected Writings of Edward Sapir in Language, Culture, and Personality* (D. Mandelbaum, ed.), Berkeley, pp. 308–32.

SAPIR, E. and SWADESH, M. (1939): *Nootka Texts*. Wm. Dwight Whitney Linguistic Series, Ling. Soc. of Amer. Philadelphia.

SCHAPERA, I. (1930): *The Khoisan Peoples of South Africa, Bushmen and Hottentots*. London.

—(1938): *A Handbook of Tswana Law and Custom*. London.

—(1943): *Native Land Tenure in the Bechuanaland Protectorate*, Lovedale (South Africa).

SCHAPERA, I. and GOODWIN, A. J. H. (1937): "Work and Wealth." *The Bantu-Speaking Tribes of South Africa*. (I. Schapera, ed.), pp. 131–71. London.

SCHECHTER, FRANK I. (1935): "The Law and Morals of Primitive Trade." *Legal Essays in Tribute to Orrin Kip McMurray*, pp. 565–622. Berkeley.

SCHMIDT, MAX (1920–1): *Grundriss der ethnologischen Volkswirtschafts-lehre* (2 vols.). Stuttgart.

—(1926): *The Primitive Races of Mankind*. London.

SCHMIDT, WILHELM (1937): *Das Eigentum auf den Ältesten Stufen der Menschheit*. Bd. I. Das Eigentum in den Urkulturen. Münster.

SCHUMPETER, JOSEPH A. (1948): "Keynes, the Economist." *The New Economics* (S. E. Harris, ed.), pp. 73–101. New York.

SCHURTZ, HEINRICH (1898): *Grundriss einer Entstehungsgeschichte des Geldes*. Weimar.

SEAGLE, WILLIAM (1941): *The Quest for Law*. 1941.

SELIGMAN, C. G. (1910): *The Melanesians of British New Guinea*. Cambridge.

SELIGMAN, C. G. and B. Z. (1911): *The Veddas*. Cambridge.

SELIGMAN, E. R. A. (1902): "The Economic Interpretation of History." *Publ. Am. Econ. Assn.* (3rd ser., no. 1), vol. iii, pp. 369–86.

—(1905): *Principles of Economics*. New York.

SENFFT, ARNO (1907): "Die Rechtsitten der Jap-Eingeborenen." *Globus*, Bd. xci, pp. 139–43, 145–9, 171–5.

SERVICE, ELMAN (1947): "Recent Observations on Havasupai Land Tenure." *Southwestern Jour. of Anth.*, vol. iii, 360–6.

SHARP, LAURISTON (1934–5): "Ritual Life and Economics of the Yir-Yoront of Cape York Peninsula." *Oceania,* vol. v, pp. 19–42.

SMITH, ADAM (1937): *An Inquiry into the Nature and Causes of the Wealth of Nations.* New York, Modern Library.

SMITH, MARIAN W. (1940): *The Puyallup-Nisqually.* Columbia Univ. Contr. to Anth., vol. xxxii, New York.

SPECK, FRANK G. (1914–15): "Basis of American Indian Ownership of the Land." *Old Penn* (Weekly review of the Univ. of Pennsylvania), pp. 181–96.

—(1915): "The Family Hunting Band as the Basis of Algonkian Social Organization." *Am. Anthrop.,* vol. xvii, pp. 289–305.

—(1931): "Montagnais-Naskapi Band and Early Eskimo Distribution in the Labrador Peninsula." *Am. Anthrop.,* vol. xxxiii, pp. 557–600.

SPIER, LESLIE (1930): "Klamath Ethnography." *U. Cal. Publ. Am. Arch. and Eth.,* vol. xxv, pp. 1–338.

SPIER, LESLIE and SAPIR, EDWARD (1930): "Wishram Ethnography." *U. Wash. Publ. in Anthrop.,* vol. iii, no. 3, pp. 151–300.

STANNER, W. E. H. (1932–4): "The Daly River Tribes—a Report of Field Work in Northern Australia." *Oceania,* vol. iii, pp. 377–405; vol. iv, pp. 10–29.

STAYT, H. A. (1931): *The Bavenda.* London.

STEVENSON, MATILDA C. (1904): *The Zuñi Indians,* 23rd Ann. Rep., Bur. of Am. Eth.

STEWARD, J. H. (1938): *Basin-Plateau Aboriginal Sociopolitical Groups.* Bur. Am. Eth., Bull. 120.

STITES, SARA HENRY (1905): *Economics of the Iroquois.* Bryn Mawr College Monographs, vol. i, no. 3.

SWANTON, JOHN R. (1905): *Contributions to the Ethnology of the Haida.* Publ. Jessup N. Pac. Exped., vol. V, part 1.

—(1906): "Exchange." *Handbook of American Indians.* Bur. Am. Eth., Bull. 30.

—(1908): *Social Condition, Beliefs, and Linguistic Relationship of the Tlingit Indians.* 26th Ann. Rep., Bur. of Am. Eth.

—(1911): *Indian Tribes of the Lower Mississippi.* Bur. Am. Eth., Bull. 43.

—(1928): *Social Organization and Social Usages of the Indians of the Creek Confederacy.* 42nd Ann. Rep., Bur. of Am. Eth.

TAUXIER, LOUIS (1912): *Le Noir du Soudan, Pays Mossi et Gourounsi.* Paris.

TAX, SOL (MS): *The Economy of the Indians of Panajachel* (hexographed).

TEIT, JAMES A. (1900–8): *The Lillooet Indians.* Publ. Jessup N. Pac. Exped., vol. II, part 5.

—(1909): *The Shuswap.* Publ. Jessup N. Pac. Exped., vol. II, part 7.

—(1928): "The Middle Columbia Salish." *U. Wash. Publ. in Anthrop.,* vol. ii, no. 4, pp. 83–128.

THOMPSON, J. ERIC (1933): *Mexico Before Cortez.* New York.

THURNWALD, RICHARD (1932a): *Werden, Wandel und Gestaltung der Wirtschaft. Die Menschliche Gesellschaft,* vol. III, Berlin.

—(1932b): *Economics in Primitive Communities*. London.

—(1934–5): "Pigs and Currency in Buin." *Oceania*, vol. v, pp. 119–41.

—(1937): "Ein Vorkapitalistisches Wirtschaftssystem in Buin." *Archiv. Rechts und Sozialphilosophie*, Bd. xxxi, pp. 1–37.

TORDAY, E. and JOYCE, T. A. (1922): *Notes ethnographiques sur des Populations habitant les bassins du Kasai et du Kwango Oriental*. Ann. du Musée du Congo Belge, Ser. III, T. ii, Fasc. 2.

TUCCI, GIOVANNI (1950): *Sistemi Monetari Africani al lume dell'Economia Primitiva*. Naples.

TUETING, LAURA T. (1935): "Native Trade in Southeast New Guinea." *B. P. Bishop Museum, Occas. Papers*, vol. xi, no. 15.

TURNEY-HIGH, HARRY H. (1937): *The Flathead Indians of Montana*. Am. Anthrop. Assn., Mem. 48.

USHER, ABBOTT PAYSON (1920): *An Introduction to the Industrial History of England*. Boston.

—(1949): "The Significance of Modern Empiricism for History and Economics." *The Journal of Economic History*, vol. ix, pp. 137–55.

VAISBERG, P. E. (1925): *Dengi i tseny. Podpolnyi ryok v period "Voennogo Kommunisma."* (Money and Prices. The Illicit Market during the period of "War Communism.") Moscow.

VEBLEN, THORSTEIN (1915): *The Theory of the Leisure Class*. New York.

—(1918): *The Instinct of Workmanship and the State of the Industrial Arts*. New York.

VILJOEN, STEPHAN (1936): *The Economics of Primitive Peoples*. London.

VOEGELIN, ERMINIE W. (1938): *Tübatulabal Ethnography*. Anthrop. Records, vol. ii, no. 1.

WAGLEY, CHARLES (1941): *Economics of a Guatamalan Village*. Amer. Anth. Assn., Mem. 58.

WAGLEY, CHARLES and GALVÃO, EDUARDO (1949): *The Tenetehara Indians of Brazil, a Culture in Transition*. New York.

WALKER, K. F. (1943): "The Study of Primitive Economics." *Oceania*, vol. xiii, pp. 131–42.

WARNER, W. LLOYD (1937): *A Black Civilization, a Social Study of an Australian Tribe*. New York.

WEBER, MAX (1927): *General Economic History* (transl. by F. H. Knight). New York.

WEDGEWOOD, CAMILLA H. (1933): "Report on Research in Manam Island, Mandated Territory of New Guinea." *Oceania*, vol. iv, pp. 373–403.

WEEKS, JOHN H. (1913): *Among Congo Cannibals*. London.

WEST, ROBERT C. (1948): *Cultural Geography of the Modern Tarascan Area*. Pub. No. 7, Inst. of Social Anth., Smithsonian Institution, Washington.

WESTERMARCK, EDWARD (1908): *The Origin and Development of the Moral Ideas* (2 vols.). London.

WHIFFEN, THOMAS (1915): *The North-West Amazons*. London.

WILLIAMS, F. E. (1936): *Papuans of the Trans-Fly*. Oxford.

WILLIAMSON, ROBERT W. (1924): *The Social and Political Systems of Central Polynesia* (3 vols.). Cambridge.

—(1937): *Religion and Social Organization in Central Polynesia* (R. Piddington, ed.). Cambridge.

WILSON, G. L. (1917): *Agriculture of the Hidatsa Indians, an Indian Interpretation*. U. of Minn. Studies in the Soc. Sci., No. 9.

WILSON, GODFREY (1938): "The Land Rights of Individuals among the Nyakyusa." *Rhodes-Livingstone Papers*, No. 1.

WOOTTON, BARBARA (1938): *Lament for Economics*. London.

MAP OF TRIBAL AND PLACE-NAMES: I. Polynesia; The Americas

INDEX of Tribal and Place-Names

MAP OF TRIBAL AND PLACE-NAMES: II. The Old World

NUMBERS *Designating Tribal and Place-Names*

1 Samoa; Satapaitea
2 Niue
3 Tonga
4 Tongareva
5 Pukapuka
6 Mangaia
7 Society Islands; Tahiti
8 Marquesas
9 Ingalik
10 Tlingit
11 Haida
12 Tsimshian
13 Kwakiutl
14 Puyallap-Nisqually
15 Chinook
16 Klamath
17 Tolowa-Tututni
18 Yurok
19 Modoc
20 Achomawi
21 Yuki
22 Nomlaki
23 Wintun
24 Patwin
25 Maidu; Nisenan
26 Miwok
27 Chumash
28 Eskimo (Copper)
29 Eskimo (Central)
30 Eskimo (Caribou)
31 Chipewyan
32 Shuswap
33 Lillooet
34 Flathead
35 Blackfoot
36 Gros Ventre
37 Wishram
38 Shoshoni
39 Shasta

40 Paviotso
41 Yokuts
42 Havasupai
43 Tübatulabal
44 Paiute
45 Mono
46 Cochiti
47 Halchidoma
48 Mohave
49 Kaveltcadom
50 Walapai
51 Apache
52 Yuma; Maricopa
53 Navaho
54 Hopi
55 Zuñi
56 Acoma
57 Tewa
58 Pima
59 Crow
60 Sioux
61 Plains Indian
62 Taos
63 Jemez
64 Santo Domingo; Sia
65 Comanche
66 Arikara
67 Hidatsa
68 Mandan
69 Dakota
70 Omaha
71 Ojibway (Chippewa)
72 Chippewa (Ojibway)
73 Timiskaming
74 Menomini
75 Montagnais-Naskapi
76 Algonquin (Algonkian)
77 Penobscot
78 Iroquois

79 Cherokee
80 Creek
81 Caddo
82 Natchez
83 Coastal Indians (*Gulf of Mexico*)
84 Florida Indians
85 Tzintzuntzan (Tarascan)
86 Aztec
87 Mitla
88 Oaxaca
89 Popoluca
90 Panajachel
91 Haitians
92 Kogi (Kagaba)
93 Bush Negroes
94 Guiana Indians; Arekuna; Guinau; Maionkong; Otomac; Oyapock River Peoples; Warrau; Waiwai
95 Taruma
96 Makusi
97 Karahone
98 Boro
99 Menimche
100 Witoto
101 Inca
102 Tenetehara
103 Siriono
104 Pilagá
105 Toba
106 Chaco; Choroti
107 Selk'nam
108 Alacaluf
109 Ona
110 Yaghan
111 Berber

112 Bambara
113 Dogon
114 Mandingo
115 Lobi
116 Peul; Toucouleur
117 Dioula; Téguessié
118 Mossi
119 Tallensi
120 Gola; Kpelle
121 Mende
122 Kru
123 Ashanti
124 Akan
125 Dahomey
126 Yoruba
127 Gbari
128 Nupe; Agaie; Bida
129 Yakö
130 Ibo
131 Wabena; Clemba
132 Kasai Tribes
133 Batetela
134 Upper Katanga
135 Lamba
136 Lozi (Barotse)
137 Ba-Ila
138 Ba-Venda
139 Bushmen
140 Hottentot
141 Pondo
142 Kaffir
143 Basuto
144 Swazi
145 Zulu
146 Sotho
147 Thonga
148 Lovedu
149 Thonga
150 Bemba
151 Nyakyusa

152 Bahima (Ankole)
153 Gussii (Kissii)
154 Kikuyu
155 Akamba
156 Baganda
157 Hima
158 Hima
159 Nuer; Sungu
160 Dodoth
161 Acholi; Tirangori
162 Lango; Kokir
163 Didinga
164 Azande
165 Kazak
166 Badaga; Kota; Kurumba; Toda
167 Mannan; Paliyan; Periyan; Urali
168 Vedda
169 Naga (Sema, Lhota)
170 Li (Hainan)
171 Andamanese
172 Kelantan and Tranggann (*Malaya*)
173 Malayan Negrito
174 Borneo; Dyak (Siang)
175 Kalinga
176 Ifugao
177 Negritos (*Philippines*)
178 Palau
179 Yap
180 Mardala
181 Deiri
182 Yantruwuntu
183 Australia (*N. W. Cent. Queensland*)

184 Lunga (Kimberley Division)
185 Daly River Tribes
186 Murngin
187 Yir-Yoront
188 Tanga
189 Manam
190 Wogeo (*Schouten Is.*)
191 Jabim; Siassi
192 Papuans
193 Keralai
194 Busama (*Huon Gulf*)
195 Kiwai
196 Koita Motu
197 Massim
198 Admiralty Islands; Manus; Usiasi
199 Ponape
200 New Ireland; Lesu
201 Amphletts; Dobu; Trobriand Islands; Kuboma; Sinaketa
202 Buka
203 Bougainville (Siuai)
204 Ontong Java
205 Guadalcanal
206 Rossel Island
207 Tikopia
208 Malekula
209 Banks Islands
210 New Hebrides
211 Uvea
212 New Caledonia
213 Fiji
214 Maori
215 Chuckchee
216 Koryak

*INDEX**

* The Appendix (pp. 507-31) and Bibliography (pp. 532-47) are not included in the entries of this Index.

THE NORTON LIBRARY

Richardson, Samuel. *Pamela.* Introduction by William M. Sale, Jr. N166

Rilke, Rainer Maria. *Letters to a Young Poet.* Tr. by M. D. Herter Norton. N158

Rilke, Rainer Maria. *Sonnets to Orpheus.* Tr. by M. D. Herter Norton. N157

Rilke, Rainer Maria. *Translations from the Poetry* by M. D. Herter Norton. N156

Rostow, W. W. *The Process of Economic Growth.* New intro. N176

Russell, Bertrand. *Freedom Versus Organization.* N136

Russell, Bertrand. *The Scientific Outlook.* N137

Salvemini, Gaetano. *The French Revolution.* Tr. by I. M. Rawson. N179

Simms, William Gilmore. *Woodcraft.* Introduction by Richmond Croom Beatty. N107

Sitwell, Edith. *Alexander Pope.* N182

Spender, Stephen. *The Making of a Poem.* New intro. N120

Stauffer, Donald A. *The Nature of Poetry.* N167

Stendhal. *The Private Diaries of Stendhal.* Tr. and ed. by Robert Sage. N175

Stovall, Floyd, Editor. *Eight American Authors.* N178

Strachey, Lytton. *Portraits in Miniature.* N181

Stravinsky, Igor. *An Autobiography.* N161

Tourtellot, Arthur B. *Lexington and Concord:* The Beginning of the War of the American Revolution. N194

Toye, Francis. *Rossini:* A Study in Tragi-Comedy. New intro. N192

Ward, Barbara. *The Interplay of East and West:* Points of Conflict and Cooperation. New epilogue. N162